AUTONOMOUS REGION

GREAT KHINGAN MOUNTAINS

HEILONGJIANG

★ Harbin

Changchun ★

JILIN

Shenyang ★

LIAONING

NORTH KOREA

Sea of Japan

JAPAN

ngzhao asery
★ Huhehaote
aotou
Dalateqi
BEIJING MUNICIPALITY
Beijing ★
TIANJIN MUNICIPALITY
Tianjin ★

SHANXI

HEBEI
Shijiazhuang ★

SOUTH KOREA

uan
Taiyuan ★

Yellow R.

Jinan ★
SHANDONG
Qingdao ★

Yellow Sea

Xi'an ★
ANXI

Zhengzhou ★

HENAN

JIANGSU

ANHUI

Changzhou
Wuxi
Nanjing ★
Hefei ★
Yixing ★
Suzhou ★
Shanghai ★
SHANGHAI MUNICIPALITY

HUBEI

Yangzi River

Wuhan ★

Huangshan
Tunxi
Hangzhou ★

East China Sea

qing

ZHEJIANG

Nanchang ★

Changsha ★
Shaoshan

HUNAN

JIANGXI

Fuzhou ★

FUJIAN

Taibei ★

iyang

GUANGXI

HUANG A.R.

GUANGDONG

Guangzhou ★
Shenzhen ●
Hong Kong ●

TAIWAN

PACIFIC OCEAN

★ Nanning

Haikou ★

HAINAN

South China Sea

PHILIPPINES

CHINA'S FAR WEST

Also by A. Doak Barnett

Modernizing China: Post-Mao Reform and Development
(editor, with Ralph N. Clough, 1986)

The Making of Foreign Policy in China:
Structure and Process (1985)

U.S. Arms Sales: The China-Taiwan Tangle (1982)

The FX Decision: "Another Crucial Moment"
in U.S.-China-Taiwan Relations (1981)

China's Economy in Global Perspective (1981)

China and the World Food System (1979)

China and the Major Powers in East Asia (1977)

China Policy: Old Problems and New Challenges (1977)

The United States, China, and Arms Control
(coauthor, with Ralph N. Clough, Morton H. Halperin, and Jerome H. Kahan, 1975)

Uncertain Passage: China's Transition to the Post-Mao Era (1974)

A New U.S. Policy Toward China (1971)

The United States and China: The Next Decade
(editor, with Edwin O. Reischauer, 1970)

Chinese Communist Politics in Action (editor, 1969)

Cadres, Bureaucracy, and Political Power in Communist China
(with a contribution by Ezra Vogel, 1967)

China After Mao (1967)

The United States and China in World Affairs
(editor of manuscript by Robert Blum, published posthumously, 1966)

Communist China: The Early Years, 1949–55 (1964)

China on the Eve of Communist Takeover (1963)

Communist Strategies in Asia: A Comparative Analysis of
Governments and Parties (editor, 1963)

Communist China in Perspective (1962)

Communist China and Asia: Challenge to American Policy (1960)

Communist Economic Strategy: The Rise of Mainland China (1959)

A. DOAK BARNETT

CHINA'S FAR WEST

FOUR DECADES OF CHANGE

WESTVIEW PRESS
Boulder • San Francisco • Oxford

Cover photos: top row, from left, *valley on the road from Yaan to Kangding; street scene in Xiemachang; Muslim women in Linxia;* second row, *Tibetans along Tagong's main street; Kunming street scene; a Chinese landlord near Xiemachang, 1948; a young peasant woman in high heels pulls a farm cart near Xiemachang;* third row, *a Han Chinese family in Lanzhou; Baotou steel mill; Kunming skyscraper; view of Nanshan on the road from Urumqi;* bottom row, *terraced mountains near Lanzhou; a Kazakh woman in the Tian Shan in 1948; Xining street scene; Wudangzhao lamasery*

Copyright © 1993 by A. Doak Barnett

Published in 1993 in the United States of America by Westview Press, Inc., 5500 Central Avenue, Boulder, Colorado 80301-2877, and in the United Kingdom by Westview Press, 36 Lonsdale Road, Summertown, Oxford OX2 7EW

Library of Congress Cataloging-in-Publication Data
Barnett, A. Doak.
  China's far West : four decades of change / A. Doak Barnett.
    p.   cm.
  Includes index.
  ISBN 0-8133-1773-8 — ISBN 0-8133-1774-6 (pbk.)
    1. China, Northwest—Economic conditions.   2. China, Southwest—Economic conditions.   3. China—Politics and government—1949–
4. China—Description and travel.
HC428.N6B37   1993
330.951'405—dc20   93-4194
                                                                                 CIP

Printed and bound in the United States of America

The paper used in this publication meets the requirements
∞ of the American National Standard for Permanence of Paper
for Printed Library Materials Z39.48-1984.

10   9   8   7   6   5   4   3   2   1

Contents

Maps

Acknowledgments

I AM DEEPLY INDEBTED to more institutions and individuals than I can possibly acknowledge by name for their assistance and support, which made this book possible. I must mention a few. The Committee on Scholarly Communication with the People's Republic of China (of the National Academy of Sciences, Social Science Research Council, and American Council of Learned Societies) made a research grant to me that covered the bulk of my costs during my research in 1988, and they also assisted in my discussions and negotiations to arrange my itinerary and travel in China. I wish to thank especially Mary Bullock, then director of the Committee on Scholarly Communication, Michel Oksenberg, of its National Program for Advanced Study and Research in China, and staff members Kyna Rubin and Caroline Reeves.

The Chinese Academy of Social Sciences was my principal host organization in China, and as such it assisted me in innumerable ways, arranging my travel, communicating my requests to several local host organizations in China, providing escorts for many of my trips, and setting up a large number of interviews and visits to institutions. I am indebted to a great many individuals at the Academy, including several of its leaders, particularly Li Shenzhi and Zhao Fusan, and many staff members. I wish to thank here especially those staff members who were most directly involved in making arrangements for me and accompanying me on my journeys: Lin Di, Wu Yu, and Tsao Dapeng. For a period of about a month, my host organization in Shanghai and throughout the Yangzi valley region was the Shanghai People's Association for Friendship with Foreign Countries, which financed my stay in that region. I wish to give special thanks to Li Shoubao, as well as his son Li Yaping, who arranged my schedule and accompanied me on my travels. In addition, in every place that I visited, leaders and staff members of the local Academies of Social Sciences or Foreign Affairs Bureaus helped me in a great many ways; they are too numerous to mention by name. However, I would like to thank, specifically, Zhang Xiangrong, the young member of the Chengdu Academy of Social Sciences who accompanied me for almost a month during my travels in Sichuan Province. I am also grateful to the hundreds of people whom I interviewed all over the country who patiently answered my questions; this book is, above all, about what I learned from them as well as about what I observed on my travels. I wish to express my sincere appreciation to Vivian Hogan and Jean Schlessinger, who typed my manuscript. I also wish to thank the Paul H. Nitze School of Advanced International Studies of Johns Hopkins University, in particular Dean George R. Packard, for continuing support of my work after my retirement in 1989. Finally, I wish to express my appreciation to those at Westview Press who helped to produce this book: Susan L. McEachern, acquisitions editor; Jane Raese, production editor; Sarah Tomasek, copy editor; Polly Christensen, art director; and Patricia Isaacs, cartographer.

A. Doak Barnett

Note on Romanization

THE BASIC SYSTEM used in this book for romanization of Chinese names and terms is Pinyin, which the government of the People's Republic of China adopted for use in China starting January 1, 1979. (The only exceptions are a few Chinese names best known in the West in other romanized forms.) For the benefit of readers who are more familiar with the Wade-Giles system, the Wade-Giles form is given in parentheses for some names. (My earlier writing on west China, contained in *China on the Eve of Communist Takeover,* used the Wade-Giles system.)

A.D.B

CHINA'S FAR WEST

Prologue

I N THE LATE 1940s, I had an extraordinary, and perhaps unique, opportunity to journey to virtually every part of China, from 1947 through 1949, as a Fellow of the Institute of Current World Affairs and correspondent of the Chicago Daily News Foreign Service. My assignment was to analyze and write about the current situation and trends in China. It was a fascinating task because the last years of the 1940s were a watershed in modern Chinese history—a period in which the Nationalist regime collapsed on the mainland and the Communist Party assumed power and established a new revolutionary regime. What I wrote at that time became the basis of a book entitled *China on the Eve of Communist Takeover* (originally published in 1963 by Praeger Publishers and reprinted in 1985 by Westview Press in its Encore Reprint Series).

Four decades later, in the late 1980s, I had another remarkable opportunity, also unique in many respects: to retrace my steps and revisit virtually all of the places about which I had written in the 1940s. Once again, my travels took place during a watershed period. The year 1988 was a high point of China's post-Mao "decade of reform," during which Deng Xiaoping, Zhao Ziyang, and others set China on a new course, which had begun to transform the country. It was also the eve of a major economic and political crisis—a by-product of the rapid change and reform of the previous decade—which reached a peak in 1989 and culminated in the calamitous massacre near Tiananmen Square in the middle of 1989.

My aim in 1988 in revisiting the places I had seen four decades earlier seemed in some respects to be simple but in reality was extremely complex and difficult: I set out to assess, in an impressionistic and personal way, the nature and extent of the political, economic, and social changes that had occurred during the previous few years and the general progress of modernization over four decades, especially in many of China's remotest areas, during the tumultuous period of Maoist rule as well as the decade of Deng's reform. This book is a report on some of the things I observed and learned, focusing especially on China's far western provinces.

Trying to understand China has been a lifelong commitment for me. I was born in Shanghai in 1921, spent my childhood there, and began systematic study of the country when I was in college. Most important, I have been professionally engaged in this task in a variety of jobs in journalism, government service, and academia ever since World War II. Throughout these years, I have written and edited 20-odd books about China and U.S.-China relations, but I am less impressed by what I have learned over the years than about what I still must try to learn to understand China. One thing I certainly have come to know is that because China is so huge and complex, and because it has been undergoing constant and turbulent changes throughout the modern period as the Chinese people have grappled with the enormous problems of development and modernization, one must be extremely wary of generalizations about the country that are not rooted at least partially in study, observation, and experience at the grass-roots level. Unfortunately, the images of China prevalent in the West have too often lacked such a basis.

*   *   *

The dominant stereotypes of China in the United States, and in most Western countries, have been strikingly volatile and have varied tremendously over the years. American views have been especially changeable, and, in frequent pendulum swings, they have varied between extremely naive, idealized perceptions of the country and inordinately negative, hostile opinions about it. Some of these oscillations have reflected real events and trends within China, but, too often, China seems to have existed to a large extent in the eyes of foreign beholders, and frequently the changes in American views of China seem to have been shaped in large part by domestic American politics and attitudes rather than the realities in China. U.S. reactions have tended, repeatedly, to distort and exaggerate trends in China, portraying them as a Manichaean contest of good and evil and seeing them in black and white terms. As in most countries, the situation in China has rarely been all black or all white; almost always it has been some shade of gray.

For reasons that I have never fully understood, it seems to have been particularly difficult for many Americans to grasp the complexity of the forces at work in China and to view trends at any particular time in some sort of historical perspective in order to achieve a balanced and realistic view of the country. The most recent examples of excessive fluctuation in American opinions about China were the swing toward euphoric optimism about the country "going democratic and capitalist" in the late 1970s and 1980s up to 1989 and the deep pessimism and excessive negativism about the country after the Tiananmen crisis of 1989, when a great many Americans concluded that China had abandoned reform and was returning to an old form of totalitarianism. In both instances, American views greatly oversimplified and distorted China's complicated realities.

*   *   *

I do not claim to possess any unique insights into "the truth" about China. All that I can claim is that I have been engaged in the search for an understanding of the country for a long time. Before describing what I observed and learned during my 1988 travels throughout China, including west China (the focus of this book), let me briefly summarize some of the basic historical and personal perspectives that have influenced my attempts to understand trends in modern and contemporary China over the years; they were part of my intellectual baggage as I began my travels in 1988.

I have always viewed China as one of the most important nations in the world because of its past and its potential. It is not only the world's most populous country—and territorially one of the four largest in the world—it has had the longest continuous history of any still-extant polity. Starting well before what is called the Christian era in the West, China developed one of the greatest cultures and civilizations in history, the achievements of which were, during most of Chinese history, among the most advanced anywhere. For two millennia, the Chinese viewed their society as being the "center of the world," dominated what is now called East Asia, and had an enormous cultural, political, and economic influence on all the areas on its periphery. The Han Chinese, the country's dominant ethnic group, were almost constantly threatened by non-Han groups from Inner Asia, and periodically the country was conquered by one or another of these peoples. Yet the strength of China's culture and civilization was such that eventually almost all of these conquerors were assimilated into the Chinese political system and into Chinese society—or were expelled.

However, China has been experiencing a major and continuous crisis ever since the midnineteenth century, and during this time it has undergone more profound changes than in any other period of the previous two millennia. This crisis started in the late Manchu (Qing) dynasty period, when a process of internal dynastic decline, similar to many in the past, coincided with an unprecedented challenge from abroad after the Western imperialist powers led by Great Britain forcibly "opened" China. In earlier centuries, dynastic decline had led to changes in Chinese rulers without fundamental alterations in the traditional imperial system, but since the midnineteenth century the changes have been much more far-reaching and fundamental. From the 1840s on, myriad Western influences flowed into the country through foreign "concessions," "treaty ports," and spheres of influence. The agents of change included not only foreign military forces and diplomats, but also traders, missionaries, educators, and doctors. Gradually, these external influences helped to undermine the basic legitimacy of China's rulers and subverted the Confucian values on which the traditional system had been based. The impact of the West set loose powerful new forces that began to change the economy and society as well as the polity.

It did not take long for China's rulers and political elite to realize that the West posed a major threat to the viability of the country and its political system. Eventually, many saw that the challenges facing them were to somehow modernize China, catch up with the West technologically and economically, redefine the Chinese polity, and try to find a proper place for China in the international community. These, therefore, have been basic Chinese goals ever since the nineteenth century. But the Chinese have found it extraordinarily difficult to achieve these aims for many reasons; the strength of deeply embedded traditions and the huge size of the country have been among the most fundamental. In the midnineteenth century, Qing dynasty leaders first tried simply to fend off Western influence. When that failed, members of China's elite then made several attempts to reform the traditional system, most notably in the 1860s, 1890s, and the first decade of the twentieth century. But these also failed. The Manchu dynasty was fatally weakened by a series of huge revolts, including the Taiping Rebellion in (1850–1864), as well as by escalating Western (and Japanese) pressures that became most intense around the turn of the century. In 1911, the dynasty finally collapsed, and China disintegrated.

From 1911 until the late 1920s—and in some respects until the late 1940s—most of China was ruled by local warlords, and there was no strong central government. During this period, two mass-based revolutionary movements developed, the Guomindang (Kuomintang; the Nationalist Party) and the Communist Party. In the mid-1920s and again in the 1930s, they collaborated briefly, but when the Nationalists' revolutionary army was on the verge of success and the Guomindang was preparing to establish a new regime in Nanjing, it turned on the Communists and forced them underground; subsequently, the Communists developed their own revolutionary army in rural bases.

From 1928 until the Japanese launched a full-scale invasion of China in 1937, the Guomindang regime made significant progress toward modernizing parts of China, and it was the main focus of nationalist aspirations and hope for the future of most Chinese. However, the Guomindang was never able to unify the country, most of which continued to be dominated by local warlords. Moreover, it suffered from serious internal factionalism, and it failed to address basic problems of landlordism and poverty in rural China. During the 1930s and 1940s, the Communists, by exploiting the Nationalists' weaknesses in the countryside and appealing to anti-Japanese nationalism, rapidly built up their power.

The Guomindang's weaknesses began to be apparent even before the Sino-Japanese War. Then, the full-scale assault by Japan forced the Nationalists into underdeveloped areas of southwest China and again set in motion disintegrating forces. The impact of the war was devastating. Ultimately, runaway inflation and pervasive corruption undermined the Nationalists' support, and the vacuum that the war created in much of rural China provided the Communists with an opportunity to build a strong Party and army in rural areas. These trends laid the basis for the Communists' success in the open civil war that followed World War II, and by 1949 the Communists were victorious and had established a new regime.

*   *   *

I lived through much of this tumultuous period in China. Obviously, the end of the Qing dynasty and the start of what was called the Republican period were before my time, but I felt a link even to that period: My father had arrived in China as a YMCA secretary in 1910, the last year of the old imperial regime, and my family lived in Hangzhou until 1921, the year in which I was born and my family moved to Shanghai. The Chinese Communist Party was founded that same year, only a few blocks from where I grew up. Our household was infused with lore about the final years of the Qing dynasty and the start of the Chinese efforts to modernize China during the Republican period. Throughout my childhood in Shanghai (which was my home until 1936), what I observed inevitably affected greatly even a foreign child such as myself. Part of the intellectual and emotional baggage that I have carried with me in studying China ever since then has consisted, therefore, of impressions and memories of what I saw and heard in Shanghai—and in visits to other cities in central and north China—as a child and teenager. These included memories and impressions of many different kinds of interactions (both good and bad) between foreigners and Chinese, of the echoes of warlord conflicts, and of the impact of the rise of the "radical" Nationalists and their takeover of the Yangzi valley, especially as it affected Shanghai. I took for granted the prevalence of extreme poverty, which seemed at that time to be an almost immutable fact of life in China, even in areas where the foreign impact had been great, but at the same time I shared, even as a boy, the widespread enthusiasm for the efforts that were started under the Nationalist regime to develop the country and bring it into the modern world.

Some of my strongest memories are of the impact of Japanese aggression (the Japanese attacked Shanghai in 1932, almost immediately after their 1931 invasion of Manchuria) and of the growing sense of Chinese nationalism at that time. Even though I was too young to understand fully all that I saw and observed in the 1920s and 1930s, the cameo images in my mind, rooted in memories of those years, remained with me and provided one baseline for judging later trends in China when I returned after World War II. My fundamental and most lasting impression of China in those early years was of a country struggling to survive in the face of the mounting threat from Japan but also trying hard to move toward modernization in the face of almost insurmountable obstacles.

I began to study China in a formal way in the early 1940s, in college, but I was not able to progress very far: Because of World War II, my class at Yale was "accelerated," and immediately after graduation I joined the Marine Corps and then served in the Pacific. However, at the end of World War II, my Marine unit moved from Okinawa to Qingdao. I was then able to revisit Shanghai, and my latent interest in China was strongly rekindled. Thereafter, I was "hooked." I returned to Yale for a brief period to study international relations, focusing on China, as well as to study the Chinese language (this time I studied Mandarin; what I had learned as a child was the Shanghai dialect, and I had forgotten much of it). Then, when I was offered an opportunity to go to China in 1947, I jumped at the chance.

My experiences in China in the late 1940s can best be described as total immersion. Although I spent some time investigating and writing about national political and economic developments, seen from the vantage point of major cities such as Nanjing (then the capital), Shanghai, and Beijing (then called Beiping), I spent most of my time in more distant places in China's interior. My travels took me to all but two of China's provinces. For one extended period I settled into a Chinese village in Sichuan Province and studied local government and politics. I visited almost all of the semiautonomous, warlord-ruled provinces, met the local leaders, and wrote fairly detailed profiles of their regimes. Finally, in late 1948, I flew to Beijing to watch the Communists' takeover and then spent six months observing how they consolidated power and organized their new regime. What I learned between the fall of 1947 and the late summer of 1949 provided another baseline—perhaps the most important one in my experience—for judging subsequent developments in China. More specifically, what I learned in my visits to all of the provinces in west China in 1948 provided me with my starting point for trying to judge continuity and change in that region when I revisited the western provinces in 1988.

                    *   *   *

The China that I wrote about in the late 1940s was a disintegrating country engulfed by revolution and civil war, which resulted in the Communist victory in 1949. After their takeover, the Communists, led by Mao Zedong, rapidly reunified the country—for the first time in decades—and set China on a course of forced-draft economic development. In the early years, China's modernization was impressive in many respects. The Communist regime rapidly built a large industrial base. The Party also, however, established what was, for China, an unprecedented totalitarian political system. Political power penetrated the grass roots of Chinese society and intruded into ordinary people's lives more than under any regime in China's history. The Communists were ruthless in their treatment of all those they labeled enemies, and, through a series of convulsive mass campaigns, they kept the country in almost constant turmoil. Starting in the late 1950s, moreover, Mao, who was fearful (with good reason) that revolutionary fervor in China was declining, launched the country on several campaigns that proved to be complete disasters. The Hundred Flowers campaign of political liberalization was followed by a harsh Anti-Rightist Campaign, which punished and alienated much of China's intelligentsia. The Great Leap Forward and communization of agriculture led to economic disaster, and China experienced a

Communist version of a great depression, the consequences of which took many years to overcome—and resulted in unprecedented splits in the Communist Party's leadership.

Finally, in 1966, Mao initiated his last hurrah, the so-called Cultural Revolution, and China entered a period of political chaos from which it had not totally recovered by the time Mao died in 1976. For about two years, from late 1966 through the end of 1968, there was a breakdown of Party and government rule: The Party's radicals and military leaders assumed power, and the People's Liberation Army (PLA) was compelled to take over both Party and government functions for a period of time. The effects of that disaster are still felt in China today. Future historians will have to pass judgment on the Maoist era as a whole. It began impressively, unified the country, and propelled China toward modernization more vigorously than any previous regime in Chinese history. But the costs of its achievements were enormous: During the latter years of Mao's rule, China experienced one disaster after another, and many of the problems confronting the country's rulers today are rooted in the failures of that period.

*   *   *

Throughout the Maoist era, I continued to study China, but mainly from a distance, first in Hong Kong and later in New York and Washington, D.C., with short stints in Cambridge, Massachusetts, and Honolulu. Like other Western specialists on China, I spent endless hours reading Chinese Communist writings and interviewing Chinese émigrés, in Hong Kong and elsewhere, and talking with foreign visitors who were able to go to China during those years when Americans could not. It was possible to learn a good deal about the nature of the Chinese regime and trends in the country from this kind of political archaeology, but I, like others, began to see China as an abstraction, until it was possible to visit the country once again.

Access to China for Americans began to improve immediately after President Richard M. Nixon's trip and the resulting U.S.-China "opening" in 1972, and I made my first return trip in the winter of 1972–1973 with a delegation from the National Committee on United States–China Relations. Thereafter, I was able to visit China regularly and to travel fairly widely, visiting major cities in many parts of China (including, besides Beijing, cities such as Shanghai, Shenyang, Changchun, Tianjin, Hangzhou, Guangdong, Xi'an, Chengdu, and Kunming). For me, China began to be, once again, a real place populated by live people coping with enormous but understandable problems. However, throughout the 1970s, there continued to be very serious constraints on what foreigners could see and learn. China's ideological and political controls remained tight, and these controls severely inhibited almost everyone—even individuals whom I knew well—from speaking frankly or revealing their true feelings. This began to change, slightly, during the Hua Guofeng interregnum after Mao's death, but the political relaxation was still limited.

Then, dramatic changes began in late 1978 when Deng Xiaoping achieved political primacy and started China on a new reform course. The disastrous effects of the Cultural Revolution had convinced Deng and many others that far-reaching changes were urgently needed in China's basic system, especially its economic system. Ideologically, the call went out for nondogmatic pragmatism; the dominant slogans were "seek truth from facts" and "practice is the sole criterion of truth." Beijing, abandoning Maoist isolationism, adopted a new "open policy," and the growth of China's foreign economic relations took off. Foreign trade expanded rapidly, and Beijing started substantial borrowing abroad, encouraged foreign investment, established special economic zones, and gave preferential treatment to export-oriented coastal areas. The open policy led to a large flow into China of ideas and people as well as goods and capital. Within China, agriculture was decollectivized, and family-based farming was revived. This strategy rapidly transformed a crucial sector of China's economy—one that still employed the majority of the Chinese population—and stimulated extraordinarily high rates of agricultural growth. Eventually it led to the very rapid development of collective and private industries in rural areas.

The effects of rural reforms provided the foundations for broader reform efforts. In the urban industrial economy, change was slower and more difficult, but it proceeded nevertheless, especially from the mid-1980s on. The regime took steps to increase material incentives to managers and workers and tried to impose greater accountability and discipline on enterprises. It decentralized a great deal of decisionmaking, granting new powers both to local governments and to enterprises. The scope of state planning was gradually cut back, and marketization of the economy increased substantially. Little progress was achieved, however, in raising the efficiency of large state enterprises, and only a start was made toward price reform, an essential step for genuine economic transformation.

The steps toward political reform were much slower and less far-reaching. In fact, relatively little was done to initiate major structural innovation that could move the country toward genuine democratization. Despite some calls for major political reforms, Deng and most others of his generation clearly feared rapid political changes, and they insisted on maintaining the essentials of a one-party authoritarian system. Nevertheless, some significant political changes occurred, and their impact was substantial, altering the political climate in the country and the relationship between the regime and the population.

Among the most important developments was the sweeping generational turnover in the leadership, in which young technocrats were promoted to high positions (although not to the very top ranks in Beijing, where a small group of old revolutionaries retained ultimate power). Some attempts were made to cut and rationalize the bureaucracies. The role of ideology was eroded, and old dogmas lost their force. The Party reduced its direct intervention into economic matters. The importance of laws—particularly economic laws—was stressed, and a legal system of sorts began to take shape, although it had relatively little effect on criminal law and the treatment of dissidents. Decisionmaking was increasingly influenced by advisers and experts working in China's growing research establishments. Representative bodies began to deal seriously with some policy issues, and, even though they remained rubber-stamp organizations in many respects, they were, for a period of time, significant sounding boards of public opinion. Journalists pushed the limits on press freedom considerably beyond the boundaries that had previously existed. Intellectuals, as well as officials, engaged in spirited debates over economic policy. And the flow of information on important and controversial issues grew significantly. More broadly, political and ideological controls were loosened. And the regime's intervention into ordinary people's lives decreased significantly. In this period, average standards of living more than doubled. This created rising expectations, which exerted increasing pressures on the leadership. An important trend toward increasing social pluralism was evident, most of all in the economy but affecting other sectors of the society as well. In short, even though relatively little structural political change took place, the general trend was from an extreme form of totalitarianism, which had been characteristic of the Maoist era, to a looser form of authoritarianism.

Deng and China's other reform leaders did not have any blueprint for reform, but, once started, the reform process developed a logic and momentum of its own, and in the years between 1978 and 1989, the country began a historic transformation. Not surprisingly, there was substantial opposition within the leadership to many reform policies, and the country's bloated bureaucracies resisted change. As a result, the course of reform was erratic: There were cycles of advances and retreats. Spurts of economic growth and reform were followed by periods of retrenchment, and periods of political liberalization provoked conservative backlashes and campaigns against "spiritual pollution" and "bourgeois liberalization." Nevertheless, despite all of the obstacles and the setbacks, during the decade before 1989 China began to undergo profound change. In the late 1980s, China was clearly in the forefront of economic reform within the Communist world. Moreover, with an average annual gross national product (GNP) growth rate of close to 10 percent, it also was in the forefront of Third World nations in the pace of its development. China was not "going capitalist," as some in the West believed, but it was moving rapidly toward a new kind of market socialism. And even though its leaders opposed Western-type democracy, they did seem prepared to move toward a liberalized form of authoritarianism, significantly different from the totalitarianism of the Maoist past.

*   *   *

Throughout the 1980s, these trends hypnotized me, as they did most other China specialists, and as the changes unfolded and China became increasingly open to foreigners, I found that it was possible to study China in new ways, ones unthinkable in the Maoist era. For me, new opportunities presented themselves first in Beijing, where I discovered that both political leaders and academics were now willing to discuss more openly and frankly many questions that had been completely out of bounds in earlier years. In 1983 and 1984, I seized the opportunity that this new openness provided and interviewed a wide range of knowledgeable Chinese (including then-premier Zhao Ziyang) about how Chinese foreign policy—and policy in general—was made. The results of these interviews were sufficiently illuminating that I decided to put my conclusions together in a small book titled *The Making of Foreign Policy in China: Structure and Process* (Westview Press, 1985). I then began to explore whether it might be possible, in the new situation, to undertake a study of conditions and trends in China at the grass-roots level, as I had done in the 1940s.

Starting in 1985, a number of close colleagues and friends began to urge me to see if I could undertake a project that would take me back to all or most of the places that I had written about in the 1940s and then write another book on the model of *China on the Eve of Communist Takeover*, comparing conditions in the 1980s with those I had observed in the 1940s. I found this idea tempting, but at the start I was wary of it. I knew that, at best, it would be a formidable and exhausting task. However, ultimately I succumbed to the temptation. In 1986, I applied for financial support to the Committee on Scholarly Communication with the People's Republic of China (CSCPRC). I was delighted to hear in mid-1987 that I had been awarded a grant, and I immediately set about the fairly complicated process of planning and making the necessary arrangements to carry out my project in China in 1988.

During the summer of 1987 I made a trip that I regarded as a kind of warm-up for my more extensive expeditions in 1988. The Shanghai Institute of International Studies had invited me to lecture in that city, and they offered me the opportunity, following my lectures, not only to meet and interview local Shanghai leaders (including then-mayor Jiang Zemin and ex-mayor Wang Daohan) and to investigate the progress of reforms in Shanghai, but also to make a trip through two provinces—Zhejiang and Jiangsu—accompanied by a member of the institute, Ding Xinghao, who was a longtime friend. That trip whetted my appetite for further travel throughout China's hinterland. We traveled by boat, car, and railway, visiting Wenzhou (already famous as the area in China that had gone the furthest in developing private enterprises), Ningbo (which had embarked on grand plans to develop a major new port), Fenghua (Chiang Kai-shek's birthplace, which had been refurbished as a new tourist site), Wuxi (a rapidly modernizing midsize city, long famous for its textile industry but now developing more high-tech industries), and Nanjing (the former Nationalist capital). My visits to these cities convinced me that it was now possible to learn a great deal about economic and political developments at the grass-roots level, and the progress of reform, because of the new openness. I was also able to sharpen my questions and hone my interviewing techniques in preparation for my project in 1988.*

Although my basic aim in planning this project was to do many of the things that I had done during 1947–1949, I fully recognized that I could not try to do them in exactly the same way. In my travels during the 1940s, I had been entirely on my own. Even though at that time it had been necessary to obtain permission for visits to some out-of-the-way places, either from local warlords or officials in Nanjing, for the most part I simply went where I wished, when I wished, without any formal hosts or escorts. Wherever I went I simply asked to interview anyone of interest to me, including the top local leaders, and with very few exceptions my requests were granted. I encountered almost no serious obstacles to meeting and talking with people of all sorts, including ordinary citizens everywhere, and I was able to poke and probe into the nooks and crannies of the society, throughout the country. In the 1940s, that approach worked.

In the late 1980s, however, it was clear that I could not do what I wished by simply exploring the country on my own. Although it was again possible for Westerners of many sorts to wander without escorts or elaborate prearrangements over a good deal of China, traveling by air, train, car, and even bicycle, it was clear to me that I could not expect, if I traveled this way, to gain access to the kinds of institutions I wished to visit or to meet the kinds

---

*I was able to make return trips to China, following my 1988 project, in the fall of 1989, the fall of 1990, the fall of 1991, and two trips in 1992, which enabled me to judge the impact of the Tiananmen massacre in Beijing in June 1989. I do not attempt, in this book, to analyze in detail the retrogressive trends in China during 1989–1990. Here, I will simply say that although my post-Tiananmen visits highlighted the tragedy of Tiananmen and the resulting serious setbacks in the reform process in China, they convinced me that the conservative, octogenarian leaders who were still in control in Beijing would not be able to halt or reverse the powerful forces for change that were released during the 1980s. These are the forces that most impressed me in 1988 and that are described in this book.

of people I was determined to see. To undertake serious research—or serious reporting—it was now imperative to have a designated host organization willing and able to open doors to other organizations and to help make arrangements for interviews not only with government and Party officials but even, in most areas, with academics, journalists, or others. This was also true for most Chinese who traveled around the country: They, too, needed to obtain formal introductions to visit organizations and meet officials when they visited places distant from their home base.

I decided to ask the Chinese Academy of Social Sciences (CASS) in Beijing to be my host organization. It seemed to be the most appropriate organization for a person with my interests, and during the 1980s I had developed many friendships with its leaders and researchers. CASS quickly agreed, but I suspect that later, as planning progressed and they had to wrestle with the extremely complicated problems of helping to arrange my travels, they may have had very mixed feelings about their original decision. Nevertheless, after I presented my proposed itinerary to CASS, Lin Di of its Foreign Affairs Office, with the help of several young scholars on the staff of the Academy's Institute of American Studies, proceeded to obtain the necessary travel permissions and to communicate my requests to individuals and institutions all over China. They later told me that this involved some of the most complicated and difficult problems that they had encountered in arranging any of the U.S.-China academic exchanges.

The program that I proposed called for two major periods of travel and study during 1988, the first from mid-February to mid-May and the second from mid-September to mid-November. My plans called for returning to the United States in the summer, mainly to catch my breath and reflect on what I had learned in the spring but also to have time to attend a conference in Moscow. The Moscow trip proved to be more useful to my research than I anticipated because it provided an invaluable comparative perspective on developments in China. Already, in 1988, the Soviet Union was considerably ahead of China in introducing political reform, but economic changes in the USSR lagged very far behind those that I was able to see in China.

I decided, in planning my itinerary, that during the first major period of my project I would make Beijing my primary base, and from there I would make three separate forays into different interior areas of northwest and southwest China, returning to Beijing between them. Even though I gave particularly high priority to assessing developments in remote areas of China, my stays in Beijing in 1988 were important to my overall objective. There I was able to interview a wide range of leaders, officials, and academic specialists about national policies, problems, and prospects. Among the most valuable of these in 1988 were the interviews I had with many of China's leading economists and economic administrators, individuals who were playing a major role at that time in defining, and debating, the country's economic reform policies.*

*   *   *

Economic reform was at a critical juncture in 1988. China had reached a halfway point, with no clear agreement on where to move next. Throughout the year there were intense debates in Beijing, in which the men I met played key roles, about whether the next stage of economic reforms should give priority to price reform, ownership reform, broad enterprise reform, or enterprise management reform. Because of the lack of consensus, for a period of time policy was virtually stalemated. During this period, moreover, the side effects of past reforms were creating mounting problems, the most serious of which, in terms of their social and political impact, were rising inflation and growing corruption, especially in China's major eastern cities. (In response to these trends, Beijing decided in late 1988 to adopt a stringent economic austerity program, which was clearly needed but exacerbated many of China's short-term problems. All of these developments were a prelude to the political crisis in 1989, which culminated in the Tiananmen massacre.)

My time in Beijing spent learning about broad trends affecting the economy, and about the thinking of experts on economic reform, provided me with essential insights and data on the national context in which I would later judge local situations as I traveled around China. My interviews in Beijing also included some with leading reform-minded officials and academics who were pushing at that time for meaningful political reform: Bao Tong, Huan Xiang, Su Shaozhi, Yan Jiaqi, and others. What I learned from them also provided me with valuable background information and insights that formed part of the basis on which I judged Party and government trends at the local level throughout the country.

In 1988, even most of China's leading proponents of further political reform called not for sudden attempts to democratize the system but for gradual, incremental, political reforms. And there was considerable support, among reform-minded academics as well as political leaders on the forefront of political reform, for the idea of "neoauthoritarianism," conceived of as a short-term period of paternalistic, liberalized, authoritarian rule, preliminary to more extensive democratization. A few intellectuals called for more far-reaching political reforms, however, and after the Tiananmen tragedy, the thinking of many reform-minded Chinese—particularly those who left China—was radicalized, although many, both within China and abroad, still

---

*I interviewed, among others, Ma Hong, Gu Mu, Liu Guoguang, Gao Shangchuan, Wu Jinglian, Li Yining, Du Rensheng, Dong Furen, Wu Mingyu, Sun Shangqing, and Zhang Zuoying.

My second trip took me to the southwest, to China's most populous province, Sichuan. While there, I also traveled to the faraway area that had been Xikang (Sikang) Province in 1948 but had subsequently become the Ganzi (Garze) Tibetan Autonomous Prefecture of Sichuan. I flew to and from Sichuan, but during my month there the rest of my travel was on the ground: a little of it by train, but most of it by car. I spent more time in Sichuan than in most other places for several reasons. With a population of over 100 million, Sichuan is in many respects more like a major country than a province, and I felt that it obviously deserved more than ordinary attention. Moreover, I had a special feeling about Sichuan because in 1948 I spent several months there, traveling over much of the province and also into adjacent Xikang (Sikang). At one point I settled into a small village north of Chongqing, where I did an in-depth study of village government and politics—one of the most memorable and valuable experiences I ever had in studying China. My first post-1949 return visit to the province had been in the 1970s, when I visited the provincial capital, Chengdu, but I learned little at that time. This time, I was determined to learn much more, and I was not disappointed.

My travels in Sichuan Province in 1988 took me to Chongqing and areas to its north, to the city of Zigong (formerly Ziliujing) in the central south, to Chengdu and the nearby prefecture of Wenjiang, and to Kangding and the Ganzi grasslands area in the west. In contrast to most of western China, where the population is very sparse, Sichuan—except for its westernmost, minority-inhabited prefectures of Ganzi, Aba, and Liangshan—is a place of wall-to-wall people, an incredibly crowded area where the population is jam-packed into small, intensely cultivated, agricultural valleys and into densely populated cities. Sichuan was a fascinating place to study the complex crosscurrents in China in the 1980s: the forces of modernization that clearly were beginning to transform the economy and society; the persistence of deep-rooted traditions that made the process of change extremely complicated; the distinctive local efforts to promote reform (when Zhao Ziyang was provincial Party first secretary, Sichuan had been one of the first areas to start agricultural reform); and the inevitable new impediments and stumbling blocks that made reform increasingly difficult as it proceeded.

The one serious disappointment I had in Sichuan was my inability to obtain permission to spend a period of time in Xiemachang, the village where I lived in 1948. I requested permission to do so, but word came back from CASS that "Professor Barnett will have access to all places mentioned in his proposal except Xiemachang north of Chongqing due to its closure to foreigners." I was baffled by this response, so I enlisted the assistance of Han Xu, then the Chinese ambassador in Washington, who was about to return to Beijing to attend a Party Central Committee meeting; he agreed to press for permission for me. He did so but was unsuccessful. Indirectly, I heard that the military authorities in Chengdu had blocked my request, but it was only after I reached Chongqing that I learned definitely that this was the case. However, after I reached the city, local Chongqing authorities agreed that I could visit Xiemachang briefly, even though I could not stay there, so I took up this offer.

Xiemachang turned out to be virtually unrecognizable; from the medieval village that I had studied in 1948, it had been transformed into a small modern town with a number of up-to-date factories. I could identify only a couple of old buildings that dated to the 1940s. How many of the people I had met in 1948 still lived there, I do not know. I met only one old man, a shoemaker, who could discuss the pre-1949 years with me, and he did not remember meeting me—nor did I recall meeting him. (I saw no signs of military activity in the area, which made the army's veto of my request to stay for a period in Xiemachang particularly difficult to understand.) My frustration about Xiemachang was counterbalanced, however, by the opportunity I subsequently had to do extensive interviewing about the structure and functioning of the local Party and government in several other places: in Chengdu (where I focused on provincial-level organs), in Zigong (where I discussed in detail the government of the local municipality), and in Wenjiang (where I gathered an enormous amount of information about the prefecture and subordinate units including a county, a township, and a village).

In some respects, the highlight of my stay in Sichuan was the opportunity I had to revisit the city of Kangding and the grasslands area of Ganzi. This was one of my most adventurous expeditions, in 1988 as it had been in 1948. It also was instructive in a special way because it provided fascinating and convincing evidence of the extent to which the process of modernization was reaching into even the most remote parts of China.

My third trip, in the spring of 1988, was to Xinjiang (Chinese Turkestan), China's westernmost region, which is the homeland of most of the country's Uighurs and Kazakhs. I flew to Urumqi (formerly Tihwa), capital of the region, because I did not have time to make the long rail trip, which I would have preferred. But from Urumqi I was able to make two trips by car to outlying Uighur and Kazakh areas. As in the other areas that I visited in northwestern China, I was both startled and impressed by the extent of change since my 1948 visit.

After my stay in Xinjiang, I first flew to Lanzhou, to conduct additional interviews with Gansu's leaders (including its governor) and to visit the Hui center at Linxia in the south. I then traveled by train from Lanzhou to Xi'an in Shaanxi and then to Taiyuan in Shanxi. The latter had been ruled by Yan Xishan, one of China's most notorious warlords, when I visited it in 1948. In 1988, Taiyuan, though still subject to authoritarian rule, impressed me as being much more loosely controlled than it had been when Yan had been in charge. From Xi'an, I flew to Beijing and from there back to Washington, D.C.

reached Chongqing that I learned definitely that this was the
~ver, after I reached the city, local Chongqing authorities agreed
~visit Xiemachang briefly, even though I could not stay there, so I
~s offer.
~ang turned out to be virtually unrecognizable; from the medieval
~I had studied in 1948, it had been transformed into a small mod-
~ith a number of up-to-date factories. I could identify only a cou-
~uildings that dated to the 1940s. How many of the people I had
~B still lived there, I do not know. I met only one old man, a shoe-
~) could discuss the pre-1949 years with me, and he did not re-
~eeting me—nor did I recall meeting him. (I saw no signs of mili-
~y in the area, which made the army's veto of my request to stay for
~Xiemachang particularly difficult to understand.) My frustration
~nachang was counterbalanced, however, by the opportunity I sub-
~ad to do extensive interviewing about the structure and function-
~local Party and government in several other places: in Chengdu
~cused on provincial-level organs), in Zigong (where I discussed in
~overnment of the local municipality), and in Wenjiang (where I
~n enormous amount of information about the prefecture and sub-
~nits including a county, a township, and a village).
~respects, the highlight of my stay in Sichuan was the opportunity I
~isit the city of Kangding and the grasslands area of Ganzi. This
~f my most adventurous expeditions, in 1988 as it had been in
~so was instructive in a special way because it provided fascinating
~ncing evidence of the extent to which the process of modernization
~ng into even the most remote parts of China.
~ trip, in the spring of 1988, was to Xinjiang (Chinese Turkestan),
~sternmost region, which is the homeland of most of the country's
~d Kazakhs. I flew to Urumqi (formerly Tihwa), capital of the re-
~use I did not have time to make the long rail trip, which I would
~rred. But from Urumqi I was able to make two trips by car to out-
~ur and Kazakh areas. As in the other areas that I visited in north-
~hina, I was both startled and impressed by the extent of change
~948 visit.
~y stay in Xinjiang, I first flew to Lanzhou, to conduct additional
~with Gansu's leaders (including its governor) and to visit the Hui
~inxia in the south. I then traveled by train from Lanzhou to Xi'an
~i and then to Taiyuan in Shanxi. The latter had been ruled by Yan
~e of China's most notorious warlords, when I visited it in 1948. In
~yuan, though still subject to authoritarian rule, impressed me as
~h more loosely controlled than it had been when Yan had been in
~om Xi'an, I flew to Beijing and from there back to Washington,

playing a major role at that time in defining, and debating, the country's economic reform policies.*

       *   *   *

Economic reform was at a critical juncture in 1988. China had reached a halfway point, with no clear agreement on where to move next. Throughout the year there were intense debates in Beijing, in which the men I met played key roles, about whether the next stage of economic reforms should give priority to price reform, ownership reform, broad enterprise reform, or enterprise management reform. Because of the lack of consensus, for a period of time policy was virtually stalemated. During this period, moreover, the side effects of past reforms were creating mounting problems, the most serious of which, in terms of their social and political impact, were rising inflation and growing corruption, especially in China's major eastern cities. (In response to these trends, Beijing decided in late 1988 to adopt a stringent economic austerity program, which was clearly needed but exacerbated many of China's short-term problems. All of these developments were a prelude to the political crisis in 1989, which culminated in the Tiananmen massacre.)

My time in Beijing spent learning about broad trends affecting the economy, and about the thinking of experts on economic reform, provided me with essential insights and data on the national context in which I would later judge local situations as I traveled around China. My interviews in Beijing also included some with leading reform-minded officials and academics who were pushing at that time for meaningful political reform: Bao Tong, Huan Xiang, Su Shaozhi, Yan Jiaqi, and others. What I learned from them also provided me with valuable background information and insights that formed part of the basis on which I judged Party and government trends at the local level throughout the country.

In 1988, even most of China's leading proponents of further political reform called not for sudden attempts to democratize the system but for gradual, incremental, political reforms. And there was considerable support, among reform-minded academics as well as political leaders on the forefront of political reform, for the idea of "neoauthoritarianism," conceived of as a short-term period of paternalistic, liberalized, authoritarian rule, preliminary to more extensive democratization. A few intellectuals called for more far-reaching political reforms, however, and after the Tiananmen tragedy, the thinking of many reform-minded Chinese—particularly those who left China—was radicalized, although many, both within China and abroad, still

---

*I interviewed, among others, Ma Hong, Gu Mu, Liu Guoguang, Gao Shangchuan, Wu Jinglian, Li Yining, Du Rensheng, Dong Furen, Wu Mingyu, Sun Shangqing, and Zhang Zuoying.

felt that only incremental political reform had much chance of success in the near term.

In Beijing, I also spent considerable time and effort trying to get a feel for how the rapid development and the reforms of the 1980s had affected the Chinese capital and what the quality of life for ordinary people in the city was like as a consequence. I will not try to disguise the fact that in judging the impact of "progress" in Beijing I had a strong bias. As a boy I had fallen in love with traditional Beijing on my first visit to it during the summer of 1934, and, after making the city my principal headquarters in China during 1947–1949, I had decided that, even under civil war conditions, it was the most attractive and seductive city in the world. When I first revisited Beijing in the winter of 1972–1973, it impressed me as being an extremely gloomy place: Stalinesque buildings had desecrated its main streets, and the heavy hand of Maoist totalitarian control made it seem lifeless.

However, during several subsequent visits, especially during the 1980s, I had seen the city come alive. By the late 1980s, Beijing's appearance had been transformed by a remarkable building boom, and large numbers of sleek modern apartment and office buildings had sprouted in different parts of the city. Traffic jams clogged the roads, and a highly visible foreign presence had altered the atmosphere in fundamental ways. Beijing was beginning to sound, look, and feel like other world metropolises, and, as in many such cities, while modernization and development raised living standards and unquestionably brought many benefits to ordinary citizens, the cost of such progress was substantial and the quality of life suffered. The charm of old Beijing had virtually disappeared; the hassles involved in daily living had multiplied; and it was easy to sense growing irritation and discontent with the social effects of rapid change, the erosion of traditional values, the frictions created by increasing generational differences, and uneasiness about the impact of outside influences (including Western pop culture).

*   *   *

I began my travels from Beijing in 1988 in the cold of midwinter. My first trip covered much of northwest China, a remote region that had been dominated by local warlords and was extremely underdeveloped when I had last seen it in 1948. On this segment of my travels, I made all of the longer journeys by rail and all of the shorter ones by car. I visited, in sequence, the Baotou region of central Inner Mongolia; the mixed Han and Hui Muslim area of Ningxia; the Alashan territory in western Inner Mongolia; Gansu Province, including the famous Hui center at Hezhou (Linxia) in the south; and Qinghai Province, including the Han-dominated area in the east and the Tibetan area near the lake from which Qinghai got its name. I then returned to Beijing by air.

My second trip took me to the southw[...] ince, Sichuan. While there, I also travele[...] Xikang (Sikang) Province in 1948 but h[...] (Garze) Tibetan Autonomous Prefectur[...] Sichuan, but during my month there the r[...] a little of it by train, but most of it by car[...] in most other places for several reasons. [...] lion, Sichuan is in many respects more lik[...] and I felt that it obviously deserved more t[...] I had a special feeling about Sichuan beca[...] there, traveling over much of the province[...] kang). At one point I settled into a small v[...] did an in-depth study of village governm[...] memorable and valuable experiences I eve[...] post-1949 return visit to the province had[...] the provincial capital, Chengdu, but I lear[...] was determined to learn much more, and [...]

My travels in Sichuan Province in 1988[...] to its north, to the city of Zigong (formerly[...] Chengdu and the nearby prefecture of We[...] Ganzi grasslands area in the west. In co[...] where the population is very sparse, Sich[...] minority-inhabited prefectures of Ganzi, A[...] wall-to-wall people, an incredibly crowd[...] jam-packed into small, intensely cultivat[...] densely populated cities. Sichuan was a fa[...] plex crosscurrents in China in the 1980s:[...] clearly were beginning to transform the eco[...] of deep-rooted traditions that made the pro[...] cated; the distinctive local efforts to prom[...] was provincial Party first secretary, Sichuan[...] start agricultural reform); and the inevital[...] bling blocks that made reform increasingly [...]

The one serious disappointment I had in[...] tain permission to spend a period of time in[...] lived in 1948. I requested permission to d[...] CASS that "Professor Barnett will have acce[...] proposal except Xiemachang north of Cho[...] eigners." I was baffled by this response, so [...] Xu, then the Chinese ambassador in Washi[...] to Beijing to attend a Party Central Commi[...] for permission for me. He did so but was [...] that the military authorities in Chengdu had[...]

only after[...] case. How[...] that I cou[...] took up t[...]

Xiemac[...] village tha[...] ern town [...] ple of old[...] met in 19[...] maker, w[...] member [...] tary activ[...] a period [...] about Xi[...] sequentl[...] ing of th[...] (where I [...] detail th[...] gathered[...] ordinate[...]

In som[...] had to r[...] was one[...] 1948. It [...] and con[...] was rea[...]

My th[...] China's [...] Uighurs[...] gion, be[...] have pr[...] lying U[...] western[...] since m[...]

After[...] intervie[...] center [...] in Shaa[...] Xishan[...] 1988, [...] being r[...] charge[...] D.C.

Left:
The entrance to Xiemachang's covered, arcaded main street. Lined with traditional shops, it was the only real street in 1948.

Below:
One of Xiemachang's numerous specialized markets, situated adjacent to the village center. Held on regularly scheduled days, they were attended by peasants and traders from all over the township (Xiang) and from more distant places.

Above left:
A tenant farmer and his family,
wearing clothing typical of the
entire region in 1948. Their
poverty was like that of the
majority of Sichuan peasants
at that time.

Above right:
Planting rice and carrying water
using age-old methods, 1948.

Right:
A Chinese landlord near Xiema-
chang, Sichuan, 1948.

The only two 1948-vintage buildings that I saw in 1988 were at the entrance to the 1948 arcaded main street, now gone. A medium-sized high-rise is in the background.

Xiemachang's new main street in 1988. Public buildings, stores, and small factories superseded traditional structures.

Right:
An elderly shoemaker in a
modern side street in Xiema-
chang in 1988. He was the
only person I met who could
discuss memories of 1948.

Below:
The attire of this young peasant
woman, who is pulling a cart
with farm produce, dramati-
cally symbolizes the differences
between 1988 and 1948.

*   *   *

In September, I again flew to Beijing, to start the second major part of my project. (My wife, Jeanne, joined me for the first six weeks, and apart from providing good company, she added an important dimension to my trip because she was able to conduct separate interviews with people concerned with women's and religious issues, two areas in which she had a special interest and knowledge.) From Beijing, we traveled by train all the way south to the Yangzi valley. Our major stops included Tianjin and Qingdao. In 1948, I had investigated Tianjin's industry and foreign trade, which were crippled at that time by the effects of China's civil war. In 1988, Tianjin not only was one of China's most important economic centers, as it had been in 1948, but its industry had expanded enormously. It had been greatly damaged by the great Tangshan earthquake of 1986, but by 1988 it had largely recovered, and an impressive process of rebuilding was under way. It also, like most places along the coast, was attempting to take full advantage of China's new open policy and was energetically soliciting foreign investment and trying to promote foreign trade. By this time virtually every city along China's coast was preoccupied by the task of expanding foreign economic relations, I was to learn as I traveled down the coast.

Qingdao was a city that I had known as a boy, from summer vacations that I had spent there; I had also lived there briefly as a U.S. Marine in 1945. My last pre-1949 stop there had been in 1947. At that time, Qingdao was a center of only limited industry (some of its industry dated to the period of German control, which lasted from the late nineteenth century until World War I). In 1988, however, I learned that its industrial base was vastly larger than it had been in the 1940s. The city still had a unique German flavor, and its beaches still attracted large numbers of vacationers (now mainly Chinese rather than foreigners), but its atmosphere was very different from what I remembered from the past. It was now working hard to be accepted as a big league player among China's industrial cities, and like other coastal cities it was trying to increase its trade and attract more foreign investment.

Until I reached Shanghai, the Chinese Academy of Social Sciences had been responsible for major arrangements for each segment of my trip. During most of October, however, my host organization in Shanghai, and on the trips that I made from there through Jiangsu, Anhui, and Zhejiang provinces, was the Shanghai People's Association for Friendship with Foreign Countries. Its head, Li Shoubao, was a friend whom I had first met in the 1940s, and he took time from his very busy schedule to accompany us throughout most of the Yangzi valley region. (After he had to return to Shanghai, his son, Li Yaping, became our traveling companion.) I had a very special feeling about Shanghai, because it had been my real hometown for the first 15 years of my life. I had stopped there many times in later years, in

1945 and in 1947–1948, and thereafter, from 1972 on, I had again visited it frequently. Shanghai is a unique place. Even those who are repelled by its mixture of Chinese and Western ways, its Brooklyneselike dialect, and its commercialism and hectic pace of life agree that there is no other place quite like it. It has long been China's largest city, its biggest industrial center, and its leading port for foreign trade. In addition, it has been China's most cosmopolitan city and a major intellectual and cultural center as well. Shanghai's factories, technicians, and skilled workers have played a major role in industrializing other parts of China ever since the 1940s, and it was Shanghai entrepreneurs and workers who fled to Hong Kong during 1948–1949 who were the main developers of industry in Hong Kong. In the Maoist era, Shanghai was an anomaly in many respects, a place of great contradictions. On the one hand it was the prime symbol of "bourgeois" influences from the West and therefore was considered by Maoists to be dangerously subversive. On the other hand, it was a hotbed of nativistic radicalism and was the headquarters of the Party's most "leftist" leaders—the "Gang of Four"—during the Cultural Revolution.

In 1988, my local hosts arranged for Jeanne and me to interview not only the top city leaders but also a wide range of working-level officials, academics, businessmen, journalists, religious leaders, women's leaders, and others. I also visited several types of factories and talked at length with their managers. And I explored virtually every part of the city and its suburbs. I was not surprised, but nevertheless was impressed, by the enormous expansion of modern industry—and by what I sensed to be a new vitality and energy in the city life. When I had visited Shanghai in the 1970s, during the twilight of the Maoist era, it had seemed to me to be shabby, run-down, inward-looking, and dispirited. It was still suffering the aftereffects of the Cultural Revolution. In 1988, it had come alive. Like all of coastal China, it was "on the move." Shanghai's shops were full of goods, and its population enjoyed a living standard well above that in most of China. Many old industries were modernizing. A major building boom was under way, and I could see its old cosmopolitan traditions reemerging.

Yet Shanghai was obviously still a city in economic trouble. Although a progressive attitude dominated among its top leaders, its bureaucratic establishment resisted change. Its huge state enterprises were in serious trouble, changing at only a glacial pace, if at all; most were extremely inefficient, and many were losing money. Enormous housing and transportation problems, requiring huge new investments, plagued the city, and much of the city's industrial equipment was outdated.

The local leadership was trying to cope with these problems—with some success—but needed much greater capital to do so effectively. One basic reason that they were short of capital was the fact that the city had to contribute a huge percentage of the revenue to the central government's budget. For years, Shanghai had been Beijing's largest source of taxes—a kind of fiscal milk cow for the national treasury. However, the leaders I met in Shanghai outlined ambitious plans for projects to attack all of the city's problems, and these proved to be much more than pie-in-the-sky or idle daydreaming.*

From Shanghai, we journeyed, by train and car, through much of the Yangzi valley, making stops in Jiangsu Province at Suzhou, Wuxi, Changzhou, Yixing, and Nanjing, in Anhui Province at Tunxi and Huang Shan, and in Zhejiang Province at Hangzhou. I was really astonished by much of what we saw. Even though this region had long been one of the most economically advanced areas of China, and in the Maoist era had developed substantially, in the 1980s its economy took off like a rocket, in a very new way, and the results were highly visible. The countryside had been transformed, in large part as a result of decollectivization. Signs of rural prosperity could be seen everywhere. Among the most dramatic symbols of the new prosperity were the peasant houses: Old-style farmhouses had virtually disappeared and had been replaced by large, spacious, multistory brick dwellings. (In some areas these looked, from a distance, almost like suburban areas in the West.) Throughout the region, in both urban and rural areas, there had been an amazing growth of small and medium-sized factories, classified as village and township enterprises, collective enterprises, or private enterprises; these had become by far the most dynamic sectors of the industrial economy. Not only in suburban areas but throughout much of the countryside in this region I saw such industries everywhere and visited several of them; they, even more than the new housing, symbolized the far-reaching changes that the reform policies had produced.

The cities in this region were also being rapidly transformed. The appearance of high-rise modern buildings was altering urban skylines. The spirit of entrepreneurship, which had been characteristic of this region before 1949 but had been suppressed for more than three decades, was reviving throughout the region. The mood of smaller cities in the area was even more dynamic and innovative than that of Shanghai, partly because these cities lacked the monstrous bureaucracies and huge state enterprises that dominated Shanghai. But Shanghai nevertheless was the engine for much of what was taking place. Virtually all areas in the Yangzi valley had developed relationships of either dependency or symbiosis with Shanghai. The entire region, moreover, was turning its attention outward in a fairly dramatic way,

---

*By 1991, Shanghai's leaders had embarked, with central Party and government support, on a huge development program centering on the development of Pudong—across the river from old Shanghai—which they hoped would help Shanghai become the dynamo for rapid development of the entire Yangzi valley and a major international center of trade and finance, as it was before World War II.

and its producers were increasingly export oriented. It was clear that the Yangzi valley was rapidly becoming integrated into the Asian-Pacific trading community. (In this, it was second only to the coastal area of south China, centered on Guangdong Province—with its special economic zones and the Pearl River delta—but also including Fujian Province and Hainan Island, which in 1988 was broken off from Guangdong and made into a separate province.)

*   *   *

My original plan had called for flying from Shanghai to Wuhan, the principal industrial center of central China, located on the Yangzi River a little less than midway between Shanghai and Chongqing. This was the only part of my entire itinerary that I was compelled to cancel because of insoluble transportation problems. But I learned some interesting things even from my abortive attempt to reach Wuhan. I took off from Shanghai's Hongiao Airport in a small Chinese-made prop plane (a Yun-7), jam-packed with about 50 Chinese passengers (I was the only foreigner), but within a few minutes we learned that the pilots could not lock the plane's wheels in place, either up or down, so, while the co-pilot tried frantically to lock them with a hand crank, the principal pilot turned the plane back toward Shanghai, where we finally made an emergency landing, with much excitement and full mobilization of all the airport's fire trucks and disaster paraphernalia. We did not know until we touched the ground whether the co-pilot's cranking had worked, but fortunately it had, and we avoided a disaster. I and the other passengers (except for some who gave up right away) spent the next three days at the airport and three nights in nearby hotels, all the while mystified by what was going on. Meanwhile the company owning our airplane (a local branch airline called the Dongfang—the East or Orient—Airline) first tried, unsuccessfully, to obtain a missing part and then attempted, also without success, to find a replacement airplane.

Our airline, however, did arrange for overnight stays in nearby hotels (a different one each night) and paid for them; the accommodations were simple, but I found each place interesting. We first stopped at a small Chinese hotel near the airport, then in another semimodern but rather seedy army-run hotel in a remote suburb of Shanghai. Neither I nor my Chinese fellow passengers could ever obtain any reliable information on whether or when we might be able to depart again. By the fourth day, when the waiting passengers had dwindled to less than a dozen, I crossed Wuhan off my itinerary and decided to go directly by train to Changsha, the capital of Hunan Province (the home province of Mao and many other early Chinese Communist leaders); it proved to be a long (from 5:55 P.M. one day to 8:07 P.M. the next) but interesting trip.

In Changsha, I was again impressed, as I was repeatedly in most areas that I visited in China in 1988, by the remarkable changes that had occurred since I had visited the city in 1948. Changsha was now much more modern and developed than I had remembered it or expected it to be. After numerous interviews with local people, however, I decided that even though the reforms of the 1980s had had a significant impact on the city, and on Hunan Province as a whole, the ghost of Mao still hung over the area much more than in any other place in China that I visited. There were monuments to Mao, and many other reminders of his association with the city, in numerous parts of Changsha; in some of my interviews, moreover, I sensed that at least some local people were much less enthusiastic about repudiating Mao, and Maoism, than people in other parts of China generally were. (I was reminded of a visit I had made not long before to the Republic of Georgia, in the USSR, where I found that local people tended to be very critical of Moscow but much less willing to denounce their fellow Georgian, Stalin, than people elsewhere were.)

However, when I made the mandatory one-day pilgrimage to Mao's birthplace, in Shaoshan, I found that his childhood home and the nearby museum focusing on his life, which millions of people had visited in the 1960s and 1970s, were now almost empty. In most of China in 1988, my impression was that Mao had almost become a nonperson, and his slogans and writings appeared to have been virtually forgotten, at least temporarily. In several cities, I visited state bookstores, where I found, to my astonishment, that his books had disappeared from the shelves. Sic transit gloria! The fickleness of history struck me especially forcefully because when I had visited Chiang Kai-shek's birthplace in Fenghua in 1987 I had been amazed to see that his home had become a major political shrine, and a special hotel had been built to accommodate Overseas Chinese visitors to it. (By 1990, however, it appeared that the muse of history might be playing capricious games again: In the aftermath of the Tiananmen disaster, there were some signs of what seemed to me to be a perverse revival of interest in Mao among some young people who were most critical about the leaders responsible for the Tiananmen massacre, and I read reports of an increase in the number of visitors to Mao's birthplace in Shaoshan.)

*   *   *

After leaving Changsha, I embarked on another long train journey, south to Guangdong, and I made its capital, Guangzhou, my base for the final weeks of my project. From Guangzhou, I made my final foray into west China, flying to Kunming, capital of Yunnan Province, and from there I made a long trip by car to the city of Gejiu, China's "tin capital," located near the border of Vietnam. When I had made my previous visit to Kunming, in the 1970s, it was obvious to me that the city had developed a great deal since I had first visited it in 1949. But it was also obvious that it had not recovered from the demoralization and destruction inflicted by the Cultural Revolution, and it seemed to be a fairly lifeless place. In 1988, by contrast, I was impressed by how much Kunming had been revitalized and modernized during the 1980s. Like Changsha, the city's appearance had radically changed as a result of a building boom: Tall, modern, high-rise office and apartment buildings now soared in many parts of the city. Changes in Yunnan's countryside were less striking but impressed me as being significant, nevertheless. The long trip that I made to Gejiu took me through some of the poorest rural areas that I had seen anywhere during my travels in 1988, but even there I saw many signs of the creeping spread of modernization and the acceleration of development When I reached Gejiu I found that the changes were so great that I could not recognize the place.

I spent my final days in China in 1988 in Guangzhou and adjacent areas including Shenzhen, China's most rapidly developing special economic zone, and then I exited China via Hong Kong. In the 1980s, Guangdong had become China's most dynamic and fastest-growing province. There were many reasons for this, including the area's traditional self-assertiveness and distinctiveness, its long contacts with foreign countries, and its past experience with trade. But there were many other more important reasons for its explosion of entrepreneurship and remarkable dynamism. Most important, undoubtedly, was its proximity to Hong Kong, which had developed in the years after the Communist takeover on the China mainland into one of the world's most successful examples of free enterprise and freewheeling trade and entrepreneurship. Beijing's decision, soon after its adoption of an open policy, to encourage Guangdong—and Fujian Province as well—to take the lead in expanding foreign trade and trying to attract foreign investment opened up unprecedented opportunities for south China.

Still another reason for Guangdong's success was the fact that Beijing gave preferential treatment, and many special privileges, not only to the special economic zones in Guangdong and Fujian, but also to the two provinces as a whole. One of the most important advantages was that the taxes that they were required to pay to the central government were incomparably lower than the levies imposed on all of the other coastal provinces. As a result, more foreign investment flowed into south China—most of it into Guangdong—than into any other area of the country. Small and medium-sized collective and private industries developed at a breakneck pace, faster than anywhere else. The area's economy turned outward and was oriented basically toward Hong Kong and the world economy, to an extent impossible for other areas of China, and the region's foreign trade rose at an extraordinary pace. To many Chinese elsewhere, Guangdong became a symbol of how to "get rich" fast—a place that was envied, imitated, and admired, but also resented, by others.

By the late 1980s, the economic interactions, and symbiotic relationships, between Hong Kong and Guangdong—and much of the rest of south China as well—had gone far toward creating a new economic region where international boundaries were blurred. Two-way travel, trade, and investment were creating economic bonds that seemed to foreshadow not only the integration of Hong Kong into China in 1997 but also the emergence of what could be called an area of "greater China" encompassing Hong Kong, south China, Taiwan, and perhaps other Chinese areas abroad as well. In effect, the influence of the "Hong Kong model" was spreading throughout the region. Hong Kong had become the engine of economic growth in south China and the funnel for powerful external influences emanating from the entire industrial world.

Hong Kong was a place that I had known for a great many years, yet in 1988 I was again awed by its seemingly limitless kinetic energy. When I first visited Hong Kong, in 1947, it was still a sleepy colonial town; it had little industry and depended mainly on its traditional entrepôt trade. Then, in the 1950s and 1960s, when I lived there for six years, I was impressed by how, given half a chance, Chinese businessmen could become world-class entrepreneurs. At the time of the Communist takeover in China, many of Shanghai's textile barons, together with many of their skilled workers, migrated to Hong Kong, and in a few years these new arrivals really industrialized the economy of this British colony—much as Westerners and Japanese had industrialized Shanghai earlier in the century. In repeated visits to Hong Kong in subsequent years, I was constantly astounded by the pace of its growth and development; the face of the city seemed to change almost entirely every two or three years. By the late 1980s, Hong Kong's population was approaching 6 million. It had become one of the most important centers of trade, finance, and industry in East Asia and was playing a very significant global role as well. It also acquired the look of such a center. The downtown area, on Victoria Island, now consisted of tightly packed, extremely modernistic skyscrapers; the city resembled most world capitals but was more modern and futuristic. Comparing it to New York, I would say that downtown Hong Kong in the 1980s combined Wall Street, central Manhattan, and Fifth Avenue and seemed more modern than any of these areas.

In 1988, there was rising uneasiness in Hong Kong about its future, as the 1997 date for its retrocession to China (agreed upon in a Sino-British pact signed in 1984) crept nearer. Even though Beijing had pledged not to change Hong Kong's basic economy and social system for half a century, many Hong Kong residents had little confidence in this promise (especially after the Tiananmen tragedy in Beijing), and large numbers of those belonging to the most talented managerial and professional groups were migrating elsewhere (and thousands of others were trying to make arrangements to make a move later, nearer to 1997). There also was a sizable outflow of capital from

Hong Kong. Yet many people (including many Japanese and Western investors) still believed that the place had an important future, so as local experts and money flowed outward, there was new investment and an infusion of some new people into the colony. Moreover, even though some of Hong Kong's own investors had serious doubts about future trends in China, their involvements on the mainland were so great it was difficult to see how their ties with south China could be severed. By the late 1980s, there were many more workers employed by Hong Kong companies who were located in south China than there were in the colony itself, and the Hong Kong dollar was rapidly becoming the major medium of exchange in Shenzhen and beyond. However difficult the transition to Chinese rule would be in 1997, the intertwining of the economies and interests of Hong Kong and south China appeared to be irreversible.

Shenzhen, just across the border, had been a mere farming village when I first saw it in 1949, peering with binoculars across the border to watch the arriving Communist troops raise their flag above the village for the first time. It was still not much more than a village throughout most of the Maoist era, even though it became the place where most foreign visitors had to walk across a small bridge to enter Chinese territory. Shenzhen's transformation in the 1980s, after it was made a special economic zone, was nothing short of astounding. By 1988, its business center was dominated by tall, modernistic skyscrapers, and the center of the city had begun to look very much like Hong Kong. Shenzhen had become the undisputed headquarters of freewheeling and freebooting entrepreneurship in China. One consequence was a rapid, almost runaway, pace of economic development; another, however, was an equally rapid spread of popular Western culture accompanied by rampant corruption and prostitution.

Similar trends were visible—although in less extreme forms—in Guangzhou, and throughout Guangdong Province as a whole. It was by no means new for Guangzhou (Canton) to be one of China's major metropolises; it had had this status for centuries. However, when I first visited it in the 1940s, it had little modern industry. My memories of it in those days are dominated not by symbols of modernity but by images of old-fashioned, mold-covered, arcaded shops and buildings of a kind that were characteristic of most of southern Asian cities in that period. By the late 1980s, although some of the oldest areas of the city still looked like they had in the 1940s, much of the city had been modernized and looked increasingly like Hong Kong. The transformation of Guangdong's surrounding countryside was what was most astounding. Throughout the Pearl River delta, thousands of small new factories had been established, and millions of farmers had shifted from agriculture to industrial work—and other nonfarm employment. Even so, the local labor force was unable to meet the demand for nonfarm employment, and huge numbers of peasants and workers had migrated to Hong Kong from other areas of the country. Moreover, virtually all of those who still lived and worked in the countryside had built large and comfortable new houses, and the majority enjoyed a standard of living that would have been unimaginable in rural areas of China before the 1980s.

I observed, also, how the influence of Hong Kong, Shenzhen, and Guangdong was spreading inexorably into neighboring areas. It was strongest in adjacent provinces such as Hunan, but I found that even in some very remote areas of the country south China was exerting a new and growing influence. In many places its impact rivaled—and in some it appeared to have surpassed—that of Shanghai, which for decades had been the most important source of modernizing influences reaching other parts of China.

By the late 1980s, it was evident that a broad belt of coastal China would play a pivotal role in the economic development of the entire country and would be given special treatment by Beijing to do so. Both on their own initiative and with the urging of national leaders, these areas were turning increasingly outward, developing a strong export orientation, and stepping up their efforts to solicit foreign investments and loans. This entire coastal zone seemed destined to be rapidly integrated into the East Asian and world economic system. But coastal provinces were also expected to assist less-developed interior provinces in eventually catching up economically.

Beijing's adoption of a so-called coastal policy codified these ideas. China, it was said, consisted of three zones or "fronts," one along the coast, one in the middle of the country, and one in the far west. Modernization and development were expected to take place most rapidly in the coastal area and then "trickle down" to the second and third zones. There was a plausible logic behind this policy, but it clearly created new problems, and by 1988 there were widespread complaints about the resulting inequities.

All over China, people I met in 1988 believed—and accepted that it was inevitable—that two coastal areas would continue for the indefinite future to be in the forefront of China's development: south China and the Yangzi valley. Few if any people expected Guangdong to catch up with Shanghai in large-scale heavy industry, but a great many people felt that because of its proximity to Hong Kong, Guangdong would be in the forefront of economic reform in China and would enjoy advantages over Shanghai for some time to come. It was already clear that competition between Shanghai and Guangdong was intense and that this was likely to have a significant impact on the future of the entire Chinese economy. The gap between the entire coastal region and the country's midsection and far west also seemed destined to increase. (My own guess was that Beijing would eventually be compelled to modify its coastal policy in order to respond to the dissatisfaction over the inevitable inequities that resulted from it.)

*   *   *

In 1988, I learned a great deal about all of the places that I visited. The next task that I faced was to determine how best to communicate to others at least some of what I had learned. The first thing I did was review all of my notes. When I did so, and in the process put together some simple statistics on exactly what I had done during the year, I was flabbergasted by the figures.

Altogether, I traveled (in rounded figures) 17,500 miles within China in 1988. Of this total, 9,000 miles were on the ground—5,500 by train and 3,500 by car.* My travels in 1988 took me to 19 "provinces" (that is, provinces and provincial-level autonomous regions and municipalities) plus Hong Kong. I made working visits to, and interviewed people in, 47 cities, towns, and villages (of the total, 25 were large cities; the other 22 were medium-sized or small cities, towns, or villages), and I stopped overnight and slept in 32 of the 47. In every city in which I stayed, I made a point of making a careful and extensive tour, with local map in hand, of the entire urban area. In addition, I passed through or by, and therefore at least obtained glimpses of, hundreds of other urban centers and thousands of miles of countryside.

I interviewed a total of close to 800 people of many kinds and took notes during virtually all of these interviews. This number does not count the hundreds of casual conversations that I had. My visits took me to many institutions of numerous sorts. These included 30 factories (of varying sizes and types); 12 farms (some engaged in agriculture, others in animal husbandry); more than 30 religious institutions (lamaseries, Buddhist temples, mosques, and Protestant and Catholic churches); and more than 25 academic, research, and educational institutions. I also met quite a few journalists. I was able to visit a wide range of minority areas, including four inhabited by Hui Muslims, four Tibetan areas, three Mongol areas, two inhabited by Uighurs, two Kazakh areas, and one inhabited by Yi people. Everywhere I went I carried with me small notebooks that fit into my jacket pocket, and in them I made detailed notes on my interviews and entered observations and reflections on what I saw. Altogether, these notes filled more than 4,600 pages in 44 notebooks. Almost everywhere, also, I obtained some locally published materials, and in every region, province, and city I obtained detailed local maps. I also carried with me a fully automatic camera and used it to make a photographic record of almost all the places I visited. Later I used these pho-

---

*These figures were comparable to those for my travels during the entire two years that I spent in China in the late 1940s. During 1947–1949, however, most of my travel to remote areas in China had been on the back of open mail trucks, and I had spent more than a week hiking, eight days riding horseback, and several days riding old-fashioned donkey carts. In 1988, I did not try to make any long trips to places that could not be reached by some sort of modern, enclosed vehicle.

tographs, together with my notes, to refresh my memory of places as well as people. Many years earlier, I had learned that it is virtually impossible for a single individual to make a full and detailed written record of a trip and also produce professional photographs, but in 1988 I discovered that with a fully automatic camera I could at least keep a useful visual diary.

These statistics do not reveal very much about my travels, except that my journeys were extremely busy and exhausting. More important was the kind of people I was able to interview. From the time I started planning my project, I knew that to achieve my objective it would be essential to interview a very wide range of knowledgeable people. In preparation for my project, therefore, I began in 1987 writing letters to try to impress upon my host organization, CASS, that the success of my project depended fundamentally on my being granted access to local political leaders, and a wide range of other specialists and institutions, in every place that I visited. I tried, as best as I could, to mention specific people as well as specific places that I wished to see, but this was extremely difficult because I simply did not know who the key people were in most remote places. I had to depend heavily in most instances, therefore, on the judgments of CASS, which passed on my requests and tried to obtain local cooperation in setting up the kinds of visits and interviews that I wished. Each place I was to visit was requested to prepare a tentative program and schedule, which I could discuss with them after I arrived.

*   *   *

Once I started my travels, my basic modus operandi followed a fairly consistent pattern. Upon reaching a city or town, I would immediately discuss in detail with my hosts the program that they had put together prior to my arrival. Almost invariably, it was necessary thereafter to negotiate, to modify the program and add interviews and visits to those already planned. Usually I had substantial success in such negotiations, but rarely did I have complete success. My escorts from CASS played an essential role in this process as well as in making travel and other arrangements. They also served as interpreters when needed. I conducted some interviews in Chinese myself, without interpretation, but in others I relied on my escorts to serve as interpreters partly because it made it much easier for me to take full notes during the interviews—which was especially important when I interviewed high political leaders. For different segments of my travel, CASS provided me with three different escorts (I will have something to say about each of them later). However, in Sichuan, Guangdong, and Yunnan, I relied entirely on local Academy staff members.

Although CASS faced an enormous challenge in trying to arrange what I requested, generally it was able to set up most things I had asked for. But this was not always the case. There were clearly limits to what any research organization in Beijing could accomplish by letters and telegrams to organizations in other parts of the country. CASS had no line authority over local academies, each of which functioned essentially as an independent entity, even though most maintained significant ties with CASS. It had even less influence, and no control, in its dealings with local government foreign affairs bureaus. Arranging my program in each place I visited therefore required a great deal of negotiating, both before and after my arrival. The interactions between representatives of CASS and the key people in local academies and foreign affairs bureaus were interesting to watch. They involved subtle processes that I perceived only dimly. However, I often sensed, rightly or wrongly, that local organizations were signaling to my CASS escorts that in return for their cooperation in assisting me it would not be unreasonable for them to expect return favors of some sort from CASS. There were inevitable tensions between CASS and the local organization. One recurring problem resulted from the fact that local organizations often tried to charge the highest possible prices for the services they provided to me (in 1988 virtually every organization in China that had any contact with foreigners was obsessed with finding ways to earn foreign exchange) while CASS consistently tried to keep within bounds the research costs of all foreign scholars involved in exchange programs carried out under its aegis.

Neither CASS nor most local academies seemed to have much real clout when requesting access to leaders who worked primarily within the Party apparatus or the military establishment, whether in Beijing or in local areas. The main links that academic institutions had with higher authorities were usually with government agencies rather than Party or military organizations. The effectiveness of the local academies in arranging interviews with top local leaders, especially Party and military leaders but even civilian leaders as well, depended very much on the kind of personal ties they had with such leaders or with key members of their personal staffs. In provincial and other local governments, the gatekeepers controlling access to the top leaders were generally their secretaries-general plus their foreign affairs bureau chiefs and personal secretaries. Often the ability of my local hosts to arrange interviews for me with top political leaders depended on the degree to which they not only had good contacts but also were prepared to expend some political capital to arrange such interviews with leaders who were obviously extremely busy.

Despite all the difficulties of making arrangements, everywhere I went (with only one exception) I was able to meet and interview at least one top government leader. At the regional, provincial, and municipal level, this was in some instances the chairman, governor, or mayor, and in others it was the senior deputy, usually the so-called executive (*changwu*) deputy. At lower levels in the system, I was almost always able to meet the top government leaders. However, I had much less success in meeting top Party and military leaders, but I was persistent and did meet some. My insistence on trying to meet top leaders was based not simply on the fact that they were important sources of information but also because I wished to judge for myself the characteristics and qualities of the new leaders who had emerged all over China in recent years, to compare them to local leaders I had met in earlier years.

Besides meeting some top leaders, I had numerous interviews everywhere with officials responsible for particular fields of activity that were of special interest to me. The largest number of these were individuals responsible for economic affairs, who worked in local planning commissions, economic commissions, economic structural reform commissions, and departments or bureaus responsible for industry, agriculture, and foreign economic relations. In every factory and farm that I visited, I talked at length with the resident managers, and in factories I also spoke with the chief engineers. Because of my long-standing interest in Chinese bureaucracies, I also interviewed quite a few officials specifically about the organization and functioning of the government and the Party, trends in personnel policies, and the progress, if any, in political reform. At the provincial level, government secretaries-general and personnel officers were particularly informative about these matters. From such interviews, I gathered a considerable amount of data about local government in almost all of the regions, provinces, and larger cities that I visited as well as in the more than 20 prefectures, counties, townships, and villages where I conducted interviews.

In almost all the places I visited, I also talked with people dealing with education; in larger cities, these included university leaders, professors, other intellectuals, and some students as well as education officials. Wherever I could, I also talked with local journalists. In a few places I was able to meet young writers, sociologists, and women's leaders. And throughout west China, I spent a great deal of time interviewing representatives of minority and religious groups in addition to government and Party officials dealing with them.

The fact that my interviews covered such a wide range of people, in so many places, made it possible for me to learn a tremendous amount about the areas I visited—more, in fact, than I had anticipated. However, I was acutely aware that what I learned on many subjects was inevitably fragmentary and partial. Even though my probing of those I interviewed was extremely intensive, because of the limitations of time I was unable to follow up on many critical questions and issues. Often I simply had to leave a subject hanging because I was unable to find time to return to it and probe more deeply. My contacts, moreover, were overwhelmingly with members of China's elite. I was able to meet quite a few ordinary workers and peasants—members of China's *laobaixing*—but fewer than I had in 1948, when I had made longer stays in the countryside and in some cities.

Furthermore, I cannot claim that I really got to know many of the people whom I met. In some of the major cities in east China, I was able to talk with some old friends, including individuals I had first gotten to know in the 1940s; my conversations with them were qualitatively different from the formal interviews that I had with most other people. But in remote interior areas I encountered almost no one whom I had met in the 1940s. Most of those I specifically asked about had died or retired or simply disappeared. (In all of west China, only two persons I met claimed to have remembered me from my 1948 visit, and I did not remember meeting either of them.) I believe that it is no exaggeration to say that my opportunity to meet and talk with so many people in so many parts of China was unique in some respects and that I was able to obtain insights from my many interviews that could not have been obtained any other way. At the same time, I was fully aware that what I was doing could, in many respects, be best described by an old Chinese saying: "*Zouma guanhua,*" meaning "viewing the flowers from horseback."

I was extremely fortunate in the timing of my project. In 1988, the majority of people I interviewed were remarkably open and frank and eager to talk. Political controls in China had been greatly loosened since the start of reforms in 1978. Even though there were major ups and downs in the process of liberalization during the 1980s, it was very evident to me that there was much less fear on the part of most people of the Party's enforcers of orthodoxy or its policemen, and there were many fewer inhibitions about speaking one's mind than had been the case in China for decades. I had observed this trend developing throughout the 1980s, and I believe it reached a peak in 1988 and early 1989, before the Tiananmen crisis. If I had planned to carry out my project either a couple of years earlier or a year later, it probably would not have been possible to do what I did.

                              *   *   *

I returned to the United States in late 1988 exhilarated by what I had seen and learned and eager to start writing about the whole experience. Then, a few months later, the Tiananmen massacre shocked the Chinese people and the world. The conservative Party elders proceeded, after the crisis in June 1989, to try to tighten ideological and political controls throughout China. Like most China specialists, for many months I was totally preoccupied with the June tragedy and its aftermath, and I put on hold my plans to write a book. For a while, in fact, I was uncertain whether I should postpone my writing indefinitely or even abandon the idea of a book, for two reasons. First of all, I did not know how far the political repression and purging in China would go and could not help but ask myself whether writing a book about my experience in 1988, under the conditions existing after Tiananmen, might have damaging consequences for all those who had assisted me and perhaps even for those who had granted me interviews. Second, I was uncertain, as most observers were, whether the impact of the crisis in China might be so profound that what I had learned about the country in 1988 would soon become obsolete or irrelevant.

However, on reflection I decided that there were important reasons to proceed with my plans to write about what I had learned. I concluded that the post-Tiananmen crisis in no way reduced the value of attempting to compare China in the 1980s with China in the 1940s and to identify long-term trends, major changes, and important continuities. Moreover, after some months had passed I came to the conclusion that the conservatives who emerged to the top in Beijing would simply be unable to turn back the clock in any fundamental way. Following the 1989 crisis, these conservative leaders pursued policies that were both regressive and repressive, and the result was a serious setback in China's development and reform process. However, it gradually became clear, to me at least, that in many respects the effects of what they were trying to do were superficial and likely to be temporary.

Apart from Zhao Ziyang and a small group of his closest associates who were purged, the majority of the regime's reformers and new technocratic leaders kept their jobs; they seemed to be simply waiting for leadership changes that could put the country back on the course of active reform. The worst repression was targeted on those intellectuals and students (and some workers) who were most directly involved in the demonstrations during 1989. Although Beijing attempted to impose tight new ideological and political controls on intellectuals, and all media, the effects, in my judgment, were superficial. Most intellectuals simply pulled in their horns and refrained from stating their views publicly, but many of them continued to be remarkably frank, in private, in condemning conservative leaders and many of their policies. They, too, seemed to be holding their breath and waiting for the Party's conservative elders to die, hoping that when this happened more active reform would be resumed.

On the basis of judgments such as these, I concluded in 1990 that I should start writing the book. But almost immediately I confronted another dilemma: I had gathered so much data that it would be impossible to include all of my findings in a single volume. What would be necessary, I decided, was to deal separately with what I had learned about three major regions of China: the most advanced, dynamic, and rapidly changing coastal regions of China; the major interior provinces in the middle of the country; and the country's far western regions, which are the most underdeveloped parts of the country and unique because of their minority populations.

After a good deal of soul searching, I decided I would first write a book on China's far west; this volume is the result.

It would be easy to argue that the logical starting point should have been China's coastal provinces because they are the most advanced, rapidly changing, and dynamic areas of the country and they will clearly take the lead in China's modernization and reform as it moves toward the twenty-first century. A case could also be made that the three major interior provinces that I studied—Sichuan, Shanxi, and Hunan—are more important than areas in China's far west; each is an area of special interest and significance, and together they have a population approaching 200 million, which is more than that in most major nations. My decision to focus first on China's least-developed, minority-inhabited, outlying provinces may, therefore, seem quixotic, but I nevertheless decided that there were good reasons for doing so. These are by far the least-known areas in China; even the majority of Chinese know little about them, and to most foreigners they are terra incognito. I therefore decided that adding to knowledge about them could help to fill a serious gap in understanding China as a whole.

Second, I decided that precisely because these regions have been so remote, and are so backward, relative to most of the rest of the country, describing the changes that I observed in them in the four decades since 1948 could provide especially useful insights into the strength and pervasiveness of the forces for development and modernization throughout China in the years since the 1940s. Because these areas had been hardly touched by the twentieth century when I first visited them, I found that the evidence of recent trends toward modernization was particularly striking. Third, I felt that although the reforms of the 1980s were obviously having their greatest effect in coastal provinces, what I learned about the implementations of the reform policies in the western provinces provided important indicators of both the force and outreach of the reforms and the difficulties, obstacles, and limits to reform in the country as a whole. This was so partly because of the obvious special difficulties of carrying out reform in these outlying areas.

*   *   *

Having explained why I decided to focus this book on China's far west, I should also make clear what kind of a book it is—and is not. I would call it a combination of travelogue, scholarship, journalistic reporting, and personal reflections—a kind of Chinese bouillabaisse (or, perhaps, chop suey!). In some respects, it is clearly a travel book, although it is not designed for casual tourists. I describe in some detail all of the places that I visited. It is an account of my own odyssey—or rather odysseys, since it is based on my travels in both 1948 and 1988—and of my own intellectual journey in search of a better understanding of China. But in some respects it is also a commentary on China's odyssey—that is, its long and difficult path toward modernization. It is hardly a conventional travel book: It contains far too much economic and political data, presented in either a scholarly or journalistic way, to fit that genre. I would say that in some respects it is a scholarly study and in others a journalistic account—and yet, in many respects, it is neither. I tried to invent a term that would describe the kind of amalgam of scholarly and repertorial approaches that I have used. The phrases that came to mind were academic reporting and journalistic research, but both sounded so dull that I quickly abandoned them, and in fact I abandoned any attempt to find a concise label to describe the book. Simply stated, the book is an account of my wanderings through China in search of greater understanding of China's path to modernization and reform and an attempt to identify both continuities and changes in the 1980s compared with the 1940s.

The book consists of eight substantive chapters plus some reflections at the end. Essentially, I have tried to write a profile of each area that I visited, making it as well rounded as possible given the limitations of the data that I gathered. Each of these profiles contains a little historical background, including what I learned in each area about the period of the Communist takeover, which took place soon after my 1948 visits. But my primary focus is on recent trends and the contemporary situation. In many places, I comment specifically on the situation in 1988 compared with that in the 1940s, but I do not attempt to give any full picture of the situation in the earlier period. Readers curious about what I learned in the 1940s can read, if they wish, my previous book on that period, *China on the Eve of Communist Takeover.*

Even though my aim has been, in each profile, to present as broad a portrait of an area as feasible, there are many gaps, some of them serious, which were inevitable because of the limited period I was able to stay in each place. All of the chapters are based essentially on my on-the-spot interviews and observations. I could have tried to do library research to supplement what I learned in China, but this would have taken a long time, and I decided against it. Therefore, what I myself saw and heard is what the reader gets in this book.

I will confess, without apology, that the book reflects certain of my own personal and idiosyncratic interests. Because of my own academic and journalistic past, I devote a great deal of attention to the political economy of each area that I visited.

I suspect that some readers may feel that the book contains an excess of statistics. I recognize that statistics are often extremely boring and that it is not always self-evident what they mean. I have nevertheless included many numbers, not because I am hypnotized by statistics—I, too, am often bored by them—but because I believe that generalizations, particularly about economic matters, that do not have some statistical backing are highly questionable. Moreover, contemporary Chinese leaders and bureaucrats are so obsessed with statistics that one really cannot understand the country without knowing a good deal about the world of numbers in which they live. I grew up in a China where definite statistics were a rare commodity, and one of the most common Chinese expressions was *chabuduo,* meaning "approximately." In recent years, however, the Chinese have swung to the other extreme, and they seem almost to reify numbers. Statistics are now used almost universally in China to evaluate people's performance and to judge the success or failure of the regime's policies. Wherever I went I was given specific figures on virtually everything that I inquired about, and I have included many of them in this book. Readers who are allergic to statistics, or whose eyes simply glaze over when confronted with numbers, can simply skim them and read the conclusions or generalizations that I draw from them.

As to the reliability of these statistics, my advice to readers is to treat them as useful clues to reality but not as the embodiment of the "gospel truth" about anything. I myself have wrestled sufficiently over the years with the task of understanding Chinese statistics to know that even when they are extremely useful they may not be totally reliable; all of them require careful analysis and interpretation. In my opinion, there has not been widespread deliberate falsification of statistics in China in recent years. However, the weaknesses of the country's statistical system have resulted in many inaccuracies. Moreover, to understand what any set of Chinese statistics really means, one needs to know a great deal about the precise definitions on which they are based, and during my travels in 1988 it was often impossible for me to clarify this. Moreover, I have not even attempted to translate monetary figures, given in Chinese yuan (Y), into U.S. dollars. My reason is that I am convinced that converting yuan figures to U.S. dollar figures on the basis of official exchange rates seriously distorts reality and greatly undervalues the yuan figures. Until there are reliable studies of the "purchasing power parity" of Chinese currency, I believe that it is far better to leave most figures in their original form.*

My profiles also contain a substantial amount of data on Party and government matters, including bureaucracies on local levels. This is another subject that has long been a special interest of mine.† I believe—or at least hope—that much of the information that I provide relating to central-provincial relations, local leadership, the interrelationships among different bureaucracies, the ties between different regions in China, and other political matters is sufficiently illuminating about the basic patterns of governance in China that it will be of interest to most readers. I suspect, however, that

---

*An unclassified CIA report in June 1991 pointed out that if yuan figures were converted to U.S. dollars at official exchange rates, China's GNP in 1988 was only US$307 billion. One U.S. Census Bureau estimate based on purchasing power parity (PPP), however, put China's GNP that year at US$837 billion. Another estimate the CIA report cites (a "Penn World" estimate) put the PPP of China's GNP in 1988 at $2.53 trillion. Further studies may produce different figures. But I have no doubt that converting yuan to dollars at official exchange rates greatly understates the yuan's value. (See Central Intelligence Agency, *The Chinese Economy in 1990 and 1991*, July 1991, pp. 15–16.)

†My writing on the subject includes *Cadres, Bureaucracy, and Political Power in Communist China* (Columbia University Press, 1967).

some of the details I present about the organization of bureaucracies will be of interest mainly to specialists on Chinese politics. I have included such details, nevertheless, for several reasons: because I myself have had an interest in Chinese bureaucracy for so many years myself, because I believe the details will be of value to other specialists, and because I felt an irresistible urge—a kind of Marco Poloitis—to record what I learned. My advice to readers who are not interested in such details is to skip them and move on.

I have devoted substantial space in all of the chapters to discussion of minority groups: their situation, the nature of the present regime's policies toward them, and the state of Han-minority relations in each area that I visited. My attention to these subjects requires no apology or special explanation. Interest in ethnic issues is now intense, worldwide, and I have little doubt that information on China's minorities will be in the forefront of the interests of many readers of this volume. But for those who know little about China's minorities, perhaps a few introductory comments are required.

Compared to some other multinational countries, China is relatively homogenous. Most of the country is populated by Han Chinese, who make up roughly 92 percent of the country's total population. In this respect, China is quite different from countries such as the former USSR, where minorities constituted a much larger percentage of the population (in the USSR, they made up almost half the population). However, even though the 92 million members of minority groups constitute only about 8 percent of China's population, many of the minority groups in China are very sizable: Eighteen of the 55 recognized minority groups have more than a million members, and 9 have more than 4 million.* Moreover, the importance of China's minority groups is magnified by the fact that they occupy a large part of the country, including many areas of major strategic importance in the northwest and southwest. The five large areas in China that are classified as provincial-level autonomous regions (Xinjiang, Inner Mongolia, Tibet, Ningxia, and Guangxi) include 45 percent of Chinese territory, and official Chinese publications state that all minority autonomous areas in the country (including minority prefectures, counties, and so on) occupy more than 60 percent of the country's land area.

---

*Chinese figures for the total minority population in China vary. In 1988, Zhao Niannian, deputy minister of the Nationality Affairs Commission, stated that the total was 85 million. However, some publications use a 92 million figure for China's total minority population, based on 1990 census data published by Beijing; the census figures for the largest groups in that year were as follows (rounded): Zhuang—15.5 million; Manchu—9.8 million; Hui—8.6 million; Miao—7.4 million; Uighur—7.2 million; Yi—6.6 million; Tujia—5.7 million; Mongol—4.8 million; and Tibetan—4.6 million.

In recent years, American and European interest in China's minority areas has focused mainly on the Tibetan Autonomous Region—and to a lesser extent Xinjiang. Tibet, in particular, has received extensive press coverage in the West, which has highlighted Tibetan resistance to Chinese repression and the Dalai Lama's wish to achieve autonomy. However, little has been reported about the situation in most of the other minority areas in China, which I visited and describe in this book.

*   *   *

I cover a wide range of subjects in this book, but I do not in general try to test in conventional academic fashion any major hypotheses or put forward any grand theory. The basic framework of the book was determined by my travels, and the reader is therefore asked to meander, as I did, both geographically and intellectually, over a lot of territory. Nevertheless, wherever I went I searched for information and insights relating to a broad range of questions in my mind. Many of these were extremely specific—about the economy; reform policies; local leadership; the government, Party, and military establishment; transport and communications; the media; education; public health; living standards; problems such as inflation and corruption; social conditions; generational change; ethnic relations; and many others. Before I started on my travels, I formulated several pages of specific questions, which then provided a framework for many interviews during my travels. There is no need to list all of these questions here; they will be apparent, in each chapter, from what I learned and describe.

However, all of my specific lines of inquiry were related to two broad and fundamental sets of questions that, as I noted earlier, were the raison d'être of my project.

The first set of questions concerned the extent and nature of change—and of continuity—during the four decades from the 1940s to the late 1980s. To what extent had modernizing influences penetrated these remote areas? Had they begun to transform the areas fundamentally? And if so, how? Or had the far west remained basically premodern, as it was in the 1940s? What now is the mix of old and new? My main baseline for trying to make judgments relating to these questions was the situation that I observed in 1948.

My second set of questions concerned the effects of Beijing's reforms during the 1980s on these areas. What were the attitudes in China's far west toward the reforms? Which reform policies were being implemented, and which were not? How much, if at all, had the reform begun to change these areas? I had no personal standard against which to assess the progress of reform between 1978 and 1988 in these particular areas since I had not seen most of the areas in the period just before the reform started. I therefore had to rely on what local people in the areas told me. I did feel that I had some basis for judging the plausibility of what I was told, however, since I had studied China continuously—and had visited many other parts of China re-peatedly—during the 1970s and 1980s.

Let me make one final comment, concerning whether readers should re-gard what I have written as contemporaneous or historical. When I started writing this book in 1989, that question simply did not arise, and I wrote in the present tense. Even now, I believe that the present tense is still valid. De-spite the fact that immediately after the Tiananmen crisis China was differ-ent in some respects from the China I observed in 1988, I do not believe that most of what I learned on my travels in 1988 has become outdated in any major way. China obviously has not stood still since 1988; it never does. The period following the Tiananmen crisis was an interim, transitional one. In contrast to most of the 1980s, when the pace of development and reform was extremely rapid, Chinese policies in the immediate aftermath of the di-saster in 1989 did not move forward so rapidly—in fact they have moved backward in some respects, but only temporarily. The reform policies were not basically reversed, and by late 1990 there were signs that the economic reforms were being revived and making progress again. Then, in early 1992, Deng Xiaoping called for accelerated economic reform and growth, and as a result the pace of economic change was faster than it was before 1989.

My decision to put what I had written in the past tense was essentially a technical one. Since most of the statistics I report are now several years old, I felt that for the sake of accuracy I had to use "was" rather than "is" in de-scribing the situations that these statistics reveal. I remain firmly convinced, nevertheless, that what I describe in the book still reflects present-day reali-ties.

Enough of preliminaries. I hereby invite readers to accompany me on my journey to China's far west. The starting point will be Inner Mongolia.

CHAPTER ONE

Steel City in Inner Mongolia
BAOTOU

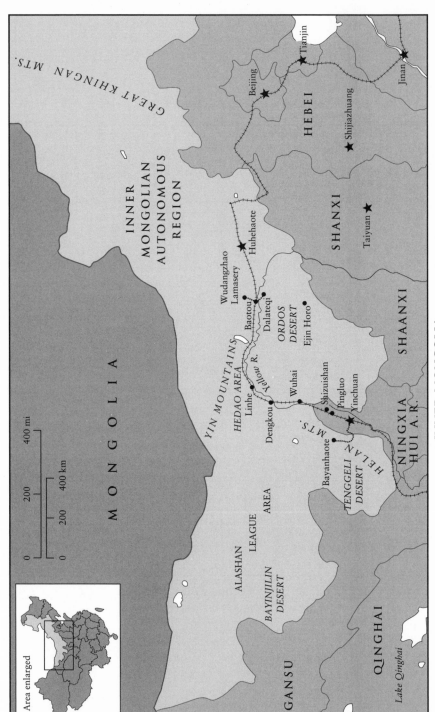

INNER MONGOLIA

I T WAS A BRISK February day, chilly but not unusually cold, when I set
out from Beijing's main railway station for Inner Mongolia. I was starting
the first leg of a five-month odyssey during which I would retrace routes all
over remote parts of China that I had traveled four decades earlier. I still
have vivid memories of the bitterly cold weather of the last trip—memories
of bleak, frozen landscapes, sheepskin-clad Chinese and Mongols, and
clouds of vapor created by snorting steam engines and the breath of ordinary
people. This time I took with me ample cold-weather gear: a very heavy
overcoat, thermal underwear, and warm boots. I am not quite sure why I
made the perverse decision to start my travels in 1988 by going first to Inner
Mongolia in the dead of winter; perhaps it was simply because I had made
my first major foray into China's deep interior 40 years previously to this
frozen part of the country. As I rode to the station with Wu Yu, the young
woman from the Chinese Academy of Social Sciences who was to be my escort during the first month of my travels in west China, I felt a growing excitement, plus a little apprehension. Five months of constant travel and intensive interviewing lay ahead, and I was not sure how I would cope with the
inevitable physical, intellectual, and psychic pressures. I had been 26 years
old when I started my travels in 1947; now I was 66.

The Beijing railway station presented a scene of utter chaos—something I
was to become very familiar with, but not totally inured to, during the next
few months. In 1988, China was still in the railway age, and despite considerable expansion of its rail system, the rapid growth of travel had all but
overwhelmed the system. Almost 4 million passengers traveled by train in
China every day, and in peak periods as many as three-quarters of a million
had to stand, according to Chinese officials responsible for the rail system.
Citizens of every conceivable status and occupation thronged the Beijing station, where 210,000 passengers a day were handled in peak periods, and the
station attendants—among the most irritating of petty bureaucrats in a
country run by bureaucrats—were arrogant and indifferent to all of our requests for information. Nevertheless, we finally located train number 263 to
Baotou, settled into our "soft-berth" compartment, and started on time, at
3:15 P.M., on the 521-mile overnight journey; our train was scheduled to arrive at Baotou at 7:56 the next morning.

When traveling by train, in China as elsewhere, I sometimes felt that I was
in a cocoon, at other times in a time capsule. I always enjoyed the secure feeling of being sheltered from the elements yet able to see the world go by from
the window, and I learned a great deal from being thrown into intimate contact with strangers. Our soft-class compartment had four bunks (two upper
and two lower berths); each had a couple of pillows, covered by small

changeable towels, and a quilt. A tiny bed light made reading possible, although it was difficult. Only small luggage could go under the lower bunk; large suitcases had to be hoisted onto a high platform above the door leading to the car's corridor. Males and females were mixed, but no one was embarrassed about this since virtually everyone slept in daytime clothing. The car was well heated; however, the noise pollution from the compartment's "radio" speaker, which blared announcements and music well into the night, was irritating. Fortunately, though, in contrast with earlier years, the loudspeaker carried no political or ideological slogans. Occasionally we listened to matter-of-fact announcements made by train attendants, but mainly there was nonstop music of various sorts plus entertainment. The most popular programs were *crosstalk,* a comedy form in which glib, fast-talking men made fun of each other's and of society's foibles.

*   *   *

During the next few months, I was to have dozens of conversations with train-compartment mates of almost every conceivable sort; most of them spoke with remarkable frankness about their lives, ways of thinking, problems, and hopes. This time, our compartment mates were two young men, dressed in Western clothes but rustic in their general demeanor and appearance. They were representing a state factory north of Beijing, making one of their periodic trips to Baotou to purchase synthetic fiber used to manufacture clothing. In 1988, the number of enterprise purchasing agents and salesmen who, like these young men, were traveling the length and breadth of China was surprising to me; their numbers had multiplied rapidly in recent years as commercialization and economic competition in China had grown. On this trip I also talked with a variety of other passengers when I explored the entire train, including both its hard-seat and hard-berth cars. One who was particularly interesting was a forestry expert who told me about his work; he was engaged in building shelterbelts in Inner Mongolia.

I also began to get acquainted with Wu Yu. She proved to be a delightful traveling companion. The daughter of a teacher of the Chinese language in Fujian Province, she had enrolled in Fujian Teachers' College and majored in English. After graduating in 1985, she had a lucky break of the kind most young college graduates in China now yearn for. Because of her knowledge of the English language, she was selected to work in the Chinese Academy of Social Sciences (CASS) in Beijing. Her ultimate hope, she told me, was to do graduate work in sociology and concentrate on women's issues. Although only 25, she was married but had no children and was in no hurry to become a mother. She was in many respects naive, in a refreshing way, but she nevertheless was an able, articulate, hardworking young woman and already was experienced in the complexities of arranging travel and interviews for foreign scholars in China. As we traveled together, I learned much from Wu Yu

about the attitudes and hopes of young intellectuals and also about the difficulties of their daily living. (She and her husband shared three rooms with
two other young couples.) She told me a great deal about the hassles of com-
muting, shopping, cooking, and working, but she was philosophical about
them, and she impressed me as being basically an optimist.

Although a few passengers on our train were people of education and relatively high social status, the majority were workers, peasants, and low-
ranking cadres. All were packed, sardinelike, into close quarters; Chinese,
who are used to a lack of space and privacy, seem to find these conditions
more bearable than most foreigners do. In the hard-seat cars, there were five
unpadded seats in each row, three on one side, two on the other, but many
passengers had to stand, some of them for hours. In the hard-berth cars, the
compartments were open, and each side had three tiers of bunks; passengers
brought their own bedding. Each car had a toilet at one end. Ours, which
was typical, had a filthy, uncomfortable, squat, seatless commode, and there
was no toilet paper. The small washbasin was hardly usable. One soon
learns in China that these toilets should be used only as a last resort. The
train also had a dining car, where we had a quick supper at 5:00 P.M.; it was
jam-packed, and getting food was a matter of survival of the fittest. The
food was hardly worth the effort. The rice was of poor quality; the meat
dishes were fatty, greasy, and unsavory; and everything was expensive by
Chinese standards—double or triple what the cost would be in an ordinary
city restaurant. But I was able to buy a bottle of good beer (which has virtually replaced tea in China in recent years), which helped to wash down the
unappetizing food. I was charged roughly double what the Chinese were,
and I soon learned that this had become standard for hotel rooms, train
tickets, and virtually everything else in China because everyone seemed determined to acquire foreign exchange in any way possible. (Even at the price
I paid, however, the heavily subsidized train travel was cheap: My ticket to
Baotou cost Y 102, whereas Wu Yu's was Y 50.80. For most passengers,
hard seats cost only Y 15.20 and hard berths only Y 25.00.*)

*   *   *

During the three hours of daylight before winter darkness settled in at
about 6:30 P.M., our train climbed to the northwest from the flat, brown,
dusty north China plain, through Badaling Pass (to which thousands of tourists, Chinese and foreign, trek to see the Great Wall), and then through

---

*Y stands for yuan, the Chinese dollar. The exchange rate between the U.S. dollar and the
yuan has varied; during 1988 it was generally close to 3.7 yuan for each U.S. dollar. But as I
noted earlier, in a footnote in the Prologue, the foreign exchange value of the yuan does not reveal its true purchasing value in China.

Nankou Pass before reaching higher ground in the area beyond the wall, formerly called *kou wai*—"beyond the pass." As always in midwinter, the land in north China looked bleak and lifeless, but I could nevertheless see that much had changed since I had last made this trip. On the plain, the fields were much larger; many of the peasants' homes were now constructed of bricks; trees paralleled the rail lines in many places; and I could see numerous small factories, not only in towns but also scattered throughout the countryside. As we climbed up through the passes, the landscape was dominated by jagged, bare crags. Then dusk descended, followed by ink-black darkness, and by 7:30 P.M. most passengers, including my compartment mates, went to sleep. Using a small, battery-run, travel light that I had brought with me, I tried to read but soon gave up and simply lay back and ruminated about my last trip to Baotou in late December 1947 and early January 1948—and about what lay ahead.

In late 1947, China was in the midst of a bitter civil war, which had not yet engulfed (although it soon would) Beijing (then called Beiping) or the areas of Hebei, Chahar, and Suiyuan through which the train from Beijing to Baotou (Paotow) ran.* Construction of this line was started soon after the first Sino-Japanese war (at the turn of the century) by the Chinese themselves, and it reached Baotou in the early 1920s. In the 1940s, the railway was well run; in fact, it was less crowded and more comfortable in 1947 than it was in 1988. My destination, Baotou, was at that time the end of the line. Along the way I made stops in Zhangjiakou (Kalgan), capital of Chahar, and Guisui (Kweisui), which is now called Huhehaote, a city that then was the capital of Suiyuan Province and now is capital of Inner Mongolia. In 1947, I made much of the trip in daylight, and I still remember well the winter landscape—hills and valleys all covered with a light dusting of snow. After traveling over Nankou Pass we followed a valley northwest to the geographical basin containing Zhangjiakou and then turned southwest on the plain that paralleled the Yin Mountains and the outer loop of the Great Wall to the north Shanxi coal mining and industrial city of Datong (Tatung), which also lay in a basin surrounded by mountains. From there, the line turned into the eroded Fengzhen (Fengchen) highlands, where the rolling hills looked like tremendous waves; then we passed through the Great Wall again to Jining (Chining); and finally we turned westward and followed the Guisui plain, at the foot of the Daqing (Taching) Mountains, to Baotou.

From the time that it was first built, this railway had brought increasing numbers of Han Chinese into the region, fundamentally changing its charac-

---

*In this paragraph, I give, in parentheses, the transliterated forms of place names used in the 1940s.

ter. Well before 1949, the entire railway zone, as well as the irrigated land west of Baotou and north of the Yellow River, had become essentially a Chinese area, extending the Han heartland of China into southwest Inner Mongolia. Even in the 1940s, this zone could well have been called Outer China, despite its location in Inner Mongolia. In 1947, what was then Suiyuan Province (but is now part of Inner Mongolia) was ruled by Fu Zuoyi (Fu Tso-yi). I did not meet Fu on my trip, but I did later, in Beiping. He was one of the ablest pre-1949 warlords and was widely respected, even by the Communists. Later he became the top military commander in Beiping, and in early 1949 he negotiated an agreement with the Communists that resulted in the peaceful surrender of the city. His personal impact on the province was strong. The route to Baotou was heavily militarized in 1947: There were stone and brick pillboxes at every bridge and station as well as on many high mountain ridges adjacent to the line, and one could see barbed wire and trenches at frequent intervals. Thousands of troops—many of them cavalry—moved through the zone, and a heavily armored train moved up and down the line to protect and, if necessary, repair the line.

Until December 1947, this area had been relatively placid compared with many other war zones, but it so happened that my travel coincided with a major Communist effort to disrupt rail transport throughout north China. During my trip to Baotou, an attack between Zhangjiakou and Datong halted traffic for a day and a half—delaying my train for 13 hours—and on my return trip we were again delayed for several hours when a bridge was destroyed between Zhangjiakou and Beiping.

One of the greatest contrasts between 1988 and 1947 was the demilitarization, or civilianization, of society, not only in the area I went through on this trip, but also, I was to discover in the months ahead, in most of west China. I saw no signs of military forces or activities anywhere on my 1988 Baotou trip. Although a significant number of military units were stationed elsewhere in Inner Mongolia, none were visible in the major civilian areas that I visited. One could argue that this was unremarkable four decades after the Communists won the civil war. Yet having seen the area when military forces not only were ubiquitous but constantly intruded into ordinary people's lives, I found this simple but fundamental change striking.

There was one moment on my 1988 trip when I wondered whether everything was as peaceful as it seemed. A little after 5:00 A.M., when our train had stopped outside of a small town, a fist-size rock suddenly shattered our compartment window and crashed into our room. A train policeman, who immediately rushed in and then arranged for us to move to another compartment, apologized profusely; he speculated that it was probably the work of juvenile delinquents. I was skeptical at the time and was suspicious that the incident might have had some political cause. We were in a Mongol area, and I could not help but wonder whether it was an anti-Han act. (It could not have been motivated by antiforeignism: I was the only foreigner on the train, and no one outside could have seen me in our darkened compartment.) But in retrospect I decided that his explanation was plausible. During 1988, the Chinese press carried many reports of juvenile delinquency as well as a rise in crime generally—the result, in part, of rapid social change and loosened control. During the rest of the trip, I encountered no overt sign of anti-Han feelings in Inner Mongolia, and, in all my travels in the west during subsequent months, no comparable incident occurred.

                              *   *   *

Dawn arrived about 6:00 A.M., and as we neared the end of the trip I began to get a sense of the remarkable changes that had occurred in this area since the 1940s. In 1947 when my train had approached Baotou, I could see, even though it was dark, that Baotou was surrounded by sparsely populated, barren land. We debarked, on that trip, at a very small train station and traveled by donkey cart to the city wall. The city wall had already been closed for the night, but it was opened to let us in. We had gone directly to the best inn in town, the Tai An, which was a small, crowded, clamorous place, typical of traditional Chinese inns (it evoked images of what I imagined an Elizabethan inn might have been like).

As we approached the city in 1988, I could see that, although the landscape still appeared to be poor, desertified, and fairly bleak, the modern world had caught up with Baotou; even in the suburbs we began to pass numerous modern factories. Finally we ended our journey at a large modern train station.

We were met by two officials from the Municipal Foreign Affairs Bureau, which was to be my host organization. Every Chinese city of any size has such a bureau, and they all belong to a national network, affiliated loosely with the Foreign Ministry in Beijing. One of their functions is to deal with visiting foreigners. (Throughout the following months, wherever there was a local Academy of Social Sciences, its leaders were my hosts, but they existed only in large cities, mainly provincial capitals, and everywhere else the local foreign affairs bureaus managed my visits.) My Baotou hosts whisked us by car from the rail station to the Qingshan Guest House, formerly a state guest house for officials only but now one of the two best hotels in town. En route, from the car window, I had my first glimpses of modern Baotou, which had become a large, sprawling metropolis.

Immediately after reaching the hotel, we discussed my program—based on suggestions that I had sent ahead through the Chinese Academy of Social Sciences in Beijing. It did not include many things that I had asked for, so I proceeded to suggest modifications—a ritual that I was to go through dozens of times in the months ahead. Nevertheless, within two hours of my arrival I began to explore Baotou and its environs, to interview local officials, and to learn everything I could about modern Baotou—and Inner Mongolia in general. In the next few days, I was able to interview more than 30 officials, enterprise managers, and journalists, some individually and some in groups. My interviews included ones with a deputy mayor (the mayor was out of town), his secretary-general, and leading officials from several government commissions (for economics, planning, agriculture, education, and minority affairs) and bureaus (for personnel and urban construction) as well as an editor and reporter from the *Baotou Daily*. I toured the entire city by car (something I insisted on doing in every city that I visited during the next five months) and visited three factories. I also made two trips outside of the city, one to a lamasery north of Baotou and one to the south, to the headquarters of the Dala Special Banner (Dala Teqi). Overall I was greatly impressed by the astonishing development that had occurred since my last visit. Even though, in 1988, Baotou still seemed remote from China's capital—and from the major cities of coastal China—it had become a major, modern industrial center.

Starting in the 1950s, Baotou had developed into what was by far the largest and most developed city in the Inner Mongolian Autonomous Region. Its population was now considerably larger than that of the region's capital, Huhehaote, the only other large city in the region (which in the 1940s had been double Baotou's size and had been somewhat more modern). Essentially it was a transplant—a Han Chinese enclave, with industry built by people who had come from other parts of China—and it contained almost nothing to remind one of Mongol history or culture or even of contemporary Mongol society, which still predominates in the more remote grasslands of Inner Mongolia.

*   *   *

In area, the Inner Mongolian Autonomous Area is now the third largest provincial-level unit in China (after Xinjiang and Tibet). Encompassing about 463,000 square miles, it is larger than many countries (Egypt, for example) and stretches roughly 1,800 miles in a huge arc curving from northeast China toward the southwest. On one side it borders on the Mongolian People's Republic, which is slightly larger in area but has less than a tenth of its population; on the other side it touches seven Chinese provinces—Jilin and Liaoning in the northeast; Hebei and Shanxi in north China; and Shaanxi, Ningxia, and Gansu in the west. As of the late 1980s, it had the following 112 administrative units: 8 units classified as prefectures (most of them called *leagues*), 16 cities (4 of them treated as prefecture-level units and 12 of them as county-level), 72 county-level units (more than 50 of them called *banners* and the rest regular counties), and 16 districts within cities.

Topographically, most of the territory incorporated into Inner Mongolia belongs, along with Outer Mongolia, to the vast Mongolian plateau, which is a part of the huge "Inner Asian" area of steppes and deserts that stretches from Asia almost to Europe. The plateau in Inner Mongolia, which averages about 3,000 feet in elevation, contains great expanses of grassland, which are rich in the east and somewhat poorer in the north and west. It is China's most important pastural area, producing large numbers of sheep, goats, horses, camels, and cattle. This is where most of China's Mongols live. The majority engage in animal husbandry, although many of those living near Chinese-inhabited areas are semisedentary and do some farming; even on the grasslands a few trading centers have developed. To the south of the Mongolian plateau, the Langshan mountain range stretches into the Yinshan range; compared with many of the highest areas in China, these are not particularly impressive, but many peaks rise to almost 5,000 feet and some to about 6,500 feet. Further east is the Daqing range, which is parallel to, but south of, the Yinshan; Baotou lies at the foot of the Daqing.

To the northeast of Baotou is a large desert area and the Great Khingan (Hinggan) Mountains. West of Baotou, and north of the Yellow River bend, is the area called Hedao (Hotao), which is roughly 40 miles wide and 100 miles long. The land in this region adjacent to the Yellow River is well irrigated, and it is one of the most productive agricultural areas in west China. Its complex irrigation network began to be built long ago, but most of it has been developed in its modern form in the past 100 years or so. Most of Inner Mongolia's agriculture is concentrated in the Hedao region west of Baotou and on the plain stretching from Baotou to Huhehaote. This agriculture is important to the region's economy, but the value of its output is only a tiny fraction of the total output in the entire territory—which is not surprising since only about 3 percent of the region's total territory is cultivated. South of the Yellow River is the Ordos, famous as a place where, centuries ago, Han Chinese and invading nomadic groups often met and clashed. Several other deserts occupy much of the southwest of Inner Mongolia; one of the largest is the Alashan Desert (about which I will have more to say later).

The history of Mongolia—both Inner and Outer—was, until recent times, part of the dramatic and incredibly complex history of what French scholar René Grousset termed the "empire of the steppe." Starting well before what is called the Christian era in the West, numerous nomadic Turkic, Mongol, and Tungusic tribes fought among each other in this region and periodically produced strong leaders whose forces expanded east, west, and south into the surrounding sedentary, agricultural areas in China, central Asia, India, Persia, and Russia. Over the centuries, many of these tribal groups conquered parts—and a few conquered most—of what is now China. They included the Turkic Xiongnu (Hsiungnu), or Huns; the Mongol Xianbi (Hsien-pi); the Mongol Ruan Ruan (Juan Juan); the Turkic Tujue (Tu Chueh); the Khitan Mongols; the Kerayit and the Naiman (often labeled Turko-Mongol groups); and the Mongols led by Genghis Khan. The wars with these tribal peoples are an important part of the Chinese historical memory. Even today, people in Baotou have not forgotten that as early as the Qin and Han dynasties the Xiongnu periodically headquartered in what is now the Ikh Zhao (also romanized as Yikezhao, Ih Ju, or Yeke Juu) area of Inner Mongolia near Baotou.

Present-day Mongols are most aware, however, of the history of Genghis Khan and his successors (especially Kublai Khan), who in the twelfth and thirteenth centuries unified the most important tribes, embarked on wars of conquest, and established one of the largest empires in history. These Mongols achieved control of all of China, overthrew the southern Song rulers, and established the Yuan dynasty, which lasted from 1279 to 1368, when the Chinese revolted and established the Ming dynasty. They also extended their dominance throughout Central Asia and Russia to Europe. In the seventeenth century, another tribal people, the Tungusic Manchus from the northeast, conquered China. They incorporated the Mongols into their new Qing empire (1644–1911), replacing the Ming dynasty, and converted the old Mongol tribal units into leagues and banners that have continued to today, even though they have metamorphosed into administrative units little different from other Chinese prefectures and counties.

The separation of Inner Mongolia and Outer Mongolia, when viewed in the broad sweep of history, took place relatively recently. Before the rise of the Manchus, the Mongols themselves were split, with the Khalka Mongols controlling Outer Mongolia and a variety of tribes competing in Inner Mongolia. Then, from the seventeenth century on, Mongolia was a focus of Sino-Russian rivalry, and after the fall of the Manchu empire the Russians supported first Outer Mongolia's autonomy and later its independence, which both the Chinese Nationalists and Communists ultimately accepted, the former in 1945 and the latter in 1950.

During the past century, Inner Mongolia, in contrast to Outer Mongolia, has been increasingly controlled and populated by Chinese and absorbed into the Chinese polity. For a brief period, in the 1930s and 1940s, the Japanese supported an autonomous Inner Mongolian regime, Meng Jiang (Meng Chiang) under De Wang (Teh Wang). And between the end of World War II and 1949, several local Mongol regimes, including one under the tutelage of the Communist leader Ulanfu, were established. Once the Chinese Communists achieved power, however, they rapidly established firm control over all of Inner Mongolia, and they converted the Mongol regime led by Ulanfu—which they had sponsored since 1947—into a new Inner Mongolian Autonomous Region. Over several years, from 1949 to 1956, they enlarged the region, step by step, to include the Mongol areas that had belonged to the provinces of Rehe (Jehol), Chahar, Suiyuan, and Ningxia (Ninghsia). In all essentials, the new Inner Mongolian Autonomous Region was organized like other large provinces, although certain of its administrative and other policies differed because it was given the status of an "autonomous region."

In short, Inner Mongolia became one of China's 29 provincial-level units (not counting Nationalist-ruled Taiwan). (These units included 5 large minority-inhabited regions, 3 large municipalities, and 21 regular provinces— to which 1 additional province, Hainan, was added in the late 1980s when it was split off from Guangdong.) Like other autonomous regions, Inner Mongolia was granted certain special privileges and rights relating to language, culture, political representation, and financial support. However, it remained under strong central control and—partly because of increased Han migration—was assimilated into the national polity and national economy to an unprecedented degree.

*   *   *

Chinese policies toward all minority regions fluctuated over time. Conciliation during most of the 1950s was followed by more repressive policies in the 1960s, which culminated in widespread violence during the Cultural Revolution, when Red Guards launched brutal attacks on all religions and destroyed thousands of religious institutions. This created widespread bitterness. There was some Mongol resistence to Chinese rule, but, as far as is known, there was no very significant organized opposition in Inner Mongolia comparable to the rebellion in Tibet in 1959 or even dissidence comparable to that in Xinjiang, which in 1962 led to an exodus of Kazakhs to the Soviet Union.

In the late 1960s, during the Cultural Revolution, the size of the region was drastically contracted, with large portions of its territory transferred to adjacent provinces in the northeast and to Ningxia and Gansu in the southwest. Officials in Baotou (and, later, others in Alashan) gave me several explanations for this: The changes were dictated, I was told, by both political and defense considerations. These officials acknowledged that one major reason was worry about possible Mongol political opposition during that chaotic period; in effect, Beijing adopted a policy of divide and rule to achieve tighter control. Then, at the start of the post-Mao reform period in the late 1970s, these areas were returned to Inner Mongolia in 1978, reportedly (and plausibly) in response to the Mongols' desire for unity. Han-Mongol relations clearly improved thereafter as a result of the more conciliatory policies adopted by the government, starting in the late 1970s.

The population of the region grew rapidly during these years. By the late 1980s it exceeded 20 million (in 1986 it was 20.29 million). However, by Chinese standards this was still relatively small; in fact, only Tibet, Qinghai, Ningxia, and Xinjiang had smaller populations. At the same time that its population was growing, it was becoming increasingly Han Chinese in its composition, and by the late 1980s only about 3.4 million of its inhabitants were Mongols. Even though this Mongol population was almost double that in the Mongolian People's Republic (the total population of which was just over 2 million), by the end of the 1980s the Mongols in Inner Mongolia accounted for only 17 percent of the total population of the region. Today, therefore, the Mongols are a minority—in fact, a very *small* minority—in their own autonomous region. As a percentage of the total local population, the percentage of minority people in Inner Mongolia is smaller than the percentage of minorities in any other of China's autonomous regions.

Although modern industrialization had begun to transform the region in important ways, most of the population still worked in rural areas. In 1986, of a total work force of 8.6 million in the region, 4.97 million worked either in farming (mainly Chinese) or animal husbandry (mainly Mongolian) or other agricultural-type jobs (fishing, for example); the number of people employed in industry had risen to 1.47 million—about 40 percent of them in Baotou alone—but they amounted to only about one-sixth of the total work force. However, by 1986 industry accounted for 62 percent of the value of the region's gross agricultural and industrial output (Y 12.63 billion out of Y 20.36 billion) whereas animal husbandry and agriculture together accounted for just over 35 percent (Y 7.2 billion); the rest was accounted for by construction, transportation, commerce, and other occupations.* Somewhat surprisingly, however, national statistics indicated that in 1985 Inner Mongolia ranked thirteenth among all Chinese provincial-level units in per capita consumption.

Statistics for the region as a whole obscure the fact that by the 1980s there were really two Inner Mongolias: One was the relatively small railway zone stretching west to the outer edge of the Hedao area, which contained most of the region's agriculture and industry and was populated mainly by Han Chinese; the other consisted of the vast, thinly populated steppes, grasslands, and desert areas, which continued to be the homeland of most Mongols. Because the latter areas are so large, there are now only about 17 people per square kilometer (roughly 6.6 per square mile) in the Inner Mongolian region as a whole; only Tibet, Qinghai, and Xinjiang are more sparsely populated.

Because of its immense pastoral areas, Inner Mongolia has long been China's most important producer of animals and animal products. In the 1980s, it shared with Xinjiang the distinction of raising the largest number of sheep and goats (Inner Mongolia raised 25 million in 1986, almost three-quarters of them sheep), and it rated at the top in its herds of horses and camels,

---

*In most of the places that I visited in 1988, local officials gave me up-to-date statistics, usually for 1987. For Inner Mongolia and Baotou, however, most of the figures I obtained were for 1986 or earlier years.

which totaled 1.82 million and 274,000 respectively in 1986. It also raised over 6.7 million cattle and draft animals, but seven other provinces or autonomous regions, mainly in China's major agricultural areas, exceeded this figure.

*   *   *

My trip to Baotou did not take me very far into "real Mongol" areas, although on two short expeditions out of the city I did visit the fringe of these areas. In Baotou itself what I saw was the modernized economic heart of new Outer China in Inner Mongolia. In this newly developed extension of Han China, I was astonished to see how much modernization had transformed the city since my visit four decades earlier. Over the years, I had watched many cities throughout East Asia evolve from traditional urban centers into strikingly modern metropolises, and I had watched especially closely the growth and modernization of many industrial cities in eastern China, so I was prepared to see major changes even in this remote part of China. Moreover, I knew, even before my trip, that Baotou had become an important steel center. Yet even though Baotou still lags behind the major cities on China's coast, to say nothing of those in countries on China's periphery, I was unprepared for what I saw; Baotou had been transformed in ways that far exceeded what I had expected.

In 1947, Baotou was a very traditional, fairly primitive small town of just under 80,000 people crammed into a walled area. Although it traces its origins to the Warring States period (fifth to third century B.C.), it did not have a long history as a walled town. In Qing times, it was still a small settlement, called Donghe. Its present name—Baotou—was adopted later and was derived, I was told, from a Mongol word meaning "place where there are many deer." Before the nineteenth century, it had been classified as a village. Then, in 1809, it was upgraded to the status of a town (*zhen*) and in 1865 it became a county seat. Not long before my previous visit, its status had been upgraded to that of a city, in 1938. By the late 1940s, its population reached 78,000, but it still had the atmosphere of a small town. Then, after the Communist takeover, it finally acquired the status of a municipality of prefecture rank, in 1953, when the central government designated it as a major base for future industrial development.

When I visited Baotou in 1947, it still had the atmosphere of a small and remote nineteenth-century town. The city wall was perhaps 15 feet high, which was not very impressive in comparison with most other Chinese county seats. There were no modern buildings; almost all the shops, homes, and other buildings were one-story structures with traditional sloping tile roofs. Only two streets in the entire town were paved. Scattered throughout the town were bazaars and caravansaries, all of which had courtyards filled with camels and bales of wool. Most people dressed as they had for centuries; the majority wore lambskin jackets and fur hats to protect themselves from the bitter cold. Local officials were proud that they had a tiny electric plant, a primitive telephone system, and a small running water system, but these served just a few members of the local elite. The largest modern industry in the town consisted of three small factories producing leather, flour, and tobacco; the most important of these, the leather factory, produced only 50 cowhides and 50 sheepskins a day, by simple handicraft methods.

By 1988, the population of Baotou Municipality had grown to 1.67 million; slightly more than 1 million of these lived in urban areas and about 660,000 lived in the countryside. The size of the municipality had expanded as the population had grown. In 1988, it covered 3,856 square miles—more than three times the size of Rhode Island—and it contained, in addition to its main urban areas, two important mining areas as well as sizable rural farm areas. Following the lead of most other major Chinese cities in recent years, it had expanded its territory to integrate fairly large rural areas with its core city. The municipality as a whole was divided into three city districts (Kundulun, Donghe, and Qingshan, all located in the city proper) and one suburban district as well as the Shiguaigou coal mining district, the Baiyun Ebo (Bayan Obo) iron mining district, Guyang County, and the Tumete Right Banner (a total of eight units).

Urban Baotou, which lies just north of the Yellow River and the Baotou-Beijing railway, had developed into two distinct cities. To the east, the "old city," now called Donghe District, had grown on the site of the original walled town, and it contained about 330,000 people (close to four times Baotou's 1947 population—in an area only slightly larger than the original town). The city wall was gone, but quite a few pre-1949 buildings still stood in the old city; however, many modern buildings, some of them several stories high, gave it an entirely different appearance. All of its main roads were paved; the city was entirely electrified; and it contained a considerable number of light industrial manufacturing plants. The old railway station still existed, but it had become a subsidiary stopping point; the large main station was now just south of the "new city." I found only one old building that I remembered from my 1947 visit; it was the Tai An Inn, where I had stayed. (It was no longer an inn—it had been divided into several family apartments.) All the camel caravansaries had disappeared; the only thing resembling them were a few auto and truck junkyards.

The new city, which had been built slightly more than six miles to the northwest of Donghe, consisted of two districts, Qingshan and Kundulun, which together contained about double the population of Donghe. The buildings in these districts were entirely new, constructed since the early 1950s on formerly desertified grassland. This part of the city had become a sprawling modern metropolis, with broad avenues laid out in a regular pattern. Some avenues were six lanes wide and lined with a few scraggly trees that were fighting for survival in an inhospitable environment (most of the city was still bare, dusty, and brown). Lining the major avenues were quite a few interesting and even colorful five-, six-, and seven-story buildings, and throughout the city there were large numbers of squat but well-built and not unattractive four- or five-story brick apartment houses. (Apartment houses of this sort have proliferated through all modern Chinese cities in recent years, and, because they are so common, I will hereafter refer to them simply as "standard apartments.")

The new urban districts of Baotou were planned and built in the 1950s, after the city was designated by Beijing (in 1953) as an "industrial base." They were designed, with Soviet assistance, by the National Institute of Design in Beijing, which at that time was under the Ministry of Building Construction (but later was incorporated into the Ministry of Urban and Rural Construction and Environmental Protection). Soviet advice obviously had a major influence on the planning and, therefore, on the nature of the city that evolved; basically, Baotou was modeled on the "new" cities that the Soviet Union had built from scratch. The plan worked out in the 1950s was a comprehensive one, which included specific plans for roads, housing, electricity, water, gas, and so on. When I interviewed officials from the Baotou Urban Construction Bureau—men who had been involved in local city planning since the start—they stressed that although Soviet experts supervised the general planning, Chinese planners did much of the work and modified the Soviet model substantially to fit local circumstances.

Qingshan District, where my hotel was located, lay close to the foothills of the mountain range to the north of Baotou. Laid out in regular streets, on an axis oriented northwest to southeast, it contained many large housing estates and also parks, schools, hospitals, restaurants, department stores and shops, company headquarters, and government offices. It was also the site of the city's TV tower and a large workers' "cultural palace." Kundulun, oriented east-west, had many similar buildings, but it was dominated by the city's large factories, above all by the Baotou Iron and Steel Corporation, the preeminent enterprise in the city. The most impressive street in the municipality, which bisected Kundulun, was the six-lane Iron and Steel Avenue, where phalanxes of bicycle commuters, as well as city buses and company cars, filled the streets in the early morning and late afternoon rush hours, going to and from the steel company.

*   *   *

Baotou was not only much larger and more modern looking than I had expected; a total transformation had occurred since 1947. The city looked well built, clean, and more like eastern cities than an outpost in Inner Mongolia. People appeared healthy, well fed, and well clothed. The free markets scattered throughout the city were full of goods and of customers—much fuller than the larger state stores. The clothes that people wore now consisted mostly of Western-style garments. Both men and women were, to a surprising degree, dressed fashionably, in clothes comparable to those worn in Beijing or Shanghai; in fact, as is often true of "provincials" in other countries, many people in Baotou seemed to be more self-conscious about fashion than the more sophisticated and jaded residents in eastern cities. Women wearing high heels and men wearing elevator shoes were common, for example. As I was to learn as I traveled throughout west China in the months to follow, the spread of fashions in clothing—as well as other fads and, more important, new ideas and values—was testimony to the outreach of the country's new modern communications system—and especially to the TV revolution that occurred during the 1980s.

Not surprisingly, in light of the city's rapid growth, a large part of Baotou's population consisted of people who had come from other parts of China, especially from more modern provinces in northeast and north China, starting in the 1950s. Recent migrants made up about four-fifths of the municipality's urban population, I was told. This migration had clearly ended the area's isolation and had been a major factor contributing to the modernity of local clothing, food, and general life-style.

I was also told that numerous Chinese who had recently migrated to Baotou from other areas still regarded it as a fairly backward and remote place—which did not surprise me—and that many of them yearned to return to their home cities in the east. It appeared to me, however, that the younger generation, born and brought up in Baotou, had put down roots in the city and regarded themselves both as modern urbanites and as local people. (They were not regarded as such, however, by many Chinese visitors from the east, including my escort, who seemed to view most, if not all, of Baotou's residents of all ages as provincials rather than genuine big-city people.)

As in many other areas of China—including provincial cities and towns as well as rural areas—there had been a notable revival in the 1980s of many old social customs and practices. One night at my hotel, a wedding banquet was held for a young man and woman—both from a local factory—who had married that day. The bride was dressed in red, high-heel shoes, attractive slacks, and a colorful silk jacket and had multicolored spangles in her permed hair. The groom wore a fancy Western suit and elevator shoes (the estimated cost of the latter: Y 100). Invited by relatives of the bride and groom, the guests at the banquet filled six tables, each of which had 10 seats. One local person told me that he estimated that the cost for the food, liquor, wine, and so on was about Y 150 a table—or Y 900 for the six tables—a huge amount of money in relation to the budgets of ordinary Chinese. Much of this, however, was paid for by guests' contributions of money, given in traditional red envelopes to the couple's relatives. The climax of the affair came when the bride and groom circulated among the tables and, together, toasted and bowed three times to each guest—and to interested bystanders as well, including me. As I observed the proceedings and watched the young couple, I said to myself at one point: How different these young people seemed from those I met in "old Baotou" in the 1940s. At another point, however, as I reflected on the costly conspicuous consumption that the banquet represented, I thought to myself: Plus ça change, plus c'est la même chose.

Almost nothing that I saw in Baotou reminded me that the city belonged to Inner Mongolia, but some things I heard did. Three of the officials I met were Mongols. They seemed to be almost totally Sinified, but they were eager, nevertheless, to tell me about the Mongol history of the area and about the four *buluo*—tribes, converted later by the Qing rulers into banners—that had inhabited the area: the Tumete (Tumet), Ulate, Erduosi (Ikh Zhao), and Ulanchapu (Ulanqab). However, very few members of these groups remained in Baotou Municipality. This was not really a new situation, though. Even 40 years previously, very few Mongols lived within Baotou. (During my visit in 1947, I was told that only 400 Mongols lived within the town; officials in 1988 gave me a somewhat larger number, 3,323, for the number of Mongols living in the town in 1949.) Nevertheless, in the late 1940s, because of its caravansaries, numerous camels, and visiting Mongols, Baotou still had a definite Mongol flavor. By 1988, the Mongol population within the city totaled 28,842—considerably more than in 1947 but now less than 2 percent of the total population. Most of them were so completely Sinified that it was impossible to identify them as Mongols on the street. (Actually, in 1988 the number of Hui Muslims—29,584—living in Baotou exceeded the number of Mongols; the city's population also included about 10,000 people of Manchu origin.)

The Mongols in Baotou had been largely assimilated into the Han-dominated work force; roughly 10,000 had become factory workers—more than four-fifths of them as employees in state enterprises (2,000 worked for the steel company alone) and the others in collectives, with only a handful in private enterprises. Despite their small numbers, the Mongols were well represented in Party and government positions; almost 2,000 held cadre jobs, mainly in the government—a number slightly greater as a proportion of all cadres than their proportion of the total population. They were particularly well represented—in fact overrepresented—in top political positions. The mayor, a deputy mayor, the head and a deputy head of the local people's congress, and the head and a deputy head of the local People's Political Consultative Conference were Mongols, I was told. Current national policy required that certain government jobs be reserved for minority leaders in areas such as Baotou, even though Han Chinese predominated in the population. Within the local bureaucracies, more than 100 Mongols had the status of "county-level" cadres. Mongols were much less well represented, however, in the top posts of the Party—which was still the main center of important decisionmaking. Within the highest levels of the local Party, only one Mongol held a leading position, that of a deputy Party secretary. It appeared to me that the roles of many Mongols in the government and Party were mainly symbolic. However, their symbolic functions were not unimportant—particularly in relation to Baotou's links with other parts of Inner Mongolia and with Mongol-inhabited areas elsewhere. From what I was told, it was clear that contacts with other Mongol areas were substantial and increasing; recently, for example, Baotou had hosted a number of visitors from Outer Mongolia, including the ambassador to China of the People's Republic of Mongolia.

*   *   *

I was not able to learn very much about local politics in Baotou, or Inner Mongolia as a whole, in 1988; in fact, I learned much less in this respect than I had in 1947. However, I did learn one thing that confirmed what I had believed to be the case, namely that the relatives of Ulanfu, who for decades had been the leading Mongol leader in the Chinese Communist Party, played extremely influential roles. I was told that Ulanfu's third son, Wu Jie, was Baotou's mayor and that his first son, Bu He, was chairman of the autonomous region.

The term *autonomous* is really a misnomer for regions such as Inner Mongolia. Everything I learned indicated that Inner Mongolia (including Baotou) had been more fully integrated into the Chinese body politic in the years since the Communist takeover than it had ever been in the past—much more than when Fu Zuoyi ruled Suiyuan Province. Real power obviously was monopolized by Han Chinese. When I talked to local officials, moreover, it became clear that even though Baotou was subject to the authority of the region's leaders in Huhehaote, the direct influence of the central government on Baotou was particularly strong because it had become a major industrial city. When I asked local officials why—in light of the fact that the Mongol population was such a small minority—the region, including Baotou, was classified as an autonomous minority area, they said, simply, that it was for "historical reasons," and when I asked what, in practical terms, autonomy meant, they said that its most significant feature was the fact that preferential treatment was given the Mongols in many respects.

The structure of the Party and government in Baotou was virtually identical with that in other large Chinese cities, although, as in all minority areas, special bodies had been established to deal with minority affairs. I was told that, altogether, Baotou had over 3,000 administrative cadres working in 30-odd government bureaus and commissions. The total number of government employees, however, was many times that number. For example, officials I interviewed from one bureau said that although the bureau had only

82 staff members there were about 7,000 people working for units directly managed and supervised by the bureau. The total number of Party members in the municipality as a whole in 1988 was 87,000; this figure amounted to more than 5 percent of the population—a percentage similar to that in most other areas of China.

I was interested in learning anything I could about what effects recent national trends toward decentralization, personnel reform, and political liberalization had had on Baotou, and this was a subject I explored in my conversations with Deputy Mayor Zhang Zhiyu and many others I interviewed. I concluded that the effects were by no means insignificant, but not nearly as far reaching as in some other parts of China. In both political and economic reform, Baotou clearly lagged behind east China—particularly the coastal areas—and the changes that had occurred had affected economic policy more than political affairs. The municipality had taken few moves, as of early 1988, toward "separating Party and government" (a high priority aim of national reform)—although progress had been made in "separating Party and management" in enterprises.

Some authority for managing Party and government personnel affairs had been decentralized, but not a great deal, and mainly to the regional government in Huhehaote and to local enterprises in Baotou rather than to the municipal government. However, the municipal government had acquired somewhat greater power to control personnel appointments. In Baotou, I was told, all appointments of cadres of county level and above still required approval by the regional government, and the local Party Organization Department still controlled the appointment of all Party cadres of bureau level and above who held either Party or government posts. However, the role of the government's Personnel Bureau had been increased somewhat, and it now handled all administrative matters relating to low-ranking cadres, both those who were Party members and those who were non-Party cadres. At the same time, some of the Personnel Bureau's authority had been decentralized to enterprises, and this was a change of considerable significance. The bureau still set cadre quotas and salary levels, made decisions on rewards and punishments, and handled transfers and promotions, but, bureau officials themselves stressed, they were no longer involved in managing the day-to-day business affairs (*yewu*) that affected the personnel management of enterprises; responsibility for many decisions on personnel had been transferred to managers of enterprises.

I was impressed by the evidence of a considerable turnover of personnel in the 1980s, in which younger, more technocratic officials had replaced old cadres in both Party and government units as well as in enterprises. I did not obtain any detailed statistics on these personnel changes in Baotou, as I did later in most other areas that I visited, but it was nevertheless obvious that a major generational change had been taking place. Moreover, local officials asserted, since they had ended the old 24-grade ranking system in 1983 and shifted to a ranking system based on the positions that cadres held, they had tried to relate work and salary more directly than in the past to performance (although I had no way to judge the real effects of this change).

* * *

I obtained some insights into the generational change in the leadership, and into differences in generational outlooks, in an unexpected place. One afternoon, I visited Baotou's Old Cadres Activities Center, where I chatted at length with eight retired cadres. Such centers, built all over China during the 1980s, were established in part to minimize resistance to sweeping personnel changes that had resulted in millions of retirements.* Baotou's center for re-tired cadres was located in an attractive new building that had been com-pleted in 1986; it had a full-time staff of 8, assisted by 16 part-time workers, and it served over 5,000 retired cadres, most of whom were in their sixties. (Normal retirement age for cadres, though variable in practice, was 60 for men and 55 for women.) Retired cadres were classified into four groups on the basis of the periods in which they had acquired full cadre status: (1) be-fore July 1937, (2) between July 1937 and August 1945, (3) between August 1945 and October 1949, or (4) after 1949. The most important dividing line, I was told, was 1949, but all these cadres appeared to have equal access to the center's recreational and educational facilities and programs. The building had a library, a reading room, a music room with musical instru-ments, game rooms, and so on, and it offered classes in Qigong (a special kind of traditional exercise stressing breathing, which was enjoying a major revival in the late 1980s), the game majong, chess, and music, among other things. The current rage, I was told, was disco dancing; dancing sessions with free instruction were held every Thursday evening and Saturday after-noon, and they were said to be well attended.

The retired cadres I met were all men in their sixties, the majority of whom had come to Baotou in the 1950s, soon after its "liberation," and they in-cluded a former deputy mayor and a former secretary-general of the city. They seemed delighted to reminisce about their revolutionary experiences and careers, which they discussed with more than a touch of nostalgia. They argued among themselves, in a good-natured fashion, about the differences between those of them who had worked openly in "liberated areas" and those who had been a part of the underground in "white areas" (mainly in Nationalist-held cities). Cadres who had worked in both of these areas

---

*By the late 1980s, the Chinese government supported more than 20 million retired cadres and workers, at an annual cost of over Y 30 billion.

agreed that the rank-and-file Party members in liberated areas, mostly of peasant origin, had fought against Japanese oppression mainly for food and survival, not primarily for ideas, and that Party members in white areas had tended to be better-educated and more influenced by ideas. However, they differed on whether those in the "red" (that is, "liberated") areas were simple-minded or just practical and whether those in white areas were more intelligent or simply more utopian. They agreed that some Party leaders, including Lin Biao, had tried to exploit these differences.

What was most interesting to me, however, was their attitude toward recent trends in China. They talked with what seemed to me to be a real sense of guilt about the Cultural Revolution. One said: "It was a disaster. At the time, we were too simple-minded and thought that the Party would correct its mistakes. We just did what top leaders told us and did not speak up and express other ideas, partly because Chairman Mao approved of what occurred. A country should not be ruled by one man." Talking about the younger generation, all of them seemed to recognize that there were huge differences in attitudes between young and old cadres, and in general they said that they approved of the changes. One said: "Younger people in China today are more liberated in their thinking than we were. They are ready to try new things. They know more than we did and are trying to achieve more." All seemed to be philosophical, rather than resentful, about the emergence of younger, better-educated leaders. Although all of these old cadres had come to Baotou from other areas of China, they were proud of the city's development and talked at length about the great economic changes since 1949. But they expressed concern that current policies giving preferential treatment to coastal areas would seriously harm interior areas.

They had good reason for this concern. Despite its impressive development since the 1940s, Baotou clearly lagged behind eastern provinces in the 1980s. This was particularly true in regard to reform—not only political reform but some aspects of economic reform as well—and many people in Baotou feared that they could fall far behind eastern China in their overall pace of development. The current deputy mayor and his secretary-general, as well as other officials I met, made this fairly clear in their conversations with me. They were frank in admitting that compared to eastern provinces they were followers and not leaders ("We are not an experimental area"), and they were still "studying," rather than actually implementing, many reform policies. Some said that they would wait until central policy—and directives from Beijing to Baotou specifically—became clearer before carrying out difficult reforms. At one point a journalist said to me that central policy had changed so often that Baotou's officials could not be sure how long any policy would last, and therefore the tendency was to wait and see. This attitude did not surprise me greatly; in many respects Baotou was still far from the mainstream of change in China, and I sensed that most of the individuals I met, in contrast to many officials and entrepreneurs in coastal areas, were extremely cautious and unwilling to stick their necks out.

*   *   *

In its economic relationships with higher authorities, Baotou—unlike most underdeveloped areas in west China but like most industrialized areas in the east—had long been a net contributor of funds to higher authorities. Even though it was still very dependent on the state (especially the central government) for most of its investment capital, it nevertheless provided large amounts of money for the budgets of both the regional and central governments. According to figures given to me by municipal government officials, Baotou collected Y 427.5 million in revenue in 1987, mostly from taxes on enterprise profits and other industrial and commercial taxes, but of this it transferred Y 180 million (42 percent) to higher authorities—Y 147.6 million (34.53 percent) to the regional government and Y 32.4 million (7.58 percent) to the central government. The expenditures of the municipality totaled slightly more than Y 300 million, of which close to Y 250 million was covered by the tax revenues that it collected and retained; the rest came from subsidies from higher levels of government.

The regional government in Huhehaote, I was told, had a budget of close to Y 4 billion, of which about half was provided by Beijing and Baotou. I do not know how accurate these figures were—they came from municipal officials rather than officials in the regional government—but I had no doubt about the main point these officials were trying to make to me, namely, that the region was highly dependent fiscally on Beijing and Baotou. This pattern of fiscal dependency was characteristic of virtually all the underdeveloped provinces and regions of west China. Baotou's situation—that is, its fiscal surplus and its contribution to higher levels of government—was an exception and was more like that of industrial areas in east China.

In the military sphere, as I noted earlier, what struck me most, in contrast to what I saw on my previous visit, was the absence of any visible sign of military personnel or facilities. Local officials emphasized that military affairs in the region were basically the responsibility of Beijing—and to a much lesser extent Huhehaote—and they indicated that most of the "main force" units of the PLA were stationed far from Baotou, nearer to the Sino-Soviet border. Baotou, which constituted a military subdistrict, was mainly responsible, I was told, for local recruitment and some military training. Even granting that the local military responsibility was very limited, I was surprised not to see any overt evidence at all of a military presence.

I asked my hosts to tell me something about Baotou's economic links with other areas of China. During the 1980s, there was considerable emphasis in national policy on the need to develop "horizontal" ties between different cities and regions in China, but as of 1988 this clearly had not developed very far in Baotou's case. Inner Mongolia—including Baotou—was considered to be part of China's "second front"—the group of provinces located between the coastal areas and the far west—and local officials told me that there were special relationships of various sorts that had developed between it and the north China provinces of Hebei and Shanxi as well as with the municipalities of Beijing and Tianjin. A number of cooperative agreements had been signed, I was told, that linked commissions, bureaus, and departments in all of these areas. Baotou also had agreed to formal "sister city" relationships with Shijiazhuang and Zhangjiakou—both in Hebei—which involved some cooperation in developing resources and some technology transfers (although I could not judge how significant these were). But Baotou's most important ties, both political and economic, were obviously vertical and linked it to Beijing via Huhehaote; in addition, its economic relations with Tianjin, its main sea outlet, were vitally important, as they had been in the past. Baotou still had many significant links, not surprisingly, with the Mongol grassland areas to the northeast and southwest, but these seemed to be less important, relatively speaking, than they had been when Baotou was a frontier trading post. Its most important economic relationships now followed the railway eastward.

*   *   *

By the 1980s, Baotou's main raison d'être was its role as a major new industrial area and above all as a steel center. It was the growth of industry that had transformed the city into a modern metropolis. Starting in the 1950s, modern industry had developed virtually from scratch, on the initiative of the central government as a result of Beijing's decision in 1953 to build Baotou into a major industrial base. However, its development had had its ups and downs. The first surge of growth was in the 1950s, when, I was told, more than Y 4 billion of "investments in fixed capital" (almost all from the central government) flowed into the city. Its steel mill was one of the key projects in China's first Five Year Plan, and Soviet experts and equipment played a crucial role in its construction. In addition, many factories, and numerous technicians and laborers, were transferred to the city from more developed areas, particularly northeast China.

Then, in the 1960s following the Sino-Soviet split, when Mao's policy stressed the need to industrialize China's so-called third-front areas, which were more remote from China's international borders, Baotou's growth slumped; the slowdown in its development lasted until the 1980s. During this period of almost 20 years, local planners said, only about Y 1 billion was invested in fixed capital in the city. However, a second period of rapid growth began in 1979, and during the decade of the 1980s another Y 2 billion or so had been invested in fixed capital in Baotou. Overall, the total investment in fixed capital in Baotou between the early 1950s and the late

1980s amounted to roughly Y 7.6 billion, over 80 percent of which, local officials estimated, had come from the central government and less than 20 percent of which had come from the regional and municipal governments and local enterprises themselves.

As a result of this investment, by 1987 Baotou had 888 factories, and the annual value of its gross industrial output had increased more than 330 times compared to 1949, rising from Y 10.4 million to Y 3.437 billion. In the same period, the number of workers had risen to over 590,000. The overwhelming majority, almost 386,000 (more than 65 percent), worked for state enterprises. However, the number working for collective enterprises (which in the 1980s was one index of economic reform) had grown substantially, to over 185,000 (31 percent of the total). Only about 19,000 (3.22 percent) worked for individual enterprises, but this number was slowly beginning to rise.

Because of the city's industrial development, by the late 1980s the population of Baotou enjoyed a comparatively high standard of living, well above that in most areas of west China though still lower than in many eastern industrial cities. A survey in 1987 determined that the average per capita income in the municipality's urban areas was Y 890. In 1988, according to preliminary statistics, the average wage of workers in state enterprises in Baotou was almost Y 1,400 (which was about the national average for such enterprises). This figure did not include the value of government subsidies for housing, food, and so on, which, if included, would probably more than double that figure.*

Residential housing in Baotou was, by Chinese standards, comparatively new and spacious. Three young people I talked to, including one bachelor, told me that each of them had an apartment of roughly 40 square meters (about 430 square feet), which was far larger than they could have expected in cities such as Beijing or Shanghai. In recent years, the local diet had improved substantially and had become increasingly varied. Because Baotou obtained most of its food from fairly distant areas, several items were still rationed, including grain (the standard ration was between 27 and 37 *catties* per person per month, depending on one's occupation, age, and so on), vegetable oil (just under one-half a catty per person), and pork (recently 1 to 1.5 catties per person).† I was told by an official responsible for food policy, which includes food distribution, that there were no real shortages of food in

---

*Nationally, according to Beijing's statistics, average per capita consumption in China in 1988 was Y 639, but there was still an estimated total of 70 million people—6 to 7 percent of the population, most of whom were living in remote areas of west China—whose incomes were still well below the poverty level, defined by the Chinese at that time to be Y 200 per capita per year.

†A catty is a Chinese measure equal to one-half a kilogram, or 1.1 pounds.

the municipality. Reportedly, most people bought at least 20 to 30 percent of their food, including perhaps 60 percent of their vegetables, at free markets, and some residents relied primarily on free markets for most of their purchases. Free market prices for food, I was told, generally were 10 to 15 percent above state prices, but the quality was much better. People were eating more rice, as well as seafood, despite the cost of transporting these items from distant areas.

There was no rationing of cloth or clothing. Demand for consumer durables far exceeded supplies. There were widespread complaints, in fact, that Baotou was not allotted enough color TV sets to meet the local demand. Rising expectations, and the strong and growing demands for material goods, especially among the young, dismayed some of the older people I met. One elderly official condemned, with some emotion, the erosion of old values as a result of growing materialism and consumerism, and he blamed the trend on the impact of TV. "It is like opium," he said. "Everyone wants a color TV, and some people buy a refrigerator just for decoration. They no longer have noble goals." What a contrast, I thought to myself, to the situation in the 1940s, when the goal of most people in this remote area was simply survival.

*   *   *

Even though economic reform in Baotou was still in its early stages and obviously still lagged well behind that in most of east China, everyone maintained that the reforms that had been implemented had given a much-needed stimulus to the city's economy in the 1980s. And after hearing many statements about how Baotou lagged in reforms, I was surprised, when I asked about special reforms, to learn how much at least some economic reforms had begun to take root. Various forms of the so-called manager contract responsibility system—*chengbao zhidu*—had been introduced; some efforts had begun to try to separate Party and government from enterprises; and enterprise managers now enjoyed at least somewhat greater authority than previously to make decisions regarding personnel, management, and the use of capital. One official told me that roughly 70 percent of the city's enterprises—mainly medium-sized and small ones rather than the largest ones—had already adopted the factory director responsibility system (*changzhang fuze zhidu*). Of these enterprises, 30 to 40 percent were under a particular kind of contract system (*changzhang chengbao zhidu*) in which the manager's responsibility and authority were increased substantially and the manager had to assume greater risks of punishment for nonfulfillment of contracted targets. Under this system, I was told, the managers in some enterprises now had supreme authority even over Party affairs, as well as over production, and often one man—generally a technical expert—was both manager and Party secretary. This doubtless involved a far-reaching change in the places where the system had been implemented; it sounded, in

The Baotou city wall. In 1948, Fu Zuoyi's troops constantly manned the city wall and closed the gate at night; Chinese Communist forces were not far away.

A Baotou cityscape. In 1948 the entire city, a county seat, consisted of traditional one-story buildings; there were almost no signs of modernity.

Two of Fu Zuoyi's soldiers on guard
outside Baotou's city wall, 1948.

A friend from Beijing and I mount camels
in a traditional Baotou caravansary.

In subzero winter weather, Bactrian camels together with Han Chinese and Mongols bundled up in sheepskin clothing crowd an open-air market.

Standard worker apartment buildings now house most of Baotou's working popula-tion; similar apartment dwellings dot cities throughout west as well as east China.

Modernistic buildings like this, built in the 1980s, line Baotou's main ave-nues; they are much more colorful than Mao-era or pre-1949 struc-tures.

Right:
A Han Chinese technician, an adminis-
trator, and my young escort stand
in front of part of Baotou's huge
steel mill—built by engineers from east
China with Soviet assistance.

Below:
Modern young Han Chinese women
shop for clothing at an open-air market
in Baotou; they try hard to keep up with
current fashions.

A donkey cart on the road to the Wudangzhao lamasery, north of Baotou.

Wudangzhao lamasery: a magnificent Qing-dynasty Mongol lamasery north of Baotou. Lamaism is reviving but lacks the fervor of the past.

Right:
A huge dune at the start of the
Ordos Desert, south of Baotou.
This desert stretches to the
horizon and far beyond.

Desertified fields on the road to the Dala Special Banner, south of Baotou.

fact, less like a separation of the Party and enterprises than a merger of Party and enterprise management—but of an entirely new kind, in which technical specialists instead of old-style organizational men held the key positions.

As elsewhere in China, mandatory planning (that is, the setting, by planning agencies in Beijing, of specific targets that enterprises had to meet) had been reduced. This reduction had had more effect on medium-sized and small enterprises than on large ones such as the iron and steel company—as I will discuss later. However, the figures given to me, if correct, indicated far-reaching changes affecting a large percentage of Baotou's industrial enterprises. In the two main categories of planning in effect—mandatory and guidance—only about 10-plus percent of the value of gross industrial output (mainly that of the iron, steel, and aluminum industries) remained subject to old-style mandatory central planning, I was told by local officials; under this system the government provided all or most of the raw materials and controlled the use of all of the output. By 1988, local officials said, an additional 20-plus percent or so of the gross value of industrial output was subject to "guidance planning," in which the government made strong "suggestions" but gave enterprises considerable authority to modify them. Enterprises subjected only to guidance planning had to purchase most or all of their raw materials on the market but then could sell much—and, in some cases, almost all—of their products on the market. Local officials went on to say that more than 60 percent of Baotou's industrial output was now basically "marketized"; that is, this much of the output came from enterprises not subject to either mandatory or guidance planning—enterprises that bought their own raw materials wherever they could and sold their output on the market (they admitted, though, that most markets were still subject to extensive government regulations).

I was surprised, and, frankly, slightly skeptical, about these figures. They indicated a much higher degree of decontrol than I had expected or that really seemed plausible to me, especially for an economy dominated by the steel industry, but there was no way that I could independently check the figures. My guess was that the share of the economy under state planning continued to be larger than these figures suggested, perhaps considerably larger. Nevertheless, what I was told convinced me that a significant process of decontrol and marketization had begun and that local officials strongly favored it.

Officials said that there had been some efforts to develop a local labor market, and increase labor mobility, but they admitted that not much real progress on this had been made. They recognized the importance of developing a real labor market but stressed the difficulty of doing so. Workers were rarely if ever fired, they said, in part because no unemployment insurance system existed to assist them. The highest number of workers fired in any one local enterprise, I was told, was 30; this was in a large cotton mill that had about 10,000 employees.

The Baotou government had formulated plans to decentralize overall supervisory authority affecting a large number of enterprises from the municipal level to the city district level. However, they had barely begun to implement this. One official said, "speaking frankly," that "many factories are theoretically under the district, but really they are still supervised by the municipal Party and government."

All the Baotou officials I met fervently wished to be granted, under China's new open policy, greater authority to make their own decisions about starting enterprises that required the use of foreign exchange. As of 1988, however, their authority in this respect was extremely limited. Baotou itself could initiate only those projects involving a maximum of US$2 million of foreign exchange; this was a very low ceiling compared with those set for the major industrial areas along the China coast. In general, Baotou's direct links to the outside world were still very limited. It exported some of its products, but its total foreign trade was still relatively small. Foreign visitors, especially investors, were few and far between. (At my hotel, the leading one for foreigners, I saw only four non-Chinese—two Austrians and two Japanese.) In the entire city as of 1988, I was told, there were only two joint ventures involving people from outside China (in both cases, these people were Hong Kong entrepreneurs); one was an electronics factory and the other was a taxi company. Several of the city's largest enterprises had recently imported new foreign machinery; one notable case was the Number One Machinery Company, which had purchased machines from West Germany. Many other factories wished to import new machinery, but to date most had been unable to do so.

I heard numerous criticisms—some overt and blunt, some muted and subtle—of Beijing's current policy favoring coastal areas. One official, for example, said: "In Inner Mongolia, experts disagree with the 'coastal policy.' They think the central government should treat all three 'fronts' in China equally. The west has rich resources, and its development is good for the country, but our technical development is still weak, and we think the central government should give equal priority to the west. ... Supposedly, the 'coastal policy' will last to the end of the century, and if so it unfortunately will increase the gap between the west and the coast." Another said bluntly: "I do not agree with the priority given to coastal areas; it will make the west relatively more backward. National policy is sometimes wrong."

Baotou's leaders felt largely left out of China's increasing economic interaction with the outside world. They also clearly were concerned—and frankly stated their concern—about the difficulties and problems they were encountering in trying to implement reform. "It is not easy to mesh reforms with the present system," one top official said. "Part of the reason is that successful changes in one part of the system are impeded by a lack of change in others, and so much of the present system is not adequate."

When I asked—as I did in interviews with a number of people—what, when one looks at Baotou's overall economy, the most pressing problems were, and what problems looked most serious for the period ahead, I received several answers. The deputy mayor declared that Baotou's basic problem was "to catch up with other big cities." Many people gave answers that reflected resentment about what was felt to be discrimination under the coastal policy. However, many cited very specific problems. One was inflation, which by 1988 had become a major problem throughout China, causing widespread dissatisfaction. Somewhat to my surprise, however, I was told that the inflation rate in Baotou was significantly lower than in Bejing and many other large cities. Nevertheless, fluctuations in food prices were causing worry. Unemployment was also cited as a growing problem. It was officially estimated to total roughly 25,000, or close to 5 percent of the labor force. This figure sounded low to me, and I suspected that it understated real unemployment, but it was regarded as high for China. Unemployed workers were mainly supported by relatives, I was told, but the government had initiated some training programs for them.

Everyone recognized that, even with the reforms that had started, rigidities in planning and poor management continued to pose absolutely fundamental problems; they were particularly troublesome in a place such as Baotou, where large state enterprises dominated the economy. The burden of direct and indirect subsidies given to the population was also very heavy—amounting to about a quarter of all local budgetary expenses, I was told. The burden of transferring over two-fifths of the revenues collected in Baotou to a higher government was also heavy, and it was resented by at least some people. And it became clear when I talked to enterprise managers that modernization of the city's industrial equipment—much of which was aging and outdated—was badly needed.

*   *   *

Despite all the problems, however, the size of Baotou's industry was really impressive—at least to one who had first seen the city when it had only three tiny factories. The decision made in the 1950s to build Baotou into a major center of industry was based principally on its proximity to major iron and coal resources; not surprisingly, the city's iron and steel complex had become the foundation of its economy. However, I was impressed also by the variety of its industries. Its 888 factories encompassed more than 15 fields, including several branches of metallurgy, machine building, energy, construction materials, chemicals, textiles, and other types of light industry, including electronics. Metallurgy and machine building were preeminent, together accounting for 60 percent of the gross value of the municipality's industrial output. The

Baotou Iron and Steel Corporation, which local officials said was the fifth largest steel enterprise in China (ranking behind Anshan, Wuhan, Baoshan in Shanghai, and Shijingshan in Beijing), together with a smaller company called the Dongfang Iron and Steel Works, made Inner Mongolia one of China's top nine steel-producing "provinces" (this list included Shanghai and Beijing, which had administrative status equal to that of provinces), although its output was still far behind that of Liaoning (which produced almost 11 million tons) and Shanghai (which produced 8 million). Baotou's aluminum plant, with a capacity of 25,000 tons of ingots (which it planned to expand to 80,000), was one of the eight largest ones in the country. Baotou was the largest producer in China (and was said to rank high worldwide) of "rare earth." Its two big machinery plants produced a wide variety of machines, tools, mining and oil drilling equipment, and vehicles. The city also had plants producing copper, chemicals, tractors, valves, auto accessories, windmill generators, solar energy batteries (widely used on the Mongol grasslands), and a great variety of consumer goods.

Although many of its factories were fairly large, the Baotou Iron and Steel Corporation was in a class by itself, and its role in the local economy was so great that in many respects Baotou had clearly become a "company town." Visiting this enterprise was therefore high on my list of priorities, and my host arranged for me to spend a half day visiting the furnaces and mills at its huge, sprawling main production center. While there, I talked at considerable length with its top management, including its general manager, Zhang Guozhong (a technician who also was the company's chief engineer), and the Party secretary, as well as other key technical people, the leaders of sections dealing with planning and personnel, and others. The general manager chaired my briefing session, and it appeared to me that he outranked the Party secretary, at least as far as production decisions were concerned; he called on many others at the meeting to provide details on their areas of expertise. The briefing that they gave me on the company's history, development, production, and future plans was thorough.

The initial decision to build an iron and steel complex at Baotou was made in 1951, I was told—well before China's first Five Year Plan began—because of the known resources nearby. In the 1920s, a geological survey team of Chinese and Swedes had first located iron at Baiyun Ebo, a little over 90 miles due north of Baotou. More iron was discovered there in the mid-1940s, but none was exploited at that time. Soon after 1949, a team of experts spent three years surveying the area and concluded that the iron reserves at Baiyun Ebo totaled about 1 billion tons (a figure that subsequently was raised to 1.2 billion), making it one of China's richest iron deposits. Also nearby were several large areas of coal deposits, which, the company manager said, had reserves second only to those in Shanxi Province. The nearest coal mine, at Shiguaigou, roughly 30 miles northeast of Baotou, was especially important, but the company also used coal from a large deposit about 185 miles to the west, and recently another large deposit had been discovered near the Yellow River (where plans called for building a huge coal-fired electric plant, which I believe they said would ultimately have a capacity of 2.4 gigawatts).

The company was formally established in 1954; construction started in 1956–1957 with Soviet aid (Russians drew up the original designs); and in 1960 the first open-hearth furnace was constructed—just before the Sino-Soviet split. It took a long time to get large-scale production under way. Major production of steel ingots finally began in the 1966–1968 period, more than a decade after construction had begun.

While the Baotou government's public relations personnel waxed lyrical when describing the company's industrial empire, which they labeled the "pearl on the prairie" and the heart of China's "grasslands steel city," the technocrats running the company, even though they were obviously proud of their huge complex, were more matter-of-fact in describing it, which they did largely with statistics. The statistics were impressive, however. By 1988, the company had three large open-hearth blast furnaces, three 50-ton converters, and five major rolling mills, a blooming mill and ones producing heavy rails, steel I beams, seamless pipe, wire, and welded pipe. The company also produced a little, but not much, alloy steel. The most important original equipment had been purchased from the Soviet Union, but after 1960 much of the equipment was Chinese-made, and recently some has been imported from West Germany, Japan, France, and the United States.

The company expected that output in 1988 would total 2.5 million tons of pig iron, 2 million tons of steel ingots, and between 1.1 and 1.2 million tons of steel products (about 17 percent of the steel product output at Anshan, China's largest producer). These figures were far larger than they had been a decade previously; the average annual increases in the company's output since 1979 had been 18 percent for iron, 14 percent for steel, and 13 percent for steel products.

The value, in yuan, of the company's output in 1988 was expected to reach close to Y 1.2 billion (which compared with Y 480 million in 1978 and Y 1.16 billion in 1987); this total would account for roughly one-third of the expected gross value of output of all industry in Baotou (but would still amount to only about a quarter of the value of the steel output at Anshan). Under the company's management, there were 92 organizational units, of which 37 were factories and 7 were mines. The factories' floor space totaled over 32 million square meters (344 million square feet).

The manager outlined for me the company's ambitious plans for expanding output. The target for production of steel products by the end of China's next Five Year Plan, I was told, was 3 million tons, and its target for the end of the century was 5 million. To support this expansion, Baotou Municipality also had ambitious plans to increase its sources of electric power. Already, its own power sources totaled 520 megawatts from three plants—310 megawatts from its Kundulun plant, 200 megawatts from its Qingshan plant, and 10 megawatts from a small plant in Gonghe—and it also obtained additional power from a 100-megawatt plant in Wulanshan, 58 miles from Baotou. Local officials also hoped, as noted earlier, to increase their supply substantially from the planned plant scheduled to be built at the newly discovered coal deposit near the Yellow River. (According to published reports, in the first phase of its development this power plant would build four 330-megawatt generators, and its target was to have a capacity of 5 gigawatts by the end of the century—more than any power plant in Asia at present.)

The size of the company's work force also put it in a class by itself among Baotou's enterprises. In 1988, the total of its employees of all kinds was 71,437—roughly one-eighth of the municipality's work force. If one included family members, the number of people supported by the company was much larger, of course. Most of its employees had come from other parts of China. Of the total, roughly 4,000 were classified as engineers and technicians, 3,000 as managerial and administrative personnel, and the rest as ordinary workers. About 2,000 of the employees were Mongols. The average wage for the entire company in 1988 was roughly Y 1,700 (not counting subsidies), which was a little above the average of state enterprises in general but was lower, I was told, than the level of wages in the Anshan, Baoshan, and Shijingshan plants, although some employees in Baotou received extra benefits for long service in a remote area and for having obtained higher education. For example, one technician I met who had worked in Baotou with the company for 20 years received an extra Y 20 a month, and I was told that university graduates were given an automatic bonus of Y 8 a month.

Like all large state enterprises in China, the Baotou Iron and Steel Corporation was what Chinese referred to as a "small society" that managed its own housing, schools, hospitals, and recreational facilities. The company itself had 32 large housing blocks, with space totaling 1.44 million square meters (15.49 million square feet). It operated a large educational system of its own, which included 8 kindergartens, 28 primary schools, 12 regular middle schools, 10 other middle schools for workers, a spare-time "university" for workers, several training institutions for senior technicians, and medical and teacher training institutions. The company also operated a major iron and steel research institute and published its own newspaper. Medical institutions operated by the company included three "hospitals" and a nursing home. (By 1988, Baotou Municipality as a whole had 37 institutions classified as hospitals, which together had a total of 7,000 beds.) In sum, the company provided almost all the services needed by employees, and they therefore were almost totally dependent on the company in every respect.

Breaking this pattern of *danwei* (unit) dominance became, in the 1980s, one of the basic objectives of China's reformers, but there had been little progress at all toward this end in this huge company.

The reform policies adopted by Beijing in the 1980s clearly did not ignore the special challenge posed by huge state enterprises of this sort, but the impact of the new policies on such enterprises, throughout the country and not just in Baotou, had so far been relatively small. This company had implemented one form of the contract responsibility system, under which it had signed a contract guaranteeing achievement of some specific production targets in the period through 1990; the contract also specified definite levels of profits and taxes and set targets for technical improvement. In theory, if these targets could not be achieved, the company would be fined and its employees' wages reduced; if they could be surpassed, the company would be authorized to use the above-target profits for reinvestment and increased salaries and benefits to workers. In 1987, I was told, the company's profit was well above the target (Chinese planners tended to set targets that were achievable without great difficulty); the company kept Y 50 million to Y 60 million as above-target profits, and roughly half of this was used for reinvestment and half for increased wages, salaries, and benefits (the central government continued to regulate how much could be used for each purpose). How all of this operated in practice was difficult to judge on a short visit. However, if this company operated like most huge state enterprises in China, as I assumed it did, the changes, though significant, may not have been as great as they appeared on the surface.

I did receive the strong impression that as a result of recent reform policies the manager and other technical specialists were clearly in charge of production, and the Party secretary's role appeared to have been significantly reduced. The general manager maintained that he had acquired much more flexibility than in the past, and that this had helped to account for rising profits. According to his figures, in 1987 total profits and taxes paid to the state had amounted to Y 340 million (close to 30 percent of output value), which compared, he said, with Y 50 million in 1978. In spite of all that I was told about changes, my impressionistic judgment was that the Baotou Iron and Steel Corporation, like most large state enterprises in China, was probably still very inefficient and that many problems posed great obstacles to real change. The company was clearly overstaffed by Western standards. Moreover, although I carefully recorded what I was told about the company's profits, I viewed the figures with some skepticism; in 1988 many of China's largest plants were operating at a loss. Although I had no expertise relating to steel production, the company's equipment appeared to my layman's eye to be old and outdated (perhaps comparable to the equipment at Anshan but far less modern than the Japanese-made equipment at Baoshan, both of which I had previously seen). The general manager expressed a very strong desire to upgrade the company's equipment, and I could see why. Despite the reform policies in the 1980s, most large Chinese enterprises similar to the steel company in Baotou still operated for the most part under direct state planning—unlike China's growing cooperative and private sector—and this made me doubt that reform had gone as far as some of the data given to me suggested.

In 1988, the Baotou Iron and Steel Corporation still operated under the "dual leadership" of the Ministry of Metallurgical Industry and the equivalent provincial-level organs. The latter, I was told, had gradually been given somewhat increased responsibility, and apparently this had allowed the company to have somewhat greater flexibility in making decisions. However, this obviously had not changed the basic fact that state planning, not the market, still regulated the company. Of the company's output target set by the state, 90 percent still had to be sold to the state, I was told—mainly through materials bureaus. However, 10 to 15 percent of the actual output of the company was above quota, and the company itself could sell this part of the output—which varied between 120,000 and 180,000 tons of steel products a year (in 1987 it was 150,000 tons)—on the market, mainly through state-supervised steel markets established by materials supply organizations, but some of it directly to other enterprises and factories. In state-supervised markets, the range of permitted prices was regulated by the government (and varied by province), but in general it was said to be about double the state prices. Eventually, according to the plans of China's reformers, a much larger percentage of the output even of the large state enterprises would be marketized, but for the Baotou Iron and Steel Corporation the attainment of this goal still seemed in 1988 to be fairly far in the future.

*   *   *

Following my visit to the iron and steel complex, I tried to learn something about other industry in Baotou by visiting two smaller factories. One was a producer of enamelware. Although the number of its employees, 1,070, was sizable, it was categorized as a medium-sized state enterprise. Founded in 1958, in 1988 it had seven workshops and produced 162 different products. It was not capital-intensive—only Y 3.48 million had been invested in fixed capital in the factory over three decades—but the gross value of its output had risen fairly rapidly in recent years, from Y 4.9 million in 1985 to Y 5.5 million in 1986 to Y 6.9 million in 1987, an increase of over 40 percent in two years. Profits had reportedly risen even more rapidly, from Y 396,000 in 1985 to Y 891,000 in 1986 to Y 1 million in 1987. Average wages had risen about 30 percent in the same period, but they still averaged only Y 960 a year in 1987—much lower than wages in the iron and steel company. The most interesting recent change, in the case of this enterprise, had been its increasing involvement in foreign trade. In its early years, the output had been sold almost entirely within Inner Mongolia; by 1987, not only had its domestic markets been broadened, but 65 percent or more (by value) of its output was exported, mostly to Southeast Asia but a little to Outer Mongolia and the USSR and even a small amount to the United States.

The director and technicians whom I met in this enamelware factory seemed to me to be fairly old-fashioned types (they were all clad in Mao suits, which no longer seemed to be very common in Baotou), but they attributed most of their recent success to the new reform policy. The factory had introduced the responsibility system, under which targets had been set for the factory as a whole as well as for each of its seven workshops and for each worker; they said that this system had effectively increased incentives and productivity. The reform policies also had led them to reduce the number of management personnel a little, although not by much, from 15 to 13 percent of the total number of employees. They also stressed that they were trying to base increased incentives on technical skill and productivity. Perhaps the greatest change, it seemed to me, was their adoption of new marketing methods, especially to promote exports.

The third factory that I visited was an individual (*geti*) private leather factory, one of the largest such factories in Baotou, which was located in a villagelike area in a poor suburb of Kundulun District. The development of small private businesses (as well as cooperatives, many of which were semi-private) had been one of the most striking new trends in China in the 1980s. This trend had advanced most rapidly in China's coastal regions, but it had begun to affect even remote places such as Baotou. By 1988, Baotou had about 30,000 small "individual household" enterprises, I was told. This figure did not include about 10,000 itinerant peddlers, buyers, and sellers from other areas, especially southern cities, among whom traders from Wenzhou in Zhejiang Province were most numerous. The overwhelming majority of the individual household enterprises in Baotou were engaged in commerce or the provision of services. Nevertheless, the number of small "factories" (many of which were just small production shops) had risen to roughly 5,000. They were organized and represented by a citywide association (a sort of guild), with subunits in each district. The government had encouraged private production by these small entrepreneurs by granting them tax exemptions or tax reductions and by providing them with low-interest loans.

The leather factory that I visited was regarded as a model business. Organized in the early 1980s by a well-off peasant family from an area near Baotou, it had developed into a very profitable enterprise. One member of the family, who clearly was the moving spirit, described to me its origin and development. He and one of his brothers, he said, were inspired by the government's encouragement of individual enterprise, so they took a trip, at their own expense, to Shanghai, Jiangsu Province, and Zhejiang Province to investigate possibilities. They decided that there was a demand for leather products, which seemed to be a logical thing to produce in Inner Mongolia. On their return trip, they met on the train, by accident, a man from Henan who knew something about leather products, and this serendipitous encounter led them to invite him to visit Baotou. On the basis of his advice, they decided that they would establish a small factory, and the two brothers and their father managed to pool Y 24,000 (Y 8,000 each) as start-up capital. Purchasing tanned leather from the Baotou Foreign Trade Bureau, they started making gloves and jackets. They were tax-exempt at the start (but in 1988 no longer were), and as they grew they obtained low-interest loans from the local Agricultural Bank and began buying leather directly from the Ikh Zhao Mongol area about 60 miles from Baotou, transporting it to the city by truck.

By 1988, when I visited the factory, it had become a thriving business. Although the buildings and facilities were old-fashioned and simple—in fact, fairly primitive—their operation had expanded to the point where their fixed capital totaled Y 120,000 and their working capital (leather, raw materials, chemicals, and so on) amounted to Y 180,000. They had 67 employees (of whom 10 were family members; the rest belonged to relatively poor households nearby), and the wages that they paid averaged Y 80 to Y 100 a month (although the wages of a few were as high as Y 240). They produced 21 different products, including men's and women's leather jackets, ordinary gloves, large cyclists' gloves, and leather ties. The gross value of their output in 1987 was Y 260,000, on which they paid a 5 percent product tax and a 7 percent tax on profit (a rate that they said would rise as output grows), and in 1987 their net profit, after paying production costs and taxes, was over Y 40,000. Initially, they sold their products through Baotou department stores (at one of them, they obtained permission to set up a special counter), then through several outlets in large enterprises in the city (including the Iron and Steel Corporation), and subsequently through more distant outlets, the most important of which was the Beijing Friendship Store, where some foreign businessmen were buyers. The ex-peasants running this business were obviously, and understandably, proud of their entrepreneurial success. Private enterprises of this sort still played only a very small role in Baotou's overall economy, but there was little doubt that the potential for development was substantial, and local officials said that the government's policy was to encourage their development.

*   *   *

Industrialization had obviously been the main engine of modernization in Baotou. Agriculture had played only a minor role, yet it too had undergone some modern development. In the municipality as a whole, there were, in 1988, 467,000 acres of cultivated land (much of which was very poor land, however) and 1.17 million acres of grassland pasture (also mostly dry and poor). Creeping desertification made most of the area unpromising for agriculture. Nevertheless, the municipality had achieved self-sufficiency in vegetables, which were grown mostly in the suburbs, where farmers used plastic sheeting that allowed cultivation during most of the year (except in the coldest months of January and February—the period when I made my visit). In addition, local farmers grew a little wheat, corn, and sorghum, but not much, and most of the output of these crops was consumed by its producers. The city basically depended, therefore, on grain purchased from other parts of China, which the municipality's Bureau of Grain arranged through the equivalent bureau in Beijing's Ministry of Commerce. Local production of sunflower seeds provided only a small fraction of the city's need for vegetable oil, so it too had to be purchased elsewhere. Animal and meat production was also small; local production supplied only 10 to 15 percent of Baotou's meat requirement, although the municipal Agricultural Commission hoped to double this eventually to over 30 percent. Baotou purchased most of its beef from Inner Mongolia's grassland areas and most of its pork from Shandong and Sichuan provinces. The household contract responsibility system had been implemented throughout the city's rural areas (even, I was told, in modified form in most of its state farms) and, local officials maintained, it had stimulated increased output, in Baotou as elsewhere in China. Agriculture was still subject to "guidance planning," but I was told that peasants were able to make their own decisions on most matters, and many were now trying to diversify production and shift from grain to more remunerative cash crops.

I did not visit any farms producing crops (it was the wrong time of year), but I did visit the Yellow River Dairy Farm, a state farm established by the city's Agricultural Commission, which operated with some of the characteristics of a factory. When I talked with the farm's leaders, it appeared to me that, as in the Iron and Steel Corporation, the director now exercised more authority than the Party secretary, a significant change from the past (which the farm leaders themselves pointed out to me). The director and other leaders, dressed in either Western-style clothes or good Mao-style suits, did not in any way look like, or act like, traditional Chinese peasants. The director, in particular, impressed me as being an intelligent, well-informed, energetic entrepreneur.

Established in 1957, this state farm, which was located in a suburb on the edge of the Yellow River a few miles south of the city, included (as of 1988) more than 20 square miles of territory, within which roughly 1,700 acres were used to grow fodder and about 1,000 acres were pastureland. About 400 acres were wooded. The farm was, in one sense, a territorial subunit of the city as well as a farm. Its population totaled 3,900 people, who belonged to about 1,000 households; 2,400 of them were farm employees. The more than 1,200 cows on the farm produced about 3,500 tons of milk annually. As a result of diversification in recent years, the farm also had about 50,000 chickens, producing over 300,000 kilograms (more than 661,000 pounds or 330-plus tons) of eggs a year; it also operated two brick factories and managed an enclosed area in the river that produced carp (with technical help from experts sent from Beijing under the State Council's "Spark Program," organized to provide technical assistance to underdeveloped areas).

The milk produced by the farm was pasteurized with French-made machinery, packaged with "soft packaging" that used French technology, and sold in the city through two sales outlets maintained by the farm itself. Its sole competitor was a smaller farm that had only one such sales outlet. The director said that before 1978 the farm had lost money, but now, as a result of reforms, its profits—though varying annually—were generally over Y 200,000 a year.

From what I was told, it appeared to me that recent reforms had had more impact on this farm than on some factories in the area and had brought significant changes in organization, decisionmaking, and operations. The management and Party organizations still coexisted, in parallel, but the director and his office seemed to exercise the most important authority. The management organization, which was called a *changbu* (farm department), was headed by the director and two deputies, both of whom were appointed by the municipality's Agricultural Commission. Under them was a staff of over 60, organized into six sections, which included the director's office and three sections handling planning, accounting, and production; interestingly, they described the Party Committee Office and a Security (*baowei*) Office as if they too were part of this structure, subordinate to the director. Important production decisions were made at Production Management Meetings (*sheng-chan bangong huiyi*), which were attended by over 20 people, including top management personnel and the heads of the farm's 17 production units (each of which was considered to be an "independent accounting unit," led by a "responsible person"—*fuzeren*—and two assistants). These meetings took place two or three times a month.

The Party's organization was headed by the Party secretary and one deputy; they were appointed by the municipal Party Committee, but, I was told, the government's Agricultural Commission played a role in choosing and supervising them. Altogether, there were 132 Party members on the farm (3-plus percent of the population and 5.5 percent of the employees), organized into 12 branches (one of which was a "general branch"), each with its own committee. The Party's top body, a five-man standing committee, consisted of the secretary, his deputy, and three others, and it met only irregularly—rarely more than once or twice a month—to consider major issues relating to general policy and to deal with personnel management, propaganda, and Communist Youth League affairs.

The farm director stressed—with the Party secretary present, nodding his agreement—that before the reforms, the Party secretary's power had greatly overshadowed that of the director, but now the reverse was true, and the Party was much less involved in enterprise affairs related to production. In the process of reform, the farm had reduced its staff by about a quarter, from over 80 to roughly 60 (of whom about 40 were the main operating staff and more than 20 were what Westerners would call support staff).

Reforms also had had a significant impact on the way the farm's production activities were carried out. Whereas needed capital formerly had been allocated to the farm by the municipal Agricultural Commission, the farm itself was now required to obtain such capital, either from its own earnings or from loans. The introduction of the responsibility system had changed the farm's methods of operation. Two forms of the system, each managing 600 cows, were now practiced; each, the director said, had strong and weak points. One was called the "collective responsibility system." Under this system, targets were set not only for the entire farm (that is, for all the members involved in this system) but also for each of the three levels under it: the "branch farms," the production teams (*shengchan banzu*), and individuals. Targets for each level were determined largely by the next higher-level authority. If the targets were exceeded, units and individuals received increased income, and, in theory at least, penalties were imposed if targets were not achieved. Most employees worked under this system. Their average basic wage, I was told, was Y 80 a month (Y 960 a year)—about the same as at the enamelware factory that I visited—but year-end bonuses often were substantial and amounted to as much as Y 200 to Y 300 a year. The director said that the farm's output of those working under this system was of high quality but that because they used modern methods and faced rising production costs it tended to be less profitable than that under the other system, which was called the "household responsibility system." Under the second system, individual households contracted to handle a specific number of cows for a 10-year period. The profit per cow tended to be higher under this system, but the manager said that the "quality of the work" was often lower (for example, the milk was less pure) in large part because of the inferior hygiene. The manager refrained, however, from labeling either system as "the best"; he intended to continue using both.

*   *   *

I spent most of my time in Baotou trying to learn about the municipality's economic development, for obvious reasons. Data on industrialization and economic growth provided the most revealing indexes of the dramatic transformation that had occurred in Baotou in the course of its modernization during the previous 40 years. However, I also tried to learn something about other fields in which far-reaching changes had taken place, including education and communications.

Although in 1947 Baotou had a number of primary schools, there were only three middle schools and no postsecondary educational institutions in the city. By 1988, the size of its educational establishment was impressively large, even though the quality of education admittedly lagged far behind that in China's major eastern cities. (Even in East China there was growing concern about the qualitative shortcomings of the educational system.) I did not find time to visit any schools in Baotou—as I did in many other places I visited—but the deputy head of the Education Bureau briefed me on the educational system and on some of its problems.

Baotou, in 1988, had 632 primary schools. The majority (548) were government-run primary schools, most of which had five-year programs, but the program in some of the 84 factory-run primary schools was six years. A total of 165,500 students attended these schools. (There were 116,400 students attending schools under the Education Bureau and 49,100 attending factory schools.) The bureau stated that almost 98 percent of all children of primary-school age (ages 7 through 12) in the entire municipality attended school. In rural areas, the percentage was lower. The bureau also claimed that 80 percent of the graduates went on to middle school (a figure that seemed high to me). There were 130 middle schools in the municipality, with 116,500 students. Some of them included both junior and senior middle school courses, but most offered only a three-year junior middle school program. Factory schools were particularly important at this level; they totaled 47 and had 45,200 students—which compared to 83 government schools, with 71,300 students. Since 1983, there had been an increasing emphasis, I was told, on vocational middle schools, which totaled 36: Eleven of these gave full-time vocational training and 25 had a curriculum that was "half vocational."

Of the middle schools, three were minority schools: one in Kundulun, for Mongols (which included both junior and senior middle school programs and which taught in two tracks, one in the Mongol language and the other basically in Chinese but with Mongol taught as a second language); one in Gonghe for Hui Muslims; and a third for another small minority group.

During the 1980s, many new textbooks were introduced, I was told, to "try to raise levels to world standards"; all of them were provided by the Education Commission in Beijing (although the Inner Mongolian authorities sometimes added materials of particular local relevance). Materials on science and technology had been increased, and materials on politics and ideology had been cut back, although the schools still taught courses on subjects such as social development, law, dialectics, and political economy that were heavily political and ideological (albeit less so than a decade previously). The shortage of qualified teachers was a fundamental problem, as was true in most of China but especially in outlying provinces. A large percentage of the teachers were graduates of teacher training institutions or colleges in north and northwest China.

Local officials put considerable stress on the fact that Baotou had also developed higher education. In many respects it was noteworthy that there were any institutions at all at this level, but clearly the city was still backward in postsecondary education. Just under 4,200 students attended regular institutions above the high school level, and these were, admittedly, less than first-rate. Baotou had developed three regular institutions of higher education, an Iron and Steel College with 2,105 students, a Medical College with 957 students, and a Normal College for teachers with 1,125 students. It had no general or "comprehensive" university, however. In addition to the three colleges, there were seven adult institutions of "higher education" in the city, including the Baotou Workers' University; altogether they had 3,400 students. Some major factories ran postsecondary institutions for workers.

The institutions of higher learning in Baotou had not acquired any real national standing. China's best universities and colleges were concentrated in Beijing, Shanghai, Tianjin, Wuhan, Guangzhou, and some other large provincial capitals; even most of those in interior provincial capitals were not regarded as first-rank institutions.

Baotou was proud of the fact that by 1988 it had developed 33 scientific research institutes, with scientific and technical personnel (broadly defined) totaling over 50,000. The best ones, I was told, were those dealing with research on rare earth, iron and steel production, and metals. In this area, too, there was some basis for local pride; in national terms, however, the majority of Baotou's research institutions did not have much standing. The best of them were preoccupied with applied research associated with particular local industries or factories. Baotou had neither a local academy of sciences nor an Academy of Social Sciences (as provincial capitals did), and therefore its links to the major national research networks were relatively weak. Nevertheless, its research establishment, as well as its educational system, had helped to propel it into the modern world.

The municipality had nine libraries as well as several movie houses. This also represented "progress," but my strong impression was that interest in cultural matters was low, which I did not find surprising in this newly built city that had been rapidly created as a center for industrial production in a very remote area of the country. Intellectually, Baotou was obviously far from the mainstream of national life; the local scene was dominated by officials, managers, and technicians, and the city lacked—as far as I could judge—any significant group of intellectuals or any well-developed cultural life. Nevertheless, remembering the situation in the 1940s, I found the expansion of applied research as well as basic education quite impressive.

*   *   *

The communications revolution that had occurred in recent years seemed even more remarkable to me. In 1947, Baotou was, and its population *felt,* extremely isolated, despite its rail connection to the east. It did have, even then, one small local newspaper and a small telephone system used by officials and a few businessmen. But most of the population knew little about national trends, to say nothing of world affairs. Few citizens read the news, and, in the pretransistor age, virtually none had radios. In 1988, I discovered that Baotou—like almost all of China—was blanketed by modern media, especially the electronic media, which informed them in an unprecedented way about both national and international developments. The media were still controlled by the Party and the government, but in 1988 the controls were much looser than in earlier years (or than they became immediately after the Tiananmen crisis in 1989).

There was still only one major newspaper in the city—the *Baotou Daily.* Its staff of editors and journalists totaled 73, and its daily press run was 61,000. Its editor asserted that it reached 1 in 15 people in the city itself and close to 1 in 30 in the municipality as a whole. I did not find these figures to be very impressive. They suggested that the paper was less important in reaching the population as a whole than in serving the city's political and economic elite. National newspapers, such as *People's Daily,* also circulated in Baotao and were required reading for the local elite, but my impression was that most local people had relatively little interest in them. The *Baotou Daily* was the official organ of the municipal government, I was told, but it also served, in effect, as the Party's organ. (There was no other local Party paper.)

Reformist winds of journalistic change had reached Baotou, but only as a very mild breeze. I discussed with the paper's young editor, who impressed me as being able, and one of his reporters the nature of the paper's reporting. They stated that they had increased reporting on people's complaints and on issues of concern and special interest to the population as a whole, and they said that they were trying to educate people about the reforms and their relevance to the realities of their lives. They gave me several examples of their own "investigative reporting" (which was useful but not particularly audacious, it seemed to me) on matters such as corruption, the use of influence by relatives of officials to get housing and jobs, the difficulties of making specific reforms work, and problems created by inflation. However, my overall impression was that they still had relatively little independence—although they obviously wished for more—and in contrast to some of the really innovative papers and journals elsewhere in China, they, like Baotou's political leaders, were essentially followers, not leaders. Although the editor seemed to be both bright and energetic, there were obviously severe limits on what he could do. At first, I thought the reporter accompanying him might prove to be an interesting maverick, partly because he wore a natty beret that made him look like an unconventional Left Bank type of intellectual, but when he later interviewed me for the paper he turned out to be an extremely dull, uninformed, naive, and completely unskilled reporter. The beret had misled me.

In addition to the *Baotou Daily,* there were eight papers published in the city by large enterprises. However, none was a daily; most published only one, two, or three times a week. As house organs, they were less informative about national affairs than the *Baotou Daily.*

In Baotou, it seemed clear, it was not the press that had created the communications revolution—that is, the explosion of information made available to ordinary people—that clearly had taken place in the 1980s, even in this remote place. Modern electronic media now reached far more people, and, it seemed to me, they had become a much more powerful instrument of change.

Since China manufactures huge numbers of radios, many of them small and inexpensive, virtually every family in Baotou had at least one radio, I was told, and the airwaves (long-wave, short-wave, and FM) were crowded with programs. What I found most remarkable, however, was the prevalence of television. By 1988, the market for radios in China was almost saturated, and the demand for, and production of, TV sets approached that of radio sets. In 1986, China produced 15.9 million radios and 14.6 million TV sets. As the production of TV sets had grown, black-and-white sets had fallen out of favor, and people now wished to have color TV. By 1987, China's output of color TV sets had surpassed 6.7 million, and it was estimated that in 1988 the demand for such sets would be 12 million. Official statistics indicated that the number of TV sets of all sorts in China exceeded 100 million in 1988—roughly 1 for every 10 persons in the population, or about 1 per 2.5 households; in many large cities, ownership was close to universal. (Ownership of radio sets exceeded 250 million.) Although I was not able to get statistics on the number of TV sets in Baotou—as I did later in most of the western cities and provinces I visited—officials told me that "most families" owned TV sets, and I found this to be very plausible.

My hotel room in Baotou contained both a radio and a color TV set (this, I was to discover, had become standard, even in small hotels, over most of China), and I carried with me a good short-wave radio. Although I did not have a great deal of time to use them, I made a point of trying to watch a little TV before or after dinner and to listen to the radio late at night. The variety of radio programs that I heard was extraordinary: The airwaves were full of news, commentary, feature programs, and language lessons as well as music of all kinds (Chinese popular music, Chinese opera, Mongol songs, Western classical music, jazz, pop, and rock—a great deal of rock). On short wave, I listened not only to VOA and BBC but also many other foreign stations (most of them broadcast not only in their native language but also in Chinese and in English), and I marveled at how, from a remote corner of Inner Mongolia, I could lie in bed and listen to broadcasts from Moscow, Tokyo, Australia, France, Germany, the Netherlands, India, and other places. Radio Moscow seemed to have the strongest signal in Baotou.

From all that I was told, I concluded that by 1988 TV had a far greater attraction than radio, most of the time, for a majority of ordinary Chinese. Baotou had its own TV station—the tower of which was by far the tallest structure in the city. It was run by the municipal government's Broadcasting and TV Bureau. It did some programming of its own, but a great many of its programs were ones relayed from the national broadcasting network, headquartered in Beijing; these included the 7:00 P.M. national news (carried by TV stations all over China), a wide variety of entertainment (including many Chinese and foreign soap opera serials, some of them from the United States but many from other countries), educational programs, and live coverage of major national meetings and events. These programs brought the outside world into the houses of huge numbers of ordinary Chinese who did not even have a radio a decade ago, and they carried images that highlighted—and often idealized, explicitly or implicitly—the way of life in big cities, both in China and in other countries. TV also carried a great deal of advertising, mainly for consumer goods—especially consumer durables, but also luxury foods and beverages—which had helped to stimulate the growth of consumerism in China. Most important, TV was clearly promoting, both consciously and unwittingly, the rapid spread of new ideas, values, fads, and fashion. Many of the results were visible on Baotou's streets.

                              *   *   *

In 1988, I was determined not only to learn about Baotou itself but to try to visit some nearby Mongol areas. This had not been possible in 1947–1948, partly because of the winter weather and poor roads but most of all because of the militarization of the area as a result of civil war. In 1988, I was able to make two trips, one to the north and one to the south.

My first trip was to Wudangzhao Lamasery, about 47 miles to the northeast of Baotou. Our travel time, by car, was roughly three hours each way. It was a bitterly cold day when we started out, and, even though I had bundled up in my best cold-weather gear, by day's end I was chilled to the bone. The road immediately north of Baotou was spectacularly good; it was well paved and had six lanes (three each way). A short distance later, however, the road narrowed to two lanes; the paving was still good as far as the coal mining town of Shiguaigou (roughly two-thirds of the way), but thereafter it steadily deteriorated and eventually became a rocky dirt road. For the last few miles, in fact, there was really no road at all; we drove over solid ice on a small frozen stream. At one point the ice almost defeated us, and we had to mobilize local help to pull us out of a frozen rut. To me, the road symbolized both the inexorable spread of modern influences, which all over China were reaching out from industrial cities into the hinterland, and the fact that in many remote areas of the country these modern influences tended gradually to peter out the farther one went away from the major cities.

There were not many motor vehicles on the road; the few we passed were mainly trucks. More numerous were the donkey carts, two-wheeled vehicles with rubber tires. Their drivers were clad in traditional padded clothes, sheepskin overcoats, and fur hats. The topography was flat at first, and then we climbed into hills. The landscape was extremely bleak, yellow-brown, and dusty; there were virtually no trees visible, and because it was midwinter there was little vegetation of any sort on the ground. We could see, though, that despite the poor soil some of the land was farmland, because a few dry, wispy stalks were visible. Some of the areas we passed were pastureland; I was told, though, that the grasslands were also poor in this area because of continuing desertification. As we climbed into the rolling hills, we passed scattered villages and individual homes, mostly traditional ones built of mud brick, with tile roofs, although a few were more modern and had been built of hard-fired brick. Sheep and goats grazed near almost all the houses. The countryside looked very poor, although perhaps this was caused in part by the winter bleakness. At one point, we passed an ancient remnant of the Great Wall next to the road; this segment, which was built of yellow mud brick and was only 10 to 15 feet tall, was said to date from the Eastern Zhou (Chou) dynasty—the Spring and Autumn period and the Warring States period (722–221 B.C.).

We stopped at Shiguaigou, a coal mining town. This town was essentially "new," I was told; it had been relocated to its present hillside site after a 1958 flash flood had washed away the old town. There was nothing attractive about it, but in some respects the town clearly was modern and relatively prosperous. Five mines were located nearby, and I could see some mine entrances on the hillsides near the road. It was prosperous because the miners were relatively well paid. The average wage, I was told, was about Y 200 a month, or Y 2,400 a year—higher than most workers' wages in Baotou. A public square occupied the center of the town. On one side was the leading local restaurant. We stopped there, on our return trip, and had a big-city kind of meal, which was bountiful but gastronomically miserable. On the other side was the town's theater, used for movies, meetings, and—recently—dancing. I was flabbergasted to see that the movie currently being advertised was an American film featuring breakdancing, and a poster on the auditorium wall advertised a breakdance festival a few days later. This import from the United States, I learned, had become a major fad not only in the Baotou area but in many remote areas of China. I had to admit to local citizens that I knew less about breakdancing than they did.

Wudangzhao Lamasery rested a little over 15 miles beyond Shiguaigou in a small valley surrounded by low hills. Its name, local people said, referred to the fact that the areas inhabited by five Mongol tribes intersected there. The monastery was a remarkable example of Tibetan architecture, and in recent years the government had begun to promote it as a tourist site. On the cold winter day of my visit, however, there were only a half dozen visitors, all of them Overseas Chinese. The lamasery had enjoyed a religious revival of sorts, local people said, but I did not see much evidence of its vitality as a religious institution and felt that it probably was only a pale reflection of what it had once been.

Before touring the lamasery, I visited with a Mongol lama in his home; seated on an elevated, rug-covered *kang* (a combination bed and stove), we discussed the area and the lamasery. He was an elderly man who had first come to Wudangzhao at the age of seven, and he was now a member of the lamasery's Management Committee, which, under the Baotou Minority Affairs Commission, was responsible for its administration.

The lamasery was located in Sumuxiang (a township), the governmental seat of which was in a small village adjacent to Wudangzhoau. Sumuxiang was part of Guyang County, an area belonging to the Baotou Municipality. The area originally had been populated almost entirely by Mongols, but by 1988 there were only a few more than 800 Mongols, and about 20,000 Han Chinese, in the township. Han migration had obviously swallowed up the area and had Sinified virtually everything but the lamasery itself.

Many of the lamasery's main buildings were constructed in the eighteenth century, when the Qing emperor, Qian Long, provided funds to build monasteries in many Mongol areas. At its peak, in the late Qing period, the lamasery was said to have about 1,200 lamas (monks), and it served as a major religious center. Its decline started early in the twentieth century, I was told, and by the late 1940s the number of its lamas had dropped to about 300. During most of the Qing period, it was the seat of at least one Living Buddha. The seventh (and last), who had close links with the Nationalist regime (and reportedly controlled his own military forces and dominated the Shiguaigou area), died at the start of the 1950s and thereafter the Communist regime did not permit the choice of any successor. After 1949, the decline continued, but with ups and downs. The worst period, local people said, was in the late 1960s and early 1970s, during the Cultural Revolution, when young Red Guards—some from Baotou, some from the local area—attacked and severely damaged the lamasery and persecuted the lamas. (At the peak of the Cultural Revolution, Red Guards attacked virtually all religious institutions of all kinds all over China.) All the lamas were forced out of Wudangzhao, but a few stayed in the area and took up farming.

Repair of the buildings began in 1975, and then the revival of the lamasery as a religious institution took place after 1978 when Beijing began its major reforms and adopted a new conciliatory policy toward religion. However, in 1988 the number of lamas still did not compare to what it had been at the lamasery's peak, but, significantly, some young men were again being recruited and trained. At the time of my visit, Wudangzhao had only a few more than 30 regular lamas, 5 of them Tibetans and the rest Mongols, most of them quite old. (They all were able to read and speak Tibetan.) In addition, however, there now were more than 40 young apprentices, all Mongols, who had been recruited—by the Inner Mongolian Religious Association and the Baotou Minority Affairs Commission—from throughout Inner Mongolia and were in training there, studying in the Tibetan language. The lamas were paid Y 38 a month by the government, which also provided some funds for repairs and maintenance; the rest of the lamasery's income came from fees charged everyone except Mongol and Tibetan believers who visited the place.

The lamasery had been repaired and repainted and was in good shape. It included eight large buildings, each of them two or three stories high, and a number of two-story living quarters for the lamas. Most of the largest buildings had been built in the Qing period. The construction of one started in 1749, and it was named by Qian Long in 1756; it was a place for study and examinations. A large central building, which had a hall about 10 meters (almost 33 feet) high, was called the Philosophy College. Another three-story building contained a large hall, with rug-covered platforms and square columns, in which the lamas read scriptures; a special seat for the Living Buddha was located at its rear. Other buildings contained gilt statues of various sorts, and in one there were photos of a previous Living Buddha and of the Banchan (Panchen) Lama (but there was none of the Dalai Lama).

The architecture, typically Tibetan, was strong, stolid, and impressive. The white stone walls slanted inward, as did the windows. There was a great deal of color, especially red but also yellow, green, and blue, on the columns and roof eaves as well as on the rugs that covered the floors, platforms, and columns. The lamas were dressed in deep red robes.

Although a few traditional prayer wheels were visible, I saw little religious activity at the lamasery. A few resident lamas were reading scriptures and chanting, but there were no pilgrims or ordinary believers such as I had seen in large numbers in earlier years in lamaseries such as the one at Kumbum in Qinghai. I was told that at certain times of the year there was a sizable flow of religious pilgrims, especially in the summer, when the number of visitors at any one time could total 2,000 to 3,000; most of them were ordinary Mongols who were still believers, but some of them were visiting lamas from other Mongol religious institutions. Wudangzhao had no formal organizational ties with any other lamasery, but local lamas said that there were frequent two-way visits between their lamasery and leading ones elsewhere: Kumbum, at Taersi; Labulong (Labrang), south of Xiahe in Gansu; and the leading temples in Lhasa. Most lamas at Wudangzhao visited all of these at some time during their lives, I was told. Two-way visits between Wudangzhao and Outer Mongolia had resumed on a small scale.

At Wudangzhao, the restoration of buildings, the revival of worship, and especially the renewed recruitment and training of some younger apprentice lamas symbolized China's relatively moderate, tolerant, post-1978 policies toward religion as well as Beijing's effort to repair relations between Han Chinese and minorities (although Tibet proper, where there was increasing agitation for greater autonomy or even independence, clearly was an exception to these trends in many respects). However, Wudangzhao also symbolized both the steady Sinification of Mongol regions near the main areas of Han settlement, the long-term weakening of religion, and the decline of many religious institutions in west China as a result of the spread of modernization and secular values in these regions.

*   *   *

My second trip out of Baotou was to the south, across the Yellow River, about 40 miles to the town of Shulinzhao, which lay beyond the borders of Baotou Municipality. This was the headquarters of the Dalateqi—the Dala (Dalad) Special Banner—on the edge of the Ordos Desert. Dalateqi was part of the Ikh Zhao League (Meng) and was a major stopping point on the route to the league headquarters in Dongsheng (Eastern Victory) County, which was roughly 65 miles from Baotou. A little beyond that, I was told, is the spot where, Mongols now believe, the remains of Genghis Khan have rested, in Ejin Horo (Ejina, Altan Xinet, or Yijing Huoluoqi) Banner. A few miles to the east of Dalateqi, at Salaqi, was the headquarters of the Tumet (Tumd, or Tumete) West (Right) Banner.

The Ordos Desert begins, according to conventional wisdom, right after one crosses the Yellow River car bridge; this modern structure, built in the early 1980s, was just a few miles south of Baotou. From there on, the signs were in both Chinese and Mongol. A new railway bridge was under construction, parallel to the road bridge, to serve a line that would connect with a large new coal mining area being developed within the Ikh Zhao League, near the border between Inner Mongolia and Shanxi Province, at Zhen Ge. The main highway in the region, which we traveled, crossed the Ordos and led to Xi'an and beyond.

The Ordos is a very large area of about 33,200 square miles. It lies on a plateau that varies between 3,200 and 4,000 feet in height, and a sizable part of it consists of a Sahara-like sand desert. The Yellow River curves around it, on its east, north, and west. In ancient times, a fairly large population inhabited the Ordos, raising animals and growing grain, but over the centuries the area was steadily desertified, and in the modern era the population has been sparse and confined to scattered settlements.

By the 1980s, two major paved roads crossed the Ordos; the one going south from Baotou, which we traveled, crosses a large desert area, touches at the town of Yulin (located where a southern portion of the Great Wall parallels the south side of the Ordos), then goes to Yan'an (Yenan) and south to Xi'an. In earlier years, this was a primitive rocky road, but it was paved with financial help from the central government in the early 1980s—when the river bridge was built—and I was told that it is now a two-lane paved highway all the way to Xi'an. The other main highway crosses the Ordos east to west, leading to Ningxia, where it turns south to Yinchuan and ultimately goes to Lanzhou. These roads have not resulted in much of an increase in population, however; to most Han Chinese, and to many Mongols as well, the Ordos continues to be regarded as an extremely forbidding region because of its two large sand deserts—the Kupuqi (or Kobq), which covers over 4,090 square miles in the north, and the Maomusu (Muus), which encompasses over 10,690 square miles in the southeast.

Going south from Baotou, our road at the start was—like that to the north of the city—a six-lane Chinese version of a superhighway, but soon after the Yellow River toll bridge (the toll: Y 2), it narrowed to two lanes, and it steadily deteriorated as we approached Dalateqi. The wind velocity rose immediately after we crossed the frozen Yellow River, where some trucks were traveling on the ice, and the swirling dust and sand created a desert atmosphere, even though we were still some distance from real sand desert. For several miles we traveled through poor, desertified farmland and pasture area, in a region that local people called "Ordos pasture." There was not much vegetation; Yellow River water was not far away, but it was too costly to pump water that far. We passed many flocks of sheep, herded by sheepskin-clad shepherds, whose appearance evoked memories of what I had seen in 1947. There were virtually no passenger cars on the road, but truck traffic was quite heavy. Most of the trucks carried coal, and along the road there were numerous small huts, run by private entrepreneurs; they served food and beverages to the truck drivers, who sometimes paid their bills with coal.

Halfway between the river and our destination, we were met by three Dalateqi officials who had come to escort us to the town. They were observing an old Mongol tradition, but instead of galloping toward us on horseback they were riding in a Toyota sedan. Virtually all local leaders in the area had recently purchased cars, my hosts said, and the press in Baotou had published several articles criticizing poor counties and banners for buying too many new cars, arguing that often it was mainly for show and was both unnecessary and wasteful.

I had no idea what kind of a town Shulinzhao would be, but I suppose I expected to see one that at least had a strong Mongol flavor. Instead, it turned out to be a very Chinese place. The main road was lined with small private shops, stalls, and open markets, run mainly by Han Chinese who were selling goods purchased from all over China. People were well dressed, and most younger people wore Western-style clothing, some of it, even here, following the latest Chinese fashions, although many older people still wore Mao suits, traditional padded clothing, or sheepskin-lined jackets.

I was welcomed in the town by six local officials. They were young—five of them were in their fifties and one was younger—but, to my surprise, they were mostly Han Chinese (only one of the six was a Mongol). The six included the Dala Special Banner Party secretary (a Han Chinese) and the chairman of the Banner Government (a Mongol). All five of them impressed me as being bright, articulate, and eager to brief me on both Dalateqi and the Ikh Zhao League to which it belonged. The Ikh Zhao League, a unit equivalent to a prefecture, had its headquarters, as I mentioned earlier, in Dongsheng County, some distance away. The league administered eight units; the county was one, and the other seven were banners equivalent to counties, of which Dalateqi was one. (The others were Jungar, Ejin Horo, Uxin, Otog, Otog Front, and Hanggin.) Originally, my host explained, banners were based on tribes rather than territory, but many years ago they had been given clear territorial boundaries. I expected that here, in an important banner in an important league, I would finally feel as if I was really in Mongol territory, but I was wrong, and the reason soon became clear. As of 1988, the population of the entire league was overwhelmingly Han; of the 1.1 million total population, only about 120,000, or a little over a tenth, were Mongol. In Dalateqi, Han dominance was even greater; of the banner's total population of about 300,000, only a tiny minority—about 9,000, or 3 percent— were Mongols, and more than 290,000 were Han. As in the area north of Baotou, Han migration had transformed this region's character.

Once again I asked local leaders why, in light of such overwhelming Han dominance, the area was considered to be an autonomous minority area. The answer, again, was that it was because of "historical reasons" and that because this had traditionally been a Mongol area, Beijing's policy was to accord them special treatment and give them special privileges. The law required certain government posts to be filled by Mongols, and although the local Mongols were very Sinified, and the Han language (Hanyu) was generally used in daily life, either Mongol or Chinese could be used in government meetings.

Dalateqi was obviously a poor area. Nine-tenths of its population— 270,000 of its 300,000 inhabitants—worked in agriculture or animal husbandry (many now did a little of both), and the rest were mainly shopkeepers, teachers, and government officials. However, because of subsidies from superior levels of government, average living standards were higher than one might have expected. According to the banner's official statistics, the average

per capita annual income in the area in 1987 was Y 404 among those engaged in agriculture and animal husbandry and Y 900 among those living in
urban areas.

Approximately 700 people work for the banner government. Its chairman
was, as the law required, a Mongol, but of his five deputies, four were Han
Chinese and only one was a Mongol. In the Party organization, the secretary
and two of his deputies were Han, but the two other deputies were Mongols.
However, I was told that among the 700 or so government employees more
than a quarter of all ordinary cadres were Mongols—a figure many times
their percentage of the entire population.

Dalateqi's economic dependence on subsidies from higher levels of government fit the pattern that—I would soon learn—was characteristic of west
China. Local leaders told me that in 1987 the banner government's regular
budget expenditures totaled Y 16 million. It collected Y 7.7 million in revenue, and, although in theory, they said, this was supposed to be shared with
both the Inner Mongolian Autonomous Region and the central government,
in practice, to make it possible for Dalateqi to cover its deficits, both the regional government and the central government let the banner keep most of
its revenue and also gave it regular subsidies, which totaled close to Y 10 million in 1987. In addition, they said, the banner received some other special
subsidies from above, outside of its regular budget, to support educational,
cultural, and economic development, especially projects that benefited the
Mongol minority.

This trip obviously did not satisfy my desire to see a "real Mongol area." I
learned more about how Han China has steadily extended its outreach into
remote areas than I did about the characteristics of the predominantly Mongol areas of Inner Mongolia. However, I did get a glimpse of one of China's
great sand deserts. To reach the desert, we drove due south of Shulinzhao
through a desperately poor area, where we passed only one real village. The
road steadily deteriorated and eventually petered out—as the road north of
Baotou had—until it was nothing more than a cross-country track. Finally,
as at Wudangzhao, we had to drive over a frozen streambed, which seemed
totally out of place on the edge of the desert. The only other vehicle in sight,
a crawling tractor, had broken through the ice and blocked the track ahead
of us, so we got out of our car and walked the last half mile to the desert's
edge. The sand dunes were spectacular. One rose 40 to 50 feet immediately
above us, and the dunes stretched as far as the eye could see. I felt a little like
an explorer in the Sahara—until my host told me that in recent years the
Baotou government had made a major effort to develop this as a summer
tourist spot. In the tourist season, the government provided camels that gave
rides up and down the dunes, and some Baotou residents brought food to
have picnics overlooking the sand wilderness.

I suppose that what struck me most forcefully on my trip to Dalateqi was something that I had recognized intellectually but had really not fully grasped before my 1988 trip—namely, that sizable areas of Inner Mongolia, including the most developed ones not only in the railway zone but also in areas adjacent to the Yellow River and the territory near large cities, had been populated by Han Chinese and Sinified to a large degree.

*   *   *

My trip to Dalateqi was the final activity on my itinerary in the Baotou area. The following day, I left by train for Yinchuan, capital of Ningxia. The train route from Baotou to Yinchuan followed the Yellow River around its great bend and then turned south. This line had not existed when I visited the area in the 1940s. In 1948, I traveled to Yinchuan (which was then called Ningxia City) from Lanzhou in the west. That trip had been an adventure. To reach Ningxia, I had traveled several days on the back of a mail truck (the only transport available) on very rough unpaved roads, and to cross the Yellow River we had to hoist the truck onto a flimsy raft. Along the way, my evenings were spent in traditional Chinese inns, located in old towns untouched by any modernity. Now, not being as young as I once was, I looked forward to a trip that would be much faster and more comfortable.

However, before starting the trip I once again had to fight a small battle with the Chinese bureaucracy—the kind of battle that still makes travel in many remote areas of west China something of a challenge. In Beijing, I had been told that it was impossible to buy a through ticket all the way to Lanzhou, with stops at Baotou and Yinchuan; all that I could purchase was a ticket for the first leg of the trip. But in Baotou the railway ticket seller said that they could not issue soft-class tickets to Yinchuan because such tickets were totally controlled by Beijing; it was a classic Catch-22 situation. I told my hosts that I would be delighted to go hard class, but they insisted that this was very inappropriate for a "foreign guest" such as myself. They frantically telephoned to get help from the Academy of Social Sciences in Beijing, and the head of the Baotou Foreign Affairs Bureau also wrote a special letter for me to carry and show to the train attendants, but nothing produced a guaranteed berth. After arriving at the station, my local hosts engaged in some complicated finagling and long palaver, and finally the train attendants reluctantly assigned me and my escort to a compartment, which we shared with a middle-aged Chinese gentleman and his young daughter. As we left Baotou, a light snow began to fall—a fairly rare occurrence because it is so dry in that area—and I settled in for another overnight trip. My destination was the Ningxia Hui Autonomous Region and, beyond it, the Alashan region of western Inner Mongolia.

CHAPTER TWO

Han and Hui

NINGXIA

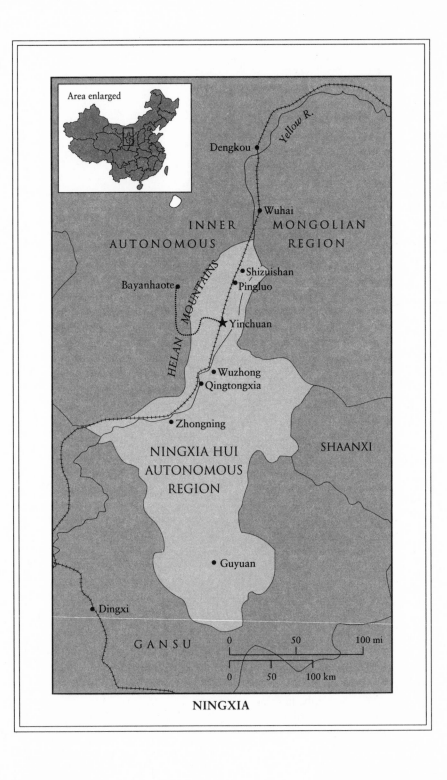

NINGXIA

F ROM BAOTOU, China's interior trunk line goes west and then south to one of China's main concentrations of Muslims, in the Ningxia Hui Autonomous Region. My train left Baotou at 9:16 A.M., and the 317-mile trip took slightly over 10 hours; we arrived at 7:30 P.M., just 19 minutes late, at Ningxia's capital, Yinchuan.

West of Baotou, the line closely parallels the great bend of the Yellow River, south of which is the Ordos Desert. As we passed through the irrigated agricultural region called Hedao, our train stopped periodically at many small and some medium-sized towns, including Wulateqiang, Linhe, Dengkou, and Wuhai. Wulateqiang, capital of the Ulate (Urat) South Banner, rests on the edge of Inner Mongolia's largest body of water, Lake Wuliangsu (Ulansuhai Nui). From there, both the river and the rail line turn south; the most important city in this area is Linhe. Further on we stopped at Dengkou, which is located on the edge of another desert, called the Wulanbuhe. From there we crossed over the river to the east, proceeded south to the twin cities of Wuhai, crossed back to the west, and went south to Yinchuan.

The light snow that was falling when we left Baotou had deposited a thin white blanket on both fields and mountains to the north, and the late February weather was cold, between 10 and 20 degrees Fahrenheit. The snow continued falling during our entire trip, becoming somewhat heavier toward the end. The accumulation did not exceed two to three inches; even that much was somewhat unusual in this dry Inner Mongolian area, however. During parts of the trip, the main Baotou-Yinchuan highway paralleled the rail line, and some local roads were visible, but vehicles were few and far between, and at times the roads were obliterated by the snow.

Most of the countryside looked very bleak in the cold of winter; some of the region, especially in the Hedao area, has good agricultural land, but the snow-covered fields looked desolate, and many areas appeared to be extremely sparsely populated pastureland or wasteland. Most of the small towns where we stopped had a kind of frontier atmosphere; often large open spaces separated the buildings, giving the towns a very different appearance from the crowded urban centers of east China. One-story brick houses predominated, but in larger towns there were some multistory structures. Compared to the pre-1949 traditional towns that I had seen in remote western areas, the changes were substantial. The towns no longer looked like remnants of traditional China: They had a modern, or at least a semimodern, appearance.

Telephone, telegraph, and power transmission lines along the rail line were almost always visible, and we could see factories in most towns. Mod-

95

ern communications and industry had spread throughout this region, where none at all had existed before 1949. I was also astounded to see virtual forests of TV antennae in almost every town, even in many rural areas. The people on the station platforms were well dressed, mostly in "modern" and Western clothing that peeked out from under the heavy overcoats in which everyone was bundled for protection against the penetrating cold. Some men wore Mao suits but many wore Western-style clothing. Elevator shoes—that is, shoes with higher-than-normal heels—were worn by many men. This new shoe style, introduced only very recently, was popular, I was told, because almost all the women preferred tall men. Many women were quite fashionably dressed; a sizable proportion wore high-heeled shoes, which were introduced in this area in the early 1980s, according to my compartment mates.

The first fairly large town where we stopped west of Baotou was Wulanshan, a county seat; from the train we could see its large power plant and cement factory. Further on we halted at Wuyuan County, an important trading post linking Baotou with both the Hedao agricultural area and the Mongol grassland. Wuyuan had been connected by road to Baotou long before the rail line was built in the 1950s, but the railway had increased its importance and spurred its growth. Still further on we stopped at Wulateqiang, where we glimpsed Lake Wuliangsu; this town was the main gateway, I was told, to the Hedao region. A sizable town, with many factories, it had become a major transportation hub for roads leading east, northeast, and northwest.

Hedao is crisscrossed by irrigation canals that are linked to the Yellow River. These canals were built centuries ago, but they have been improved in recent years. Hedao is clearly the most important crop area in Inner Mongolia; in fact, it is the only important agricultural center west of Baotou until one turns south and reaches the Ningxia plain, where there is another important well-irrigated area. Although the Yellow River has often been called "China's sorrow" because it has flooded so frequently over the centuries, its water has neverless been the lifeblood of Han civilization in the west. Hedao is more heavily populated, and economically better off, than adjacent areas. However, even though some of the farmhouses visible from the train had obviously been built recently and were constructed of hard brick, many were very traditional, old-style building, built with unfired brick. In the dead of winter, even this relatively prosperous region looked fairly forbidding.

After turning southwest, the train stopped at Linhe. I learned a little about this town from my compartment companion, who lived there. A county-level town, it was the headquarters of the Bayannur League. We could see its downtown area, marked by several multistory modern buildings, as well as a fairly large industrial area on the edge of the town. Most living quarters were long, one-story brick structures that generally were divided into six family apartments, each of which, my companion said, usually had double or triple the space of apartments in eastern cities. The comparative spaciousness of living quarters, I was told, was common in the modernized towns in west China; although such towns lacked many of the amenities of those in eastern China, the sparse population and ample land had some advantages.

Further on we crossed the Yellow River at Dengkou (its Mongol name was Bayangol). This, too, was a county-level town of considerable economic importance. Thereafter, we paralleled what appeared to be a partly desertified area. Some of it might have been pastureland—clumps of grass were visible through the snow—but we did not see many houses. However, power and telegraph lines were still visible in most places. Soon we entered an area that seemed to be a mix of pastureland and cropland. Our main stops in this stretch of the trip were at two stations in the twin cities of Wuhai. Haibowan (Wuhai East) appeared to be a small, widely dispersed, industrial center, with the same frontier atmosphere that had struck me in many earlier stops. Across the river, Wuda (Wuhai West) was smaller, and appeared less modern or industrialized, but even there most of the structures were well built and adorned with TV antennae.

*   *   *

We entered Ningxia soon after leaving Wuhai. Fog as well as snow made visibility very poor, and for a while the snow-covered landscape appeared to be a real wasteland. But soon thereafter we reached the Ningxia plain. Despite the snow and fog, I could see that this flat, irrigated area was relatively prosperous. The fields in the farms were surprisingly large, and the landscape was punctuated with modern-looking brick villages separated by considerable distances. Before we reached Yinchuan, our final major stops included: Shidanjing, where a branch rail line led west to the salt-producing lake and town of Jilanta (Jartai); Shizuishan, a large coal center and one of the four principal industrial cities in Ningxia; and Pinglou and Xidatan, two smaller industrial towns with a frontier-like atmosphere. (At Xidatan, even the local mosque supported a very large TV antenna!)

It is not difficult to understand why most Chinese from east China still view this entire area as remote, backward, and fairly forbidding—an area to be avoided if possible. Yet what struck me most on the trip was how much the area had developed during the previous four decades. In 1948, when I had traveled to Ningxia from Lanzhou by mail truck, not only had it taken me three days on unpaved roads to reach Yinchuan (then called Ningxia City), but the towns where I stopped had had no electricity, virtually no modern communications, and no industry or other signs of modernity. By 1988, it was clear—even from my superficial initial impressions in the railway zone—that despite the area's frontier atmosphere the region had been incorporated into "China proper" much more completely than ever in the past and that it had been significantly modernized. Even from the train it was obvious that transportation, electrification, communications, industrialization, improved housing, modern clothing, television, and many other aspects of modern life had begun to alter the region in fundamental ways.

The relative comfort of train travel was one obvious change. As I peered out at the snow-covered countryside, I was grateful for the comfort and warmth of the train. This was especially true in my soft-berth (first-class) cabin, but even passengers in hard class did not have to endure the hardships of traditional travel. The train was often jerky; on this route, it used steam engines (sensible in a region with huge coal deposits). Otherwise it differed little from the electrified line north of Beijing. The inside temperature was fairly low (50 to 60 degrees Fahrenheit), but like my Chinese traveling companions I dressed warmly, in thermal underwear, and was protected from the elements. Almost all of the passengers in my car were on official business. I was told that first-class travel by Chinese private entrepreneurs had recently been restricted (though, I learned, by no means totally ended); the reason, my fellow passengers said, was a clampdown on such travel following a train murder in another part of China several months earlier. Hard class, as always, was crowded with passengers of all kinds. Many were ordinary workers and peasants.

Train fares were still a remarkable bargain (subsequently they were raised substantially). My soft-berth fare was Y 68.50, and the fare for my escort, Wu Yu, was half that. (If we had taken hard seats, our fares would have been Y 20 and Y 10 respectively.) These were fares that most people could afford. The food was far from memorable, but it was better than the food on the Beijing-Baotou trip. I found it interesting that pork was excluded from the menu as a gesture of sensitivity to Ningxia's Muslims. But, even though Muslims are not supposed to consume alcohol, beer rather than tea was the drink of choice, and it was consumed in large quantities by young Muslims as well as others.

Service on the train had been unaffected by Beijing's reform policies, and bureaucratism was in command. The women attendants were, if possible, even more arrogant than those on the Beijing-Baotou trip. And the bathrooms were even worse than usual: They were abominably dirty, with an overpowering smell of urine, and seemed more like outhouses than modern bathrooms. The train's broadcasting speakers carried recorded music of many sorts—Chinese and Western, traditional and modern. As on the trip to Baotou, what entertained passengers the most were periodic comedy programs of crosstalk, which evoked gales of laughter. Most were so rapid-fire and colloquial that I could not understand them, but I asked fellow passengers to explain some of the ones that they considered most hilarious. In one, two men made raucous fun of themselves, each trying to outdo the other in boasting about his own virtues. In another, two men ridiculed Japanese formality and ritual, including the custom of constantly bowing. (During my subsequent months of travel, I encountered, much more frequently than I expected, anti-Japanese attitudes, usually in unsolicited comments about the Japanese lack of openness, their formality, arrogance, and unreliability, and their reputed crass commercialism; such comments often were made by young Chinese who had never had any personal contacts with Japanese.)

*   *   *

During most of the day-long trip, I conversed, as I did on every train trip I made in China, with as many fellow passengers as possible—in my compartment, in the train's corridors, and in the dining car as well as in hard-class cars that I visited. My conversations were with people of very varied backgrounds. They were usually casual conversations, and mostly nonpolitical, but they nevertheless provided illuminating, albeit fragmentary, insights into ordinary lives, attitudes, problems, and the clash of modern and traditional values.

For most of the trip my cabin mates, in addition to my escort from CASS, were a 59-year-old chemist, returning to his home in Linhe, and his 20-year-old adopted daughter, who he had taken under his wing after her parents (relatives of his) had been killed in the great Tangshan earthquake of 1976. The chemist, who once lived in Tangshan, had worked first, as a very young man, for a military research organization there, during the 1950s and the 1960s, and then was employed by an army-run chemical plant in Wuhai until the plant had closed. Thereafter he did not have any regular employment for a while, but finally he returned to Tangshan and resumed work there, this time as a consultant to a military-run factory—until the great earthquake. In that cataclysm, almost all of his immediate relatives had been killed. It was a terrible tragedy, with hundreds of thousands of casualties. Eventually, however, he and other survivors picked up the pieces of their lives, and he resumed consulting for a factory. Shortly before I met him, he had been assigned by his factory to work in Linhe under the State Council's "Spark Program."

He was extremely enthusiastic about the program and gave me his version of its origin and organization. It had been initiated in 1983, he said, and began full-scale operations in 1984, under the central government's Commission on Science and Technology, working with comparable local commissions. The program recruited retired scientists from the national Association of Science and Technology, assigning them to assist local development projects that used local capital and resources in relatively underdeveloped areas of the country. The basic purpose was to help accelerate the spread of modern technology in relatively simple form to spur increased production in remote areas. His assignment, he said, was to spend two years helping to develop two projects in Linhe; one was to improve the production of a confectionery using sunflower seeds, and the other was to reprocess into usable products discarded plastic sheeting (now used by farmers throughout much of China, especially to cover vegetable plots). His salary came from a

Tangshan research unit, as its contribution to the development of a backward area. (Wu Yu described a different but comparable program under which Beijing organizations, including CASS, annually sent groups of perhaps 10 to 20 people—sometimes more—to teach prospective or actual teachers in normal schools and middle schools in remote areas. Her understanding was that the Party's General Secretary Hu Yaobang had personally initiated the program in 1986. CASS groups, she said, had gone to Henan Province.)

The chemist told me something about his family. His natural daughter was married, and her husband, also a chemist, had recently become a private entrepreneur manufacturing a kind of Chinese medicine reputedly useful for treating cancer. His adopted daughter, accompanying him, was not yet married. Although age 20, she seemed much younger. She was beginning to worry, she coyly told me, about becoming a spinster; if she did not marry by age 24 or 25, she said, she could easily become an old maid (*lao guniang*). (Wu Yu, herself 25 and already married, interjected that this danger point was not approached until after age 26 or 27 in Beijing.) The chemist's adopted daughter had completed junior middle school but had not gone on to senior middle school. Few of her classmates had, she said, because they "had not studied hard enough" to pass the exams. In her own case, there were also other reasons. Her mother "did not want me to go on," and in junior middle school she had suffered frequent headaches during her last year, which she blamed on schoolwork.

Instead of continuing school, she had gone to work in a sugar beet factory in Wuhai, together with some of her friends. To some degree she envied girls she knew—mainly from farm families—who married and did not have to work (although many, she said, earned a little money processing goods at home for local factories). On balance, though, she said that she wanted to continue to work, but she also wished to get married. However, her mother did not want her to "marry up"—that is, marry a better-educated person—because she felt that the social gap would make life difficult for her. But one problem was that most young men just wanted to find an obedient, traditional girl as a wife, she said. Moreover, she added: "I do not know how to find a husband myself, so I must rely on my [adopted] parents' help and advice. I would not dare to decide, myself, to go out with boys; there would be too many rumors." The only girls she knew who had found their own husbands had married classmates or fellow workers, but "I do not know any good-looking young men in my factory." (Wu Yu intervened, again, to say that things were different now in Beijing. Most young people were less concerned about differences in social background, although, she acknowledged, many educated people were still reluctant to "marry down" by choosing less-educated partners. But a girl could date anyone, and many found their own husbands.)

I was struck by the contrast between this young woman factory worker, who was entrapped in many respects by traditions supported by her mother's attitudes, and Wu Yu, the modern young intellectual. Yet even the factory workers' attitudes were obviously influenced somewhat by modern media, which transmitted new ideas and values. During our trip, she spent a great deal of time reading Chinese magazines, including several issues of one called *International Photography*, which was full of photographs revealing life abroad; they included photos of leggy, stylish women and many appealing advertisements for Western-type consumer goods—things absolutely taboo in the Maoist era. We discussed fashions. She, like young women all over China, was very style-conscious and regularly read fashion magazines (several of which promoted fashion ideas from the West, Japan, and Hong Kong as well as Shanghai and Guangzhou, China's two main competing fashion centers). Both she and her chemist father asserted that women in Linhe and Wuhai had ample money to buy good clothes, and she insisted that they were just as fashionable as their counterparts in Beijing or elsewhere. Hedao, they maintained, had a long tradition of using cosmetics, which was revived in the 1980s (they also said that there was one special local tradition that encouraged gold teeth because they were considered very fashionable).

Among the others with whom I talked on the train, one was a Shanghai man—another transplant to the west—who, in contrast to the chemist and his daughter, was anything but a booster of the area. Following his graduation from one of Shanghai's leading universities, this man had been victimized during the Cultural Revolution—"struggled against" and beaten (he showed me scars on his face)—partly because he had refused to denounce his father, who once had worked for the Guomindang. He was then "sent down" to spend many years in a remote Ningxia village. Just three years before I met him, he had finally been rehabilitated and recruited to be a lecturer at Ningxia University, and his wife had come from Shanghai to join him. Their primary goal, he said, was to return permanently to Shanghai, but he saw no immediate prospects for doing so. Throughout China in 1988 there were still thousands of intellectuals with histories similar to his, and on my travels I heard more than a few of their personal stories. Many who had been sent to the west still longed to return to the east. As a result of Deng's reforms, which had loosened political controls and permitted increased mobility, a growing number were able to do so. This Shanghai man was still hoping that he could arrange such a transfer.

*   *   *

Snow was still falling gently when we arrived at the main rail station in Yinchuan, located in its "new city"—which had not existed at all in 1948. I was greeted cordially by a deputy chairman from the Ningxia Academy of Social Sciences, my host organization, who, accompanied by an aide, met me at the station. After working our way through a chaotic crowd, typical of China's rail stations, we sped by car—too fast over icy roads—to a guest house in the "old city," a little more than six miles to the east. Once reserved for Party and government officials, the Number Two Guest House still accommodated officials but was now also used as a regular hotel for both foreigners and well-to-do Chinese travelers. The hotel was unspectacular, but nevertheless I found it to be an attractive place; it consisted of several low buildings that were connected by covered walkways and surrounded a central courtyard. Stylistically, it represented rampant eclecticism, combining many different architectural elements: traditional Chinese (old-style curved tile roofs), Muslim (pointed arches), and modern Western (atrocious white statuary in the courtyard framed by a looming factory smokestack in the background). My rooms—a living room and bedroom—were large and comfortable, with all the modern appurtenances of a good hotel, including color TV. The interior decoration was in a style quite popular in China in the 1980s, which I decided to label "modern, provincial, Chinese Victorian." It was characterized by red velvet-and-lace curtains, scenic photos, and overstuffed sofas with doilies. I had a quick but excellent meal consisting of several small dishes. One was bêche de mer (sea slugs); the inclusion of this dish on my menu confirmed a rule that I had learned in China 40 years earlier, namely, that the more distant one is from the sea, the more likely one is to be served this difficult-to-obtain, expensive specialty—a delicacy that many Westerners abhor but that I had learned to enjoy.

I then sat down to discuss the itinerary and schedule for my visit with my hosts, including the Academy president (a Chinese Muslim, or Hui, from Yunnan Province who had spent two decades in Ningxia) and the deputy president, who had met me at the station (a Han Chinese from Shanxi Province, who after graduating from Beijing University, where he had specialized in the study of minority affairs, had spent the past two decades working in Inner Mongolia and Ningxia). We agreed fairly rapidly upon a program that mixed interviews and visits—and packed an impressive number of both into a relatively short period of time.

In the ensuing days in Yinchuan, I interviewed, fairly intensely, more than 40 people—some of them in groups—including Ma Yingliang, a deputy chairman of the regional government;* several other key members of the re-

---

*In Yinchuan, as in Baotou, the Party secretary and chairman of the government were both absent, attending meetings in Beijing. This was true in a number of places I visited in 1988, and at first I was highly suspicious that they probably were present but simply did not want to see me. Eventually I decided that in most cases they really were in Beijing; local leaders, I learned, do spend a considerable amount of time traveling to the capital, and some important national Party and government meetings were taking place in Beijing at the time of my travels.

gional government, including its secretary-general and staff members deal-ing with organizational matters, personnel, and finance; a group of Acad-emy scholars specializing in local history and Ningxia's economy (including its population, industry, agriculture, and economic reform); individuals knowledgeable about journalism and education; a group of government offi-cials responsible for minority and religious affairs; local township leaders; a local farmer in a suburban area; the manager and staff of a local factory; and religious leaders in two mosques. Bit by bit, I tried to piece together a profile of Ningxia in 1988 and to ruminate about how it had changed since 1948.

*   *   *

Ningxia's boundaries have changed many times in recent decades, but it always has remained one of China's smallest provincial-level units. In 1988, only Hainan, split off from Guangdong as a separate province in 1988, and China's three provincial-level municipalities—Beijing, Shanghai, and Tian-jin—were smaller in area. Ningxia's population, totaling 4.24 million at the end of 1986, also was one of China's smallest; only the Tibetan Autonomous Region and Qinghai Province were smaller.

When I had visited Ningxia in 1948, it was a major stronghold of Hui Muslim political power—as it had been for most of the first half of the twen-tieth century. A large percentage of China's Hui population inhabits a belt of territory that stretches across much of northwest China and includes parts of Ningxia, Gansu, and Qinghai. The Hui in this arc are the descendants of in-termarriages, centuries ago, between Han Chinese and Muslim groups who migrated to China from the west, starting as early as the seventh and eighth centuries (in the Tang dynasty); most of these Muslims, it is believed, came from central Asia and the region between Afghanistan and Arabia. The term *Hui,* according to some sources, was derived from the first syllable of the Chinese name for the Uighurs, a Turkic group converted to Islam. But, un-like many Turkic and other Muslim groups in China, including the Uighurs and Kazakhs in Chinese Turkestan (Xinjiang), the basic language of the Hui is Chinese.* The Hui people have been Sinified in many respects. However, as faithful—and in the past often militant—believers in Islam, and as a group with a racially mixed ethnic background, most have differed in appearance from Han Chinese and have maintained many distinctive customs. In the

---

*In this discussion, I will use the terms *Hui* and *Han* both as adjectives and collective nouns. Here I refer to the Chinese language as *Hanyu;* actually, the terms used by the Chinese language are varied. *Putonghua*—which means common speech—is a general term used throughout China at present for spoken Mandarin (standard pronunciation), but in west China when I dis-cussed questions relating to language, the term most frequently used by my interlocutors was *Hanyu,* which means the Han language.

eyes of both the Hui themselves and the Han Chinese, they have been a distinct ethnic group. Traditionally they have observed Muslim taboos against
eating pork, smoking, and drinking. They have worshiped in mosques (in
services using archaic Arabic) and they have faithfully observed Muslim fes-
tivals such as Ramadan. Yet in other respects they have been at least partially
assimilated into Han Chinese culture, to a greater extent than other Muslim
groups in China whose native languages are not Chinese.

The history of relations between the Hui and Han peoples in northwest
China has been a turbulent one in many periods. In the nineteenth century, in
fact, there were several major Muslim revolts in both northwest and southwest China, most of them (although not all) led by Hui; these contributed
significantly to the decline of the Qing dynasty. And, in the late nineteenth
century and early twentieth century, certain Hui clans with the name of Ma
emerged as powerful military and political leaders, and eventually they
achieved dominance in much of the northwest. Ma, which means, literally,
horse, is one of the most common Hui surnames. Some people have attributed its prevalence to the fact that many of the Hui's ancestors were famous
for their horsemanship, but the most common explanation I heard from Hui
leaders I met was that it derived from the name Muhammad.

The Ma clans that achieved predominance in this century had roots in a
Gansu town called Hezhou (now called Linxia) and in Gansu's former Taohe
County. They rose to prominence first in Gansu and then expanded their
power into adjacent areas. Ultimately, one branch dominated Qinghai and
another controlled Ningxia.

One of the first of these Mas to emerge as a powerful local leader in the
late nineteenth century was Ma Zhaoan. Influenced by the Yellow Turbans,
an anti-Qing secret society, he fought with some success against the Manchus but was defeated by Zuo Zongtang (Tso Tsung-t'ang), the Chinese
statesman who pacified the northwest in the 1870s. Zuo then reached an
agreement with the Mas and appointed Ma Anliang, one of Ma Zhaoan's
sons, as governor of Shaan-Gan (Shaanxi-Gansu).

Subsequently, two of Ma Anliang's protégés, the brothers Ma Qi and Ma
Lin, achieved dominance in Qinghai and started what was, in effect, a small
dynasty of their own. Ma Qi was governor of Qinghai from 1921 to 1931.
Ma Lin succeeded him and held the post, formally at least, until 1938. Real
power gravitated, however, to two of Ma Qi's sons, Ma Bufang and Ma
Buqing, who were born in Hezhou. Ma Bufang formally became governor of
Qinghai in 1938 and held that post until the Communist takeover in 1949.
Ma Buqing, his elder brother, served under him.

Another branch of the Ma family, with roots in Taohe County and
Hezhou, rose to power in part because they supported the Empress Dowager
against the Westerners who attacked China after the Boxer Rebellion in
1900. Two of them, Ma Fulu and his younger brother, Ma Fuxiang, steadily

accumulated military and political power, and both produced powerful heirs. Ma Fuxiang, born in Taohe, was especially successful. Following the overthrow of the Qing dynasty in 1911, he and close relatives extended their military control over a broad area encompassing much of what later became the provinces of Suiyuan, Ningxia, Qinghai, and Gansu. Ma Fulu, his elder brother, was killed while fighting during the Boxer Rebellion, but his son, Ma Hongbin, rose to be acting governor in Gansu in 1930–1931, and, even though he was soon ousted by a coup, he continued to command important military units in the area. However, Ma Hongkui, the son of Ma Fuxiang, eventually overshadowed his cousin, Ma Hongbin. Starting as a military commander under his father in 1913, he served for a while under Feng Yuxiang (the famous "Christian General"), but then he built his own power. In 1931, he succeeded his cousin as governor of Gansu, and in 1938 he became governor of Ningxia, where he ruled for a decade and a half. (Briefly, in 1948, he was the top leader in both Ningxia and Gansu.)

As the civil war in China reached its climax during 1948–1949, Ma Hongkui in Ningxia and Ma Bufang in Qinghai were among the last rulers to put up strong resistance to the Communists in northwest China. However, in 1949, when the Communist victory was in sight and both faced defeat, they fled China. Ironically, at the end of Ma Hongkui's reign, his cousin, Ma Hongbin, took over as governor of Ningxia, and, accepting the inevitable, he negotiated a surrender and peaceful transfer of power to the Communists. He was rewarded with a job in the new regime.

*   *   *

When I visited Ningxia in 1948, Ma Hongkui was still governor. A huge man weighing over 240 pounds, he looked more Han than Hui, but he was extremely proud of his authoritarian Muslim regime. Even though he claimed to treat Hui and Han people equally, and in some respects did, his warlord regime and personal army were riddled with relatives and other Hui Muslims. His hatred and fear of the Communists, who for many years had controlled Yan'an and other areas in nearby Shaanxi, seemed to motivate everything he did. He used crude methods of conscription to mobilize virtually all young men in the province for extended military service (as long as they were useful). His regular military forces and his Peace Preservation Corps units included roughly 100,000 men—about a seventh of the province's total population at that time—and most other able-bodied men were included in the so-called Self-Defense Corps, a militia force numbering about 120,000. Ma was particularly proud of his cavalry troops and frequently put them on display to impress visitors, including me. (The only person I met in Ningxia in 1988 who claimed to remember my visit in 1948 was a former soldier who said he had seen me at a military show put on by Governor Ma.)

Ma built an elaborate apparatus for political and economic control. The result was a strong and extremely oppressive police state. He boasted to me that his government maintained maps and charts showing every household in the province; his government, he claimed, knew where every individual was at all times. Everyone was required to carry an identity card, with thumbprint or photograph, and no travel was allowed without a permit. At 6:00 each morning, all able-bodied men, civilian as well as military, were mustered for anti-Communist indoctrination sessions. Every 10 to 15 households had a leader responsible for reporting all arrivals, departures, and significant events. Wrongdoers were punished swiftly and severely. Flogging was common, and executions occurred almost daily.

The economic burden of this militarized police state was enormous. Taxes were very high, and price controls were strict. Despite an abundance of good irrigated land in the province, rural poverty was evident everywhere. It was caused in part by the shortage of young men to do farm work and in part by the heavy tax burden. I saw almost no signs of real modernization in Ningxia in 1948. Ma and his relatives ran a monopoly enterprise, the Fu Ning Company, of which he was inordinately proud, but it was merely a trading company and did little to develop industry. Ningxia City had one tiny electric generator and a primitive hand-cranked telephone system, which were comparable to those in Baotou; they served a small group of officials and merchants in the capital city. But existing factories were really no more than workshops. Ma took pride in his efforts to develop some modern schooling and to promote extensive tree planting. However, the atmosphere, economically as well as politically, was oppressive; this was mirrored in the glum, sullen expressions of almost everyone I saw when I drove through a large part of the province.

The final demise of Ma Hongkui's regime and the establishment of Communist power occurred rapidly in 1949. The account I received from Ma Yingliang (when I met him in 1988 he was one of the deputy chairmen of Ningxia's government and also a member of the regional Party's standing committee), supplemented by the accounts of several local academics, may have been self-serving in some respects, but their story was a plausible one. When defeat was imminent, I was told, Ma Hongkui transferred his wealth to Hong Kong and then departed from Ningxia by air with only a few immediate family members (on September 1, 1949, according to my informants). Ultimately, he settled in California. After his departure, one of his sons reportedly took charge briefly, but then he too fled, on September 17, the same day the Communist general Yang Dezhi (later to become PLA chief of staff) is said to have led his forces into Ningxia. Two days later, according to the chronology given to me, several local generals started negotiating with the Communists in Zhongning County in the south. The outcome was decided when Ma Hongbin decided to switch allegiance; an agreement for a transfer of power followed quickly, and Ma was co-opted to be a deputy to Yang in the local Military Control Commission established for the takeover period. Some serious fighting continued in Wuzhong County, but before long the leader there also negotiated a peaceful turnover and was co-opted into the new regime. (In 1988, this man still served as a deputy chairman of the Gansu People's Political Consultative Conference.) Some of Ma's military forces were absorbed into the PLA; they included Ma Hongbin's 81st Army, transformed into the Number Two Independent Northwest Army, under the PLA. But many other units were demobilized.

The Ma family's personal base of power and their police-state apparatus rapidly crumbled, according to my informants, who were in Ningxia at the time. This, they said, was because of deep and widespread resentments about Ma's policies, which I thought was understandable in light of what I had observed in 1948. Nevertheless, some strong guerrilla resistance continued, but my informants claimed that only 3,000 to 4,000 people were involved. (My guess was that this may have understated the number.) In any case, it took a major "campaign to clean out bandits" in the winter of 1950–1951 to eliminate this resistance. The basic strategy, Deputy Chairman Ma explained, was to kill only the most intransigent resistance leaders, forgive others, and co-opt as many as possible with offers of jobs. A large number of officials who had worked for the Ma regime—including many of his relatives and commanders—were given positions (albeit subordinate ones) in the new regime. Several still worked for the Ningxia government in 1988 (examples cited included deputy heads of the Water Conservancy Department and the Office of Consultants). Clearly, however, in Ningxia as elsewhere in China, the Communists destroyed, fairly rapidly and effectively, the political and military base of the old regime and built an entirely new power structure. The local Military Control Commission, headed by Yang Dezhi with Ma Hongbin as a deputy, lasted in Ningxia for only three months, I was told, from September 23 to December 23, and then it was replaced by a civil government. If these dates are accurate, the transition was more rapid than in many other places in China. The Party then brought in many outside cadres from other regions. In subsequent years, there was no real sign, to my knowledge, of any reemergence of autonomous Hui political power in Ningxia. However, the Party trained large numbers of local Hui as Party cadres and gave them high positions, mainly in the government bureaucracy rather than in the more powerful Party apparatus.

*   *   *

I talked with Deputy Chairman Ma Yingliang at considerable length one afternoon and into the evening, over a dinner that included not only the best roast lamb I had ever eaten but also shredded camel hump, an exotic but delicious dish. Ma exemplified the new kind of local Hui leadership cultivated

after 1949 by the Communists, and he also impressed me as being a good example of the new breed of able, relatively young, technocratic leaders promoted in the 1980s. He was well informed and his concerns were more on
economic development and problem solving than on old ideological dogmas.

Deputy Chairman Ma (who was a Hui but no relation to Ma Hongkui)
was in his fifties when I met him. Son of an uneducated peasant, he had
grown up in a farming village but got a lucky break when he was admitted to
a school giving free education—one of the so-called Helan schools established by Ma Hongkui for poor boys. However, the Communists arrived before he completed school, and he immediately "joined the revolution" in
1949, at age 18. The Communists enrolled him in one of their first training
classes for local cadres; of his group, which consisted of about 1,200 young
persons, roughly one-third were Hui Muslims. They received six months of
training. Ever since then, Ma said, the regime's policy had been to select and
train local cadres roughly according to their proportion in the population.
Ma soon joined the Party, in 1950, and immediately was assigned to a job in
government administration. This was the start of a long career during which
he dealt mainly with economic matters. Unlike many of China's new technocrats, he never obtained a college education, but during his career he attended various training institutions and was "educated through experience."
He impressed me as being very competent, and he was extremely open in discussing almost all of the issues and problems that I raised.

Others I met discussed with me the evolution of the leadership in Ningxia.
What became clear was that, as a matter of policy, the Chinese Communists
had promoted minority cadres to numerous leading government positions in
Ningxia, as in all minority regions, but Han Chinese continued to dominate
the top positions in the Party apparatus. Tracing for me the succession of top
Party and government leaders in Ningxia since 1949, local Academy experts
pointed out that all but one of the chairmen of the regional government had
been Hui; the one exception had been Kang Jianmin, a Han Chinese who
headed the local government as well as Party and military leadership during
the Cultural Revolution. In contrast, all but one of the Party's first secretaries (recently called, simply, Party secretaries) had been Han Chinese. The one
exception was Yang Jingren, a Gansu native who rose to be one of China's
top Hui leaders after 1949 and headed both the Party and government in
Ningxia in the 1960s, following the ouster from the government chairman-
ship of another prominent Hui leader, Liu Geping, who was accused of "local nationalism"—that is, a preoccupation with Hui interests. (Liu later rose
again, then fell again, in nearby Shanxi Province during the Cultural Revolution.)

It was not possible, in the time I had, for me to delve very deeply into
Ningxia's political history after 1949. However, from what I did learn, it was

clear that, like the rest of the country, it had experienced all the traumas of the many mass campaigns of the early 1950s, followed by the Great Leap Forward in the late 1950s and culminating in the Cultural Revolution in the 1960s. Serious Hui-Han tensions surfaced in the late 1950s and early 1960s and again, in an extreme form, during the Cultural Revolution, in the late 1960s and early 1970s. What struck me in 1988, however, was the degree to which—despite the turbulence of those past periods—the appearance of things and the general atmosphere in Ningxia, at least in Yinchuan and nearby areas, seemed to be, as far as I could judge, characterized by normalcy, stability, and relative political relaxation. I judged this to be largely the result of the reforms and the economic development that had occurred in the 1980s. I saw no obvious signs of Han-Hui tensions. It was possible that some still existed, latent and under the surface. However, I gradually was convinced that the active "affirmative action" policies carried out in Ningxia, as well as in many other areas, in the 1980s—which involved a great deal of reverse discrimination in favor of the Hui—had gone quite far toward healing the most recent wounds and repairing the most visible damage that had been inflicted by rampaging Red Guards during the Cultural Revolution. Perhaps the mending process had been made easier because the Hui had not been singled out in the Cultural Revolution as the sole targets.

The impact of Red Guard persecution and destruction obviously had hit the Hui very hard at that time, but the Red Guards were not simply anti-Hui; their targets included all other religious groups and, in addition, most intellectuals and Party and government bureaucrats—Han as well as Hui. This made it possible, and in many respects logical, for leaders in the 1980s to blame "leftism," not just "Han chauvinism," for the excesses in the 1960s and 1970s. The relatively relaxed atmosphere in Ningxia also reflected, I felt, the gradual trend, all over China during most of the 1980s (up to 1989), toward depoliticalization of ordinary day-to-day affairs, a loosening of ideological and political controls, and a general secularization of society—following the ideological extremism of the late Mao period. In any case, the political climate in 1988 was very different from—and much better than—that when Ma Hongkui had ruled.

None of the recent trends had produced any signs, as far as I could see, of significantly increased pressures for greater real autonomy from Beijing or of centrifugal forces weakening ties to the center. On the contrary, Ningxia seemed to me in 1988 to be much more closely linked to, as well as dependent on, "the center" than it had been in earlier years; some of the reasons for this I will note later.

*   *   *

As a political and administrative unit, Ningxia has had its ups and downs—to put it mildly. When first established as a province in 1928, it was created from a merger of a sizable chunk of Gansu (inhabited by both Han and Hui people), and a large Mongol area inhabited by the Alashan Mongols as well as another adjacent Mongol banner. The relationship between the Ma regime in Ningxia and the Mongols beyond the Helan Mountains was uneasy, often strained, and at times very tenuous; when I was there in 1948, the Alashan Mongols enjoyed a high degree of de facto autonomy, even though they were theoretically still part of Ningxia.

In 1954, Ningxia was suddenly abolished as a province, and most of it was reabsorbed by Gansu. I never heard a very good explanation of why this occurred, but my guess is that it was a move to strengthen Han political control over the Hui. Then, in 1958, Ningxia was reestablished, this time as a new provincial-level Hui Autonomous Region but with a much smaller territory. The Mongol areas it once contained were split off and merged into the Inner Mongolian Autonomous Region. A decade later, another major reorganization took place. In the fall of 1968—during the Cultural Revolution—a decision was made to carve up Inner Mongolia, and the Alashan area was returned to Ningxia. Different local officials and scholars gave me several explanations for this change, but the most convincing was that in this chaotic period Beijing was especially concerned about possible opposition and separatism in Mongol areas, so it divided Inner Mongolia to facilitate tighter political control over the Mongols. From 1969 to 1978, therefore, Ningxia again administered a large Mongol area. But, after the end of the Cultural Revolution, I was told, the Mongols in the west lobbied Beijing to reunite their area with Inner Mongolia, and then Beijing "persuaded" Yinchuan to agree, so that in 1978 Ningxia once more lost its Mongol areas and again became a small administrative unit inhabited almost entirely by Han and Hui.*
Somehow, it seemed to me, Ningxia appeared to have retained its sense of identity through all of these changes; its core Han-Hui area was not greatly affected by most of the changes.

In 1988, Ningxia's territory totaled a little over 25,000 square miles—about the size of West Virginia. This was less than a quarter of its size in the 1930s, when—in theory at least—it ruled vast Mongol areas, and it was less than 1 percent of China's total territory in 1988. In sum, it was a Lilliputian spot on the map of China.

Ningxia's population was also diminutive. Totaling 4.24 million in 1986—the latest year for which I obtained official statistics—it was estimated by local officials to have grown to about 4.29 million at the start of

---

*The precise dates of these changes varied in different accounts that I heard. Some said that the division of Inner Mongolia took place in 1969 instead of 1968 and that the enlargement of Inner Mongolia was in 1979 instead of 1978. Perhaps the decisions were made in the earlier years cited and effectively implemented in the later years.

1988. This 1988 figure was almost six times what it had been estimated to be in the late 1930s, and it was almost 70 percent above its population three decades earlier, in the late 1950s. Small as it was, it had grown rapidly in recent years partly because of natural growth (the Muslims had not been subjected to birth-control policies as strict as those applied to the Han), but, equally important, because of a large influx of Han Chinese sent to develop the region economically.

Although Ningxia is still thought of in the popular mind in China as a primarily Muslim region—as the name, Hui Autonomous Region, suggests—the population actually has been predominantly Han throughout the modern period. It still is predominantly Han, although what I learned suggested (if the statistics I received were correct), somewhat to my surprise, that the proportion of Hui had actually increased since the late 1940s, despite the large, continuing influx of Han Chinese from other provinces. In 1948, local officials had told me that, of a total population of 760,000 (not counting the Mongols), three-quarters were Han Chinese and one-quarter (about 190,000) were Hui Muslims. Statistics for 1986 indicated that the number of Hui had grown to 1.37 million, and they now made up close to a third of the total population. These figures suggested that the number of Hui people was more than seven times what it had been four decades earlier, which seemed highly questionable. Although improved public health, lower death rates, and relatively loose policies on birth control may have contributed to the rapid growth rates, I suspected that figures for earlier periods must have been too low. There seems to be little doubt, however, that in recent years the number of Hui has grown a great deal, and even though they remain a minority, they now appear to make up a larger proportion of the population than in the pre-Communist period.

Administratively, Ningxia as of 1988 was divided into 4 cities, 16 counties (4 of which were administered by municipalities), and 46 towns (*zhen*). The 4 cities, Yinchuan, Shizuishan, Wuzhong, and Qingtongxia, all located in the north, had developed into the region's major economic centers. Han Chinese made up by far the largest part of the population in these municipalities, which accounted for roughly 40 percent of the region's total population. Han Chinese were dominant in most other urban areas as well. The municipality of Yinchuan, for example, had a total population of about 700,000—with 390,000 in three core urban districts and the rest, roughly 310,000, in its two counties—and, of the total, only 15 percent, even including residents in rural areas, were Hui Muslims, and almost 85 percent were Han Chinese (a handful of people belonged to other minorities). Even though Han and Hui were mixed to some degree throughout the region, the Hui really predominated only in certain areas of the south, especially in Jingyuan, Tongxin, and Haiyuan counties (there were large Hui minorities in the southern counties of Guyuan and Xiji as well). Close to two-thirds of

Ningxia's Hui population lived in these southern counties, which generally tended to be less developed and poorer than Han-dominated areas in the north.

In retrospect, it seems rather remarkable that the Ma clans of Hui origin, representing a minority in the total population, were able to dominate the region as long as they did and to establish so autonomous a local regime. A major factor, clearly, was their control of strong independent military forces. Since the Communist takeover and the destruction of the old regime, the Han role has more accurately reflected their predominant numbers and their greater economic power as well as the stronger controls—military, political, and economic—exercised from China's capital. As stated earlier, the old local military forces were eliminated right after 1949. The periodic administrative changes affecting Ningxia also reflected—and strengthened—central control. From 1949 on, Beijing not only imposed a new political structure but also appointed all of the region's top leaders. In Ningxia as elsewhere, moreover, there was a dramatic proliferation of bureaucratic structures, all vertically linked to the capital. And, as Ningxia developed, it became heavily dependent, fiscally, on Beijing's subsidies.

*   *   *

In the early years after 1949, when the top authority in northwest China was a powerful Military and Administrative Committee (similar committees were established in all but one of the major regions of China at that time), it looked as if political decentralization might be far-reaching and long-lasting. Headquartered in Xi'an, this regional structure, which had authority over Shaanxi, Ningxia, Gansu, Qinghai, and Xinjiang, was predominantly military at the start but gradually built up government bureaucracies exercising considerable power. The leaders in Beijing soon had second thoughts, however, about such decentralization. In 1952, they changed the regional bodies to Administrative Committees, with reduced functions, and in 1954 they abolished them. In 1955, they also abolished the Central Committee's regional Party bureaus. These were briefly revived in 1961 but abolished again in 1967, and since then nothing like them has reappeared.

When I asked Ningxia officials why there were not any regional Party or government bodies coordinating affairs in northwest China, and whether such coordination was desirable or needed, their answers were emphatic. "Both the center and the provinces," one official said, "now prefer to deal with each other directly. The regional bodies may have been useful before, but they are not necessary and would actually be unhelpful now." From the 1960s on, Yinchuan, therefore, no longer has had any special governmental or Party relationship with Xi'an or any other northwestern city; its main chain of command has tied it directly to Beijing.

Military affairs are an exception to this, however. The Northwest Military Region's headquarters in Lanzhou has continued to exercise overall responsibility for military affairs throughout the region, and the Ningxia Military District has continued to operate under it. Lanzhou had been a major coordinating center for political as well as military affairs in all northwest China during the last days of the Nationalist regime, but, under the Communists, its coordinating role had been limited to the military establishment. Officials I met in Ningxia emphasized, moreover, that control of crucial military affairs is highly centralized and exercised mainly by the Central Committee's Military Affairs Commission in Beijing, which has direct authority over the PLA's "main forces;" they said that the size and role of "local forces" has diminished substantially, at least in Ningxia.

Leading Ningxia government officials also asserted that, in 1988 at least, the Ningxia Military District performed only very limited functions, such as providing logistical support to regular forces, organizing conscription, and managing the People's Armed Police and that it was primarily the Ningxia region's Party Committee rather than its government that dealt with military affairs ("the Ningxia government has *no* responsibility for the Military District," one official said, in what clearly was an exaggeration.) Actually, the Ningxia government regularly provided substantial support—including grain supplies and housing—to military units. No special liaison bodies were required, I was told, because there were effective informal working relations between military authorities and the government departments. The local needs of the military were estimated annually (based on past allocations, with some adjustments), and government departments included the military's requirements (for example, for grain) in their own economic plans.

The Ningxia leaders played down the significance of regional economic cooperation. They said that in the northwest there had been no efforts to organize any really strong special body to coordinate regional cooperation. However, they acknowledged that there had been a number of cooperative efforts on specific projects, mainly on an ad hoc basis. For example, they said, Ningxia and Gansu had engaged in negotiations, which were continuing in 1988, about a possible new Yellow River dam near the Gansu border that might eventually develop a hydroelectric capacity of 1.6 gigawatts. In addition, meetings were held quite frequently involving economic administrators and/or bureau-level officials from two or more northwestern provinces. Surprisingly, they did not even mention the annual meetings of the northwestern governors and regional chairmen, which I later learned were being held annually. Leaders I met in some other northwestern areas put considerably greater emphasis on the value of these regular regional meetings among top leaders. I do not know why Ningxia's leaders underplayed the significance of such efforts at regional cooperation. Perhaps they were uneasy about being overshadowed and outcompeted by larger provinces and regions and preferred to deal directly with Beijing and with major trading partners in the east.

Because it is connected by rail to both Baotou and Lanzhou, Ningxia quite naturally viewed its trade ties with them as extremely important. However, its basic financial ties linked it to Beijing. And in conversations with me, Ningxia officials emphasized that, in their view, the trade and technical relationships that were likely to be most significant for its future economic development were those they had been developing with Shanghai and other coastal areas. Several talked of Ningxia's "special relations" with Shanghai, and some said—half jokingly but half seriously—that they liked to think of Yinchuan as a "little Shanghai." At the start of the 1980s, I was told, when the State Council ordered economically advanced cities to help underdeveloped areas, it specified that Shanghai should help Ningxia, and since then there had been an increased number of transfers of technology, growing trade, and other forms of economic cooperation that had developed with the support of local economic cooperation offices (under municipal Planning Commissions) in both Shanghai and Yinchuan. These trends had resulted in a sizable number of Shanghai technicians and workers moving to Ningxia. Yinchuan also had developed useful "sister city" ties with Ningbo, in Zhejiang Province, and Shenyang, in Liaoning Province. The strengthening of these ties with eastern cities was more important to Ningxia, local officials said, than efforts to coordinate policies among northwestern provinces—which in many respects were their competitors in dealing with Beijing and the eastern provinces.

*   *   *

The recent development of modern transportation and communications had been one basic factor, Deputy Chairman Ma emphasized, that made it possible for Ningxia to develop stronger ties with, and strengthen its orientation toward, both Beijing and coastal areas. In the 1940s, he pointed out, it took 10 days or more to go from Ningxia to Beijing (via Xi'an) to attend meetings; by the late 1980s, it took just a little more than an hour by plane or about 27 hours by train. Moreover, he said, good telephone, telegraph, and TV links had fundamentally changed the situation, and he implied that these worked against a regional orientation and for closer links with the eastern areas.

Ningxia's great financial dependence on the central government clearly was another basic factor (perhaps the most basic one) helping to explain why local leaders seemed to be preoccupied with their fundamental economic relationships with Beijing rather than with any theoretical potential benefit from expanded ties with neighboring provinces. The fiscal facts of life clearly imposed great constraints, moreover, on any temptation to try to increase local or regional autonomy, political or economic. (This was true, I learned, in all the western provinces.)

The Ningxia government's secretary-general discussed with me the region's budget and later provided me with some published budgetary figures. I did not totally understand the financial relationships that he described (central-provincial economic relationships are extraordinarily complex in China), but he, and his statistics, made the basic situation fairly clear. The Ningxia Tax Bureau (under dual leadership of central and regional governments) collected all revenues, most of which came from industrial and commercial taxes and profit taxes on the profits of state enterprises. Then, after taxes had been collected, he said—and here I became slightly confused by what he told me—Ningxia kept all of certain tax receipts, kept a part of others, and remitted a large part directly to the central government, which then returned some to Ningxia and—most important—added large subsidies to the region.

The bottom line was that, in recent years, Ningxia's own retained revenues had paid for less than a third of its expenditures, and central government subsidies had paid for more than two-thirds. Official statistics for 1986 showed, for example, that in that year local government expenditures (including those of both the provincial-level regional government and subordinate governments) totaled Y 1.202 billion. Revenues that Ningxia collected and kept for its own use totaled Y 366.13 million. Central government subsidies totaled Y 824.17 million. There was, therefore, on paper only a small budget deficit of Y 11.84 million (under 1 percent of expenditures), but the real deficit was the difference between the usable local revenues and actual expenditures—which was made up by central government subsidies—and this amounted to 69 percent of expenditures. (I was told that whereas they could not yet give me final official figures for 1987, total expenditures were roughly the same as in 1986 but that Ningxia's own contribution had risen to about Y 400 million and the central government subsidies were therefore slightly reduced.)

I learned as I continued traveling through China in 1988 that Ningxia was an excellent illustration of one basic fiscal pattern in China: The central government provided large subsidies to all the economically backward interior provinces, and to make this possible it took from certain advanced coastal provinces a very high percentage of the taxes they collected. Areas such as Ningxia obviously had very strong incentives to be responsive to Beijing—it paid their bills.

The organizational as well as fiscal links to Beijing that had developed since the Communist takeover tied areas such as Ningxia to the center in an unprecedented way. Many reforms adopted in China in the 1980s were aimed at decentralizing the economy and granting local governments as well as enterprises increased decisionmaking authority. These trends had had an enormous impact on China's coastal provinces, but in northwest China decentralization appeared to me to have much more limited effects. As of the time of my 1988 visit, I did not see that they had altered the basic economic dependency of the western areas in any fundamental way.

                                     *   *   *

Because I had long had a strong interest, dating to the 1940s, in local Chinese political leadership, organizations, and bureaucratic structures and had written a good deal on those subjects over the years, I was determined to learn what I could in a limited time about both the political leadership in Ningxia (especially the roles of Hui people in it, four decades after the demise of the Ma warlord regime) and about the structures of the local bureaucracies of both the government and the Party (to see both how they differed from the past and whether recent reforms had had much impact). I was able to learn a little, but less than I would have liked; to probe deeper would have required a lot more time.

Everyone with whom I talked agreed—which was no surprise to me—that the Party Committee of the region was still the highest local authority. Its top leaders—the secretary and deputy secretaries—were formally elected by the local Party Congress, but, it was acknowledged, this was a pro forma endorsement of proposals made by the Central Committee's Organization Department. Beijing had not yet shown any willingness to give up its control of key Party appointments of top provincial-level leaders. But Ningxia officials asserted that the local Party organization now decided whom to appoint to lesser positions; moreover, they said, since the 13th Party Congress (held in the fall of 1987), some local authority over appointments had been shifted from the Party to the government.

In 1988, the Standing Committee of the Region's Party Committee had nine members—a secretary, four deputy secretaries, and four others. The top leader, the secretary, was a Han Chinese from Jiangsu Province, but of the other eight, five were Hui Muslims, which was a remarkably large representation. Following the 13th Party Congress, Beijing had called for steps to "separate Party and government" and to reduce parallel organizations. Since then, I was told, two of the local Party departments had been abolished: the Rural Work Department and the Urban Work Department.* Both of these departments had duplicated the work of government organs dealing with economic matters. However, the Party still retained its most important political organs: the Organization Department, the Propaganda Department, and

---

*Although Ningxia had an Urban Work Department before 1987, not all provinces had a department of this name.

the United Front Work Department as well as a Policy Research Office and a General Office.

In the government, the top leadership group consisted of six people: the chairman of the region (a Hui from Liaoning) and five deputy chairmen. Of the six, only one deputy chairman (an expert on light industry, who had come from Jiangsu) was a Han Chinese. Of the four Hui deputy chairmen, three were local people (one from near Yinchuan, one from Wuzhong, and one from a mountain area in the south), and the other, a woman, came from Nanjing, in Jiangsu. Of the six, five were still in their fifties or early sixties; all of the five had joined the Party about the time of "liberation," so they had no preliberation Party experience.

In some parts of the bureaucracy, the role of technocrats from Jiangsu and Liaoning, two of China's most developed areas, was notable. (In subsequent travels, I learned that in many other interior provinces as well, technical and professional experts from coastal provinces were playing an extremely important role in local economic development.) But local people predominated, and, surprisingly, the Hui were actually "overrepresented" in top positions (that is, overrepresented in proportion to their share of the total population), even in the Party. This was true, I was told, even at the county level; 7 of Ningxia's 16 counties had Hui magistrates. However, it was not true among the rank-and-file cadres in the Party and government, where the portion of Hui (about a seventh of all cadres) was less than half of their proportion in the total population.

The government secretary-general of the region, another Ma (Ma Jixing), spent a long time patiently answering my questions about local government personnel and bureaucratic structures. As of 1986 (official statistics for 1987 on virtually everything had not yet, it seemed, been certified for public use), Ningxia had a total of 129,691 "state cadres."* This was between four and five times the number of state cadres in Ningxia three decades earlier, I was told (the total in 1958 had been 28,000); this fact provided one revealing index of the explosive growth of the bureaucracies in Ningxia during the period of Communist rule that resulted from both the regime's pervasive political intervention into all aspects of society and to its attempt to manage all facets of a rapidly growing economy. State cadres accounted for a little over 3 percent of Ningxia's population in 1986—slightly above the average.

Just over two-fifths of Ningxia's state cadres in 1986 were Party members (55,964, or 43 percent); the rest were non-Party cadres (although another

---

*This category included all Party and government officials and functionaries, at all levels, who were on the state's payroll. It did not include local rural cadres who were not paid by the government or many people working for state enterprises who did not have "state cadre" status; if these categories were included, the figures would be much larger.

20,629, or almost 16 percent, of state cadres were members of the Young Communist League, most of whom would eventually become Party members). I did not obtain any figure on the total Party membership in Ningxia; if it paralleled the national average of 4 to 5 percent of the population, it might have been close to 100,000; if so, the proportion of Party members who were state cadres was unusually high.

Among the rank-and-file members of the bureaucracies—the people with whom the population as a whole came into most frequent contact—the Hui were poorly represented. Of all 129,691 state cadres in Ningxia in 1986, only 18,459—a little more than 14 percent—were Hui, which was well under half of the Hui percentage of Ningxia's population. Several factors probably helped to explain this fact. Compared to the Han, a disproportionate number of Hui lived in rural areas, and, partly because of this fact, the average levels of both their incomes and education tended to be lower than that of Han Chinese—despite conscious efforts by the government to narrow the gaps. One can only speculate about whether Chinese leaders—remembering Hui political domination under the Ma regime before 1949—deliberately limited Hui participation in the lower levels of the bureaucracies (while co-opting a disproportionately large number of Hui into high-level positions). I suspected that they did. But I obtained no evidence to support this supposition, and conceivably economic, educational, and other factors provided sufficient explanation.

Not surprisingly, women were underrepresented among Ningxia's cadres. This has been a consistent pattern throughout China, and I expected the underrepresentation to be even greater in an area with many Muslims. Actually, the number of women cadres—34,486, or close to 27 percent of the total—was proportionately greater than I expected. It was larger, in fact, than in some other places in China. I could only guess at how many were Hui, but my impression was that they were mainly Han Chinese.

At the summit of the regime, Secretary-General Ma said that there were, in 1988, 3,286 state cadres holding provincial-level positions in the regional Party apparatus, top governmental organs, and the leadership of major mass organizations as well as in the 38 "first-level" bureaucratic organizations in the official table of organization (T.O.) for the provincial government. This turned out to be a rather narrow definition, and it did not reveal the total number of people working at the provincial level. I was told that first-level organizations included only certain units, authorized by the central government, with specified staffing levels; many other organizations were not included in that list, and the provincial government had considerable flexibility, I was told, in staffing these units.

One of the aims of national political reforms during the 1980s had been the "streamlining" of the bureaucracies to reduce the number of units and the number of people working for them. Since 1983, the secretary-general said, Ningxia had responded to calls for such reform by cutting the number of first-level organs by almost a third, from 55 to 38, and by reducing the number of provinicial-level cadres working for these organizations by almost a fifth, from more than 4,000 to 3,286. On paper, these cuts were significant.

I had no way of judging, however, what the real effects of such cuts had been; many times in the past, similar efforts in China had had only very limited effects. Sometimes, in fact, the effects had been no more than cosmetic. I suspected that in the bureaucracies in Ningxia the retirement of old cadres and the promotion of younger, better-educated, more technically qualified individuals had had a greater impact than the organizational cuts. Many leaders I met belonged to the rising group of technocratic leaders; I found them to be very different from typical leaders in the Maoist era.

It seemed to me that bureaucratic organizations, except at the top, had been—as of 1988—only marginally affected by reform. They clearly were still greatly overstaffed and very inefficient. Imperial China invented bureaucracy; the Nationalists further expanded the bureaucracies; and the Communists inflated them to an unprecedented and gargantuan size. It will take a great deal of reform, implemented over many years, even to begin to change the bureaucracies in fundamental ways, if, indeed, that is possible under any regime. In virtually all countries, including the United States, reform of bureaucracies reminds one of Sisyphus pushing his rock up the mountain. In China, the task is especially daunting.

*   *   *

To understand how China is governed, it is essential to know something about the bureaucratic structures of government because bureaucracies intrude on virtually every aspect of people's lives. Every provincial-level government in China is, in essence, a duplicate of the central government. The structures have been adapted and modified in minor ways to fit local conditions, but, generally, there are no major structural variations. However, the minor adaptations are sometimes of interest; so too are the different ways in which local officials describe their bureaucracies. Trying to obtain an understanding even of the general structure of the bureaucracies is often like peeling off the successive layers of an onion: It takes time and patience. I decided nevertheless to ask Secretary-General Ma to explain Ningxia's onion to me.

Ma started by explaining that in the regional government, first-*level* units could be grouped into five *categories:* (1) units directly under the region's chairman; (2) first-category comprehensive (*zonghe*) units; (3) second-category management (*guanli*) units; (4) third-category supervisory or monitoring (*jiandu*) units; and (5) units directly under the central government. Units had different labels: commissions (*weiyuanhui*), departments (*ting*), bureaus (*ju*), offices (*shi*), and so on. Over time, however, the distinctions had become blurred, and the labels in many cases had become interchangeable, although some of the commissions still had broader coordinative functions than the departments and bureaus.*

The secretary-general's five categories of units seemed to me to mix apples and oranges. In this respect, they differed to a considerable extent from the categories, based on so-called functional systems (*xitong*), generally used by the Chinese Communists in recent years. The categorization by *xitong* has grouped units into several very logical systems: organization and personnel; political and legal affairs; cultural and educational affairs (including health and sports); agriculture and forestry; industry and communications; finance and trade; military affairs; and foreign affairs (plus—within the Party— united front work, women's work, and youth work). Although the groupings described to me in Ningxia partially reflected such functional divisions, they were based in part on other criteria (hierarchical status, breadth of function, relationship to central and regional authority, and so on), but they seemed to mix units in a fairly illogical way. I did not have time to try to explore the reasons for this.

The more the secretary-general talked about the government, the more complicated and confusing the picture became. The first-level units listed for

---

*Lists of organizational units are undoubtedly dull to most people, but to me they are interesting indicators of the scope of government responsibilities and the complexities of the bureaucracies that deal with almost all aspects of society. The specific organizations in Ningxia's government in 1988 that were considered to be first-level units included the following: (1) units under the Chairman: General Office, Foreign Affairs Office, Office of Consultants (*canshi shi*); (2) comprehensive units: Planning Commission, Economic Commission, Finance Department, Science and Technology Commission, Price Bureau, Industry and Commerce Management Bureau, Statistics Bureau, Labor and Personnel Department, Family Planning Commission, Civil Affairs Department, Minority and Nationality Affairs Commission, and the Commission on Staffing (*bianzhi weiyuanhui*, which I decided simply to call the "T.O. Commission"); (3) management units: Heavy Industry Department, Light and Textile Industry Department, Coal Industry Department, Materials Supply Department, Transport and Communications Department, Agriculture Department, Water Conservancy Department, Farm Management Bureau, Rural Construction Management Department, Township Enterprise Bureau, Forestry Department, Animal Husbandry Bureau, Weather Forecasting Bureau, Grain Bureau, Commerce Department, Department of Foreign Economic Relations and Trade, Education Department, Health Department, Publication Management Bureau, Broadcasting and Television Department, and Sports Commission; (4) monitoring and supervision units: Public Security Department, Judiciary Department, Investigations (*jiancha*) Department, and Auditing Bureau; and (5) units directly under the central government: Metallurgy Bureau, Electronics Bureau, Railway (branch) Bureau, Post and Telegraph Bureau, and Geology and Minerals Bureau.

The ancient Gu Lou. In 1948 this structure marked the center of Ningxia's provincial capital, then called Ningxia city.

*A typical city street in the
provincial capital, lined
with shops, open markets,
and peddlers; the soldiers
and bicycles were the only
signs of modernity.*

*A traditional two-wheel ox
cart; the huge wheels were
built to travel deeply rutted
mud roads.*

In 1988 the Gu Lou was still standing but was no longer the center of the modern city, now called Yinchuan, which had grown in several directions.

A major department store and shops in the business center of Yinchuan. The shoppers look more like those in Shanghai than those in pre-1949 Ningxia.

A modern apartment house in Yinchuan; its individual apartments are more spacious than similar ones in east China cities.

A textile factory in Yinchuan. Women workers predominate in light industry but most workers in heavy industrial factories are men.

me (discussed earlier) actually totaled 45* and covered only part of the government structure, he explained. In a category of second-level units, there were 10 more organizations—a mix of seemingly important and relatively unimportant ones. In theory, I was told, the regional government had greater authority to decide on the structure and staffing of these second-level units, but I could see no logic to the inclusion of such important organs as the Tax Bureau in this category, together with such minor units as the one dealing with the underground shelters that had been built during the Maoist period for defense against alleged threats at that time.

My briefers then proceeded to discuss several other groupings of organizations. One consisted of fairly specialized units run directly by the central government and not included in the first-level units; these included the Earthquake Bureau, Bureau for Testing Commercial Products, and Reserve Materials Bureau. Another grouping included all of Ningxia's branches of national banks and financial institutions, including the People's Bank of China, Bank of China, Construction Bank, Agricultural Bank, Industrial and Commercial Bank, and Insurance General Company. Still another category consisted of so-called general companies performing certain administrative and coordinating functions in special fields, covering petroleum and chemicals, metallurgy, construction materials, and medicine. Some of these oversaw numerous factories and thousands of employees. To obtain a comprehensive picture, one also would have had to add the following: courts and procuratorates, academies and other research organizations, educational institutions, and military-related bodies.

Stated bluntly, despite my intense interest and the patience with which the secretary-general and his staff spent the better part of an afternoon explaining Ningxia's bureaucratic structure to me, I left the discussion overwhelmed by a huge number of trees and still not able to see the forest very clearly. However, the data provided to me highlighted several things that anyone interested in China's government must recognize. The bureaucracies in all local governments, including Ningxia's, had grown enormously since the 1950s. This growth reflected the great expansion of all government functions, but it also revealed that even in remote areas of west China local governments were integrated into the national system much more than ever in the past. Locally, as in Beijing, there was a government organ to deal with virtually everything. As the secretary-general said to me: "The regional gov-

---

*When earlier the secretary-general said to me that first-level units had been reduced to 38, he may have excluded 3 units directly under the chairman as well as 5 units directly under the central government. His specific list of comprehensive, management, and monitoring and supervisory units totaled 37 (one less than the figure of 38 that he used earlier).

ernment must have bodies dealing with everything that the central government deals with, except things like state security [counterintelligence]."*

By 1988, I concluded, the national reforms initiated in China in the early 1980s had not had any fundamental impact on the structure of the bureaucracies in Ningxia. They had, however, resulted in very significant leadership changes and in some limited cuts in the bureaucracies, but Ningxia's bureaucracies still penetrated every sector of society, and they still functioned in many respects as branches of the central government, tied vertically to equivalent organizations in Beijing as well as to local leadership bodies. It seemed clear to me that until the processes of decentralization, decontrol, and social pluralization—which economic modernization and reform in the 1980s had fostered—go much further, reform of the bureaucracies could be no more than partial, at best, and the task of "debureaucratizing" Chinese society (to say nothing of "democratizing" the political system) would be extremely difficult. It will take many years, even under favorable conditions. My sense, however, was that the new kind of technocratic leaders I met in Ningxia would try to push efforts to streamline and rationalize the bureaucracies and would probably recognize the necessity for greater pluralization of the economy and the society.†

*   *   *

As the previous comments suggest, structural reform of the bureaucracies was still in an early stage and structural reform of the basic political system had really not yet begun in Ningxia in 1988.‡ Nevertheless, the general political and social climate impressed me favorably. As best as I could judge, in

---

*The secretary-general continued: "We do not have to have exactly the same units as Beijing does. Sometimes we have two organs dealing with one ministry (for example, we separate agriculture and forestry), and sometimes it is a reverse (for example, we have not yet separated machine building and electricity, though we may do so in the future). But with just a few exceptions, we must have some unit to handle every field. Sometimes the difference between us and Beijing is simply because we lag in following changes that they have made."

†Later, reviewing my notes on what the secretary-general and his staff had told me, I realized—and was baffled by the fact—that they had not even mentioned any local Commission on Economic Structural Reform. Ningxia by 1988 must have had such a body—as other provinces and the central government did. Their failure to mention it to me may have been inadvertent, but I could not understand why such an important body had been overlooked. I wondered to what extent it indicated that economic reform was not their highest priority or preoccupation. In developed coastal provinces that I visited, the desire to show that they were at the forefront of reform was much more evident and I was told a good deal about the work of these commissions responsible for economic reform.

‡By "structural reform" of the basic political system, I mean pluralization and democratization leading to competing policies and parties, a free press, the choice of top leaders by elections, and so on.

comparison to both the Mas' pre-1949 authoritarian warlordism and Mao's post-1949 brand of totalitarianism, the general atmosphere in which ordinary people lived and worked seemed to me to be relatively depoliticized and relaxed. I encountered almost no ideological sloganeering. Neither military nor police controls were much in evidence; the apparatus of coercion obviously still existed, but in 1988 it did not appear to impinge on day-to-day life to the extent it had in earlier periods.

The population, it seemed to me, was preoccupied with practical problems of daily life. Living standards had obviously risen substantially in recent years; the improved quantity and quality of clothing, housing, and health care were evident everywhere. People were concerned about growing inflation and corruption, but less so, it seemed to me, than in eastern cities. People's horizons were much broader than they had been in earlier years because of the spread of modern communications and the development of electronic media, especially TV. For better or worse, expectations clearly were rising rapidly, and many people, especially youths, looked to other countries rather than to China's own past for models and standards for comparisons. I sensed an uneasiness about the future because many of the reforms being promoted by Beijing created new problems and uncertainties, but I saw less evidence of social unrest than I expected to see after a decade of complicated and rapid social change, which, nationally and especially in major eastern cities, had resulted in mounting problems.

Overall, what impressed me most in the capital city, Yinchuan, and in those parts of the region as a whole that I was able to visit (I was not able to see Ningxia's poorest areas in the south) was the striking evidence of rapid economic development and modernization. Since my previous visit in the 1940s, Ningxia had catapulted from an isolated, traditional existence into the modern world.

Images from my 1948 visit were still engraved on my mind. At that time, none of the roads were paved. Virtually all buildings were old-fashioned, one-story structures with curved tile roofs. The inns where I stayed were primitive. Because people lacked electricity, their lives were diurnal; few nocturnal activities were possible when the only light was from dim kerosene lamps, and almost everyone went to bed soon after darkness fell. En route to Ningxia, the only real sign of urban development and modernization that I saw were new gray brick facades constructed in front of shops facing the highway in major towns; they had just been completed on the orders of Ma Hongkui, who, expressing a personal whim, had decided that all merchants were required to build such facades simply to spruce things up. And, in every town, including Ningxia City, I saw old men wearing traditional gowns, aided by small boys, who were using little spades to smooth out ruts in the mud roads, also on Ma Hongkui's orders. Ningxia City in the late 1940s was a small, premodern provincial town, not much different from county towns except that it was larger and boasted a sizable city wall (the city's front gate looked a little like a miniature Beijing Tiananmen). The city's other landmarks included the four-story Gulou (meaning "old building") near the center of town; a large "palace," called the Jade Emperor Pavilion; and the North and South Pagodas (both of which were ancient—the one to the north reputedly had been built during the Tangut Xixia Kingdom, which had ruled the Ningxia area from the eleventh century to the thirteenth century). Apart from these landmarks, the town consisted of undistinguished, old, gray one-story buildings that lined both sides of unpaved streets.

*   *   *

When I arrived in Yinchuan in 1988, the "gateway" to the city was no longer an old city gate (the wall was gone); it was now a large, modern railway station on the edge of the "new city." This modern urban part of the city, which did not exist in the 1940s, was connected by a broad boulevard to the edge of the "old city," roughly 10 miles to the east. As in Baotou, even the old city appeared largely new: Lining its wide paved streets were many modern, multistory public buildings, offices, and apartments. Although the city wall had been torn down, the main south gate remained; so too did Gulou, the Jade Emperor Pavilion, and the pagodas, preserved as historic sites. One area in the southwest still had some traditional one-story houses, but the general ambiance in the city was modern.

Just south of my hotel (which was located on what had been one of Ma Hongkui's parade grounds), the main east-west thoroughfare (Liberation Avenue) stretched the length of the old city. Lining it were many new government buildings, a sports stadium, a restored Catholic church, the main post and telegraph office, Gulou and the Jade Emperor Pavilion, and East Wind Theater (located on the site of Ma Hongkui's government guest house, where I had stayed in 1948). To the north and west were sizable parks, containing recreational lakes. A large, clean, and not unattractive industrial area lay to the northeast; its broad streets were laid out in a regular square pattern, and it was filled with factories and modern four- or five-story apartment buildings for workers. At the western edge of this area was a handsome new municipal government building (resting on the spot, I was told, where Ma Hongkui's main office had been located and where I must have interviewed him—although I did not recognize the area) as well as a very modernistic new Science and Technology Building. Further north, where the city petered out, the North Pagoda rose. A handsome, well-restored cluster of religious buildings surrounded the pagoda, but only six monks lived there as caretakers: It clearly was a historic site and not an active religious center.

The business and shopping center of the old city was south of Liberation Avenue, where New China Avenue and several other bustling streets were lined with shops and department stores, all of which were well stocked with a wide variety of goods. These streets, framed by plane trees (sycamores) along their sidewalks, were filled with quite fashionably dressed young women and men, mainly walking or riding bicycles. Automobile traffic was light; it was sufficient to make the city seem modern, but there were no traffic jams like those that, by the late 1980s, plagued eastern cities. On the eastern edge of the old city, another broad avenue—Sun Yat-sen (Sun Zhongshan) Street—went south, past the main municipal government building, to the old south gate, outside of which were Yinchuan's main open square for public meetings, a large mosque, and a modern intercity bus terminal.

The new city lay 10 miles to the west, and it was connected by a broad avenue—in fact, by two broad avenues, both lined with tall, thin trees—poplars, I believe. Along these roads there were some spaces of undeveloped land, but dotting the way were many new public buildings, some factories, a few shops, a College of Education, and a large new Islamic Cultural Center. The center, which was still under construction, was being financed with a large grant (equivalent to US$1.9 million, I was told) from Muslims abroad; the main donor was said to be an organization called the World Islamic Association. The new city was open, sprawling, and laid out in a regular checkerboard pattern. The buildings were, and looked, very new. Its main thoroughfare was a broad, central, east-west avenue—Xixia Road—and the city had grown outward from it. Xixia Road was lined with many new modern buildings, quite a few of them high rises; these included the regional Party headquarters, some government offices, the main railway station, Ningxia University, the Number Two Minority Nationalities College, and other educational institutions. Also along this avenue were the region's TV station, a large Workers' Cultural Palace, hospitals, department stores, the headquarters of some large enterprises, restaurants, and so on. Numerous factories and workers' apartments lay to the north and south. And to the west, a highway led toward Alashan Mongol territory. After exploring all of Yinchuan, my main reaction was one of astonishment at how the traditional city I had seen in the 1940s had been converted into a new and modern urban center. The principal visual reminders of the past were the remaining historic landmarks.

*   *   *

Yinchuan served, as it always had, as the economic as well as political and administrative center of the region. The new railway and the nearby Yellow River provided links to the northern and southwestern fringes of Ningxia, and a network of reasonably good paved roads, built or greatly improved since 1949, linked it to the east and south. By 1988, almost 4,500 miles of paved roads reached most of the region; they connected with major highways to Baotou, Lanzhou, Xi'an, and north Shaanxi. Branch roads now led to all counties, and secondary paved roads reached all townships, I was told, even those in the south.

Topographically, and economically, the northern and southern areas of Ningxia are very different. The broad, alluvial Ningxia plain in the north has for centuries been a very productive agricultural area, and in the years since the Communist takeover it has developed also into a significant industrial base. Despite low rainfall, the plain's web of canals, some of them built as early as the Qin dynasty and many dating to the Han period, were gradually improved, and they provided a reliable water supply, which made possible high yields in many crops. Spring wheat and rice were the main ones; others included millet, sorghum, soybeans, cotton, tobacco, and hemp. The growth of modern industries, most of them developed since 1958 when the railway was opened, created a new industrial zone, which, like the railway, paralleled the river. The principal industrial centers were the four main cities mentioned earlier.

The south of Ningxia is largely mountainous; some fairly high mountains, the Liupan range, are to the west of and parallel to the Qingshui River, which flows north into the Yellow River. In the late 1980s, this area still had the heaviest concentration of Hui people, and the area continued to be mainly agricultural (with spring wheat as the main crop), although it contained some pastoral areas. Guyuan was its largest urban center and its commercial nexus. In many respects, I was told, Guyuan was linked more closely to southern Gansu (to which it once belonged and which still almost surrounded it) than to the Ningxia plain.*

                        *   *   *

In 1948, Ningxia had no large-scale modern industry. By 1988, even though it still did not belong on any list of the major industrial areas in China, it nevertheless contained a fairly impressive and comprehensive industrial base. The financing for industrialization had come largely from the central government, and most of the equipment and skilled personnel had been transferred from east China, but by 1988 its diversified industry could provide many of the region's requirements for further development.

There were three periods of rapid industrial growth in Ningxia, according to its planners. The first was during 1958–1960, after completion of the railway, at the time of the Great Leap Forward. The second surge, which was stronger, was during 1966–1974 and was a direct result of Mao Zedong's "three-front" (*sanxian*) strategy of shifting industry to interior areas. The

---

*In the past, when the Mongol-inhabited grasslands and deserts west of the Helan Mountains were part of Ningxia, these constituted a distinctive third region, by far the largest one geographically, but this was no longer true in 1988.

third, and most important, period of development started in 1978 when Deng Xiaoping initiated his reform policies that spurred accelerated development throughout most of China.

Local officials and scholars in Yinchuan provided me with a range of statistics, some published, some not, about the local economy. In interviews on economic topics, my interlocutors in Ningxia, as in most areas I visited in 1988, frequently referred to little red notebooks. Many of these notebooks used by officials I interviewed in Ningxia contained published statistics through the year 1986, but some contained only handwritten figures, which were more up-to-date. I was not able, in the time available, to clarify the basis for many of the figures given to me (sometimes it was not even clear to me whether statistical series were in constant or current yuan). Later, comparing the figures for 1986 that I obtained in Ningxia with statistics published by the State Statistical Bureau (SSB), I discovered that some of the SSB figures in current yuan were considerably higher than those given to me in Ningxia. I was not sure why. Even without knowing the precise meaning of the figures I was given, I found them very useful as rough indicators of growth; this was particularly so because in many cases they provided statistical series, covering many years (which were unavailable in the SSB annual publications that I later checked), and from them I was able to get a sense of the growth over four decades.

These statistics showed that the gross value of industrial and agricultural output increased almost 20 times from 1949 through 1986, rising from Y 191 million in 1949 to Y 402 million in 1957, Y 987 million in 1970, Y 2.088 billion in 1978, and Y 3.655 billion in 1986.* These figures—that is, those for "gross value"—inflate the numbers a great deal because of double counting, but they nevertheless give a very useful indication of trends.

Industrial development accounted for the lion's share of this growth. By 1986, the value of industrial output, broadly defined, reached a level more than 200 times that of 1949. Measured by gross value of output, it rose (according to the figures I received in Ningxia) from Y 12 million in 1949 to Y 42 million in 1957, Y 200 million in 1960, Y 530 million in 1970, Y 1.44 billion in 1978, and Y 2.57 billion in 1986. (An article published in Beijing in 1988 contained figures fairly close to the figures I received in Ningxia; the article stated that Ningxia's 1987 industrial output was Y 2.74 billion.) Per

---

*SSB statistics showed Ningxia's gross value of industrial and agricultural output in 1986 as Y 4.253 billion, and it showed the "national income" for the region that year as Y 2.231 billion. As I have noted, I am not certain why the SSB gross value figure was higher than the one given to me in Ningxia. Perhaps the SSB's figure included some military production that the Ningxia figures did not, but even if that were the case it would not fully explain the differences.

capita industrial output rose, according to local Ningxia figures, from Y 10 in 1949 to Y 605 in 1986.

In 1957, on the eve of the first important period of Ningxia's industrial growth, agriculture still accounted for 90 percent and industry for only 10 percent of the gross value of industrial and agricultural output. However, on the basis of gross value calculations, the output of industry had surpassed that of agriculture by the start of the 1970s, and the Ningxia statistics provided to me indicated that by 1986 70 percent of the gross value of industrial and agricultural output was accounted for by industry and only 30 percent by agriculture. The SSB statistics on gross value of industrial and agricultural output in Ningxia differed from those I received in Yingchuan, but they indicated comparable proportions between industrial and agricultural output in 1986. The SSB figures were Y 2.837 billion, or 67 percent, for industry and Y 1.416 billion, or 33 percent, for agriculture. However, the SSB's "national income" figures for Ningxia in 1986 showed that only when the output value of other nonagricultural activities—construction, commerce, and transport—were added to those of industry was the output of "industry" (including these other nonagricultural sectors) close to twice that of agriculture. As noted earlier, the figure for Ningxia's 1986 "national income" was Y 2.231 billion, of which industry accounted for Y 827 million, or 37 percent, agriculture for Y 828 million, or 37 percent, and construction, transport, and commerce for Y 580 million, or 26 percent. In any case, even though the picture varied somewhat, depending on which set of statistics one used, all of the output figures clearly showed a quite remarkable economic transformation in Ningxia in the three decades after 1958—from a premodern rural economy to a significantly industrialized modern economy.

This transformation was revealed in other statistics as well. By 1986, the total number of factories in Ningxia reached 1,716. The growth of the number of factories paralleled, as one would have expected, the growth of industrial output. In 1949 there were 293 "factories" in Ningxia (most of them, at that time, were simply workshops); the number increased to 310 in 1957, to 597 in 1970, to 1,072 in 1978, and to 1,716 in 1986. In 1986, 34 of the total were classified as large and medium-sized (10 large and 24 medium-sized), all of which, by Chinese definition, were big. Many of these had been started when plants—or parts of them—were transferred to Ningxia from coastal China. During the "three-front" period of the late 1960s and early 1970s, more than 20 large and medium-sized factories were transferred, I was told, from other areas. Most of them had later been expanded.

*   *   *

In 1986, the main foundation of the region's industrialization consisted, I was told, of 450 state-owned enterprises, which included all really large factories; their gross output in 1986 was Y 1.97 billion, which accounted for roughly three-fourths, by value, of all of Ningxia's industrial output. However, one result of the reform policies of the 1980s was a significant expansion of collective industries, which had been the fastest-growing sector during the decade of reform after 1978; their number almost tripled during those years. By 1986, there were more than 1,200 industrial collectives in the region, with a gross industrial output of Y 448 million, a little more than a sixth of Ningxia's total industrial output. Of that output, Y 95.38 million came from rural township industries, which—though still relatively underdeveloped compared to those in coastal areas—were growing the fastest of all. There still were almost no private industries in Ningxia, although private enterprises in commerce and services had expanded rapidly in the 1980s.

The balance in Ningxia between "heavy industry" (producing raw materials and capital goods) and "light industry" (consumer goods) still reflected, in the late 1980s, the stress that had been placed on the former during the period of Mao's three-front strategy. In 1986, heavy industry still accounted for roughly two-thirds of the gross value of industrial output. Nevertheless, Ningxia's industry had been gradually diversified and included, by 1986, in addition to basic energy, 10 broad industrial sectors. The leading ones, in order of importance, were coal, machine building, chemicals, and metallurgy, followed by food processing, light industry and textiles, construction materials, and clothing.

By 1986, roughly 184,000 people in Ningxia worked in state-owned mining and manufacturing enterprises (64,000 in mining, about 90 percent of them in coal mining; 120,000 in manufacturing, of whom almost 40,000, or a third, were in machine building). In terms of physical output, Ningxia in 1986 produced 13.27 million tons of coal, 33,000 tons of aluminum, 38,000 tons of sugar, roughly 380,000 rubber tires, almost 6,000 small tractors, 1,500 lathes, and 38,000 wool blankets. All these were significant figures for a region that had a total population of just over 4 million—and had possessed virtually no modern industry even in the 1950s.

The impact of industrialization had been greatest and most visible in a few key urban areas. Ningxia's four main cities, mentioned earlier, accounted for over four-fifths of its total industrial output in 1986; Yinchuan alone provided roughly 40 percent, Wuzhong and Qingtongxia (located immediately adjacent to each other) about 30 percent, and Zhizuishan more than 10 percent.

* * *

I chose to spend more time in Ningxia interviewing people about the economy than in actually visiting factories, but I did visit one: the Number Two Wool Factory, which was one of three major wool textile plants in Yinchuan. Construction of this factory began in 1979, with assistance from Beijing's Ministry of Textile Industry (which directly controlled it at first but later transferred control to the region); it started producing in 1983. By 1988, it had more than 1,500 employees (mainly women—70 percent from places other than Yinchuan), working in six large workshops, manufacturing several types of wool cloth, mostly of high quality. In 1987, the factory produced 850,000 meters of cloth, and the gross value of its output was Y 18 million. I toured four of its workshops, and they looked not only large but also clean and quite modern. When I said that this was my impression, the manager and his staff responded that their factory really was not very large compared to some similar factories elsewhere and that technologically it still lagged seriously behind the best wool factories in Shanghai, Wuhan, and Huhehaote; they urgently needed, the manager said, to acquire new machinery. The one thing about the factory that really disturbed me was the noise pollution. I thought that the decibel level was intolerable, and I said so to the manager, remarking that, in my opinion, it would probably lead to a great deal of deafness among the work force. The manager acknowledged that this was a major problem, but he stated that he was compelled to give priority to increasing production and therefore had to postpone dealing with environmental and similar problems until later. Chinese workers, I ruminated, were doubtless destined to repeat many of the difficulties experienced in the early days of the Industrial Revolution in the West.

This wool factory clearly had benefited from Beijing's recent reform policies—especially the open policy—which encouraged enterprises, even in remote areas, to try to look outward. The manager had been able to seize the new opportunities offered by this policy, even though the central government had given much less authority to Ningxia—and most of its enterprises—to engage in foreign economic activities than the eastern provinces of China enjoyed. When it first started, the factory had obtained all of its raw wool through allocations made by its parent ministry in Beijing, but starting in 1986 it began to import some wool from abroad, with foreign exchange provided by the Ningxia government. In 1987, it then was permitted to use some of the foreign exchange that the factory itself earned from exports to purchase wool from abroad. As a result, by 1988 it was importing from foreign countries about 45 percent of the wool it needed (mainly from Australia); foreign exchange provided by the Ningxia government was used to buy 25 percent; and foreign exchange that the factory itself earned and retained made up the other 20 percent. Of the 55 percent of its wool that it obtained domestically, 30 percent was purchased in Inner Mongolia and Xinjiang by the factory's own buyers and only 25 percent was allocated to it by the state.

Diversification of the factory's markets had paralleled the widening of its raw material sources. By 1987, it was selling about a fifth of its output abroad and keeping 25 percent of the foreign exchange it earned. With some of its foreign exchange (what was left after importing wool), the manager had recently purchased two new machines, one British and one Japanese, and the factory was negotiating for additional purchases of new equipment from Britain, West Germany, and France. The manager's priority goal was "renovation" (that is, modernization) of the plant's technology and equipment and his target was to use this new equipment to raise the enterprise's output in the immediate future by about 40 percent, raising it to 1.2 million meters a year, and in the longer run to raise the figure to 1.7 million meters—double the 1987 output.

This enterprise reflected some of the competitiveness and dynamism that Beijing hoped to stimulate through its reform policies, and I could sense the pressures exerted on such enterprises, and on local governments, to set ambitious goals, accelerate growth, and catch up with more advanced producers. Many enterprises producing consumer goods, such as this wool factory, seemed to be responsive to the new pressures and opportunities; however, many large, state-owned heavy industries were clearly not, some of them because their managers opposed the new policies, some of them because they encountered seemingly insuperable obstacles in their efforts to change.

*   *   *

Ningxia's leadership impressed me as being intelligently forward-looking, and Deputy Chairman Ma and others spoke to me at length about some of their development plans and objectives. These plans continued to stress the priority of increasing output of energy and heavy industry. They made a strong case for doing so, but it seemed to me that consumer goods were being given insufficient attention.

Development of energy resources and electricity had provided the underpinnings for Ningxia's development from the late 1950s on, and the region's leaders obviously counted on it doing so in the period ahead. The development of coal and hydropower had been of great importance in Ningxia's initial modernization, and because of the Yellow River's large hydropower potentialities and Ningxia's rich unexploited coal resources, the potential for further development was large. The deputy chairman said that they had confirmed coal resources in Ningxia totaling 30 billion tons, and they estimated that the reserves exceeded 200 billion tons, which if confirmed, he said, would make Ningxia fifth in China in coal resources. By 1988, Ningxia had increased its electric generating capacity to about 920 megawatts; its electric consumption was roughly 2.5 billion kilowatt-hours in 1986, and I was told that its power output might reach close to 3.5 billion kilowatt-hours in 1988.

Most of the region's electricity came from four large power stations, one hydro and three thermal (using coal). The biggest were at Qingtongxia and Dawukou. A large percentage of Ningxia's coal output was converted to electricity because this was easier to move than coal itself. The regional government's energy goals for the Seventh Plan period (1986–1990) were ambitious. Four "key" projects (which obtained large central government support) included the following energy projects: Daba Power Plant (first stage goal: 600 megawatts; ultimate goal: 2.4 gigawatts); a large new coal mining base across the river, east of Yinchuan (which would produce 10 million tons annually); and an oil refinery in Yinchuan that would purchase crude oil mainly from Gansu and Xinjiang and refine about 500,000 tons a year. The fourth "key" project in the plan was a new railway (over 310 miles long and running from south Ningxia to Baoji in Shaanxi) that would be electrified. Besides these four major projects—all of which were regarded as of "national importance" and were "guaranteed to be completed"—many related projects were under way. One, for example, was a very large chemical fertilizer plant, with a planned output of 300,000 tons—a carryover from the Sixth Plan.

The basic strategy for Ningxia's future development was stated succinctly by Deputy Chairman Ma. "We will continue to develop our energy and use it to process raw materials and build heavy industry," he said. "Because we have large reserves of coal, we will expand its production, and because we are on the Yellow River we will build several hydro stations. Our transport is backward, so we will convert coal to electricity. With our power, we will increase processing of raw materials. So Ningxia will be an energy base and heavy industrial base in the future."

Ningxia's planners expressed regret, however, that they had lagged—and in the future might lag even more—in the development of high-technology industries. In electronics, they said, Ningxia had only five medium-sized factories; they would like to develop more, but they doubted that they would soon be able to do so. The main problem, they said, was a serious shortage of qualified personnel—not only people with technical skills but also those with sophisticated marketing knowledge.

*   *   *

Beijing's reform policies clearly had had some impact on Ningxia, not only in rural areas (where the effects of decollectivization were far-reaching) but also, in a more limited way, on its urban industrial economy. The fairly rapid growth of collectives, and the increasing marketization of plants such as the wool factory I visited, illustrated some of the consequences of reform. Yet my overall impression was that the reforms had barely begun to have very significant effects on the large and dominant state-owned heavy industrial enterprises. Some local Ningxia specialists—like their counterparts I met in Baotou—themselves stressed that the region was lagging far behind coastal areas in many aspects of reform, and they were disturbed by this fact. Intellectuals in Ningxia told me that there was intense continuing debate on what the next steps should be in reform, and some were pressing for much more far-reaching reform.

Serious reform efforts affecting industry began rather late in Ningxia, I was told. From 1984 on, some limited steps were taken to delegate to enterprise managers more decisionmaking authority regarding planning, personnel, finances, materials procurement, and marketing, and in 1986 the first moves were made to implement, gradually, the manager contract responsibility system (*chengbao zhidu*). However, I was told, although this system had been adopted in many smaller factories, by the end of 1987 only 13 of Ningxia's large and medium-sized enterprises were operating under the system. Even though managers in theory acquired under this system the right to fire inefficient employees, in reality they, like managers elsewhere in China, generally did not—and really could not. As one official said: "We first need an unemployment insurance system." But as a result of the reforms, factories could retain a sizable amount of their profits—usually 20 to 30 percent of profits in larger factories, I was told—and this had helped to spur "reinvestment" within these enterprises. At least 50 percent of retained profits had to be reinvested, local people said. Attempts had been made to improve workers' incentives through wage increases and bonuses, and these had had some beneficial effects.

I myself heard some of the argumentation going on among local scholars over reform priorities. It reflected the continuing debates in Beijing. One Ningxia economist, a conservative, argued that the *chengbao* system should be the main thrust of reform for some time. Another argued strongly, however, that priority should be given to reform of the ownership system and that much greater encouragement should be given to private enterprises. This man cited a recently organized private enterprise that made auto parts in Helan County near Yingchuan as a success story and an example of what was needed. Another man stressed the need to take further steps to "separate the Party from both government and enterprise operations"—a process that had begun but was far from complete.

I listened with interest to these different views (in 1988, most of the people I met seemed to feel that they could express individual opinions openly—which was less true throughout China immediately after mid-1989). Yet I concluded that—as several local people said to me—reform would probably continue to be relatively slow in Ningxia. One scholar argued that this was in part because of strong conservative tendencies, locally, and because of resistance from old-style bureaucrats, but he believed that it was also because people had seen so many policy shifts take place in Beijing that they were wary about the direction of national policy in the future and therefore felt that a go-slow policy was prudent.

*   *   *

Although industrialization had brought about the greatest economic changes in Ningxia, agriculture—the traditional foundation of the local economy—clearly had also done quite well in recent years. Even though the share of agriculture in the value of gross industrial and agricultural output had dropped from over 90 percent to roughly 30 percent, the gross value of agricultural output had nevertheless grown impressively. In the 1950s, it had more than doubled, and then, after a period of stagnation following the Great Leap Forward, it had more than doubled again in the 1970s and 1980s. The gross value of agricultural output in 1986 was Y 1.086 billion, more than six times that in 1949, I was told, and even in per capita terms it had increased by over 70 percent, from Y 150 in 1949 to Y 256 in 1986.

As of 1988, Ningxia had 2.27 million acres of cultivated land, and local Academy specialists estimated another half million acres were arable but still not cultivated. The region also had 7.5 million acres of pastureland, primarily in the mountains, 350,000 acres of forest area, and sizable fishing areas, but animal husbandry, forestry, and fishing were much less important in the rural economy than farming was.

In the 1980s, according to local specialists, not only had decollectivization had a fairly dramatic impact on peasant's incentives and output, but increased agricultural "inputs" and other improvements had also had very positive effects. The percentage of agricultural land effectively irrigated rose from 19.4 percent in 1952 to 23.5 percent in 1986. These figures included southern areas, most of which had much less irrigation than northern areas did, so the proportion was much higher in the north. The application of chemical fertilizers per *mou* (one-sixth of an acre) increased dramatically between 1978 and 1986, from a little less than 19 pounds to more than 52 pounds. In the same period, the use of electricity in agricultural areas (especially for pumping water) almost tripled, rising from 7.9 to 18.2 kilowatt-hours per *mou;* this was relatively high for China. However, perhaps as a result of the return to family farming, mechanization had actually declined in that period: The percentage of cultivated land "tilled by machine" dropped from 35.1 percent in 1978 to 23.5 percent in 1986.

Ningxia's main crops continued to be, as they had long been, spring wheat and rice, but output of other grains and cash crops (including corn, sorghum, millet, soybeans, cotton, tobacco, and hemp) had increased. In 1986, Ningxia's 728,000 acres of wheatland produced over 700,000 tons (averaging almost 355 pounds per *mou,* or just under a metric ton per acre) and its 128,000 acres of riceland produced over 420,000 tons (averaging 1,216 pounds per *mou,* or more than 3.2 metric tons per acre*). The rural north was much more productive and prosperous than the rural south, however. Not only was the north the main center of high-yield rice, its wheat fields

*These figures are from national statistics.

also tended to be more productive. The overall figure for the average wheat yield obscured great regional differences: In some good irrigated land, it was as high as 660 pounds per *mou,* and in some poor mountain areas it was as low as 110 to 132. The latter areas, in the south (which I did not see), continued to be among China's poorest areas.

*   *   *

Winter is hardly the best time to visit farm areas anywhere, and perhaps this is especially so in northwest China. However, I wanted to meet some rural people, so my hosts arranged two trips into the countryside for me, the first to Yinxing Xiang, a township (*xiang*) in a suburban area, and the second to Lajiahu Cun, a village in nearby Yongning County. In Yinxing, we first met the township head and discussed the area and local government, and then we visited a dairy farmer. The township was not particularly large—19,610 people, belonging to 4,047 households in 75 "natural villages" (*ziran cun*).* Roughly half of the residents were Hui and half were Han. Before the 1980s, it had been a commune, divided into eight brigades. Then in 1983 it was converted back into a *xiang* (the precommune form of organization) and the brigades became "administrative villages" (*xingzheng cun*).

The number of persons working for the township government was not large for an area with almost 20,000 residents; nevertheless, under the government were subunits to handle all of the major functions and services required by its rural population. In 1988, the township had 46 employees (most were full-time cadres, but a few were temporary employees) who worked in three management *shi,* or offices (their titles were General Management Office, Enterprise Management Office, and Family Planning Office) and eight *zhan,* or working stations (the titles of the stations were Agricultural Technology Management Station, Agricultural Machinery Station, Veterinary Services Station, Hydropower Station, Economic Management Station, Forestry Station, Vegetable Production Station, and Finance Station). At the same level as the government, Party affairs were run by the local Party Committee, which supervised a Young Communist League branch and the local Women's Association. In each of the township's eight administrative villages, there was a Party Committee and a Village People's Committee (*cunmin weiyuanhui*), which had special responsibilities for mediation and family planning, plus an organ called the Economic Association, which dealt with broad economic affairs. Each natural village had a head (*dui zhang;* this title was a hangover from the old commune's production teams).

---

*A natural village is a cluster of households that is an economic unit but not necessarily an administrative unit.

At the township level, Yinxing ran 19 township enterprises, and scattered throughout the township were 65 collective enterprises and over 1,100 individual enterprises. If 60 percent of a rural family's income came from nonfarming activity, I was told, it was classified as an "individual enterprise." The most notable recent development—made possible by the reforms in the 1980s—had been a shift by quite a few farmers from growing crops to producing milk. Others had recently found new employment as railway workers and itinerant peddlers.

I visited one of the dairy farmers, in a natural village that was 90 percent Hui (unusually high in this area). The farmer was a Hui Muslim, 56 years old and named Ma (what else?). He had decided in 1981 (very early in the reform period) to shift from growing grain to producing milk. Using his own savings and a loan from the local credit cooperative, he paid Y 1,500 to buy one cow, which soon produced two calves. With a second loan he purchased two more calves, and soon he was in business—and had rapidly become a successful entrepreneur. Altogether, he said, it took Y 4,000 of his own savings and Y 5,500 in loans (which he repaid rapidly) to become a dairyman, but thereafter he did not need to buy any more cows; in fact, he sold some. In 1988, he had ten milk cows and five calves.

Starting in 1982, this dairyman first sold his milk to a pasteurizing plant in Yinchuan, but in early 1988 the local village had established a small plant to produce powdered milk, so thereafter he sold his milk to it. In recent years, his annual output had averaged between 110,000 and 130,000 *jin* (a *jin*, or catty, is 500 grams, or 1.1 pounds). His gross annual income, he said, had recently averaged over Y 30,000; his production costs annually were close to Y 20,000, so his profit was somewhat more than Y 10,000 each year. (Rounded figures, given in 10,000s—*wan* in Chinese—always arouse one's suspicions about accuracy because there is a long tradition in China of giving figures in *wan* without great concern about precise facts, but this man seemed to be eager to give me the real facts. However, clearly his figures were not precise.) His operation was now categorized as a "specialized agricultural enterprise" and he was labeled a "10,000-yuan farmer." He was obviously prosperous. I talked with him and his family in his quite comfortable farmhouse, which was well equipped with consumer durables, including a TV set. A few years earlier, when I had seen farmhouses with modern appurtenances of this sort, I suspected "Potemkinism," but this was clearly not phony; I saw many similar peasant homes throughout China in 1988.

The township head told me that in his area of jurisdiction most peasants were doing well; about 40 percent of all households in this immediate area, he said, had reached the level of "10,000-yuan households." This label was based on "calculations that included their fixed capital assets," the township head said; I stated that I did not fully understand what this meant. He went on to say that the figure was about 15 percent if one considered only current net income (the 15 percent figure was more plausible, I thought). In any case, this township clearly was fairly well-to-do.

Living standards in Ningxia—at least in the areas I visited, especially in the Yinchuan region—were dramatically better than I remembered them from 40 years ago. People dressed much better, looked healthier, had better housing, and were rapidly acquiring many modern consumer durables (a development of the 1980s). Food, clothing, and other goods seemed to be in plentiful supply in the areas I saw, and they were very much in evidence in all the bustling free markets scattered throughout Yinchuan City. Although Ningxia was still in the "boondocks" in some respects, I decided, because of the way the streets, the buildings, and the people looked, that it was not completely ridiculous when local boosters said that Yinchuan aspired to be a "little Shanghai."

* * *

Because it was in the boondocks, Ningxia's leaders and officials were obviously worried—justifiably—about Beijing's policies giving preferential economic treatment to China's coastal provinces. They feared that even if Ningxia continued to make real progress it would not be able to keep up with the development of China's eastern provinces, in part because of its inability to develop foreign economic relations to the same extent that coastal areas could but also, more basically, because of its relative backwardness in education and shortages of skilled personnel.

Ningxia's leaders were obviously eager to expand the region's foreign trade, attract foreign investments, and promote joint ventures. Like leaders I met in virtually all parts of China, they had come to feel, in the 1980s, that taking full advantage of China's open policy was essential to further development; in fact, they seemed to regard this as a kind of touchstone for modernization and an open sesame for accelerated growth. The regional government had therefore established the necessary organizational infrastructure to promote its foreign economic relations. By 1988, there were, in Yinchuan, not only a Bureau of Foreign Economic Relations and Trade (with offices in Tianjin and Guangzhou) but also a general Import Corporation, an International Economic and Technological Cooperation Corporation, and an International Trust and Investment Corporation. There were also in Yinchuan branches of 10 national import and export companies, a branch of Beijing's Council for the Promotion of International Trade, and also branches of several other national organizations dealing with transport, inspection, and packaging as well as branches of the Bank of China and the People's Insurance Company.

Ningxia had invited quite a few foreign businessmen, I was told, from the West, Japan, and Islamic countries to visit the region. And its foreign trade had grown quite rapidly—from a very low base—rising in some years by as much as 20 percent. Ningxia enterprises had imported some new technology and equipment (for example, Japanese machinery for an aluminum plant and machinery for a plant to manufacture pumps). They were pleased that UN-related organizations had supported, with personnel and limited funds, a number of small projects in the region, mainly ones relating to agriculture and animal husbandry; these had involved the World Bank, FAO, WHO, UNESCO, and UNICEF. In addition, several European countries had assisted—or were considering assisting—a number of small projects with loans as well as technical assistance. These included ones relating to apple growing (Italy), milk production (Denmark), and animal husbandry (West Germany). Discussions with several Islamic countries were proceeding on expanded economic cooperation.

Yet top Ningxia officials were unsatisfied and felt, rightly, that all of this was still of only limited significance. Ningxia still had relatively little authority, compared to coastal provinces, to make decisions regarding foreign economic relations. Moreover, it simply was not competitive with areas such as the Yangzi valley and Guangzhou, and they acknowledged that it was very difficult to interest foreigners in their small remote corner of China. When I was in Yinchuan, the only foreign businessmen in my hotel were six Americans from Ohio helping to install machinery that they had sold to a factory that would produce insulation materials. Deputy Chairman Ma said to me that so far only one real joint venture had gotten into operation in Ningxia; it was a Chinese-American enterprise established to produce environmental testing equipment.

                              *   *   *

Ningxia's concern that it might be relegated to the sidelines in China's opening to the outside world was equalled by its worry that it would not be able to keep up with China's general technological development because of the weaknesses of its educational system. The information I obtained on education in Ningxia was limited, but it was enough for me to understand the causes for their concern. As always, in examining anything, judgments depend on what one uses as a basis of comparison. Compared to the pre-1949 period, Ningxia had, by 1988, made quite remarkable progress in educational expansion. But compared to education in more advanced areas—and to what the region needed—its school system was still seriously deficient.

In 1948, at the time of my previous visit, Ningxia had had only 68,000 students in primary schools and 1,900—a pitifully small handful—in middle schools in all of the province. By 1986, primary school enrollment totaled close to 682,000 and there were almost 259,000 regular middle school students, of whom more than 59,000, or a little less than a fourth, were in senior middle schools. In addition, almost 12,000 students attended agricultural and other vocational schools, and there were more than 10,000 in specialized secondary schools (which taught at a level between regular middle schools and higher educational institutions and provided some special training in engineering, agriculture, medicine, economics, science, politics and law, and art).

These numbers were impressive in some respects, but Ningxia's officials themselves went out of their way to point out to me the weaknesses of their educational system. One basic problem, they said, was the low quality of teaching. Deputy Chairman Ma decried the fact that only 60 percent of primary school teachers and 50 percent of middle school teachers could meet even the minimum standards set for their positions—and these standards, he admitted, were not high to begin with.

The structure of the educational system was like that of a steep pyramid that narrowed greatly at the top. Most children in both urban and rural areas started primary school, but only a few made it through senior middle school. Of the more than 963,000 students in both primary and secondary education, 71 percent were enrolled in six-year primary schools, 21 percent in three-year junior middle schools, and just over 8 percent in regular senior middle schools, vocational schools, and specialized secondary schools.

Beyond middle school, the pyramid almost became a needle. By 1986, Ningxia had eight "institutions of higher learning," but their enrollment was extremely small. The eight included Ningxia University (classified as a "comprehensive university"), a Technology College, two with the title of Normal College (for teachers' training), an Agricultural College, a Medical College, one called an Educational College, and China's Number Two Nationalities Institute. In one sense, the fact that Ningxia had any higher education at all (there was none before 1949) could have been a legitimate source of considerable pride, but I did not sense much pride about the region's higher education. Instead, I heard many expressions of concern about the shortcomings of these institutions, which clearly were regarded as inadequate to meet the region's needs. According to official statistics, the total enrollment in all eight institutions was between 7,000 and 8,000, and they graduated less than 2,000 students a year. Moreover, all those I asked about the flagship institution—Ningxia University—seemed to view it, with some embarrassment, as a very backward institution.

To try to remedy serious shortages of skilled personnel, the Ningxia government in recent years had sent about 1,500 students annually to universities elsewhere in China, but it had a problem inducing them to return. Up through 1986, I was told, as few as 100 or so came back in some years. In 1987, however, as a result of a very special effort to guarantee them good jobs and working conditions, between 400 and 500 returned.

Efforts had also been made to strengthen local research institutions in Ningxia, although few of these could aspire to very high national ranking. By 1988, Ningxia had established several dozen research institutions with more than 5,000 staff members. I had no time to learn about most of them, but I did learn a good deal about one: the Academy of Social Sciences, an independent body informally linked to the national Academy in Beijing. Although its roots traced to 1964, it had been established as a separate academy only in 1982. In 1988, it had a staff of 144, of whom 111 were professionals. The most interesting work it was doing related to local history (especially Hui and Xixia history), Islamic studies, and area studies on the Middle East. Some of its staff members impressed me as being serious and able scholars; at least a few of the others, however, seemed to be old-fashioned holdovers from the past.

The lag in education in Ningxia clearly affected the Hui more than the Han. This was not, it seemed to me, the result of deliberate policy. On the contrary, what I learned convinced me that the government's policy was to make special efforts to support the education of the Hui. A total of 98 special primary schools and 14 special middle schools had been established specifically for Hui students—even though there were no linguistic reasons for doing so since the Hui Muslims, unlike many minority groups, spoke Chinese as their native language. In many regular schools, also, there were special classes—in effect, remedial classes—for Hui students whose previous education was under par. The government provided free tuition and subsidies amounting to Y 12 to Y 15 a month for many poor Hui students, especially in the south. Hui students were admitted to higher education with lower examination scores than those required of Han Chinese. And, I was told, the government tried to obtain the help of Muslim religious leaders to urge Hui parents to enroll their children in school.

Despite such efforts, however, the Hui population in Ningxia was still poorly educated compared to the Han Chinese. Although they constituted a third of the population, and at the primary school level made up 30 percent of all schoolchildren, they constituted only 16 percent of those attending middle school and higher educational institutions. One study in 1987 showed that in nine cities and counties that were surveyed, more than half of the Hui children between the ages of 6 and 11 were not in school, and 30 percent of those aged 12 to 14 were illiterate. Ningxia's Education Bureau estimated that more than half of all Hui people in the entire region between the ages of 14 and 40 could not read. One basic reason for this rather dismal picture was doubtless economic; in very poor areas, especially in the south, many Hui kept their children at home to work. Possibly—although no one emphasized this to me—cultural factors may also have been involved: It seemed to me that the regular institutions of education paid relatively little attention to Hui traditions and religious beliefs.

*   *   *

The problem of Hui education was obviously only one aspect of the complex, multifaceted problem of Han-Hui relationships. One of my goals in revisiting Ningxia was to get some sense of the state of these relations 40 years after the Communists had ousted the pre-1949 warlord regime of the Mas. One thing that struck me right away was that Yinchuan *looked* less Muslim—and more modern. In 1948, a larger number of Hui men sported beards and wore black or white skullcaps, and most Hui women wore hoods covering their heads except for oval openings for their faces. In Yinchuan in 1988, few could be easily distinguished by their clothes; the population seemed to have become increasingly homogenized in some respects, partly Sinified and partly Westernized. In the countryside, however, this was much less true; I concluded, moreover, that the change in appearance could be misleading. Most Hui in Ningxia had by no means been completely assimilated into Han culture, and they continued to retain their distinct identity.

During my stay, I visited mosques and one Hui village and discussed a range of matters relating to the Hui, and Han-Hui relations, with the religious and governmental leaders I met. Islam, I concluded, was very much alive in Ningxia; in fact, after a period of severe repression in the 1960s and 1970s, it appeared to have experienced a significant revival.

The destruction of places of worship and suppression of religious practices by young Red Guards during the Cultural Revolution were considerably worse than I had realized. But since 1978, the government had not only tolerated but in many respects had actively assisted the revival of religion in Ningxia, and the government's official "affirmative action" policies, which discriminated in favor of the Hui in many fields, also seemed to have gone further than I had realized—by placing Hui in high-level government positions, giving them preferential treatment in education, and so on. The aim, obviously, had been to try to repair the serious damage done to Han-Hui relations during the Cultural Revolution. Both Han and Hui people I met told me, frankly, that there was—not surprisingly—a residue of Hui resentment about past treatment, but, as best as I could judge, recent policies had helped to normalize relations, and I saw few obvious signs of ethnic conflict or tension.

I felt that there doubtless were some continuing resentments and tensions under the surface. Not only were the Hui still disadvantaged, economically and educationally, but real power, at the top of the local Party, remained in the hands of Han Chinese and Sinified Hui, and Beijing was not likely to tolerate any revival of "local nationalism" in Muslim areas. Signs of such "local nationalism" in the early 1960s had led to purges in Ningxia. However, I did not sense that there was any nostalgia among the Hui I met for the kind of Muslim warlordism that existed before 1949, and I felt that most of the Hui with whom I talked genuinely felt that Beijing's policies in the 1980s had improved their situation compared to earlier periods. For those I met, this improvement was symbolized above all, I think, by Beijing's new policies that permitted the revival of Islamic religious practices.

The Hui in northwest China are Sunni (Xunyi) Muslims. They are divided into many subgroupings, and, I was told, in Ningxia there were five major groups or sects: More than 300,000 belonged to each of the two largest sects; there were about 200,000 in each of the third and fourth largest; and only 100,000 or so belonged to the smallest sect.* Their differences, it was explained to me, did not involve many significant doctrinal divergencies; they were "simply rooted in history." The sects venerated different historical leaders, and their religious services varied somewhat. As in much of the Islamic world, each mosque apparently operated essentially as an independent institution, although there were significant ties between mosques of the same sect or "order." They were essentially self-supporting and selected their own religious leaders. In earlier years, many had regarded Hezhou in Gansu as a very special place (referring to it as a kind of Mecca—though not really in a strict religious sense, since there is only one real Mecca for all Muslims). In the 1980s, visits to Mecca had resumed; more than 30 people from Yinchuan applied to go, and 18 actually went, 16 of them self-financed and 2 with financial help given by Iran. The Hui in most of west China still had a reputation of being good Muslims: They were fairly strict in their observance of Islamic laws and faithful in their worship, although many young men, I learned, no longer observed all traditional taboos.

Before the Cultural Revolution, according to official statistics, there were about 1,800 mosques in Ningxia. Then the fury of the rampaging Red Guards wreaked havoc; one official said to me that "almost all mosques were destroyed or seriously damaged, and all that were not were converted to secular uses." Thousands of Muslim religious leaders were subjected to "political struggle"; some were killed, many injured, and all were denied the right to hold services. Looking back, both Hui and Han agreed that it had been a major disaster.

---

*These sects (jiao pai), I was told, included the following: the Gedimu (also called the Laojiao, or "old teaching" group), the Zheheliye (a Xinjiao, or "new teaching" group), the Yihewanli (a "new, new teaching" group), the Hufeiya (the Chinese name for the Khufiyya group—another "new teaching" group), and the Gadelinye (or Qadariyya, also a "new teaching" group). These are by no means the only groupings, however. Later, in Gansu, one Hui leader told me that the Laojiao had three subgroups, or factions (menhuan): Zeherenye, Gaderenye, and Hufurenye. He asserted that, of these, Zeherenye (which may be the same group as the Zheheliye, although I am not sure) was the most powerful one and in Ningxia had its main centers in the south, in three counties—Guyuan, Xiji, and Haiyuan (all in Guyuan Prefecture), where some especially important mosques are located. (Since I am no expert on Islam, the romanized forms of sect and faction names are my transliterations of Chinese names; experts may use different forms.)

In light of that fact, the reconstruction of mosques since 1978 seemed quite remarkable. With a combination of local contributions and government financial support, old mosques that were worth repairing had been repaired, and many new ones had been built. By 1988, according to both Han and Hui officials with whom I talked, Ningxia had 2,090 operating mosques; this was more, they emphasized, than before the Cultural Revolution.

*   *   *

The first mosque that I visited, Nanguan, was a large new one; it was 1 of 38 operating within Yinchuan City in 1988. Most mosques in Yinchuan were new; only 7 had survived the Cultural Revolution. Nanguan's construction began in 1980 and was completed in 1982. I was told that it served an area with more than 2,600 Hui households. I met some of its leaders, including one of its Ahong. (This title was derived from the Persian word *akhun,* local people said; its meaning in China was the equivalent of *imam* or *mullah.*) Altogether, this mosque had 13 Ahong, of whom 7 were called "teaching Ahong." The responsibility of an Ahong, in addition to conducting services, was to train others. Young students, who generally started their training at age 13 or 14, were called Mala (this mosque had more than 20). After four to six years of study, in which they concentrated on the Arabic language and the Koran, they could become apprentices (Xiang Lao), at about age 18. After having this status for roughly three years, they then were required to pass an examination to become an Ahong.

Nanguan held five regular services a day, all in Arabic; attendance at most of them was not very large—about 30 to 50 people—but at some, especially on Fridays, as many as 300 people attended, and on special occasions, especially during Ramadan, the number could be "in the thousands." Most regular attendees, they acknowledged, were older people, many of them retired. Almost none understood the archaic Arabic used in the services, but they nevertheless could follow the ritual (as many Roman Catholics do when services are in Latin).

I asked whether Party members could be active participants in religious services. The answer was ambiguous. One Hui official, himself a Party member, said: "A Party member cannot *believe* in religion, but he can attend services without believing. Many Hui are Party members; in fact many are high officials. Their 'Party life' is different from the 'Hui life' of ordinary people. Some occasionally attend services, but not many do in normal time. However, in periods such as Ramadan, many do."

This mosque—as well as all others that I learned about—was essentially self-supporting, and members' contributions paid the salaries of the Ahong. Even the building of the mosque was paid for mainly by more than

Y 200,000 in contributions from ordinary people; the government had given about Y 100,000.

In Yinxing Township, which I visited, there were nine mosques. In the natural village where I met a dairy farmer, the old mosque had been destroyed during the Cultural Revolution but later rebuilt. In the 1980s they tore it down and built a new and better one. The dairy farmer said that he had contributed Y 2,000—a substantial amount—to the construction fund, even though, he admitted, he attended services only a few times a year. Services in the village were normally attended by 50 to 60 people, but on major occasions 90 percent of the village went. However, the people I met agreed that relatively few young people attended regularly. When I asked why, I was told that one major reason was that many young men could not attend because they drank and smoked.

The most interesting mosque that I visited was one in Lajiahu Village in Yongning County. Built in the sixteenth century (during the Ming dynasty), it had been reconstructed three times. Part of it was destroyed during the Cultural Revolution, so it was closed from 1969 to 1979, but it was re-opened in 1979. It was again rebuilt in 1987, mainly with private donations but with Y 165,000 from the government. Its annual budget, which varied between Y 30,000 and Y 35,000, came entirely from local contributions, leaders at the mosque said. Attendance at services in this mosque was comparatively large; often up to several hundred people attended even ordinary services, and as many as 15,000 came—and filled its courtyard—on special occasions. More than 20 Ahong and over 30 Mala were residents at the mosque.

On my visit I was accompanied by an official from the county Bureau of Religious Affairs, who was a Hui but also a Party member, and I feared that I would simply see an arranged "show." Instead, I had an experience that was quite moving. I met and talked with a sizable group of Ahong and Mala. They were lively, open, very willing to talk, and also curious and eager to ask questions. I still have a vivid memory of the scene: We met in a fairly dark room but light from a window illuminated their faces, and I was reminded of a chiaroscuro painting by Rembrandt. The group included many young men as well as old men. They were frank in discussing past persecution. The senior Ahong, an 88-year-old man with a wonderful bearded face, showed me scars from his Cultural Revolution injuries. Both the older and younger men seemed extremely interested in the outside world. They were very aware of the Islamic universe outside of China, and they had received visitors (arranged through the All-China Islamic Association) from the Middle East and South Asia. One Ahong had visited Mecca in 1986. They asked if I would like to observe their 4:30 P.M. service, and I immediately accepted the invitation. After removing my shoes, I stood quietly in the back of the mosque to observe. The vitality and reverence of the service genuinely impressed me.

Although the regime's permissive policies in the 1980s had encouraged a religious revival, it was evident that the region's Party and government were still determined to monitor religious affairs closely, and they maintained an apparatus for effective political control. In the Ningxia government, two bodies, the Nationalities Affairs Commission and the Religious Affairs Bureau (which were really identical, with one office and the same staff of 40) were responsible for dealing with Hui affairs. They reported to equivalent bodies in Beijing, and under them in Ningxia were similar bodies in all counties and municipalities. Their budgets and functions appeared to be limited, however. Mainly, I was told, they tried to ensure that other bureaucratic bodies in Ningxia implemented the regime's policies toward minority and religious affairs—including its affirmative action policy—and to see that religious groups were properly informed about and supportive of government policies. They also acted as ombudsmen in relations among Hui sects as well as between Hui religious leaders and the regime. Their most obvious political function was to provide, in cooperation with the Ningxia branch of the All-China Islamic Association, the political "education" (that is, indoctrination) of leading Ahong.

Each mosque's management committee (generally consisting of 3 to 5 people) selected a representative to serve at the local level on the Islamic Association's committees (each of which generally had about 10 members) and at the regional level more than 2,000 leading Ahong, representing all important mosques, selected an operating committee of 249 members, which met annually. A major function of the lower-level organizations was to hold regular "study" meetings for the top Ahong of all mosques; these were generally held either biweekly or monthly. I had no way of knowing how tight or loose the political controls were. My impression was that in 1988 the controls may have been quite loose. However, I had no doubt that the mechanisms for control were ones that could tighten the screws if higher authorities instructed local leaders to do so.

Nevertheless, my overall impression of Han-Hui relations in Ningxia in 1988 was that even though the memory of past conflicts, and especially resentment about persecution during the Cultural Revolution, had by no means disappeared, relations had improved significantly and, on the surface at least, they seemed quite relaxed and normal. The leadership's decade-long policy of preferential treatment for the Hui seemed to have paid off for both the Hui and for Han Chinese.

Another impression of mine was that modernization and economic development were gradually narrowing the social gap between Hui and Han and were defusing some old social conflicts, especially among the young. However, most Hui of all ages still observed the taboo against pork (almost all institutions ran two canteens, with different food), but when it came to smoking or drinking, apparently many young Hui men were less orthodox than their elders and violated religious rules. Intermarriage had increased some-what, I was told, but Hui parents still tended to oppose it, even in urban ar-eas, and it was still said to be uncommon in rural areas. Han men who mar-ried Hui women generally eschewed pork at home but made up for this abstinence when they were away from home. Two Han men I met who had Hui wives told me that this was true in their cases; they were willing to ac-commodate their wives' religious sensitivities, but they were not prepared to deny themselves entirely the most popular meat in Chinese cuisine.

Overall, comparing Ningxia in 1988 to what it had been like four decades earlier, I was not really surprised to see major continuities, especially in the legacy of Islam.* What did surprise me, however, was how much things had changed. The progress that had been made in modernization and economic development was much greater than I had expected. Ningxia was still re-garded by most Chinese, with considerable justification, as a relatively back-ward region, but I was impressed by how hard it was trying to catch up. Al-ready, it was a very different place from the one I had seen in 1948.

---

*Apart from Islam, no other religion seemed to play significant roles in Ningxia. In 1988, ac-cording to the Bureau of Religious Affairs, there were—in the entire region—only 20,000 or so people classified as Buddhists, served by about 100 monks and nuns; about 1,000 Catholics at-tending four churches; and a few more than 1,000 Protestants attending three churches. I visited one Catholic church, where Belgian priests had once worked; there I had a poignant conversa-tion with a lay leader who showed me some new religious paintings that parishioners had painted to replace ones destroyed during the Cultural Revolution. Several dozen believers at-tended daily mass, he said, and several hundred came on Sunday.

CHAPTER THREE

Alashan Mongols

BAYANHAOTE

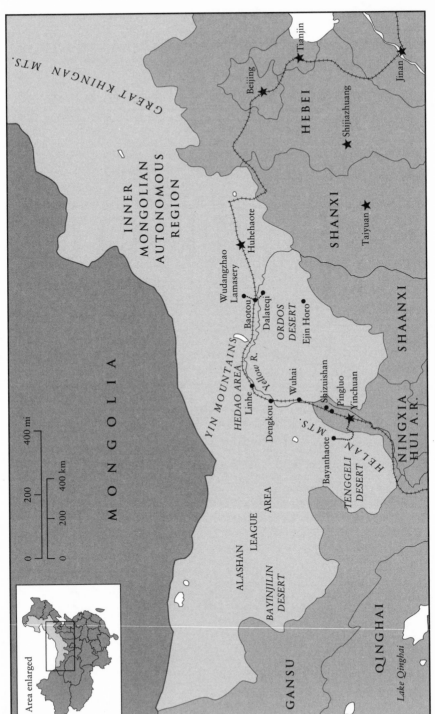

INNER MONGOLIA

M Y NEXT DESTINATION, after Ningxia, was Alashan, which lay to the west of Yinchuan and beyond the Helan Mountains. A Mongol area that had been nominally part of Ningxia in the 1940s, it now was the southwestern corner of Inner Mongolia.

Alashan was one of the remotest areas that I had visited in 1948. Located at the edge of the huge Tenggeli (Tengger) Desert, Dingyuanying, the headquarters of the Alashan Special Banner, had seemed to be on the edge of nowhere four decades ago. It was a poor, dusty, little oasis village, and, like many faraway places that I have visited in the Mongol-Turkic Central Asian steppes, it seemed exotic and in many respects romantic; this was in part simply because of its remoteness but also because it conjured up the past and symbolized an unfamiliar way of life. Even the name Alashan had—to my ear at least—a euphonious, sonorous, romantic quality, evocative of Ali Baba or Shangri-la. The Alashan Mongols had enjoyed an unusually close relationship with the leaders of China for several centuries, but, like all Mongols, they had not forgotten Genghis Khan's empire, and when I was in Alashan I found it easy to summon up images of the Mongols' past.

In 1948, visiting Alashan had not been easy. Few foreigners traveled to the area, and permission to enter was required from both Ningxia's governor and the prince ruling Alashan. I discussed the trip with Ningxia's governor, Ma Hongkui, and he agreed to introduce me to Da Wang, the hereditary ruler of the Alashan Mongols. (The "Wang" in his name meant prince or king in Chinese.) Da Wang happened at that time to be visiting Ningxia City. Relations between Ma and Da Wang were complex and fragile: Although Alashan was ostensibly under Ningxia's jurisdiction, as Chinese maps indicated, in reality it was essentially autonomous. Later, when I asked Da Wang to characterize Alashan's relationship with Ningxia, his noncommittal reply was that it was merely "adjacent." Nevertheless, the introduction was made, and Da Wang invited me to visit his headquarters at Dingyuanying, about 70 miles west of Ningxia City. We made the trip together, partly by jeep, partly on horseback. There was an unpaved road, which at times consisted simply of a track, but much of it was impassable for vehicles when I was there. In Dingyuanying, I was the guest of Da Wang; there were no hotels or even good inns, so I stayed in his simple guest house.

Da Wang was the tenth (and last) Wang of the Alashan Mongols. According to specialists on the area's history whom I met in Ningxia in 1988, in the late seventeenth century (during the Kang Xi period of the Qing dynasty), a powerful Mongol leader based in what is now Xinjiang began a campaign to try to unify the Mongols. Another Mongol tribe (called, in Chinese, the Hesuotebu), based in Qinghai, resisted, and the leader of a part of this tribe

149

declared his loyalty to the Qing court and asked the Qing ruler for aid. In 1686, the emperor, Kang Xi, agreed to help, so he allocated this Mongol group a large area of good pastureland west of the Helan Mountains, which has been their headquarters ever since. Three years later, in 1689, they were designated a "special banner" (*tebie qi,* or *teqi,* for short). As a special banner (one of only two in China), Alashan enjoyed a special relationship with Beijing's "Colonial Office" (Lifan Yuan) and maintained a direct link with it (instead of being subordinate to a league, as banners normally were). For the next three centuries, the Alashan Mongols continued to have this arrangement with China's leaders in which they were granted considerable autonomy.

*   *   *

In 1948, at the time of my visit, Alashan was largely insulated from the revolutionary currents that agitated many other Mongol groups in north and northeast China following World War II, when several independent movements were spawned. Da Wang, who had assumed the title Wang after his father's death in 1931, had spent much of his youth in Beijing (then Beiping) and, thoroughly Sinified, he was loyal, up to the last, to China's rulers in Nanjing and, later, Beijing. He was an unassuming person but very popular locally and was known for his penchant for dressing nattily in a Chinese army officer's uniform; he was also known for his avocations and hobbies—horsemanship, hunting, and photography. Da Wang had a reputation for being progressive and modern. Although he maintained a small Chinese-style "palace" in Dingyuanying, it was unpretentious and he lived very simply in a separate one-story brick building. Local inhabitants were nevertheless proud of their palace—Wangyefu—which was noted for its bright red columns and Beijing-style architecture. In fact, they often called Dingyuanying simply Wangyefu, and some referred to their town as "Little Beijing." (The propensity of those who live in out-of-the-way places in China to compare their localities to either Beijing or Shanghai testifies to the unique, but very different, status of these two great cities in China.)

Dingyuanying in 1948 was really only a tiny town with a mixed Mongol and Han population of about 7,000. Resting on a high slope just to the west of the Helan Mountains, and shaded by tall trees, it consisted mainly of one-story mud houses; there was almost no trace of modernity. When I rode by horseback outside the town to visit nearby Mongols living in yurts (*ger*)—traditional round, felt huts—I saw a way of life that had changed little since the days of Genghis Khan.

The population of the entire Alashan area was estimated at that time to total about 120,000, and it was spread very thinly over the grasslands and deserts that were part of the steppes. Most Mongol herdsmen, I was told, still lived essentially in isolated, family-based units, moving frequently in search of good pasturage. In 1948, Alashan was barely touched by either the civil war or the revolution sweeping China—or by modernization.

In 1988, I was particularly eager to revisit this remote area to see to what extent it had been brought into the twentieth century. My curiosity was heightened when, as I was preparing for my trip, I learned that even though large areas of China had by then been opened to visits by foreigners, Alashan was still closed. I therefore had to request special permission to visit the area. Eventually CASS sent me word that my visit had been approved but that higher authorities (not identified) had specified that I could "not stop during [my] travel between Yinchuan and Alashan Zuoqi [Alashan Left Banner]." I was also informed, later, that under no circumstances could I take any photos when going over the mountain pass between Yinchuan and Alashan.

The Ningxia Academy of Social Sciences provided me with a car for the trip, and one of the Academy's deputy presidents, Chen Yuliang, accompanied me. Chen proved to be an excellent traveling companion and a scholar very knowledgeable about Mongol history and society. He was an enthusiastic Mongolphile, genuinely empathetic with the Mongols we met, and throughout our trip he briefed me about Mongol life and customs. His special knowledge of deserts and desertification, about which he talked to me at length, changed the way I looked at the wide variety of desiccated wilderness area that I encountered in west China.

*   *   *

The trip to Alashan, which in 1948 had taken a full day, this time took a little under two hours by car. The two-lane road we traveled had been paved in the 1950s, and it was smooth the entire way. In our Japanese-made sedan, we rode in real comfort. Our car heater kept us warm, even though the weather outside was very cold and became progressively colder as we went west. It was about 20 degrees Fahrenheit when we started, but then dropped, over the next couple of days, to 5 to 10 degrees in the daytime and 5 degrees below zero at night.

After leaving Yinchuan's "new city," we passed rapidly through a small suburban area of mud houses, most of them built around courtyards, and then our road paralleled an area of poor farmland for quite awhile. Thereafter, the road went straight west toward the southern end of the Helan Mountains, through flat, barren territory. I would have called the terrain simply desert, but Chen explained to me that such terrain was known locally as *huangmo*. *Huangmo* meant desert, he said, in the sense of wasteland, but desert of a special kind: Basically it consisted of desertified grassland, and even though it was extremely dry it had enough sparse vegetation to allow some camels, sheep, and goats to graze. The Chinese in this area, Chen said, use three terms to describe three quite different types of desert. In Alashan, large sand deserts, with huge dunes reminiscent of the Sahara, were called *shamo;* these covered large areas in the western part of Alashan. Rock and pebble deserts were called *gebi* (*gobi*); large areas of this kind of desert were located in the northwest, in the Ejin Horo Banner.

Between Yinchuan and the mountains, we passed the ancient tombs of the rulers of the Tangut Kingdom of Xixia. The Tangut Kingdom, of Tibetan origin, ruled this area from the eleventh century to the thirteenth century (1038–1227). Located far off the road to our right, the tombs looked like large brown beehives. They had not yet been disturbed by tourism, but I wondered how long this would last. There were virtually no houses in this area, but the penetration of modern influence was symbolized by telephone, telegraph, and some electric lines, which were visible almost everywhere. Just before we reached the mountains, we passed a remnant of the Great Wall, reputedly built during the Ming dynasty.

Soon after the road entered the snow-covered mountains, it went through a pass near the southern edge of the Helan range. The origin of the name Helan, according to Chen, was still debated, but it may have come from a word meaning "handsome horse" in the language of the Xiongnu (Huns) who lived in this area before either the Tanguts or the Mongols. I was reminded by Chen that I was forbidden to take pictures, which of course made me particularly alert to look for something that would explain why. I assumed that it might be because we were to pass near secret military sites. Unfortunately, my curiosity was not satisfied. Although we did see, quite far in the distance to our right, one sizable military compound consisting of brick-made barracks surrounded by a wall, I saw only a few uniformed soldiers there and no sign of military equipment. I could only speculate about whether the ban on photography was because there were other, less visible, military installations—or something else nearby that the regime did not wish foreigners to see. (Many of China's most important nuclear and missile facilities had been built in the northwest, but most of the important ones that I had read about were in Gansu, Qinghai, and Xinjiang, and I was not aware of any in Alashan.)

Once through the pass, the road descended a long slope, with broad treeless vistas, and then we entered an area of dun-colored *huangmo.* Chen said that centuries ago there were excellent grasslands on both sides of the Helan Mountains but the area had been steadily desertified over the centuries. Soldiers in the garrison that was stationed in the Alashan area during the Qing period had developed some farms, which exacerbated the desertification. In the area beyond the mountains, we passed occasional Mongol houses called *buming;* the majority were built of mud, but a few were more substantial brick structures. Most were far from the road, and they were widely separated. I saw that some had windmill-run electric generators, a recent innovation. There were few vehicles on the highway—only an occasional jeep or bus. A strong wind raised thick clouds of brown dust, which made visibility poor, but occasionally we could see, to our left, the high sand dunes of one of China's largest deserts, the Tenggeli Desert. A second, the Bayinjilin (or Badain Jaran), lay to the northwest, and a third, the Wulanbuhe, to the northeast. At one point, on the edge of the desert, we passed an oasis town shaded by trees; its water came from the mountains, Chen said, and its inhabitants grew some grain. Further on, we passed one sizable factory, distant from the road. Chen said that it was a potassium-producing plant.

*   *   *

Our destination was the same town that I had visited in 1948, which was the headquarters of the Alashan Mongols. But it had a new name. What had been called Dingyuanying in 1948 was now called Bayanhaote (Alazuoqi or Bayanhot). The old name had connotations that the Mongols resented, so the Communists had changed it after their takeover. Dingyuanying had been the traditional capital of the Alashan Mongols; now Bayanhaote served as the headquarters of both the Alashan League (a recent creation) and the Alashan Left Banner (one of three banners making up the new league).

When we were still some distance from the town, we were met on the road in traditional Mongol fashion (as I had been met on my trip to a Mongol area south of Baotou) by two official greeters: the chairman of the People's Congress of the Alashan Left Banner (who was a Mongol) and the head of its Foreign Affairs Bureau (who was a Han Chinese). The People's Congress chairman was a genial man who welcomed me with enthusiasm. He was pleased to tell me all about his personal history. He was 58 years old and had been born in a pastoral area. He had moved to Dingyuanying at age eight, he said, to attend the first primary school that Da Wang had established there. Subsequently he attended middle school in Lanzhou, and, right after the Communist takeover, he was sent to study in Beijing's Nationalities Institute, graduating from it in the early 1950s. He was an accomplished greeter—a great talker who was very helpful—but I later learned that he did not have much political clout. The substantive briefings given to me in Bayanhaote about Alashan's polity and economy were presented by others who exercised more real power.

Within a few minutes of arriving at Bayanhaote I was astounded to have a visitor knock on the door of my hotel room; his arrival answered my basic question about whether Alashan, despite its remoteness, had been brought into the twentieth century. The visitor, a young reporter from the local Alashan TV station, came to my hotel room with a video tape recorder and asked to interview me for the local TV news! (I was interviewed for local TV in several large cities that I visited in 1988, but I certainly had not expected this in Bayanhaote.)

I soon learned that Bayanhaote, though still a relatively small town, bore little resemblance to the old Dingyuanying. Like Baotou and Yinchuan—

though on a much smaller scale—it had become a bustling, modern, urban center. The town's population had grown to roughly 40,000, almost six times its size in 1948. Roughly 82 percent, about 33,000, were now Han Chinese; moreover, virtually all of its 7,000 or so Mongol inhabitants had adopted Chinese clothing and looked essentially Sinified.

Like Baotou and Yinchuan, Bayanhaote now had an "old town" and "new town" that constituted the town's two administrative districts. Even most of the old town looked fairly new and modern. There were a few reminders of the past, though: Da Wang's palace (which was still undergoing reconstruction to repair damage wrought during the Cultural Revolution), a major monastery called Yanfu Si (which had been damaged, but not very seriously, during the Cultural Revolution and was already completely repaired), Da Wang's former home (now a school), one short street of former officials' homes (looking very run-down), and a few areas where old mud huts still predominated. But the center of the town was now bisected by a paved, four-lane avenue lined with multistory office buildings, and it boasted a large modern movie theater. Traffic on the avenue was light, but it included buses and autos as well as bicycles. The segment of the avenue that led to the new town passed the Alashan TV station and tower and then entered an area that looked entirely modern. In this area, the avenue was fairly grand for a small town, and it was lined with a mixture of public buildings, including the offices of the Party and government, and modern apartment houses, many of which were five or six stories high.

Near the end of the avenue was a large statue of a camel. It was the city's logo. The town was called "Camel City," my host explained, because, even though camels no longer came into the city, the Alashan area raised more camels than any other area in China. My hosts' exuberant boosterism reminded me of some small towns in the United States that proudly proclaim that they have the world's biggest of this or the best of that. Not far from the statue, there was an area of large, very modern-looking houses that were the homes of high-ranking cadres; they would not have looked out of place in an American suburb. In another direction was the guest house/hotel where I stayed. This building, designed to accommodate what they hoped would be an increased flow of outside visitors, was remarkably modern and comfortable and was decorated in the same "modern, provincial Chinese Victorian" style as my hotel in Yinchuan, and it actually was an even more commodious place.

During my stay in Bayanhaote, I was superbly entertained at three memorable banquets and participated (along with virtually the entire local population) in celebrating the traditional Chinese Lantern Festival (the fifteenth day of the first moon). I also trekked to the huge dunes of the nearby sand desert (this time traveling by car instead of riding horseback, as I had in 1948), visited the Yanfu Lamasery, and toured one local factory of which the Alashan government was particularly proud.

I spent most of my time in Bayanhaote, as I did everywhere, interviewing as wide a range of people and visiting as many places as I could, but it was not all work and no play. The most notable play consisted of eating, and I will not soon forget the banquets given to me. The pièce de résistance at one of them was a delicious whole roasted lamb, with crisp skin similar to that of Peking duck. This was unique in Alashan; it was an "invention," I was told, of Da Wang, who had acquired a taste for roasted duck when he was in Beijing and decided that there was no reason that lamb could not be cooked in a similar fashion. Another banquet featured a whole boiled lamb; the climax of that affair was the serving of thin, noodlelike slices of lamb's tail, consisting of pure fat, which the Mongols present sucked in and swallowed without chewing. Having once suffered a major coronary attack, which had made me acutely aware of the effects of cholesterol, I demurred, claiming an allergy to lamb's fat, a claim that my host could not understand but accepted with good grace.

At all three banquets, those attending were a mixture of Mongols and Han Chinese, but Mongols predominated, even when the primary host was a Han official, and the ritual and etiquette followed Mongol customs. The meals involved a fairly elaborate ritual, including the presentation of a blue silk scarf from the host to the guest (me) and many special kinds of toasts in which the host and guest drank from the same cup of liquor. I was carefully briefed by Chen about these customs beforehand, and I believe I did not commit any egregious faux pas. There was a great deal of drinking, mostly of *bai jiu* (a strong, clear, grain liquor) but we were also served a local alcoholic drink flavored with a special herb that came from the Helan Mountains. There was also a great deal of boisterous singing of local folk songs. The Mongols are great singers, and I was told that more than 300 traditional songs were widely sung. One of my tablemates said that he could sing more than 100 from memory, and another said that he knew more than 70.

I was favorably impressed by how easy and relaxed the relationships between Mongols and Han Chinese seemed to be. This appeared to be the case not only at social occasions but also in my interviews, in all of which both Mongols and Han Chinese participated. The most authoritative officials I interviewed were Han, but I had no sense that the Mongols present resented the authority exercised by these "outsiders." Moreover, even though many Han Chinese had traditionally viewed Mongols as culturally inferior, the Han officials I met in Bayanhaote—all of whom had worked there for many years—seemed genuinely to respect, and to identify themselves with, the Alashan Mongols.

On the night of the Lantern Festival, Han Chinese and Mongols participated together in an unselfconscious, rollicking, and noisy celebration on the streets that was reminiscent of Mardi Gras. Masked, gaudily costumed revelers, carrying a remarkable variety of lanterns, danced to the accompaniment of loud percussion music and wound their way through crowds that filled the main street. Not only did Mongols mix easily with Han Chinese, but officials mingled with the hoi polloi in a very uninhibited way. In the dark, almost no one on the streets except my dinner host was aware of my presence, and I was able to watch all the activities without others seeing me.

*   *   *

As always, I learned a good deal about the local situation from casual conversations and observation, but also, as usual, most of the hard data that I gathered came from systematic interviewing of knowledgeable officials and others. I interviewed more than 30 people in Alashan. Much of what I learned, however, came from separate interviews with two leading officials, both Han Chinese, who (with the help of several aides, both Han and Mongol) talked with me at length. One was a deputy chairman of the Alashan League Government, a man named Chen Jinyong; the other was a deputy secretary of the Alashan League Party Committee named Gao Menghun.

Chen, a native of Sichuan, had grown up in Chengdu and was a graduate of the Engineering Department (with a specialty in machine building) of Chongqing University, class of 1960. Immediately after graduation, he had been assigned to teach at a technological college in Huhehaote, capital of Inner Mongolia, for five years. Then, in 1965, he was assigned to a salt plant in Alashan where he worked first as a technical expert and then as chief engineer and finally as plant manager. He became deputy chairman of the Alashan League, with responsibility for economic affairs (including industrial development) in 1983. Chen impressed me as a very able individual, strongly committed to Alashan's development—a technocrat of the new breed in China.

Gao, from Hebei Province, was older and had the demeanor of a more traditional Party organization man, but, having worked in Alashan for 34 years, since the mid-1950s, he too was very knowledgeable about the area and seemed to identify himself closely with it. From the two of them, and the staff members accompanying them (ten came with Gao!), I pieced together a picture of how Alashan had changed in the years since my previous visit.

I started by asking a few questions about recent history. When I inquired about the process of Communist takeover (which had occurred soon after my 1948 visit), my informants were pleased to provide me with many details—only a few of which I will record here. In the final days of Ma Hongkui's rule in Ningxia, I was told, the "brotherly relations" between him and Da Wang became increasingly strained. Ma, who was much more determined than Da Wang to resist the Communists, apparently wanted to occupy Alashan with his military forces to strengthen his position against the

Communist army. He refrained from doing this, however, and instead sent one of his relatives to try to convince Da Wang to cooperate in fighting the Communists. Da Wang was not convinced. Sensing that a Communist victory was imminent, he decided instead to position himself for a peaceful transfer of allegiance. Just before the Communist forces entered the region, some minor skirmishes took place, I was told, between Ma's troops and Da Wang's Peace Preservation Corps. Then, immediately after the Communist forces arrived in Ningxia, Da Wang sent a representative to negotiate with General Yang Dezhi about a "peaceful liberation." An agreement was rapidly reached, and Da Wang was later rewarded by being appointed deputy governor of Ningxia; subsequently he became a deputy chairman of the Inner Mongolian Autonomous Region.

The Communist Party proceeded, gradually and cautiously, according to Deputy Party Secretary Gao, to build up its organization in Alashan. At first it sent a small group of a half dozen or so Party members—all, reportedly, persons knowledgeable about minority affairs, and all approved, according to Gao, by Da Wang before they came. They set up a Working Committee that cooperated with Da Wang but also began to recruit and organize Party supporters. Gradually they established low-level working groups in each *shumu* (township-level administrative units in the Mongol-inhabited areas). Organizational work proceeded in parallel in both the Alashan Special Banner and the Ejin Horo (or Ejina) Banner to the northwest.

The first Party Committee in Alashan was established in 1952. Over time, however, it went through various institutional permutations as Alashan itself was shifted among various administrative jurisdictions. When Ningxia was abolished in 1954 and most of its territory was incorporated into Gansu Province, Alashan became an autonomous prefecture (*zizhi zhou*) under Gansu; at that time, a prefectural Party Committee was established. In the late 1950s, when Alashan was transferred to Inner Mongolia, it was first placed administratively under the Bayaneer League. Even though the local Party organization at that time had the title of Party Committee (*dangwei*), it was in fact a branch (*paichu jigou*) of the Inner Mongolia Party Committee. Then, when Inner Mongolia was divided and Alashan was returned to Ningxia, in the late 1960s, an Alashan Party Committee was reconstituted, and it functioned continuously thereafter, even after Alashan was returned to Inner Mongolia in the late 1970s. Finally, when a league government was established in Alashan in 1980, with jurisdiction over three banners, a League Party Committee was organized and three lower-level committees were established in the banners. The jurisdiction of the league government and Party covered a very large area: It included all of the Alashan territory as well as that of the Ejin Horo Banner. The original Alashan Banner was divided into two parts at that time: an Alashan Left Banner, headquartered in Bayanhaote, and an Alashan Right Banner, to the west, with its headquarters in the village of Ehen Hudag. The Ejin Horo Banner, in the far west, had its headquarters at a place they called Dalankebu (although on my maps it was simply called Alashan Right Banner).

I asked how the tumultuous political campaigns that had swept China during the Maoist period, from the 1950s through the 1970s, had affected Alashan. The details about this will have to be sorted out by some future historian, but my impression—from what I was told—was that every major Chinese political and economic campaign during those years did, in fact, have a significant impact on this remote area. In Alashan, as elsewhere, the rampages of the Red Guards during the height of the Cultural Revolution wreaked great destruction on religious institutions and historical sites. In Bayanhaote both Yanfu Lamasery and Wangyefu Palace were damaged, although neither was destroyed, as so many other lamaseries and public buildings in the west were. I did not learn exactly how many Mongols in Alashan were victimized at that time or which groups bore the brunt of the attacks, but one knowledgeable individual told me that Da Wang was a primary target of persecution and that his mistreatment had later led to his death in Huhehaote at the height of the Cultural Revolution. This same individual, a Han Chinese, estimated that "several tens of thousands of Mongols" throughout Inner Mongolia were casualties (either killed or injured) during that calamitous period—although he could not vouch for the accuracy of that estimate. He also stated that there had still been intense Mongol bitterness in the late 1970s as a result of persecution during the Cultural Revolution, but he also maintained that Han-Mongol relations had subsequently been repaired quite successfully, as a result of the regime's conciliatory policies after 1978.

*   *   *

Because of my limited time, I could not pursue many historical questions that interested me; the main purpose of my interviews was to learn as much as I could about the situation in 1988. As of 1988, the territory of the Alashan League totaled more than 104,000 square miles—about the size of Italy. This was more than a fifth of the territory of the Inner Mongolian Autonomous Region and was more than four times the size of adjacent Ningxia. The Alashan Left Banner, headquartered at Bayanhaote, covered 31,039 square miles—roughly the size of Maine—and accounted for about 30 percent of the league's territory.

More than two-thirds of all of the league's territory consisted of sand desert and rocky *gebi*. The sand deserts, sometimes referred to simply as the Alashan Desert, actually consisted of the three separate deserts that I described earlier. Altogether, they covered about 30,000 square miles and made up a little less than 30 percent of the league's territory. Local leaders proudly claimed that Alashan's sand deserts were China's second largest—exceeded in size only by the Taklimakan (Takelamakan) in the Tarim Basin in southern Xinjiang. They believed that their three deserts made up the fourth largest sand desert area in the world.

Rocky *gebi* occupied an even larger area: more than 42,000 square miles, mainly in the territory of the Ejin Horo Banner. The league's remaining 35,000-plus square miles or so were classified as grasslands. However, of the grasslands, only 69 percent were said to be usable for pasturage (the rest was too dry) and the majority of the area was classified as *huangmo,* or semidesert. The best pasture area was that in the uplands of the Helan Mountains. (In Alashan Left Banner, 58 percent of its 31,000 square miles was classified as grassland and 42 percent as sand desert.)

The population in this topographically inhospitable corner of China had remained relatively small, totaling a little over 150,000 people in the entire league, according to the statistics I was given. What surprised me most about the figures was how few Mongols there were in the league. Like many areas in west China, Alashan had been steadily Sinified as a result of Chinese migration. By 1988, Han Chinese greatly outnumbered Mongols in the league as a whole. They accounted for close to 73 percent (110,000) of the population and the Mongols made up only 23 percent (35,000); the rest were mainly Hui Muslims. These figures revealed that although the overall population had not grown a great deal—actually by less than I had expected—since my 1948 visit, the Han population had grown more than I expected. The Hans were now clearly predominant in Bayanhaote and other towns and villages in the Alashan Left Banner. However, in the west, the population rapidly thinned—and became more Mongol. In the east, the Alashan Left Banner had a total population of over 115,000 (over 76 percent of the league's total), whereas the Alashan Right Banner contained much fewer (23,000, or 15 percent) and the Ejin Horo Banner contained only 14,000, or 9 percent. In short, Han migration had changed the demographics of the eastern part of the league, where the population was now clearly predominantly Han. The western deserts and grasslands remained essentially Mongol but were extremely sparsely populated.

From what I was told not only by officials but by others with whom I talked, the Alashan area was now much more effectively integrated, administratively, into the Chinese polity than it had ever been in the past. Moreover, it was apparent that modernizing influences had had a significant impact not only in Bayanhaote (where I myself could see the effects) but also on more remote grassland areas.

Alashan's past relationship to Beijing as well as to Ningxia had been—as I noted earlier—fairly loose, and the area had been almost untouched by modernity in the 1940s. During the Nationalist period, for example, the Guomindang was never able to develop an effective Party apparatus in this area (I am not sure that it even tried). At the time of my 1948 visit, government administration seemed to be minimal and largely traditional; the Mongol population was still predominantly nomadic; there was virtually no modern transport or communications; and there were almost no urbanized areas of any sort. After the Communists had established their Party organs throughout the area, government administration was substantially expanded and brought more into line with that elsewhere in China (although some old Mongol titles of local government units were retained); an increasing number of Mongols became semisedentary; a network of simple roads was built; modern communications (including TV) extended to most of the area; and small towns grew even in the grasslands.

As of 1988, Alashan League, an administrative unit equivalent to a prefecture, supervised—as mentioned earlier—three county-level banners, which were divided into 40 *shumu* (equivalent to *xiang,* or townships) and 8 towns (*zhen*). The *zhen* included the main administrative and economic centers; among them were the settlements at two large salt mines and a major coal mine. *Shumu* populations were small—often a thousand or less in the west and only slightly larger in the east, where some had several thousand inhabitants. Below the *shumu,* the *gacha* were the Mongols' administrative equivalent of Chinese villages (*cun*). At the lowest level, families were grouped into *haote,* each consisting of perhaps 3 to 10 families. (The *haote* were not administrative units but were one of the bases for allocating pasturage.)*

By the 1980s, there were Party committees in Alashan not only at the league level but also in all three banners, all 40 *shumu,* and all 8 towns as well as at the two largest salt plants; at the *gacha* level there were Party branches. Altogether there were more than 6,000 Party members in the league (close to 4 percent of the population—about the same percentage as elsewhere in China); of this total, more than a third (over 2,000) were Mongol (a figure somewhat above the percentage of Mongols in the total population). Roughly three-quarters of the league's 6,000-plus Party members were in the Alashan Left Banner, which reflected its share of the league's total population.

The percentage of the Mongol population belonging to the Party—close to 5 percent—was high, but the top Party leader, the secretary, was a Han Chinese, as was true in virtually all minority areas in the northwest. Nevertheless, Mongols were well represented within the leadership; three of the four deputy Party secretaries were Mongols.

---

*In the 1940s, Alashan Banner had been divided into 36 administrative units called *baga,* and Ejin Horo had 5 *baga;* after 1949, the key unit became the *shumu*—of which there were 6 in Alashan. Apparently, the *baga* were absorbed into and replaced by the *shumu,* although this was never clearly explained to me.

The Party's top leadership body, its Standing Committee, had 8 members—the secretary, his deputies, and 3 others. Roughly 100 cadres worked in the central apparatus under the Standing Committee. Some Party reforms had been implemented. The committee's economic subunits had recently been abolished, reducing the principal organs to 5: a general office, departments for propaganda, organization, and united front work, and a policy research office. The Party organizations in the banners were similar, but smaller; for example, roughly 50 cadres worked for the Alashan Left Banner's Party Committee. Party committees in the *shumu* typically had about 10 cadres working for them, I was told; in the *gacha,* personnel worked for the Party only in their spare time.

The league government was described to me as being "basically the same as prefectures elsewhere, except that its organs dealing with minority affairs are more important." However, following national policies that call for governments in minority areas to be headed by individuals representing the largest minority group, the chairman of the league government—who concurrently was a deputy Party secretary—was a local Mongol. More than 200 cadres worked for the league government, and the government of the Alashan Left Banner also had about 200 cadre employees; *shumu* governments generally had 18 to 20 government cadres.

In theory, top leaders in both the Party and government in Alashan were chosen by elections, which had been introduced in the late 1950s. Local leaders insisted on telling me in detail how the elections were carried out: In remote *shumu,* they said, cadres went out into even the most distant areas with mobile ballot boxes. It seemed evident to me, however, that reforms had not yet altered in any fundamental way the post-1949 pattern, namely a system of one-Party rule combined with formalistic symbolic elections. The choice of key leaders obviously was decided from above, not below. Nevertheless it appeared that Mongols had been drawn fairly extensively into government jobs and were participating in the work of government in unprecedented ways. Yet at the same time, the overall authority of the Han Chinese had been strengthened at the top; Alashan was much less autonomous than it had been in the days of Da Wang.

*   *   *

The development of modern transportation and communication, starting in the 1950s, had been an extremely important factor in extending the outreach of Party and government authority as well as in fostering economic development and the growth of small towns. Only one short rail line had been built within the league—a branch line connecting the salt plant at Lake Jilantai (also called Lake Jartai)—the largest salt lake in the area—with the main Baotou-Yinchuan line. And in 1988 the only well-paved highway was the main road linking Bayanhaote to Yinchuan. However, a network of gravel roads had been built; they included ones going north to Jilantai, Shizuishan, and Wuhai and west to the Ejin Horo Banner (and then to Gansu). As a result, trucks had replaced camels and horses as the main carriers of heavy cargo. The league hoped before long to pave the road to Wuhai, which connected with a much better road to Huhehaote. In addition, I was told that there were now roads of some kind—some gravel but many only dirt tracks—to most *shumu* except for a few in very remote places called "central areas" by local people. In large part because of improved transportation, there were now small towns (in most cases really small villages) in each *shumu*, I was told—even the two in sand desert areas. These contained the Party and government organizations, schools, veterinary stations, supply and marketing cooperatives, credit cooperatives, gasoline depots to supply trucks and, in a few places, "movie theaters."

Electric lines had been extended to a few of these villages, but not yet to the majority of them. However, in a great many places where no such electric supply existed, many households had purchased small windmill generators. In fact, league officials estimated that perhaps 60 percent of all those households in the league that did not have a regular supply of electricity had purchased these little generators. I myself saw a number of them.They typically cost about Y 1,500—and therefore were said to be affordable for the majority of Mongols—and they could produce 105 to 110 watts, just enough to power an electric light and a TV set. These generators obviously had had some fairly revolutionary effects on ordinary people's lives in distant places and had greatly expanded connections between Alashan's remote pastoral areas and the rest of China—and the outside world. The government had built TV relay stations at frequent intervals along major roads; each of these, I was told, had a coverage of about 15 miles on both sides of the roads. One official estimated that by 1988 about 70 percent of the league's entire territory could receive TV programs (another put the figure at 90 percent); officials also claimed that in Alashan Left Banner 50 to 60 percent of all households owned TV sets. The percentage was lower in areas further west.

The Bayanhaote TV station operated three channels: Two rebroadcast programs from Beijing's number one and number two channels, and one was a local channel. The local channel also carried rebroadcasts from Huhehaote, most of which consisted of local Inner Mongolian news, but it also initiated some programs itself in Alashan (including the interview with me!). I was told that the league and all three banners had their own radio broadcasting stations. I never was able to identify these among the many stations I could pick up on my small traveling radio, but I did hear programs from a remarkable number of medium- and short-wave stations, including some programs in the Mongol language.

The official governmental communications links between the league (and its banners) and Huhehaote, Beijing, and the rest of the country had im-

Mongols in a courtyard in Yanfusi (Yanfu lamasery). This lamasery and the "palace" of the ruler, Da Wang, were the major buildings in the dusty town of Dingyuanying (now Bayanhaote).

My companions on a horseback trip to the edge of the Tenggeli Desert.

Above left:
An old Mongol woman, her face illuminated by the sun, seated inside the door of a yurt. Near Dingyuanying, in 1948.

Above right:
A typical Mongol yurt (ger) on the grasslands near Dingyuanying.

Right:
A Mongol lama at Yanfu lamasery, 1948.

Lamas celebrating Spring Festival in 1988 at Yanfu lamasery, which had recently been refurbished after damage wreaked during the Cultural Revolution.

The modernized center of the old town of Bayanhaote (formerly Dingyuanying), transformed by modern buildings, clothing, and transportation.

The principal boulevard in Bayanhaote's new town—a far cry from the 1948 village.

On the edges of modern Bayanhaote are some areas with mud houses that are similar to those that made up all of Dingyuanying in 1948.

proved enormously in recent years. Telephone connections were said to be good, and because travel—via Yinchuan—to Huhehaote and Beijing still took considerable time, a great deal of Party and government business was done by telephone. Quite a few documents were sent by telegraph. Routine documents, of course, still went by mail. A special telephone line had recently been established, I was told, for official use between government bodies in Bayanhaote and those in Huhehaote. Although no telex links had yet been established, planning was under way to introduce them. The greatest innovation, which pleased local leaders the most, was a procedure for arranging what the league deputy chairman called live TV "dialogue meetings" involving officials from the league (and all three of its banners) and officials in Huhehaote. These procedures had been tested once and worked satisfactorily, I was told, and they expected to use this channel for conferences fairly frequently in the future.

These new electronic means of communication permitted much more rapid handling of important official business. The printed word continued, nevertheless, to serve many of its old roles, but it seemed to me that the print media were in many respects less influential, or at least had less outreach beyond the Party elite, than radio and TV. National newspapers such as the *People's Daily* reached Bayanhaote three or four days late. The national Party organ continued, however, to be a paper that local cadres and others had to read to keep abreast of authoritative Party statements emanating from Beijing. More up-to-date news was carried by the small *Alashan Newspaper* (*Alashan Bao*), which was published on Wednesdays and Saturdays, but its circulation was small; its normal print run was 3,800 copies in Chinese and 850 in Mongolian.

*   *   *

When I compared Alashan in 1988 with the way it was in 1948, it was obvious to me that improved transportation and communication had played a really crucial role in the economic development and modernization of the area; their development was paralleled by the introduction of small-scale modern industry into an area where none had existed before. Living standards were clearly substantially higher than in the past; I could see the results myself in Bayanhaote. In 1948, poverty had been obvious and general: Even in Dingyuanying almost all houses then were built of mud brick, clothing was poor, the population was generally illiterate, and health problems were very visible (trachoma being a primary one). In 1988, the majority of residents in Bayanhaote appeared well dressed and well fed, and many lived in modern apartments. I was not able to see how people lived in the distant grasslands or in small *shumu* villages, but the claims of local officials that the lives of Mongols in the hinterland had also improved significantly were plausible to me, and local government statistics supported their claims. Even in pastoral areas, most Mongol families reportedly had built small homes and—as noted earlier—a large number had acquired television sets. Many—perhaps most—were still seminomadic, owned transportable yurts, and moved from pasture to pasture during part of the year. However, they settled down during the coldest winter months, I was told, and in the *shumu* villages they had access to some health, veterinary, educational, and other services.

Official statistics indicated that in 1986 the average per capita income in the league as a whole was Y 517. This was somewhat higher than the central government's estimate of per capita income for all families throughout the entire country, which was Y 424. The estimate of per capita incomes of the urban population in Bayanhaote was higher—about Y 800 a year. Incomes were lowest in "poor northern areas." However, many pastoral Mongols were said to be quite well off, in part because of relatively favorable prices for animal products.

Animal husbandry remained the primary occupation of most of Alashan's Mongols. In the entire league, the amount of cultivated land was less than 22,000 acres; in short, pastureland predominated throughout the territory. Animals raised by Mongols were mainly sheep, goats, and camels. In my conversation, however, it was the camels that they most wanted to talk about. The number of camels in Alashan—all of them double-humped Bactrian camels—had once reached a peak of about 200,000, my informants said, but subsequently—because of the desiccation of some grassland areas—the number had declined to about 150,000, the level in 1988. Despite this drop, Alashan remained the leading camel-raising area in China, with close to 30 percent of the nation's total. Inner Mongolia as a whole contained more than half the 504,000 camels in China. Because the use of camels for transport had declined greatly as trucks had taken over in most areas, they were now used mainly to produce wool; the output of camel wool that was marketed averaged 700,000 to 800,000 catties a year—roughly 350 to 400 metric tons. In addition, some camel leather was produced, and some of the most affluent Mongols ate camel meat. Although local pride focused on the camels, in fact goats and sheep were almost 10 times more numerous, and they had increased more rapidly—by a factor of 5 since 1949. (Local statistics indicated that in 1988 there were 1.5 million animals of all kinds in the league, compared to 310,000 in 1949.)

In the 1950s and 1960s, animal husbandry in Alashan, as in all of Inner Mongolia, had been collectivized and communized. I did not learn how this was accomplished or exactly what changes had taken place and what the costs had been. I am still not wholly clear, therefore, about exactly how collectivization really operated in the grasslands. However, the people I met said that despite the increase in animals, collectivization had adverse effects on incentives in this area, as it did elsewhere in rural China. In any case, in the 1980s it was abandoned. Decollectivization began in Alashan in the early

1980s, and subsequently—about 1985, I was told—the household contract responsibility system (*chengbao zhidu*) was introduced. It had been generally implemented well before my visit in 1988.

One knowledgeable local person described the evolution of the reforms in two stages. Stage one, he said, applied to animals. Under collectivization, although individual households raised the animals, they owned very few; most animals were owned by the *shumu*. When the contract responsibility system was introduced, the *shumu* sold most animals to individual households, at low prices, and each household signed a contract to pay annually a specific amount of money per head to the *shumu*. Stage two applied to the land. In effect, most grazing land also was contracted to households, which then made annual payments for its use. Under the resulting system, there were definite boundaries not only for each *shumu* but for all subordinate units and groups, including the small informal groups called *haote* and the individual households, although enforcement at the lowest levels was not very strict, it was said. However, each *shumu* retained control of some land; households whose pastureland was hit by bad drought could apply to use this *shumu* land. Although this bare bones description did not reveal a great deal about how the system worked, it appeared that the Mongol herdsmen in this area had benefited very concretely from the policy of decollectivization, which had been the centerpiece of economic reform in Alashan—as in rural China as a whole—during the early part of the 1980s.

*   *   *

Even though animal husbandry had developed substantially in recent years, the most notable economic change had been the development of modern industry. There was literally not a single modern factory in the area when I visited it in 1948. In Dingyuanying at that time, a few—but very few—households engaged in traditional handicraft work such as weaving rugs and making silver-lined Mongol bowls. In contrast, by 1988 the output value of mining and industry far exceeded—in fact, was more than double—that of animal husbandry and other traditional rural work. There were, I was told, 102 state-owned factories and mines in the league—56 of them in Bayanhaote. This figure did not include small township or "individual" (mainly single-household) enterprises. (If all these were counted, the total of all enterprises in the league was more than 800.) Salt production was a major activity. Previously, salt had been produced by nonmechanical means and transported to Wuhai and Dengkou by camel. Since the Communist takeover, salt output had been greatly expanded and modernized. The largest modern plant was one at Lake Jilantai, about 60-odd miles north of Bayanhaote. It had started operation in 1975, and by the late 1980s it was producing, with modern equipment, about 700,000 tons a year. This plant's output was shipped on a special railway to Wuhai and then was sold in more than a third of China's provinces. Roughly half of it was for industrial use and half for consumption.

Coal mines also had been developed. The best ones were in the Helan Mountains and produced high-quality Tai Xi coal. Alashan coal output was just a little over 1 million tons a year in 1988, but plans called for increasing it fairly soon to 2.4 million and selling it throughout western Inner Mongolia. This coal output was insignificant in national terms, but it was important locally. Alashan also had developed modern chemical factories, the most important of which was the potassium plant that I had passed en route to Bayanhaote; it produced about 60,000 tons a year.

The majority of state-owned enterprises in Alashan, however, were in manufacturing. Many of them—most, I believe—were in fields using animal products. I visited one, which made rugs, blankets, and heavy wool cloth (using mainly sheep wool but some camel wool as well). Begun in 1956, the factory had 112 employees at the start; by 1988, the figure had risen to more than 1,200. Seventy percent of them were Han Chinese, 16 percent Mongols, and most of the rest were Hui Muslims. It purchased its wool directly from supply and marketing cooperatives in the *shumu* on the grasslands and trucked it to Bayanhaote. Its annual output, at the time of my visit, was—in round (very round) numbers—10,000 square meters of rugs, 100,000 of blankets, and 100,000 of heavy wool cloth (principally for overcoats). Output value, I was told, was Y 7.8 million; of this the profit tax took Y 1.77 million, which was remitted to the government. The factory was partly traditional, partly modern or semimodern. The rugs, of which they were most proud—and justly so—were entirely handmade, however. They were extremely attractive, with beautiful designs, and obviously were of high quality; I was sorely tempted to buy one but blocked the impulse. The rug makers, mainly young girls, generally spent a month to make a 9-by-11-foot rug.

China's open policy had had some impact on this factory, but mostly indirectly. Four-fifths of the factory's rug output was now exported to Hong Kong, Japan, the United States, and Western Europe, but all of these sales were made through Inner Mongolia's foreign trade organizations, which obtained the foreign exchange. The manager in Bayanhaote hoped to be able in the future to sell at least some rugs directly to buyers abroad.

All of the factory's blankets and wool cloth were made by machines. Although a few of the machines were relatively new, many were quite old (probably most would have been considered obsolete by any really up-to-date factories in modern industrial cities), and the manager said that he was eager to purchase newer machines. What a Western textile production specialist would have had to say about the factory I do not know. As for myself, remembering the little mud town I had visited in 1948, my own reaction was that it was quite remarkable, and even though some of the factory's production was really only semimodern, it symbolized to me in many respects the changes that had occurred in Alashan.

In addition to Alashan's 102 state factories, about 700 small township enterprises (*shumu* and *gacha* factories) had been developed in recent years throughout the League. In addition, more than 40 small coal mines were in operation at the *shumu* level. The league government intended to encourage further growth of nonstate enterprises, including plants processing goat hair and other animal products, brick kilns, gypsum- and potassium-producing facilities, and so on.

The basic economic statistics provided to me highlighted how even a modest degree of industrialization can greatly raise the productivity of a backward but developing area. I was told that in 1987, of the gross value of the Alashan Left Banner's agricultural and industrial output, the output of industry and mining accounted for 70 percent and that only 30 percent came from animal husbandry, agriculture, forestry, and sideline production. Even though modern industry in Alashan was not large, it represented a large change from the traditional economy I had seen in the 1940s.

Fiscally, the league and its banners were, like most areas in the west, very dependent on subsidies from higher levels of government. The league government's outlays in 1987 totaled Y 110.4 million, I was told. Of this, the expenditures made by the league government itself accounted for Y 71.4 million, and it gave Y 39 million as subsidies to its banners (Y 17 million to the Alashan Left Banner, Y 12 million to the Alashan Right Banner, and Y 10 million to the Ejin Horo Banner). The league's own revenues, which it collected and was able to retain, totaled only Y 67.4 million, my informants said. Its overall deficit was therefore Y 43 million. Subsidies of that amount came from the Inner Mongolian Autonomous Region, much of which the league then simply passed on to the banners. The banners' own revenues were very small, and consequently their expenditures were largely financed by subsidies from the league. For example, Alashan Left Banner's own retained revenue amounted to only a little over Y 12 million; its expenditures were close to Y 30 million, and therefore its subsidy from the league—totaling more than Y 17 million—covered almost 57 percent of its outlays. Such subsidies, mostly originating from the central government and passed through the Inner Mongolian Autonomous Region, obviously were essential for Alashan's development. However, they created a pattern of basic dependency that would be difficult to change.

Alashan still seemed far off the beaten track. I saw remarkably few vehicles, for example, on the road from Yinchuan to Bayanhaote, and the wasteland through which we traveled was so sparsely populated that it seemed almost empty. Nevertheless, Alashan clearly had been brought into the modern world since the 1940s. The town of Bayanhaote had been transformed; modern communications had made the population very aware of political, economic, and social trends (and fashions) elsewhere in China and even abroad; and Alashan's economic and cultural as well as political links with other areas had greatly expanded. These changes pulled Alashan in several directions. Politically and financially, its most important connections were obviously with Huhehaote and Beijing, but its main trade and other day-to-day economic relationships were still with Ningxia and Gansu. Except for its northeastern areas, Alashan Left Banner's crucial economic ties were with Ningxia. However, the northeastern part of the Banner was oriented more toward other areas of Inner Mongolia because of the rail line to Wuhai, Dengkou, and then to Baotou. In the west, the trade and economic ties of the league's other two banners—the Alashan Right Banner and the Ejin Horo Banner—oriented that area mainly, as in the past, toward Gansu Province.

Alashan's links with Outer Mongolia (the People's Republic of Mongolia) to the north had atrophied many years earlier and were almost nonexistent for a period of time. However, in the 1980s contacts were reestablished and Alashan's leaders hoped to develop direct cross-border trade. Two years previously, I was told, the league's leaders, after obtaining Beijing's approval, had met officials from Outer Mongolia at the border and proposed designating two places for direct cross-border trade. But as of early 1988 Ulan Bator had not yet approved of the idea. I had little doubt that before long such trade would resume on a significant scale.

Beijing's reform policies of the 1980s had created new hopes and plans for the future in Alashan as well as in other parts of China. The league's basic strategy for future development of its local economy was summed up for me by the government's leading planner in fairly simple terms: further develop industry and mines whose products can be marketed outside of Alashan (salt, coal, chemical raw materials, and processed animal products); encourage expansion of small township enterprises; and use a substantial part of the net income from industries and mines to improve animal husbandry.

League officials believed that by using modern methods it should be possible to improve the productivity of at least some of the grasslands substantially. On my 10-mile trip from Bayanhaote to the edge of the sand desert (part of which took us on a gravel road and part of which took us on a rough track over wasteland), my host pointed out to me one fenced area with superior grass that had been seeded by an airplane. I was told that this area was kept as a reserve for use only when drought had desiccated nearby areas. They hoped to expand the area seeded by air. Local officials saw little prospect, however, of greatly expanding or improving agricultural crops. They expected, therefore, that Alashan would continue to meet most of its grain needs by purchasing quotas allocated to it by the central government and shipped in from other parts of China, via either Ningxia or Gansu.

The introduction of mechanized industry has been one key factor in starting Alashan on the road to modernization. It had made possible rising productivity that clearly had improved the general standards of living. Equally important, however, in terms of both raising productivity and the quality of life had been the development of education and public health.

*   *   *

As I mentioned earlier, in 1988 the problems and weaknesses of China's educational system were a major national issue and strong criticisms were being voiced in Beijing and elsewhere about the relatively low level of investment in education, the poor quality of many schools, and the general lag in achieving the high-quality education needed for modernization. The critics decried the shortcomings of education even in China's most developed provinces; their criticism had greater validity, obviously, for the country's underdeveloped regions. On my brief visit to Alashan, I had no real opportunity to judge the quality of local education, but I presume that it was fairly low. Nevertheless, I could not help but be impressed by the quantitative progress that had been made since the 1940s toward at least laying the foundations of a modern educational system and spreading literacy and basic knowledge in an area where the population had been almost totally uneducated at the time of my previous visit.

I remember seeing only a couple of small schools in Dingyuanying in 1948, and official statistics indicate that at that time there were, in the entire region now belonging to Alashan League, a total of only six primary schools (with 30 teachers and 675 students, 139 of them in two schools for Mongols), and one junior middle school (with 59 students, 8 of them Mongols). The League Party deputy secretary told me that, according to their records, in 1949 Mongolians made up 43 percent of all of Alashan's population but only 270 of these Mongols were literate. Since then the quantitative expansion of Alashan's educational system, "from kindergarten to higher education," had unquestionably been impressive. In 1988, according to Alashan League officials in charge of education, the league had 22 kindergartens; 80 primary schools; 30 middle schools (of which 11 included both lower and senior middle school levels); and "several" vocational schools, which taught at roughly a senior middle school level. The system also included 6 postsecondary institutions, which they categorized as higher education; these included 1 normal school (which taught at a level between middle school and university); 1 "advanced" teacher training institution; 3 specialized post–middle school institutions; 1 "TV university"; and 1 post–middle school worker training institutions. None of these was really a college-level institution, but they did provide some new kinds of postsecondary school training. The total number of students in the League (broadly defined), local officials said, was 46,768, close to a third of the entire population. Of these, 19,089 were primary school students, and they claimed that, depending on the area, between 95 and 98.6 percent of primary school age children attended school. They also asserted that 16,275 students (a surprisingly high figure, which I questioned) attended middle schools or their equivalents. The rest— over 10,000—included those involved in all other types of institutions.

Although teaching at most schools in Alashan was in the Chinese language (which was not very surprising in light of the fact that 73 percent of the league's inhabitants were Han Chinese), a sizable number of schools taught either in the Mongol language or in both Mongol and Chinese. Schools using the Mongol language as the basic language of instruction included 8 kindergartens, 16 primary schools, and 7 middle schools (including 3 senior middle schools). Schools with "half-Mongol, half-Chinese" instruction included 3 kindergartens, 24 primary schools, and 5 middle schools. Enrollment figures showed that the proportion of Mongol students in the system as a whole (8,509, or 18 percent of all students) was somewhat below the Mongol percentage of the total population. However, at the middle school level, only 14 percent of all students attended Mongol-language schools; clearly, the leadership's preference was to train most people at the middle school level—including most Mongols—in the Chinese language. It may also have been the preference of many Mongol students themselves because most jobs for which middle school graduates were eligible required the use of the Chinese language.

The number of Han Chinese who learned the Mongol language had declined in recent years, education officials said, and this was a cause for some concern. Previously, Mongol had been the only second language offered in local Chinese schools; now other languages were offered, and Han Chinese students generally opted to study a Western language (usually English) instead of Mongol. Really usable knowledge of English was still rare, however. None of the officials or scholars who hosted me in Bayanhaote could speak English, as had also been true of my hosts in both Baotou and Yinchuan. But those I met told me that a great many young people were working hard to learn English, by listening to lessons on radio and TV as well as studying it in schools. The passion to learn English existed all over China in 1988; knowledge of English was one of the most useful keys to a modern life and to personal advancement.

College-educated individuals were very scarce in Alashan, as I expected, but I was surprised to learn that in 1987 the league had sent 203 students to study in universities or colleges elsewhere—more than 40 each to Yinchuan and Huhehaote and more than 20 each to Shanghai and Tianjin. None in this group had gone to Peking, they said, which I found curious. In Alashan, as in Baotou and Yinchuan, the problem of inducing these students to return was serious, even though cadres' salaries and perquisites were relatively high. Alashan was classified as a category 11 wage area—the highest level in the national salary scale for cadres. In effect, cadres in Alashan and other remote areas received what in the United States would be called "hardship pay." A government clerk I met in Bayanhaote told me he earned Y 150 a month—far more than a clerk in eastern cities could earn—and he had a fairly spacious apartment and owned a color TV, a refrigerator, and a washing machine. I was told that an educated person who stayed in Alashan 15 years earned Y 43 a month more than if he or she worked in Beijing. Moreover, salaries went further in Alashan because the local price level was estimated to be perhaps 20 percent below Beijing's. Yet educational officials admitted that because of Alashan's remoteness, most easterners were reluctant to move to the area, and local youths often opted to leave if they had the opportunity to do so.

The improvement of medicine and public health in Alashan had paralleled the development of education. In the late 1940s, in the entire area now belonging to the league, there were only two health stations (which together, I was told, had five beds!), and the population was served by 12 doctors of traditional Chinese medicine, all residents of Dingyuanying. By 1988, Alashan had 56 medical and health institutions of various sorts, and there were more than 800 medical and health personnel scattered throughout the league. Most of these institutions were small clinics (reportedly every *shumu* had one), but in Bayanhaote there were two sizable hospitals, one using Western medicine (located in a clean, modern, three-story building), and the other using Mongol medicine; together they had about 300 beds. Although 500 of the 800 personnel were said to have received some sort of medical training, there were still only a few fully trained doctors; 6 of these were "class two" doctors (in the national system for classification of medical personnel), 2 of whom were qualified in Western medicine, 1 in Chinese medicine, and 3 in Mongol medicine. There were, however, no "class one" doctors. Clearly the system was still not capable of offering medical care in any way comparable to that available in eastern cities; nevertheless, the government had succeeded in extending the outreach of at least simple medical health care to much if not most of the population.

*   *   *

The development of transportation, communication, industry, education, and medicine since the 1940s had set Alashan on at least the early stages of the path to modernization and had integrated it into the Chinese polity more than I had expected. Modernizing influences had obviously had a large cultural impact as well, but I did not find it easy to judge exactly how great this impact had been. In Bayanhaote, as I noted earlier, the signs of Sinification of the Mongols in the town were very apparent. All young Mongols I saw wore the same Westernized clothing that local Han Chinese now did. The only Mongols I saw wearing traditional clothes were the lamas, most of them elderly men, at Yanfu Lamasery in the center of Bayanhaote. I visited the lamasery, where I was served traditional Mongol beverages (including red brick tea with milk) and food (boiled lamb) as well as some Sinified Mongol food including rice embedded with lamb chunks and grapes. (I was told that Mongols in this area had incorporated rice into their diet more than a hundred years ago.) The old lamas with whom I talked said that they regularly ate traditional *tsamba* (ground, baked barley) with tea. But, they said, very few ordinary people in the league's towns ate *tsamba* anymore; instead most generally ate Chinese food. In the grasslands, however, this apparently was not so: In remote areas meat and milk were reportedly still basic staples in the diet of ordinary people.

Several persons emphasized to me the strong cultural impact of television as a carrier of Chinese—and modern—influences. I had no doubt that they were right. Yet even in Bayanhaote I did not feel that the Mongols with whom I talked had lost their sense of identity or been de-Mongolized, even though many of them obviously had been partially Sinified. Their personal manner (characterized by a relatively open, hearty style of dealing with people) and their self-conscious preservation of distinctive customs (including the unique banquet rituals and the enthusiastic singing and drinking that I had observed) made even those Mongols who were most Sinified seem to be quite different from their Han colleagues. I had no doubt that the Mongols in grassland areas retained their cultural distinctiveness to an even greater extent.

In broad terms, however, it seemed to me that there clearly had been major cultural changes. One was the apparent decline in the influence of religion and of the roles of lamas and lamaseries, which traditionally had played a central role in Mongol life and culture. My visit to Yanfu Lamasery was on the day of the Lantern Festival, the customary end of New Year celebrations. Thirty-odd red-robed lamas (the senior ones wearing elaborate gold-colored hats) carried colorful silk standards, played ancient musical instruments (mostly trumpetlike instruments, varying in length from about 3 feet to almost 10 feet), and performed a highly ritualistic ceremony in the courtyard of the 250-year-old lamasery (in which the largest building had been built, I was told, in 1742 and given its name by Emperor Qian Long in 1760). Many of the participating lamas, I was told, were men who worked most of the time at secular jobs elsewhere and gathered together mainly for special celebrations. My strong impression was that even though this lamasery seemed to be somewhat more alive than that of Wudangzhao, north of Baotou, it did not appear to be a very vital religious institution or to attract much popular attention. Very few ordinary townspeople attended the New Year celebration in the lamasery; in fact, while it was going on, a steady stream of young people passed in front of the lamasery on their bicycles without so much as a glance at the ceremony.

Like the overwhelming majority of religious buildings in China, Yanfu Lamasery had been attacked and damaged by Red Guards during the Cultural Revolution. However, the exterior of most of its buildings—which were a combination of Chinese-style and Mongol-style structures—had survived Red Guard depredations, and the damaged interiors had been repaired quite rapidly after 1978. In the early 1980s, also, some of the lamas had returned from elsewhere. As of 1988, the lamasery had between 10 and 20 lamas, mostly old, who were permanent residents, and 35 to 40 others, some of them younger, who were affiliated but spent most of their time on the grasslands raising animals. This was only a pale reflection of former times: In the late 1940s more than 200 lamas had been resident there, and in the nineteenth century, I was told, the number had been much higher.

According to the lamas with whom I talked, traditionally each large lamasery in the area supervised or controlled several smaller ones. In fact, they said, eight large lamaseries had controlled all the rest in Alashan; Yanfu itself used to control a sizable number of other lamaseries. But this was no longer the case.

In the Alashan area as a whole, most lamaseries had been destroyed or badly damaged during the Cultural Revolution. In Alashan Left Banner, 13 (including the 8 leading ones) had recently been rebuilt or repaired. Of these, two were most important because they were the seats of Living Buddhas. The top-ranking Living Buddha in the area was based at South Lamasery (Nan Si). In his late thirties, this man had obtained an advanced degree from a Japanese university. (They thought it was a Ph.D. but were not sure.) Actually, he spent most of his time at Huhehaote, where he was a university professor. The other Living Buddha was resident at North Lamasery (Bei Si), a little more than 20 miles from Bayanhaote. This lamasery had been completely destroyed but then was fully rebuilt. The Living Buddha there, a man in his midfifties, was a member of the National People's Congress. Occasionally he spent some time at Yanfu Lamasery (which no longer had a permanent Living Buddha). As members of the Yellow Sect of Buddhism, they—and all lamas in Alashan—recognized both the Banchan (Panchen) Lama and Dalai Lama as important religious leaders, but, I was told, in Alashan the Banchan was regarded as being the more important one. The ninth Banchan had been the last to visit Alashan, they said; he came in the 1930s. The tenth Banchan reportedly had never come to Alashan.

All in all, my impression was that in Alashan, as in the area north of Baotou, there now clearly was official toleration and some support of religion (the government had provided financial support of lamaseries in the 1980s to repair much of the damage—both physical and psychological—done in earlier years) but that religious institutions were no longer the key institutions that they once had been. How much their decline had resulted from past persecution, especially during the Cultural Revolution, and how much had been the result of inexorable forces of modernization and secularization, was something I could not judge. I suspected that it resulted from both. In any case, my strong impression was that in contrast to Yinchuan, where I sensed a real revival of Islam, religion in Alashan still seemed to me to be in decline. How long this had been so, I did not know. My guess was that it had been under way for many years. Conceivably, under changed conditions, there could be a revival. (Reports from the Lhasa area of Tibet indicated that Lamaism there was by no means in decline; in fact, there was much evidence of increased religiously inspired political activity in the 1980s.)

*   *   *

On my last night in Bayanhaote, before returning to Yinchuan (after which I immediately departed for Lanzhou), I reflected not only on what most impressed me in what I had heard and seen but also on two things that surprised me because they were unexpectedly less salient than I had assumed they would be. I had expected to hear much more than I did about inflation and corruption. When I left Beijing, inflation was already a primary concern for almost everyone, and criticism of corruption was mounting. But I heard relatively little about either in Alashan. I did not attempt to draw any sweeping conclusions from this. However, I did conclude that although inflation was clearly a problem, its economic impact in Alashan was somewhat less—and therefore appeared to be less of a preoccupation—than in eastern cities. I had no way at all of judging whether this was also true of corruption or whether I heard little about it simply because the situation inhibited expression of criticism of corruption to a foreigner.

I also had expected to see more evidence than I did of the coercive apparatus of the state, including a larger and more visible military presence and more police than I actually observed. I had presumed that the ban on photography during my trip to Alashan might have been related to the presence of military installations in the area. I had also assumed that because of the area's ethnic mix the police might well play a more obvious role than in eastern areas and that in a remote and restricted area there might be closer surveillance of a foreigner. However, I found the presence of both the army and the police to be extremely unobtrusive. In the "new town" part of Bayanhaote I saw a handful of military men, and—as noted earlier—I observed one army installation on the trip from Yinchuan to Alashan, but my overall impression was that the entire region had been demilitarized, at least compared to the situation I had observed in the 1940s. I was also struck by how seldom I saw policemen of any kind; at no point did I feel that I was under tight political surveillance. I had no doubt that, in this area as in others, the regime had the ability to bring to bear—probably rapidly if necessary—substantial police and/or military forces to maintain order. But in 1988 neither the army nor the police seemed to intrude very much into ordinary lives or day-to-day affairs.

CHAPTER FOUR

Corridor to the West
GANSU

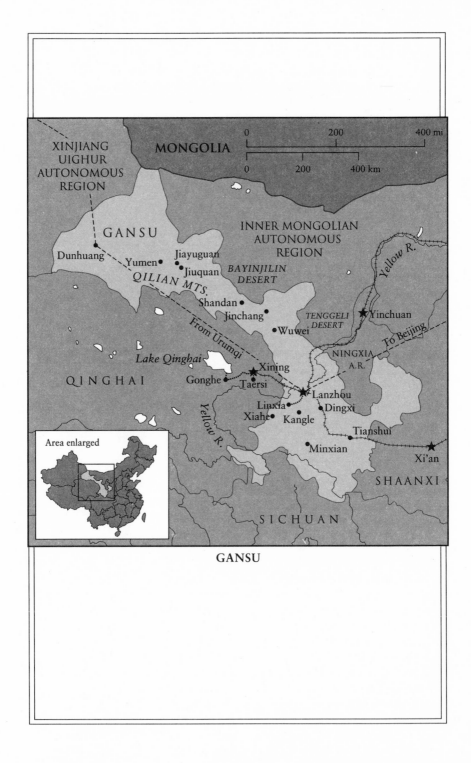

GANSU

ꜰᴛᴇʀ Nɪɴɢxɪᴀ, my destination was Lanzhou, capital of Gansu Province, historical corridor to the far northwest, and one of China's poorest provinces. The rail line from Yinchuan to Lanzhou is awesome. For much of the route, it cuts through a vast expanse of desolate territory, mainly wasteland and deserts.

Forty years ago, when I had made the trip in reverse, from Lanzhou to Yinchuan, I had traveled in the cab of a Dodge mail truck (Dodge trucks seemed to be the favorite of Chinese drivers at that time). The rear of the truck was piled high not only with mail but also with local peasants who had paid a small fee to the driver to sit on the mailbags and ride part of the way. For reasons that I never learned, these passengers were called "yellow fish." The unpaved road had taken me through extremely poor, but fairly heavily populated, agricultural areas, and on the three-day trip I had spent two nights in traditional Chinese inns in small towns that were totally lacking in any sign of modernization—towns where life went on essentially as it had centuries before.

This time, in 1988, the rail trip from Yinchuan to Lanzhou was much shorter and more direct. It took us ten and one-half hours (from late morning to early evening) to cover the 291-mile route; that was not exactly speedy by the standards of the world's most modern trains (we averaged under 30 miles per hour!), but it was a great deal more comfortable as well as faster than the three-day trip I had made in 1948. Encapsulated in a moving modern oasis, we looked out on largely barren, and extremely sparsely populated, areas of wilderness.

The trip began inauspiciously. As usual, travel arrangements had involved frustrating hassles. My Yinchuan hosts confronted the same bureaucratic obstacles as my Baotou hosts had. It was impossible, the rail authorities in Yinchuan told them, to get definite soft-class reservations because the train originated elsewhere. (The idea of computerized ticketing systems had certainly not reached this part of China—in fact, virtually no Chinese transportation had modern ticketing systems in 1988.) The local Academy of Social Science people then pulled every conceivable string available to them and, finally, to their great relief (personally I was not particularly concerned and would have been delighted to go by hard class, but their "face" was involved) they obtained reservations for compartment 13. After my young CASS escort and I had blithely boarded the train, on time, and taken our seats, we were immediately told by a snarling young train attendant that our reservations were invalid; only she had the right to make such assignments, she asserted. There followed, before our departure, much palaver and heated argument between my Academy hosts and this woman.

By this time I had concluded that the further west one went by rail, the more arrogant and stubborn these train attendants were. I decided that I would be stubborn, too, so with the moral support of both the Academy deputy president who saw us off and the two young men who were our compartment mates (they were purchasing agents from a department store in Baotou), we simply claimed squatters' rights and refused to move. It worked, and ultimately the train attendant agreed—very grudgingly—to recognize our seat assignments. Thereafter, however, in an obvious spirit of revenge, she provided us with absolutely no services of any kind. Our treatment in the dining car was even worse: The food was abominable and service was nonexistent. I decided that the only sensible way to respond to the situation was to adopt a traditional, passive, Daoist philosophy, assuming a posture of *wu wei*—doing nothing and accepting the inevitable.

                              *   *   *

Immediately after leaving Yinchuan, the train wound its way for a while through dry, brown farmland that was covered with a thick haze of dust. But then, for about four hours, the topography was mixed: There was some farmland, some eroded loess areas, some *huangmo* wasteland with scattered patches of grass, and some extremely barren and desertified land, interspersed with occasional oasislike settlements. For much of the way, roads of a sort paralleled the rail line; a few were paved but most were gravel. Traffic was very sparse: We saw only an occasional truck, crawling tractor, or bicycle and passed only one passenger car. However, electric and telegraph lines crisscrossed even very barren areas almost the entire way.

Not long after we had left Yinchuan, the population quickly thinned out. We periodically passed small, isolated villages and towns, but there were long distances between them. However, even in this remote and poor area there were signs of modernization and development. In a few of the bigger towns, there were some fairly large factories, and in smaller settlements there were quite a few township factories. Most of the towns, and quite a few villages, looked relatively new, with many of their buildings made of hard brick. In some of the smaller villages, however, most of the houses were still old-fashioned and made of mud brick. In only one area, a little more than two hours from Yinchuan, were there villages that looked completely traditional, with almost all the houses built of mud brick, and even these had quite good tile roofs, in typical traditional curved style. I was astonished to see many TV antennae not only in towns but in rural areas all along our route as well. The only sign of any military presence that I observed on the entire trip was one walled army installation containing barracks.

At about 3:00 P.M. the train entered an area where the rail line closely paralleled the Yellow River, which lay to the east and flowed through a deep, eroded gorge backed by mountains. At the bottom of this gorge, on the edge of the river, there were a few tiny farming villages, but to the west lay a huge desert with very large sand dunes.

The train then plunged directly into the desert and went straight over a sizable area of large, rolling sand dunes. The train conductor, speaking on the intercom system to the Chinese passengers (I was the only foreigner aboard, as had been the case ever since I had left Beijing), asserted with pride that no other rail line anywhere in the world traveled directly over such a large area of sand dunes. For many miles, grass was planted on both sides of the line in a unique checkerboard pattern consisting of open squares that were each one to two feet in size. This, the conductor stated, was a desert-control method devised by Chinese experts in the late 1950s and was the only way that construction of this line over the sand dunes was possible. Many foreign experts, he said, had come to study this system. I marveled at the enormous amount of human labor that must have been required not only to build but also to maintain this huge grass grid designed to tame nature and keep the desert at bay. For millennia, the Chinese ability to mobilize laborers on a mass scale to build public works of all kinds had been awesome. It still is.

We traveled through sand desert for more than two hours. The dunes were not continuous, however; some areas appeared to be mainly *huangmo* wasteland or rocky *gebi*. Other areas were eroded loess. But we kept returning to desert dunes. Throughout this entire region, the population was—not surprisingly—extremely sparse, but electric and telephone lines and roads were visible most of the way, and we did pass occasional remote towns and villages, including the town of Gantang near the Ningxia-Gansu boundary. There the railway divided, one branch going to Lanzhou and the other to Wuwei, which is located on the Lanzhou-Urumqi rail route.

The poverty of this area was evident, yet even in the most benighted regions there were some evidences of the impact of modernization. Power and communications lines were ubiquitous, and there were quite a few factories—more than I expected. And, as I stated earlier, the prevalence of TV antennae constantly astonished me. There were forests of antennae in almost all towns, with only one or two exceptions (that I saw), but what was even more surprising is that I saw them in most rural areas as well.

Almost all the people we could see from the train window—mainly people at train stations—appeared well clothed, many of them in fashionable dress. Following the lead of coastal China, most wore modern clothing. What young women tended to regard as most fashionable, it became clear, were red jackets, tailored slacks, and red-leather high-heel shoes. Elevator shoes were common on men. The contrast with the 1950s was striking. At that time almost everyone, even in cities in this part of China, wore traditional Chinese cotton padded clothing and cotton shoes, and during my summer visits straw sandals were the norm in almost all rural areas. Traditional Chinese clothing of this sort had virtually disappeared. And instead of padded clothes, most people—certainly in the cities—wore thermal underwear to protect themselves from the bitter winter weather.

After leaving Gantang in the late afternoon, we again passed through a few areas of large sand dunes and then entered an area of desertified grassland, with scattered flocks of grazing camels. On this part of the trip we passed only a few widely spaced mud houses, some of which had been abandoned. Then, for a while, we went through a wild area of "moonscape"—a forbidding and uninhabited region where the eroded face of the land had been, probably for millennia, torn and scarred by extremely powerful natural forces. The landscape reminded me of similar landscapes that I had seen in remote Iranian areas on a flight from Kabul to Tehran in the late 1950s—as well as of certain badlands in the United States.

Near the end of the day, we briefly went through an agricultural area, but then, after stopping at the Gansu town of Jingta, we again entered a bleak region of rolling hills covered with desertified grasslands, punctuated by occasional mud villages. When dusk and then night descended, we could no longer see the landscape but we could sense it from the laborious climbing of our train; our steam engine puffed hard for a long stretch and then accelerated on a long downhill slope as we began the last stretch to Lanzhou. The night was black, but we could see electric lights not only in all of the towns but even in some villages. This, too, was a striking change from the past, when there had been no electricity at all in western China outside a few of the largest cities, and even there electric lighting was scarce.

*   *   *

As on all of my train trips, I found numerous opportunities to talk with fellow passengers. This time they included the usual mix of people, ranging from high officials to peasant *laobaixing*. However, about half of our soft-class car—the only such car on the train—was filled with military officers of fairly high rank, several of whom were eager to talk with me. These officers had come from Beijing and were going to attend a military conference in Lanzhou. They exuded authority, and everyone else treated them with obvious deference, yet—in contrast to many military men that I had encountered in the region in the 1940s—they had the bearing of professionals and were neither arrogant nor overbearing. However, most ate their meals in their compartments, avoiding the unpleasant crowding and confusion in the dining car, and they maintained a certain aloofness toward all civilians on the train.

One of the officers was particularly interesting to me. The son of a Hui farmer in Ningxia (his father had moved to try farming in Ningxia to escape a drought in Henan), he had done well in local Ningxia schools, and, by dint of superior performance in national examinations, he had been admitted to China's best-known university—Beida (Beijing University), where he had majored in Chinese history. After graduating, he had joined the PLA—something that very few university graduates ever considered in the late 1940s—and during his first 10 years served as a correspondent for an army newspaper. Then he was assigned to engage in "military research." Still in his forties, he was at the time I met him on the staff of the National Defense University in Beijing, engaged in research on reform of the PLA's educational system; he and others involved in this task, he said, were drawing on foreign as well as Chinese experiences and models. He was what I would call a "military intellectual," one of a new type of young, professional officers brought to the fore in the reform period of the 1980s. He impressed me as being very intelligent, sophisticated, articulate, and thoroughly modern. (Even though he was Hui, he smoked and drank beer—although he told me that he observed Hui prohibitions against pork.)

The other officers on the train varied in age, background, and the work they did, but they, too, all spoke like professionals—and all were obviously accustomed to privileged treatment. Their uniforms, for example, were of cloth that was of unusually good quality. One was accompanied by his wife, who was wearing a fairly elegant fur coat. They did not try to disguise their ranks (although all wore only single stars on their shoulders), and they were fairly frank in stating that they looked forward eagerly to formal reestablishment of ranks—which had been abolished in the Maoist era—and the restoration of insignia, scheduled to take place later in the year. All in all, they struck me as being very impressive representatives of the emerging generation of military officers.

As I mentioned earlier, our companions in the train compartment were two young "businessmen"—purchasing agents for a state enterprise in Baotou. Both were extroverts, extremely friendly and talkative. They insisted that I share their tea and peanuts, and they were eager to discuss anything and everything. Both were around thirty years old, each was married, and each had one child. They were traveling to Lanzhou to purchase washing machines for their department store, which was located in Baotou's old city. With almost no prodding from me, they proceeded to tell me all about their lives, finances, families, and aspirations. It was apparent that they enjoyed jobs that permitted travel on expense accounts. I asked them where they planned to stay in Lanzhou, and they said that as usual they would find a place after they arrived. Lanzhou was full, they said, of small Chinese-style hotels, and no reservations were normally needed. Rates were about Y 10 to Y 20 a night. The two men had only very slight interest in national affairs of any kind, including the forthcoming National People's Congress session. The only trend that caused them real concern was inflation. Although it had not yet hit them very hard personally, they were very worried about it.

In 1988, I found young men like this traveling in large numbers all over China. As a result of the recent reforms, and growing commercialization of the economy, a new kind of young business class was emerging. Many, like these two young men, were business representatives of state enterprises, but an increasing number were entrepreneurs representing collective or private enterprises.

When we arrived at Lanzhou station at about 10:15 P.M., the scene was one of near-chaos. This was typical, I learned, of rail stations in most of China's large cities. The explanation was simple: As a result of the increasing, and only partially controlled, mobility of a growing segment of the Chinese population, China's rail system was overloaded to the point of being almost overwhelmed. At the Lanzhou station, masses of travelers pushed and jostled each other to exit through a very narrow gate, where the attendants collected used tickets. They then emerged onto a large plaza filled with another raucous mass of people, some soliciting taxi passengers, others promoting small local hotels, many simply waiting. The station plaza at Lanzhou, as in many other big cities, was filled with transients, many of them job seekers.

*   *   *

I was met at the station by a staff member of the local Academy of Social Sciences named Lo—a young Gansu native who had recently graduated from Lanzhou University (a philosophy major, he had studied Western as well as Marxist thought). This young man immediately escorted me in an Academy car halfway across the city to the Friendship Hotel. Although it was dark, I could immediately see that Lanzhou, even more than Yinchuan or Baotou, had become not just a modernized city but a large, modern metropolis.

The Friendship Hotel was a fairly massive, but undistinguished, government-run hotel with two main buildings. The front structure had been built in the 1950s to house Soviet experts. The rear building, where I stayed, had been built later but in the same ponderous style; during the Cultural Revolution it had served as headquarters for the Red Guards and then in the 1980s was modernized and converted into a commercial hotel. My first impression was that, despite its cavernous and gloomy atmosphere, it was a truly modern hotel. I soon learned, however, that its modernization was only skin-deep in most respects. It operated clearly in a prereform "socialist" mode. With only a few exceptions, its service personnel were even more slothful than in most other government-run institutions. What the hotel needed, obviously, was a shaking up by some entrepreneur from Hong Kong or a Western country. (In many parts of China in the 1980s, such entrepreneurs had helped to create joint-venture hotels that functioned in ways very similar to good hotels in the rapidly developing countries of East Asia or in the West.)

The morning after my arrival, I began, as I did on all of my visits, with a discussion of my program. I was surprised—in fact, somewhat shocked—when my hosts outlined for me what appointments and visits had been initially arranged. They were extremely few. I concluded that no one with any clout in the Academy—or in the local government or Party organization—had given any real attention to my visit. Not disguising my dismay, I reiterated in fairly forceful terms the requests that I had made earlier and ticked off a large number of people and institutions that I wished to visit. I was insistent—politely but forcefully—that it was essential that I see many more people and institutions than had initially been scheduled, and eventually my persistence paid off. Before I left, my program in Lanzhou and elsewhere in Gansu turned out to be highly successful, and I was able to interview a very wide range of people, including the governor.

By this time in my travels in 1988, it had become apparent to me that to meet the kind of people I felt it important to meet I had to be insistent, and at times stubborn, without being unpleasant or arrogant. In my previous three stops, although I had had many fruitful interviews with second-level government leaders (and in Alashan, with a deputy leader of the Party), I had not been able to meet with many of the very top officials. In each place, I was told that the top government leaders were in Beijing. At first I was very skeptical about whether they really were absent, but eventually I concluded that they in fact were in Beijing (a National People's Congress session was soon to convene). Actually, however, in many cases the second-level leaders I met—especially the executive deputy governors—proved to be able men carrying a great deal of responsibility, and many of them may well have provided me with more useful information than some of the very top government and Party leaders would have. But I nevertheless was very eager to meet the top leaders so that I could see what sort of men they were in order to draw some comparisons between them and local leaders I had met four decades earlier.

From the kind of access that I was given as I traveled through west China, I drew several conclusions, which subsequent experience confirmed, about the kind of treatment that a visitor such as myself could expect as well as conclusions about the factors that determine how a visitor is treated. To have access to top political leaders in China, or even to very important bureaucrats, it is absolutely essential to have a reputable official sponsoring organizational unit (*danwei*), and much depends on how influential one's sponsoring organization is. It was logical, for many reasons that I mentioned earlier, for me to have the national Academy of Social Sciences as my sponsor. Not only did the Academy have close relations with the U.S. Committee on Scholarly Communication with the People's Republic of China, whose grant made my trip possible, but I had personally gotten to know several top Academy leaders, who offered to help arrange what I wished. They obviously tried their very best. However, it was also obvious before long that there were limits to their ability to open doors in the provinces. Their leverage in dealing even with local academies, all of which were independent organizations, had its limits, and it depended a great deal on what personal ties (*guanxi*) people in Beijing had established with particular provincial academies.

Beijing's clout in dealing with local governmental foreign affairs bureaus was even more limited. Even though the national Academy had the status of a ministry in China's bureaucratic hierarchy, it could only make requests to these local bodies and then hope that they would be responsive and cooperative. As my travels progressed, I learned that some local Academy leaders had very close relationships with top Party and government officials in the provinces whereas others did not. The degree to which they could—or would—open doors for me also depended on their willingness to expend some political capital in asking for interviews on my behalf. Provincial government and Party secretaries were surrounded by "gatekeepers"—as high-ranking leaders in most countries are—and anyone wishing to arrange meetings with them had to go through the members of their personal staff office—especially the head of the governor's or Party secretary's immediate staff office and his personal secretaries.

It also became clear to me, as my travels progressed, that the treatment that visitors receive depends to a very large degree on local perceptions about their importance. These perceptions reflect deep cultural feelings that assign great importance to official rank. I was generally treated as an academic of seniority, in part because the Academy portrayed me as such but also because local leaders had been well briefed on the fact that four years earlier, in 1984, I had had a long personal interview with Zhao Ziyang (then premier and in 1988 general secretary of the Party); this interview had given me a great deal of "face." I was frequently introduced to local officials as "the American professor whom Zhao had met in 1984." Nevertheless, it also became apparent to me before long that in the provinces most top leaders were not inclined to give me the kind of access that they were prepared to give to high-ranking foreign diplomats or officials whose visits were sponsored by the Foreign Ministry (or other bodies of comparable rank). This was no surprise, and, in fact, I would not have wanted to be treated like a foreign official. They obviously felt that it was appropriate to arrange meetings with government leaders, but they were much less inclined to arrange meetings for me with top Party leaders or local military people. Everywhere I went, I kept reiterating my desire to meet Party and military officials as well as government leaders, and I did meet a few, but fewer than I hoped to see. My treatment in this respect was by no means atypical. Very few foreigners are given access to top Party leaders outside of Beijing, and the few outsiders who are given access to local Chinese military leaders are generally foreign military men (or civilians closely linked to military organizations).

My experience in Gansu illustrates all of these generalizations. As I said earlier, the program that had already been arranged for me when I first arrived was extremely disappointing—in fact, it was one of the least satisfactory of any place I visited. Yet by the time I left Gansu (I made two separate visits during 1988 to the province) the local Academy had been able to arrange a highly rewarding series of interviews and visits, including very fruitful meetings with more than 30 leaders and a variety of other kinds of people not only in Lanzhou but also in the prefecture of Linxia in the south. In Lanzhou, one highlight was an extremely illuminating dinner meeting that I had with the governor of Gansu together with his principal deputy governors, his secretary-general, and two of his closest advisers. Among the most fruitful of my other interviews in Lanzhou were meetings with leading economic planners from both Gansu Province and Lanzhou Municipality, key officials responsible for Gansu's minority affairs, leading members of the Lanzhou Personnel Bureau, faculty members and graduate students from the Northwest Normal College, and a very able group of young scholars from the local Academy of Social Sciences. A memorable trip to Linxia fulfilled a desire I had had ever since the 1940s to visit this very important base of the Muslim Ma warlords and of Islam in northwest China. While there, I spent a full day in nonstop interviews with the young head of the prefecture, and many other local officials, who briefed me in great detail about all aspects of Linxia's development.

*   *   *

Much of what I saw and learned in Gansu and Lanzhou impressed me. In the years since my visit in 1948, Lanzhou had been totally transformed from an old-fashioned, medium-sized provincial capital into a large, modern, industrial metropolis, and modernization had reached beyond it, deep into the province. But the enormity of the problems facing Gansu's leaders also impressed me. These leaders were still confronted with the task of somehow overcoming some of the worst poverty in China. Part of Gansu clearly had entered the modern world, but much of it was still lagging very far behind.

When I had visited Lanzhou in 1948, the city was not only the capital of Gansu Province but also the seat of the Northwest Political and Military Affairs Administration. This regional structure was headed at that time by General Zhang Zhizhong (whom I met on my visit)—Chiang Kai-shek's top representative in the northwest; Zhang was an extremely urbane and very influential leader. On several occasions he negotiated on behalf of the Nationalists with the Communists. His responsibility at that time covered four provinces: Gansu, Ningxia, Qinghai, and Xinjiang. (In recent years Shaanxi has been included as part of the northwest, but it was not in the 1940s.)

Lanzhou itself in 1948 was a fairly dreary place, a sprawling traditional city—or really a very large town—with not many signs of modern development. It still was, as it had been for centuries, a place of great strategic importance, militarily and politically. However, its economic importance had declined and was not nearly as great as it had been in earlier centuries. Gansu

Province in 1948 seemed extremely remote from the main currents of development in China, and it obviously was one of the most desperately poor areas in the country. In 1948, I was not able to stay very long in Gansu and consequently was unable to probe deeply below the surface of the local situation. When I met General Zhang, we mainly discussed political development in the northwest as a whole, not the local situation. One of my aims in seeing him was to ask his help in obtaining permission from the warlord rulers of Qinghai and Ningxia to visit their provinces, and Zhang did use his good offices to convince Ma Bufang in Qinghai and Ma Hongkui in Ningxia to approve my visits. My visit in 1988 was much more useful, and I was able to learn a great deal about both the city of Lanzhou and Gansu Province.

People in Lanzhou—both officials and ordinary individuals—like to remind visitors of Gansu's strategic importance, historically, as the gateway from China to Central Asia; the Silk Road led from Xi'an to the West. They also take pride in claiming that the geographical center of China is in Gansu. (In this respect, they remind me of Kansans who like to point out that the geographical center of the United States is three miles north-northwest of Lebanon, Kansas.) Whether one accepts Gansu's claim depends on what part of East China you measure from; moreover, virtually everyone in China views Gansu not as being in the center of anything but as a province in the very remote west, far from the economic and political centers of the country.

There is no question, however, about Lanzhou's, and Gansu's, strategic importance historically—an importance derived from geography and topography. The Gansu corridor has from ancient times been the key route to the far west and to Central Asia. It is a peculiarly shaped passageway, stretching roughly 1,200 miles to the northwest from Lanzhou to Xinjiang, with forbidding mountains on the west and south, bordering Qinghai and Sichuan, and with menacing deserts to the north and east, bordering Inner Mongolia and Ningxia. Although most of the corridor itself is dry and inhospitable, and, like almost all of the northwest, suffers frequently from natural disasters of major proportions, it prospered in early years from the fact that it was by far the best route to Central Asia—and therefore was the place from which, starting many centuries ago, camel caravans traveled the fabled Silk Road all the way to Asia Minor.

Gansu's governor told me, with great pride, about recent archeological discoveries that prove that there was an early society—a slave society—in the Gansu area 7,000 years ago. Local boosters argue that this proves that Gansu was "one of the cradles of Chinese civilization." In any case, a well-known type of local pottery, Yangshao, was indisputable evidence that there was a thriving neolithic culture in the area. Starting at about the time of the Zhou and Qin dynasties (well before the start of the Christian era in the West), Gansu began to be gradually incorporated into Chinese culture and society. By the time of the Han dynasty (206 B.C. to A.D. 220), virtually all of present-day Gansu came under effective Chinese control. The Great Wall was extended along Gansu's northern flank as far as Yumen in the far west of the corridor, and important Chinese garrisons were stationed in the area. These garrisons provided protection for both Chinese and other traders, and trade on the Silk Road thrived.

Following the end of the Han dynasty, the region entered a period of conflict and decline. Then, however, during the Tang dynasty (A.D. 618 to 907), especially during its early years, Gansu and the Silk Road enjoyed another great period of development and prosperity. The Chinese I met in Lanzhou in 1988—including the governor—compared Gansu's entrepôt role in those early centuries, especially during the Tang dynasty, with the role played in later centuries, particularly during the Ming dynasty, by cities such as Yangzhou, located in central China at the convergence of the Grand Canal and the Yangzi River. They argued that the decline of overland trade, which accelerated when China's maritime trade began to grow, was one of the most basic reasons for Gansu's subsequent decay.

With some ups and downs, Gansu's fortunes clearly did decline greatly in later centuries, but there were numerous reasons for this, including frequent conflicts between Han Chinese and other ethnic groups (Uighurs, Tangut Tibetans, Mongols, Hui Muslims, and others), numerous and very destructive wars and rebellions, and, periodically, terrible natural as well as human disasters. One of the most terrible human disasters occurred when Genghis Khan—as well as his immediate successors—laid waste to much of Gansu in the thirteenth and fourteenth centuries, with effects that lasted for centuries. The province recovered somewhat during the Ming dynasty, but not completely, and during the late nineteenth and twentieth centuries it was badly ravished again, this time by huge Hui rebellions, Chinese campaigns of repression, warlord conflicts, and natural disasters. During most of the Republican period, Gansu was very isolated and poverty-ridden, even though it did reemerge briefly in the midtwentieth century as a significant strategic center, first when Soviet aid to the Nationalist regime during World War II flowed by truck down the Gansu corridor to Lanzhou and subsequently during the civil war of the 1940s when Chiang Kai-shek made it the Guomindang's headquarters for northwest China.

During World War II, the Communists' Shaan-Gan-Ning Border Area* reached into eastern Gansu, and in the postwar period the Red Army gradually expanded its area of control into the province. Finally, in 1949, General Peng Dehuai's forces, supported by troops under General Nie Rongzhen and

---

*At that time, this area's name was romanized as Shen-Kan-Ning; the name refers to Shaanxi, Gansu, and Ningxia provinces.

others, defeated the two Ma warlords; they captured first Xi'an (in Shaanxi Province) and then Lanzhou and established the Northwest Military and Administrative Region (MAR). Headed by Peng and dominated by the First Field Army (the headquarters of which was in Xi'an), this MAR—as well as the Central Committee's Northwest Party Bureau (which was also located in Xi'an)—gradually consolidated Communist control in the northwest. At that time, the northwest was redefined to encompass five provinces: Shaanxi, Gansu, Ningxia, Qinghai, and Xinjiang.

*   *   *

Starting in the early 1950s, the central government, which was determined to push forward the modernization of China's interior provinces, began to pour large investments into Gansu, much of it into the city of Lanzhou, and this marked the start of the first major period of Gansu's industrialization. By the end of the 1980s, a part—although by no means all—of the province had been profoundly changed. In fact, by the 1980s there were, in economic terms, really two Gansus, one urban and one rural. The level of average per capita income of all of the province's urban inhabitants, I was told by local officials, was, by the 1980s, rated as the sixth highest among China's provinces (which astonished me). However, its rural population was still, as in the past, rated as the poorest in the country.

Militarily, Lanzhou continued to be a key center—the headquarters of the Communists' Northwest Military Region. Politically, Gansu's post-1949 history paralleled that of other provinces in many respects, but because of the poverty of the area and the legacy of past Han-Hui conflicts, Gansu's leadership faced many special problems. Partly because of worries about Muslim "localism," Beijing's appointments to the top Party and government leadership posts in Gansu tended to be dominated by outsiders, particularly men from Shaanxi (especially from the northern Shaanxi area centered on Yan'an—although some prominent appointees also came from the eastern part of Gansu that had once been part of the Shaan-Gan-Ning Border Region). The dominance of outsiders seemed, however, to stimulate even stronger localist responses. As a result, the leadership in Gansu was more unstable during the Maoist period than "average" provinces; it suffered, for example, from more frequent purges of Party secretaries. Apparently because Beijing feared that Hui leaders might try to regain political power, the Party seemed determined to limit their roles, and on more than one occasion local purges focused on Hui cadres. Toward the end of the Maoist period, the impact of the Cultural Revolution was especially severe in Gansu; some provincial leaders, including a number of military leaders, opposed the extreme radicalism of the time, but with only limited success.

In certain respects, however, Gansu's experience from the late 1950s to the late 1960s was quite comparable to that of most other provinces. It, too, experienced all the great mass campaigns, most of them inspired by Mao Zedong, that kept China in almost constant turmoil. Then, in the 1980s, after Deng Xiaoping initiated his national reform policies, Gansu—like most of the country—entered a new period of rapid growth and development, described to me by people in the province as "by far the best years since the 'golden age' of the 1950s and the First Five Year Plan."

The results of development since the 1950s and of the decade of reform and development were very visible when I visited the province in 1988. This was especially true in Lanzhou, which was totally different from the city I had visited 40 years previously. In 1948, Lanzhou was an old-fashioned provincial city and, in Chinese terms, was only a medium-sized urban center with a population of just over 200,000. It had no really modern industries; in fact, it did not even have any train connection, and trucks were still fairly rare and cars even rarer. The Lanzhou that I returned to in 1988 had become a huge industrial center, with over two million inhabitants, and the city was now dominated by an immense industrial complex—or perhaps one should say several industrial complexes.

                    *   *   *

The heart of Lanzhou, as of 1988, was located on the south bank of the Yellow River, which in this area flows west to east and is fairly shallow, narrow, and sluggish. The river is useful as a supplier of the city's water, but not for much else: It is not navigable near Lanzhou. Barren, low mountains almost surround the city on both sides of the river. They protect the basin in which the city lies, and they help to make Lanzhou's winter climate milder than that of most northwestern areas. When I made my first 1988 trip to Lanzhou, in February, some days were mild but others were quite cold, and light snow dusted the city and mountains around it. When I returned in May, it was much milder.

Lanzhou is now classified as one of China's largest municipalities. Its boundaries had by 1988 been extended to include large areas of the countryside, and its total area had grown until it encompassed 5,375 square miles (more than four times the size of Rhode Island). It was administratively divided into five urban districts and three rural counties. The latest published population statistics provided to me (for 1986, I believe) listed the municipality's total population at 2.28 million, of whom about a half—1.127 million—lived in urban areas and the rest in the countryside. Local experts told me that they believed the population had by 1988 actually risen to about 2.4 million but that it was still roughly one-half urban and one-half rural.

In Lanzhou, academic specialists whom I met praised the national policy (labeled the policy of "cities managing counties"—*shi guanli xian*) of creating enlarged municipalities by incorporating rural counties as well as urban districts under unified municipal administration. Local experts believed that this had led—as intended—to improved economic planning and coordination that benefited both rural and urban areas.* In Gansu as of 1988, there were 15 prefectural-level administrative units (that is, prefectures, autonomous prefectures, and prefectural-level municipalities) but only 5 expanded municipalities of the new type had so far been established (Lanzhou, Tianshui, Bainingshi, Jinchang, and Jiayuguan). Local scholars favored extending the system to the entire province, eliminating prefectures and attaching all counties to municipalities.

During my two stays in Lanzhou in 1988, I visited all of its urban areas. They varied considerably in function and appearance as well as in flavor. The largest and newest part of the municipality lay in the eastern part of the city. Built almost entirely since 1949, it looked—and in some respects clearly was—very modern, although many of its buildings, built in the 1950s, were stodgy, uninspired structures with a "Moscow modern" look. Lanzhou's huge modern railway station was located on the southern edge of this area. A broad and quite grand avenue (Tianshui Road) cut straight north from the station; to the east of it was a large educational and research district, where Lanzhou University, the institutes affiliated with the Chinese Academy of Sciences, and many similar institutions were located.

Further north, Tianshui Road intersected with one of Lanzhou's several major east-west boulevards at a large circle; this boulevard led west into the business and governmental center of the city. Halfway to this center was "East is Red" Square, used for major celebrations and public gatherings.

Throughout the eastern part of the city were numerous modern buildings. Many of them were 5 or 6 stories high—some even higher—and most were built of brick or other kinds of dark masonry; the majority were institutional headquarters or large state-run apartment houses. The overall appearance was modern and clean but also antiseptic and drab; however, the trees that had been planted on both sides of the major streets somewhat relieved the dullness. Interspersed among the Maoist-era buildings were an increasing number of Western-type high-rise skyscrapers, some of them rising 10 to 15 stories. Built in the previous few years, during the construction fever that swept China in the mid-1980s, these high rises were mainly of light-colored construction material, and many were quite pleasing to the eye architecturally; quite a few could well have blended into recently built areas in Euro-

---

*These specialists hoped, in fact, that this system would soon be expanded even further in Gansu. They were impressed especially by the experience of Jiangsu and Liaoning provinces, where the system had been carried to its logical conclusion and prefectures had been eliminated so that all counties were attached to and included under municipalities.

pean or American cities. One concentration of post-Mao high-rise buildings was located around "East is Red" Square. Several structures there, including the Science and Technology Palace, which had a novel spiral tower with a circular room on top, was architecturally very interesting. One 15-story office building had the kind of clean vertical lines that would not have looked out of place in central Manhattan.

The most dynamic central part of the city—where the old Lanzhou of 1948 had been located—lay slightly to the west. This area was a mixture of old and new. The main shopping and business districts were located there, in an area crisscrossed by a grid of streets that, though narrower than the main new boulevards, were nevertheless much broader than the traditional, pre-1949 streets. Lined with shops interspersed with office buildings, the streets in this area were filled with well-dressed pedestrians of all ages, and motor traffic was quite heavy, so the area had an extremely lively atmosphere. On the eastern fringe of the shopping district was a small area of very traditional small alleys, where Hui Muslims predominated. It was one of two areas in the city where Hui people were most in evidence; the other was across the river. To the north, adjacent to but south of the river, were more major public buildings, including both the provincial government (located in an old Chinese-style yamen compound) and the offices of the municipal government. Along the river ran a very attractive riverside boulevard, with several parks abutting it; two major bridges crossed the river in this area (there were others in different parts of the city).

The southern part of what was old Lanzhou was more nondescript. I was eager, however, to tour it so that I could try to find the guest house where I had stayed in 1948 and to locate the office where I had interviewed Zhang Zhizhong. This guest house had been called, rather grandly, the Northwest Mansions (Xibei Daxia). When I inquired about whether it still existed, I was surprised to learn that it was still well remembered because it had been the leading "modern" hotel (it was, in fact, only semimodern) in Lanzhou before 1949. I had remembered it not as a grand building but rather as a fairly drab, two-story, dormitorylike structure. When I saw it again, I discovered that my memory was accurate. It seemed curious to me that its existence as a hotel had not been totally forgotten by the people of the town because the building had been converted in the recent past into a Party school run by the Railway Bureau. The fact that such a lackluster building had acquired a lasting reputation was testimony to how little there was in pre-1949 Lanzhou that was worth remembering. I also searched for Zhang Zhizhong's old headquarters, but it had disappeared; in its place was a large military hospital.

*   *   *

To the west of the old city was another urban area, similar in some respects to the one on the eastern edge of the city; it, too, was predominantly "Maoist modern," and most of its buildings were far from impressive. Through this area, another wide boulevard went straight toward the west, passing the Friendship Hotel where I was staying. Several miles beyond it the road entered a huge industrial area filled with factories interspersed with massive blocks of workers' apartments, all of them several stories high. The factories were of diverse sorts, and many were very large, but the skyline was dominated by Lanzhou's oil refinery and petrochemical complex. Smoke and smog hung over this industrial area—air pollution had become a major problem that worried local leaders a great deal—but the general ambience was not totally unattractive. Few factory districts in any country are really attractive, but I was impressed that this area was less grimy than a great many I have seen elsewhere. It certainly was far less unattractive than early industrial cities in the West, and it was not bad at all compared with many contemporary industrial districts in other countries. The streets were generally quite wide, and most were lined with trees. Workers' apartment buildings were well built and clean; from the outside they looked quite good. (I did not have time to visit inside any of these apartment buildings, but I had done this in many other Chinese cities, and if these were similar, I would guess that inside they were relatively cramped and austere—even though local Lanzhou statistics indicated that workers' apartments were somewhat more spacious than comparable apartments in most east China cities.)

The majority of Lanzhou's population lived south of the Yellow River, but there were also two important urban areas north of the river. One was in the east, directly across from the center of Lanzhou. It was far less modernized and looked a good deal poorer than most areas south of the river; it was in this area that I saw the most evidence of Muslim culture and customs. I visited—although I did not enter—several mosques and saw a considerable amount of religious activity at all of them. In one place I encountered a lively commotion on the street outside a mosque and was told that it was a celebration of a leading Ahong's birthday; it was attended by several dozen other Ahong and Mala.

In most of Lanzhou, however, I saw relatively few traces of Muslim culture. The reason, I soon learned, was obvious. The total number of Hui people in Lanzhou Municipality was estimated in 1988 to be only about 20,000—less than 2 percent of the total urban population of the municipality. Even though Lanzhou is *the* major municipality located in the Muslim belt in the northwest, it is very much a Han Chinese city. Despite this fact, official public policy continued to pay a great deal of attention to the Hui population (in ways that I will discuss later in more detail): Among other things, the government had given substantial help in the 1980s to repair or rebuild old mosques and to construct some new ones. Among the new ones was a fairly spectacular structure—a circular building in a Chinese architectural style but of unusual design, with a conical roof—which was still under construction in the central part of the city.

North of the river but further to the west was another newly built area. It, like the area northeast of the railway station, was the site of numerous research and educational institutions, including the Gansu Academy of Social Sciences, which had recently moved into a new headquarters building in that area.

Knowing that Gansu was classified as one of China's poorest (probably *the* poorest) provinces (which local leaders emphasized), I kept looking, as I toured Lanzhou, for visible signs of extreme poverty of the kind that I had seen throughout northwest China in the 1940s (and also in most of eastern China during my childhood in the 1920s and 1930s): emaciated and dirty beggars, people with ragged clothing, and obvious signs of health problems such as skin sores and trachoma. I saw almost none of these in Lanzhou Municipality. Among the job seekers and refugees crowding the railway station plaza were some who looked obviously poor, but even they were not emaciated like those I remembered from the pre-1949 period. On Lanzhou's streets I saw only a handful—about half a dozen—adult beggars or ragged street urchins, but almost everyone else I saw was quite well dressed and looked reasonably well fed and healthy.

I was initially baffled by the discrepancy between what I saw and the Chinese data I obtained from official publications and from articles I had read that openly acknowledged poverty to be a major problem in China, especially in west China areas such as Gansu. Official Chinese statistics indicated that in all of China in the early 1980s, roughly 100 million Chinese (about 10 percent of the population) were still categorized as living below China's extremely low poverty income line (Y 200 a year). By 1985, this reportedly had dropped to about 70 million (6 to 7 percent of the population) in part because rapid economic development in the 1980s had significantly raised incomes and in part as a result of increased government relief efforts, supervised by a newly established State Council Poverty Relief Office but carried out mainly by local relief institutions. By 1988, there were said to be over 37,000 welfare institutions in China. Many of them were governmental, but the majority were reportedly run by local neighborhoods and collectives. The central government officially acknowledged that as many as 50 million people in China's rural areas still suffered food shortages and that 20 million of these people lived on the borderline of starvation. To help such people, the government in 1988 reportedly spent about Y 1 billion on relief, of which almost Y 300 million went to the 20 million people facing the most dire food shortages. Moreover, Beijing officials estimated that about 1 in 10 Chinese in 1988 suffered some type of malnutrition resulting from diet deficiencies.

In light of all this, I expected to see substantial visible evidence of poverty in the capital of China's poorest province. Yet I did not. In fact, I saw fewer obviously poor people in Lanzhou than one sees regularly in the streets of Washington, D.C., where the city's homeless men and women are highly visible. I thought long and hard about the reasons for this and searched for answers; by the end of my visit I concluded that there were several explanations. (My conclusions were reinforced by data I gathered in subsequent months.) One basic explanation was that the overwhelming majority of the poorest people in China live in extremely remote rural areas, most of them in areas far from modern transportation—especially in remote mountain districts and particularly those inhabited by isolated minority groups. Another explanation was that the government's welfare efforts had substantially reduced the prevalence of the most extreme and visible poverty, especially in major cities, even in relatively poor regions of the country. Despite the significant loosening of travel restrictions as a result of the reform of the 1980s, the government was still able to deter (at least in 1988) most rural poor people in remote areas from flooding into some large cities. In China as a whole, however, the mobile population had increased greatly and rapidly during the latter part of the 1980s and probably reached at least 50 million by 1988. (By the end of the 1980s the number was estimated to be considerably larger.) It was fairly clear that in major cities the government was quite successful in assisting the poorest groups and in keeping most indigents off the street.

I concluded, however, that the most important of all the reasons why I saw little poverty in cities such as Lanzhou was that most of these cities—and their immediate suburbs—had benefited greatly from the rapid economic development that had occurred even in the Maoist era but especially during the reform period of the 1980s. In the 1980s, living standards of both rural and urban areas rose, but urban areas still enjoyed a substantially higher standard of living than that prevalent in the poorest rural areas. Official statistics indicated that nationally the gap between average income in urban areas and those in rural regions had narrowed somewhat in the 1980s but continued to be quite large. The gap was especially striking in Gansu, where, as I noted earlier, average incomes in urban areas placed it in the upper third of China's provinces whereas average income in the province's rural areas placed it at the bottom of all provinces in China.

Life in the suburbs of most major Chinese cities had improved especially rapidly during the 1980s as a result of both recent economic reforms and—most important—rapid rural industrialization, mainly in the form of collective, township, and village industries. I wondered whether this was something I would see in Lanzhou's suburbs, and I did. Northeast of the city, on the southern edge of the Yellow River, many signs of new prosperity were apparent. Intensively cultivated plots of vegetables (grown under plastic sheeting) and apple orchards were interspersed with bustling and obviously well-off villages. The majority of peasant housing appeared to be new, and most houses were built of hard bricks; some of the houses were very colorfully ornamented. Many villages were developing into small towns, and in them were numerous nonfarming enterprises, including small manufacturing plants and service industries (including transportation units that owned several trucks); these were mostly owned, I was told, by prosperous farmers.

On the north side of the river, to the west, in an area famous for its peach orchards, the air of prosperity was even more palpable. When we were en route to the Academy of Social Sciences headquarters, my young local escort mentioned in passing that a cousin of his was a farmer in this area, and at my request we made an unannounced visit to his peach orchard and home. The cousin, who was in his thirties, and his pretty wife had a remarkably comfortable brick house that was built around a courtyard and was well appointed with modern furniture, a television set, a tape recorder, and other modern household appliances. He and his wife and their small children were all dressed in good-quality Western-style clothes (in contrast, his mother, who lived with them, wore very traditional padded jackets and trousers). He impressed me as being an extremely urbanized young man: His farming forebears would have had great difficulty identifying him as one of their own. It did not take long, however, driving further outside of urban Lanzhou to reach quite bleak, arid areas where a great many people were obviously poor.

*   *   *

The transformation of Lanzhou from a backward, premodern provincial city into an industrial metropolis was the result of deliberate central government policy. Starting in the 1950s, Beijing directed large investments into Gansu, and a great deal went to Lanzhou. However, a substantial amount was also invested in a few other provincial cities, the majority of which were located in the Gansu corridor, where a major effort was made to develop mineral resources, hydropower, and, above all, heavy industry—especially petrochemicals and mining. Although most of the province remained agricultural, the province's gross economic output was, by the late 1950s, dominated by industry. By the time of my visit, in fact, industrial output accounted for close to three-quarters of the gross value of Gansu's total agricultural and industrial output and Lanzhou Municipality alone accounted for almost a half of the province's industrial output. The figures that I was given on the economies of both Gansu and Lanzhou highlighted how dramatic the economic transformation had been. According to officials in the Gansu government, in 1987 the gross industrial output value of agriculture and industry in the province totaled Y 18.6 billion; of this total, industry accounted for roughly Y 14 billion whereas agriculture accounted for only Y 4.6 billion.* The value of Lanzhou's gross industrial output was Y 6.452 billion in 1987, and it was projected to reach roughly Y 6.5 billion in 1988. It accounted, therefore, for close to half of the total industrial output, by value, of the entire province.

Statistics that Lanzhou's officials gave me on the population of the municipality and on the number of factories there provided other very revealing indicators of the degree to which the city had been transformed from a premodern provincial town into an industrial powerhouse. When I had visited Lanzhou in 1948, its population was estimated, as I noted earlier, to be about 200,000. But by 1988 it was estimated to be roughly 2.4 million. About half of the municipality's residents lived in the city proper. Some of the increase had resulted from the expansion of the municipality's boundaries. Some was the result of a "natural increase" in the population: Local Academy specialists said that in the 1980s family planning had been loosened, and this had contributed to the population growth. However, by far the most important factor leading to the municipality's expanding population had been government-encouraged migration of workers and technicians from other parts of China to Lanzhou to help industrialize it. These migrants had come mainly from more advanced areas of the country, especially Shanghai and the lower Yangzi provinces, the northeastern provinces in what formerly was called Manchuria, and the Beijing-Tianjin area. In some cases, the migrants accompanied factories that were transferred from other areas to Gansu and Lanzhou. In other cases they came separately but were integrated into the developing industrial structure.

In 1948, I had seen almost no evidence of industrialization. The government's records now show that there were at that time 56 factories in the city, but all of them were small. The factories included an electrical plant, some wool factories, and several miscellaneous establishments that produced items such as water pipes and swords. By 1986 (the latest year for which I could obtain statistics on this subject), Lanzhou had 1,146 sizable factories (including both state-owned and collective enterprises). Among them, heavy industries, mainly state owned, were overwhelmingly dominant. A total of 327 "large and medium-sized" state enterprises accounted for 91.5 percent (by value) of the municipality's total industrial output, and 819 collective industrial enterprises accounted for 8.5 percent.

---

*Beijing's State Statistical Bureau figures were somewhat higher than those that I obtained in Gansu: They showed the province's total agricultural and industrial gross output value in 1986 to be Y 20 billion, of which industry accounted for Y 14.4 billion and agriculture for Y 5.64 billion. I do not know why the State Statistical Bureau's figures for 1986 were higher than those of the Gansu Provincial Government for 1987. Unless otherwise noted, however, throughout the discussion that follows I will use figures that Gansu and Lanzhou planners gave to me.

*   *   *

The development of modern industry in Gansu, not only in Lanzhou but also in the other cities where industry had been developed in the Hexi corridor, which stretched to the northwest, began in the 1950s after the central government decided to give considerable priority to the creation of a new industrial base in this remote area. In the ensuing four decades, this development went through several phases. In the 1950s, Beijing's decisions, made in the context of its planning for China's first Five Year Plan, were directly related to its broad national strategy stressing heavy industry. Beijing called for very large investments in Gansu mainly to develop raw materials production, other heavy industry, and power plants (with a special emphasis on hydropower), which, among other things, could support other industrial efforts elsewhere in the country. Of the 156 "key" Soviet-assisted projects built throughout China in that period, 14 were located in Gansu.

Subsequently, Gansu's economy, like that of China as a whole, was seriously damaged by the failure of Mao's Great Leap Forward and by the sudden withdrawal of Soviet technicians in 1960 and the abrupt ending of Soviet aid. (Moscow's technicians left Gansu "almost overnight," I was told). The natural disasters and political disruptions of the post-Leap period inflicted further damage. Some factories were forced to halt all production for several years in the early 1960s.

Then, during the late 1960s and early 1970s (during China's third and fourth Five Year Plans), Gansu experienced a second period of rapid industrial growth. Once again, the central government invested large sums of money in the area and transferred to it large numbers of factories and technicians from coastal areas. The rationale for this was provided by Mao Zedong's "three-front strategy," under which, for both strategic and economic reasons, Mao called for concentrating major development efforts in China on the so-called third-front region in China's interior, which included parts of Guizhou, Sichuan, Gansu, Qinghai, and Ningxia as well as the western portions of Henan, Hubei, and Hunan. Particularly high priority was given to military-related industries. However, because of inadequate—in some cases virtually nonexistent—feasibility studies, extremely ill-considered choices of plant locations, and great haste, the industrial development in much of this period was very wasteful and created serious long-term problems, which continued to plague the region in the late 1980s. I was told that the government was still actively trying to carry out a major process of industrial "readjustment." The aim was to raise the efficiency of plants that had been built in that earlier period—to make them economically viable—and in at least some cases this required relocation of factories. In addition to the disruptive effects of Mao's three-front policy, politics obtruded again, at the height of the Cultural Revolution in the late 1960s, which disrupted Gansu's economy as well as its politics, as it did elsewhere in China.

The third period of rapid industrial development was initiated after Deng Xiaoping's reform policies started in 1978. It got well under way in Gansu in the early 1980s and continued throughout the decade. Local leaders stressed that because these reform policies were much more economically rational than earlier policies, they had had a much greater impact than previous development efforts on people's lives and had raised living standards substantially.

In sum, the course of local development from the 1950s into the 1980s was an erratic one, with some very impressive accomplishments and some extremely serious failures. The Gansu leaders whom I met recognized—and discussed in detail why—they still faced some extremely serious economic problems. Many of these problems were very intractable ones, inherited from the past, and were still a long way from solution. Others were the result of the rapid development in the 1980s, and they illustrated the truism that whenever rapid change occurs, the solution of one set of problems brings to the fore a new set of problems.

On the plus side, it was evident that by the late 1980s Gansu had acquired a very large—albeit geographically concentrated—industrial base, which in size was impressive by any standards, particularly in comparison to the 1940s. Extensive geological prospecting had taken place starting in the 1950s and had proved that the province had large resources of raw materials, which provided a very solid potential for continuing development. By the late 1980s, the top leaders in the province consisted, predominantly, of a new kind of well-trained technocrat, knowledgeable about and firmly committed to rational economic development of the area. These leaders had formulated ambitious plans for future development. A start had been made, also, in implementing structural reform of the economy, which Beijing was actively promoting at that time, and the reforms had had some positive results.

However, the problems facing the province were still enormous. As noted earlier, one fundamental problem was the continuing, great gap between urban and rural areas. Even though some significant efforts had been made to improve agricultural life, a large portion of the rural population remained extremely poor. The province's industry also was badly out of balance because it was overwhelmingly dominated by heavy industry and continued to be weak in its ability to produce consumer goods. Even though the province's economy was growing at a fairly impressive rate in the 1980s—a rate that exceeded the national average, in fact, according to local officials—it continued to be relatively backward compared to China's most advanced coastal areas, and Gansu's leaders were acutely aware of this. Rail and air transport now linked the major cities of Gansu with the rest of China, but transportation within much of the province was grossly inadequate, and local leaders, as well as people from other parts of China, still viewed most of the province as remote, isolated, and out of China's mainstream.

The province was very dependent, financially, on the central government, and one of its basic problems was a severe shortage of both capital and technical skills. Efforts to take advantage of China's new open policy by expanding Gansu's economic interactions with the rest of the country and the outside world had really just begun, and local leaders were seriously concerned that Beijing's policies giving preference to coastal provinces could well put Gansu even further behind those provinces. In implementing Beijing's reform policies, Gansu—like most interior provinces—was making some progress but still lagged substantially behind the coastal provinces in many respects. I was told that conservatives in the provincial bureaucracy still strongly resisted many of the efforts being made by the new technocratic leaders in the province to introduce reforms, whereas some local intellectuals were strongly urging the government to move faster and further toward economic restructuring. But implementation of some reforms was relatively slow.

Almost everyone I met, including not only the governor and numerous other officials but also local academics and journalists, spoke enthusiastically about the province's ambitious plans and about the goal of making Gansu "the economic center of the northwest." They all acknowledged, however, that Xi'an and Shaanxi Province were economically still ahead of Lanzhou and Gansu and that as of 1988 Xi'an rather than Lanzhou was really the most important center in the region.

The overwhelming majority of those I met were unquestionably "modern" in their outlook, technocratic in their inclinations, and committed to economic development of the region. It seemed to me that the tone of the local regime was set in many respects by the provincial governor, a man named Jia Zhijie. Jia, a man in his fifties, impressed me as being an able and forward-looking leader. Born in Jilin Province in the northeast of China, he graduated from the Northeast Normal College, was subsequently selected for training in the Soviet Union, studied Russian in Beijing's Foreign Language Institute as preparation, and then spent five years (1955–1960) studying machine building at the Moscow Petroleum College. (Much later, in 1980, when he was still a factory manager, he had visited the United States. He spoke some English, which he taught himself.) For more than two decades, Jia's career was primarily that of a technical and managerial specialist in the petroleum industry. Following his return from Moscow, he was assigned to the Lanzhou Petroleum Machinery Plant (later renamed the Petroleum and Chemical Machinery Works) and rose to be manager of the enterprise. Then, when major changes in Gansu's political leadership began to be made, starting in 1983, he became a deputy secretary of the Gansu Province Party Committee, in charge of economic work. In 1986, he was appointed acting governor, and he then became governor in 1988.

The executive deputy governor of the province, who also participated in my meeting with the governor, was a man named Yan Haiwang. He had had a similar career. Born in Zhengzhou, in Henan Province, he was trained as an architect at the Harbin Engineering College in northeast China. His first assignment after graduation was as a technical expert in a construction company in Gansu, and eventually he rose to be manager of the company. In 1983 he was appointed director of the Provincial Construction Bureau, a post that he held for four years, and then in 1987 he was appointed a deputy governor. There were four other deputy governors, I learned, and three of them had had careers as technicians or academic specialists; one had headed an iron and steel plant, another had served as an agricultural expert, and the third, a woman, had been a researcher in the local Academy of Sciences' Institute of Industry. (The one deputy governor who was not a technical specialist was a Hui Muslim.) Gansu's Party secretary, Li Zeqi, was also a technocrat, I was told, who managed a copper plant for many years and then became director of the Department of Light Industry of the province; he was selected Party secretary in 1983.

This kind of leadership was vastly different from that characteristic of the Maoist era. Not only were the new leaders much more oriented toward problems of modern economic development, but they were also far better qualified than earlier leaders to cope with such problems. The governor, the executive deputy governor, and the others I met all seemed to me to be both forthright and realistic in the way in which they looked at the enormity of the problems facing them, the obstacles to rapid development, and the drag created by old attitudes and conservative tendencies within the bureaucracy. From them, and others, I was able, by the time I left Gansu Province, to piece together a picture of the economy of Gansu that greatly increased my understandings of both its accomplishments and its problems.

*   *   *

The area of Gansu Province, as of 1988, was more than 175,000 square miles; this meant that it was the seventh largest provincial-level territorial unit in China and that it had an area that was slightly larger than that of California. By 1988, its population was just over 21 million. Located in the heart of the northwest region, where so many of China's minority groups live, it has a population with a complex ethnic mix. However, I was surprised to learn the extent of dominance, numerically, of Han Chinese. In 1988, the Han Chinese accounted for more than 92 percent of the total provincial population, whereas the minority groups—totaling about 1.5 million—accounted for less than 8 percent. Moreover, the minority population was divided into 41 different ethnic groups. Ten of these were numerically significant. Close to two-thirds (980,000) of all the minority peoples in the province were Hui Muslims. The Tibetans (with 320,000 people in the province) were the second most important group. As I discussed earlier, before 1949 the Hui Muslims had played a major political role in the province—as well as in the region as a whole—but by the late 1980s they no longer did. (However, as I will explain later, they still did exercise significant political influence in some local regions of the province, such as Linxia Autonomous Zhou.)

Despite its industrial development, Gansu continued to be predominantly rural. Figures for 1986 (the latest that I could obtain) indicated that the labor force in the province totaled 9.63 million. Of this total, 5.6 million (almost 60 percent) worked in agriculture (including animal husbandry and forestry as well as farming) and 1.17 million (about 12 percent) worked in industry. The rest were in construction, services, government work, and other kinds of work. Overall, the rate of GNP growth in the province had been quite impressive: In the previous five years, I was told, it had averaged 13.5 percent—exceeding the national average. However, as I stressed earlier, the benefits went more to urban dwellers and industrial workers than to people in the countryside, and the gap between the two economies remained distressingly large.

Paralleling the development of basic industry in Gansu in the years after 1949, transportation and communication links to other parts of the country had been greatly improved, but internal transport links were still inadequate. Before 1949, Gansu had lacked virtually all forms of modern transportation. However, by the late 1980s Lanzhou had become a major transportation hub for all of the northwest. New railways linked it to Sichuan Province in the southwest (via Baoji), to the eastern provinces (via the Longhai Railway), to Urumqi in Xinjiang in the far northwest, and to north China (Beijing and Tianjin) via Ningxia and Inner Mongolia. Also, there were regular (although not wholly dependable) air flights to many other major Chinese cities, including Beijing, Shanghai, Xi'an, Urumqi, Taiyuan, Chengdu, and Guangzhou. However, within Gansu, even though roads of a sort now linked all the major economic regions of the province, only a beginning had been made toward developing the kind of transportation network required for broad modernization.

Within Gansu, there were enormous differences in the level of development and general conditions in different administrative as well as economic subregions. This fact confronted the leadership with major problems. The subregions could be defined in various ways. Administratively, Gansu, as of 1988, had 14 prefecture-level municipalities and prefectures, under which were 86 counties and county-level cities. The 14 included 5 municipalities (Lanzhou, Tianshui, Yumen, Jiayuguan, and Jinchang),* 7 regular prefectures (*diqu*), and 2 autonomous prefectures (*zizhi zhou*).

The creation of enlarged municipalities—to replace prefectures—was a stated goal of the provincial leadership, but, as in so many other things, the province encountered difficulty in changing the system and lagged behind eastern provinces in this respect. By 1988, as noted earlier, only five of these enlarged municipalities had been established. Officials and academics who were most reform-minded in Gansu urged a more rapid implementation of this policy because they believed that it not only would improve economic planning and coordination of the areas belonging to municipalities but also would help to promote a "commodity economy," that is, one in which market forces rather than administrative economic management would eventually predominate. This idea of enlarging municipalities had begun to be developed in China years earlier, but it was first promoted in an energetic way during the early 1980s, during the sixth Five Year Plan. It took root most rapidly in China's three provincial-level municipalities (Beijing, Shanghai, and Tianjin) and in two of the country's most advanced provinces, Liaoning in northeast China and Jiangsu in the central part of coastal China. In some places, as many as 5 to 10 counties were incorporated into enlarged municipalities.

Economic experts in Gansu's Academy of Social Sciences argued that, in their judgment, the experience in eastern provinces and cities demonstrated that the new system of enlarged municipalities clearly contributed in a very positive way to reform and also accelerated development. One scholar pointed out that by 1988, Jiangsu, which was now entirely under the new system, contained 11 such enlarged municipalities and that some of them, individually, had gross output value as large as, or almost as large as, some provinces, including Gansu. They also cited statistics that indicated that in some of these enlarged municipalities the rural counties now contributed perhaps as much as 60 percent of the total output of the municipality. Everything they had learned about the experience in the eastern provinces had convinced them, they said, that Gansu Province should push ahead and try to implement the new system more broadly. However, they acknowledged that it would be difficult to do so because of Gansu's relative backwardness and poverty. Up through 1988, they told me, only 13 of Gansu's 86 counties had been incorporated into its five enlarged municipalities (3 in Lanzhou, 5 in Tianshui, 3 in Bainingshi, and 1 each in Jiayuguan and Jinchang). These

---

*Published lists include these five. In Lanzhou, officials and scholars discussing the five included Bainingshi but not Yumen; I do not know if these two names refer to the same place.

Gansu scholars felt that the provincial government should implement the new system throughout the province as soon as they could.

*   *   *

Both the government economic planners and the local academics whom I met spent considerable time analyzing for me the economic subregions of the province, and almost all of them agreed that it is possible to identify five distinct economic regions. One, the central region, included not only the municipality of Lanzhou (which, as emphasized already, is the province's largest industrial center) but also Dingxi, one of the poorest agricultural areas of the province. Dingxi is largely mountainous and is very dry, with extremely low annual rainfall. It has access to the Yellow River and its water, but the cost of pumping river water to irrigate cropland is prohibitively high, so most farmers are at the mercy of the weather. The second region, Longnan (South Gansu), borders Sichuan and Qinghai and lies to the southwest of Lanzhou. This region has a somewhat higher rainfall and also has access to the water from several tributary rivers that join the Yangzi in Sichuan, so farming conditions are somewhat better. It also contains a sizable area of pastureland at higher altitude, where animal husbandry is feasible, and it contains some forest areas. The third region discussed with me was Gannan, in the far south of the province. A very mountainous and poor area, with primitive transportation and very little industry, its local economy relies heavily on animal husbandry and somewhat on forestry.

The fourth region discussed with me was Longdong (East Gansu). Much of it lies high on a plateau, where rainfall is somewhat more plentiful than in Dingxi. Farming conditions are therefore slightly better, but it too is relatively poor, in part because of its lack of modern industry and transportation. The province's current economic plans call, however, for building a second railway through this region to Ningxia, which would help to promote local economic development in the region. The fifth region discussed was Hexi, which clearly rates right after Lanzhou Municipality as the second most prosperous region in the province. Stretching northwest along the railway zone on the way to Xinjiang, it includes much of the best agricultural land in the province as well as several major cities where industry has developed. Although rainfall in the Hexi area is low, the growing season is fairly long, and the region is fed by three rivers. On the basis of extensive irrigation, it has become an important "commodity grain base"—that is, an area able to produce a significant grain surplus and thus able to provide grain to other areas. Strung along the corridor are several significant cities, all of which have developed some industry or mining: Wuwei, Jinchang, Zhangye, Jiuquan, Jiayuguan, and others. Apart from Lanzhou, the Hexi corridor has become the second most important base for the province's economy because of its good irrigated cropland and the industrial and mining cities that have developed in the region.

In sum, as of the 1980s Lanzhou Municipality and the Hexi area had developed a fairly impressive economy, but in all the other regions there were enormous problems. Provincial leaders recognized that they had to find means to use the resources of the two most prosperous and developed areas to attack the problems of poverty and underdevelopment in the three poorest regions—which actually make up the larger part of the province's territory.

Despite all of the province's problems, many people I met there expressed considerable confidence and optimism about the potential for the province's future development. A primary explanation for such confidence and optimism, I learned, was the judgment of everyone that the area had such rich mineral and hydroelectric resources that it was "inevitable" that it would be able to develop a much more modern and larger economy in the future. One enthusiastic official, when talking with me, compared Gansu's potential with that of California!

According to Governor Jia, since the 1950s prospectors have discovered significant deposits of more than 60 minerals in the province. Deposits of 23 of these minerals in Gansu, he said, were now estimated to account for as much as a fifth of China's total deposits, and the deposits of 10 of them were believed to be the largest in the country. Major development of deposits of copper, nickel, lead, aluminum, and several nonferrous metals had already taken place in various parts of the province. As of 1988, moreover, provincial planners estimated that the potential hydroelectric capacity of Gansu was 14.26 gigawatts, of which 2.1 gigawatts had been developed (more than half of this developed capacity was at Liujiaxia hydroelectric station). It was development of this power that had made possible the growth of a number of major heavy industries, some of which were large users of electricity.

                    *   *   *

Analyzing the structure of the province's industrial and mining enterprises, the top economic planners I met emphasized that both the central government and the provincial government had given priority, for many years, to the production of power, raw materials, and heavy industries—rather than to consumer goods industries. The governor, when describing the relative importance of different industrial sectors and the way these reflected state priorities, listed, in order of importance, the following: energy (especially hydropower), petroleum refining and petrochemicals, alloy metals, and machine building. Lower on the list of priorities were cotton textiles and other light industries (including woolen textiles), cement, and plate glass. By 1988, however, the governor and provincial officials in general had recognized that the underdevelopment of light industries producing consumer goods was a major weakness in the local economy. They all stated that one new priority was to try to remedy this fairly soon, but at the same time they admitted that so far they had made relatively little progress in this respect. It seemed clear that the primary emphasis on heavy industry was likely to continue.

As I stated earlier, almost everything I learned highlighted the fact that Gansu's industrial economy was badly unbalanced—with excessive emphasis on large-scale, state-owned heavy industry. In 1986, according to official national statistics on Gansu, the province had a total of 122,800 industrial enterprises, the gross output of which totaled more than Y 14 billion, but 117,000 of these enterprises were small ones at the village level and below. The really modern industrial economy was dominated by roughly 5,800 major urban industrial enterprises, which accounted for more than nine-tenths of all of the province's industrial output.* Although 4,389 of these were collective enterprises, they accounted for only about 10 percent of total output. In contrast, 1,437 state enterprises accounted for about 90 percent of the total output of the major urban industrial enterprises. The breakdown of these urban industrial enterprises, moreover, indicated that 2,549 (44 percent) were classified as heavy industry, and these accounted for three-quarters of gross industrial output, by value. Light industrial enterprises were more numerous (there were 3,282 of them) but they produced only one-quarter of the value of urban industrial enterprises. Moreover, among heavy enterprises, just a few dominated the economy. In fact, 61 heavy industries that were officially classified as "large" accounted for 47 percent of the industrial output of the major urban enterprises; another 99 "medium-sized" enterprises (many of which were quite large by most standards) accounted for 22 percent; and the remaining major urban industrial enterprises accounted for only 31 percent.

Figures on employment provided another measure of the high degree of domination by state-owned heavy industry. Of the 913,000 workers and staff members of industrial enterprises in Gansu (those above the village level), more than 775,000 worked in state-owned industrial enterprises, whereas only 137,000-plus were employed by collective enterprises. The breakdown of the 913,000 by type of industry shows that 670,000 were em-

---

*Different breakdowns of the major industrial enterprises added up to different totals—5,831 or 5,286.

ployed in heavy industrial enterprises and only 243,000 worked in the field of light industry.*

Even these figures may well have understated the degree to which state-owned heavy industrial enterprises dominated Gansu's economy because, I was told, they excluded industries that were strictly military. From the 1950s on, Gansu was developed into a major center for the production of certain military-related products. It played a role in the development of both nuclear and missile capabilities in China. Before my 1988 visit, I had tried to learn what I could from Western sources about developments in these fields, and it was possible to learn quite a bit. However, when I visited Gansu I discovered that it was virtually impossible for a person such as myself to learn anything on the spot. Not only was information about industries of this kind shrouded in extreme secrecy, but the civilian officials I met all firmly maintained (I could not be certain whether they were correct, but what they said sounded convincing) that they themselves had very little detailed knowledge about nuclear, missile, and related matters. They repeatedly stressed that military industries in Gansu operated under their "own system," directly administered from Beijing. In answer to questions I asked, they acknowledged that the provincial government maintained statistics on both military and industrial production in the province, but they also stated that the figures that they had given me covered only civilian industries—plus that portion of military industry that had recently been shifted to the output of civilian goods.

Shifting the production of defense-related factories from military goods to civilian products was a major national priority in China in the 1980s—partly because Beijing in the early 1980s was determined to cut back its military budget but partly because Chinese leaders recognized that there were large unused capacities in many military industries.†

------

*Some of the above figures came from national statistical sources. Local Gansu planners gave me slightly different figures for the year 1987 for some categories. Of the total industrial output of Y 14.01 billion (including township enterprises) in 1987, they said, Y 10.09 billion (72 percent) was from heavy industry and Y 3.92 billion (28 percent) from light industry; Y 11.67 billion (83 percent) came from state-owned enterprises and Y 2.34 billion (17 percent) from collective and township enterprises. They said that *their* figures indicated that there were about 4,900 important enterprises above the village level; however, they said that 160 of them—61 "large" ones and 99 "medium-sized" ones—were dominant.

†A survey in the late 1980s indicated that defense factories in "third-front" areas accounted for about 50 percent of "China's industrial and scientific capacity"—an indication of how much was invested in such industries in remote areas under Mao's policies of the 1960s and 1970s—but the survey also indicated that, despite continuing major efforts to shift from military to civilian output, about 30 percent of the capacity of military industries was still not effectively utilized. However, the output of civilian goods by military industries had risen greatly, and by 1985 it exceeded 40 percent of the total output of defense industries; by the end of the decade that figure exceeded 60 percent.

In Gansu as elsewhere, the policy of encouraging defense industries to shift to production of civilian goods was taken seriously and was being implemented; the provincial government had established a Military Industry Office to monitor and coordinate this shift. The provincial statistics given to me did include, as I stated earlier, the value of civilian products produced by defense industries. But no one I met could—or would—give me overall output figures on the production of military industries in Gansu. Several provincial officials did say, however, that in Gansu the shift to civilian production had been slower and less far-reaching than in some other areas.

More than one person noted that one serious general economic problem in Gansu was that even though the province had a substantial number of well-qualified technical specialists, a very large proportion of them worked for defense industries controlled by organizations in Beijing, or for research institutes responsible directly to Beijing's Academy of Sciences, and that these specialists made relatively little contribution to the province's civilian industries. Efforts had been made, I was told, to involve scientists and technicians from military-run factories and institutes in the civilian economy—for example, they had been mobilized to help develop new factories producing TV sets and some other kinds of consumer durables—but a great many specialists still paid very little attention to local civilian needs. This, local people felt, put Gansu at a definite disadvantage compared to coastal provinces. Local economic officials also complained that too much of the research being done in institutes within the province still focused mainly on subjects on the priority lists of national (especially military) institutions rather than on problems that preoccupied local leaders, for example, much of their work was related to atomic energy and high-energy physics and long-term problems such as desertification and so on. Although Gansu officials were willing to acknowledge that all of these fields were important, they stressed that they did not contribute very directly to the most pressing immediate economic problems faced by the local civilian economy.

*   *   *

Local officials also discussed with me a range of problems that, they said, were the direct result of the huge role played by the central government in the provincial economy. These problems continued despite the fact that there had been a trend in the 1980s to decentralize decisionmaking to the province. The predominant local view, I felt, was that the central government still controlled too much of the local economy, too directly, despite decentralizing trends. In the municipality of Lanzhou, for example, of the total value of civilian industrial output, enterprise directly administered by the central government controlled almost 50 percent (by value) whereas enterprises administered by the provincial government controlled about 30 percent and enterprises administered by the municipal government controlled only about

20 percent. Although the statistics on Lanzhou's industrial output covered all of these categories, the ability of municipal planners to manage and handle the economy was severely restricted by the fact that so much of industry was not directly under their control. The provincial government faced comparable problems, and to try to improve the coordination among all three types of industries, the provincial government had established a special office—the Economic Cooperation Office. But, it was acknowledged, this office had relatively little authority, and to the degree that there was any effective coordination, it was largely "voluntary" and based on "personal relations" (*guanxi*). Both municipal and provincial officials were obviously not satisfied with this situation because it made their problems of planning and management extremely difficult and in some respects almost impossible. They obviously felt that there should be much greater decentralization and were quite willing to say so.

Gansu's economic subordination to, and dependence upon, the central government was highlighted, also, by the budget figures that I obtained. Like all western provinces, Gansu depended on large subsidies from Beijing. I obtained conflicting figures, however. According to Governor Jia, Gansu's provincial revenues in 1987 totaled about Y 2.2 billion and its expenditures totaled roughly Y 3.3 billion. The difference, he said, was made up mainly by central government subsidies and investments—plus the capital flowing into the province from China's coastal province and a small amount of capital coming from international organizations such as the World Bank. However, the head of the Comprehensive Planning Section of the provincial Planning Commission said that in 1987 revenue was Y 2.2 billion and expenditures were Y 2.6 billion and that the shortfall of Y 400 million was made up by a central government subsidy—but he also said these figures did not include some important items paid for by Beijing.

Fiscal relationships with Beijing were both complicated and changeable. Before 1983, the governor said, most major, basic civilian industries in Gansu, including the biggest petroleum and petrochemical enterprises, power plants, and nonferrous metal factories, "belonged to the province." Then, in 1983, nine major enterprises in these fields were transferred to the control of the central government. Before 1983, he said, the province had control of between Y 700 million and Y 900 million of the profits from these industries, although much of this had to be paid to the central government. Following the shift of control in 1983—which, the governor said, was made "because these enterprises were so important to the national economy and to macroeconomic control"—the central government, in compensation to Gansu for the province's loss of control over these industries, had given an annual subsidy of Y 240 million to Gansu and had also permitted the province to keep about Y 500 million a year of the commodity taxes that it collected from enterprises within the province. The net result was that Gansu's fiscal situation had really not changed very much, he said, at least immediately. Nevertheless, officials in Gansu felt that their dependency on Beijing had been increased—which they viewed as a "contradiction" to the stated national policy of increasing decentralization of the economy—and they obviously did not like the change.

From several officials in Gansu I learned that the province was continuing its efforts to persuade Beijing to increase its local authority—but that they were also trying to convince Beijing to give more financial support to the province. Shortly before I interviewed Governor Jia, I learned that he and one of his deputy governors—together with governors and deputy governors from Qinghai and Ningxia—had met (between sessions of the National People's Congress in Beijing) with two national economic planners, Yao Yilin and Tian Jiyun. During this meeting they had lobbied not only for more generous financial support for development in the northwest but also for a specific proposal that would involve a readjustment of financial relationships. They proposed that their provinces be allowed to sell one-half of their output of key resources on national markets at negotiated prices, which they had estimated would bring them about Y 1.5 billion a year more in income. They could then use this income for local investment, thereby lowering the amount of investment funds they would have to request from Beijing. (I was told that what they really would have liked was an arrangement in which they could sell all of their resources at negotiated or market prices, enabling them to obtain about Y 3 billion more in income, but they decided that it was more realistic to ask for half a loaf rather than a full loaf.)

No decision had yet been made on this matter, I was told, but they were still hoping for a favorable response. Governor Jia emphasized to me that western governors also strongly supported further price reform, in part because they believed it would result in higher raw material prices that would clearly benefit their provinces. (In contrast, some leaders in coastal provinces feared that because further price reform would lead to increased prices for essential raw materials from the west it could greatly complicate their problems.) Gansu's leaders also had some doubts about whether they were being treated fairly in comparison to other western provinces, especially those classified as autonomous regions. These areas were receiving more generous subsidies from Beijing because of the national policy of giving special treatment and special subsidies to all minority-inhabited areas. Because its minority groups were smaller, in proportion to its total population, than those in the places labeled autonomous regions, Gansu did not obtain comparable treatment.

*   *   *

Nevertheless, despite some causes for complaint, Gansu's leaders clearly recognized—and were very willing to acknowledge openly—that central government investments were what had made possible the province's past economic development and that a continued flow of investments by Beijing to the province would be essential to its future economic development. The level of central government investments in Gansu was still very large. Most continued to go into mining, power, and heavy industries, but in the recent past a substantial amount had been earmarked for development of agriculture—to try to get at the root cause of poverty in the area. Zhao Ziyang, after a visit to northwest China in the early 1980s, had decided to allocate sizable investments to three rural areas—two in Gansu and one in Ningxia. Under this program, Y 200 million a year was promised for a 10-year period; much of this was to be used to expand irrigation, but some was designated to increase terracing and planting to control erosion. Of the amount specifically assigned to Gansu for agricultural development, the bulk was to be used in two areas: the province's poorest area, Dingxi, and also its richest agricultural area, Hexi. Investment in the latter was justified as a means to strengthen it as a "grain base," which could step up its assistance to the entire province, especially the poorest areas of the province. (In the late 1980s, the province still suffered an annual grain deficit of about one million tons. Most of this deficit was made up by purchases of grain from other parts of China, on the basis of central government allocations, but a small amount of wheat was provided free by Beijing to certain of the poorest areas in the province.)

In the 1980s, the increase of investment in rural areas, plus the reforms of agriculture, had improved the lot of some of Gansu's peasants, but the prevalence of rural poverty remained a fundamental problem. In the early 1980s, Gansu had implemented decollectivization, which introduced the household responsibility system. This had clearly had very positive effects, I was told (and believed), and the new rural development projects supported by the central government also had begun to help. But many areas of Gansu were still so poor that the struggle to eliminate poverty had only begun to make significant progress.

There were a few really bright spots. For example, in the area around Jiuquan, in the Hexi region, average annual per capita rural income had risen substantially and reportedly had reached Y 735. However, rural per capita incomes in all of Gansu still averaged only about Y 302 in 1987, according to provincial officials. This figure represented some progress: In 1979, the average for the entire rural population had been Y 101. However, even the figure in 1987 was still not much above the national poverty level of Y 200. In 1988, 46 of Gansu's counties—over one-half of the total—were classified as the poorest areas, and the average rural income in these counties, I was told, was expected to be under Y 200 a year. In some other counties in the middle of the province there had been a certain amount of improvement during the 1980s; rural incomes in them had risen from an annual average of Y 72 in the early 1970s to Y 270 in 1987, and provincial planners said that they hoped that it would be possible to "basically solve the problems of food and clothing in these counties by the start of the 1990s." The overall picture, however, still was very discouraging; it was clear that at best it would take a long time to turn the situation around. (Almost all Chinese figures on average rural incomes are fairly rough estimates. The ones I was given were based, I was told, on sample surveys plus official estimates of the value of the grain harvest and other sources of peasant incomes.)

The extreme poverty in many of Gansu's poorest rural areas was particularly troublesome because of the contrast to some of the more advanced and more affluent parts of the province. The inequities were striking. The average "regular income" (which includes wages and bonuses but not extra income) of wage earners in cities and towns in Gansu in 1987 was Y 1,557 (the sixth highest, I was told, of any Chinese province). One reason it was high was that the wage levels in Gansu were based on the scale for eleventh-category areas—the highest in China—because it was a remote and developing area. The figure on the average per capita urban income in Gansu—taking account of nonworking dependents of wage earners and other nonworking people—was of course lower, but it was still fairly impressive. In 1987 it was estimated to be Y 861. In fact, this probably underestimated the real level because the figure was based only on statistics covering regular income and it did not include extra income from spare-time activity or moonlighting in second jobs. A large percentage of the urban population did have some income aside from their regular wages. (Two officials asserted, however, that they believed that the average incomes of people in coastal China were understated even more and were substantially higher than those in Gansu; they argued that in coastal China people had much larger opportunities to earn extra income.)

Rural development in Gansu was constrained by the limited amount of really good land, but according to local officials the province still had land that could be developed—if the necessary funds were available. Altogether, I was told, Gansu had 8.7 million acres of cultivated cropland in 1987, with about four-fifths of it planted in grain and about one-fifth in cash crops and vegetables. In addition, it had very large areas of pastureland—at least 33 million acres. Planners estimated that perhaps as much as 10 million *mou* (close to 1.7 million acres) could be, in theory, added to the cultivated land in the province if water could be made available, but that was a very big if. Because of the high costs, nobody expected that there could be a rapid expansion of cultivated areas.

In Gansu, as elsewhere in China, a major effort had been made in the 1980s by the provincial government to encourage the development of rural township enterprises. This effort had produced some significant results, but local planners themselves stressed that the level of local rural poverty made it extremely difficult for peasants who wished to start enterprises to find the necessary capital and expertise to do so. As a result, they said, Gansu lagged seriously behind coastal provinces in this respect. In 1983, when the development of township and village enterprises was in its early stages, the value of their output was only about Y 500 million. By 1987, according to the governor and other officials, it had reached Y 3.3 billion.* They expected that the figure for 1988 might be Y 4 billion. The contributions of rural industrial enterprises had risen to the point where they were by no means insignificant. These small enterprises had become an important source for jobs. By 1987, they employed about a million people—more, actually, than major urban factories. However, the government was by no means satisfied with the pace of their growth.

Population transfers, not only to rural industry within Gansu but also to other provinces, were regarded by provincial leaders—and provincial planners—as another important means to try to relieve poverty in rural areas. In addition to the total of about one million people in the rural labor force who had been shifted to township enterprises by 1987, it was estimated that about a million more had migrated during the 1980s to work in other provinces. Many had gone to Xinjiang, Qinghai, and even Tibet to help raise cotton and to mine gold; others had moved to coastal provinces and to Beijing to become construction workers. I was told that there was no specific provincial plan to promote a certain level of out-migration but that some counties did have specific plans, and provincial leaders made clear that they actively encouraged—and supported, in whatever ways they could—all efforts to find employment for unemployed rural workers either in Gansu or in other parts of the country.

*   *   *

Even though in the early 1980s the Gansu government carried out rural reform and from the mid-1980s on had given increasing attention to rural development, the major concerns of most of the provincial officials I met in 1988 focused above all on reform of the urban, industrial economy. Beijing's leaders had shifted their priorities to urban reform starting in 1984–1985, and Gansu had tried to follow suit. It was clear that the provincial government was making genuine efforts to implement most of the reform policies that had been articulated by leaders in Beijing up to that time. I spent many hours, therefore, trying to learn as many details as I could about the local implementation of reform and the impact of reforms up until that time. It became clear to me, however, that, in general, implementation of reform poli-

---

*This figure included township and village enterprises of all kinds. The figure for collective industrial township enterprises was Y 2.34 billion.

cies was relatively slow in Gansu—at least by comparison with the most dynamic coastal provinces. The poverty of the area was obviously a fundamental reason. Another reason, though, which several people I met discussed, was the fact that reform was greatly complicated by the strength of local conservatism (what some people referred to as "feudal thinking") in the bureaucracies. Perhaps the most fundamental difficulty, though, was that in Gansu the industrial economy was so dominated by large state-owned heavy industries, which were particularly resistent to change, that local leaders and agencies were severely restricted in what they could do because of the intrusive role of the central government and the province's heavy financial dependence on Beijing.

One major thrust of China's economic reform policies, starting in the early 1980s, had been toward decentralization of economic decisionmaking (to give both local government and individual enterprises greater control over their operations and to make them more accountable). Gansu's governor discussed this with me in general terms, and top planning officials from both the Gansu and the Lanzhou planning commissions discussed in some detail the changes that had occurred in the planning process. After hearing all that they had to say, I concluded, however, that the changes, though not insignificant, were still quite limited.

At the height of the Cultural Revolution, in 1968, the local planning commission had been disbanded and was replaced, I was told, by an Office of Production Planning Control, which had a small planning section (later made into a somewhat larger office). But in 1971 the Planning Commission was restored and rapidly resumed its old functions. Before the reform process began, the setting of production and other targets, in Gansu as elsewhere, was carried out through a process that was called "two downs and two ups." Gansu planners emphasized—contrasting the situation at that time with the one that developed in the 1980s—that in earlier years all the initiative really came from the top, specifically from Beijing, where the state Planning Commission issued (usually in the fall of each year) preliminary target figures for the coming year, which were then sent to each province (and each ministry), which in turn allocated the targets to lower administrative and sectoral units. On the basis of these preliminary control figures, lower units made their own proposals to the center, which—after national planning conferences that balanced local and sectoral plans—sent revised targets downward. The new target figures were again worked over by local units, after which they sent their final "proposals" to Beijing, where central planners did their final balancing and defined final targets. In theory, Gansu planners said, the process was supposed to be completed for any year by the end of the preceding year, but in practice, although the general outlines of plans usually had emerged by then, a great many specific targets were not finally defined until well into the new plan year.

According to Gansu planners, after the reforms were introduced the process was simplified somewhat. Now, they said, the process was supposed to start with proposals formulated by the provincial authorities. In Gansu, they said, these were decided in the course of a number of conferences involving both provincial officials and officials from lower levels, and subsequently they were sent to Beijing, where national planners held conferences to balance all provincial and ministerial proposals. The targets that emerged from this process were then passed down, as approved targets, to the local level. They said that this new procedure actually did eliminate one step in the previous process, and they also maintained that it did increase the scope for local initiative—at least in theory. In practice, however, local and provincial planners acknowledged, they still had to base their proposals mainly on two things: (1) their performance during the previous year and (2) the long-term targets that had been set by national and provincial authorities. This fact, plus Gansu's economic dependency on Beijing and Beijing's control of heavy industry, made it appear, to me at least, that although local input into the planning process may have increased somewhat, it was still far more limited than local leaders hoped for.

Nevertheless, I concluded that local people took the planning process more seriously than they had when in the past it was clear that they had almost no control over it. Locally, fairly large bureaucracies were engaged in planning. For example, the Planning Commission of the Lanzhou Municipality had a staff of 83, at the time I was there, working in 12 divisions or offices, of which 6 were called "comprehensive" (which included units dealing with basic construction, labor and wages, materials planning, and comprehensive planning plus a general office and a research office) and 6 were categorized as "specific" units (including ones that dealt with industry, agriculture, finance and trade, science and technology, energy, and resources). However, it seemed clear that decentralization had not gone anywhere near as far in Gansu as it had in some coastal provinces.

Another focus of reform efforts in the 1980s, nationally, was what was called the "separation of Party and government" (and the "separation of government and enterprises"). The stated purpose was to reduce ideological and political distortion of economic decisions by giving greater decision-making power to experts and technical specialists—rather than to the political generalists in the Party and the government. One specific proposed change, given special emphasis after the 13th Party Congress, called for the abolition of the economic departments within Party committees, which had operated in parallel with the top economic decisionmaking bodies in the government. During much of the Maoist era, these Party departments had exercised as much or more power in managing the economy as the agencies of government directly responsible for doing so. On one of my visits to Beijing in 1988, I had interviewed Bao Tong, Zhao Ziyang's top adviser on political reform, and he had stressed to me the vital importance, in his view, of this particular reform. In Gansu, when I asked the leaders and bureaucrats what, if any, progress was being made in implementing this reform, I was told that although they "planned" to abolish the economic departments of the Party, this had not yet been done—and nobody could provide any very clear estimate of exactly how or when it would be done.

Another national priority of economic reform, starting in the early 1980s, was the objective of diversifying industry and accelerating the expansion of light industries that could better serve consumer needs. Trends in this direction had already gone quite far in China's eastern industrial areas. However, in Gansu as of 1988 this change was still in an early stage. Light industry still accounted for only 25 to 30 percent of the value of total industrial output, and although this was significantly larger than the percentage in 1979 (which had been 18 percent), local leaders recognized that it was still far below what it ideally should be.

*   *   *

Progress in some other areas of reform seemed to be having a greater effect on Gansu. There definitely had been, local officials said, a significant shift from "mandatory" plans to "guidance" plans, affecting many commodities—in fact, affecting the majority of the economy. In addition, there had been a significant acceleration of the trend toward commercialization. I was not able to obtain all the statistics I wished for on these trends, but municipal planners in Lanzhou asserted that "a large majority" of the output of municipal-controlled industries was now "sold on the market." (As stated earlier, however, these did not include the largest centrally controlled industry in the city.) Moreover, they said, whereas Lanzhou's industries had formerly obtained almost all of their key raw materials from state allocations, by 1988 they obtained "close to one-half" of their steel requirements and needs for many other important materials from markets rather than from state materials supply agencies. (In 1987, I was told, 57,000 tons of Lanzhou's steel needs came from state supply channels, and 47,000 were purchased on various markets.)* Overall, Gansu provincial planners asserted, by 1988 the percentage (by value) of goods produced in the province that were handled through markets and came under guidance rather than mandatory planning exceeded the amount subject to direct planning and state allocations. However, they acknowledged, large state industrial enterprises, especially those in heavy industry, were still subjected to a great deal of direct planning, with

---

*The most important markets for materials, however, were still supervised by the state, and although prices were allowed to float to reflect supply and demand, the state still set maximum limits.

the state supplying most of their raw materials and taking most of their products. Economic specialists at the local Academy of Social Sciences estimated that between 30 and 40 percent of the economic output of Gansu Province was by 1988 at least "partially marketized and under guidance rather than direct mandatory planning." They emphasized, however, that this was far less than in coastal provinces. One scholar, making this point, cited a particular coastal city where, he said, 90 percent of the economy was already "either completely marketized or under loose guidance planning."

Like many of the most reform-minded people elsewhere in China, these academics clearly favored larger and more rapid steps toward reliance on market forces rather than on planning, and they decried the side effects of China's transitional multiple price system—because they tended to create a distorted "negotiating economy" rather than real markets with serious competition and because they opened up huge opportunities for corruption. Direct planning still controlled more of the output of Gansu's economy than was the case in many other provinces, and this created "a great many contradictions" between Gansu and the central government, they said. I heard strong complaints about the unrealistic levels set for many prices, about the fact that even when things were supposed to be under guidance planning many planners tended to blur the distinction between such planning and mandatory planning and often intervened more than was justified, and in general about excessive intervention from above. In short, although Gansu had begun moving slowly toward a more market-oriented economy, it still had an extremely long way to go.

The same was generally true about Gansu's efforts to implement another important reform policy—a diversification of the ownership of industry. Both local planners and local academics in Lanzhou expressed admiration— and envy—of the progress that had been made in coastal provinces in these efforts, particularly the rapid development of collective industry and of rural township and village enterprises but also, to a lesser extent, the development of private enterprises. Everyone in China, it seemed to me, was acutely aware of the role that these new kinds of enterprises were playing in making the economies of coastal provinces so dynamic. Virtually everyone with whom I talked in Gansu positively approved of the idea of rapidly expanding such industries in their province, but these individuals acknowledged that local shortages of capital and skills—as well as "conservative thinking"—continued to pose formidable obstacles.

Discussing collective industrial enterprises, both officials and academics in Gansu differentiated between three different types. A small number of "old collectives" were enterprises that had been established in the 1950s and 1960s (many of them had developed initially from handicraft cooperatives). More important, however, were urban collectives that had been organized during the 1980s—mainly from 1983 on—in city neighborhoods. Many of these employed children and relatives of factory workers as well as unemployed workers of other kinds. Some had grown into fairly large factories. The third—and in many respects most important—type of collective consisted of rural township enterprises. Although a few of these had existed before 1983, they had had a "weak economic base," and the real development of them was from 1983 on. Many of the first two types, I was told, were really more like state enterprises than private enterprises; one local expert called them "semistate enterprises." However, many of the third—and most successful—type were acknowledged to be much closer to real collectives or even to private enterprises.

By 1987, the gross output value of rural collective township industrial enterprises in Gansu was Y 2.34 billion; they therefore already accounted for about one-sixth of the total industrial output of the province. In Lanzhou Municipality, the gross output value of all kinds of urban and rural collective enterprises rose from Y 180 million in 1980 to Y 540 million in 1986, but rural township collective industry (the output of which was Y 41 million in 1980 and Y 155 million in 1986) accounted for only about 23 percent in 1980—and 29 percent in 1986—of the value of output of all collectives in the municipality. In 1986, however, the pace of growth of township enterprises in Lanzhou increased somewhat, and in 1987 the output of such enterprises reached Y 203 million—a 30 percent increase in one year. But this did not at all satisfy local planners; they told me that they were determined, therefore, to try to speed up the growth of such township enterprises. They were frank in stating that, in many respects, their model was the coastal provinces, where they saw such enterprises playing a critically important and dynamic role.

Another reform policy that Gansu had begun to implement was that of leasing some state enterprises either to individuals or to groups or to other state or private enterprises. Experiments with this policy had begun in Gansu during 1981–1982, but according to local journalists its implementation slowed during 1983–1986 because of "opposition from conservatives" who labeled it "capitalistic." However, after "considerable debate," it was actively promoted again, starting in 1987. In 1987, I was told, 2,849 sizable state enterprises—some industrial, most commercial—had been leased, usually after competitive biddings, to individuals, groups, or other enterprises. The leases were generally for three to five years. Some people described the leased enterprises as "privately managed but still state-owned." The capital needed by those who wished to lease such enterprises often came from bank loans. This trend toward leasing was extremely interesting and potentially quite important. However, Lanzhou's planners stated that so far only 2 percent of the municipality's industrial enterprises had been put under leases; most of the leased units were commercial enterprises, not industries.

From what I was told, it appeared that greater changes had taken place in the structure of commerce than in the structure of industry. Local officials asserted that, apart from some large state stores, by 1988 "most shops" were either leased or privately owned. That may have been an exaggeration, but I had no doubt that major changes had taken place. Lanzhou's planners said that the municipality had (as of 1986) about 24,000 shops and other enterprises engaged in trade and services, employing 95,000 people. Of these, they said, roughly 19,000 were individual (*geti*) enterprises—many of them simply individual peddlers—employing 27,000 people (which meant that the "average private enterprise" had only one or two people in it). However, these small enterprises handled about a sixth of the city's commercial turnover, I was told.

*   *   *

At a national level in 1988, an intense debate was under way in Beijing over what reform measures should be given priority in the next phase of national economic reform. Different reformers were pushing for either price reform, or ownership reform, or enterprise management reform. This debate had swung, temporarily at least, in favor of those pushing enterprise reform, most of whom were fairly cautious reformers. As a result, national policy in 1988 was stressing implementation of the manager contract responsibility (*chengbao*) system in industrial enterprises. Talking with me, both Gansu provincial officials and people at the municipal level emphasized that they were following this national trend. They asserted that "the main priority of reform in this period is the introduction of the contract responsibility system." However, they also admitted that in enterprise reform as in many other areas, Gansu lagged behind more advanced areas. As of 1988, their main accomplishment in this respect, they said, had been the selection of quite a few new, younger managers for state industrial enterprises. Some had been chosen by competitive bidding. With the new system, these younger managers assumed "manager's responsibility" by signing contracts (usually for three to four years) with supervising government industrial bureaus. In these contracts, they committed themselves to achieve certain definite targets—for profits, output, increases in productivity, the quality of product, technical renovation, additional investments, and so on. Under such agreements, the managers were authorized to keep and use a defined percentage of targeted profits as well as above-target profits, but they were liable for penalties if they failed to achieve their contracts' targets. Generally, managers also signed contracts with their employees, but from the government's point of view the crucial contracts were the ones that the managers had to sign with government bureaus. In medium-sized and small enterprises, I was told, profit taxes levied by the government generally amounted to 55 percent of total profits; of the remainder retained by the enterprise (45 percent), 20 to

30 percent could be used for bonuses and wage increases and 20 percent could be used for welfare, while 50 to 60 percent had to be reinvested. (The percentages were defined by the government.)

Most large enterprises not only had to pay a profit tax (of about the same level) but in addition were subject to an "adjustment tax." This, I was told, took account of the unequal effect on different enterprises of "irrational" prices—set by the state—for both raw materials and end products. Generally, according to my informants, the profit taxes plus other levies on larger enterprises amounted to about 70 percent of total profits, and the remaining 30 percent left to the enterprises were allocated to different uses in about the same proportions as those allowed for smaller enterprises.

I was not given any statistics on how many enterprises had fully implemented "management reform," nor did I have an opportunity in Gansu—as I did many other places—to interview managers in factories where such reforms were already in effect. My impression, however, was that implementation had been relatively slow and that the *chengbao* system was in many instances viewed with very mixed feelings, by local planners and enterprise managers as well. It had, I was told, stimulated production to a certain extent, by increasing incentives (through wage increases and bonuses), but—because so many prices continued to have very little relationship to real values—the effects in many instances tended to exacerbate economic inequities and imbalances. Moreover, because of the key role still played by government bureaus in negotiating and monitoring enterprise contracts, in reality the results often tended to limit and distort—rather than to stimulate—market competition.

Local experts were critical of the continuing shortcomings of the wage system as well as the irrationality of the price system. Some new wage policies had been introduced, but, they said, repeating a standard refrain, "more slowly than in many other regions." Most wage differentials still had very little to do with productivity, I was told, and this remained "a large problem." For example, in many mining enterprises, wages were said to be unjustifiably low. In contrast, in many processing industries they reportedly were much too high. In the petroleum industry, they said, wages were unfairly high. Such inequality, they said, resulted from "irrationalities" and required urgent correction.

I asked whether, as a result of recent reforms, any enterprises had begun to fire redundant or inefficient workers and whether any failed enterprises had gone bankrupt. Not surprisingly, my informants said that in Gansu, as in most of China, very few workers had actually been fired (the firing of a few at one Lanzhou power plant was the only example they were able to cite). And Academy economic experts said that there had been "no case of formal bankruptcy by a state enterprise." "If a state enterprise was on the verge of bankruptcy," they said, "the government either loaned it money or arranged for its merger with another enterprise." This did not apply, however, to private and collective enterprises. There had been quite a few failures of such enterprises, but they did not have any statistics on how many.

In many of the conversations I had, Gansu leaders, and academics and journalists as well, showed obvious concern about the relatively slow pace of reform in their province. What they feared was that if they lagged in reform and also were put at a disadvantage because of the preference that Beijing's "coastal strategy" was giving to provinces in the east, the result could well be a steady widening of the gap between Gansu and more developed regions. I also sensed some concern about rising inflationary pressures—which by early 1988 had become a major national preoccupation—but, it seemed to me, people in Lanzhou did not appear to be as worried about this as people in eastern cities such as Beijing and Shanghai were.

*   *   *

Beijing's coastal strategy was a sensitive subject. The people I met rarely raised it themselves. However, I frequently did, and invariably my questions evoked expressions of serious concern. The trend in Beijing's policy seemed, to people in Gansu, to be moving step by step toward giving unfair advantages to eastern provinces. Beijing's "open strategy" had been adopted in the late 1970s; the coastal policy was not explicitly formulated until considerably later. The establishment of "special economic zones" in the early 1980s was followed by a progressive expansion of the number of coastal areas granted special rights and privileges to solicit foreign investment and promote foreign trade. In 1985, the privileged areas were expanded to cover most of China's coastal areas, and then in 1987 Zhao Ziyang finally spelled out the coastal policy and called for the areas along China's coast to orient themselves increasingly toward the international economy, to step up their production of exports and to do everything they could to expand foreign investment and trade. At the same time, Zhao and other leaders emphasized that the coastal areas should actively assist China's interior areas to speed up their development as well. Essentially, the idea was a Chinese variation of the trickle-down theory. The coastal areas would develop faster, but the benefits would—in theory—rapidly flow to interior areas as well. A new kind of "three-front" concept emerged from this period—one that was very different from Mao's. It envisaged differential rates of economic development in three major parts of the country: the coastal areas, the middle provinces, and the far western regions and provinces.

At each stage in the evolution of both the open policy and the coastal policy, there was considerable debate and controversy in China, but Deng Xiaoping was unwavering in his commitment to the basic idea of opening China to accelerate its economic development and work toward a much closer relationship with the international economy. In the late 1980s, Zhao was equally firmly committed to the idea.

From the start, China's interior provinces had many justifiable fears about the possible consequences of these new policies, and before long virtually all of these provinces began lobbying in Beijing to try to convince the central government to expand their rights to solicit foreign investment and promote foreign trade. Beijing did, step by step, grant somewhat greater authority in these fields to various interior provinces, although their treatment varied tremendously. However, in the 1980s none of them was granted anything like the authority that was given to certain coastal provinces, and this fact—combined with their natural disadvantages (being poorer and more remote)—meant that most of them had great difficulty in trying to interest foreign business in their areas.

Some of the Gansu officials I met tried to take an optimistic view—or at least tried to give the impression that they were taking an optimistic view—of the long-term benefits that could come to provinces such as theirs as a result of these policies, but it was nevertheless clear that they were worried about the possible adverse effects on the interests of almost everyone in west China. Governor Jia said to me, "We are concerned that priority to coastal development could result in less development in the interior." But he was one who made some effort to try to put the best face on the situation. He said:

> Emphasizing coastal areas is only part of the policy. The interior provinces also have a lot to do. We must promote production of raw materials. And if it is possible to develop increased "horizontal connections" with the coastal provinces, then we should be able to accelerate joint efforts. The policy does not mean that the central government will increase its investment in coastal areas; those provinces should rely on themselves in this respect. The aim is to promote prosperity in the entire nation, but considering that China is so vast, economic development is bound to be uneven. Some places must take the lead and will get rich first, but they will promote further development in the interior.

Some of the local Lanzhou journalists I met were pessimistic about the possible impact on the west of the coastal policy, but one—who belonged to the optimists' camp—stated: "The central government's idea is that coastal provinces should produce more for the international market, and this should improve our ability—we in the interior—to serve the local Gansu market (which in the past obtained about 70 percent of its goods from coastal provinces), and therefore this should stimulate local industry here. We are confident about our long-run future because we are so rich in resources."

When I asked specifically about Gansu's international connections, almost everyone bemoaned the province's slowness in developing foreign trade and attracting investment, and they all favored a much more energetic effort to move in these directions—though they recognized that it would be extremely difficult to attract foreign businessmen. Gansu's foreign trade in 1987, I was told, totaled only US$120 million—which was still small, even though it was larger than in the past. Although quite a few foreign businessmen had been invited to visit Gansu, and I was told about some of their visits, the results had been slim. Without giving specific figures, local officials said that very few foreign investments or joint ventures had so far been consummated. (One of the few specific ones they mentioned to me was a joint venture with a Japanese corporation for the development of a food packaging factory.) The World Bank had become involved in Gansu and had initiated several quite significant projects in the province. However, I met no one who was not relatively pessimistic about the prospects for attracting large-scale private investment or rapidly increasing foreign trade. Yet I did see some signs that a few people from abroad were at least looking into the situation. In my own hotel, I met and talked with a dozen foreign businessmen, who were all Europeans (mainly Italians and French). However, I did not sense much enthusiasm among them about the climate for foreign business in Gansu.

*   *   *

Gansu's "horizontal" economic ties with China's coastal provinces were, however, increasing fairly rapidly, I was told, and the provincial government obviously was very actively searching for new domestic sources of technical expertise and capital. In return for help from more advanced provinces, they were offering to assure them access to badly needed raw materials. This kind of horizontal cooperation was something that Beijing was trying strenuously to encourage and promote. As a result, new forms of collaboration between enterprises as well as governments in different regions of the country were developing.

I was told about new "economic cooperation groups," each of which involved two or more enterprises, based on agreements under which the Gansu partner provided factory space and facilities, raw materials, and labor and the partners from more advanced parts of the country provided capital and technical expertise. Profits in such enterprises were shared. My informants said that such cooperative agreements began to be promoted seriously in Gansu in 1987—later than in some other parts of the country. Local journalists told me that, as of 1988, seven particularly important agreements of this kind had been finalized. One was an agreement with an enterprise in Shanghai for producing TV sets. Another involved cooperation among several Chinese factories to produce appliances (in this case, a Japanese corporation was also involved, providing technical assistance). Still another agreement involved collaboration in the petroleum field with an enterprise in Luoyang, Henan. Several people said to me that, in their opinion, Lanzhou's most important economic ties with any other area were those that it had with Tianjin. The rail link that went via Baotou to Tianjin made Tianjin the

One of Lanzhou's major boulevards; modern high-rise buildings line multilane modern avenues.

A major petrochemical complex, one part of Lanzhou's recently developed industrial base.

Below:
Most Hui Muslims still look quite different from Han Chinese. They are now a very small minority in Lanzhou.

Above:
A young and prosperous Han Chinese farmer with his wife, child, and mother. Their home, which is filled with modern appliances, is in a Lanzhou suburb.

Right:
A futuristic modern tower in Lanzhou with a winding staircase leading to a circular room on top.

A traditional Hui village on the road from Lanzhou to Linxia, with women wearing typical hoods (the men wear caps). Such villages had changed little since 1948.

A bird's-eye view of Linxia, a remarkable enclave of modernity. Most of the modern city was built in the 1980s.

A busy market street in Linxia, filled with a mixture of Hui Muslims and Han Chinese. The white-capped man is a typical Hui. The crawling tractor has multiple uses in urban as well as rural China.

Top:
Modern Islamic architecture on a public building near the business center of Linxia.

Middle:
One of Linxia's famous animal markets, which were first organized many centuries ago. This one deals in sheepskins.

Bottom:
A Hui mosque in Linxia built in modified Han Chinese style; it was crowded with people, including Ahong and Mala, when I visited it.

most important outlet for Lanzhou's foreign trade. Next in importance, I was told, was Shanghai, with which Lanzhou had very extensive economic ties as well. In addition, I was told, Guangzhou was gradually becoming of greater importance.

The governor—and other officials as well—discussed with me their views about the evolving mechanisms for regional cooperation in the northwest. I had learned a little about them when I was in Ningxia, but I learned more during my visit in Gansu. Some of the examples of cooperation I was told about were primarily ad hoc. A good example was the meeting, which I mentioned earlier, involving Governor Jia and the governors of Ningxia and Qinghai, in which they tried, early in 1988, to lobby top planners in Beijing to give the three provinces greater authority to decide how and where to sell their raw materials. It seemed to me that top leaders in Gansu saw substantial potential benefits from further developing this type of collaboration (more so, I felt, than did the officials I met in Ningxia).

Some of the forms of cooperation that had been developing were institutionalized in varying degrees. All five of the provinces categorized as members of the northwestern region (Gansu, Shaanxi, Qinghai, Ningxia, and Xinjiang) had established, under their provincial governments, "Economic and Technical Cooperation Committees." In Lanzhou, the staff of this committee totaled between 20 and 30 people, I was told. Comparable committees had been established in each of the other provincial or regional capitals. Academy experts in Lanzhou said to me that the main function of these committees was simply to establish liaison and that their ties were fairly loose. However, they did provide a mechanism for discussion of some of the important common interests among the five northwestern provinces and regions, including their basic problems of poverty, their heavy dependence on raw material output and sales, and their fiscal dependence on the central government for subsidies. In Gansu, I sensed a growing recognition of the need for increased collaboration to coordinate efforts to deal with such problems.

Each province in the northwest also had, I was told, an Economic Cooperation Office (in Lanzhou, it was identical to the Economic and Technical Cooperation Committee and was located in the same office). The main function of these offices, as described to me, was to do everything possible to expand horizontal ties with other parts of China.

The Academy specialists felt, however, that by far the most important mechanism for coordination in the region—albeit a fairly informal and loose one—was the annual meetings held among the five chairmen and governors in the region together with key people on their staffs including deputy governors and heads of important departments. I was told that these meetings had resulted in a number of useful agreements on economic and technical cooperation. One Academy scholar asserted to me that "of the several regional coordination groups in China, this one in the northwest is considered to be the most successful one." They told about some of the subjects that they had discussed. One important recent topic had been the possible implications for development in northwest China of the completion—scheduled to take place soon—of the rail line connecting China with the USSR via Xinjiang.

Governor Jia also mentioned to me a Yellow River coordinating body, directly under the State Council; its headquarters, he said, was in Zhengzhou (in Henan). A comparable body had existed even before 1949. Its primary function was to determine allocations of water from the Yellow River. Jia thought that it would be very desirable for this body to acquire broader developmental functions, comparable to those enjoyed by the special units dealing with the Yangzi River. Jia also stated that, under the State Council, there was a body (which I had never heard about) called the Three Fronts Office (*sanxian bangongshi*). He said that one of its responsibilities concerned the "readjustment"—and, if necessary, relocation—of factories in the northwest that had been built in unsuitable locations during the 1960s (often because of a lack of adequate feasibility studies). He went on to indicate, however, that in his opinion the actual importance of the office had been limited and that it did not itself make specific operational decisions. (I wanted to follow up and ask about this office when I was in Beijing but never had the opportunity to do so.)

Even though those with whom I talked obviously felt that it was desirable to expand cooperation among northwestern areas and believed that there was a real possibility of doing so, no one I met favored the creation of any really strong regional mechanism. Although they recognized that they had some important common problems and interests, they were acutely aware of the fact that the regions and provinces in the northwest were also very much in competition with each other—in competition for investments from Beijing, for support from coastal provinces, and for investment, trade, and assistance from abroad. Lanzhou obviously regarded Xi'an as its major competitor in many respects—and felt that one objective of Gansu should be to overtake and surpass Shaanxi in economic terms. There were also, in addition to shared interests, some obvious sources of tension and disagreement among these areas in the northwest. One, for example, was the resentment felt by Gansu (and also, I was told, by Shaanxi) about the fact that they received subsidies that were less generous than those of other areas in the northwest because they did not have minority groups in their population that were as large or as significant.

It was apparent to me that, in a basic sense, Gansu's leaders felt that their primary economic orientation was, and would have to be, mainly toward Beijing—much more than toward its immediate neighbors—but that they were very ambivalent about their relationships with China's capital. On the one hand, as I noted earlier, they desired and hoped for as much financial support from "the center" as possible. On the other hand, they wanted to maximize their local authority and achieve as much flexibility as possible. In viewing their interests, moreover, the majority of those I met seemed to look to the coastal areas as being more important to their economic development than adjacent competitive provinces. As one scholar put it to me: "Clearly, our natural economic relations are with China's developed coastal areas."

No one I met favored the reestablishment of powerful regional bodies in the northwest comparable to the regional Party and government organs that had existed in the early 1950s. No one wished to see reestablished the regional Party bureau that functioned in the early 1960s, or the dominant Military Region authority that emerged to dominate the whole region during the Cultural Revolution. "Not only are such bodies not necessary," one leading local journalist said to me, "they would, by overcentralizing authority, be a major obstacle to economic development."

*   *   *

I thought that most of the people I met in Gansu—both officials and non-officials—were quite realistic, in 1988, when they tried, at my request, to add up their accomplishments and their problems. There was widespread, legitimate pride in many accomplishments, but there was also obvious worry and concern about formidable long-term problems. On the plus side, what they tended to emphasize was the fact that in four decades the province had built, from scratch, a major industrial base. It had tried to attack and alleviate the worst problems of rural poverty, it had significantly raised living standards (especially in the 1980s and most of all in urban areas), and it had at least begun the process of economic reform. However, on the negative side, virtually everyone was frank in recognizing that the province still faced some of the worst problems of poverty—particularly rural poverty—of any part of China. Its industrial structure was very unbalanced, with far too much heavy industry and too little light industry; it was too dependent on external financial support; it had barely begun to expand its foreign economic relations; its reform efforts were lagging behind those in eastern provinces; and in general its economy was still extremely inefficient.

Despite all the problems, I found these people's view of the future basically optimistic because of the large resources that had been discovered within the province. However, I also heard a number of officials and scholars discuss, with great frankness, many extremely serious and difficult problems that will pose great obstacles to development in the future: the shortages of skilled technical personnel in the civilian economy, the weaknesses of the basic system of education, and some disturbing recent demographic trends.

In regard to technical and research personnel, I was told that by 1988 Gansu had a substantial pool of well-qualified specialists—36,000 was one figure that they used—but everyone said that this was far fewer than the province needed (and was far fewer than those in advanced provinces).

Moreover, on several occasions people discussed the problem that I mentioned earlier, namely that not enough of the skilled people in the provinces were working on basic economic development since so many of them were involved in military organizations and military research institutes.

The demographic situation in Gansu, as it was described to me, presented a mixed picture. According to official statistics, Academy scholars said, the local rate of natural population growth had dropped significantly in the 1960s, to a figure just over 1 percent a year—which is an impressively low rate for an area with a primarily rural population characterized by great poverty. Moreover, local experts told me that they estimated that the increase in the province's "working-age population" should be slower in the 1990s than it was in the 1980s. However, Academy scholars expressed very serious concern about what the real population trends in the period ahead might be. One research study carried out by the Academy, which was based on survey data, raised a lot of serious questions about the validity of the official data. The survey data indicated not only that the past rates of increase may have been somewhat higher than the official statistics indicated but also that during the reform years of the 1980s the trend actually had been upward again, in considerable part because of the effects of the reform. According to the data collected during this study, the annual rate of overall population increase in Gansu was 1.2 percent in 1978 but then rose to 1.41 percent in 1984 and 1.52 percent in 1986. The average family size for the entire province rose from 5.07 in 1982 to an estimated 5.4 in 1988. Moreover, the 1988 figure, which melded statistics on both rural and urban areas, understated the degree to which the rate had increased in rural areas. In some rural areas, the family size had risen to 5.9. (In contrast, figures for China as a whole indicated that the average family size had dropped to 4.7 in 1987— and was considerably lower than that in major cities.)

The explanation for such trends in Gansu, the principal author of the study said to me, were several. Studies showed that after the implementation of rural reforms, peasants generally felt that they needed more labor to cultivate their family farms (this was true in many other areas of China as well). In Gansu, also, government controls over population growth had been significantly loosened during the reform period. Moreover, those who conducted the study concluded that the low level of rural incomes in Gansu tended to reinforce old "feudal ideas," including the strong desire for sons. I was not surprised to hear that trends of this kind were disturbing to leaders in the province: If the upward trend in population growth could not be contained and reversed, it would eat away much of the benefit of future economic growth. It seemed likely, therefore, that the government would before long try to tighten up its control of population.

*   *   *

In the field of education, the picture I obtained in Gansu was similar in some respects to what I had seen in the other northwestern provinces that I had already visited, but in certain respects it had advanced further. The progress made since 1949 had been impressive, quantitatively, but the shortcomings of the educational system were still very serious in relation to the province's need for future modernization and development. In the 1940s, not even basic primary education reached most of Gansu's population, and in the entire province there were only three institutions of higher education, I was told. In contrast, by the mid-1980s the system had expanded enormously. By 1986, a total of 2.66 million students attended primary schools, and 1.09 million were enrolled in regular middle schools. Impressive as these statistical measures were, however, the educational officials I met were the first to emphasize that the quality of education was far lower than it should be—and, as in so many fields, they tended to compare their situation with that in coastal provinces, and they frankly acknowledged that Gansu lagged far behind those areas.

By the late 1980s, Lanzhou had developed several quite good university-level institutions. None of these were really in the very top ranks of universities in China, but several of them were clearly respectable institutions. Among the province's 17 "institutions of higher education," which among them enrolled more than 30,000 students, the leading one was Lanzhou University (a so-called comprehensive university—one with special strengths in several scientific fields). It had grown out of a small college established early in the second decade of the twentieth century, I was told. As of 1988, it had more than 5,000 students and a faculty totaling more than 2,000. It granted Ph.D.s in several fields. The Northwest Minorities Institute, another leading institution of higher learning in the province, had developed into one of the country's most important universities for minority students—perhaps the most important one outside of Beijing. A third institution of major importance to the educational system in the province was the Northwest Normal Institute, which was the main teacher training college in the province. The origins of this college could be traced, I was told, to World War II, when faculty members from several Beijing institutions of higher learning moved to northwest China after the Japanese had taken over north China. In 1988, this normal university had about 5,000 students (including a handful of Ph.D. candidates) and over 1,000 faculty members. Most of its graduates were assigned to teach in middle schools throughout Gansu Province.

I had one interesting conversation with several faculty members and graduate students from the Northwest Normal Institute, and they discussed with notable frankness what they considered to be the most important trends and problems affecting their institution. Reorganized in the 1950s, on the model of comparable Soviet institutions, the school was attempting to change again in the 1980s and to introduce more "flexible" and "realistic" programs based mainly on Western (especially American) experience. It had carried out 10 faculty exchanges with Western countries, including 2 with the United States—with the University of Connecticut and Towson State. They told me that within the institute the role of the Communist Party had been significantly reduced and that the president's authority had been greatly strengthened. Political courses had been reduced as well, to about 15 percent of the curriculum (measured by the allocation of students' time). About 50 percent of the faculty still belonged to the Party, but only about 8 percent of all students were Party members, I was told. However, a sizable number of others were members of the Young Communist League.

During the 1950s, faculty members for the Northwest Normal Institute had been recruited from all parts of China, but thereafter most of them were graduates of Gansu institutions. The faculty members enjoyed preferential salary levels and very favorable promotion policies, they said, which were deliberately designed to attract scholars from elsewhere—as well as to keep at the university ones who had earlier come from other provinces. But because of Gansu's remoteness, it was difficult, they acknowledged, to attract good outsiders. Moreover, their graduates were often reluctant to accept assignments to schools in poor, remote Gansu counties. Some faculty members were critical of the curriculum, saying that it gave inadequate preparation for real-life teaching, and they told about efforts that were being made to adjust the curriculum so that it would be more relevant to the real needs of those assigned to teach in poor, rural middle schools.

Although the number of students in Gansu's institutions of higher learning was still relatively small, in higher education it really was not very far behind the majority of other provinces; in fact, it probably was ahead of some. But at the bottom of its educational system, basic-level education was lagging badly. Even though the figures that I cited earlier for 1986—2.66 million students in primary schools and 1.09 million in middle schools—symbolized great change from the past, when analyzed carefully the figures proved to be less impressive than they seemed on the surface. I was told that only about 80 percent of children of primary school age in the province started school and that of those who started, only about 40 percent reached the fifth grade and only 20 percent went on to middle schools. Of the 1.09 million students in middle schools, only about a fifth were enrolled in senior middle schools. Provincial educational officers estimated that only two-thirds of primary school teachers met even the relatively low, minimum standards for qualification of such teachers, and official government estimates of adult literacy in the province put the figure at only slightly above 50 percent (compared with a national estimate of about 75 percent or more).

Those with whom I discussed these problems stressed—and I thought that they were doubtless right—that the fundamental reason for such backwardness in basic education was the prevalent poverty in the province's rural areas. All indices of educational achievement in Gansu's rural areas were very low and this pulled down the overall provincial averages. Provincial leaders were acutely aware of these facts and seemed genuinely committed to improving the situation. But even though many felt that with greater efforts the improvement of basic education could be accelerated (more rapidly, perhaps, than general economic improvement), nevertheless everyone acknowledged that the economic backwardness of rural Gansu would probably hold back, for a long time, the development of its educational system.

*   *   *

The only research organization with which I had substantial contact in Gansu was the local Academy of Social Sciences. It had been established, formally, as a separate institution in 1978. As I noted earlier, my first impression of the Academy was not particularly favorable because of the poor way, it seemed to me, my visit had been organized before my arrival. However, before I left, I had met and talked with a number of its leading scholars—most of them relatively young (for the most part in their forties and early fifties)—and I changed my mind. I concluded that the Gansu Academy had a very competent staff engaged in some research projects of real significance. With 128 employees—92 of them professionals—belonging to six research institutes (for economics, agricultural economics, society and law, philosophy, history, and literature), it was focusing its research mainly on local history and society, which seemed sensible to me, but it was also conducting five "national projects" (many of which also dealt with Gansu's problems).

Among the projects that they described to me were ones on economic development in the entire northwest China region, political reform at the county level in the province, political reform in one particular prefecture (Wuwei), rural social development in the poorest areas, the history of the Shaan-Gan-Ning area during World War II, the development of township industries in Gansu, ancient literature found at Dunhuang, and population and family trends in Gansu. Some of these studies had been undertaken in response to requests by provincial Party and government leaders, and Academy scholars believed that the results were given serious attention by many provincial leaders, including the provincial Party secretary and governor. The Academy also published two journals: *Social Sciences* and *Research and Development*. Its international exchanges were limited, but were beginning to develop, and several of its scholars had established useful contact with scholars abroad.

In my conversations with Academy scholars, they discussed a number of their studies and their long-run implications. I also was interested in getting their views on pressing immediate problems. I asked them their views about inflation. They said that by 1987 the inflation rate in Gansu had risen above 10 percent in the cities (actually it might have been somewhat higher than that) and that ordinary people had become alarmed because food prices were rising even more than the rise in the general price level. Some of the scholars were critical of the government for not having adopted a more effective antiinflationary policy. For example, they said, it would have been possible to have a more rational and effective policy to keep under control the cost of essential agriculture "inputs" such as fertilizer; they said that some attempts were made to do this, but they were not effectively implemented. They also decried what they called the "pork price crisis," when pork prices had suddenly risen to a very high level even though, according to some surveys, the availability of pork was actually 98 percent of what it had previously been. They blamed the crisis on speculation and a growing "inflation psychology" in many urban areas. In short, they did not play down the problems and risks of inflation as much as some of the officials I met did. One scholar said: "Controlling inflation of daily necessities is *the most* important immediate problem facing the State Council."

The majority of young scholars I met in Lanzhou impressed me as being intellectually lively, articulate, and fairly outspoken in discussing most of the issues that I raised. This clearly reflected the liberalizing trends that predominated in China in 1988. "Intellectual freedom," one Academy scholar said to me with real conviction, "is much greater than in the past, and there are really no very serious restraints on our research at present. Moreover, if you focus on local and regional issues, you can do research on what you choose—although you must first complete the work assignments under the annual plan assigned to you, which generally take about one-half of one's working time. The ideological and political atmosphere in the Academy has changed greatly in recent years, partly because we researchers are relatively young." Others present agreed and described how the treatment of intellectuals had improved during the 1980s: Salaries, grades, and titles all had been adjusted upward.

I also found that the journalists I met in Lanzhou were quite well informed, articulate, and remarkably frank in discussing issues of all kinds. I had one long session with six journalists—five men and one woman—who, among them, were engaged in newspaper, radio, and TV work. We discussed an extremely wide range of topics, on most of which they had at their fingertips some relevant and significant data. They were very willing to give me, also, their personal opinions and to criticize existing conditions and policies. After obtaining their views on many economic and political issues, I asked them to brief me on the development of modern media in Gansu. In response, they gave me the following statistics. In 1988, Gansu had a total of 47 newspapers, both large and small (including ones published by major enterprises). Some of them were dailies, but many were issued less frequently. Their total circulation was estimated to be about 2 million, roughly 1 per 10 people in the province.* The main audience for most newspapers was in the cities. My impression was that radio broadcasting actually reached a larger and more dispersed and diverse audience, including most people in rural areas. There were 15 radio broadcasting stations in the province, I was told (5 medium-wave and 10 FM, the latter mainly operated by counties). Officials and journalists estimated that there were about 2 million radio receiving sets in the province (a figure that included some radios that also had cassette players). In addition, the province had 72 wired broadcast systems; in these systems, county personnel rebroadcast materials from other areas but also initiated some themselves, and programs were piped to speakers throughout the local area being served. I was told that the local estimate was that, altogether, the coverage of all radio stations (including the wired systems) reached more than half (52 percent) of the entire population.

Everyone agreed, though, that the most significant development during the 1980s had been the growth of television. TV coverage had, it was claimed, actually surpassed that of the radio (which I found to be extraordinary, if true). Gansu, I was told, had six TV broadcasting stations—one provincial station and five at the prefectural level—and officials estimated that by the end of 1986 more than 710,000 TV sets (roughly one for each five to six households, and a much higher percentage in cities) had been purchased within the province (and the figure had risen substantially since then). One official, who should have known, estimated that the geographical coverage of TV in Gansu now reached 60 percent of the population.

The figures cited earlier for the outreach of print journalism were not very impressive. Perhaps this was understandable in light of the area's demographics. It was obvious that the circulation of newspapers in poorer rural areas, where the level of literacy was low, tended to be small, and such areas covered much of the province. The figures on the outreach of modern electronic media—both radio and TV—were very impressive, however, in Gansu as in other places I visited in 1988. And in the case of these media, I thought it was especially remarkable in Gansu because so much of the province is rural and poor.

*   *   *

---

*Gansu's five leading newspapers, I was told, were the *Gansu Daily* (*Gansu Ribao*), which was said to have a circulation of about 260,000; the *Lanzhou Evening News* (*Lanzhou Wanbao*), with a circulation of 120,000; the widely read *Literature Newspaper* (*Wenshi Bao*), with a national circulation of about 400,000; the *Children's Paper* (*Shaonian Wenshi Bao*); and the *Peasants' Daily* (*Nongmin Bao*). Also published in Lanzhou was a kind of *Readers' Digest* (*Duzhe Wenzai*), with a very large national circulation.

I could sense, in Gansu as in other parts of China, that the communications revolution was reinforcing many other trends leading toward looser political controls, freer discussion of issues, and a shift away from ideology—and toward nonpolitical and pragmatic concerns. All of these trends contributed to an important change in the political atmosphere, even though so far relatively little structural change in the political system had taken place.

Of all the political trends that I observed, perhaps the one that struck me most forcefully, in Gansu as well as other provinces, was the degree to which there had been a sweeping change in the leadership at almost all levels. Clearly a major generational turnover—which involved a change in the type of leadership from relatively ideological men to relatively pragmatic men—had in fact already taken place in Gansu (as in so many other places I visited) between the mid-1980s and 1988. However, as I probed the situation in Gansu I gradually came to the conclusion that although at the provincial level the turnover had been far-reaching, at the local level there had been fewer changes in Gansu—so it seemed to me—than in some other areas that I visited.

Not surprisingly, the personnel changes had not been free of problems. I heard numerous complaints about the obstacles to reform posed by the "conservatives" who still held many positions in the bureaucracies. Nevertheless, my feeling was that at the higher levels of the government and Party in the province, the changes had been quite spectacular. But the new leaders at that level still had to confront subtle dragging of feet by people at lower levels. On more than one occasion, people I interviewed talked about the fact that reforms stalled and slowed in Gansu between 1982 and 1986 because of opposition by conservatives and bureaucrats. Thereafter, apparently, some of the impediments to reform weakened, and the process speeded up.

With almost everyone I met, I discussed questions relating to political structure, leadership, and the bureaucracies. By the time I left I had learned a good deal not only from the governor himself but from a wide range of provincial and municipal officials as well as from local journalists and academics. Some of the most detailed and interesting data I obtained about the bureaucracies came from an official from the Lanzhou Personnel Bureau.

Major leadership changes in Gansu really began, he said, in 1983–1984, at the urging of Beijing. In a fairly short period of time thereafter, a large number of "younger, better-educated, and more professional" (and also less ideological) cadres were installed at almost all levels. These changes were strongly applauded by everyone I encountered—even people who were critical of many other things. The local journalists I met were very enthusiastic about the personnel changes. They also were frank in stating their criticisms of the characteristics and attitude of leadership during the late Maoist period. The following comments were typical: "The cadres had too much power; power was too centralized." "The tendency of most leaders—especially Mao—was wrong; although one must recognize that Mao played an important historical role, it would be wrong now to swing from one extreme to the other." "Old leaders tended to be simple revolutionaries, lacking education, and unprepared to deal with new problems." "Even after major personnel changes, the persistence of 'conservative' [that is ideological-dictated] attitudes continued to be a problem, slowing reforms. Many thought of socialism just in terms of large state enterprises, and they opposed collective industry, labeling it capitalist, and they were against the opening to the outside world. Some also opposed the separation of Party from government and enterprises. Gradually, however, they were influenced by the rapid changes in the coastal provinces, where reform resulted in faster development."

In Gansu, the big push to appoint new, younger leaders (mainly technocrats) to high positions began, I was told, in 1983 when "organizational reform" (*jigou gaige*) got under way at the provincial and municipal levels. It continued in 1984 and was extended to lower levels. At the start, the provincial Party Committee established a "guiding small group" (*zhidao xiaozu*), which, after intensive investigations and surveys, recommended specific leaders; their choices then obtained pro forma approval by the Provincial People's Congress. In Lanzhou, the Party Committee went through the same process. In late 1983 the top leadership bodies selected new leaders for the municipality, its five districts, and its three counties. In 1984, the process was extended to the township level. In each case, the initial focus was on selecting the heads and deputy heads of organizations—not only the top government bodies but also the subordinate departments, bureaus, and so on. Changes at lower levels came later. The process of selecting new leaders at all levels was still going on in 1988.

As I mentioned earlier, in my long meeting with the governor and his top lieutenants I asked them to tell me about their own personal histories. After all of them had done so, the governor told me, with a good deal of satisfaction, about other changes taking place in the provincial leadership. On the day in which we met, he said, there had been a meeting of the provincial People's Congress at which a new slate of 42 top provincial leaders had been approved. Analyzing the new structure of the leadership of the province, Governor Jia said that the top leadership group consisted of 49 people: the governor, 5 deputy governors, the secretary-general, and 42 others. Of the 42 who had been approved that morning, every one of them was in his fifties or younger, Jia said. Most of the new appointees replaced leaders who had been considerably older.

Any sweeping generational change of this sort inevitably involves problems and risks, but the Chinese leadership (inspired by suggestions made by Deng Xiaoping) followed remarkably shrewd—and sensible—policies in the 1980s to minimize the opposition from the old leaders being retired. In

Gansu, I was told, many of the retired leaders (some people said "most" of them) were shifted to various kinds of positions that were less active or powerful, but still had considerable prestige, in the People's Congress, the People's Political Consultative Conference, the Party Advisory Commission, and various other research, consultative, and advisory organs. Moreover, following national policy, the government made a special effort to ensure that retirement salaries and other perks were attractive. A variety of special governmental and other institutions were established to assist retired cadres.

As a result of national reform policies, I was told, in Gansu the power of the provincial government leadership did increase, gradually, in relation to the Party's power. Nevertheless, from all I learned there was no question that the greatest power still rested in the Party apparatus and the military establishment rather than in the government. I was not able to obtain much detailed data on personnel changes in the Party and military hierarchies, but I was told that a comparable shift to younger and more professional leaders had taken place within them as well as within the government.

*   *   *

I tried to learn, as I did in every place I visited, what the relationships were between and among the leaders of the government, Party, and military, and I obtained some fragmentary data that illuminated this in some respects. In Gansu, as elsewhere, I was strongly impressed by how much—according to what everyone told me—the military operated as a separate "system." The Lanzhou Military Region was the PLA's headquarters for all of northwest China. It was described by civilian leaders as being "*wholly* under the central Beijing authorities." The governor himself stressed to me the importance of the separation, in day-to-day operations, of the government and the military establishment. Several other civilian leaders also emphasized that all regular military forces, such as army groups (*jituan jun*), were under direct central command. I was also told that the leaders of the Military Region had relatively few formal relationships or links with the local Party and government structures. However, from what I learned it also seemed quite clear that the military did have a substantial political influence, locally. Moreover, it would be surprising if any Chinese leaders have forgotten the times when the military forces took direct control, when it was necessary, to ensure order during crisis situations—such as the Cultural Revolution. In Gansu the military, "at that time controlled everything in Gansu, including both the Party and the government." However, I was told that in 1988 the commander of the Military Region was not a member of—or very directly involved in—most of the work of the provincial Party Committee. (I found that to be surprising and intended to double-check what I was told, but I was unable to do so.)

The Gansu Military District, also headquartered in Lanzhou, operated under the "dual leadership" of both the Military Region and the civilian provincial authorities. The provincial government's Arms Services Department (*wuzhuang bu*) was one of the key bodies providing linkage and liaison. However, it appeared to me that the Military District also operated in a way that was separate in most respects from the civilian authorities. Nonetheless, everyone stressed that "liaison was close." The District's commander was a member of the provincial Party Committee, and the provincial Party secretary was political commissar of the Military District. The governor himself did not, he said to me, have any direct organizational link to the military, but it was obvious that he had very effective informal links, through the Party. The governor was one of the deputy secretaries of the Party Committee. The governor noted, in talking with me, that in many provinces the executive deputy governor (the *changwu* deputy governor) also belonged to the Party Committee, but this was not the case in Gansu in 1988. There were some special bodies in Gansu that dealt with certain aspects of the civilian-military relationship at the governmental level. For example, under the provincial government there was an Office of National Defense Industry, responsible for supervising those local defense plants that had already shifted to civilian production.*

The government provided necessary resources to the military, but this, I was told, did not require any special liaison mechanisms since it was based on long-established procedures and practices, generally adjusted annually through ad hoc consultation. The other side of the coin was that the military provided emergency and other help to the government when needed, especially in times of natural disasters. I received the impression that in such situations all relevant organizations cooperated closely on an ad hoc basis; people said that there was no need for a well-structured permanent liaison organization for this purpose. Most of those I met stressed the separation between the military establishment and the government more than they did the cooperative relationships between them.

*   *   *

---

*Academy scholars, in talking with me, differentiated between enterprises exemplifying four different types of military-civilian industrial relationships: (1) military plants producing military products for the PLA, (2) former military plants that had been shifted to the control of civilian government institutions—including "most" electronics plants, (3) factories producing both military and civilian products (the civilian output of which was the responsibility of the Office of National Defense Industry), and (4) cooperative arrangements between military and civilian factories. Academy scholars stated that in Gansu the most significant shifts of production from military to civilian products had occurred "mainly" (one scholar said "only") in military factories that had "excess" capacity.

Although relations between the military establishment and civilian organizations—both the Party and the government—did not appear to be extremely close or intimate—at least in regard to day-to-day matters—this was not the case with the relationships between the Party and the government. However, during the 1980s period of reform, some changes were beginning to take place in these relationships as well. Traditionally, especially in many periods during the Maoist era, the Party totally dominated the government and, in fact, intervened in almost all governmental matters. At times, the overlap of governmental and Party positions was so great that it was difficult to distinguish between the two hierarchies. This obviously had begun to change, however, and, following the 13th Party Congress in 1987, all local areas were instructed to implement the new policy of "separating" Party and government and enterprises to give the latter greater authority. The Party was instructed to pull back from its day-to-day intervention into government affairs—particularly economic affairs.

I was naturally interested in learning as much as I could about how this new policy had been implemented and the extent to which it had changed the situation in Gansu Province. I was told that this was the "direction" (*fang xiang*) of policy, but when I probed deeper it seemed that relatively little had yet been done to carry out the policy in concrete terms. Plans had been drawn up to abolish, at all levels within the provincial Party apparatus, three important economic departments: (1) Industrial and Transportation Work Department (*gongye jiaotong gongzuobu*), (2) Finance and Trade Work Department (*tsaizheng maoyi gongzuobu*), and (3) Rural Work Department (*nongcun gongzuobu*)—but no clear timetable had been set for carrying this out. No specific plans at all had been drawn up to abolish the Political and Legal Committee (*zhengfa weiyuanhui*), which was responsible for public security, the courts, and so on. In Gansu, Party committees at all levels except at the very bottom thus still had six major subunits: a General Office (*bangongshi*); three key departments dealing with traditional Party organizational and ideological work, namely, the Organization Department (*zuzhibu*), the United Front Department (*tongzhanbu*), and the Propaganda Department (*xuanchuanbu*); a Policy Research Office (*zhengce yanjiushi*); and an ad hoc Bureau for Old Cadres Work (*laoganbu gongzuoju*). The lack of specific plans and timetables to carry out some of the internal political reforms within the Party, which were being urged by the principal advisers to Zhao Ziyang, seemed to me to suggest that at the local level in Gansu these reforms were encountering opposition—or at least foot dragging.

Another important change called for by reform leaders in Beijing, after the 13th Party Congress, was the abolition of the Party's so-called "fractions," or "core groups" (*dangzu*). These were small groups of Party leaders, directly appointed by higher Party authorities (rather than being chosen by local Party members and committees), that existed at high levels in virtually all government organizations and other non-Party groups under the control of the Party. Party fractions had long been one of the primary mechanisms for highly centralized control within the Party, and they had enabled the top Party leaders to exercise very tight discipline not only over government units but also over mass organizations and so on. Party reformers in Beijing who were in favor of a process of decentralization and democratization within the Party insisted, therefore, that these core groups be abolished. When I asked leaders in Gansu whether they had abolished them, their answer was, "no, not yet." Moreover, they said that their intention, at least initially, was to abolish only the core groups in economic agencies of the government. In these agencies, also, their plan was not simply to abolish the old units but to replace them with "Party Work Committees" (*dangde gongzuo weiyuanwei*). Although they said that these committees would be smaller and less powerful than the old units, it sounded to me that they would probably serve some of the same functions.

All of this made it fairly clear that not much basic "structural" political reform had yet taken place even within the Party in Gansu Province. However, my strong feeling was that all of the changes that were taking place in the province would create mounting pressures for further political reform, which I believed would almost inevitably increase over time—not only as a result of the pressures exerted by economic development, social changes, and the communications revolution, but also because of the sweeping generational change in the leadership that had already taken place and was continuing.

After interviewing officials at the provincial level, I turned my attention to trends affecting the municipal Party and government and lower levels. The data given to me on leadership of Lanzhou Municipality presented a picture similar (though not entirely identical) to that of the provincial level. There had been sweeping changes in the leadership—almost a clean sweep—of Lanzhou's Party and government, starting in 1983 and continuing in subsequent years. By 1988, I was told, there was only one individual still in office who had been serving in a top position before 1983. The average age of the new municipal leaders had dropped to about 49. The Lanzhou Party secretary was an engineer from northeast China, with a background similar to that of the technocrats who had taken over at the provincial level. Of his five deputy secretaries, two of whom were local people and three of whom had come from other parts of China, the level of education had risen, but not as much as among leaders at the provincial level. Four of the deputy Party secretaries had education at the level of at least specialized, postsecondary schools (*da zhuan,* a level above regular middle schools but below universities). And the careers of four of the five had been in economic work—two in industry, two in agriculture. Trends in the municipal government had been similar. The mayor, like the top municipal Party secretary, was an engineer from the northeast, and two of his four deputy mayors—both of them engineers, and one of them a woman—had come from provinces other than

Gansu. Their careers, too, had been in industry. (Of the 11 people identified to me as the top municipal Party and government leaders in Lanzhou, only 1 was a Hui Muslim; the others were all Han Chinese.)

I did not have time to gather detailed data on leadership changes at lower levels, under the municipal government, but the officials I interviewed told me that the changes there also had been sweeping and that "most" heads and deputy heads of commissions, bureaus, and offices, as well as top county, district, and township leaders, had been replaced by new people. The majority of new appointees were said to be better educated and to possess specialized technical or economic skills of some sort. Virtually all of them were younger than the people they replaced. For example, the average age of top county leaders, in the counties under the municipality, was now between 30 and 40—much lower than it had been previously.

*   *   *

As I continued to probe, however—particularly in my long interview with officials from the Personnel Bureau of Lanzhou—I concluded that although changes at leadership levels had been sweeping, the turnover of rank-and-file bureaucrats had been less far-reaching and the structure of the bureaucracies at lower levels had changed relatively little. Moreover, although a few reforms in the personnel system had been implemented, they mainly affected personnel in enterprises, rather than Party and government bureaucrats, and the fundamental personnel system had apparently not yet been significantly altered.

One objective of reform in China in the 1980s was what was called a "streamlining" of the bureaucracy—that is, organizational rationalization and a reduction in the number and size of bureaucratic units to increase their efficiency. My strong impression was that in Gansu the effects of this had been minimal. As of 1988, the table of organization of the Lanzhou Municipal Government included 47 offices, commissions, bureaus, and other regular units. Although the officials of the Personnel Bureau who briefed me did not have with them a printed copy of a table of organization, when they learned of my interest in bureaucracies they insisted on describing each of the bodies in the table of organization.*

———

*The listing that they gave me was similar to, but not identical with, that which I received in other places. Like the data I obtained elsewhere, it highlighted the fact that local governments had bodies to manage and deal with virtually every conceivable economic and social activity. Although my trip notes contain details on all of the 47 major governmental units that my informants discussed with me, I will not list them here but will note some of the main points local officials stressed in their discussions with me. However, I believe that neither this list nor those I received elsewhere were really complete. An official Chinese government publication in 1989 listed a total of 76 commissions (committees), offices, departments, and bureaus that *provincial*

The officials from the Municipal Personnel Bureau asserted that although central government regulations stipulated that provincial and municipal governments should generally have between 30 and 40 bureaucratic units, they were given some authority to adjust this number. A large city with a population of over a million, they told me, could have more than 40 if the central government authorized it, and in practice different provinces and municipalities varied somewhat. To obtain authorization for adjustments in local organization and personnel, local leaders had to deal with the Ministry of Labor and Personnel in Beijing. In the Lanzhou government, the Personnel Bureau had a special office to monitor compliance with the center's authorizations regarding local organizational structures and personnel strengths. (The name of this unit was Bianzhi Bangongshi, which I decided to translate loosely as the "Table of Organization Office," or, for short, "T.O. Office.") They emphasized to me, as officials elsewhere had, that local governments had to be capable of dealing with almost all of the diverse tasks that the central government dealt with, although the actual scope of responsibilities in particular fields varied greatly by area and therefore tables of organization could be and were adapted for local situations. The officials pointed out several instances in which Lanzhou had more than one body to deal with a particular field that in smaller cities would have only a single organization responsible for it.

The number of cadres working in the 47 aforementioned bodies in the Lanzhou Municipal Government in 1988 was 5,970, I was told. My briefers did not have with them statistics on how many of these were members of the Party; they explained that the management of Party members was the responsibility of the Party Organization Department, not the government's Personnel Bureau. However, they guessed that between 40 and 50 percent of all of these cadres working in the government were members of the Party.*

The number of "state cadres," whom the Personnel Bureau was at least theoretically responsible for managing, was much higher. The total, I was

---

governments can have; although obviously not all provincial governments include all of them. I suspect that the governments of provinces I visited may have had some units that were not on the lists provided to me. Municipal governments (such as that in Lanzhou, which I discuss here) are obviously not identical to those at the provincial level, but in large municipalities they are similar. See *The Provincial Bureaucracy: Functions and Structure*, in Joint Publication Research Service Report, "China," JPRS-CAR-91-062, November 7, 1991.

*Later I was given a figure for the number of cadres employed by the Gansu Provincial Party Committee. The total, my informants said, was 443, and they worked for the Party Committee's 10 major units: General Office, Organization Department, United Front Department, Propaganda Department, Industrial and Transportation Work Department, Finance and Trade Work Department, Rural Work Department, Political and Legal Committee, Bureau for Old Cadres Work, and Policy Research Office. I did not receive any comparable figure for the Lanzhou Party Committee, but I assume that it was smaller.

told, was 54,000. This figure, the Personnel Bureau officials said, included all cadres paid by the government and belonging to the regular cadre system in Lanzhou Municipality, including its subordinate districts and counties. (The number included some cadres working for industrial enterprises—although, as a result of recent reforms, enterprises had assumed direct responsibility for a large number of their cadres. The figures did not include ordinary factory workers.)

This was the theory. However, I learned that—as is often the case in China—the longer you discuss a question, the more complications you learn about, and theory and practice often diverge. In practice, I was told, the Organization Department of the Party Committee continued to be responsible for selecting the top bureaucrats—that is, heads and deputy heads of units—in virtually all government as well as Party organizations and it also still selected some leading cadres in major industrial and other enterprises. However, its responsibilities had been reduced; before 1982, I was told, this Party organization—with the cooperation of the Personnel Department—had selected *all* state cadres. The most important recent change had been the transfer of power to make many appointments in enterprises to factory managers.

Even though one objective of recent reforms had been to strengthen the government vis-à-vis the Party, from what I learned it was evident that although this had happened to some extent, in many respects the Party was still clearly dominant in the field of personnel decisions. It did not, however, have the total monopoly that it once had. Another objective of reform was to grant greater autonomy to enterprises and cut back the intervention of Party and government into management; it appeared to me that significant progress had been made in that direction.

*   *   *

Elaborating on their generalizations about the personnel system, the official talking to me then proceeded to provide further details on how the cadre system in Lanzhou worked as of 1988. The more I learned, the more complex it appeared. Of the 54,000 state cadres in the municipality, the Party Organization Department really chose only about 1,700 of them—the highest-ranking cadres (of "county level" and above) in the Party, government, and other units. (Of the 1,700, roughly 200 were enterprise managers holding this rank.) The government's Personnel Bureau now was responsible for choosing the majority of state cadres of lower ranks. This division of responsibilities applied to appointments down to and including the counties and townships. The Personnel Bureau also handled many practical matters affecting even the higher-ranking cadres selected by the Party Organization Department. The Organization Department managed the career dossiers of all the high-level cadres it selected; however, the Personnel Bureau supervised the dossier system for lower-ranking cadres. But they did not, my briefers said, really keep physical control over most of them; generally the dossiers were kept by the units in which cadres worked.

Enterprise managers, I was told, with expanded rights to appoint cadres, now appointed about 17,000 cadres working in economic enterprises. Plans had been drafted, also, to give managers the power to chose *all* their own personnel. In practice, however, only managers in factories that had already adopted the manager contract responsibility system were authorized to choose their own deputies and staffs (and even they usually would consult with the government industrial bureaus with which they were associated before making important appointments).

Policies and procedures for recruiting new cadres had not, so far, changed very much. Personnel Bureau officials discussed with me four different sources of cadres: (1) graduates of universities, professional middle schools, and *da zhuan* schools (who were given assignments by the Personnel Bureau—except for those who were assigned to teaching and other educational jobs by the Educational Bureau); (2) demobilized soldiers (every year some left the army and were given cadre assignments by the Personnel Bureau); (3) individuals promoted within their own units or transferred from other units; and (4) cadres recruited by "open recruitment." The last category was an innovation: Under it, authorities advertised for certain jobs and selected from among the applicants. But as yet not many people were selected this way. In general, the number of new rank-and-file cadres selected every year was quite limited, I was told, because the bureaucracies were already overstaffed.

In earlier years, my briefers told me, all promotions had required approval by the Personnel Bureau but this was no longer true. Units could now promote some of their own employees, but in doing so they were supposed to follow guidelines defined in official regulations. Transfers from other cities were now possible; however, they had to be negotiated between the units involved. Moreover, to move to Lanzhou and obtain an official residence certificate (*hukou*), approval had to be obtained from the Lanzhou Personnel Bureau. Some open recruitment was now possible—not only by certain government units but by enterprises. I was told that this was still largely "experimental." Most of the experiments had been at the township level, but local governments were beginning to try to select more people in this fashion. In the 90 townships under the municipality, recently about 170 to 180 cadres had been selected through open recruitment. However, no cadres at the county level or higher had yet been recruited in this fashion.

In 1988, reformers in Beijing were discussing plans to introduce a formal civil service (*gongwuyuan*) system. Lanzhou's officials told me that they had read documents discussing this but that they had not even tried to draw up concrete plans about possible local implementation. "We want to wait until we receive instructions and regulations [from Beijing]," they said.

The old cadre ranking system had undergone some changes in the 1980s. Under the old system, 30 grades were generally used in Gansu, I was told. This system had been replaced in 1985 with one that reduced the number of ranks to 10. New rank titles were based on job titles.* The salary system for cadres seemed to me to be an accountant's nightmare. The monthly salary of an individual cadre was calculated, my briefers said, on the basis of four components: (1) a basic salary (*jiben gongzi*), which amounted to Y 40 a month for everyone; (2) a rank-based salary increment (*zhiwu gongzi*), which varied greatly, starting at Y 7 a month for the lowest-rank cadres and rising to well over Y 100 a month for high-ranking cadres (two specific examples were cited: Y 53 for a deputy division chief and Y 103 for a division chief); (3) seniority pay (*gongzuo nianling gongzi*), amounting to Y 0.5 a month for each year's service (for example, a cadre with 10 years' service obtained Y 5 a month in seniority pay); and (4) bonuses for good performance (*jiangli gongzi*), which in theory varied according to the efficiency of one's work. The first three components were fairly standard and automatic, with little reference to performance. It was the fourth that was designed to provide new incentives for superior work. However, local officials admitted that the idea of incentive pay based on efficiency went against the grain of the egalitarian impulses of most cadres and therefore encountered resistance. In reality, I was told, almost all cadres were paid an identical "bonus," amounting to Y 10 a month, and very few received any additional payments for good performance.

*   *   *

Reflecting on all that I was told about political—mainly bureaucratic—change and reform in Gansu, I concluded several things. One was that there had, in fact, been a sweeping and rather remarkable change in the top leadership, at almost all levels, in which older cadres had been replaced with younger and better-educated people. This generational change really had altered, it seemed to me, the characteristics of the leadership and had placed in power men (very few women were involved) who were definitely more pragmatic,

---

*Under the new system, my informants said, the grades for government cadres were (1) ordinary office worker (*banshiyuan*), (2) section member (*keyuan*), (3) deputy section chief (*fukezhang*), (4) section chief (*kezhang*), (5) deputy division chief (*fuchuzhang*), (6) division chief (*chuzhang*), (7) deputy department chief (*futingzhang*), (8) department chief (*tingzhang*), (9) deputy governor (*fushengzhang*), and (10) governor (*shengzhang*). These had become generic terms, and people with different titles at lower levels had equivalent status to particular titles among these 10. For example, I was told that the rank of a township head was equivalent to that of a provincial section head, the rank of a county magistrate was equivalent to that of a provincial division head, and the rank of a prefectural head was equivalent to that of a provincial department head.

as well as more technocratic, and far less ideological than most of their pre-decessors. However, I also concluded that there had been relatively little change in the staffing of rank-and-file cadre positions in most bureaucratic organizations and that the process of altering the basic personnel system had barely begun. The latter did not surprise me. Real reform of huge bureaucra-cies is an extraordinarily difficult task anywhere—and perhaps particularly in China because of its long bureaucratic traditions, which had survived from the imperial period through both the Republican and Communist periods. But I felt that the pressures for additional change would continue. As one official from the Personnel Bureau said to me, Lanzhou was in a "transitional period" and there were "many difficulties" and "contradictions between old and new." The system therefore had only been "partially re-formed." Later a different interlocutor said to me bluntly: "There has been no basic change in the personnel system in government." This was an exag-geration, but it was probably not very far off the mark: Systemic change was beginning but had not gone very far.

Although I spent a great deal of my time in Lanzhou interviewing officials, I was able to find time to see every part of the city as well as large areas of the suburbs and countryside. With a map in hand, I drove throughout all sec-tions of the city. I also was able to see the industrial area that stretches both east and west of Lanzhou—on my train visits from Ningxia and to Qinghai. Twice, also, I drove the long route between Lanzhou and its airport.* Earlier I described the layout and appearance of the city. On the trips to and from Lanzhou's airport, I got a feel for the kind of arid, bleak territory that covers much of Gansu. The area was obviously very poor. There were quite a few sizable villages located between the bare hills and eroded loess canyons, however. Their houses were made mainly of mud brick. Fairly long distances separated the villages. I saw no machinery in the fields, and the plowing was

---

*After visiting Lanzhou in March 1988, I returned to Beijing, then spent a month in Sichuan Province, returned to Beijing again, then visited Xinjiang, after which I revisited Lanzhou in May. My second trip to Lanzhou involved a bit of excitement—which by this time I was begin-ning to expect on many Chinese trips. Leaving Urumchi by air at about 7:30 one evening, we flew over the magnificent Tian Shan peaks (including the memorable Bogda Ola). We were told that we would make one stop at Dunhuang (which we had not known) and arrive at the Lanzhou airport around midnight. However, our "short stop" at Dunhuang—scheduled to be 40 minutes—turned into two and a half hours. The reason, we were told, was that the pilots "could not get the electrical system working" on our turboprop plane—a statement that created considerable alarm among all of the passengers (which included a large number of Japanese tourists plus two Russian glaciologists as well as many Chinese officials). Eventually the pilots did get the propellers turning—how, I do not know—and we flew on, arriving at Lanzhou's air terminal (a small structure, not nearly as grand as the terminal in Urumqi) at 2:00 A.M. We then drove directly into the city—a route of about 50 miles. Although I saw little of that stretch on this nighttime trip, I had seen it on my previous flight out of Lanzhou.

being done with mules. It was apparent that the land was very difficult to farm. In the distant hills, there were numerous manmade caves; they were used, I was told, for shelter from violent rains that usually came in late summer. There were few signs of modernization in this area, even though it was so near to Lanzhou.

*   *   *

The place in Gansu that I most wished to visit was Linxia Prefecture; formerly called Hezhou, it is the most famous Hui Muslim area in northwest China. I had learned a little about it in 1948 because it was a native place of the warlord Mas who dominated the northwest. Then, in 1988 in Beijing, my curiosity was further stimulated by Professor Fei Xiaotong, one of China's leading sociologists, whom I had first met in Beijing in 1948. When I visited him again at Beijing University in 1988, he talked at some length to me about Linxia, which he had visited several times and regarded as one of the most interesting centers of local entrepreneurship that he knew. I therefore scheduled a trip to Linxia to learn what I could about Han-minority relations in the region and also to see for myself what Fei was talking about when he waxed so enthusiastic about local entrepreneurship in the region.

As I stated earlier, Gansu's population is now overwhelmingly Han Chinese, but parts of the province are important minority areas, and Hui Muslims are the dominant minority group in the province. Before my trip to Linxia, I obtained a briefing on the minorities in the provinces, and on current minority policies, from the head (a Hui Muslim) and the deputy head (a Han Chinese) of Gansu's Minority Affairs Commission and learned what I could from other knowledgeable people in Lanzhou—both Han and Hui. The commission head and his deputy were old-timers, but they impressed me as being both well informed and forthright, and I learned much from them. I also learned some from other knowledgeable people in Lanzhou—both Han and Hui. On some matters, my informants differed.

I received several different figures for the total minority population of Gansu as of 1987. Most of the figures were between 1.6 and 1.7 million.* Whatever the correct figure, the minority population accounted for less than 10 percent of the total provincial population—probably between 7 and 8 percent. Most minorities lived in designated minority areas, including 2 autonomous prefectures, 1 autonomous municipality, and 19 autonomous counties.

The provincial government kept statistics on 40 different groups classified as minorities. Hui Muslims were, as stated earlier, by far the largest and most

---

*The lowest figure given to me was 1.5 million. The highest was 1.8 million.

important group, totaling 980,000. It was estimated that about 80 percent of all Hui people in Gansu worked in agriculture, but the 20 percent said to engage in "business" played influential roles in a number of parts of the province. The largest single concentration of Hui Muslims was in Linxia Hui Autonomous Prefecture, located southwest of Lanzhou, but there were also sizable concentrations in several other places, including an autonomous Hui county (Zhangjiachuan) in Tianshui Prefecture to the south and in 11 minority townships in Pingliang Prefecture (most of whom lived in Pingliang County) in the southeast. Outside of these concentrations, it was estimated, roughly 320,000 Hui were scattered throughout the province (including the 20,000 or so in Lanzhou), and reportedly there were a few in virtually every county.

The second largest minority group in Gansu consisted of Tibetans, who totaled about 320,000. They were concentrated in the far southwest, beyond Linxia, in Gannan Tibetan Autonomous Prefecture. The spiritual center of this area was Labulong (Labrang) Monastery, which some Tibetans categorize, together with the principal monasteries in Tibet proper and Kumbum in Qinghai, as one of the main headquarters of Lamaism. (Labulong is only a few miles from Linxia; I very much wanted to visit it but simply did not have the time.) In addition, to the north of Lanzhou there was a Tibetan autonomous county at Tianzhu, in central Gansu, near the Inner Mongolian banners of Alashan and Ejin Horo, which formerly had belonged to Gansu. Most of Gansu's Tibetans raised yaks and other animals in a traditional fashion.

The third largest minority in Gansu was the Dongxiang (literally "east country" people). Like the Hui people, they were Muslims, but they spoke a different language (related to Mongol) and they were culturally distinct. The Dongxiang in Gansu totaled 240,000; this number accounted for almost nine-tenths of all Dongxiang in China. The majority of them in Gansu lived in or adjacent to Linxia.

Each of the other six "important" minorities, according to the Minority Affairs Commission, had 10,000 or fewer people in the province. Some of them, though, despite their small numbers, were the largest concentrations of those particular minorities in the country. The 10,000 Yugu (Yugur) people lived mainly in the Hexi corridor region, south of the Qilian mountains (especially in the Yugu Autonomous County), in the area of Shandan. They were said to account for 97 percent of all Yugu in China. The 8,500 or so members of the Baoan (Bonan) minority group were located in and near Linxia. They were said to account for 92 percent of all members of this minority group in China. Other "significant" minority groups in Gansu, according to members of the Minority Affairs Commission, included 10,200 Tu people (a Lama Buddhist group, linked with the Tibetans and Mongols, but with a distinctive language); more than 9,000 Manchus (originally from northeast China, but now almost totally Sinified); about 6,400 Mongols (mainly in the Subei Mongol Autonomous County in the far northwest, in Jiuchuan Prefecture); over 4,000 Sala (Salar), another group of Muslims, with a distinctive language related to that of the Uighur, who had come to Gansu from Qinghai (where the majority of Sala still lived); and about 2,400 Kazakhs, concentrated—like the Mongols—in Jiuchuan Prefecture in the far northwest, in an autonomous county (the Aksai Kazakh Autonomous County).

In view of the relatively small percentage of Gansu's total population made up by minority peoples, the degree of attention given to them struck me as being quite remarkable. I had no doubt that one basic reason was the fact that historically there had been such bitter conflicts between Han Chinese and minority groups (especially Hui Muslims and Tibetans). In Gansu, as in Inner Mongolia and Ningxia, local people, when discussing Han-minority relations, frankly acknowledged the seriousness of conflicts in the past but asserted—fairly convincingly, I thought—that relationships had improved substantially in the 1980s. Here, as in Ningxia, many people referred to the 1950s as "a golden era" and said that the situation deteriorated thereafter, reaching its nadir during the Cultural Revolution in the late 1960s and early 1970s, which everyone described as a period of total disaster. In Gansu as elsewhere, during the Cultural Revolution most mosques and lamaseries were attacked; many were destroyed, and most others were damaged. There was deep bitterness about the persecution that took place at that time. However, according to both Han and Hui people with whom I talked, relations between the two groups began to improve very substantially starting at the end of the 1970s as a result of the regime's new policies. The basic attitude of the government toward religious and minority groups changed at that time, they said, and from then on the government introduced a wide range of measures that granted minority peoples preferential treatment. The stated aim was to try to overcome the legacy of past discrimination and persecution and to raise the economic and educational levels of minority groups, which, everyone frankly acknowledged, still lagged seriously behind those of the Han majority.

*   *   *

Both Hui and Han cadres involved in minority affairs—and also local journalists and academics—described for me, in some detail, many of the "affirmative action" policies implemented in Gansu. The foundation of the new policies, they said, was a major change in official policy toward religion. My informants all maintained that the regime now not only tolerated but actually encouraged many religious practices and activities—for the first time in many years—and the government was giving financial support to rebuild and repair religious buildings. In addition, a major effort was being made to expand the role of minorities in government and to improve their economic and educational opportunities.

State regulations required that in any administrative area labeled "autonomous," the head of government plus the chairman of the local People's Congress and People's Political Consultative Conference should be minority cadres. My informants maintained that, in addition, although the deputy heads of these organizations were not required to be members of minority groups, in a great number of cases they were. They acknowledged, however, that at the top levels of local power, Han Chinese still dominated the Party. Only very rarely did members of minority groups rise to the very top within the Party apparatus. Generally, though, minority peoples had emerged into significant jobs in both government and Party at levels below the top. General local policy, I was told, called for ensuring that at least 30 percent of all government and Party cadres in autonomous areas be members of minority groups, and my briefers maintained that actual figures tended to be larger than this. In fact, they said, about 38 percent of all "leading cadres"—in government and Party—in the autonomous areas throughout the province were minority cadres. They stated, in passing, that minority cadres in these autonomous areas who achieved the rank of "section head" or higher were paid higher salaries than equivalent Han cadres. It seemed obvious to me that, compared with the past, the participation of minorities in government had expanded significantly. Nevertheless, the statistics indicated that they were still politically underrepresented. In autonomous minority areas, members of minority ethnic groups still accounted for less than a third of all cadres, whereas they accounted for over a half of local populations in such areas.

Although the officials I interviewed did not have easily available figures on the total number of cadres—and minority cadres—in the province, they were prepared to make an estimate of them. They estimated that there were about 400,000 cadres in the province and that of these about 40,000—or roughly 10 percent of the total—were minority cadres (and they estimated that about half of these were Hui). If correct, these estimates indicated that minority cadres were growing in number and now were represented proportionately to their share in the population. This was much less true at the provincial level. Discussing members of minorities at that level, the officials in the Minority Affairs Commission said that at the highest level of the Party there was one minority cadre (a Tibetan); he was a deputy Party secretary in the Provincial Party Committee. And at the highest level in the government, there was one minority cadre (a Hui Muslim) who had become a deputy governor. Both of these men belonged to the Party Standing Committee. In addition, about 20 minority cadres had risen to government positions with the rank of bureau or department chief (all but 5 of these were Hui).

Gansu officials expressed some resentment of the fact that neighboring autonomous regions, such as Xinjiang, received larger subsidies from the central government than Gansu did. Nevertheless, Beijing did give Gansu Province very substantial funds earmarked for minority peoples. Most of these subsidies were passed on to local governments in minority autonomous areas within the province. Between 1979 and 1986, I was told, subsidies given to minority autonomous areas within the province totaled about Y 700 million; most of these funds were designated for investment to develop water conservancy, animal husbandry, and other economic purposes or for projects relating to culture and education. It was estimated that roughly two-thirds of this total was channeled via the provincial government, whereas perhaps as much as one-third went directly to minority areas from the central government. In 1988, special subsidies to minority areas totaled roughly Y 80 million, they estimated.

My briefers discussed with me—and decried—the fact that the educational level of all minority groups, including the Hui, still lagged badly behind the Han population. They estimated that, compared to Han children, 14 percent fewer Hui children of school age actually started primary school. There were fewer schools—in proportion to population—in minority areas than in areas populated by Han people—largely because so many of them were in remote and poor areas. As of 1985, I was told, in all of the province's minority areas there were roughly 2,600 regular primary schools, with about 200,000 students, but at the middle school level there were only 118 regular middle schools, with approximately 70,000 students. Moreover, even in minority areas the majority of schools still taught in Hanyu (Chinese). To encourage minority students to attend school, the government reportedly exempted minority children at the primary level from all tuition and book fees (which for other students amounted to about Y 10 a semester). Although there was no such blanket exemption at the middle school level, I was told that subsidies were given to many poor students in middle schools—both Han and minority. The subsidies reportedly varied, but in some cases covered about half of the fees each semester. Even though most schools taught in Chinese (which was not surprising in view of the fact that not only the Han population but also the members of the largest minority, the Hui, were native speakers), in recent years some efforts had been made to develop schools that taught in the other minority languages.

As of 1988, I was told, there were close to 50 "minority people's schools" (*xiaoshu minzu xuexiao*) in the province that taught in minority languages—about 30 at the primary level and 17 at the middle school level. In these schools, subsidy policies were comparable to those in other schools. And, starting in 1981, a system of special boarding schools had been established in some minority pastureland areas (called *muju jishuzhi xuexiao*), which taught in both minority languages and Hanyu (with the former the basic language in primary schools and the latter the main language in middle schools). These schools borrowed texts from Tibet, Inner Mongolia, and

Xinjiang for use, respectively, in schools for Tibetans, Mongols, and Kazakhs in Gansu. I was told that by 1988 there were 84 such institutions in the province—75 primary schools and 9 middle schools. These were located in Gannan Prefecture, where they had started, and in four county-level autonomous areas (the Aksai Kazakh, Subei Mongol, Sunan Yugu, and Tianzhu Tibetan counties). In these schools, tuition and books were free, and students were given subsidies for food—Y 10 a month for primary students and Y 15 a month for middle school students.

For members of minority groups wishing to enter institutions of higher learning, the point average required to pass entrance examinations was lowered by 10 points to 20 points—10 points for the largest minority groups such as the Hui and 20 points for smaller groups such as the Dongxiang, Baoan, and Yugu. The Northwest Minority Institute—which was designed mainly to train minority cadres—had more than 2,000 students, who came from all over the northwest, and its graduates were assigned, after graduation, throughout the entire area. Two other special institutions of higher learning for minorities—both religious institutions—were developed in the 1980s, with government support. The Lanzhou College of Scripture (Jingxueyuan), established in 1984, taught the Koran and other Muslim scriptures in Arabic; it had more than 40 students. The College of Buddhist Studies (Foxueyuan), established in 1985 at Labulong Monastery in Xiahe County, had more than 60 students.

My ability to probe deeply into Han-minority relations in Lanzhou and Gansu was obviously limited. However, my strong impression was that the regime's conciliatory policies of the 1980s had, as claimed, definitely improved relations between ethnic groups, and these relations appeared in general to be calm and "normal," at least on the surface. I assumed that in this region—as in others in China where there have been conflicts between different ethnic groups in the past—there must be some continuing strains and tensions under the surface—not only because of past conflicts but also because the minority groups are still obviously poorer, less educated, and less politically powerful than the majority Han Chinese. However, I saw virtually no evidence, myself, of these strains and tensions. Even among the Hui Muslims, who obviously had lost a great deal of political power since the 1940s, I saw nothing to indicate that there was any nostalgia for leaders such as the Ma warlords who had dominated the region before Communist takeover. I could not help but wonder whether some Hui still resented the great change in their political fortunes and perhaps still had a longing for a return to greater power and glory; if there were some who felt this way, they concealed it from me.

*   *   *

Finally, after many conversations and briefings in Lanzhou, I was able to fulfill my long-standing desire to visit Linxia, to see for myself this homeland of the Ma warlords and focal point of Islam in that area.* I made the trip to Linxia by car from Lanzhou with two pleasant traveling companions—my escort from CASS and my host from the Lanzhou Academy of Social Sciences—plus a driver.† The route to Linxia was 112 miles (a 224-mile round-trip), and it took three and a half hours each way. The road was a narrow, two-lane macadam highway, generally smooth but with periodic rough patches. It climbed up over some quite high mountains just outside of Lanzhou and then descended into a long valley that continued most of the way to Linxia. We started climbing while still in Lanzhou's suburb, winding through a narrow valley in which a tiny rivulet fed postage-stamp size plots of wheat growing in brown loess soil (*huangtu*). The road then climbed up and up, into the mountains, twisting on hairpin turns or clinging to mountainsides, below which there were precipitous drops into small valleys, framed by terraced fields. Near the top the terrain was extremely rocky and bare. Lo thought that the pass that we went through was about 5,500 feet high, although our driver thought it was somewhat lower. On the other side of the pass, we again went over rather scary hairpin turns for a while but then cut southwest through a long valley, interspersed only occasionally by low hills, that led toward Linxia. Work was under way to construct a tunnel through the mountains; when completed, hopefully within a year or so, I was told, it would cut the travel time significantly—and doubtless have far-reaching effects on the entire region.

Once we had gone through the pass and entered the long valley leading toward Linxia, we entered real Muslim territory. Not only was the population predominantly Hui, but the appearance of the area was very traditional and very Muslim—almost Middle Eastern. It clearly was a very poor area. The

---

*Several Hui men with whom I talked in different parts of northwest China said to me that the most important Hui centers in the region, in their view, included Linxia (which many still referred to as Hezhou); several places in Ningxia, including Yinchuan and three counties in southern Ningxia that had major mosques; and Xining in Qinghai. Of the three, however, Linxia seemed to be regarded as the preeminent one by most people.

†By the time I made this trip, my initial escort from CASS, Wu Yu, who had accompanied me on my travels throughout Inner Mongolia, Ningxia, and Qinghai, had been replaced by a somewhat older man from CASS, named Tsao Dapeng. Tsao accompanied me on my travels to Xinjiang, Gansu (my second trip), Shaanxi, and Shanxi. The son of a manufacturer of high-quality artist's paper in Shanghai, Tsao was an extremely literate man, much more interested—it seemed to me—in history, literature, and aesthetics than in politics. He was looking forward to retirement in the near future and planned to pursue his personal interests full time. My other companion, a Gansu Academy staff member named Lo (described earlier), was a recent graduate of college.

highway ran right through the middle of numerous old-style villages. Almost everywhere tall trees—mainly poplars—lined the road. We saw only a few new peasant homes; most homes were old, mud-brick and plaster structures. Many had mud-walled enclosures. Most roofs were flat—although a few had Chinese-style, sloping, tiled roofs. All along the way we passed numerous open markets full of goods. We also passed many small mosques. There were a number of "modern" buildings in township centers; most were two-story shops with open fronts. But along most of the way the atmosphere was essentially traditional, and for me it evoked the past. It brought back memories of the trip I had made by truck in 1948 from Lanzhou to Xining in Qinghai. The majority of the villages that I saw in 1988 were similar to the Hui villages that I had seen on that earlier trip. The main difference, and the principal reminder that this was a trip in the 1980s, not the 1940s, was the road itself, which was a ribbon of modernity that stretched the entire way, on which trucks and crawling tractors were mixed with donkeys and old-fashioned carts.

*   *   *

When we arrived at Linxia, a bustling little modern city surrounded by low hills, my immediate impression was of a modern transplant that had suddenly sprouted from the traditional countryside. It was a fascinating and unique mixture of both old and new.* On our arrival, we were taken immediately to a comfortable, modern, guest house, and within minutes we were greeted by La Mingzhi, the head (*zhou zhang*) of the Linxia Hui Autonomous Prefecture (*zhou*). La presented me with an English-language name card, on which he used the title "governor"; in view of the size and significance of many prefectures, this title may not have been totally inappropriate, but it is not the title generally used in English. I spent all that afternoon and evening and the next morning in nonstop conversation about Linxia with La and many of his officials. The more I learned about the prefecture, the more it interested me, and I was almost as fascinated by the young "governor" as I was by the place itself.

La was a kind of local Horatio Alger. Round-faced, plump, and amiable, he seemed boyish in many respects, but I found him to be articulate, dynamic, enthusiastic, and a charged-up booster of "his prefecture," and he clearly was in charge of everything going on within it. He was in his late for-

---

*In the 1940s, I personally saw only one small town in all of China—Beipei, north of Chongqing—that gave me the same sense of being a remarkable oasis of modernity set in a traditional countryside. I was told at that time that there were a few others, principally towns supported by Overseas Chinese in Guangdong Province. However, as I traveled throughout the country in 1988, I kept discovering towns of this kind in many parts of the country.

ties, and he had risen to his position as chief of the prefecture the previous year, 1987.

A local Hui Muslim, La had been born in a nearby village. His father was a blacksmith throughout his life, but in 1958—during a campaign against "feudalism"—he had been accused of counterrevolutionary activity. Eventually, during the post-Mao period, he had been able to have this label removed, and he was still living, aged 74. La's success in his career was in spite of this "feudal and counter-revolutionary family background."

La began working at age 19, before he had completed middle school. His first job was that of a bank clerk, and in this position—held for six years—he helped to "issue loans," he said. The next six years he worked as an "archivist" in "legal work" (*sifa gongzuo*). Even though he knew his father's political difficulties would work against him, La decided in 1972 to try to join the Party, and he was accepted. In 1974—a year, he said, when higher authorities called for more rapid promotion of young minority cadres—he was assigned to be a Party secretary in a commune in which two-thirds of the commune members were minority people. There, he felt, his family background actually helped him, and he did well in the job. Three years later, he became Party secretary in another commune, in the Baoan-Dongxiang-Sala Autonomous County, where 99 percent of the commune members were minority people. The situation there was extremely complex, he said, both because of the unusual ethnic mixture (involving eight different nationality groups) and because of the prevalence of "leftist influences," but then the national shift to moderate and pragmatic policies, starting in late 1978, and the subsequent "reversal of verdicts," which removed "labels" from "bad elements," improved the political climate. Thereafter, his work attracted the attention of provincial Party and government leaders.

Gansu's provincial leaders convened an important conference in Lanzhou in 1979 to discuss rural policy, and La was 1 of 10 local Party secretaries invited to attend. His career took off thereafter. First, Linxia's prefectural leaders appointed him to be both head of the local Party's Rural Work Department and deputy head of the government's Agricultural Commission. In 1982, he became deputy Party secretary in Kangle County, and for close to a year he worked there in the local "cultural and educational system" (*wenjiao xitong*). Following that, he was promoted to the position of Party secretary in Guanghe County. Clearly targeted for further promotion, he passed an examination in 1984 to enter the Northwest Normal Institute in Lanzhou, where he studied Chinese literature under a special program that the Provincial Party Committee sponsored for cadres of county-level rank and above. Graduating in 1986, he returned to Linxia Prefecture to head a "leading group on economic structural reform" that operated under the dual leadership of the Party and the government. That same year, he became deputy head of the prefecture in charge of economic work. Finally, in 1987—the year before I met him—he became (was "elected") head of the prefecture. La did not try to disguise his pride in his career and his many successes. He also took some pride in the career of three of his brothers: One was a successful trader, a second was a school principal, and a third was receiving training in Lanzhou so that he could become involved in "foreign economic relations." His one sister, however, was uneducated and worked at home as a house-wife; her husband had a job in the public security apparatus.

*   *   *

In response to my questioning, La gave me, with tremendous enthusiasm and verve, a thorough briefing on the Linxia area and provided me with a great deal of information about local history, leadership, administration, and education, and—above all—local economic development and the problems still confronting the region.

According to La, Linxia became an autonomous prefecture in 1956 (he had on the tip of his tongue the exact date, September 19, 1956, as well as the exact date of the prefecture's "liberation," which was August 22, 1949). The urban center of the prefecture was Linxia City. Within the prefecture were seven counties, two of which had the status of autonomous counties because within them were concentrations of minorities other than Hui; these two counties were the Dongxiang and the Jishishan Baoan (Bonan)-Dongxiang-Salar autonomous counties. The other five counties (Linxia, Hezheng, Kangle, Guanghe, and Yongjing) had the status of regular counties. Three of these counties bordered on Qinghai Province. There were 130 townships (*xiang*) in the prefecture, as well as five municipal districts under Linxia. Under them were numerous villages (*cun*).

The region is quite well supplied with water. The Yellow River, which enters the prefecture from Qinghai, is fed by several local tributaries (including the Daxia River) that cross four of the counties in the prefecture. At one point on the Yellow River, a huge dam and hydroelectric power station, Liujiaxia, had been built some years previously. It supplied most of Linxia's electricity and provided electricity to Lanzhou and other parts of the province as well.

The prefecture's area, as of 1988, totaled 3,081 square miles—only a little smaller than the country of Lebanon. It is filled with agricultural valleys and mountains; the average elevation is fairly high, and a number of mountain peaks rise well above the valleys. I did not see the most mountainous area in the prefecture, but La said that the elevation of the higher areas ranged from 5,000 feet to almost 10,000 feet. The prefectural headquarters was located in the city (*shi*) of Linxia. The city had once been a part of Linxia County, which, as I said earlier, was originally called Hezhou, but by 1988 it had become a separate administrative entity. Historically, I was told, the city dated to the Han dynasty, and over the centuries it had a succession of names, including Fuhan, Daohe, and then Hezhou, before getting its current name, Linxia, in the 1930s.

As of 1988, according to La, the population of the prefecture totaled 1.502 million. Despite the fairly rapid growth of Linxia City, the prefecture as a whole remained predominantly rural. Over 90 percent (1.36 million) of its inhabitants were classified as rural, and roughly 150,000 as urban. Of the total number of inhabitants, 1.282 million were supported by agriculture and only 220,000 were supported by nonagricultural occupations. Linxia had the greatest concentration of Hui and also the largest number of Muslims of all kinds (not all Muslims are Hui) in Gansu. A total of 803,000 (53.5 percent) of the prefecture's inhabitants were Muslims; 520,000 (34.6 percent) were Hui, and the other Muslims were mainly Dongxiang, Baoan, and Sala.

La, and others I talked to as well, were full of lore about the area's local history and were well informed about the ethnic and religious roots of people in the prefecture. The area began to develop centuries ago, I was told, primarily because it was an important trading center for exchanges between the Tibetan plateau in Qinghai and the loess agricultural area of the Yellow River valley. From the start, it had a population that was engaged not only in agriculture but also in animal husbandry and trade. It was trade that made the area special, and everyone stressed that its long commercial traditions continued to have a great influence on its economy in the 1980s. From its early days, Linxia had direct links with the southern branch of the Silk Road, La said, and—most important of all—it became a major center for Hui-Tibetan trade in which the Hui people sold Chinese red tea (in the form of brick tea) to the Tibetans and in exchange purchased Tibetan horses.

La asserted that there was convincing evidence that the first Hui people to come to this area had originated from Arabic lands to the west during the Tang dynasty (starting in the seventh and eighth centuries A.D.). La acknowledged that there was still considerable debate over the roots of the Hui minority, but in his view there had been several main sources: (1) Imams who came from Arab lands and settled in this area (he said the area still held tombs of these religious leaders, who were all regarded as sages); (2) Hui people (and perhaps some Han Chinese who had come to believe in Islam) who moved to Linxia from the Xi'an area of Shaanxi because of the attractive commercial opportunities involved in Han-Tibetan trade; (3) Arab craftsmen and soldiers brought back from the west by Genghis Khan; and (4) the offspring of intermarriages among members of all of these groups. From the Tang period on, according to La, Hui people had constituted the majority of the population in this area. For all of the Hui groups, the Chinese language (Hanyu) had been adopted as their own, and this set them aside from most other Muslims, just as their religion and customs set them aside from the majority of the Han Chinese.

Each of the other Muslim groups in the area had its own spoken language (although almost all of them used the written Chinese characters). Their origins varied. La said there were two competing theories about the origins of the Dongxiang: One maintained that they had come from the west with Genghis Khan, and the other maintained that originally they had been Mongols (their language is related to Mongol) who were, somewhere along the way, converted to Islam. Almost everybody—whichever theory they accepted—apparently dated their origins to the Yuan dynasty. The Sala were said to have originally been Arab traders who came to China during the Tang and Song dynasties and then later moved to Linxia. One of the main areas in which they had concentrated—in addition to Linxia—was, and is, an area in Xunhua County, in Qinghai, next to the Gansu border. The Baoan also were said to have moved to Linxia from an area of Qinghai near the Gansu border—Tongren County—but fairly late, during the Qing dynasty.

*   *   *

Early on, Linxia became a religious center as well as a trading hub, and, in fact, in some periods during its history it was really known more as a religious center than for its trade. Before visiting the place, I had heard—in several places in the northwest—the popular saying that compares Linxia to Mecca. La himself said to me: "One could call this the Mecca of China; in fact a recent TV program used this term." Minority Affairs Commission officials in Lanzhou also had said to me: "Many people consider this a 'small Mecca' for northwest China." The comparison really is not valid, as everyone was quick to acknowledge when I questioned it: There is only one Mecca for all Muslims. Nevertheless, the saying did reflect the feeling—which still continues—that Linxia has had, and continues to have, a very special significance as a religious center.

As in other parts of the northwest, the destruction of mosques in Linxia during the Cultural Revolution was incredibly disastrous: "All mosques were destroyed," one person said to me, although I subsequently learned that what this really meant was that "almost all" of them had been either "destroyed" or "damaged." However, virtually all of them had subsequently been rebuilt, and many were now larger than they had been before. This reconstruction was financed mainly by local contributions, although the government subsidized the rebuilding of some of the larger mosques. As of 1988, there were 1,772 mosques of all sizes in the prefecture; 16 of the most important ones were in Linxia City, but virtually every township had at least one, and even most villages had their own mosques. The buildings were of two architectural types. Some were built in Chinese style, with curved tile roofs (often the minarets were like pagodas) but modified in distinctive ways. The others were very much like Middle Eastern mosques, with colorful domes. Religious life clearly was very active. I visited one large mosque,

La Wang Si, which was built in a Chinese style, and there I met several Ahong and young Mala. I was told that about 20 people attended each of this mosque's five daily services. My visit corresponded with Ramadan, and it seemed to me that most people were observing it strictly.

Traditionally, La told me, Linxia had had extensive and continuous contacts with both Arabic countries and Turkey, and these still continued to be important. Over 200 local people had made the pilgrimage to Mecca in 1987, many at their own expense. All five of the most important religious subgroups of Islam in northwest China had important mosques in Linxia, and the influence of these particular mosques extended to other areas in Gansu and elsewhere in the northwest. Many Ahong from Linxia were said to be serving in other northwestern areas. The strength of religious tradition was obviously a major reason for the continuing strength of other Islamic cultural traditions and customs in the area. Linxia was clearly one of the most "Muslim-looking" areas that I saw anywhere in China. The streets were full of men and boys wearing traditional skullcaps (mainly white); most adult men had wispy beards; and the majority of women (though not all) wore hoods (these were almost universal in the villages but not entirely so in the city; the hoods were generally white for older women and black for young women).

In Linxia's earlier days, when it was known as Hezhou, it had been a very important political center, as I have stated previously, because it was the homeland of the Mas, who had exercised such great political power in northwest China from the late nineteenth century to the 1940s. La was able, from memory, to trace in detail for me the history of the major Hezhou Ma clans who had dominated Qinghai, Ningxia, and much of Gansu for several decades. He traced the "Qinghai Branch" (which ruled that area for four decades) from the first emergence to real power of Ma Zhaoan. With the cooperation of some other Muslim groups such as the Dongxiang and Baoan (and, he said, influenced by the Yellow Turban secret society), Ma fought the Qing dynasty's armies but then ultimately reached an agreement with them; he rose to power because of that agreement. The most important Qing leader in northwest China at the time, Zuo Zongtang, made Ma Zhaoan's son, Ma Anliang, governor-general of Shaan-Gan (Shaanxi-Gansu). According to La, two brothers who became close advisers to Ma Anliang—men named Ma Qi and Ma Lin—were sent to Qinghai to pacify the Tibetans, and subsequently both of them served, successively, as governors of Qinghai. The next generation after them included Ma Bufang, Ma Buqing, and Ma Bulin. When I visited Qinghai in 1948, Ma Bufang was governor.

La then traced for me the history of the "Ningxia Mas," starting with the brothers Ma Fuxiang and Ma Fulu, who led a rebellion in the nineteenth century. They, too, ultimately became Qing generals, after supporting the Empress Dowager at the time of the Boxer Rebellion. Because of their support, the Empress Dowager turned over Ningxia to them. Ma Hongkui, the son of Ma Fuxiang, was still governor of Ningxia when I visited there in 1948. (La also said that a famous Muslim rebel in Xinjiang named Ma Zhongying came from the same extended family but had been excluded from their areas by Ma Bufang and Ma Hongkui. La said he believed one reason Ma Zhongying went to Xinjiang was because he had been excluded by his relatives. In any case, he was ultimately defeated, militarily, in Xinjiang and disappeared into the Soviet Union.)

By 1988, it seemed to me, there were only dim memories among most people in Linxia of the former political and military power of the Mas. Following 1949, the Communists had rapidly destroyed their regional power. However, as elsewhere in the northwest, the Communists at the same time tried to co-opt as many as possible of their former adversaries. According to La, as well as to other officials I had talked to in Lanzhou, many members of the Ma clan were given positions in the new regime. All of the most powerful close associates of Ma Bufang and Ma Hongkui fled the country—some to Saudi Arabia or other Middle Eastern areas and some to the United States. But some lesser figures and relatives stayed in the area, and the new regime went out of its way to try to placate them by giving some of them governmental positions.

I was told, though, that during the Cultural Revolution many of the surviving Mas in the area were subjected to severe attacks for being former landlords, reactionaries, and counterrevolutionaries—but then after the Cultural Revolution some of them had been rehabilitated. One nephew of Ma Hongkui was appointed chairman of the Linxia Prefecture People's Political Consultative Conference; he had died the year before my visit. One of Ma Hongkui's commanders had been given a civilian position in the provincial government, as head of the Department of Agriculture and Animal Husbandry of Gansu Province, and subsequently he had become a deputy chairman of the provincial People's Congress. Still another man who had served as a top official under Ma Hongkui, a Sala, continued to serve as a deputy chairman of the People's Congress of Linxia Prefecture. Another relative of Ma Hongkui was, at age 78, continuing to serve as deputy chairman of the Gansu Province Provincial People's Congress. And one of the sons of Ma Zhongying still served as a deputy chairman of the Linxia Prefecture People's Political Consultative Conference. None of these positions were ones of real power; the appointments were mainly symbolic. Nevertheless, they did represent a conciliatory "united front" approach to dealing with the Mas. La attributed this conciliatory policy in large part to Wang Zhen, a key Communist Party leader in northwest China during 1949.

While I was in Linxia, I was taken to visit the former home of Ma Buqing—an elder brother of Ma Bufeng. It was a well-preserved, elegant, traditional, Chinese-style establishment, built around a large courtyard.

Sometime after 1949, it had been converted into a Children's Science and Technology Center (which had the poetic name of "Butterfly Pavilion"). I was told about the homes of two other of the Mas. Ma Hongkui's home had been converted into a commune, and in the late 1980s several ordinary families were living in it. Ma Bufang's former house was said to be in "very poor repair"; no one offered to show it to me.

The political losers in the late 1940s, it seemed to me, were not only members of the Ma family but also Hui Muslims in general. As I noted earlier, Hui Muslims continued to be underrepresented in the 1980s in the provincial elite. However, some new younger Hui leaders who had emerged—such as La—had in many areas acquired political power at the local level, holding top positions including those of Party secretaries, prefectural government heads, chairmen of People's Political Consultative Conferences, and heads of the People's Congresses. In Linxia, I was told, of the "35 leading cadres" in the prefecture, more than half were minority cadres—mainly Hui Muslims. (This was roughly in proportion to their percentage of the total population.) However, among all the state cadres in the prefecture, Hui and other minorities were still underrepresented: They held, I was told, only 35 percent of all state cadre positions in the prefecture.

*   *   *

What La was most proud of—justifiably, it seemed to me—was the rapid economic development of Linxia Prefecture and the transformation of the city into a new, modern, urban center; the greatest changes had taken place during the period of reform in the 1980s. He was very aware, however, that progress had been much more impressive in urban areas—and in trade and industry—than in rural agricultural areas, many of which remained very poor and faced enormous difficulties.

The transformation of Linxia City had been a direct result of the reform policies of the 1980s, La maintained, and of the stimulus to trade and general economic development that the new reform policies had given. When I traveled around the city, I was startled to see how up-to-date it looked. I was told that almost everything that I saw had been entirely built—or rebuilt— during the two to three years before I saw it. It had previously had a quite traditional appearance, people said. (Actually, before 1949 most Hui lived not in the city itself but outside, in an area south of where an old city wall gate had been.) In 1984, La said, the Gansu provincial Party and government convened a special conference that adopted a plan specifically for Linxia's economic development, which called for, among other things, rebuilding the city. Thereafter, a new city was planned. Old buildings were torn down; streets were widened; and in a short period of time many new modern buildings were constructed (quite a few of them incorporated traditional Chinese or Middle Eastern architectural features into modernized structures). The plan included numerous new public buildings as well as shops and multistory apartment houses. The entire city was rebuilt quite rapidly. Almost 80 percent of the new structures were financed with local funds, I was told, although higher-level government helped with some investment.

In the center of the city was a large square or plaza, surrounded by quite interesting and attractive public and business structures. A modern "bazaar"—looking very much like a department store—was one of the most prominent structures in this part of the city. Fifteen stories high, with close to 76,000 square feet of floor space, it had been built with Y 2.45 million of private capital. (Most of it was obtained from the sale of shares worth Y 500 each.) Viewed from one of the low hills surrounding Linxia—where the prefecture head took me so that I could get a tourist's overall view of the place—the city looked very much like the newer parts of modern cities built in more developed areas of China. Almost all of the structures I could see were modern, and most of them were several stories high. However, transportation had only begun to be modernized: There were relatively few motorized vehicles, and bicycles, horses, and carts predominated.

Although Linxia's economic development had obviously begun earlier, the startling transformation of the place was a result mainly of development that had occurred in the 1980s. La and other local officials provided me with statistics that compared 1950 and 1987 and which highlighted the overall changes that had occurred in 37 years. Although the geographical size of Linxia Prefecture remained essentially the same during those years, the population of the prefecture had more than doubled, from 705,800 to 1,502,000, and the population density per square mile had increased from 228 to 490. In 1987, the gross value of output of industry and agriculture in the prefecture was more than 9 times that of 1950 (it had risen from Y 31.532 million to Y 296.219 million). Agriculture's share was still larger than that of industry, even though the most rapid development had taken place in trade and industry. In 1987, agricultural output accounted for roughly three-fifths and industry for roughly two-fifths of the total. However, industry had been developing much more rapidly. It had increased—from a very low base—77 times. (During the same period the value of the output of agriculture had increased 7 to 8 times, which was certainly not unimpressive.) There were no large industries in Linxia, but a number of small industries had been expanding quite impressively. These included ones producing carpets, clothing, construction materials, utensils, and food—in addition to electric power generation.

One of the most distinctive characteristics of the economy of Linxia in 1988 was that collective and private enterprises had grown to the point where they were predominant (in this respect, it was comparable in some ways to Wenzhou in Zhejiang Province). The latest available figures, which they gave to me, showed that of 7,111 industrial enterprises in the prefecture, which produced goods valued at Y 123.05 million, 59 state enterprises accounted for production worth Y 42 million, 40 collective enterprises produced goods worth Y 22 million, and 7,012 private and individual enterprises produced goods worth Y 59 million. Although the state and collective enterprises were the largest ones, the most remarkable figures were those for private industry, which outproduced both of the other sectors. Together, private and collective industrial enterprises produced, as the preceding figures show, almost double what the state enterprises did. This put Linxia far ahead of most of China in the process of reforming and changing the "ownership system."

Above all, Linxia's recent economic success had resulted, as had its success in earlier years, from its commerce. Although its trade was no longer based on the exchange of Chinese tea for Tibetan horses, the tradition of entrepreneurship that had begun centuries earlier was well remembered and continued to influence entrepreneurship in the area. Local leaders insisted on telling me all about the earlier trade. In the Song dynasty, I was told, a special bureaucratic unit, called the Tea-Horse Office (*cha-ma si*), was established to supervise this trade. Over the centuries, what is now Linxia steadily expanded this trade—and built its reputation for entrepreneurship. One official in Lanzhou said to me: "There is a saying—in the south there is Wenzhou, and in the northwest there is Linxia." Local officials in Linxia were very aware that in a sense they were competing with Wenzhou. La said to me that he recognized that Wenzhou was still ahead of Linxia in its development and entrepreneurship, but he was proud of the fact that the people in Linxia—like those in Wenzhou—were now traveling all over China to engage in a wide variety of trade. (In 1987, I had visited Wenzhou and had been astonished by the entrepreneurship and private and collective enterprises there. And in my earlier chapter on Baotou, I noted the presence of Wenzhou traders there.) The comparison between Linxia and Wenzhou seemed apt to me. Linxia's traders were especially active, La said, in Tibet, Qinghai, and Xinjiang, but many of them also went to major cities such as Shanghai, Beijing, Guangzhou, Shenzhen—and even to Wenzhou itself.

According to local statistics, the value of Linxia's commerce grew almost 33-fold between 1950 and 1987, from Y 10.6 million to Y 348.4 million. Moreover, during the period of reform, from 1978 to 1987, the number of commercial organizations in the prefecture grew from 1,286, employing 5,118 people, to 13,593, employing 24,222 people. Of the commercial employees in 1987, roughly one-half—12,319—belonged to "individual" trading households. The dynamism of commercial entrepreneurship was evident everywhere in Linxia City. I saw throughout the city many busy street markets (free markets), and I was told that there were more than a half dozen large specialized markets. I visited one of these, in a huge open space on the edge of town, where several hundred men—a mixture of Hui people, Han Chinese, and Tibetans—were buying and selling sheep, cattle, yaks, and sheepskins. The atmosphere of this market was what I imagined the city's ancient market, in which Chinese tea was exchanged for Tibetan horses, was like. It was easy to see how the revival of old patterns of entrepreneurship— as well as new methods of trade—had been a crucial element in Linxia's development during the 1980s.

*   *   *

Local banking also had grown during the period of reform. Between 1978 and 1987, bank deposits had increased 3.25 times, rising to Y 267.83 million, and as of March 1988, bank loans totaled Y 352.55 million—3.85 times the level of loans in 1978. Yet, La emphasized to me, one basic problem still was the shortage of capital for both private and governmental needs. Many planned projects, he said, were on hold because of the lack of capital. The prefecture was now trying actively to attract and solicit capital from China's coastal areas. La said that he hoped the prefecture could obtain some World Bank funds. He also said that he would really be delighted if he could attract any foreign investments; foreign investment was now permissible in Linxia. (Linxia City and Yongding County—the location of Liujiaxia's power station—had been classified as "open" areas some time earlier by the State Council, I was told.) However, La realized that the prefecture had little basis for hoping that it could attract much foreign investment any time soon.

Despite the critical role played in recent local development of the revival of local entrepreneurship and the mobilization of local capital, Linxia had received—and in fact had been quite dependent on—fairly large infusions of funds from higher levels of government. Like almost all areas in west China, it was therefore fiscally dependent on subsidies. It was frankly acknowledged by local leaders that the prefecture could not have accomplished what it did during the 1980s without this large outside help. In fact, it would have been in great trouble without it. Even by comparison with other areas in west China, its subsidies were large. Exactly why, I was not sure, but it was clear that provincial authorities had made a decision to give it special support.

Overall, Linxia Prefecture's total budgetary expenditures in 1950, I was told, had been Y 672,000, and local revenues that year had been Y 248,000, so its deficit had been Y 424,000. Even in that earlier period, its revenues covered only about a third of its expenditures. By 1987, all of these figures had grown astronomically. Its revenues had increased 124-fold and its expenditures 189-fold, I was told. Local revenues in 1987 were Y 30.742 million; expenditures were Y 127.297 million; and therefore the deficit was Y 96.555 million. This very large shortfall was made up by subsidies from higher authorities. In sum, such subsidies paid for roughly three-quarters of the expenditures of the prefecture—a larger percentage than in earlier years.

As La put it to me, "We are only 23 percent self-sufficient, fiscally." (My own calculation was 24 percent, from the figures I was given.) In 1987, Linxia Prefecture received more than Y 96 million in subsidies. Of this, Y 46 million was described as a "basic subsidy" from the provincial government. The rest, Y 50 million, was the sum of a variety of grants. Most of these grants were earmarked for specific programs or projects that were approved by the central and provincial governments, both of which provided substantial funds. These included specific programs for education, irrigation, and other purposes. Of the Y 50 million, La said, only Y 5 million was justified as special aid because of the minority population in the prefecture (Y 3 million of this came from the province and Y 2 million from the central government). It appeared to me, therefore, that the especially large support of the prefecture was not just because of its minority population but also because of its reputation for entrepreneurship and economic dynamism. Perhaps another reason for large provincial support was the importance of Linxia as a Muslim religious center and center of Hui culture. Whatever the real reasons, it was apparent that Linxia had been obtaining very special treatment and was making excellent use of the support that it obtained.

Nevertheless, poverty remained a major problem in some of the rural areas of the prefecture. The picture was not all grim. As I noted earlier, the overall value of agricultural output increased perhaps seven to eight times between 1950 and 1987. Grain production in 1987 was almost two-and-a-half times what it was in 1950, having risen from 129,000 tons to 309,000 tons, and edible oil output had more than doubled, from 6,374 tons to 14,254 tons. These increases had taken place despite the fact that the amount of cultivated land had dropped slightly, from 383,000 acres to 375,000 acres. In per capita terms, the drop in acreage had been even greater; the amount of land per capita had been halved, decreasing from 0.543 acres to 0.267 acres per person. Some progress in raising the productivity of agriculture had been made—despite the generally difficult conditions—by introducing more modern methods and better seeds, and over the years machinery was increasingly used on the land, I was told. In addition, electricity had been extended to all rural areas, which had helped substantially. There had been no electricity anywhere in the entire area of Linxia Prefecture before 1949, La said. It was first introduced in the city in 1953. Then, starting in 1970, it had been extended to rural areas, and by 1987 it had reached "all villages, even the poorest ones." The main source of this was the great hydroelectric station at Liujiaxia, but in addition more than 35 small stations had been built—and these were capable of being considerably expanded if capital became available. Perhaps most important, however, decollectivization and the introduction of the household contract system in the early 1980s ("we adopted it immediately and were among the first to do so") had spurred output by increasing incentives.

Yet despite the progress made, agricultural problems were still very serious. Only 30 percent of the cultivated land in the prefecture was irrigated; this was largely because of lack of funds to extend it. This was a field in which the prefectural government hoped that it might be able to get international support (from the World Bank, for example). La and his agricultural officials estimated that it would be possible to irrigate 70 percent of all cultivated land in the prefecture if funds to do so were available. Roughly a third of the cultivated land was considered to be "very poor" because of a lack not only of irrigation but of natural precipitation, and about 700,000 people in rural areas (half of the total rural population) were said to be very poor— with the lack of water being a fundamental reason. The overall gap between urban and rural incomes was, not surprisingly in view of these facts, disturbingly large. In 1987, according to local statistics, the average per capita income of the total urban population was roughly Y 500, far above that in the past and not at all bad for a remote area. In contrast, the average per capita income of the local agricultural population was only a little under Y 250, close to the Chinese poverty level.

I would have liked to learn more than I did about the local educational system, but I could not because of lack of time. However, the data I was given fit into the general economic pattern that had been described to me. La said that the figures on education that he could give me, from memory, were only very general estimates. (He said that he would be delighted to look up exact figures, but we never got around to that.) He estimated, very roughly, that Linxia's schools, at all levels, enrolled approximately 200,000 students, about three-quarters of them in primary schools and perhaps one-quarter in middle schools. Even though this was, he said, a large increase compared to enrollments in the pre-1949 period, he was concerned because they were far from achieving their educational goals, even quantitatively, but even more so qualitatively. Overall, he said, only 78 percent of the children of school age were currently attending school—a percentage far lower than it should be. This resulted, he said, primarily from the fact that in some of the most remote and poor areas—including portions of Dongxiang County—attendance rates were extremely low. In fact, he said, there were 46 villages in that county alone where there were not yet any operating schools. In education, as in economic development generally, the gap between urban areas and rural areas remained large.

*   *   *

My intensive interviewing of La and his staff eventually wore them out— and it exhausted me too. He then asked if I would like to relax after dinner by going to a movie. When I asked what the movie was, he said it was *Red*

Sorghum (*Hong Gaoliang*). I was pleased—in fact, excited—to hear that
Red Sorghum was being shown in this remote place. This film, produced by
some of the most innovative young filmmakers in China (at the Xi'an studio)
had recently won a major international prize, and in China, although it was
very controversial, it was currently the most popular film being shown
throughout the country. I had tried to see it on two recent stops in Beijing,
but on both occasions I had been told at the theater's ticket booth that it was
sold out and that I could not get a ticket for several days. So after dinner, La
and I strolled through the town and went to a commercial movie theater,
bought ordinary seats, and sat in the middle of an audience that obviously
was representative of the local population. I was enthralled by the movie. It
was a powerful story, set in rural north China during the Sino-Japanese War,
full of ambiguities and subtleties—and enlivened with violence and sex of a
kind that was forbidden in Chinese movies during the Maoist era. Seeing the
movie was a fitting climax to my visit to Linxia. (I thought the musical score
was so powerful that I immediately went out and bought a cassette version
of it; they could be purchased in almost any city in China.)

The next day, returning to Lanzhou, I ruminated on what I had seen. It
had been a remarkable mixture of old and new. Linxia was undergoing extraordinary changes but was also still strongly influenced by a powerful and
persistent tradition. I saw islands of modernity set in situations rooted
strongly in the past. The lives of many were rapidly improving, yet grinding
poverty persisted for others. However, the new had impressed me more than
the old. Linxia had definitely entered the modern world.

Two days later, I left Lanzhou by train, for north China—going first to
Xi'an, in Shaanxi, then to Taiyuan, in Shanxi, and finally to Beijing again.
On one leg of my train trip, I shared my compartment with a 70-year-old
Chinese director of an enterprise that operated three agricultural machinery
factories. This enterprise was located in Guangdong, in south China. The director had visited Lanzhou to buy steel plates and aluminum for one of his
factories. The purchases had required very tough bargaining, he said. Everywhere, now—even in his home area of Guangdong—he found that he was
constantly having to engage in bargaining: with government authorities
above, about his profit taxes; with his subordinate factory managers, about
their production targets; and with everyone from whom he bought things or
to whom he sold things. He told me a good deal about how recent reforms
had affected—or not affected—the operations of his own enterprises. In his
view, the positive effects had been significant, but considerably short of what
he thought was desirable. "Conservatives," particularly Party secretaries,
still created many obstacles to carrying out the reforms, he said.

I listened as the factory manager and a young man who shared our compartment discussed the growth of crime in Lanzhou. Crime was increasing
and becoming a very serious problem, they both agreed. They had heard of

street robberies by juveniles wielding knives. Some people, they said, now were so concerned about the problem that they tried to avoid going out at night. (The young man said that in his view the trends in Changsha, in Hunan Province, were similar.) Although I had been very aware, from reading the Chinese press, that crime was a major and growing problem nationally, I had neither seen nor heard any evidence of it while I was in Lanzhou. (I had seen some evidence of it in Changsha, however.) Everything in Lanzhou had appeared to me to be remarkably normal. Their conversation reminded me of something I knew well from many years of travel and reporting in China—and elsewhere: One cannot assume that simply by visiting a place one can learn and see all that is going on. It is easy to be misled by seeing only "part of the truth," and I was acutely aware of this throughout my travels in China. However, I reassured myself that I was trying to see and learn everything I could and was attempting to make honest judgments. This conversation reminded me of the dangers of fallibility.

CHAPTER FIVE

Blue Lake

QINGHAI

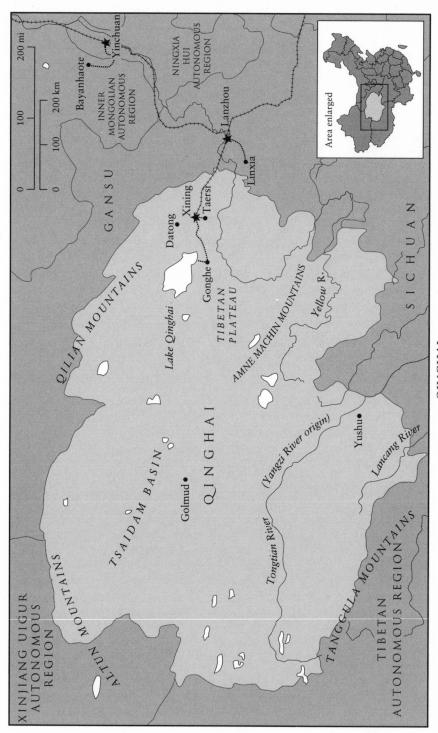

QINGHAI

Q INGHAI" means blue sea,* and the province with this name contains China's largest body of inland water, resting high in a basin on a dramatic tableland that is an eastern extension of the Tibetan plateau. I prefer the original Mongol name, Kokonor, which has the same meaning; for me, it evokes images of distant places and ancient times.

Qinghai Province is a vast, almost empty land "in the middle of nowhere"—on the "roof of the world." It has long had a reputation as a place for exiles. Bordered by Gansu, Xinjiang, Tibet, and Sichuan, it is one of the four largest administrative units in China (the others are Tibet, Xinjiang, and Inner Mongolia), all of which are located in China's west and inhabited by minority peoples. For reasons that are not entirely clear to me, Qinghai is still classified as a province instead of an autonomous region; however, almost all of its territory is divided into autonomous prefectures.

Topographically, most of Qinghai is really part of Tibet, and from its high plateau rise many towering snow mountains. The Yellow, Yangzi, and Mekong rivers all originate in these mountains. Roughly 85 percent of the province, I was told, lies at an altitude of 10,000 or more feet. As is true in many Chinese provinces and regions, the contrasts between different subregions are striking. Essentially, there are two Qinghais (although one can also identify four different economic areas, which I will discuss later). The eastern fringe of the province is inhabited mainly by Han Chinese and Hui Muslims, with the provincial capital, Xining, as its center. In the late 1980s, this part of Qinghai contained roughly four-fifths of the province's total population of almost 4.13 million, and it contains most of its farming area. The best agricultural areas are located in the valleys of two rivers, the Yellow River and one of its tributaries, the Huangshui River, both of which flow eastward toward Gansu Province. Most of Qinghai's modern industry, virtually all of which has been developed since the 1950s, also is located in this region. Parts of the Tsaidam (Chaidam) area, to the far west, were being developed as a mining and industrial area, and its principal city, Golmud, was scheduled to become a municipality soon, possibly before the end of the 1980s. Otherwise all major industrial areas are in the east. The vast expanses of the western parts of the province are sparsely populated areas of traditional animal husbandry, inhabited mainly by Tibetans. I was told that the eastern fringe of the province had a population density of almost 43 per square

---

*Qing can mean either blue or green, but blue is more appropriate here. Literally, *hai* means sea, but in this context it means lake.

mile—30 in rural areas and 96 in Xining Municipality—whereas the population density in most of the rest of the province averaged less than 3 persons
per square mile, and in most areas animals outnumbered people.

*   *   *

In 1948, when I first visited Qinghai, I knew virtually nothing about the
province. I had heard a little about the governor, General Ma Bufang, and
my objective then was to learn about Ma's distinctive regime, but the region
farther west on the Tibetan plateau was terra incognita. With two newsmen
friends (Henry Lieberman of the *New York Times* and Ian Morrison of the
London *Times*), I traveled from Lanzhou to Xining in 1948 by truck.* We
traveled over rough gravel and dirt roads, lined with poplar saplings and
willow trees, and went straight through a large number of small villages. It
was a long trip, and we had to make overnight stops in primitive, old-
fashioned Chinese inns. I still have vivid memories of the nights in those
inns, which I spent typing up notes from previous trips, pecking away at a
portable Hermes typewriter in rooms illuminated only by dim kerosene
lamps. Along the way we passed numerous Qinghai cavalrymen—who were
then famous throughout China—and the overall atmosphere of the region
was very martial. Most of the villages we saw were distinctively Hui, and
they were filled with bearded men wearing skullcaps and with women whose
heads were hooded. The villages, though obviously poor, were generally
neat and clean.

Xining at that time was a small, traditional, walled Chinese city with a
population of about 50,000. In 1948, I did not expect to see *any* signs of modernity that far west, and there were only a few, but I thought it was impressive that there were any at all in such a remote area. Ma Bufang's Qinghai regime impressed me as being one of the most energetic, disciplined, and
efficient of all the many warlord regimes that I visited that year. Although
Ma's regime was stern and completely authoritarian, both the discipline and
quality of his troops and the way in which his government's policies aimed at
economic development made Qinghai quite different in many respects from
other warlord regimes such as those under Ma Hongkui in Ningxia or Yan
Xishan in Shanxi, which in the late 1940s were characterized by extreme authoritarianism with few redeeming features.

In Qinghai, Ma Bufang had introduced some modern medicine to serve a
population among whom syphilis, trachoma, and other diseases were ram-

---

*Several weeks earlier, Lieberman, Morrison, and I had flown, independently, to Xinjiang,
where we had joined forces in our interviews and trips. We then proceeded to Lanzhou and obtained permission for the Qinghai trip from Zhang Zhizhong, the regional Nationalist leader,
and from Ma Bufang's representatives in Lanzhou.

pant. A vigorous sanitation program in Xining City set quotas for flies for everyone to kill. Reports of antifly campaigns, when circulated elsewhere in China, were often dismissed as apocryphal, but I saw many bearded gentlemen and small boys in constant pursuit of flies, for which they were paid a small fee for each dead fly by the government, and Xining's streets were among the cleanest that I saw anywhere in China's west. Ma also had established the beginnings of a system of modern education, including some free schools (the so-called Kunlun schools) for poor children, especially the Hui. Moreover, he had built a few small factories, including ones for wool washing, match making, metal working, pottery making, and the manufacture of chemicals, and had organized a semigovernmental monopoly corporation, the Huang Zhong Company, to promote commerce. All of this was impressive to me mainly because in the late 1940s one did not expect to see any signs at all of modernity in west China.

Outside of Xining, there still were almost no signs of the modern world in 1948—no paved roads, no electricity, and almost no modern vehicles of any sort. Even the city of Xining was basically a premodern town. To serve the entire provincial population—estimated at that time to be about 1.3 million—there were only 10 modern trained doctors, 1 hospital with 100 beds, and 7 health stations, and the school system consisted of only 13 middle schools and just over 1,000 primary schools with a total enrollment of a little more than 100,000. (There was no institution of higher learning of any sort in the province, although in the late 1940s about 200 to 300 students a year were sent with government subsidies to study elsewhere in China.)

In 1948, apart from seeing the Han-Hui agricultural valleys between Gansu and Xining, I was able to make only one short foray into the fringe of the Tibetan hinterland. That was a one-day trip by donkey cart (a method of travel I strongly discourage!) to Kumbum Lamasery (Taersi) at Lushar. Kumbum was a very exotic place. While there, my companions and I interviewed the Banchan Lama, who was then a lonely 11-year-old Tibetan boy surrounded by sinister-looking old advisers and enveloped by an aura of intrigue. I wrote at the time that he might well be "used in years to come as a pawn in relations between China and Tibet"—as in fact he was.

*　　　*　　　*

When I returned to Qinghai in 1988, I did not know what to expect, but I was certain that it was going to be much easier to get there. I left from Lanzhou's large, modern, hectic railway station (still accompanied by Wu Yu) in midafternoon and arrived in Xining approximately four hours later, in the early evening. From Lanzhou the rail route first paralleled the Yellow River and then the Huangshui River valley. Just outside of Lanzhou was a large, new industrial area that stretched quite far toward the west. This area was filled with factories and blocks of multistory, brick, workers' housing;

interspersed between these were small private houses, mostly constructed of plastered mud brick. Throughout China, industrial areas of this sort have grown up along the railways; most are grimy and unattractive and remind me of photographs of early industrial towns in the West. (By contrast, I was repeatedly struck by the effort within most of China's larger industrial cities in 1988 to construct avenues lined with trees and to build parks to try to beautify urban areas.)

When the industrial area west of Lanzhou petered out, the rail line entered an agricultural valley dotted with small villages, in which most of the houses were traditional, built of mud brick with sloping, shedlike, mud roofs. We passed a small modern dam, and then the line cut through an area of deep rock gorges, interspersed only periodically with small farming valleys. Just beyond the Qinghai border, we passed a sizable county town (Minhe), which had several modern multistory buildings, and then, once in Qinghai, we went through another deep gorge, with sheer rock cliffs and spectacular scenery. From there on, the route to Xining followed a river valley containing intensively cultivated fields and numerous villages.

The countryside looked much as I had remembered it from my truck trip 40 years earlier. Most village houses were built around small courtyards, and the houses were tightly packed and separated only by narrow alleys. Although there were quite a few recently built brick houses, the old peasant houses still predominated but they appeared to be in good shape. As I remembered from my 1948 trip, there were tall poplars throughout the villages and along the roads. I saw a few simple farming machines, mainly threshers, crawling tractors, and motorized plows, but most farm labor was obviously still manual. The main roads were paved, but the side roads were still almost all made of gravel or dirt. In contrast with the past, almost all traffic on the roads consisted of "modern" vehicles—trucks, buses, and especially bicycles; I saw only a handful of donkeys, which, with horses, had predominated in 1948. Perhaps the most striking symbols of new modern influences, however, were the TV antennas, which were visible almost everywhere throughout the entire valley, even in obviously poor villages. Once again I was astonished by the degree to which electronic communications had penetrated even isolated rural areas.

Another big difference between 1988 and 1948 was the apparent demilitarization of the region. In 1948, Ma's cavalry forces were omnipresent. In 1988, I saw no visible signs in the countryside on the way to Xining of military personnel or activity. There were, however, in my soft-seat train compartment, about a dozen army men, mainly high-ranking officers and their aides. Well dressed, in uniforms of fine cloth, these officers looked extremely professional, much like those I had seen on my train trip between Yinchuan and Lanzhou; they also seemed to be very accustomed to privileges. The majority of them were aloof and acted with quiet authority. A tightly knit group, they were uninterested in casual conversation with me, even though I was the only foreigner on the train, so I did not learn what they were doing or where they were going. Some of them may have been on assignments to new jobs in Xining City, but others may have been en route to Tibet or to the Tsaidam area in west Qinghai. (Most military traffic to and from Tibet goes through Qinghai, I was told, rather than through alternative routes such as the ones via Sichuan Province.)

*   *   *

My host organization in Qinghai was the provincial Academy of Social Sciences (QASS). QASS leaders were at the station when I arrived, and they met me with unusual warmth. From Xining's large, new, modern train station, they whisked me quickly by car across town to the Qinghai Guest House. This hotel was much like the one in which I had stayed in Lanzhou. It had two large buildings that dated to the 1950s, the era of Soviet aid to China; one had been used by Soviet technicians as their residence. Although somewhat smaller than the hotel in Lanzhou, it was actually more comfortable. My room not only had standard modern conveniences, including color TV and a large radio receiver, but it also had (which was somewhat unusual) ample hot water in the bathroom.

My hosts and I immediately sat down and discussed in detail the schedule of interviews and trips that they had arranged for me. I was disappointed to learn that I would not be able to see the provincial governor or Party secretary (the former was "out of town," the latter "unavailable"), but otherwise the program they had planned was excellent. It included a wide range of interviews with local leaders, including the executive deputy governor of the province and Xining's mayor as well as many other officials responsible for the economy, government administration, Party propaganda, education, and minority affairs. They had also planned several meetings with academics (mainly QASS leaders, institute heads, and leading scholars engaged in a broad range of research that covered almost all of the Academy's fields of work). Also on my schedule was a visit to one of Xining's leading factories and two trips to Tibetan areas on the plateau, one to the Kumbum Lamasery at Taersi and the other to Lake Qinghai and the nearby seat of the Hainan Tibetan Autonomous Prefecture. For once, I simply accepted the planned schedule arranged by my hosts without pressing for changes. The people at the Qinghai Academy obviously felt far removed from China's mainstream and self-conscious about their area's backwardness, but, like Avis, they seemed determined to try harder.

After a quick dinner I decided that before going to bed I would sample local TV and radio programs to see the extent to which electronic media now linked this remote area with the outside world. (In 1948, as best as I can remember, I did not see even a single radio receiver in Qinghai.) First, I turned on my TV set and caught the late evening news; it was mainly about national events but included some international news. I then watched a serial soap—a drama. It was interspersed with numerous advertisements, most of them showing Western life-styles, and the Chinese in them were all dressed in modern Western clothing. Many of them advertised consumer durables that had been unknown in China even a few years previously. (In one ad for washing machines, the song "Sonny Boy" provided the background music!) I then turned on the radio and listened briefly to many stations on both short- and medium-wave bands, in several languages. I settled, finally, on BBC and listened to it for quite a while until, exhausted, I finally decided to tune out the outside world and go to sleep. As I drifted off, though, I marveled at how the invisible TV and radio waves could demolish time and distance.

*   *   *

Within a short time after arriving at Xining, I found that I was short of breath because of the altitude. I had forgotten how high Xining—and all of Qinghai—is. My host informed me the next day that Xining, even though it is located just at the lower edge of the Tibetan plateau, lies at an altitude of 7,236 feet. Everything west of Xining is higher.

I began my interviews the next morning, but in the first break in my schedule I seized the opportunity to tour all parts of Xining by car and discovered that, like virtually all of the cities in west China that I visited in 1988, it had grown enormously and been transformed into a genuinely modern place. Xining lies parallel to, and to the south of, the Huangshui River. I started my tour at the new railway station, north of the river, and then went south over one of the city's four large new bridges into the main urbanized area. A broad avenue called National Reconstruction Road (Jianguo Lu) was the principal thoroughfare leading south, and three major avenues led westward from it. These avenues, like the entire city, were laid out on an east-west axis, and the streets of the "old city," which still constituted the urban core of the municipality, were laid out—as was traditional in Chinese cities—very regularly.

One of the three main avenues going west, which was named July 1 Road (Qiyi Lu) to commemorate the founding of the Chinese Communist army, cut through a very new urban area and then merged into a "ring road" that encircled the old city. This circular road was laid out where the city wall had once stood; only small remnants of the wall remained. Going along July 1 Road, before reaching the old city, I passed the former residence of the warlord Ma Bufang as well as the present headquarters of the Qinghai Military District and the provincial Party headquarters. The Xining Guest House, where I was staying, was located at the western end of this avenue. Further south, the main east-west avenue, called Dongguan Dajie, cut through the city's main Muslim area to the east of the old city, the Dongguan District.

Xining's Great Mosque was located in this area; it looked much as I had remembered it to be in 1948, although it was actually in much better condition than it had been then. The avenue then merged into the principal east-west thoroughfare of the old city.

The old city itself, which was surrounded by the ring road, was bisected by two other roads, which divided it into quarters. The four were named, appropriately, East Avenue, West Avenue, North Avenue, and South Avenue. The point where they met was the principal business center of the city, as it had been 40 years earlier. Next to the old city, a long north-south avenue (Yangzi Road—Chang Jiang Lu) paralleled a small tributary river that was crossed by three modern bridges; from there, four major avenues went westward, punctuated with many crossroads. This western area was almost entirely new (that is, built since 1949), and part of it had become the city's main industrial area. To the far northwest of the city was a large public park and a zoo, and another fairly large park was located further south. Surrounding the city were what appeared to be low hills—I could see them from most of the major avenues—but since the city of Xining's altitude is over 7,000 feet, these "hills" actually were quite high mountains. Only a few miles further, in several directions the mountains were even higher and were snow capped.

By 1988, the area administered by Xining City had grown to several times its 1948 dimensions, and the population of the municipality was close to 20 times what it had been when I last visited. As of 1986 (the latest year for which definite figures were given to me), Xining Municipality had a total population of almost 973,000; of these about 623,000 lived in the city itself and the rest in the municipality's rural areas.

Even in 1948, Xining had been populated predominantly by Han Chinese, but by the late 1980s, Han dominance was even greater. Of the municipality's total population in 1986, more than three-quarters (748,000) were Han Chinese. Of the municipality's minority population (totaling 225,000 or 23-plus percent of the total), Hui Muslims predominated, but even so they came to only 159,000, or 16.34 percent. The Tibetans, even though they made up a fifth of the province's total population, accounted for only about 2.5 percent (24,000 plus) of the population of Xining. Even the Tu people were more numerous than the Tibetans in the city, constituting 3.2 percent (almost 32,000). Other groups made up only a few thousand or a few hundred each (Mongols, 3,903; Manchus, 2,554; Salars, 838; and all others, 2,862).

Xining Municipality dominates the province both demographically and economically. By 1986, the municipality accounted for almost a quarter of the entire population of the province (23.59 percent of the total provincial population of 4,124,585). (Economically, as I will discuss later, Xining dominates the province to an even greater extent.) Moreover, Xining is the focal point of the entire eastern part of Qinghai, which by the late 1980s contained roughly 80 percent of the province's entire population—as well as most of its industry and cropland. Like the principal political centers in many Third World areas, the municipality of Xining had grown much more rapidly than the general region in which it was located. Between 1948 and 1988, the province's population had roughly tripled, increasing from an estimated 1,308,000 to almost 4,125,000, whereas Xining Municipality had increased close to 20 times.

During these years of growth, not only Xining but the population of the province as a whole became increasingly dominated by Han Chinese—even though geographically most of the territory of the province in the west continued to be inhabited by minorities. By 1986, 60 percent of the population in the province as a whole (2,475,000 out of the 4,124,585) were Han Chinese; 70 percent of all Han were living in places other than Xining Municipality, although most of them were in east Qinghai. Hui Muslims made up close to the same proportion of the province as of the city (565,000, or 13.69 percent, of the provincial population and 16.34 percent of Xining's population). Similarly, the 140,000 Tu made up 3.4 percent of the provincial population and 3.2 percent of Xining's population. Most striking, however, was the fact that the 811,000 Tibetans in Qinghai, who inhabited by far the largest area in the province, accounted for roughly 20 percent of the total provincial population whereas in Xining, the capital, they made up only 2.5 percent of the municipality's population. In short, the Tibetans were "out in left field": They had become a relatively small minority in an area that traditionally had been regarded as Tibetan, and they were almost unrepresented, at least in any significant numbers, in the province's capital city.

As I toured Xining, it was evident everywhere I went that it had developed into a modern city. I saw very few buildings that were left from the pre-1949 era. There were some—I have already mentioned the Great Mosque, and Ma Bufang's former headquarters—but relatively few. The city's streets, almost all of which had been old-style dirt roads in 1948, had been converted into modern, paved, and quite impressive avenues. Most of the buildings were obviously modern; the majority had clearly been built since 1949. Quite a few were multistory structures. Some of those that had been built in the 1980s were attractive modern skyscrapers. Some rose 10 or more stories. One high building under construction in the western part of the city was going to be a fancy hotel for foreigners—to be called the Xining Guest House.

The main streets of Xining were both lively and colorful. Most people were well dressed; women in particular were clearly trying to keep up with east coast fashions, and the clothes that many wore were quite chic. Quite a few women wore high-heeled shoes and tailored jackets and slacks; red was obviously their favorite color. Most local Hui Muslims, however, looked very traditional. In contrast to those in Lanzhou, the Hui in Xining dressed mostly in distinctive traditional caps and hoods, which gave the eastern Muslim part of the city a somewhat Central Asian atmosphere. And although there were not many people on the streets dressed in Tibetan clothing, there were enough to make one realize that the city rested on the edge of Inner Tibet.

Before my arrival in Xining, I was uncertain, and a little uneasy, about what the political atmosphere in the city would be. Just before I left Lanzhou, the TV news reported not only that there had been new riots in Lhasa, in which a car was burned and a police station attacked, but also that on the night of the spring lantern festival (the fifteenth day of the first lunar month) a large crowd of celebrators in Xining had gotten out of hand and several people had been killed. My arrival in Xining was just a few days after this incident. I was interested in learning more about the incident, but what I was told added little to what had been reported on TV. Local people in Xining claimed that the incident was caused not by racial conflict but by simple rowdiness, although I could not help but suspect that ethnic friction may well have been involved. However, I saw no evidence during my stay in Xining of interracial tensions, either at the central crossroads in the old city where the incident had occurred or at any other place I visited. My main impression was that the Han, Hui, and Tibetan elements in the population mixed freely and casually on the streets, and I did not see any signs of tensions among them anywhere in the city. (Later, however, when I visited Kumbum Lamasery, I talked with one Tibetan, a lama, who had just returned from Lhasa and was quite willing to talk about the Lhasa riots. He gave me more details than had been reported on the Chinese TV station. I discuss what he said later in this chapter.)

*   *   *

In Qinghai, I tried—as I did everywhere I visited in northwest China—to learn what had happened at the time of the Communist takeover, which had occurred not long after my 1948 visit. I also tried to determine whether—or to what extent—the ghosts of the old Muslim warlord regime still hung over the area. Both the Academy specialists and the local officials I met were delighted to give me their accounts of the Communist takeover, and in general they seemed well informed about what had taken place. The essentials of their accounts—as I pieced them together—were as follows.

Ma Bufang, they said, was unquestionably the most strongly committed anti-Communist leader in the northwest in the 1940s, and he was able to organize significant resistance against the Communists. However, the main fighting between his forces and the People's Liberation Army (PLA) was not in Qinghai Province but was in adjacent Gansu. Ma Bufang had tried, I was told, to create a unified resistance involving Ma Hongkui's troops as well as other anti-Communist forces in Xinjiang, but the PLA foiled these plans by severing, fairly rapidly, the links between Qinghai and both of these other places. The PLA then defeated Ma Bufang's main forces near Lanzhou, which they liberated on August 13, 1949. Ma Bufang left the northwest shortly thereafter, on August 20, local scholars told me, and then three separate PLA units from the Gansu area entered the Xining area on September 2 and 3 and soon established basic overall military control. My informants acknowledged that there continued to be resistance in some areas of Qinghai for a fairly prolonged period.

After Ma Bufang had fled, his eldest son, Ma Jiyuan, stayed behind and attempted, my informants said, to send out of the province by air the family's most valuable possessions, but the plane would not take off and he eventually had to leave without most of the plane's original contents. Although most of Ma's cavalry had surrendered near Lanzhou, according to the accounts given me, some important resistance forces in Qinghai, led by Ma Wending (Ma Bufang's chief of staff—no relative), continued fighting. However, the PLA was able to surround these forces before long, and Ma Wending, once trapped, agreed to surrender. He was subsequently given a position in the new regime; in 1988, I was told, he still was a deputy chairman of the provincial People's Congress.

Ma Bufang had a plan, according to the account given to me, for some of his remaining cavalry to "go underground" and resume resistance at a later date. This plan did not work effectively, however, and most of his cavalry surrendered. The surrender was facilitated by one of Ma Bufang's top cavalry commanders, a man named Xie Guofeng, who decided, after both Ma Bufang and Ma Jiyuan had left, to switch his allegiance. Xie was in Anhui Province at the time, but when he saw that the PLA was on the verge of victory in Qinghai he hastened to the already liberated city of Xi'an in Shaanxi and from there offered to help the Communists liberate Qinghai.

Nevertheless, my informants said, some forces did go underground and continued resistance, although not on a very large scale. It actually took until the mid-1950s, I was told, to "clean out" these "bandits." There was some fighting not far from Xining, in Datong, northwest of the capital, and also in Hualong, to the southwest. Fighting in these areas was most severe in 1951–1952. Some of Ma's old forces also went far into the grasslands and mountainous areas and continued resistance there. Two remote areas in the province where units of Ma's cavalry continued to resist were Guoluo (Golog) in the southeast and Yushu in the middle-south area. (Both areas are now autonomous prefectures.) In these areas resistance was largely ended by 1954 and was "cleaned out" by 1955.

Some remnants of Ma Bufang's cavalry survived for a while in Xinjiang Province. These, I was told, eventually left China and went into Afghanistan. Some of the most militant Kazakh cavalrymen from Xinjiang, led by Osman

Bator, first fought the PLA in Xinjiang and then fought their way down into Qinghai. There Osman's forces and the PLA clashed on numerous occasions. My Qinghai informants asserted that ultimately Osman was killed in one of these major clashes, but on this I believe they were wrong. Later, in Xinjiang, I was told that Osman had been captured in Qinghai but then taken to Xinjiang and tried and executed in Urumqi. (See Chapter 6.) After Osman's death many of the survivors of his Kazakh forces reportedly returned to southern Xinjiang, via the Tsaidam area of Qinghai, and then eventually fled to Pakistan, many of them dying en route.

Despite the fairly prolonged continuation of minor resistance—most of it by remnants of the cavalry of Ma Bufang's Hui forces and Osman's Kazakhs (and apparently not involving at that time many from the Tibetan population, although, as I discuss later in this chapter, there was an uprising of Tibetans in southeastern Qinghai in the late 1950s)—the Communists' policy in Qinghai, as in Ningxia and elsewhere, was to try, to the extent possible, to co-opt former enemies into the new regime. My interlocutors in Xining cited a number of examples of former commanders and officials who had served under Ma but then were given new positions under the Communist regime. They also cited examples of PLA officers who figured prominently in Qinghai's "liberation" and continued to hold political positions in the province up to the late 1980s.

Not surprisingly, none of these holdovers from the Ma regime were given positions of real power, and the political power of the Ma clan was effectively and completely destroyed. It was evident, from what I learned in 1988, that whereas in the late 1940s the Hui Muslims, constituting about 40 percent of Qinghai's population of about 930,000 at that time, had completely dominated the area politically before the Communist takeover, by the late 1980s they were significantly underrepresented in positions of political influence in the provincial power structure. There was virtually no possibility, it seemed to me, that they could reemerge as political leaders of the province, at least in the foreseeable future. By contrast, the Tibetans, with about a fifth of the province's entire population, seemed to fare better politically after the Communist takeover. By the 1980s, Tibetans held many leading positions in local governments administering the vast areas of western Qinghai where they were the majority ethnic group. However, they, too, held relatively few positions of significant power at the provincial level in Xining. In general, ultimate political power had been monopolized by Han Chinese ever since 1949.

*   *   *

I was impressed, however, in Qinghai as in virtually all provinces that I visited in 1988, by the profound changes that had occurred in the top political and bureaucratic leadership, especially during the 1980s when technical and economic specialists, above all engineers, had replaced old-time Party organizational men in a great many positions.

Two excellent examples of the new type of leadership were the executive deputy governor of Qinghai and the mayor of Xining, with whom I had a very long meeting that started one afternoon and extended through dinner and well into the evening. (At dinner, I should note, I had one of the best meals of Suanyangro—Mutton Hotpot—that I have ever eaten.) Both Executive Deputy Governor Bian Yaowu and Mayor Luo Kunan impressed me as being highly intelligent, articulate, open-minded, and essentially nonideological men who clearly were fully engaged in attempting to solve Qinghai's concrete economic and other problems. Together they discussed a wide range of issues relating to local governance and economic development, and I was very favorably impressed both by their commitment to modernize their province and by the intelligence with which they discussed the problems of doing so. Six of their personal advisers and staff members also participated in the meeting, and occasionally Bian and Luo would turn to them for specific data, but the deputy governor and mayor were extremely well informed and were able to discuss most questions I raised without help from anyone else.

Deputy Governor Bian was 52 years old. His family's "old home" (*lao jia*) was in Jiangsu, but he had spent most of his life in Zhejiang and Qinghai provinces. After working for six years in Hangzhou, capital of Zhejiang, he then obtained his higher education at the Shanghai Academy of Social Sciences, graduating in 1960. Assigned immediately thereafter to Qinghai, he first worked for the provincial Aquatic Products Department and then in the Department of Commerce, rising in the latter to become its deputy head. In 1985 he was promoted to deputy governor—a huge jump.

Mayor Luo, age 42, considered himself to be a native of Shanghai, where he was born, although his family *lao jia* actually was in Hunan. He graduated from East China College (Huadong Xueyuan) in 1968, with a degree in chemical engineering, and then was immediately assigned to Qinghai. From then until 1983 he had worked as a technician, first in two chemical factories and then in a factory producing "daily-use goods for minority people," where he rose to be the enterprise's director. Selected in 1983 to be a deputy mayor, he was promoted two years later, in 1985, to mayor. Luo's rise, like that of Bian, was meteoric.

Both men were quite sophisticated and worldly wise. Even before they told me that they had come from the lower Yangzi valley region, I guessed that they were from coastal China. Yet they appeared to identify themselves strongly with Qinghai Province, and they were using their considerable talents to try to accelerate its development. I felt that I hit it off with them from the start; the fact that I, too, had roots in Shanghai, Jiangsu, and Zhejiang may have helped. (Some other key individuals in the provincial leadership, whom I learned about but did not meet, had comparable geographical and educational backgrounds. The governor, for example, was a geological engineer whose career had been largely in technical positions; he had headed the Qinghai government's Bureau of Geology and Mining just before being selected governor in 1985.)

Although I did not have as much time as I wished to obtain detailed data on Qinghai Province's entire leadership, I was able to obtain a general picture of the leadership in both the Party and the government. The provincial Party Committee was unquestionably the most powerful local leadership body. But recent reforms, which my informants discussed with me, had somewhat reduced its day-to-day participation in governmental affairs. The Party's Standing Committee consisted, in 1988, of 10 people: the secretary, 4 deputies, and 5 other members. The provincial governor was one of the deputy Party secretaries, and the deputy governor whom I met was also a member of the Standing Committee. My informants asserted that the membership of these two government leaders ensured "coordination and liaison between the Party and the government."

Although there was some minority group representation on the Standing Committee, it was minimal: Eight of the 10 members were Han Chinese. Seven of the 10 Standing Committee members were "outsiders"—specialists brought in from other parts of the country—and only 3 were locally born Qinghai people. However, the majority of the outsiders had, like Deputy Governor Bian, lived and worked in Qinghai for a great many years and were therefore closely identified with the province. Of the 2 representatives of minority peoples on the Standing Committee, 1 was a Tibetan and 1 was a Salar; it was significant, I felt, that not a single Hui Muslim belonged to this supreme political body in the province. I obviously had no way of judging how local people in general felt about a leadership group of this sort. It seemed plausible to me that there could well have been some resentment about the underrepresentation of local people, especially minority groups, yet it also seemed possible that local people respected the competence of this group of outsiders who had obviously become closely identified with the province.

As is standard practice in top Party committees of this sort in China, the entire membership concerned itself with some major issues, but individual members also carried special responsibility for one or more specified areas of work. The secretary and his principal deputy (whom they referred to as the *changwu fushuji*, which I decided could best be translated as "executive deputy secretary") concerned themselves with the entire range of the Standing Committee's work, but the executive deputy secretary coordinated most day-to-day work and also coordinated and supervised propaganda and ideological work, including education. Another deputy was responsible for Party organizational affairs, especially the work of the Organizational Department under the Standing Committee but also the work of local organization departments and of the Women's Federation and Young Communist League, units subordinate to the Party. The special responsibility of another deputy, who was also the provincial governor, was "government work" in general. Still another Standing Committee member was responsible for overseeing economic work. Military affairs were handled by the political commissar of the Qinghai Military District, who was also a member of the Party Standing Committee. (One well-informed academic in Xining told me that even though the membership of the existing Standing Committee consisted of men who were relatively young and recently had been promoted to the top, there nevertheless was scheduled to be very soon—"within a month"—further major changes in the committee's membership, at which time, he thought, perhaps as many as five members would be replaced by new appointees. Why such a large turnover was about to take place, at this particular time—despite the recent large changes in the membership—he was not able to say.)

The main organizational units within the Party's top apparatus, functioning under the Standing Committee, included a general office and three key departments that dealt with organization, propaganda, and united front work. Like other provincial Party committees, this one had until recently had economic departments under it that supervised most government bodies dealing with the economy, but these departments had recently been abolished as a result of Beijing's reform policies. In this, Qinghai was ahead of some other provinces. I was told that under the provincial Standing Committee, also, there was a Political and Legal Committee (*zhengfa weiyuanhui*); according to Beijing's reform plans, my informant said, it was slated to be abolished, but this had not yet taken place in Qinghai. The Party's Policy Research Office still existed in Qinghai and was expected to continue to function. Its main responsibility was to produce reports on all important aspects of Party and government work, but I was told that in the period ahead it would focus mainly on economic problems and issues. The Party also had a Bureau for Old Cadres Work dealing with retired "Party-member cadres," giving special attention to those who had joined the Party before 1949. The Party Standing Committee also still maintained and controlled Party *dangzu* (fractions or core groups) within key government bodies—and also in organizations such as the Academy of Social Sciences. Even though Beijing's reformers were calling for the abolishment of these Party core groups, in Qinghai the Party was not considering doing this any time soon, I was told. The Party committee also continued to run its own provincial Party school.

Separate but parallel to this Party structure was the Party's Discipline Inspection Committee, operating under the "dual leadership" of equivalent committees at higher levels as well as the Qinghai Party Standing Committee; the rank of its head, I was told, was equivalent to that of a deputy Party secretary. One special Party branch was responsible for supervising the "Party life" of all cadres working in the Party apparatus at the provincial level. The total number of Party cadres working in all of these units directly under the provincial Party's top apparatus totaled roughly 1,000, I was told.

*   *   *

Within the provincial government, the top leadership group was less easy to define precisely, but Deputy Governor Bian asserted that although there was no formal "standing committee" in the government, its equivalent was a group of six individuals: the governor, four deputy governors, and the secretary-general. All of the six had risen to top leadership positions quite recently: One dated to 1982, one to 1988, and the rest had risen to the top in 1985. The governor and two deputy governors were Han Chinese, but the other two deputy governors were members of minority groups—one was a Tibetan and the other a Tu. Again, though, it was notable that there was no Hui representation at the very top level. Of the six top government leaders, two were local people and four were outsiders. The educational standards of those at the top were somewhat higher than in the Party but were nevertheless considerably lower than in coastal provinces of China. Of the six, four had had education above the middle school level, but of these only two had graduated from universities (and only one had gone on for further graduate training). The remaining two of the six (including the governor) had graduated from higher technical schools (*dazhuan*—a level above middle school but below university level).

Nevertheless, Deputy Governor Bian stressed, in the 1980s there had been very major changes in the age level and educational level of the entire leadership in the provincial government. "About 70 percent of all provincial-level leaders now have educational degrees from institutions higher than middle school," he said. This represented, he asserted, a significant upgrading of their qualifications. However, Bian also stressed that "in China, it is often difficult to determine just by tests whether or not a person is qualified for a job, and, in reality, many older cadres who have valuable experience are needed even if they lack higher educational degrees." I did not disagree with that judgment: On my travels I had met quite a few older cadres lacking higher education who impressed me as being more competent than some of the younger, better-educated ones I met.

Although Deputy Governor Bian identified who the top six provincial government leaders were, he went on to stress that many more than these six were involved in high-level decisionmaking. There were actually several different kinds of decisionmaking groups that held regular meetings, he said, and some of these involved significantly larger groups. He described three groups—or, rather, three kinds of regularly scheduled meetings—which he said were particularly important (in addition, of course, there were a great

many ad hoc meetings). The most important of all were the regularly scheduled meetings of the six top leaders. This group met formally at least fort-
nightly and more frequently if necessary; their meetings were generally called
"executive meetings" (*changwu huiyi*). A second type of important meeting
was convened at least monthly (more frequently if necessary) and involved,
in addition to the top six, a fairly wide range of other relevant leaders; these
meetings were called "production work meetings" (*shengchan bangong
huiyi*). The largest regular meetings, generally held at least every three
months (that is, quarterly), were called "general meetings" (*quanti huiyi*);
these involved most of the heads of commissions, departments, and bureaus
in the provincial government.

I had decided that, despite my deep interest in the structure of government
in China, I would not take time in Qinghai to try to piece together a complete picture of the local bureaucracy, as I had done on earlier stops. However, when local officials learned that I had a strong interest in the subject,
they insisted on briefing me in considerable detail about the organization of
the government. What they described was basically similar to what I had
learned in other provinces, with only minor variations, but, interestingly,
their categorization or grouping of units was different from that used by officials elsewhere. In Qinghai, I was told, under the governor's office (*bangong
ting*), bureaucratic units were grouped into seven categories, or "systems"
(*xitong*), with the following shorthand designations: (1) comprehensive
(*zonghe*), (2) industry and transportation (*gongjiao*), (3) agriculture and animal husbandry (*nongwu*), (4) finance and trade (*tsaimao*), (5) science and
education (*kexuejiaoyu*), (6) health and sports (*weishengtiyu*), and (7) culture and propaganda (*wenhuaxuanchuan*). These general categories are familiar to anyone knowledgeable about China bureaucracies, but this list was
idiosyncratic in some respects and illustrated the fact that although in many
ways bureaucratic organizations in China follow a remarkably uniform pattern, provincial authorities do have some latitude in modifying and adapting
that pattern to their local situation.*

I asked how many people worked in the provincial government units
headquartered in Xining. Officials were not able to give me a precise figure
without further checking, so they simply said that it was "in the thousands."
I did, however, obtain a figure for the number of "state cadres working under both the Party and government bureaucracies at all levels throughout the
province." The total, I was told, was 137,000 (this included both Party cadres and non-Party cadres). The breakdown by ethnic groups showed that

---

*Although my trip notes contained a list of the most important governmental units in Qinghai,
I will not duplicate that list here. The pattern was generally similar to that of other provinces.

even though the number of minority members working for the Party and the government was fairly impressive compared to what it had been before 1949, nevertheless Han Chinese still held a disproportionately large share of official positions. Of the 137,000 Party and government cadres, Han Chinese accounted for almost 111,900 (82 percent)—well above the three-fifths share of the population that the Han Chinese represented—whereas members of minorities accounted for 25,100 (less than one-fifth of all cadres) even though they made up about two-fifths of the total population.

Of the minority cadres, approximately 15,500 were Tibetans; this number was slightly over 11 percent of the total of all cadres, far less than the 20 percent share of the Tibetans in the provincial population. The Hui were even less well represented: Altogether there were roughly 5,900 Hui cadres in the province; these cadres constituted only 4.3 percent of all cadres, even though the Hui made up almost 14 percent of the total population. Although the Tibetans were very well represented in the local government bodies that administered the bulk of the provincial territory (as I saw for myself when I later visited Hainan), they were much less well represented in bodies operating at the provincial level. The very low figure for Hui cadres applied at lower levels as well as at the top, and this fact reinforced my strong impression that the Han-dominated power structure was still wary of the Hui population in light of the Ma clan's political dominance in the years before 1949. Hui underrepresentation may also have resulted partially from other factors, however, including their lower educational level (compared to the Han) and economic disadvantages. The large influx since the 1950s of educated Han outsiders into the province also strengthened the predominance of the Han Chinese in almost all technical and nontraditional economic fields, especially at top levels.

*   *   *

In Qinghai, as in other places I visited, I asked whether I could meet local military leaders. Although I was able to do this in some places, Qinghai was not one of them. Nevertheless, I did attempt, with some success, to get a sense of the saliency of the military presence in the province and, from the civilian leaders I met, I obtained some insights into the nature of the civil-military relationships.

Qinghai clearly has a special importance for the PLA: Even though it is not as important as some border provinces, it does have a significant strategic position as the most important route for military supplies, equipment, and personnel going from east and north China to the Tibetan Autonomous Region. I was told that much of the military traffic to Tibet relied primarily on the rail line from Xining to Golmud in Qinghai's Tsaidam region, and from the end of the rail line it went by truck to Tibet. (Some materiel went the entire way by truck.) When I made a car trip from Xining to Hainan Prefecture (which I will discuss later), I traveled over one of the main routes to Lhasa. My driver on the trip said that he had driven trucks to Tibet for more than nine years and asserted that the road was reasonably good for almost the entire 1,300-plus miles to Lhasa. The route was maintained, he said, basically by military personnel; he described the small army stations (*bingjan*), which he said were located at very frequent intervals along the route and served as hostels for truckers and other people traveling the road—civilians as well as military personnel. Driving a supply truck from Xining to Lhasa generally had taken him about 21 days in earlier years, he said. (Deputy Governor Bian told me, however, that it is now possible to make the trip by car in 5 days, and people I met in Taersi said that it generally took 4 days from there.)

In light of the fact that Xining was important as a way station on the military route to Tibet, I was very surprised, as I had been elsewhere in northwest China, that the military presence was so inconspicuous—although it was somewhat greater in Xining than it had been in Baotou or Yinchuan. Apart from the army officers who shared my train ride from Lanzhou to Xining, I saw only a few officers in uniform—some of them staying at the Xining Guest House. Moving around Xining, I did see the Military District headquarters, which was a large establishment located on July 1 Road, and just to the west of the city on my trip to Hainan I passed one sizable army barracks, although there was little military equipment visible there. All in all, the military seemed very successful in keeping out of sight.

I asked whether the local cavalry forces, which had been so famous in Qinghai in the Ma era, were still extant and of any importance. I was told that they had continued to be quite important in the 1950s and 1960s: They had helped to "liberate" Tibet at the start of the 1950s, to establish control over Qinghai Province, and to "restore order" after rebellions in Tibetan areas in the late 1950s. Now, however, few were left. In fact, I was told that only a single company (*lian*) of cavalry still existed. The province was still famous for horse breeding, though; the main centers for raising Qinghai horses were two Tibetan autonomous provinces, Yushu and Guoluo.

In discussing civil-military relations, Deputy Governor Bian stressed, as leaders I met in other provinces also had, that the military establishment was under a different "system," which was very separate from the *xitong* associated with civilian government, but that informal relationships between the civilian government and the military establishment were close. Because the military forces were not very visible to the ordinary population, and apparently did not intrude a great deal in day-to-day governance or in ordinary people's lives, their role was significantly different from—and less intrusive than—the role that military forces had played when Ma Bufang was in charge or the role that they played in certain periods after the Communist takeover (such as in the 1950s and during the Cultural Revolution).

I also tried to judge as best as I could the extent to which other coercive instruments of rule—the political-legal system, especially the police apparatus—intruded into ordinary people's lives in Qinghai and the degree to which their activities affected the general political climate. I felt that it was particularly important to make some judgment about this in Qinghai for several reasons. As I mentioned earlier, shortly before I arrived there had been a violent "disturbance" in Xining as well as another serious clash in Lhasa, both of which had resulted in deaths; I assumed that these must have had some effect on the Qinghai population, especially on local Tibetans. I also assumed that, because of Hui dominance in the past and Hui-Han conflicts in earlier years, there probably were continuing Hui-Han tensions of some sort. I was very aware, also, that Qinghai had long been known as a place to which political exiles and dissidents, and criminals of all sorts, from other parts of China were sent.*

I was extremely alert, therefore, for any overt signs of political tensions. I concluded that in general the political atmosphere, not only in Xining but also in the Tibetan areas that I visited, was remarkably "normal." Even though I continued to suspect that ethnic tensions had been involved in the Xining "incident" just before my arrival, I could not see any evidence of aftereffects. On the surface, Han, Hui, and Tibetan people seemed to mix very freely, and I saw no obvious signs of animosity.

As I had found to be the case in many other cities, the uniformed Public Security forces and the People's Armed Police were surprisingly inconspicuous. Moreover, to the extent that one can sense the extent of tension in a region from people's behavior and the expressions on their faces (both in 1948–1949 and in the 1970s, when political tensions had been high, I had seen the effects very obviously reflected in people's behavior and expressions), Xining and the other cities I visited seemed quite relaxed. However, even though I saw little overt evidence of ethnic or political frictions, I knew that it would be naive to assume that no tensions existed. In light of past conflicts, basic cultural differences, and continuing social, economic, and political inequities, which were still substantial despite the regime's efforts to reduce

---

*I had read occasional articles written by Western journalists visiting Qinghai, and most of them had highlighted its history as a destination for those sentenced to forced labor. For example, an article on Qinghai in a major Western newspaper in 1988 began: "Qinghai is the province in China with most to hide. This is China's Siberia—a land of exiles and forced labor, of lost hopes for those who have been imprisoned here or have been assigned against their will by the state to work for a lifetime." It went on to say: "No one knows how many prisoners have been shipped to Qinghai over the years, but some observers believe that forced labor camps in the province may hold tens of thousands of prisoners ... both common criminals and political prisoners deemed to be 'counter-revolutionaries.'"

them, tensions must have continued to exist. But I was struck quite forcefully by the lack of obvious signs of them.

*   *   *

In Qinghai I heard some expression of resentment by Tibetans about the behavior and political predominance of Han Chinese, but my overall impression was that Han-Tibetan tensions were much less serious in Qinghai than in the Lhasa region of Tibet. I was told, however, that the news of the recent violence in Tibet had reached Qinghai fairly rapidly and had had some local reverberations. At Kumbum Lamasery in Taersi, several lamas (monks) told me about contacts they had with Lhasa, and as I mentioned earlier I met one lama who had just returned from Lhasa; this man was dressed, somewhat surprisingly, in a leather jacket and Western-style clothes rather than the usual red robes. He said to me that Beijing's official report that only one person had been killed was simply wrong. His account of the incident was that it started when two lamas were shot and killed at the Potala, the former residence and seat of government of the Dalai Lama (what caused the shooting, he did not say) and that this resulted in riots in which he believed about 20 additional people were killed. He and others I met deplored repression in Tibet proper. However, neither he nor anyone else I talked with in Qinghai felt that incidents in faraway Lhasa were likely to provoke active rebelliousness in Qinghai.

What I learned in 1988 about relations between Qinghai and the Lhasa area of Tibet tended to confirm a conclusion that I had reached 40 years earlier—namely, that although very important linguistic, cultural, and other ties link all of the geographic areas on the Tibetan plateau, there have long been, and continue to be, important differences among Tibetan groups inhabiting different regions, and the relations between Han Chinese and Tibetans in Qinghai have by no means been the same as those in the Tibetan Autonomous Region. In the early part of this century, some Western observers differentiated between Inner Tibet and Outer Tibet (just as they differentiated between Inner Mongolia and Outer Mongolia). Qinghai was viewed as part of the former, and Lhasa and the Xigaze (Shigatse) area were the key centers of the latter.

It is valid to use several different criteria—geographic, ethnic, and political—for defining "Tibet." Geographic Tibet unquestionably includes the entire Tibetan plateau (variously called the highlands or tableland)—a vast area, most of it above 10,000 feet, surrounded by and interspersed with high mountains. This geographic definition clearly includes all of Qinghai except the eastern fringe of the province. A sizable part of Sichuan Province—the portion formerly called Xikang (Sikang) Province—also clearly belongs to the Tibetan plateau. Ethnic Tibet includes virtually all of geographic Tibet and also reaches somewhat beyond it into several areas adjacent to the plateau into which Tibetans have moved. Political Tibet, however, has varied greatly over time. Its center for centuries has been, and remains, in the area that is now organized as the Tibetan Autonomous Region. Some of the autonomous Tibetan prefectures and counties that now are part of Qinghai and other provinces adjacent to the Tibetan Autonomous Region were at times part of political Tibet, but for long periods some of these were only very loosely linked to Lhasa or Xigaze politically.

Distances separating various Tibetan areas are so great that there are very significant differences, both cultural and political, among and between regions such as the U and Zang (Tsang) areas of central-south Tibet where Lhasa and Xigaze are located; the Kham region in the east, the best-known center of which is Qamdo (Chamdo); and the Amdo region to the north, which encompasses most of Qinghai.

I was told by Tibetans as well as Chinese, both in 1948 and 1988, that Amdo Tibetans, including those in Qinghai, generally view Lhasa as quite remote, psychologically as well as geographically. Although they recognize both the Dalai Lama and the Banchan Lama as very important religious leaders, many if not most have long been oriented more directly to the Banchan, who in recent decades has had close links with Chinese leaders in Beijing and often has headquartered in either Qinghai or Beijing. The Dalai Lama, who left Lhasa for India after the Tibetan rebellion in the late 1950s, continues to be the undisputed top religious leader for most people in the U, Zang, and Kham areas, including those areas where both Tibetan rebelliousness and Chinese repression have been the greatest in recent years. Open rebellion in the period from 1954 through 1959 really began in the Khampa area in eastern Tibet and then spread to the central south; the Amdo area was much less involved. There was, however, a serious uprising of Tibetans in the Guoluo area near the Amne Machin Mountains in southeastern Qinghai in the late 1950s. In recent years, however, the rebelliousness has been greatest in the Lhasa region and nearby areas; Qinghai has been much less affected.

*   *   *

Although I was very aware that Qinghai has long been a place where criminal and political prisoners are sent, I was not able to learn much about the scope of penal forced labor in the province. There is no question that the province is the site of major forced labor camps; probably most of them are in the Tsaidam area or in other remote regions, out of sight. I discovered that Qinghai's officials were unwilling, not surprisingly, to discuss any details about these camps. However, I also discovered that the existence of "reform through labor" camps was not concealed. The provincial Reform Through Labor Department was included, overtly, in the list of local government bodies that was provided to me, and its headquarters in Xining was easy to identify from the gate sign at the entrance to its large compound on a major thoroughfare. I personally saw only one prison labor camp, which was just west of Xining on the route to Hainan Tibetan Autonomous Prefecture. It was a fairly large enclosure, surrounded by a high brick wall topped by barbed wire, with guards stationed at each corner. Seeing that it was obviously a prison of some sort, I asked what it was and received a frank reply that it was a "Lao Gao" (Reform Through Labor) camp containing a brick factory. Several local people who seemed to be credible sources (including one who had spent a long time in a labor camp) told me that as a result of the reforms of the 1980s, a large number of prisoners had been released and they believed that by the late 1980s the number of people in Reform Through Labor camps was "much smaller" than it had been in the Maoist era.

I had one fascinating conversation that brought to life what such camps meant for those victimized in them, especially during the Maoist period. Everywhere I went in China, I asked to meet and talk with some individuals who were in their late sixties or seventies and who could from their own experience discuss the nature and the scope of changes in China since the 1940s. One elderly gentleman of this sort whom I met in Qinghai reminisced at length about "then and now." Many of his observations comparing the 1980s with the 1940s were extremely interesting, and he was more than willing, in response to my questions, to discuss in detail his personal history, including the 28 years he had spent in a labor camp in Qinghai.

This individual, who was in his mid-seventies, was a Han Chinese who had been born and raised in Qinghai. He had been fortunate, he said, to have been able to attend two of the special local schools established by Ma Bufang. The first was a village-level primary school (a "Tongren school"); the second was a junior middle school (one of Ma's "Kunlun schools"), which had been established for poor children in Xining. As a result of his schooling, he said, his good fortune had continued for some years thereafter. After graduating from junior middle school, he was sent to a senior middle school in faraway Nanjing in Jiangsu Province. After graduation there, he returned to Qinghai in 1937 to teach for several years in a Kunlun middle school. Then he was one of the few local youths who were given an opportunity to attend a university. The one he attended was in Chengdu, Sichuan; he graduated from it in 1945. Returning to Jiangsu, he became a principal of a normal (teachers') school in Suzhou, and then later he became a lecturer at a university in Nanjing, rising to become an associate professor specializing in Chinese history.

Then came the Communist "liberation" in 1949, and soon thereafter came personal disaster for him. He became a target of direct political attack during the campaign against counterrevolutionaries in 1951. The reason he was victimized, he said, was that in school he had been a classmate of one of Ma Bufang's sons, and then in Nanjing he had worked as an assistant to a prominent Guomindang (Kuomintang) leader. Guilt by association, because of these links, was sufficient cause for him to be denounced and severely punished, and he was sentenced to reform through labor. The place to which he was sent was the Xiongride labor camp in the Tsaidam area of Qinghai, where he spent the next 28 years. This camp contained about one thousand prisoners, he said; all of the inmates were set to work either raising animals or farming. His years there were very *ku* (bitter). Prison life was one of great hardship. There were *no* days off. The cold was particularly hard to endure; sometimes inmates slept with the animals to try to keep warm.

After Mao's death he applied for a "reversal of verdict," and, after a long, complicated process, which he described to me in excruciating detail, he finally obtained release in 1979. He had first applied to the provincial Public Security Department, which recommended a "reversal of verdict." Even the provincial governor and Party secretary became interested in his case, he said, but the "legal authorities" would not agree and nothing resulted. After Beijing's national policy became more liberal, he applied again, this time to various national as well as provincial organizations and leaders, including members of the national People's Political Consultative Conference. Finally, he said, Deputy Premier Wang Zhen became interested in his case, and this led, ultimately, to approval of his pardon and release.

Even though this gentleman had been free for a decade and was living quite comfortably on a retirement stipend when I met him, his story symbolized the tragedy of countless intellectuals victimized during the Maoist period. Most of his adult life had been wasted. Remarkably, he remained a cultivated Chinese gentleman of a fairly traditional sort, and he still was mentally sharp and surprisingly calm and seemingly unemotional in most of the judgments that he made. He stated that he had no idea how many people had been incarcerated in Qinghai's labor camps, either in the Maoist period or recently. He said that he believed, however, that since the start of reforms, in the late 1970s, the number had been greatly reduced. In the liberalized atmosphere of 1988, this old man seemed to have few, if any, inhibitions about giving his personal opinions on anything and everything I asked him about.

His judgments about changes in China during the previous 40 years, based on what he had observed in Qinghai first in the 1940s and then in the 1980s, were extremely interesting. Like a Rip Van Winkle returning to familiar scenes after more than a quarter century of isolation in a remote and desolate place, he had been particularly sensitive to the changes. Some of the important transformations he discussed were the following.

"The changes [during the past four decades] have been tremendous. ... First of all, transportation is entirely different. When I first went to Nanjing, I spent six days going to Lanzhou by donkey, then almost seven days by truck on unpaved roads to Xi'an, then by truck to Weinan, east of Xi'an, to get the train to Nanjing. Now it is entirely different. ... Recently, also, TV has had a very profound effect. Knowledge of the world has increased greatly. We used to be very isolated. I remember in the 1930s talking to a peddlar in Dongguan, Shaanxi. He asked me where I came from, and when I said Qinghai, he thought it was someplace abroad, maybe in Europe. Even in the 1950s many people elsewhere in China confused Qinghai with Qingdao; they did not know anything about us. Even in the 1950s, many people in Guoluo in southern Qinghai did not even know where Xining was. All this has changed. TV has brought the whole world closer. ... Most households in my town (*zhen*) now have TV sets. This has ended their isolation. It has also shown people the power of science and technology, and, as a result, it has reduced superstition. It also has affected religion. In my town most people watch the news as well as many entertainment serials. TV also spreads fashions in clothing, furniture and so on. ...

"Another big change has been in education and culture. There were few schools before. I think there were only five middle schools—although I'm not sure of the exact figure—in the province. Now Xining alone has more than 40, I believe. There were practically no intellectuals here before, only a few dozen, really. Now there are many.

"A third big change has been in the economy, in production. There were no large factories here before, only one small hydrostation and a few small workshops. Now there are many; the central government has invested a lot here. ... However, agriculture has changed much less—some, but not a lot, until recently—and it is still backward. In the 1950s, people blindly cultivated areas that should not have been tilled, places without enough water, destroying pastureland. The effects were bad. At one point, harvests were less than the seed planted. ...

"Overall, judging by my own town, life has improved greatly, at least it has in my town; the living standard has risen a lot, but mostly in the 1980s. In the 1950s, from what I learned, people had enough food to eat and clothes to wear, but then in the early 1960s, because of leftist policies and natural disasters, people did not have nearly enough to eat. Really, from the 1960s to the 1980s, things were very hard; there were shortages of both food and clothing. Peasants couldn't do 'sideline' work; they would be accused of capitalism for selling eggs or chickens. But since 1978 things have been much better. Living standards have significantly increased; I can see that. This is really the only period since 1949 in which their living standards have improved.

"However, there are bad effects from all of this, too. People now try to make money any way they can, even in illegal ways. They compete to have the most ostentatious life-style. In the old days, people saved; now they spend all of their money and go into debt. They especially compete to build and furnish new houses. I estimate that two-thirds of the houses in my town are new, and two-fifths of them are large. Some are better than preliberation landlords' houses. Some peasants try to build houses as luxurious as Ma Bufang's used to be. People getting married insist on elaborate, expensive weddings. There also has been a great increase in corruption. Spending is now getting ahead of production and earnings."

The picture described by this old gentleman was consistent with what I heard from a great many others in 1988. Economic progress was leading to increased consumerism and rising expectations, but also to increased corruption and confusion about values.*

The fact that not only the deputy governor but even the former labor camp prisoner talked at such lengths about the economic changes that had begun to transform Qinghai, especially in the 1980s, was a clear indication of what was on the minds of most people I met in 1988. Economic development was the subject that the majority of people I interviewed wished to talk about. Their major preoccupation, however, was not so much the province's past achievements, even though they were proud of the progress that had been made toward modernization, but rather the degree to which Qinghai remained relatively backward compared to the more developed regions of the country and the urgent need to "catch up." The economic portrait of Qinghai that emerged from my many interviews was one of a huge, still relatively underdeveloped province struggling to overcome enormous obstacles to modernization—a province led by men who were worried that they might be left behind by the rapid changes occurring in coastal China but were nevertheless convinced that because the province possessed rich natural resources, it had the potential to move rapidly forward toward modernity.

*   *   *

---

*Deputy Governor Bian, when I asked him what he thought were the most important changes that he had seen since he arrived in Xining in 1960, mentioned, on the positive side, many of the same things that the old ex-prisoner from Tsaidam had. Bian said: "Simply stated, Xining now is totally different from what it was then. I could list 29 or 30 areas of change, but I'll just mention a few obvious ones. The city is much larger. It used to be a city of one-story buildings; now we have many tall modern buildings. Most houses here have been built since 1949. Economic output has grown greatly. A lot of people have come here from other parts of China. The cultural standard of ordinary people has risen greatly. Transportation and communication are much better. There used to be only a few bad roads, but now we have a railway, paved roads, and airline connections. Our contacts with other areas of China are much greater, especially since adoption of the 'open policy.' There are many more contacts than before. This has resulted in great changes in people's attitudes and outlooks."

The area of Qinghai is enormous, encompassing almost 280,000 square miles. It is bigger than France, and for that matter larger than any other West European nation.* As stated earlier, most of the province lies on the Tibetan plateau, but the area is so vast that, as one might expect, it consists of several subregions. Local people described these regions to me in three different ways: first, in terms of administrative divisions; second, according to geography and altitude; and third—and most usefully—according to economic regions.

Administratively, Qinghai had, as of 1988, only 1 municipality, namely Xining, the capital. But Golmud (in the Tsaidam basin), though still only a county-level city, was expected to be elevated to the status of municipality before long. The rest of the province contained 7 prefectures (5 of these were labeled Tibetan autonomous prefectures, 1 was called a Mongol-Tibetan-Kazakh autonomous prefecture, and 1 was an ordinary prefecture); and about 40 counties (several of which were either Hui or Mongol autonomous counties). Five of the prefectures as well as Xining Municipality occupied the eastern part of the province, which covered between a quarter and a third of the total territory. (The 5 prefectures included Huangnan, on the border with Gansu in the east, and 4 of Qinghai's Tibetan autonomous prefectures [TAPs]—Haidong TAP, east of Lake Qinghai and south of Xining; Haibei TAP, north of the lake; Hainan TAP, south of the lake; and Guoluo TAP, in the far southeast.) By far the largest part of the province, however, belonged to two humongous and extremely sparsely populated autonomous prefectures: the Haixi Mongol-Tibetan-Kazakh Autonomous Prefecture ("Haixi" means west of the lake), which encompassed the entire northwest part of the province as well as a sizable separate area in the southwest, and the almost-as-large Yushu TAP in the south and west. The centrality of Lake Qinghai in the province's mythology and self-image is reflected in the fact that four of the prefectural names mean, literally, east, north, south, and west of the lake.

Geographers do not all agree on how best to define the province's regions, but one common, and logical, definition differentiates the eastern, northwestern, and southern regions. The eastern plateau lies between the Qilian and Nanshan and other mountains in the north and the Bayan Kala (or Bayan Har) range in the south. This area includes Xining and five of the prefectures described previously. Most of the plateau in this area is above 8,000 feet and much of it is closer to 10,000 feet, and it is crisscrossed by mountains that are between 13,000 to 20,000 feet high. Yet this is one of the lowest areas in the province. In this area, especially just west of the lake, there is

---

*Official Chinese sources differ on Qinghai's exact size; even different publications within Qinghai gave conflicting figures. The figure given here is the one that was used most frequently. (The figure in kilometers was 720,000 square kilometers, or about 278,000 square miles.)

good pastureland. To the east, around Xining, are the areas containing most of the province's population, agriculture, and industry—much of it in low-land areas in the valleys of the upper reaches of the Yellow River and tributaries such as the Huangshui and Datong.

The southern plateau lies between the Bayan Kala mountains and the Tanggula range, which lies on the southwestern border of the province. This area's elevation averages between 13,000 and 14,000 feet, but many peaks rise to more than 20,000 feet. A cold, remote place, this area includes most of Yushu TAP and part of the Haixi Mongol-Tibetan-Kazakh Autonomous Prefecture and is inhabited mainly by nomadic Tibetan herdsmen.

The Tsaidam depression (or basin) occupies most of the northwest, between the Altai mountains to the north and the Kunlun range in west-central Qinghai. Some areas of the Tsaidam depression consist of salt marshes with interior drainage; others, in the far northwest, are true desert. The altitudes in this area are comparable to areas in the east. Administratively, it belongs to the Haixi Mongol-Tibetan-Kazakh Autonomous Prefecture. The region was almost entirely uninhabited, except for scattered Kazakh and Mongol groups, until major mineral and other resources began to be developed in the 1950s. It now has one of Qinghai's most important newly developing cities, Golmud.

Some local experts in Qinghai, when analyzing provincial regions, described them in terms of altitude, differentiating several bands of territory lying at different heights. They have good reason for doing so: One said to me, "No kind of agriculture is at all practical except in areas with good water supply that are below about 11,000 feet." Much of the province is well above this altitude.* However, some of the best pastureland lies in areas between 10,000 and 13,000 feet. The areas above 13,000 feet, I was told, are not much good for either animal husbandry or agriculture.

When I talked with economic experts from the government, they had at their fingertips fairly precise statistics on land elevation and land use in Qinghai. These figures highlighted the economic limits resulting from topography. Only 15 percent of the province is below 10,000 feet, I was told; 24 percent is between 10,000 and 13,000 feet; almost 49 percent is between 13,000 and 16,000-plus feet; and roughly 7 percent is above 16,000 feet. These economist specialists calculated that slightly less than half of the province's territory had any potential economic use at all; of the land they said was potentially useful, 96 percent was classified as territory usable for animal husbandry and only 4 percent was regarded as potentially arable agri-

---

*These and the following altitude and territory figures were given to me in meters and *mou;* I have rounded the former to the nearest 1,000 and have converted meters to feet and *mou* to acres. The percentage figures do not add up to 100 percent of the province's territory.

cultural land (and the figure might well be lower if one used standards generally used in more benign geographical areas). As of 1988, I was told, only 1.42 million acres of land in the province were actually being cultivated by the farming population of 2.5 million people (mainly Han or Hui but including some Tibetans as well as Tu and Salar); my informants estimated, however, that the total arable land was probably about 2.5 million acres, but the uncultivated 1-plus million acres would be difficult to develop. By contrast, they said, roughly 83 million acres were being actively used as pastureland, by the roughly 800,000 people (mainly Tibetan, but including some Mongols and Kazakhs) engaged in animal husbandry.

                              *   *   *

Of all the various classifications of subregions in Qinghai that people described to me, I found most useful the one presented by the head of the Long-Term Planning Division of the provincial Planning Commission. He asserted that Qinghai can be divided into four major economic regions that reflect a combination of geographic, topographic, and demographic characteristics and their impact on the economy. The Xining region, he said, was by far the most important and completely dominated the province's economy, at least in terms of its gross economic output. Although geographically small, this region—consisting of the area immediately around Xining, much of Haidong Prefecture, and part of Huangnan as well as the valleys of the Yellow River and Huangshui River—included roughly 3 million people, about 73 percent of the province's total population (roughly one-third of these were in Xining Municipality alone). The region included the bulk of the province's manufacturing plants; by far the largest number of these were in Xining Municipality itself, but there were some in nearby towns. It also accounted for most of Qinghai farm output, which was concentrated in the two principal river valleys. (Some of the economists I met maintained that one could divide this area into two regions: Xining, which dominated the industrial economy, and the surrounding agricultural areas, which accounted for most of its farming.) Local economists also felt that this region had the greatest potential for further development partly because of its great possibilities for the development of hydropower. They estimated that between the Longyang gorge, where a large dam had been under construction for some time, and the Gansu border (about 350 miles away), perhaps 19 hydrostations could be built on the Yellow River, and they estimated that if all were actually built, they might have a capacity of as much as 14 gigawatts.

The second most important economic region, they said, was the one centered on the Tsaidam basin. This region was developing fairly rapidly into a major area for mining and for industries producing raw materials. It is a large region. Until the 1950s, it was an almost uninhabited, desolate wilderness: Its population in 1949 was estimated to total only about 10,000. Then, starting in the 1950s, the central government provided substantial financial and other support. Intensive surveying of its resources took place, and steps began to be taken to exploit its potential. Surveys throughout the province, I was told, had indicated that Qinghai possessed 37 important raw materials whose deposits put the province among the top 10 potential producers in the country and that in 8 of these it ranked the highest in the country. The principal deposits of the 8 had been discovered in the Tsaidam region. The extensive salt marshes and lakes of Tsaidam, covering more than 2,200 square miles, made the region an extremely forbidding place, but because of the large resources of a wide range of minerals and chemicals, by the 1980s the government had begun to build numerous mines and small plants to process chemicals. Started on a small scale in the 1950s, development in the region accelerated after the completion in 1979 of the railway from Xining to Golmud. By the late 1980s the population of the region had risen to about 260,000.* As of 1988, major new projects under construction included a very large enterprise to produce chemicals and chemical fertilizer, which would even at its initial stage have an annual output of about 200,000 tons and ultimately could produce perhaps 800,000 tons. In the west of the basin, three oil fields were being developed, and planners hoped to build a 250-mile pipeline to connect them with Golmud and to construct a large petroleum refinery in Golmud. Central government investment was supporting virtually all of these large new projects.

Third in importance among the province's economic regions, I was told, was the region around Lake Qinghai, which included Haibei Prefecture north of the lake and Hainan Prefecture to the south, plus one county in Haixi Prefecture to the west. Even though this area was much less developed than the Xining region, and had relatively little modern industry or, for that matter, agriculture, and even though it lacked the resources that gave Tsaidam such a great potential, it was an area of excellent pastureland and its animal husbandry made it an important economic region. It had developed a few small factories, and there was some fishing in Lake Qinghai. It was also the location of a major dam that had been built on the Yellow River in Hainan TAP.

A fourth economic region, Qingnan—or South Qinghai—covered most of the south, including the two largest autonomous prefectures—Guoluo and Yushu—as well as part of Huangnan TAP in the east and a portion of Haixi

---

*Some of Qinghai's planners had for some time pushed for the extension of the railway to Lhasa, but this idea had been abandoned, I was told, because the Tanggula mountains were simply too high. The planners still hoped to connect Golmud to Xinjiang by railway eventually. The completion of the railway from Xining had facilitated a large-scale migration of labor and technicians into the Tsaidam area.

in the southwest. The remotest, highest, and coldest area of the province, this region as of 1988 had almost no industry and very little farming. For the most part, its inhabitants were Tibetan herdsmen engaged in animal husbandry. Most inhabitants of the south were poor—but not all of them. In some good pastureland areas, in fact, per capita incomes were higher than in some of Qinghai's farming areas. But the south nevertheless had many large pockets of extreme poverty that were the worst in Qinghai. The two most poverty-stricken counties in the province were Banma in Guoluo Prefecture and Nangqian in Yushu.

*   *   *

Despite recent progress, the gross economic output of the province as a whole was still very low. In fact, of all provincial-level units in China, only Tibet and Ningxia produced less. National statistics for 1985 indicated that Qinghai's total output ("total product of society") at that time was Y 5.496 billion, of which industry and construction accounted for 64 percent (Y 3.527 billion—Y 2.265 billion for industry and Y 1.262 billion for construction), agriculture 22 percent (Y 1.225 billion), and transport and commerce the rest (Y 310 million and Y 434 million respectively). Local statistics were actually somewhat lower than the national figures. In 1986, according to what I was told by provincial officials, industrial output totaled Y 2.2-plus billion (this included military industry, I was told, although local people said the military component was not large), and agricultural output was just over Y 1 billion (roughly Y 450 million from farming, Y 400 million from animal husbandry, and the rest from fisheries, forestry, and so on). Preliminary local estimates indicated that the total value of industrial output had risen in 1987 to almost Y 2.4 billion. Even though output had doubled between the 1970s and the late 1980s, it was still low.

Nevertheless, despite the realities that these figures revealed, I was genuinely impressed by how much the province had developed in the four decades since my previous visit. There was no doubt that the structure of the economy had been altered in some fairly fundamental ways and that, overall, per capita output, though still low, had risen a great deal since the 1940s.

Whereas in the 1940s industrial production and construction had been negligible, by the late 1980s these sectors accounted for about two-thirds of the value of the province's total output. The province's total work force in 1986 totaled 1.892 million. In rural areas, 1.112 million worked in agriculture, animal husbandry, and related activities. Of the nonagricultural work force, which totaled roughly 780,000, industrial and construction workers numbered about 387,000 (261,000 in industry and 126,000 in construction). In addition, roughly 74,000 people now worked in transport and telecommunications, 89,000 in commerce, 28,000 in geological work, and 58,000 in educational, cultural, and media fields, and the remainder in a variety of occupations. Although the population of the province was still predominantly rural, 22 percent of the people now lived in cities and towns. The biggest changes, compared to the 1940s, obviously were in the employment and livelihood of those in the growing urban centers.

The economic development of Qinghai from the 1950s onward depended fundamentally on central government financing. Relatively little capital could be generated locally. Although the agricultural sector was still extremely important, most of the external assistance and central government investment had gone into urban, industrial, and mining development. This was still the case in 1988. As a result, Qinghai, like virtually all of west China, remained extremely dependent financially on Beijing, and provincial experts recognized that the province would face a bleak future without large-scale central subsidies. Provincial officials gave me only a few statistics (all very rough figures) on the province's budget, but these were sufficient to make clear how dependent Qinghai still was on Beijing. They stated that in 1986 (the last year for which they could give me final official figures), Qinghai's budgetary expenditures totaled Y 1.2 billion. Its revenue from taxes (mainly the profit tax and other industrial and commercial taxes) amounted to only Y 410 million and therefore covered only a little over a third of the province's expenditures. The rest, almost Y 800 million, came from central government subsidies; Y 200 million of this consisted of funds earmarked for specific purposes, and almost Y 600 million was given as a general subsidy. As a result of recent reforms, Qinghai had acquired increased decisionmaking authority in many areas, I was told, but clearly its great financial dependence on Beijing imposed severe constraints on the ability of local leaders to consider any large projects or programs that did not have central government support or at least its acquiescence.

Even though the value of industrial output in Qinghai had grown to the point where it was more than double that of agriculture by the late 1980s, a majority of the population and the work force was still rural, and, as in earlier years, agriculture still consisted of two entirely different elements. Farming in the east, which was carried out mainly by Han, Hui, and Tu peasants—plus a few Salar—was concentrated in the valleys and nearby hillsides. Roughly 70 percent of farm output, in fact, came from the area right around Xining. In the west, farming by Tibetans was scattered and small scale. As noted earlier, provincial officials stated that even though they classified about 2.5 million acres as arable, only 1.42 million acres were actually under cultivation. Therefore in theory the amount of land under cultivation could almost be doubled, but everyone stressed that the estimated cost of doing this was so high that few people saw any prospect of increasing agricultural land very much in the near future.

My informants said that before land reform and the subsequent establishment of agricultural production cooperatives, which were organized during the first half of the 1950s, landlords dominated Qinghai's agriculture even though they constituted only 5 percent of the farming population. Farmers who were classified either as "rich peasants" or as "upper middle peasants" (that is, owner-cultivators) accounted for about a quarter of the farming population, and those classified as "lower middle" peasants and "tenant farmers" (among whom there were more Hui than Han) made up roughly 70 percent. In Qinghai, as elsewhere in China, communization was carried out in 1958, and local people all said that it had fairly disastrous results. Then, in the post-Mao era, the household-based responsibility system—or contract system—was started experimentally in Qinghai in 1980; it spread rapidly from 1981 on. By 1984 it had been applied generally in both farming and animal husbandry, reportedly with very positive effects.

The main crop in Qinghai continued to be wheat, as it had long been, but cultivation of potatoes, barley, vegetables, and vegetable oil crops was quite widespread. Although new agricultural techniques reportedly had been introduced fairly widely, in the areas that I visited farming methods still seemed to be basically traditional. I saw little evidence of mechanization—mainly small tractors. Only about 400,000 acres of agricultural land (mostly in river valley lowlands)—that is, roughly 28 percent of the total cultivated area—were irrigated, which seemed to me to be a surprisingly low figure. However, provincial officials said that their plans called for some further development of irrigation in the near future.

The proportion of the population engaged in animal husbandry in Qinghai was much smaller than that involved in farming, but the territory used for pasturage was very much larger than the cultivated area, and, surprisingly, the gross value of animal production was only slightly less than that of farming. Moreover, the value of per capita output was actually higher in animal husbandry than in farming—although there were wide regional variations. Apart from a few Mongols and Kazakhs, Tibetans made up the bulk of the 800,000 or so people dependent on animal husbandry. Although many Tibetans did some farming, the livelihood of the large majority of them depended on the raising of animals. Spread all over the vast area of south Qinghai as well as other areas such as the Lake Qinghai region, pastureland occupied more than 83 million acres of territory, well over nine-tenths of Qinghai's "agricultural land," and by the late 1980s, as noted earlier, the value of output of animal husbandry was almost Y 400 million a year, compared to roughly Y 450 million for farming. Qinghai, one of the four main animal breeding areas in China (the others being Inner Mongolia, Xinjiang, and Tibet proper), contained, in 1988, almost five times as many animals as people, I was told. Animals of all kinds totaled roughly 20 million. Of these, sheep and goats accounted for 15.7 million (sheep alone totaled 13 million). Yaks, though less numerous, continued to be extremely important to the Tibetan way of life. Totaling about 4 million, they provided transport, meat, milk, and wool. Some horses were still raised, but compared to the past, they had declined in importance.

Almost all of the changing national agricultural policies implemented by Beijing had been carried out in the Tibetan pasturelands in Qinghai as well as in the Han-Hui farming areas. These included the programs for collectivization and communization, even though these obviously meant something different in pastoral areas from what they did in farming areas. Later, in the early 1980s, the contract responsibility system was also applied in pastoral areas, and since then all herdsmen had regularly signed contracts covering both their animals and their pastureland. I was told that boundaries now divided the pastureland; in summer they often were ignored, but in winter, when good grassland was scarce, they were more important. Provincial officials estimated that about 85 percent of the Tibetans in Qinghai were still basically nomadic and lived much of the time in felt tents—this figure seemed high to me—and that about 15 percent had settled down and lived only in houses. The majority moved with their animals in the summer. I was told that although sometimes individual families moved on their own from area to area, many moved in groups consisting mainly of related families.

By the 1980s, however, small towns or settlements had developed throughout the pastureland; some of these had as many as 100 households, but in remote areas they often consisted of only 20 to 30 households. These settlements had become the centers of government, and most had "Muming Committees," equivalent to villages (*cun*) in farming areas. In each of these centers, there were at least a few cadres who worked for the government and the Party; these included, in some centers, personnel working for the provincial public security system. When government meetings were held in such centers, I was told, they usually convened in an open-air space since there were no large buildings. These settlements also served as economic centers, and some of them had both supply and marketing cooperatives and credit cooperatives.

To my surprise, official figures indicated that the average per capita annual income for the population involved in animal husbandry, in the province as a whole, was Y 459 in 1986, about a sixth higher than the province-wide per capita income of the population involved in farming, which was reported to be Y 396 in that same year.* The average income of the entire ru-

---

*The figure given to me for average farming incomes actually was higher than what I had calculated on the basis of the official figures on the rural population and on overall output of the farming population, but perhaps the official figure on the rural population, which I used for my calculations, may have included some rural people not engaged in farming. The Y 396 figure for per capita income of the population involved in agriculture was so specific that I assumed that it had some valid basis.

ral population, however, was less than half that of the per capita average income in urban areas; a recent survey of the latter had shown it to be Y 84 a month, or more than Y 1,000 a year. Compared to incomes in agricultural areas, the variations in per capita income between different animal husbandry areas was greater than that in agriculture, I was told. For example, in prosperous pastureland areas near Lake Qinghai, the per capita income of those raising animals was said to be about Y 700 in the late 1980s, whereas in very poor areas in the south it was close to Y 240. One young Tibetan-speaking Han scholar, who had specialized in Tibetan studies in the Qinghai Academy of Social Sciences, described at some length to me conditions in poor southern areas. The picture was a dismal one, largely because of poverty but also because of the persistence of superstition and old traditions, exacerbated by heavy drinking. This young scholar, who was about to leave for a six-year assignment in a poor southern area, was very interested in Tibetan culture and was clearly extremely sympathetic to the Tibetans.

*   *   *

The most striking economic change in Qinghai since my previous visit in 1948 had been the growth of a significant industrial sector, with its main base in Xining. In the 1940s, Ma Bufang had tried to introduce some modern industry, but at that time Xining had only about eight small factories, and most of these were semimodern workshops engaged in wool washing, match making, leather tanning, pottery, the manufacture of small tools, and the simple production of some chemicals. Although Xining then had a small electric plant, its power was sufficient to provide only some lighting, and almost none was used for manufacturing. Xining also had a little local telephone system, but the province was basically isolated from the rest of China.

By 1987, Qinghai had a total of 1,291 modern factories (a figure that did not include about 30,000 small township and village enterprises and workshops at the county level and below). Most of the factories were in Xining, but there were some (especially ones producing raw materials) in the Tsaidam area, and local planners hoped to develop that area into a major industrial base. Some, also, were scattered along the rail line connecting Xining and Golmud. The gross value of the output of all of these factories accounted for over 40 percent of the total economic output (the "total product of society") of the province. The core of the provincial industrial economy consisted of 45 large and medium-sized factories, virtually all in the Xining area, 15 of which were under central government control. (These 15 were classified, however, as being under "dual leadership." Beijing provided most of the investment and raw materials and set key targets; the province, or the municipality, exercised administrative supervision over the factories.)

Industrial development in Qinghai began in the early 1950s, but the first period in which there was large-scale construction of factories was during the period of the Great Leap Forward, in 1958–1960. The investment in industry, and the size of the industrial and construction work force, rose rapidly during those years, and industrial output quadrupled in the late 1950s. In the early 1960s, during the economic depression that followed the Great Leap Forward, agricultural output dropped precipitously, and this was followed by a steep decline in industrial production. Many industrial workers returned to rural areas as a result, I was told.

The local economy began to recover in 1963. Then, the greatest spurt of all in the province's industrial development occurred during the Cultural Revolution, from the mid-1960s to the mid-1970s, when, as a result of Mao's "three-front" strategy, 27 of Qinghai's most important large and medium-sized factories (of its 1987 total of 45) were established with equipment transferred from northeast China, Shandong Province, Luoyang in Henan, Shanghai, and other cities. "We have a strange saying," one local official said to me: "We prospered due to the disaster in the nation as a whole; while other places suffered, we developed here." During those years, about Y 3 billion was invested in Qinghai, according to local officials, of which roughly Y 2 billion was invested in industrial development. However, local officials acknowledged that the process was extremely wasteful and that it created many problems that Qinghai was still trying to solve in 1988. The official just quoted said to me that the transfer to Qinghai of factories (both the machinery and technical personnel to run the plants) from northeast China, coastal areas, and more advanced interior regions was too hasty and poorly planned and resulted in an "irrational production structure" that led to great waste. Of Qinghai's 45 large and medium-sized factories, 30 lacked adequate local sources for the raw materials that they needed. Their links to product end users also were very weak, and personnel from other areas experienced considerable difficulty adapting to conditions in Qinghai. As a consequence, efficiency was extraordinarily low. Despite the fact that investment in industry in Qinghai totaled almost Y 2 billion, the increase in industrial output during the same years was only Y 700 million; in short, the immediate returns on the investments were shockingly low.

After the Cultural Revolution, the next period of rapid development started when Deng Xiaoping initiated reforms in 1978. Factory output rose rapidly in the decade after 1978, and reportedly efficiency improved substantially. Many of the problems created during the earlier period of development were still unresolved, however.

During the 1980s, most of the urban and industrial reforms introduced elsewhere in China began to be implemented in Qinghai, I was told, but, as in other areas in the west, they were carried out at a slower pace, and less completely, than in the more dynamic eastern regions. Experiments with the manager contract responsibility system started in Qinghai in 1981, according to local officials, and various forms of manager contracts were gradually introduced thereafter, first mainly in small factories. Starting in 1985, the system spread fairly rapidly. In 1988, however, many large factories were still only "experimenting" with the system. Profit sharing was begun fairly early, and by 1988 many factories reportedly could keep about 30 percent of their profits for their own use, although they still had to follow guidelines set by higher authorities that limited how they could use them. From 1984 on, there were substantial personnel changes in the factories, and many younger and more technically qualified people were promoted. Numerous managers were replaced, I was told, and from 1985 on a few were "elected." Starting in 1987, steps were taken to "separate Party and management," reducing the role of Party secretaries and committees, at least as far as day-to-day production decisions were concerned. Some changes occurred in the planning process, also, which now was said to start at the bottom rather than at the top, although many targets for large enterprises were still set by government authorities. Changes in small industries and commercial enterprises were more extensive than in large industries; many second-level factories and small shops were leased to private individuals or to groups of entrepreneurs, generally for one to three years. I was told that by 1988 almost all shops in the province at the county level and below were operating under lease agreements.

Despite the reforms, many enterprises, especially the larger state-owned factories, were still losing money in 1988. This, one official said to me, was a result of "poor management" in about two-fifths of these factories, but many were unprofitable, he said, because of "national problems" such as the unrealistic price system. In sum, even though by 1988 Qinghai had built a modern industrial base—still small but nevertheless significant—of a kind that had been totally lacking in the 1940s, the problems, many of which had resulted from the unrealistic way in which industry had been grafted onto the province's economy, remained serious.

Several of Xining's major factories were described to me: its steel mill, located in the western suburb—a very large plant employing 20,000—which had been started with machinery from Liaoning in the northeast; an aluminum plant, one of the largest in China, I was told, which was built entirely in Xining and was located there because of the province's hydroelectric resources; a large wool factory, which had come from Shanghai; a mining machinery factory, transferred from Luoyang; several factories producing trucks—the "Qinghai" brand, adapted for high altitudes—and plants producing tractors, pumps, and other equipment.

*   *   *

I visited one of Xining's largest industrial enterprises, which was clearly regarded as one of the most advanced and successful in the province: the Number One Qinghai Machine Tool Factory. To my untutored eye, it looked

A 1948 view of the Great Mosque in Xining, located in the traditional Hui Muslim center of the city. It is regarded as one of the most important mosques in northwest China.

A typical Xining street in 1948. Modern influences were still very limited.

Top right: In 1988, renovated after damage during the Cultural Revolution, the Great Mosque was a revitalized religious center.

Above: In this area, beards, caps, and physical features still make it easy to distinguish Hui Muslims from Han Chinese.

Bottom right: This woman's clothing illustrates the spread of fashion and modern clothes throughout west as well as east China.

The recent modernization of Xining is illustrated by these skyscrapers, built in the 1980s, and by the modern clothing worn by most men and women.

A modern factory in Xining. Industrial development has already greatly altered the structure of the province's economy.

A monk sitting on a ledge overlooking one of Kumbum's main temple buildings in 1948. This building looked the same in 1988 as it did in 1948.

The young Banchan Lama with elderly advisers in 1948 at Kumbum, where I interviewed him.

The modern road to Kumbum, which I traveled in 1988; in 1948 I made the trip by donkey cart.

Lamas in training at Kumbum in 1988. The temples were actually in better condition than in 1948, and Kumbum was again a major religious center. And for the first time it was a center for tourism, which had ended its pre-1949 isolation.

Tibetans in a small village on the Tibetan plateau, en route from Xining to Gonghe, headquarters of the Hainan Tibetan Autonomous Prefecture, near Lake Qinghai.

Huge flocks of sheep and thousands of goats, yaks, horses, and other animals range the grasslands in Hainan Prefecture.

Lake Qinghai, China's largest inland body of water, partly frozen in winter.

quite impressive. It was a relatively modern enterprise, more attuned to and linked with the world of high technology than most local factories. I talked at length with the factory's manager and its Party secretary, both of whom were university-educated technicians, the former a man in his forties who had come from Shenyang and the latter a man in his fifties who originally worked in Xi'an. At the end of our conversation, they showed me a rather slick video presentation about the enterprise, complete with Western background music, and then we toured three of the enterprise's major production sites.

This factory had started as a small plant, with about 200 employees. It was founded in 1958 to make farm tools. Until 1965, it was "more of a workshop than a modern factory." Then, in that year, part of the equipment from the Number Two Machine Tool Factory in Qiqihar (Tsitsihar) in the northeast, together with more than 200 technicians and 400 other workers, was transferred from there to Xining and joined with the small original enterprise. By 1988 it had about 2,300 employees, almost all of them Han Chinese. A majority of the technicians and some workers had come from other parts of China, but a small group of local college graduates and quite a few local workers had been recruited in Xining itself. At the time of my visit the staff included about 500 professionals, including 176 engineers, 36 of whom were "senior engineers." The enterprise was located in a huge compound containing 10 major work sites, and, as in most large state enterprises in China, it was a self-contained "small society," with extensive housing (enough for almost all of its workers), its own primary and middle schools, a hospital and clinic, recreation facilities, and so on.

The factory produced more than 60 types of machine tools in four major categories (lathes were considered to be their most important product), which they sold in many parts of China and exported to several foreign countries, including, they said, the United States, Japan, Hungary, and Brazil. The reforms of the 1980s appeared to have had a significant and positive impact on the factory. It was operating under the dual (actually multiple) leadership of two central government bodies in Beijing, the Ministry of Machine Building Industry (later to become the Ministry of Machine Building and Electronic Industries) and the State Planning Commission, as well as the Xining municipal Economic Commission. The target set by the central bodies, which formerly had covered eight major categories relating to almost all activities, had been substantially reduced in the 1980s, although many important targets were still set from above, including the overall value of output in certain categories of products, the value of products for export, the total wage bill, the aim for total profit, taxes to be paid, technical improvements to be made, and so on. The manager asserted, however, that even in these areas the enterprise had acquired greater flexibility in making decisions within the overall targets set.

The manager contract responsibility system had first been partially adopted, experimentally, and then formally implemented in 1984. Under that system, the manager negotiated a five-year contract with the Xining Economic Commission, guaranteeing fulfillment of certain targets—mainly those set by the central bodies. The first such contract had been signed in 1986. After signature of the contract, the manager had negotiated comparable two-year contracts with workshop heads, and they had signed one-year contracts with their workers. Overfulfillment of targets brought rewards; underfulfillment resulted in penalties, at least in theory. The manager asserted that under this system, each level actually did have more scope for initiative and decisionmaking, and also was more accountable, than previously.

As of 1988, about a third of the enterprise's output was sold to "the state," I was told, and the state allocated to the enterprise the necessary raw materials for this portion of its output. Raw materials for the other two-thirds had to be obtained on a variety of markets, and these products were sold on other markets by the enterprise itself. The management described several types of raw materials markets, operating under varying degrees of state control or supervision; in most, the manager said, the state set a "standard price" but market prices could vary from this by 20 percent. Formerly, the enterprise had sold its machine tools almost entirely to the Northwest Supply Station (a state unit in Xi'an); this was still one outlet, but now it was only one of many. The manager described the enterprise's marketing methods, which included making market surveys, advertising in journals, and using a sales force of 32 people who spent much of their time traveling to scattered market centers and to other enterprises that had become customers. There was now, the manager said, fairly intense competition, which was something quite new. He considered about 30 or more other enterprises in China to be their main competitors; he specifically mentioned ones in Qiqihar (with which his enterprise no longer had any special ties), Beijing, Shanghai, and Kunming.

Both the manager and the Party secretary agreed that the Party's role in production decisions was considerably less powerful than it had been in the past, but it seemed to me, from what they said, that it was still important, even though it was now described as a "monitoring role." The enterprise's Party Committee (seven men, including the secretary and deputy secretary) had under it an Organization Department and a Propaganda Department, the enterprise's Young Communist League, the trade union, and Party branches in each workshop. There were 467 Party members among the enterprise's employees (which amounted to about 20 percent of all employees). Of these, 14 worked full time for the Party Committee. Party members filled many if not most of the key production positions, including those in the workshops. The top Party leaders (the secretary, his deputy, the head of the Organization Department, and the Young Communist League head) attended weekly meetings called "roundtables," which included the top production personnel (the manager, leading engineers, accountants, and so on). They did not regularly attend many of the other production meetings convened by the manager, however. It was impossible for an outsider like myself to judge exactly what the Party's relationships to production personnel were, but the fact that my own meeting was attended by both the enterprise manager and the Party secretary was one of many indications that the "separation of Party and enterprise" was certainly not a complete divorce. Nevertheless, the Party secretary did defer to the manager on most subjects during the course of our meeting.

In this enterprise, profit retention was important to the management, but less so, it seemed to me, than I might have expected. In 1987, I was told, the gross value of the enterprise's output was (in rounded figures) Y 25 million. Of this, Y 3 million (12 percent of the output) was profit, and the enterprise paid Y 1.8 million of this in taxes and Y 1.2 million was retained by the management.

One reason for the enterprise's success in recent years, the manager asserted, was that it had a real advantage because of its high technical level, although he admitted that their technical level was still lower than that of the best enterprises elsewhere (for example, in Shanghai). He stated that the competition in his field in China was now based more on quality than on price, and one reason for his enterprise's advantage over many competitors was that it had sent roughly 60 staff members abroad for training, to the United States, Japan, West Germany, East Germany, and Hungary. Another reason was that they had developed various forms of "cooperation" (not joint ventures but other forms of cooperation) with companies abroad. He mentioned specific companies in Germany, Hungary, and Brazil and said that one American company was currently discussing possible cooperation. Their cooperative agreements varied: Some were for the purchase of foreign equipment or for training abroad, some were for cooperation to produce and sell products in China, and in the case of Brazil the agreement was for technology transfer from the Xining enterprise to an enterprise in Brazil. The manager also discussed growing technical ties ("horizontal cooperation") between his enterprise and several others within China, including ones in Beijing and Dalian (Dairen).

*   *   *

Clearly, in the case of this enterprise the open policy implemented by Chinese leaders in the 1980s had brought tangible benefits, and the political leaders in Qinghai fervently hoped that there could be a great expansion of external economic ties. "The open policy has been a key factor in the recent development of Qinghai," Deputy Governor Bian said to me. However, when he and others discussed the specific results of the open policy and its impact on Qinghai, it became fairly clear that although the province's economic links with other parts of China had increased, Qinghai was in only the early stage of developing its foreign economic relations.

To promote trade and technical cooperation within China, not only with Beijing but with other provinces and municipalities, the Qinghai provincial government maintained offices in a number of other places. Like all provinces, it had an office in Beijing, with a staff of about 20 people who shared a building with representatives of six other provinces. The functions of these representatives were to promote increased trade contacts, keep in touch with (and, of course, lobby) central government bodies and officials, and assist personnel from Qinghai when they visited the capital. Qinghai also maintained offices in Tianjin and Shanghai, but, somewhat surprisingly, it did not have any such office in nearby Lanzhou. But local officials said that quite a few individual Qinghai enterprises maintained representatives in Lanzhou, and, as I will note later, Qinghai did regard bilateral ties with Gansu Province as being very important. Within the province, some of Qinghai's prefectures maintained offices in Xining. I saw the office of Hainan Prefecture, located in a large building on one of the city's major avenues, and I was told that there were others.

Several officials in Xining, including the deputy governor, stressed to me that they believed there should be much greater cooperation and coordination among the five provinces and autonomous regions in northwest China. Like officials I met elsewhere in the region, they told me about the annual meetings held by the top government leaders in the area, which involved the governors or regional chairmen plus some key economic and other officials. Even though these meetings, designed to promote regional cooperation, were not officially sponsored by the central government's State Council (as the Shanghai Economic Zone office was), people I met in Qinghai emphasized (much more than the leaders I met in Ningxia had) that they were important because they provided opportunities to exchange information and discuss pressing economic problems as well as to promote technical exchanges and other kinds of cooperation. Held on a rotating basis, they had been convened in Xining in 1986, Urumqi in 1987, and Xi'an in 1988. The deputy governor said that he hoped that Inner Mongolia (which generally had been regarded as a part of north China rather than northwest China) would be brought into the group; it was rumored that this was soon to take place. However, he did not think that Tibet should be included because, he said, it was oriented more toward the southwest. My impression was that Qinghai leaders had greater hopes for expanded regional cooperation than did some of the other leaders I met in northwestern areas.

Discussing interprovincial cooperation, Qinghai officials stressed that relations with certain other provinces were particularly important to them. In some respects Qinghai-Gansu relations were especially important. I was told about a top-level, bilateral meeting between leaders of the two provinces that had been held in 1987 at which there was discussion of the possibility of establishing a special, joint, governmental body at a high level to foster closer economic cooperation between the two provinces. Although this had not yet been established, there already was fairly extensive cooperation involving officials at lower levels, especially local officials in east Qinghai and south Gansu, to promote local trade. I sensed that Qinghai officials had greater enthusiasm about closer cooperation than did the Gansu officials I met in Lanzhou.

Qinghai maintained an office in Tianjin because it was the main port for export of some of the most important of Qinghai's products, including its animal products (which were transported to Tianjin by rail). Qinghai also maintained an office in Shanghai "because it is China's most important economic center." Officials in Xining said that they also regarded economic ties with Shandong and Hubei (especially the city of Wuhan) as particularly valuable. The special links with Shandong resulted in part from personal ties: The Party leader there had once been a Party leader in Qinghai. Wuhan was regarded as particularly important not only because it was a key economic center in central China but also because of its role as a strategic rail center on the Yangzi River (goods could go by rail from Xining to Lanzhou, Xi'an, Zhengzhou, and then south to Wuhan and thereafter could be shipped by boat to Shanghai). Xining also had important economic ties with Shenyang, in the northeast, I was told, because of the machine building factories and personnel that had come to Xining from there.

Intergovernmental ties with other areas in China had become increasingly important in recent years, according to Qinghai officials, but from what I was told I judged that "horizontal links" with enterprises in other regions were expanding in an even more important way, linking Qinghai's enterprises with enterprises in many parts of the country. By 1987, the deputy governor told me, more than 800 such horizontal links between enterprises in Qinghai and ones elsewhere had been established. Typically, in such arrangements, Qinghai provided raw materials needed by enterprises in east China, and in return they provided information, technical assistance, equipment, and, sometimes, capital. Although the largest "key" enterprises in Qinghai received direct support from the central government, the horizontal links between enterprises were particularly important to smaller enterprises.

Trade with other provinces, and also trade within Qinghai itself, had been boosted not only by new kinds of cooperative agreements but also by the revival of private trade. Many individual traders from other parts of China now came to Qinghai, and they traveled throughout the province, even to remote grassland areas. They played a vital role in increasing the availability of consumer goods. During the 1980s, local officials said, retail trade in Qinghai had increased to a little more than Y 2 billion a year, which they said was two and a half times what it had been in the early 1980s. Growing trade ties had begun to reduce Qinghai's isolation. Moreover, the deputy governor stressed, the open policy was having a significant impact on local attitudes, opening people's eyes to the world beyond Qinghai. More travel also had had this effect. In the five-year period before 1988, the number of tourists, including people from outside China (mainly from Hong Kong and Macao), who visited Qinghai had increased 10 times, from about 2,000 to roughly 20,000 a year. (In 1987, 11,000 of them had gone beyond Xining to visit Kumbum Lamasery, which had become the premier tourist attraction in the province.) Even though the rate of increase in tourism was impressive, the numbers were still very small compared to the rapidly increasing flow of tourists to major centers in east China. The numbers highlighted both Qinghai's continuing isolation and its strong desire to have more contact with the "outside world."

The impact of the open policy on Qinghai's economic relations with foreign countries was still relatively small in 1988. Like local leaders I met everywhere I went in China, those in Qinghai expressed a very strong hope that they could expand their foreign economic ties, and they were trying hard to do so. "Quite a few" foreign businessmen had visited Xining in the recent past, I was told (actually the number was not large), to discuss possible trade and cooperation, conduct studies, and make surveys, and a few had initiated negotiations. Some of Qinghai's exports had increased to a degree. Yet so far the results were not impressive. Not a single equity joint venture with a foreign business corporation had been started in the province, according to economic officials in Xining, and only a few enterprises, such as the machine tool factory that I visited, had developed cooperative agreements with foreign corporations. Certain UN-related bodies had given some assistance to two local projects: One was for the development of irrigation, which, when completed, would expand the irrigated area in the province by about 50,000 acres, and the other was for scientific and technical equipment. But these projects did not amount to a great deal in financial terms, either in relation to Qinghai's hopes or compared to the dramatic expansion of foreign economic relations in many coastal areas. The reasons were obvious and very basic: As one local official said to me, "Qinghai is too distant to appeal to many foreign businessmen, and we are very weak in infrastructure, capital, and trained personnel." But Qinghai's leaders still hoped that they could somehow attract greater interest from foreign businessmen.

*   *   *

One key to modernization anywhere is the development of transportation and communication. Qinghai's economic development since the 1940s would not have been possible without progress in these areas. The contrasts between 1948 and 1988 in this respect were quite impressive. Yet despite the progress made, the continuing inadequacy of transportation and communication remained a fundamental obstacle to full-scale modernization.

In 1948, there was really no modern transportation in Qinghai. The province had no railway, and no airline connection. The only "modern" road—from Lanzhou to Xining—was very primitive, surfaced partly with crushed rock and partly with dirt; vehicles using it had to cope with frequent landslides and make several difficult stream crossings. By 1988, Xining had a major rail line connecting it with Lanzhou and from that rail hub to several rail lines that linked all of northwest China to the entire national rail network. Public roads, of varying quality, now reached most of the province's cities, towns, and townships. These new links had, in a real sense, ended the kind of isolation that had existed four decades earlier. Now most of the province was at least connected by modern transport to the capital, and from there to Gansu and the rest of China. Yet transport was still backward compared to that in more advanced areas of the country.

The total length of rail lines within Qinghai was still only 685 miles. This consisted of the main line from Lanzhou to Xining, its extension to Golmud, and a spur to Datong. The once-hoped-for extension of the line to Tibet was no longer under consideration, and although the idea of building one to Xinjiang was not entirely dead, no progress was being made on it. The rail lines that did exist in the province amounted to only 2 percent of China's total rail network (of about 52,500 miles), even though the province's territory accounted for 7.5 percent of China's entire territory.

As of 1988, there were still only two commercial airports with regular service in the province—in Xining and Golmud. Another airfield, which had until recently been secret, was located in Hainan Prefecture (local officials there told me about it) but it had no regular service. I guessed that there might well be some other military airfields in the province but apparently they were not yet of any significance for commercial purposes. The only two regularly scheduled flights to and from other provinces took place each week between Xining and a few other major cities; one went to Beijing and Taiyuan on Fridays, and one went via Lanzhou to Xi'an on Tuesdays.

Between 1948 and 1988, Qinghai's road system had increased almost 17 times, from 460 miles to more than 9,874 miles, but the province still had less than 2 percent of China's total highway network. Moreover, only 6 percent of its roads were paved, although, as noted earlier, the strategic highway to Tibet—and some major roads connecting the largest population centers—were quite good.

The development of modern communications in Qinghai, which was less expensive than building roads or railways, was more impressive. In Qinghai, as in other remote provinces that I visited in 1988, I was constantly amazed by the evidence that radio and TV blanketed vast areas that in most other respects were still extremely remote and had very few other contacts with the modern world. The provincial government's Broadcasting and Television Department had energetically promoted development of both radio and TV; officials told me that for the last several years each annual budget had included very significant funds for this purpose. These officials claimed (perhaps with a degree of exaggeration, but I believe not very much) that by 1988 radio coverage of the province was close to 100 percent and that about 70 percent of the population, including residents on the grasslands, were at least within range of TV stations or TV relay stations. These relay stations, each of which had a range of about 25 miles, were scattered throughout the province. Mountains blocked TV reception in some areas, but the relay stations helped to overcome that obstacle. The government operated numerous radio stations and several TV channels, which broadcast in Tibetan as well as Chinese and carried both national and local programming.

In Xining, about 90 percent of all households owned TV sets, according to officials from the provincial government; these officials also claimed that the city ranked right near the top in China in the percentage of its TV sets that were color sets. The number of sets was smaller in grassland areas, they acknowledged, because electricity was lacking in many places. But they asserted that the number was nevertheless substantial, especially in township centers, most of which, they claimed, now did have electricity (often from small local hydroelectric stations). In the grasslands, the number of households owning small windmill generators (with enough power to run TV sets) was considerably smaller than that in Inner Mongolia, they admitted, but they said that it was slowly increasing. In Qinghai the cost of such generators varied from as low as Y 400 to over Y 1,000. Some of the windmill generators were made in two factories located within the province, but many local people felt that these were inferior and therefore preferred to buy such generators made in other provinces, even though they were more expensive.

Videocassette players also were beginning to catch on in remote areas, and some township governments reportedly provided videotapes of certain TV programs, on a loan or rental basis, to people in grassland areas. In many of the grassland areas, moreover, radio sets, operated by batteries, were quite prevalent, particularly outside the townships, and a sizable number of nomadic families were said to own them. Almost everywhere, these radios could receive numerous Chinese stations (broadcasting in Chinese, Tibetan, and other languages) and foreign stations as well.

There was no easy way to measure the extent to which radio and TV had broadened the horizons, altered the thinking, and raised the economic expectations of people in Qinghai, but everyone with whom I discussed the communications revolution agreed that the impact had been great and that it had encouraged what one person called "modern thinking."

The print media also had been significantly expanded since the Communist takeover. The Propaganda Department of the Party shared with the government the overall responsibility for developing newspapers, of which the municipal-run *Qinghai Daily* was most influential. Important local roles were also played by the Qinghai branch of the New China News Agency and the Peoples' Publishing House (which under a second name—the Minorities Nationalities Publishing House—issued materials in languages other than Hanyu). The regime also supported a network of cultural organizations and backed a local Association of Literature and Arts.

*   *   *

The development of modern education was recognized by virtually all those I met as being, if anything, even more crucial to Qinghai's modernization in the long run than the growth of modern transportation and communications. It was mainly through the spread of formal education that the regime was attempting to raise the level of literacy, general knowledge, and technical skills required for development. In this, as in other fields, Qinghai had come a long way since 1949, yet local leaders were very concerned about the distance they still had to go to meet the province's needs; educational shortcomings still posed some extremely difficult and fundamental problems.

In 1948, provincial officials in Qinghai had told me that up to that time the government had built a school system that consisted of 1,057 primary schools, with 94,000 students (an average of about 90 students per school), plus 13 middle schools, with 4,500 students. There was still no institution of higher learning in the province. In the city of Xining itself, it was claimed, roughly a third of the entire population attended school, which if true represented remarkable progress compared to most of northwest China in the 1940s. Ma Bufang was well known for his support of a special system of Kunlun schools, which had an enrollment of about 7,000 students (at all levels from kindergarten through middle school). In these schools all the needs of the students (including food and clothing) were provided free by the government. Almost nine-tenths of the students in the Kunlun schools were Hui Muslims, and Arabic was taught. Ma's stated aim was to "raise the standard of Muslim education" to create a new Muslim elite. Even though the total number of students of all kinds in the province as a whole at that time was still small (perhaps just over 10 percent of the population), and they were concentrated in Xining, I wrote in 1948 that this school system was the "most impressive development in the province" because no other warlord in northwest China had developed anything like it.*

---

*In 1988, officials from the provincial Education Department in Xining gave me considerably lower figures on the number of schools and students in the province as of 1949; their figures indicated that at that time there were 109 primary schools and 8 middle schools. I cannot explain the large differences between these figures and those I obtained in 1948, but in 1948 I did not doubt the plausibility of the figures given to me.

By 1988, Qinghai's educational system had expanded tremendously and spread all over the province. However, in my interviews on the subject (with both the Han official responsible for "general education" and the Tibetan official responsible for minority schools) it became clear that despite efforts to promote equal education, the remote minority areas still lagged quite far behind the more developed areas of the province. As of 1988, I was told, Qinghai had approximately 4,200 primary schools with 530,000 students (averaging about 125 per school), 470 regular middle schools with 250,000 students (averaging about 530 per school), plus 17 normal schools at or slightly above the senior middle school level (to train primary school teachers) with 5,400 students. There were also 165 separate kindergartens with 32,000 students (which were in addition to those attending kindergartens attached to primary schools). In the province as a whole the total number of students of all kinds—including those in postsecondary and other special schools—totaled well over 800,000; this sum amounted to more than one-fifth of the province's population in 1988. This figure was still well below that in more developed areas, but it was much higher than that in the pre-Communist period, not only in absolute terms but as a percentage of the population.

However, even local officials acknowledged that the quality of education remained low. Poor teacher training was one of the basic reasons cited most frequently. Almost all teachers in Qinghai's primary and middle schools were local people, trained within the province; few primary school teachers had themselves gone beyond middle school, and most middle school teachers had received their training at local postsecondary normal schools of dubious quality. From the 1950s through the 1970s, moreover, the education of teachers—like the education of everyone at any level in China—had been heavily loaded with ideology and politics. The situation in this respect obviously had improved in the 1980s. The regular texts were in Hanyu and were prepared or selected by educational authorities in Beijing. They were not, in Qinghai at least, significantly modified for local use, but in recent years (mainly during the early years of the 1980s) they had been extensively modified or rewritten in Beijing to reduce ideological content at least somewhat, to increase materials on science and technology, to make the "social science" content more realistic and useful, and to make the materials more relevant to students' needs.

In the curriculum in primary schools, I was told, the previous "politics" course had been converted into a course on civics, concentrating on social norms, personal behavior, and morality (especially, they said, the idea that "people need to help others"). A politics course was still a significant part of the curriculum in the middle schools, but local Education Department officials maintained that its content had been substantially changed: Politics courses no longer stressed the "Thought of Mao Zedong" but instead emphasized "general political philosophy" (dialectics) and "China's political economy." Local officials stated that "students really do not accept any more" the old ideological ideas (the implication was that they simply tuned them out). By 1988, middle school students read almost none of Mao's own writings—except for some of his poems—I was told, although certain texts still incorporated some of his ideas.

Whereas in 1948 there had been no institution of "higher education" in Qinghai, by 1988, according to local officials, there were eight institutions in this category in the province. Even though all of these eight were clearly postsecondary schools, many of them really did not deserve the label of "higher education" as the term is used in the West. The eight included two teacher training institutions (a "normal college" and an "educational institute"), mainly to train middle school teachers; a medical college; the Institute (College) for Minority Nationalities (to train cadres); a college to train specialists in animal husbandry and veterinary science; a spare-time TV broadcast "university"; and Qinghai University. All except Qinghai University were essentially special postsecondary training schools rather than institutions comparable to liberal arts colleges or universities in developed countries.

Qinghai University was a new creation; its establishment had been approved by Beijing's Education Commission only in 1988. At the start, it was simply a new name given to an old institution, formerly called the College of Industry and Agriculture. However, the provincial government was trying to develop it into a real university, and the aim was to convert it in time into a true "comprehensive" university. However, this process, local officials admitted, had really barely begun. A department of Chinese literature and a department of economics had recently been established; plans called for adding a Chinese language department in the near future and for initiating new courses in the "social sciences." But the creation of a new university comparable to major ones elsewhere in China obviously would take a long time. Altogether, I was told, all eight postsecondary institutions in Qinghai had only about 7,000 students in 1988, and they graduated less than 2,000 students a year—a tiny number to serve the province's population of over 4 million people.

Because local higher education was so underdeveloped, Qinghai in the late 1980s was sending roughly 1,700 students a year to study at universities elsewhere in China. (As I noted earlier, in 1948 the comparable number was 200 to 300 a year.) This number had been rising since the early 1970s (when national examinations for university entrance had been resumed, following the hiatus during the Cultural Revolution), and by 1988 it almost equaled the number of annual graduates from local institutions of higher learning. However, many of those sent elsewhere did not return to Qinghai because they found more attractive jobs in other places; the province provided many special incentives to try to attract them back but with only limited success.

                              *   *   *

The weakness of the educational system—especially higher education—was a primary reason that Qinghai continued to suffer from a serious shortage of skilled personnel. This shortage varied in different fields, but local leaders acknowledged that overall it was a major problem that raised serious obstacles to further economic development. The province still had to rely heavily on professional and technical personnel transferred from more advanced areas. A senior official from the provincial Science and Technology Commission briefed me on this problem. The commission supervised most of the research in Qinghai, controlled the budget for such research, and, in collaboration with the Education Department, advised provincial leaders on manpower development policy. It also handled external relations in the fields of science and technology. Administratively, this commission was entirely under the provincial government, but it followed policies defined mainly by the corresponding national commission, adapting them to local conditions.

In 1988, I was told, Qinghai had a total of about 70,000 people classified as "scientific, technical, and professional personnel," but this figure included teachers, who probably made up the largest percentage of the total. Although this figure represented a quantum leap from the number in the late 1940s (the officials to whom I talked estimated that the total in 1949 was only about 200), it was by no means sufficient to meet the province's needs. Many people included in these figures were acknowledged to be poorly educated; in fact, only about 20 to 30 percent (between 14,000 and 21,000) had received degrees from any postsecondary "college-level" institution. Of the 70,000, moreover, 70 to 80 percent (between 49,000 and 56,000) were individuals who had been assigned to Qinghai from other provinces; the better-educated among them were mostly from other provinces. Not surprisingly, the great majority (about 58,000, or 83 percent of the total) were Han Chinese, and only about one-sixth belonged to minority groups.

Because of Qinghai's pressing need for more skilled people, the provincial government was making major efforts to provide special incentives to recruit qualified people from other provinces and to attract back to the province those students it sent for higher education elsewhere. Starting in 1983, a policy was adopted under which people from other areas who came to work in Qinghai for an extended period of time were guaranteed that they later would be granted permission to return to their home provinces. The children of such people, moreover, were to be given special consideration for assignments to educational institutions in their home areas so that they could "create a base" to which their parents could eventually return. From 1984 on, a new policy permitted graduates of institutions in other parts of China to accept assignments to remote areas such as Qinghai on the basis of an eight-year contract instead of being assigned for an indefinite period, as had formerly been the practice. They could retain their residence registration (*hukou*) in their home areas. Moreover, people who had come much earlier and had lived for long periods in Qinghai could request, on the basis of health or other reasons, permission to return to their home provinces.

As in most western provinces, also, local salaries were comparatively high. Employees in Qinghai were paid on the basis of a Grade 11 salary scale (the highest in China). Some salaries, I was told, were 50 percent higher than they were for equivalent jobs in Beijing, and they were about 17 percent higher than even those in nearby Gansu. All cadres in the province, I was told, were given a special bonus of Y 8 a month because of the high altitude! Moreover, young cadres just out of college could obtain regular cadre positions in Qinghai without the probation period required in many other places, and often they started one salary grade higher than they would have in Beijing or Shanghai. In general, also, housing and other perquisites were better in Qinghai than elsewhere. But despite all of these benefits, local officials admitted, the problem of attracting people from other areas of China remained a serious one.

One of the main responsibilities of the Science and Technology Commission was to encourage "research serving economic development," and the commission supervised the work of 43 "research units" throughout the province. Only 3 of these were run directly by the commission; most of the rest were administered by various government departments. Almost all of the research, as described to me, was "applied" rather than "basic." Two examples cited were medical research on diseases or other ailments prevalent at high altitudes and the development of truck engines that could operate more efficiently at high altitudes. In addition, a number of major industrial enterprises had their own research units, and some research was being done in institutions of higher learning.

The one research institution that I received some details about was the Qinghai Academy of Social Sciences, my host organization. I met virtually all of its top leaders, institute heads, and leading scholars (one meeting included 15 of its leading scholars), and they briefed me at some length about their work as well as the "development of the social sciences" in general in Qinghai. In their account of the latter, they put special stress on the many political "twists and turns" that had affected intellectual life in the province. The story they told me was one of repeated periods of "leftist" ideological intervention into, and distortion of, research. In only two periods, they said, was there real progress in developing "practical" and relatively objective research: One was in the early 1960s and the other in the 1980s. Before the 1960s, they said, virtually all research was done within the Party and government units, and it concentrated on ideology and propagation of the Party line and current government policies. The first research institutions of significance established outside of the Party and government departments or bureaus were set up in the 1960s.

The Academy itself was formally established in Qinghai in 1978. In 1988 it had a total staff of 131 working in six institutes dealing with local Qinghai history, Tibetan studies, minority affairs in general, philosophy, literature, and economics. Its publications included one journal titled *Social Sciences in Qinghai* and another that focused on philosophy. There obviously was still close Party supervision exercised by a Party core group within the Academy, but those I met maintained that since the start of reforms in 1978, the climate for serious and objective research had been greatly improved. The bulk of their current research focused on local history, policies, and problems. Projects that I was told about included a history of Qinghai from the Han dynasty to the present; a study of Tibetan records and documents at Kumbum Lamasery, including the works of Tsongkhaba, the founder of Yellow Sect Lamaism; Buddhist studies; and research on Tibetan-Mongolian relations. Some work (mainly that done in the institutes of economics and philosophy) concerned contemporary issues. Projects in this area included ones on the meaning and significance of the concept of the "primary stage of socialism" (a hot topic in 1988 because it was used to justify many of China's reforms); the "theory of markets"; the market system in Qinghai for animal products; the problems of increasing productivity and efficiency; and the development of poor areas in the province, especially those inhabited by minorities.

Discussing the development of the intellectual and research community in general in Qinghai, they told me that by the 1980s a total of 56 academic, scholarly, and professional societies and associations that had some relevance to the "social sciences" (broadly defined) had been established in Qinghai—a great many of them concerned with matters relating directly to economic development. The number of people involved in all of the organizations in this broad field throughout the province totaled about 10,000 (roughly 70 percent of whom had come to Qinghai from other provinces). Even though I could only guess at the real nature or value of their work, I found the numbers rather astonishing: They suggested that even in remote Qinghai significant trends toward the pluralization of society were under way in the 1980s.

At least some of the Academy scholars I met impressed me as being individuals who were trying hard to produce useful research, but it was easy to sense that they felt very remote from the mainstream of intellectual activity in China. Their thinking, and the climate in which they worked, had obviously been affected—for the better—by the reform policies implemented in the 1980s, but Party officials still seemed to oversee their work more closely than was the case by 1988 in some of the major institutions in China's eastern metropolitan centers.

*   *   *

I gained additional insights into changing attitudes and ideas in Qinghai from one particularly interesting conversation that I had with four members of the provincial Party's Propaganda Department (interviews with personnel from the propaganda apparatus were rather rare in China, even in 1988). I was fascinated by much of what they told me about the Party's continuing efforts to try to influence the thinking of intellectuals and, perhaps even more important, the younger generation in general. It was evident that important changes had occurred in the Party's policies in this respect as a result of the reforms in the 1980s and the influx of new ideas from afar—including ideas from foreign countries—which in the decade of the 1980s penetrated even remote areas such as Qinghai.

The officials from the Propaganda Department told me that they had a staff of 75 people responsible for political indoctrination and "ideological matters, especially within the Party," for managing "Party life" (*dang de shenghuo*), and for exercising "supervision of education, culture, journalism, and publishing as well as education of the masses." The department had divisions and sections dealing with each of these areas and an office to promote "spiritual civilization." Operating under the supervision of higher-level propaganda departments as well as the local Party Committee, they received materials as well as instructions from above, and they used these materials to conduct regular "theoretical studies" sessions for all cadres. As in past years, much of their work was done through small "study groups" (*xuexi xiaozu*), organized in every Party and governmental unit. These, I was told, met regularly twice a week, on Wednesdays and Saturdays, for about four hours each time. Part of most sessions was devoted to lectures, part to reading assigned materials, and part—about half of their time—to discussions.

All of this sounded very much as if little had changed from the Maoist period, but then, when they described the content of the study sessions, it became clear that some of what they did was a far cry from what most propaganda units did in the Maoist era. My main briefer said to me:

> The content of study has changed greatly. Formerly, we studied mainly Mao's works, but now, because of the new reform policy, we focus on study of political economy and on philosophical issues related to reform. For example, last year [1987] one of the major texts was a report written at the Central Party School dealing with the meaning of a "commodity economy" [that is, an economy in which market forces play a major role], something people have not known about. Two volumes of Deng Xiaoping's writings—his *Selected Works* and a collection of his speeches on "building socialism with Chinese characteristics"— have also been used by us as basic texts. Starting late last year and continuing

into this year another of our basic texts has been General Secretary Zhao Ziyang's report to the 13th Party Congress. These same texts are studied all over China, although we can vary the material somewhat; for example, we pay more attention to minority nationality issues. ... But we no longer have any special study of Mao's works except for a few that are relevant to reform. The definition and content of ideology has changed ever since 1978, when a new direction was defined. Before that, politics controlled everything. The focus was on loyalty to Chairman Mao; since then the focus has shifted to what is needed to help modernization. Now the whole country has focused on economic development, and our task is to stimulate people's enthusiasm for economic reform, to discuss how to solve difficulties and overcome obstacles to reform. Because Qinghai is economically so backward, it is particularly important here to liberate cadres' minds, and most people here now do reject the former focus just on politics. Of course, there is still some class struggle in China, but now we must deal with contradictions through the legal system, not through struggle. In our study groups, at present, people have more opportunity to express their personal opinions and dissatisfactions, to criticize, and to make suggestions.

In its work among the general population, the Propaganda Department "informs people about current policies and helps them understand economic problems." For example, one propaganda cadre said: "When prices rose, and there were numerous complaints, we held many meetings to tell people why this was happening, and why it was unavoidable." Work among the masses was carried out by individual propaganda cadres at lower levels, as in the past, but also to an increasing extent through the mass media—the newspapers, radio, and TV. The department did not itself prepare most of the material used by the media, my briefers said, but gave the media "guidance," with the help of government organizations responsible for particular areas of work. TV and radio had become of primary importance not only for reaching people in cities but also—in fact, especially—reaching people in remote grassland areas. In many of these areas, radio had become the main channel of communications, they said.

The Propaganda Department was also responsible for promoting "spiritual civilization" (*wenming jingshen*) among the general population. The values and tasks promoted under this program were very different from the goals of revolutionary struggle stressed in the Maoist era. (The program seemed, in fact, to be remarkably similar in some respects to the "New Life Movement," which the Guomindang had tried to carry out in the 1930s and which had been strongly influenced by Christian missionaries' social action programs.) Certain priorities were defined in each social sector, and the Party tried to judge how effectively particular groups contributed toward their achievement. In rural villages, I was told, the priorities included promoting "social morality," reducing crime, cleaning up the environment, and helping the poor to raise their incomes. In factories, priority was given to orderly production, maintaining discipline, improving safety, protecting the environment, and studying science and technology to apply new knowledge to production. As of 1988, they said, over 2,000 units throughout the province had been honored with the title "Spiritual Civilization Units." My reaction to their description of this program was that although its emphasis was far preferable to the class struggle goals of campaigns in the Maoist era, it seemed to be largely cosmetic and hortatory in its approach and probably contributed relatively little to the solution of basic problems.

The most interesting things said during our conversation were comments made by the propaganda cadres when they talked at some length about the changing attitudes of local young people, to which, they said, they paid great attention. One cadre said:

> Many youths in Qinghai are now very active intellectually, even though they are not interested in ideology. They are now more individualistic; many have complaints, and many make suggestions. TV is especially important as a medium to educate the young. TV is very popular and has a great influence on young minds. But we try to reach them in many ways. For example, we organize competitions among youths—public speaking competitions, "knowledge competitions," and "dialogues between cadres and youths," especially at the middle school level. We sometimes arrange debates on TV, not trying to define any one correct view but to let opinions be aired.

One of the local Propaganda Department's major responsibilities now, they said, was to try to understand the thinking of young people and, through reports sent to Beijing, to give national leaders a better idea of the situation at the grass-roots level. This involved analysis of current intellectual trends and fads and the issues influencing students and other youths in Qinghai and discussion of ways of responding to them. What I was told about young people's changing ideas, as understood by these members of the Qinghai Party propaganda apparatus, was extremely interesting and highlighted the degree to which modern education, publishing, communications, and the media had altered the previously existing intellectual as well as physical isolation of the province. The ranking member of the group briefing me said:

> There have been many intellectual trends and fads among Qinghai's youths that we have observed in recent years. At one point, Freud's ideas were a fad. We did not try to ban books about Freud's thinking; in fact, we encouraged the bookstores to make them available and then organized debates on them among students. In our view, while some of Freud's ideas are reasonable, some are subjective and radical, but we did not try to set a "line"; instead we held debates in which we expressed our views but allowed students to make up their own minds. At other times Sartre and Adler were fads.
>
> A short time ago, there was a great interest in a Taiwanese writer who wrote about love affairs among youths. The whole question of romance—romantic love—has been widely discussed. There also was a debate about investigative re-

porting and about investigative reporters such as Liu Binyan. At first many young people criticized the way Liu Binyan, and also Fang Lizhi, were treated, but then they saw that they were allowed to receive awards and even to go abroad. We help young people realize that the Party's methods of dealing with intellectuals are now very different from those in the past. [It must have been very difficult to make this line of argument convincing after both Liu and Fang had fled China following the Beijing massacre in June 1989.] This year, questions relating to China being in the "primary stage of socialism" have been hot topics. Actually, Qinghai is so backward that we are in an "early, early" stage of socialism. We are so far behind Shanghai and Guangzhou, and even Xi'an, that we cannot try to follow their models; we have to develop our own model based on local realities.

Many other important issues have been of concern to youths and the Party. One, for example, relates to students who go abroad to study and do not return. This year a major report on this subject has attracted great interest. So, too, has another major report on the problems of older girls who have not been able to get married. We have not tried to organize debates on all of these subjects, be we have done so on many, and we at least try to understand such trends and let Beijing know about them.

All that the propaganda cadres told me indicated that although the Party apparatus created during the Maoist era had not really changed very much organizationally, and the Party still viewed itself as the guardian of basic ideas and values, fundamental changes in its purposes had taken place and the content of propaganda had been redefined. From promoting class struggle, the emphasis had shifted to promoting economic modernization. The Party's means of reaching people had been greatly strengthened, with radio and TV now playing critical roles, and its recognition of and tolerance of diverse points of view was considerably greater than it had been in the past. (I presume that, in Qinghai as elsewhere, all of these trends were reversed or set back in 1989, when, after the Tiananmen massacre in Beijing, the Party ideologues again tried to reimpose old-style controls, but my guess is that the setback will prove to be temporary.)

                              *   *   *

The final subject on which I focused my interviews in Xining was the regime's minority policies and minority-Han relations. Since two-fifths of Qinghai's population consisted of members of minority groups (with Tibetans accounting for a fifth and occupying the province's remotest areas, and the Hui Muslims, concentrated in the east, making up close to a sixth), Han relations with these minorities loomed large in the policies of the provincial government. Like other governments in west China, the government in Qinghai had given high priority during the 1980s to implementing special "affirmative action" (this is my terminology, not theirs) policies to overcome the legacy of past conflicts, especially the disastrous persecution of minorities during the Cultural Revolution. Genuine efforts were being made, it seemed to me, to try to raise the economic and cultural level of these groups, especially the Tibetans.

The provincial Minority Nationalities Affairs Commission in Xining had a staff of 61 in 1988, and they were divided into six divisions (*chu*) or offices (*bangongshi*), one of them dealing with "general" affairs and the others dealing with political and legal matters, culture and education, finance and economics, language issues, and the compilation of minority literature. (At lower levels, there were comparable bodies: At the prefecture level there was generally a staff of five to eight people and at the county level there were usually three to four people. In each case there were individuals designated to deal with all of these various matters.)

The commission officials whom I interviewed outlined in some detail the "special privileges" granted to minorities within the province. Of the central government's annual subsidy to Qinghai, they said, Y 31 million was earmarked specifically for development programs relating to minorities. The specific uses of these funds were determined by the provincial government and were decided upon in meetings involving officials who dealt with both financial affairs and minority affairs. Of the total, Y 9 million was allocated for special support for minority educational institutions. (At times, additional funds from both the provincial and central government were added to this basic amount for use in developing minority education.) To encourage the development of industrial enterprises in minority areas, the government gave a complete tax exemption for three years, and sometimes a partial tax exemption for an additional period of time, to new enterprises in minority areas, especially ones producing distinctive "minority goods." County governments were authorized to decide which enterprises to support, and they made recommendations to the provincial financial authorities, whose approval was required for large tax reductions. When disaster struck minority areas, special extrabudgetary help was provided, sometimes in the form of free relief funds but often in the form of reduced taxes.

Frequently, loans with relatively low interest rates were allocated to minority enterprises; in some cases the interest rate was under 1 percent (this applied mainly to enterprises producing special products for minorities). Sometimes, they were allowed to keep a higher proportion of their profits than other enterprises were. Profit retention by such enterprises could be as high as 50 percent. These policies, the commission officials maintained, had helped to raise average incomes of the minority peoples significantly, especially in the Tibetan grasslands. As a result, in some grassland areas the per capita income level was somewhat higher than in agricultural areas inhabited by Han and Hui farmers, even though many of the poorest areas in the province still were ones located in remote Tibetan regions.

For the long run, probably the most significant affirmative action policies, it seemed to me, were those related to education. Of the total of 4,200 primary schools in the province, 1,653 schools (with 186,000 students) were specifically for minority children, and I was told that at this level the percentage of minority children in schools was comparable to that of the Han population. Some of the Tibetan primary schools used the Tibetan language as their basic language of instruction, but they also taught Hanyu; in other schools, it was the reverse. However, at the middle school level the situation was different. There were only 57 minority middle schools, with 47,000 students. The statistics indicated that minority schools accounted for only 12 percent of the province's middle schools and 19 percent of their students, percentages far below the percentage share of minorities in the total population.* In middle schools, there was some use of minority languages as the basic languages, but in a great many the teaching was mainly in Chinese. In the former, there were special texts, mainly ones prepared in other regions. In higher education, there were some minority students in all of the eight postsecondary schools in Qinghai, but the largest number were in the Institute for Minority Nationalities. In addition, a special postsecondary normal school for minority peoples had been established in Hainan Prefecture. Also, some students went to study in the Minority Nationalities Institute in Lanzhou (40 to 50 a year), I was told, and some to Beijing (about 20 a year); others (about 40 a year) attended major universities elsewhere (some of which gave special first-year remedial classes for minority students). However, the total number of minority students attending all institutions of higher learning was less than 2,000.

When I visited Tibetan areas in China in 1948—in Xikang Province (now part of Sichuan) as well as Qinghai—I had been struck by the strong and widespread negative feelings that many Tibetans seemed to have at that time toward formal education: Parents often regarded educating their children as an onerous obligation, similar to military conscription for adults. In 1988, such attitudes seemed to have changed fundamentally in many areas. I was told that this was true especially in Tibetan areas near towns and in the more developed regions of the province. However, I was told, old attitudes persisted in some of the more remote and backward Tibetan areas, especially in Yushu and Guoluo. Reportedly, in these two prefectures (which contained three-eighths of the province's entire Tibetan population and in which 90 percent of the local population was Tibetan) there was still considerable prejudice against and resistance to education, and the educational system re-

---

*Some minority children attended ordinary middle schools. I never determined whether these figures included them.

mained quite backward. In the province as a whole, about 60 percent of all Tibetan children of school age reportedly attended school, I was told (this compared to more than 70 percent of all Han children who attended school).

Despite the expansion of lower-level education for minorities, literacy levels remained disturbingly low—although they were higher than 40 years ago. Officials stated that before the Communist takeover, only about 5 percent of the total minority population in the province was literate. By 1988, they said, the figure had risen to about 50 percent. But they stressed that this percentage was unacceptably low. The Tibetans were the least literate group in the province. Of all Tibetans in Qinghai, local officials said, only about 30 percent were literate, partly because the overwhelming majority of older Tibetans were still illiterate.

The minorities' representation in cadre positions in Qinghai also remained low, despite efforts to increase it. As I mentioned earlier, minorities filled less than one-fifth of all cadre positions in the province—roughly half their share in the total population—and the figure was particularly low for the Hui population. When I asked an official of the Minority Affairs Commission (himself a Hui) why the Hui seemed to be so poorly represented among cadres (with 4.3 percent of all cadres) even compared to the Tibetans (with 11 percent), he explained that the Tibetans did better because so many prefectures and counties in Qinghai were Tibetan autonomous units, where regulations required a high proportion of cadres to be members of the largest minority group. He also said that the Hui did poorly compared to the Han Chinese because many of the Hui were "culturally [educationally] more backward." I remained skeptical that these were the only reasons, however, and, as I noted earlier, I suspected that there was subtle if not overt political discrimination against the Hui because of their past political dominance.

Officials dealing with minority affairs acknowledged, in their conversations with me, that there were still frictions between the Han and Hui, rooted partly in "cultural differences," but they argued that it was limited and that its causes were more economic than political. One task of the Minority Nationalities Affairs Commission, they said, was to help mediate conflicts between and within minority groups. The commission dealt with a variety of frictions involving Tibetans, but my informants maintained that the majority of these were caused by family and economic disputes within the Tibetan population, between different Tibetan families or groups, and that generally they were not very difficult to resolve. These benign views were not surprising, coming from official sources. I certainly did not take them at face value. It seemed improbable to me that memories of past conflicts had been totally expunged, and I felt that underlying tensions must persist (even though, as I said earlier, I did not see much overt evidence of them).

In Qinghai, the Cultural Revolution had obviously been a period of extreme persecution, the impact of which was as great as it was in all other areas of west China that I visited. Local people stated that "a majority" of religious buildings in Qinghai had been destroyed or damaged. However, they said, there clearly was greater toleration in the 1980s and a religious revival had taken place—among both the Tibetans and the Muslim population. Most religious institutions had been restored, and some new ones had been built. Scholars at the Academy of Social Sciences informed me that the latest statistics showed that by 1988 there were 274 operating lamaseries in the province (with personnel totaling over 12,000) and 693 mosques (with close to 4,000 personnel). In addition, there were four Mahayana Buddhist temples, four Daoist temples, one Catholic church, and one Protestant church (both of the latter in Xining). I visited the Great Mosque in Xining (one of the most important mosques in west China), which looked much as it had four decades earlier; located in the predominantly Muslim eastern part of the city, it appeared to be very much alive, a bustling religious and community center. I also visited Kumbum Lamasery at Taersi, west of Xining, which many Tibetans say is—together with lamaseries at Lhasa and Labulong—among the most important religious centers for Tibetan Lamaism. It too appeared to be a very active place and in good condition. I was told that it had been spared destruction by the Red Guards by the personal intervention of Premier Zhou Enlai, who is credited with having protected a number of leading religious centers in China (including one that I knew very well from my childhood, Lingyin, in Hangzhou).

                                              *   *   *

My trip to Kumbum in 1988 was a pilgrimage that evoked great nostalgia. I still had vivid memories of making the trip in 1948. At that time, traveling the 37 miles or so by donkey cart took a very long day. The route followed one of the two main old-time caravan routes and went through very traditional countryside, moving gradually from ethnic China into ethnic Tibet. It was an arduous trip at that time, but seeing Kumbum made it worthwhile. The golden roofs of the large complex of buildings at the monastery, and the deep red lamas' robes, were striking in contrast to the dusty little village of Lushar nearby. The lamasery reeked of yak butter; the drone of a thousand chanting lamas filled the air; and the buildings were crowded with pilgrims from all parts of the Tibetan plateau. The atmosphere was "out of this world"—totally unlike most of China.

My trip in 1988 was quite different. My Academy hosts and I left Xining at midday and arrived back in Xining for a late dinner. In a comfortable, Japanese-made sedan, we sped along a well-paved road, first going through a long valley and then gradually climbing toward high mountains. The hills on both sides of the route were dusted with snow, and close by on our left very high, snow-covered mountains rose majestically. The countryside still looked essentially traditional. We passed a few small tractors, but most workers in the fields were making preparations for planting with the use of very old-fashioned tools, including simple wooden mallets with which they broke up clods of dirt. Many of the farmers we passed were Hui, the men wearing skullcaps and the women wearing traditional hoods. There were some signs of modernity and urbanization paralleling the route. All over even remote parts of China, where there were paved roads, modern transport brought other features of modernization. In this area I saw TV aerials in many houses on both sides of the road on the way to Lushar.

The town of Lushar had been transformed since my last visit. Instead of being a dusty little traditional village, it was now a sizable, colorful, fairly modern town—it had become a county seat—with a population of about 27,000. The population was now essentially non-Tibetan. I was told by officials at the county government headquarters that approximately 60 percent of the town's residents were Han Chinese, 30 percent Hui Muslims, and only 10 percent Tibetan. The population of the entire county now totaled about 400,000, and of these roughly half were Han, 40 percent Tibetan, and 10 percent Hui. After checking in at the county Foreign Affairs Bureau, we walked the short route to the lamasery. It was lined on both sides with small shops that were run by both Tibetans and Hui as well as Han entrepreneurs. Their main business was selling trinkets to pilgrims and to Chinese tourists. Kumbum, as I mentioned earlier, had become Qinghai's leading tourist center. There were few tourists there at the time of my visit—it was in March and the weather was quite cold—but local officials confirmed that in 1987 a total of 11,000 tourists had visited Kumbum. The local economy was now heavily dependent on this tourist business.

Kumbum Lamasery itself was much as I remembered it. As a result of recent repairs and repainting, it was actually in better shape than it had been when I saw it in 1948. It is an extremely impressive place, with a kind of Shangri-la atmosphere, and it continues to be an extremely important religious center. I was briefed in some detail on its founding and history, as well as on its current role, by scholars in Xining and people I met at Kumbum. It is located where the founder of the Yellow Sect of Lamaism—Tsongkhaba—was born. Over the centuries it was steadily expanded, and many of its present buildings were built during the Ming dynasty. Later it was further expanded with special support from two Qing dynasty rulers, Kang Xi and Qian Long. My informants gave me a long account of the numerous visits to Kumbum by past religious leaders—the Dalai Lamas as well as the Banchan Lamas—and the periods they had lived there. Kumbum rather than the traditional Banchan Lama's residence in Xigaze (Shigatse), in Tibet proper, had become the headquarters of the strongly China-oriented Banchan Lama in

the 1920s, and it remained so until after the Communist takeover. Thereafter, the Banchan Lama's residence was sometimes in Xigaze and sometimes
in Beijing (although he returned periodically to Kumbum).*

All those I met emphasized that Kumbum was still regarded as a major
place of worship for all Tibetans. However, I saw many signs that its main
orientation now was toward the Banchan Lama rather than the Dalai Lama.
Photos of the two previous Banchan Lamas hung in one of the main halls,
but I saw no photographs of any of the Dalai Lamas. In another hall, which
was a museum, there was an old auto used by the ninth Banchan Lama.
When he used it, I was told, it was drawn by animals. I did not learn whether
the authorities forbade exhibiting relics and photos linked to the Dalai
Lama. However, scholars in Xining emphasized that the principal orientation of the lamasery was now toward the Banchan Lama rather than the Dalai Lama.

In 1988, the lamasery had 560 lamas—about half the number that had
been resident there in 1948—as well as 11 resident Living Buddhas. About
10 other Living Buddhas who lived elsewhere were also closely associated
with Kumbum, I was told. Large numbers of pilgrims still visited it, but I saw
only a few. The main influx came at other times of the year, especially during
the four major religious celebrations. These occurred on the Lunar New
Year, on the fifteenth day of the fourth month, on the fourth day of the sixth
month, and on the twenty-fourth day of the tenth month. These were also
the peak periods for tourism. The pilgrims that I did see, at the time of my
visit, were acting much like those four decades earlier had: They genuflected
as they moved throughout the complex and periodically stopped to spin
prayer wheels.

I was told that the government provided some funds for the construction
and maintenance of buildings at Kumbum but that general expenses now
were met largely from income from tourism. Tickets were required for all
tourists entering the monastery. Some income also came from more traditional sources, such as the sale of religious literature and artifacts. The lamasery no longer owned land—which used to be a major source of income.

The lamasery still ran a fairly large school to train new lamas. Of the considerable number of individuals in red robes whom I saw while there, many
were young men. Some of them were mere boys. (Two other large lamaseries
in Qinghai also ran schools, I was told; in all three, teaching focused not only
on religious philosophy but also on Tibetan medicine, astronomy, and the
Tibetan calendar.) My strong overall impression was that Kumbum continued to be a very important center of active religious life—much more so than

---

*The Banchan Lama I had met in 1948 died not long after my 1988 visit to Kumbum.

the monasteries that I had visited in Inner Mongolia—yet it seemed, nevertheless, very different in many respects from when I had last visited it. The change in atmosphere, I decided, had been largely because of the development of modern transport and communications—which increased its accessibility to the outside world and exposed it to "modern influences,"—and perhaps above all by its development as a tourist center. It no longer seemed very exotic.

*   *   *

The most stimulating trip that I made in Qinghai in 1988 was one to the province's hinterland, to a grassland area near Lake Qinghai, and to the headquarters of the Hainan Tibetan Autonomous Prefecture (TAP), which I had not visited in 1948. The round trip of 220 miles took me only about one-sixth of the distance between the province's eastern and western borders, but even this short foray into the grasslands enabled me to see one of the most important areas of animal husbandry in Qinghai and to observe how the modern world had penetrated even into traditional areas, producing an intriguing mix of the old and the new.

The highway to Hainan was a good one, well paved, with two lanes that were wider than is the case on many Chinese highways; our car was a small but comfortable Mazda. We started early in the morning, leaving Xining through a new western suburban area containing numerous modern buildings. It was a cold and foggy day, and it was both windy and dusty. The wind became stronger as we went westward. I was told that in the spring and fall the wind velocity in this area of the plateau often reaches "grade eight" or higher (according to the Chinese scale for wind, this is high; I was never able, however, to translate it into miles per hour). The altitude also rose gradually as we went westward. We started at 7,236 feet in Xining, and before we reached our destination we passed a marker at Sun-Moon Pass that stated that the altitude was 3,520 meters (11,546 feet). The altitude at our ultimate destination, the town of Chabucha (Qubqa), in Hainan Prefecture, was about 10,000 feet, according to local officials there. In Xining, I had told my hosts that I was feeling the effects of altitude to some extent even there and that because I had once had a heart attack perhaps I should avoid strenuous climbing at high altitudes. As a result, they became extremely solicitous and insisted that I should "take some oxygen" with me. I did not feel this was necessary, but I acquiesced. The oxygen container looked like nothing more than a pumped-up little rubber pillow! I dutifully carried it with me, but I never tried to use it. (Eventually, after visiting a number of areas well over 10,000 feet during my 1988 travels, I concluded that I should simply ignore the altitude, and I encountered no serious problems as a result.)

The road that we traveled was the main one from Xining to Lhasa. I saw no military traffic on it, somewhat to my surprise. We did, as I mentioned earlier, pass one small army barracks. But that was all. Soon we were in territory without any real urban centers; although we went through a few small villages, none was large enough to be called a town. It was basically an area of mixed agricultural and pastoral land. We paralleled the rail line to Golmud for a while and then went alongside the Huangshui River. High snow-covered mountains lay ahead. I was told that Amne Machin (Animaqing or Anyemaqen) Mountain, which rises to 23,485 feet and is one of the highest mountains in the region, lay about 170 miles to the south.

All along the route, up to Sun-Moon Pass, there was some farmland interspersed with small villages. Tall, thin poplars lined the village lanes and farm plots. On or near the road itself were numerous signs of the penetration of modernity in this remote area. Power and telephone lines were frequently visible. In many of the villages, I could see schools and public health clinics (marked by red crosses). In the fields, we saw occasional small crawling tractors. Some farmhouses had TV antennae. On the road itself, although traffic was light we periodically passed Chinese-made trucks, occasional long-distance buses (with luggage piled on top), and a few small passenger vans, mainly Toyotas and Nissans. However, I saw only one factory on the whole way—a brick kiln. Beyond the fringe of modernity that paralleled the road, however, the countryside looked essentially traditional. Most villages consisted of small clusters of mud brick houses, and the side roads were all made of dirt. A great deal of the local transportation was by donkey cart.

The clothing that people wore in this region was mixed. The further we went, the more people we saw who wore either Mao-style clothing and "workers caps" (flat cloth caps with visors) or, in the pastoral areas, traditional Tibetan clothing. The women's dresses were very colorful, and many of the Tibetan men had old-style sheepskin coats draped over one shoulder. However, we did see some people wearing Western-style clothing, and a few of the women dressed quite stylishly.

About halfway between Xining and Sun-Moon Pass, we went through Huangyuan, a bustling county seat with a number of recently built modern buildings. This was the only real town that we saw on the entire trip. From Huangyuan we turned southwest, following a winding route through deep gorges (where the road went through numerous tunnels). Birches lined major segments of the road in this part of our trip, and occasionally I saw black-and-white magpies flying between the trees. Flocks of animals—sheep, goats, and some yaks—steadily became more numerous as we went west, but for quite a long way we continued to pass some farms in the valleys, which were watered by rocky streams fed by glaciers in the mountains. After reaching the pass, where we stopped briefly at a small tea pavilion, we entered the real grasslands. The entire atmosphere changed at that point. In all directions there were spectacular vistas, and I found the scenery—and the air—extremely exhilarating, as I had on my previous visits to grasslands areas. On the plateau beyond the pass, we went through an area where there were undulating hills visible in all directions, covered with short grass that was excellent for grazing (although it was still brown in March). Huge flocks of animals—thousands of sheep, goats, and yaks and some horses and shaggy ponies—were spread all over the hillsides. We saw animals everywhere on the rest of our route; the number was awesome. We also passed scattered Tibetan houses and a few villages; most of them were some distance from the road.

Before reaching Chabucha, we were met, in traditional Tibetan fashion, by two officials sent by the Hainan TAP, which had been alerted to the fact that we were coming. One was a Han official from Gonghe County (a part of Hainan); the other, a Mongol, was Party secretary in Daotanghe Township, which was on our route. We stopped briefly at Daotanghe, where the Party secretary showed me around the village and took me to visit the home of a prosperous local Tibetan herdsman. I had no way of knowing whether Daotanghe was "typical," but it seemed to me very much like most of the other villages that we passed along the way—although probably it was somewhat more developed and prosperous than some others.

The village center of Daotanghe had a population of approximately 400 but those living in its immediate area totaled about 3,000. The population was predominantly Tibetan but included some Mongols and a few Han Chinese. It was located in the middle of a large pastureland area on the plateau. The buildings were mostly constructed of brick, and they looked quite new; many were whitewashed. There were two schools in the village, one of which taught in the Tibetan language and the other in Chinese. The township as a whole had a population of approximately 10,000, the Party secretary told me. Apart from those living and working in the village center, all of the Tibetans were engaged in animal husbandry. In addition to the 2 schools in the village itself, there were 11 others, all fairly small, scattered throughout the township area. The top local political authority, the Party Committee, consisted of 5 Tibetan and Mongol cadres and 1 Han Chinese. The local government employed 22 cadres, all Tibetans and Mongols except for 3 Han Chinese.

The Tibetan family home that we visited was a couple of miles away from the village on a dirt track that led into the pastureland. This family was obviously prosperous; I had little doubt that it was above average. The head of the family greeted us cordially and, with his wife and four children, served us Chinese liquor (sorghum "baigan" or "baigar" imported from Sichuan), tea, and a considerable amount of food. We were fed twisted "crullers," pieces of mutton, and tsamba tea (tsamba is made from dry roasted barley), and small pellets of goat cheese. This home was very isolated—as virtually all the Tibetan homes we passed were. It was a well-built brick structure within a walled compound that held all their domestic animals. The head of the family showed me with great pride a new gasoline-powered electric generator that he had recently bought.

After this visit, we drove on to the shore of Lake Qinghai, a few miles further. This was an area of beautiful scenery and excellent grasslands. The vistas were even more spectacular than the ones we had already seen; everywhere we could see vast rolling grasslands bordered by mountains sloping down to the lake. I was told that all the herdsmen in this area had settled down—that is, they had built permanent houses and all of them had been assigned definite areas of pasturage. In some places these areas of pasturage were surrounded by low mud walls or wire fencing. However, I was told, they still moved their flocks or herds during part of the year, searching for the best pasture areas, and when on the move they lived in traditional tents. The homes that we passed were separated by great distances. I saw a few that had windmill generators. Everywhere in the distance we could see large flocks of animals tended by herdsmen, many of whom were riding shaggy ponies. Sometimes we saw only one or two herdsmen attending a flock, but at times we saw half a dozen or so who probably were tending several flocks. All wore traditional Tibetan garb. Immediately adjacent to the lake there were a few farms, but not a great many.

A cold, blustery wind blew across the water, chilling us to the bone. The lake is huge, and it was easy to understand why the Chinese call it a sea. Its area is 1,789 square miles, and its circumference is 224 miles. The part of the lake that we could see was entirely frozen. We stopped at a fishing center, the main catch of which, I was told, was yellow fish—*huangyu*—a delicious variety that is greatly prized by the Chinese. But the lake is best known for its sturgeon, locally called *luoli*, or "naked carp." There was no visible activity there: The weather was still too cold for anyone to go out fishing. (I was told about a small island at the west end of the lake, called "Bird Islet," which had become an important bird sanctuary; as a birder, I yearned to see it but unfortunately had no time to do so.)

                    *   *   *

From Lake Qinghai, we drove on to our ultimate destination, the town of Chabucha, which is also called Gonghe, the name of the county in which it is located. Our route took us through changing terrain. First, following a twisting road, we climbed through hills; animals were feeding everywhere on the hillsides. We then entered another vast grassland plateau, where tens of thousands (so it seemed to me) of yaks, sheep, and some horses were being tended by Tibetan herdsmen. A hilly, fairly dry area followed; it contained a small valley with mud villages, where the villagers raised animals, mainly sheep, and also tilled the land. Then we came to a broader agricultural plain, where farming was the major occupation; even there, though, we saw a great many animals on the hillsides and in mud corrals. Just before reaching

Chabucha, we crossed another large grassland plain, but this one appeared to be partially desertified and had fewer animals.

Chabucha was a great surprise to me. I am not sure what I had expected, but the town proved to be much more modern than I had anticipated. By this time in my 1988 travels through remote areas of China I realized that one can find scattered throughout even some of the most distant places remarkable pockets of transplanted modernization; some of them are small towns, others are actually large new cities. Almost all of them have been developed since the Communist takeover in 1949. I had seen several such places before I reached Qinghai—including Baiyanhaote, as well as Yinchuan, and Baotou—places that had, at most, been small traditional towns before 1949 but had been transformed in the past four decades. Later in 1988 I was to visit quite a few more, including Linxia, Urumqi, Turfan (Turpan), Zegong, Wenjiang, Tunxi, Gejiu, Shenzhen, and others; some of these I describe in other chapters. Chabucha proved to be one of these quite remarkable pockets of modernization, even though it was still only a small town in 1988.

I was told that before 1949 the area in which Chabucha is located was virtually uninhabited. It was a desertified area, populated mainly by wild goats and rabbits and having only about 10 agricultural households—one landlord and the rest ordinary farmers—plus a handful of Kazakhs (who had subsequently moved to the Tsaidam area, in 1953). It did, however, have a source of water, the stream that was called Chabucha, and this was the basis for its later development. I was told that the name Chabucha was Mongol and meant, according to local people, "a mountain divided in two." (Originally, the Tibetans had a different designation for the area, and their name meant: "the place where two rivers joined and in winter froze like silvery threads of silk.")

After 1949, the area was rapidly developed. I was never given a clear explanation of why this took place, but I guessed at some of the reasons. It is now located at the point where two very strategic roads, built after 1949, connect: a major road from Qinghai to Tibet proper and the road from Qinghai to Kangding (which is now in western Sichuan but formerly had been the capital of Xikang Province), from where two other roads lead to Tibet proper. At some point, an airfield was built about 10 miles from where the town is located. Until recently this airfield had been secret, but by 1988 it was an open secret. No scheduled civilian air service reached the airfield, but it was used, I believe, by military aircraft as well as by occasional top Chinese leaders who visited the area, including Party General Secretaries Hu Yaobang and Zhao Ziyang (Zhao was premier when he visited the area in the early 1980s but succeeded Hu as general secretary in 1987).

By 1983, I was told, Chabucha's population totaled close to 20,000, and by 1988 it had risen to roughly 30,000. It had become a lively and quite modern little town, with well-paved streets, electricity, and numerous modern buildings, some of which were several stories high and a few of which were quite grand, including a recently built prefectural People's Congress headquarters.

Chabucha had become the seat of three levels of government: the town (*zhen*) itself, Gonghe County (*xian*), and the Hainan Tibetan Autonomous Prefecture (*zizhi zhou*). My principal host there was the head of the prefectural government, a young Tibetan in his forties. He had been born in Kangding but had grown up in the Yushu area of Qinghai and had attended a Party school in Beijing before being appointed Hainan's prefectural head. He and his executive deputy, plus six heads of departments in the prefectural government, first entertained me at a sumptuous luncheon banquet—with 13 dishes!—that was held in a small but attractive Chinese-style guest house, a structure that was modern except that its toilet was in an adjacent outhouse. With considerable pride, my hosts told me that both Hu Yaobang and Zhao Ziyang had been entertained there. (Today, the Chinese in almost any place where a top leader has visited invariably mention the visit; I was always reminded of the "George Washington Slept Here" claims made by so many towns in the eastern part of the United States.)

After lunch, we discussed at great length the government, the economy, and many other things relating to the Hainan TAP. Local officials were obviously very proud of their prefecture, and they wanted the rest of the world to know about it. One key administrative official who managed the prefectural office told me that he was supervising a staff of people engaged in writing a multivolume history of the area; four "introductory" (!) volumes had already been completed, but that was just the beginning, he said. This man urged me to "tell Americans all about Hainan."

The Hainan Tibetan Autonomous Prefecture, which was formally established in 1953, had at the time of my visit a total population of 347,000. The Tibetans were the largest ethnic group, totaling 170,000. The Han Chinese were a close second, with 140,000. In addition, there were about 17,000 Hui Muslims, over 2,000 Mongols, over 2,000 Tu, and smaller numbers of several other ethnic minorities. Its area was divided into six county-level governments (five regular counties—*xian*—and one "special work committee" equivalent to a county), 40 townships (*xiang*), and 387 "natural villages" (*ziran cun*). At the "basic level"—in the natural villages—there were 387 "village committees"; each of these had jurisdiction over an average of 500 or so households in agricultural areas and between 100 and 150 households in pastoral areas. At an even lower level, there were 1,260 units that were called production cooperatives (*shengchan hezuoshe*), each of which was headed by a chairman and contained an average of 50 or more households in agricultural areas and 10 to 20 households in pastoral areas. Most of the co-ops in pastoral areas were said to have been originally formed from groups of close relatives, but this was no longer the case.

The Tibetan head of the prefecture's Civil Affairs Bureau asserted that the leaders of these groups were all elected and that one of the main functions of his bureau was to ensure that the elections were conducted correctly. With a small staff—9 people at the prefectural level, assisted by 71 at the county level and below—the Civil Affairs Bureau also handled marriage registrations, relief, mediation of family disputes, and a variety of other matters.

The Bureau of Culture was also headed by a Tibetan, a local man who had been educated in the Beijing Minority Nationalities Institute. With a staff of 12 (6 Han Chinese, 4 Tibetans, and 2 Hui Muslims), it had eight units directly under it and also supervised cultural bureaus at the county level. Altogether there were more than 250 people, about half of them Tibetans, who worked for the "cultural system" throughout the prefecture. The Bureau of Culture and its subordinate personnel managed or supervised a wide range of institutions and activities, including a TV relay station, a radio station, a movie theater, a library, an art center, a minorities museum, a song and dance troupe, and a sports facility. They also supervised the local press and a branch of the New China Bookstore. As always, I was impressed by the way TV and radio had spread. My informants said that both reached most of the population, although they did not provide exact statistics on their coverage. In Hainan Prefecture, the local TV relay station transmitted programs originating elsewhere, but the prefecture's leaders had plans to build a TV station of their own, and they had requested permission to do so from higher authority. The prefecture and each of its counties also had radio "broadcasting stations" (some of these may have been wired systems—although I am not sure).

The head of the Education Bureau, a Han Chinese from Guangdong Province, discussed the local school system. His bureau had a staff of 11, of whom 9 were Han Chinese and 2 were Tibetans. All of them were local people except for the bureau head. They were responsible for all schools throughout the prefecture. The system had steadily expanded, and in addition to primary schools they now had many middle schools. Not all of the townships had middle schools, but every township that contained a sizable town (*zhen*) did; the township middle schools taught in Chinese. If a Tibetan reached the middle school level and wished to study in the Tibetan language, it was necessary for him or her to attend a county-level minorities school. The bias was clearly in favor of the Chinese language—more so, it seemed to me, than in some other minority areas that I visited. (It seemed to me—from my limited observation—that most of the Tibetans I encountered in Qinghai outside of pastoral areas seemed to be Sinified to a large extent.) The most important recent educational development in Hainan Prefecture had been the establishment of a postsecondary Tibetan training institution.

The task of raising the educational level in the area, especially among the Tibetans, still posed major problems. The priority aim of the Education Bureau, its head said, was to raise the level of basic literacy, especially among Tibetans in grassland areas. He estimated that the literacy rate in the grassland areas in Hainan TAP was still only about 40 percent, whereas in agricultural areas it had risen to above 60 percent.

The economy of Hainan TAP was still based mainly on animal husbandry, but there was a substantial number of farmers and a few small industries were being developed. The prefecture contained a total of 3.8 million animals (more than 10 times the number of its human population), I was told, and my hosts maintained that their area had a larger number of animals, on a per capita basis, than any other comparable area in Qinghai. The gross value of the annual output of their animal husbandry sector, they said, was Y 70 million. The tilled land in the prefecture totaled just under 87,000 acres, which was not very much but still was significant for an area that traditionally had been almost entirely pastoral. The output value of agriculture was said to be about Y 40 million a year. I was given approximate (rounded) figures for the average per capita income of those in both animal husbandry and agricultural areas, which indicated that as a group the local pastoral population was substantially better off than local farmers: Those in animal husbandry had an average per capita income of roughly Y 600, they said, whereas the average incomes of those in farming was only a little over Y 300. (These particular figures were not entirely consistent with other data that local officials gave me, but nevertheless there was agreement among my hosts that the average incomes of Tibetan herdsmen in the area were generally higher than those of most local farmers.)

The newest sector of the economy consisted of several industrial enterprises, developed mostly in the past few years. This sector was still small, but it was making a growing contribution to the economy. Almost all local industrial enterprises were engaged in the processing of animal products. Included were two wool factories (the Number Two Provincial Qinghai Wool Factory and the Hainan TAP Wool Factory), a county factory processing hides and leathers, a Tibetan medicine factory, and several food plants processing meat, animal livers, and intestines. Local leaders had no illusions about Hainan TAP developing into a major industrial center, but they nevertheless believed—justifiably, I thought—that the processing of agricultural and animal products could gradually be expanded and could help to raise average incomes in the area.

I left the Hainan Tibetan Autonomous Prefecture—and Qinghai Province—genuinely impressed by the way in which modernizing influences were steadily penetrating into and transforming previously underdeveloped areas. It seemed to me that this process would continue inexorably. But I also left with a sense of awe about the enormity of the task of modernizing all of the outlying areas of China. My deepest foray into Qinghai's grasslands had taken me only a short distance into the vast Tibetan plateau; I could only speculate, therefore, about more distant places. The areas that I saw had changed remarkably in four decades, but they still had a very long way to go to begin to approach the level of modernization of more advanced areas in China, which were developing at a much more rapid pace. Compared to the most advanced areas of East Asia (to say nothing of the Western world), Qinghai remained far behind. But Qinghai's leaders, both at the provincial and local levels, impressed me as being determined to try to catch up. What seemed likely to me, however, was that although Qinghai would continue to move ahead, it probably would continue to lag behind, and perhaps could fall even further behind, as coastal regions, which enjoy many comparative advantages, modernize at an even faster rate.

CHAPTER SIX

Chinese Turkestan

XINJIANG

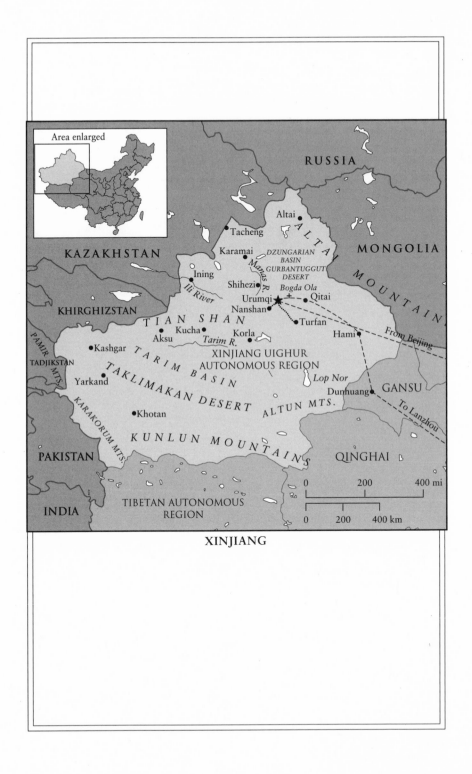

XINJIANG

M Y FINAL DESTINATION in northwest China in 1988 was the Xinjiang Uighur Autonomous Region.*

Xinjiang is often translated into English as "New Dominion" (literally *xin* means new and *jiang* means frontier or boundary). However, I have always preferred "Chinese Turkestan" or "Eastern Turkestan," the terms used for Xinjiang in many early Western writings. The last of China's outlying areas to be incorporated into the Qing dynasty's formal administrative system, Xinjiang was, historically, more associated with Central Asia than with China, and in many respects the atmosphere in parts of the region is still more Central Asian than Han Chinese. The area has had an extraordinarily colorful and turbulent history, and it is unquestionably a land of many superlatives.

It is the largest provincial-level unit in China, and its territory—almost 620,000 square miles—is greater than that of the United Kingdom, France, Italy, and the recently united Germany combined. Within its area are some of the tallest mountains in China—and the world (most of them are in the Pamir, the Tian Shan, and Kunlun ranges). It also contains the lowest point in China (Turfan, which is well below sea level) and China's largest desert (the Taklimakan). In ancient times, it was a crucial link on the Silk Road between China and the Roman world. During much of the nineteenth and twentieth centuries, it was a focal point for conflict between China and two competing imperial powers—Russia (later the Soviet Union) and Great Britain. Its position continues to be strategically very important: The region's external borders touch four states that were part of the Soviet Union (Russia, Kazakhstan, Tadjikstan, and Kirghizstan), Outer Mongolia, Afghanistan, and Pakistan, and internally it is adjacent to Gansu, Qinghai, and Tibet.

Most of Xinjiang is virtually empty. Apart from the Ili region, in past centuries the small population was concentrated almost entirely in glacier-fed oases, where deserts meet mountains. In recent years the population has grown rapidly, although it is still small for such an enormous area. When I visited Xinjiang in 1948, local officials estimated its population at that time to be about 4 million. Between the late 1940s and the late 1980s, the population rose to roughly 14 million. (It was 13.84 million in 1986.) The population has always been a complex mixture of ethnic groups; in recent centuries

---

*After my visits to Inner Mongolia, Ningxia, Gansu, and Qinghai from mid-February to mid-March, I returned to Beijing to catch up on developments in China's capital. I then spent four weeks, during March and April, in Sichuan Province in China's southwest. After that, I again returned to Beijing, and then, finally, I flew to Xinjiang in late April.

Turkic Muslim peoples have been predominant. In 1948, less than 6 percent of the population consisted of Han Chinese. Now, minority groups still make up the majority (more than three-fifths), but the Han population has increased dramatically and now accounts for almost two-fifths of the region's inhabitants.

*   *   *

Xinjiang has always been a crossroads, swept by waves of migration and invasion. Many different Indo-European, Turkic, Mongol, and Tibetan peoples have, at different times, controlled all or parts of it. As early as the Han dynasty (206 B.C.–A.D. 220), however, the Han Chinese recognized the strategic importance of the region and established garrisons in key oases. From then on, the Silk Road was the main trade route linking China with the West. This continued to be true until modern times. But the power of the Chinese empire waxed and waned over the centuries, and the imperial rulers exercised effective power in the region only in the empire's greatest periods of western expansionism, during the Han, Tang, Yuan, Ming, and Qing dynasties.

Tibetans controlled major parts of the region in the seventh century and again in part of the eighth century. In the latter half of the eighth and the first half of the ninth centuries, the Uighurs, a major Turkic group, established a local kingdom that controlled the Tarim Basin as well as parts of Mongolia for almost a century. Uighur political control continued into the eleventh century in certain areas, and in a few other areas it lasted until Genghis Khan's conquest in the thirteenth century. Starting in the eighth century, most of the population of the region was gradually converted to Islam, and its doctrines spread throughout Central Asia.

Although Han Chinese power waned at the end of the Ming dynasty, once the Manchus conquered China and established the Qing dynasty in the seventeenth century they rapidly reasserted control over key areas of Turkestan (although, like past rulers, they had to compromise with local leaders, and their control in many areas was fairly loose). By the nineteenth century, however, the Qing's strategic control weakened, and the strategic importance of the region began to decline—after Western maritime powers forcibly "opened" coastal China in the 1840s. What had for centuries been China's "front door" now became its "back door."

Nevertheless, Xinjiang continued to be a cockpit for political intrigue, competition, and conflict. Both the Russians, expanding eastward from Central Asia (and Siberia), and the British, looking north from India, competed actively for influence in the region. In the 1860s, a huge rebellion exploded in Xinjiang, led by a Muslim named Yakub Beg. His rebels conquered most of the region, but the Russians, taking advantage of the situation, occupied the Ili area in the northwest. It took years for the Chinese to reassert control.

However, eventually Zuo Zongtang (Tso Tsung-t'ang) defeated the rebels in the 1870s, and in the 1880s China recovered the Ili region from the Russians. Finally, in the 1880s, China converted Xinjiang into a regular province and incorporated it into the Chinese (Manchu) administrative system.

That was by no means the end of turbulence in the region, however. When China broke up after the 1911 collapse of the Qing dynasty, a succession of autonomous Chinese warlords controlled Xinjiang. Their power was threatened, however, when the post-1917 Soviet regime in Russia reasserted its influence in the 1920s. Then, in the 1930s there was another large revolt, led by Ma Zhongying, a Gansu Hui leader. Out of the resulting chaos, Sheng Shicai (Sheng Shih-t'sai) emerged as the leader of the province. Headquartered in Urumqi (then called Dihua), he obtained Soviet support, defeated Ma, and established a pro-Moscow regime. For some years, the Soviet Union played a very large role in the province; in fact, it stationed a mechanized regiment in Hami, at the eastern edge of the province. Then, suddenly, Sheng made a political about-face and expelled the Russians in 1942. The Russians, for their own geopolitical reasons, nevertheless continued providing military assistance to the Nationalist regime, then headquartered in Chongqing, for the war against Japan, and Xinjiang was the main route over which Soviet aid was delivered. Finally, in 1944, the Nationalists were able to reassert direct control over Xinjiang and eased Sheng out of the governorship.

When I visited Xinjiang in 1948, the Nationalists were more or less in control of part of the region but were facing imminent defeat in their internal struggle against the Communists in north China. Xinjiang at that time was still so remote from the main battlegrounds of the civil war that it remained on the sidelines in that conflict. However, it was itself heavily militarized, and Chinese control of the local population depended fundamentally on the army. The provincial regime faced two external major military threats of its own, from the north. During 1944–1945 rebels in the Ili region, along the Soviet border with Xinjiang in the northwest, had established, with Soviet assistance, the so-called East Turkestan Republic in the Ili region. They were led mainly by Uighurs but their forces included Kazakhs and others. These rebels controlled 3 of Xinjiang's 10 administrative districts. An attempt was made to negotiate a settlement, and for a brief period after the signing of a compromise peace agreement in 1946, a provincial coalition government had tried to function in Urumqi. But this government had collapsed in 1947, not long before my visit. At the time of my visit in the summer of 1948, although the Chinese and rebel forces were not actively fighting, they still confronted each other, in warlike formations, across the Manas River, northwest of Urumqi. I traveled by truck the 70-odd miles to the river, where I could see soldiers on both sides peering at each other warily, but there were no exchanges of fire when I was there.

I also traveled by truck to Qitai (Ch'it'ai), about 145 miles east of Urumqi, to visit the headquarters of the Chinese forces that confronted Mongol troops at Beidashan. In this area, a small mountain range dominated the still-undemarcated border area between Xinjiang and Outer Mongolia. Disputes over the border had led to armed clashes in 1947, and occasional military incidents were still taking place in 1948. (From Qitai, I also made a memorable trek by horseback into the nearby Tian Shan mountain range to visit Osman Bator, the preeminent Kazakh leader in Xinjiang at that time, who had only recently aligned with the Chinese in their conflicts with both the Ili rebels and the Mongols.)

*   *   *

Four decades later, in 1988, when I prepared to fly to Xinjiang in late April, I refreshed my memory about the area by rereading some of the things I had written at the time of my first trip. In 1948, Xinjiang was an extremely undeveloped area—premodern in almost every respect. Even in the capital, then called Dihua (now Urumqi), there were few signs of the twentieth century. It was a large, sprawling, dusty town, consisting mainly of one-story shops and residences. Some local people estimated its population at about 80,000; others claimed that it was over 100,000. No one—even the best-informed officials—seemed to be certain. Although the town was the center of Han power in the province, the people in its streets at that time were a colorful mixture of Han Chinese, most of whom wore very traditional, premodern Chinese clothing, and Uighurs, almost all of whom were dressed in very traditional Muslim clothing—the men wearing skullcaps and the women wearing hoods. There also were quite a few colorful Kazakhs, the men riding horses with great flair, like cocky cowboys who had come down from the hills. On the unpaved streets, there were not many modern vehicles, only a few trucks. Most of the traffic consisted of horse-drawn carts, and there were quite a few people on horseback—mainly Kazakhs, most of them wearing traditional fur-lined silk hats with large earflaps. A few gravel and dirt roads—used by trucks—connected the city with the major oases scattered elsewhere throughout the province, but the only modern transportation that connected it with the outside world was an occasional airplane flying to and from other major Chinese cities in the east. (No railway had yet been built.) The atmosphere was very much that of a Central Asian city, not that of a Chinese urban center.

The population of Xinjiang Province was estimated by local officials at that time to be roughly 4 million. (Official statistics published by the government in Nanjing in the early 1940s had placed it at 3.73 million.) Uighurs, who accounted for almost 75 percent of the total, were engaged mainly in agriculture. They dominated the oases in the south, where a very large proportion of the province's population (possibly as much as two-thirds of the total) was concentrated. The Kazakhs, most of whom were still nomadic, accounted for just over 10 percent of the population. They were concentrated in the northern parts of the province, on the slopes of the Tian Shan range, and in the Ili region. In the Ili region they occupied the grasslands, and the Uighurs and Chinese farmed the lowlands. Although Han Chinese were the third largest group, they accounted for less than 6 percent of the total population of the province. Some were farmers, but a large percentage of them were merchants and officials. The rest of the population was very mixed and consisted of a variety of groups: Dongan (another group of Chinese Muslims—2 percent); Taranqi (classified by some people as a subgroup of the Uighurs—2 percent); Kirghiz (under 2 percent); Mongols (1.5 percent); Uzbeks (under 1 percent); and several even smaller groups, including the Xibe, Solon, Manchus, Tatars, Tadjiks, and "White Russians." Virtually all of Xinjiang's population—almost 95 percent—consisted of Muslims who spoke some form of the Turki language.

In 1948, provincial officials whom I interviewed estimated that although the majority of the population was engaged in agriculture, they tilled only about 1 percent of the province's whole territory. Nomadic herdsmen, who were somewhat fewer in number, used another 5 percent of the province's land. Most of the territory was entirely uninhabited. In the entire province, moreover, there were fewer than a dozen small factories. My memories of the region were of an area that was extremely backward—but also fascinating and romantic. I vividly recalled interviews with some of the most colorful leaders I had ever met anywhere. The most memorable leader, perhaps, was Osman Bator, whom I and two companions interviewed in his yurt encampment in the Tian Shan. Everything in my 1948 visit had seemed like an adventure in a faraway place in a distant era: I traveled by truck across a trackless plain, chasing gazelles en route to the towering mountain of Bogda Ola; went by truck to the Manas River and Qitai across wilderness areas at the foothills of the mountains; climbed to a Kazakh encampment and stayed in yurts at the foot of the glacier at 14,000 feet at Bogda Ola; and rode horseback far into the Tian Shan range to visit Osman Bator.

*   *   *

When I boarded a modern airplane in Beijing in late April 1988 to make my second visit to Xinjiang, the most basic question in my mind was a very simple one: How much had all of that changed in 40 years?

I flew from Beijing to Urumqi on a Tupolev 154, a relatively new model of Soviet passenger plane that had been recently acquired by the Chinese. By the standards of the 1980s, it was less than comfortable. Configured to take 164 passengers, it was jam-packed. As is true of most planes in China, the seats were narrow and placed so closely together that there was almost no legroom. The overhead luggage compartments were tiny—only big enough for small packages. It was more comfortable, though, than the bucket-seat military transport plane on which I had flown to Xinjiang in 1948. All of the passengers on the Tupolev were Chinese except for me and several Russian technicians, who—I was told—were traveling in China to check up on the plane's performance.

The air distance from Beijing to Urumqi was 1,864 miles—considerably further than from Beijing to Tokyo. The schedule called for our leaving Beijing at 7:00 P.M. and arriving at Urumqi roughly four hours later. Actually, we left an hour late, but, because of favorable winds, the flight took only 3.5 hours. It was an uneventful flight—and also quite uninteresting because of the high altitude at which we flew and the steadily darkening skies. I had hoped to see the countryside that we traversed, but we could see almost nothing of the terrain below us—not the agriculture areas, the grasslands, or the deserts or high mountains. Dusk descended about an hour and a half after we took off, and for the rest of the trip—right up until our arrival late at night—the sky was a peculiar mixture of twilight and nighttime. The land below was pitch black; a thin strip of bright orange marked the horizon; and above that there was a wide, light blue band of sky. Right above us, the sky was inky black. (The scene reminded me of the way dusk often appears to descend in a planetarium, except that on this trip it continued for virtually our entire time in the air.)

In recent years, flying over many parts of China I had seen electric lights in many rural areas, but on this trip we saw few signs of life below until we made our approach to Urumqi. Then, we were suddenly above an area that was extremely well lit, even late at night. We landed at 11:30 P.M., Beijing time. Officially, it was also 11:30 in Urumqi, since in theory all of China was still operating on the same time as the capital. I soon discovered, however, that Urumqi operates on a double time standard. Most official schedules were given in Beijing time, but in reality everyone operated on local time, which was two hours different. Some people kept their watches on Beijing time; others set theirs by local time. This discrepancy did not seem to bother local people at all, but it was a little disconcerting for newcomers.

The airport at Urumqi was the largest and grandest of any that I saw anywhere in west China; it was comparable, in fact, to the largest ones in east China. Soviet specialists had helped to build the airfield, and its size reflected the importance of Xinjiang in Sino-Soviet relations in the 1950s, when construction of the major runways was begun, I was told. But the passenger terminal had been completed only in the 1970s. When I had flown to Xinjiang in 1948, we had landed at a tiny, primitive airstrip just outside the city. When I arrived in 1988, I asked where it was and was told that it no longer existed. The spot where it had been was now right in the middle of the city—in an area that had been totally absorbed by the city—not far from the headquarters of the regional government.

Accompanying me on this trip was a new escort from CASS, Tsao Dapeng. CASS officials may have thought that the rigors of my travels in the interior required them to provide R&R for each of their escorts after several weeks with me on the road. Or perhaps they simply wished to give different staff members the opportunity to see out-of-the-way places in the country. In any case, I was assigned a new escort for each major leg of my travels. I had met Tsao some years earlier, when he had been one of the interpreters involved in an interview I had had with Zhao Ziyang, then premier and later Party general secretary. I found Tsao to be an extremely pleasant traveling companion, even though he was remarkably apolitical and not very interested in the kinds of economic, social, and political questions that most concerned me. The son of a manufacturer of a special kind of paper used by artists, Tsao had grown up in the lower Yangzi valley but had—when I met him—lived and worked in Beijing for many years. At one time he had been interested in the possibility of joining the Communist Party, but he never did. By 1988, he was approaching retirement, and he had turned his interests and attention increasingly to his major avocations, which included traditional calligraphy, landscape painting, seal carving, singing of Chinese opera, and the playing of the two-stringed Chinese violin (*er hu*). He impressed me as being a modern version of an old-style Chinese literatus, born in the wrong century. He himself once said to me, wistfully: "There are few with interests like mine left in China anymore." He told me that he never had exhibited any of his paintings but that he continued to produce them regularly; he signed some of them with Chinese characters meaning "bewildered."

Tsao and I were met at the Urumqi airport by two men from the Xinjiang Academy of Social Sciences who were to be our local hosts for the entire time that we were in Xinjiang. After greeting us cordially, they immediately drove us to the Kunlun Hotel, about 16 miles away, to the north, in one of the new (post-1949) areas of the city.

The weather in Urumqi, which was in the sixties Fahrenheit, was considerably warmer than I had expected it to be in April. Xinjiang has a "continental climate"—very cold in the winter and very hot in the summer. I had therefore brought very warm clothing with me but found very little use for it except when I made trips into the nearby mountains. During my entire stay in Urumqi, this time, the temperature hovered in the sixties or seventies—although it was sometimes slightly warmer than seventy in the daytime and slightly colder than sixty at night. When I visited the city of Turfan (Turpan), however, I encountered weather that was like midsummer; it averaged about 85 degrees Fahrenheit while I was there.

En route from the airport to my hotel, we traveled most of the way on a very wide, modern boulevard through a built-up urban area filled with low, modern buildings, most of which were built in the 1950s and 1960s, I was told, but we also passed a few high-rise skyscrapers of recent vintage. The

Kunlun Hotel (named after one of the great mountain ranges in west China, located between Xinjiang and Tibet) proved to be a large, cavernous, building. It was much like the hotels I had stayed in while visiting Lanzhou and Xining. Its architecture was stolid—in the Soviet style of Stalin. Ten stories high, the main building had until recently been the tallest structure in the city, and originally it had been the residence of Soviet advisers and technicians. But a few years before my visit, it had been modernized and converted into a public hotel. Across the street was an impressive new building, the home of the region's People's Congress, and next door to the hotel was a "rest home" for military officers. The scene was not totally lacking in color from the past, though: A flock of sheep was grazing on the hotel's lawn.

Although the hotel was modern in some respects, its services seemed still to follow the old Soviet model. The bathroom had no toilet paper, no stopper for the tub, and no soap or towels—as was true in earlier years of every Soviet hotel in which I had stayed. Because, in times past, no Chinese hotel in the interior was likely to have these either, I had brought all of these items with me. When I started my travels in the northwest in 1988, I had no idea whether conditions would be similar to those in the 1940s, so I came well supplied with everything that had been lacking in the interior 40 years earlier. I then discovered, much to my surprise, that virtually every hotel in which I stayed in the interior—no matter how small or how remote it was—had modern equipment similar to those in coastal areas; the Kunlun Hotel was an exception.

*   *   *

Even though we arrived at the hotel, after our drive from the airport, at a very late hour, our hosts were eager to discuss the program and schedule of activities that they had arranged for us. I would have preferred to wait until the next morning, but they were insistent, so we proceeded with a long discussion, in which I began to get acquainted with the two men who would be my mentors in Xinjiang. My principal host was a deputy president of the local Academy of Social Sciences; he was a 47-year-old Kazakh named Yakub Mi-er Jahan (my transliteration). He had spent his childhood, he said, in a grassland area in the Ili region, where his father still lived and raised animals (200 sheep, 20 horses, several camels, and a few cows). He emphasized that he still has very strong roots in Ili: He visited his father there frequently, and his children returned regularly to Ili to spend their summers. Although his own early schooling had been in Ili, he passed the examination required to attend college and soon thereafter moved to Urumqi to attend Xinjiang University. He said that this institution had been the successor to one called Xinjiang College in the years before 1949 and that in the 1930s it had been the headquarters of a number of noted leftist Chinese intellectuals, including for a period the writer Mao Dun. Although my host had specialized, in his academic study, in Kazakh history, he was best known, I was told by others, for two novels that he had written, one of them set in Ili in the period right after 1949 and the other one about the life and activities of intellectuals in Urumqi. The other of my two local hosts was a Uighur named Tayerjan (Ta-yi-er-jiang); essentially he acted as a leg man, responsible for nitty-gritty arrangements. A third person in our party was an unshaven, dyspeptic Uighur driver, who was always silent unless spoken to and then responded only in monosyllables.

My hosts were extremely jovial and declared that they would do their best to be responsive to my requests. It almost immediately became clear to me, however, that they had had virtually no contact with foreigners and had almost no understanding of what I really wished to do. Although the Xinjiang Academy did seem eager to expand its foreign contacts, it obviously was ill prepared to do so. Unlike similar academies elsewhere, it did not have a foreign affairs office; four very junior staff members in its planning section had been assigned to handle foreign visitors. Since 1980, I was told, the Academy had hosted about 100 foreign visitors of various kinds; this was not an insignificant number but the majority had come in groups, so in most years there had been only a handful of visits.

I soon discovered, also, that the Academy viewed my trip as a kind of academic tourism; those assigned to help me were obviously most enthusiastic about arranging two trips outside of Urumqi, one to a mountain area called Nanshan and the other to Turfan. Before my arrival, they had scheduled very few interviews for me. Initially this dismayed me, but by persistently making additional requests I was finally able to convince them that I really was serious about my wish to meet a wide range of people. Before I left I was able, in fact, to have very good interviews in Urumqi with 25 officials and scholars, including one of the deputy chairmen of the entire autonomous region and others with key officials from the Planning Commission, Economic Commission, Nationalities Affairs Commission, and Education Commission, as well as people from many other organizations involved in education, journalism, and broadcasting and a variety of local scholars who were engaged in research on local history and economics under the Academy.

The academic tourism during my visit proved to be useful to a degree, and it was certainly enjoyable. I was able to see not only all parts of Urumqi but also one nearby mountain area and one oasis city as well as the barren areas en route to these places. I started my explorations of the region by touring Urumqi itself. This city, the capital of the Xinjiang Uighur Autonomous Region, has a spectacular setting. Located at an altitude that varies between 2,000 and 3,000 feet, it rests at the foot of numerous towering, snow-covered peaks, which are part of the Tian Shan—the Celestial Mountains.

The most majestic of these is Bogda Ola (sometimes spelled Bogda Ula), which lies east of the city. Bogda, as it is affectionately called by the local citizenry, rises to a height of 17,860 feet and dominates the entire area. Local inhabitants differ on the origin of the mountain's name. Several told me that they believed that Bogda was a Mongol word, derived from a Mongol group from Dzungaria (some of whom had at one time lived in the Urumqi area). Others argued that the origin of the name was Turki, the language of the Uighurs. Almost all seemed to agree, however, that the word meant something like "fairy." Ola or Ula, my informants agreed, came from a Turki term for mountains—used by the Kazakhs who had displaced the Mongols in this mountainous region. (The Kazakhs speak a Turkic language very similar to that spoken by the Uighurs.) The consensus, therefore, was that Bogda Ola meant "Fairy Mountain," a name that seemed very appropriate to me in light of the magical and awesome appearance of the peak. Bogda actually seems even higher than it is because it rises roughly 15,000 feet straight up above the city's level, which is right at its base. Although Urumqi's weather is very dry—averaging about 11 inches of rain a year—it is well supplied with water from nearby glaciers. It is very hot in the summer (though its nights are cool, even then) and very cold in the winter.*

*   *   *

Like all of the major cities in northwest China that I revisited in 1988, Urumqi had been totally transformed in the four decades since my previous visit. No longer a mud-colored town, it had become a very modern metropolis—although its "old city" still had a distinct Middle Eastern flavor. As the capital of the autonomous region, it was really Xinjiang's only major metropolis; it was the only city in the region classified as a "prefecture-level" municipality. By 1986 (the latest year for which I could obtain definite, published statistics), Urumqi's population had grown to more than 1,203,000. Most of the population lived in six city districts, but some were scattered throughout the one county that belonged to the municipality. Altogether the municipality encompassed 4,416 square miles. Of the total population, more than 80 percent—just under a million—were urban residents and engaged in nonfarming occupations. Although minorities—by far the largest number of whom were Uighurs—still made up three-fifths of the autonomous region's population in 1988, in the city of Urumqi itself Han Chinese constituted three-quarters of the municipality's population. The largest mi-

---

*In 1948, I had made a trek to the glacier on Bogda, which begins at about 14,000 feet, and I stayed there in a Kazakh yurt that was part of a sizable encampment. I went with several professional mountain climbers, including two of the most famous British climbers of Mount Everest; their objective was to be the first to reach the top of Bogda Ola, but they failed in that mission. My only objective was to learn something about the local Kazakhs, which I did. However, we also collected some glacier ice to take back to the city to use in martinis!

nority groups in the municipality were the Uighurs (with 12 percent of the total population), Hui Muslims (8 percent), and Kazakhs (3 percent).

The modern city of Urumqi that I saw in 1988 was much more attractive and livable than the pre-Communist city that I had visited in 1948. Near to the city center were two fairly large parks, one called "Red Mountain" (*hong shan*) and the other called "People's Park" (*renmin gongyuan*). In the former was a hill topped by a pagoda that local residents viewed as a kind of symbol or logo of the city. Both parks were obviously very popular recreation spots, and the city had recently "modernized" them by installing pool tables and video games. Not far from Red Mountain—near the center of the city—was a large office building that housed both the municipal Party headquarters and the municipal government. Two wide, tree-lined avenues, with side lanes for bicycles and pedestrians, stretched to the north. Many of the buildings in this area were of stolid Russian style. Generally, they were fairly squat—only a few stories high. Most of them were public buildings, and the majority dated to the 1950s and 1960s. One of the most impressive buildings in this section was a large, classical-style structure housing the headquarters of the Xinjiang Production and Construction Corps, the dominant economic institution in the region (which I will discuss later). Scattered among the Soviet-style edifices were some more modern high-rise buildings, which were constructed in the 1980s. To the north, the city stretched a considerable distance, and then a highway led northwest toward the nearest sizable city, Shihezi, which was roughly 95 miles away and located adjacent to the Manas River.

From the center of the city, several other large boulevards went toward the south, and they were lined with many tall, modern buildings—the tallest one rose over 20 stories. Among the most impressive of them was a recently built Economic Commission headquarters, a new office building for the State Security Bureau (still under construction), and a new hotel, called the Global Hotel, which was expected to be Urumqi's finest. In this area the new skyscrapers had all been built during the 1980s, and they looked much more modern—and Western—than the Soviet-style buildings of earlier years and the few remaining pre-1949 structures.

Directly to the east of People's Park was the main business district. It, too, contained numerous high-rise buildings mixed in with older buildings. To the south and east was the old city. Once walled (the wall had been torn down several years previously), this area contained many older buildings, yet even here there were a few high-rise office buildings and apartments. This was the main Uighur area, and in 1988 it still had a distinctly Muslim flavor. Numerous mosques, a few of them large but many quite small, were scattered throughout this entire area. The streets were crowded and lively, especially around the numerous bazaars, which looked much like those one can see throughout Central Asia and the Middle East. A little to the east was the regional Party headquarters. To the south, a highway stretched toward Turfan. A few miles along the route to Turfan, the city had built a large reservoir, and its wide canal (about 15 feet wide) was a major source of the city's water. In all the areas immediately around the core of urban Urumqi, the suburbs looked semiurban, but then the city gradually tapered off into small villages, consisting mostly of one-story mud houses surrounded by farmland.

When I had visited Urumqi in 1948, there was virtually no modern industry of any sort in the city or, for that matter, anywhere in the province. Three factories operated in the city, manufacturing clothing, glass, and animal serum, and there was one factory in Khotan. The Urumqi of 1988 still could not be considered one of the major industrial centers in China, but compared to the pre-Communist period it had developed a significant base of industry. Officials I met in 1988 told me that before 1949 industry had employed only 2,653 people in the city and that the value of its output was very small (Y 4.39 million). By the mid-1980s Urumqi's industry employed 188,000 people, and its gross output value had risen to Y 1.875 billion. The city's farms produced mainly food for local consumption—including about 25,000 tons of grain, more than 3,000 tons of edible vegetable oil, and over 80,000 sheep (which yielded close to 1,500 tons of mutton a year). Much of the municipality's farmland belonged to six state farms established in the 1950s and 1960s, which were inhabited by a population of almost 47,000 people— about a quarter of the entire farming population in the municipality.

In general, I was really amazed by how modern Urumqi appeared in 1988 compared to 1948. All the roads I saw were now paved (there were about 125 miles in the municipality), and many of them were impressive avenues. They carried substantial traffic, including numerous cars, buses, and trucks; only in the older part of the city were there many donkey-drawn, two-wheeled carts of the kind that were standard in 1948. Buildings constructed since my previous visit contained more than 10 times the space of those that existed before 1949, I was told, and about half of the new space consisted of modern "standard departments"—generally several stories high. The high-rise structures built in the 1980s had created an entirely new skyline. People in the streets were well dressed, mostly in Chinese versions of Western clothes of considerable variety and color (women clearly favored red). Only in the few older parts of the city did I see many Uighurs wearing traditional clothes, and even there I saw no Kazakhs dressed as they had been in the old days. Men in uniform (soldiers, People's Armed Police, and Public Security Police) were definitely more numerous and visible in Urumqi than in any other place that I visited in northwest China in 1988 (and I will have more to say about this later); even so, the military presence was much less obvious than it had been in 1948.

*   *   *

The first of my two trips outside of Urumqi was to Nanshan, the "Southern Mountains." Before I arrived in Urumqi, I had informed my host that one of my highest priorities was to revisit a major Kazakh area in some mountain area near to Urumqi; I was determined to do this to see how much the traditional Kazakh tribal way of life had changed since I observed it in 1948 (both at a Kazakh encampment at the foot of Bogda's glacier and at Osman Bator's headquarters in the Tian Shan, south of Qitai). Although it would not be possible to revisit those areas, the trip to Nanshan, I was told, would be a good opportunity to see another Kazakh area.

We left early one morning in a Toyota Land Cruiser, a very sturdy vehicle with multiple gears and a high undercarriage, with room for two to sit in front and three in the back. It was not a very long trip—roughly 47 miles each way. But we stopped several times, so the round-trip took a full day. En route, my Kazakh host talked at length about the organization, activities, and livelihood of the Kazakhs in Xinjiang. Although much of what he told me repeated things that I had learned 40 years earlier, he did bring me up to date and informed me about some things I had not known. The largest groupings of Kazakhs, he said, consisted of three "hordes," called *jüz*. He said that one was called the Da Jüz (the large, or great, horde—sometimes called the east horde); the Zhong Jüz (middle horde—also called north horde); and the Xiao Jüz (the small, or western, horde). (The terminology he used mixed Chinese and Turki words.) In 1948, the Kazakhs I met had not used the word *jüz* in describing various groups to me. I had heard the term used to describe Kirghiz, but this was the first time I had heard it used to describe Kazakhs.

Of these various groups, my host said, the most numerous consisted of the Zhong Jüz. Each *jüz* was divided into several *buluo* (or *bulo*), or tribes, he said. There were six of these under the Zhong Jüz, including the Kirei (Keré), the Naiman, the Auwak (Uwak), the Arghun, the Kongerat (Khongerat), and the Kupjack. Since I was not an expert on Kazakh affairs—or a linguist who knew Turki—I simply tried to translate, phonetically, the terms that he used, as I heard them; an expert might well have written them differently.

Some of the specific tribal names were ones that had been mentioned repeatedly to me in my visit in 1948. At that time, I had heard Osman Bator talk at length about the first three of these groups; he himself belonged to the Kirei, but he had talked at some length about the others. (In 1988, I was more than a little mystified to hear "Arghun" used to label a Kazakh; I had always associated this title with the Mongols.) In any case, one thing I learned in 1948 was confirmed in 1988, namely that the most important Kazakh tribes in Chinese territory had long been—and continued to be—the Naiman and the Kirei. My Kazakh host explained that every tribe was divided into subtribes. For example, the Kirei had 12 subtribes and the Naiman had 9. Below these subtribes, he said, there were at least four lower subdivisions into which groups of yurts were divided, each of which had a designated leader. In the Nanshan area, my host said, there was a mixture of Kirei and Naiman Kazakhs.

According to my host, the largest tribal divisions—especially the *jüz*—continued to be important, but the significance of many of the subdivisions, including the *buluo,* had declined in the post-1949 period. The *awul (aul),* the smallest Kazakh unit (usually with 5 to 10 households, possibly with 15), traditionally had consisted of families from the same *buluo* but this had begun to change even before 1949, and now many of the smallest units were mixtures of Naiman and Kirei. Even when a particular *awul* was not mixed, there could be members of both Naiman and Kirei *awul* grouped together under higher units.

Both my host on the trip to Nanshan and several officials from the Xinjiang Nationalities Commission, whom I later interviewed in their offices, talked to me at some length about continuities and changes in the Kazakh way of life in Xinjiang. I was told that although a few Kazakhs had entered new occupations, including agriculture, the overwhelming majority—probably over 90 percent—still engaged in traditional animal husbandry. But the rhythm of their life had changed—in some cases quite radically, in some cases marginally. Before 1949, only a few Kazakhs had owned permanent houses; most of them moved constantly (an old saying was that they "moved 40 times a year"). But by the 1980s, many of them had built permanent winter residences. Although a large number of them still were nomadic for at least part of the year, an increasing number had started some farming.

Most Kazakhs in Xinjiang were organized into "cooperatives" and then into "communes" when these institutions were established throughout China in the 1950s, but these units were generally based on the old *awul,* I was told, so real change was limited. The authorities did, though, try to assign pasturelands in a definite way to particular groups, and they enforced such limits fairly strictly. However, my informants said, whereas originally the *awul* were organized mainly on the basis of blood ties, the new units were essentially administrative ones, and many of them mixed different tribal and clan groups. Traditionally, the *awul* were generally identified by the name of their leaders, but after 1949 many were given new names. Officially the traditional Kazakh titles for various groups and leaders were abandoned, but informally they were still the names used by most local people. In the 1980s, when decollectivization occurred elsewhere in China, the old Chinese terms—*xiang* (township) and *cun* (village)—replaced the old commune and brigade titles introduced in the late 1950s. The animals owned by communes were divided up, and most were again individually owned. Assigned pasturelands also were readjusted. In practice, however, my hosts said, although pastureland borders now were fairly clear, and were usually observed in the wintertime, most people were tolerant about encroachments on their land by other groups if they were temporary and brief—particularly in the summertime. Some state farms (ranches) in animal husbandry areas continued to exist, but many of these had been broken up during the decollectivization.

*   *   *

I found all of this informative and interesting, but I was eager to see for myself how Kazakh life had changed in a "typical" Kazakh area and to interview people there. So I looked forward with great anticipation as we drove toward Nanshan, thinking that this would be an opportunity to see things myself.

The two-lane paved road to Nanshan took us first across a long, flat plain, where we passed some farming villages that looked very poor (the houses were almost all made of mud brick). We also passed a number of small, domed Muslim tombs, which I was told were centuries old and commemorated very famous Muslim leaders. Then we entered an area that consisted mostly of *huangmo* wasteland, with only very scattered habitations. From the time we left Urumqi, we paralleled the beautiful snow-capped peaks of the Tian Shan, and Bogda Ola was visible much of the way. Toward the end of the trip, we entered foothills and passed occasional clusters of very poor Kazakh houses (some of which were simple log cabins plastered with mud). Yet even in this poor area I saw many TV antennae! Finally, we entered the mountains, climbing to perhaps 5,000 or 6,000 feet. At the end, the road petered out and became gravel; at that point, snow and ice blocked vehicular travel, so we got out and walked the final stretch to our ultimate destination. (By this time in my western travels, I was beginning to think that this was standard—that is, that most roads at some point simply petered out.)

At our final destination, I discovered, there was no Kazakh encampment. I then learned from my host that the main purpose of our trip was really to see a famous waterfall, which had become a major tourist attraction! Near the waterfall were a few Kazakhs setting up a half dozen yurts, and we stopped to visit briefly with them. They were very hospitable. Sitting on rugs, we sipped tea and ate snacks and exchanged pleasantries; inside the yurt, it was snug and warm even though it was quite cold outside. But these Kazakhs, I learned, no longer raised animals: They had become "administrative cadres" responsible for handling tourists. (This area was scheduled to be opened for the annual tourist season in a couple of weeks, but they had been asked to set up some yurts ahead of time because of my visit.) I asked where the nearest real Kazakh encampments were and was told that there were no nomadic groups in the entire local area at that time of year; to reach such groups in a pastureland area now in use one would have to go considerably further, by horseback. Moreover, I was told by the Kazakhs I did meet at Nanshan that in April no nomadic Kazakhs were even near this area; nor would there be any until they moved back from fairly distant mountain pastures at the start of the summer. To say that I was disappointed is putting it mildly. I began to wonder whether my hosts might have been instructed not to take me to a Kazakh tribal area. Rightly or wrongly, I began to feel that I was getting a classic runaround.

From then on, on both our return trip to Urumqi and subsequently on my trip to Turfan, I pressed my hosts repeatedly to take me off the main route so that I could see a typical nomadic Kazakh area. For whatever the reason, I never was able to visit a major encampment on this trip. We did stop, however, at one Kazakh settlement in the foothills near the Nanshan. It was a very poor area. I stopped briefly at a small primary school there, which was in terrible shape, and spoke briefly with the Kazakh teacher and several children. But the teacher got fairly agitated when I took out my camera to take a picture and said that was not allowed. Further along on our return route, we stopped at two places to ask local people where the nearest Kazakh encampments were. In both instances, after prolonged discussion, we learned that there were some within the general area but that they were a substantial distance away; my host said that they were "too far" to visit.

Finally, after visiting Turfan, I was able to make a short visit to one "typical" area inhabited by a few Kazakhs on the outskirts of Urumqi. Turning off the main highway, our Land Cruiser carried us up into the foothills of the Tian Shan, first along a bumpy dirt road and then into a trackless area of grassland. Large numbers of sheep, horses, and camels were grazing on the hillsides, and we passed a few widely scattered Kazakh houses, each consisting of one or two rooms. The people were obviously poor. In the distance I could see a large modern chemical plant far below on the plains, near a large salt lake. The contrast between the camels grazing nearby and that distant plant was startling. We stopped to talk with one Kazakh woman and her three small children; her husband was absent. The setting was bleak. Pastureland in this area was said to be good in summer but poor during most of the rest of the year. Next to the one-room, plastered mud house was a mud-brick barn. The woman said that formerly the family had belonged to a state farm but in the previous year the farm had been broken up. The family owned 170 sheep, one horse, and one milk cow. This was less than they really needed, the woman said, but they nevertheless were considered to be a "middle-level" family. All three of her children attended primary school, but it took them between one and two hours to walk each way every school day. We also stopped at another Kazakh home near the main highway. There a colorful horseman and his daughter were delighted to have their picture taken and then put on a show of equestrian skill for us—without our requesting it. The man told me that he worked for the army, but he did not look like a military man. He wore typical Kazakh clothes, not a uniform. Perhaps he was on leave—or belonged to some kind of militia unit.

These fleeting contacts with Kazakhs fell far short of what I had hoped for, and by the time I left Urumqi, I found it hard to avoid the conclusion that my hosts had, in fact, deliberately avoided taking me to a real working Kazakh encampment. I never could make up my mind why this might have been so. Conceivably, they felt that subjecting a foreigner to the discomfort of cross-country travel was inappropriate for an academic visitor. However, other possible reasons came to mind. The Kazakhs that I did encounter seemed to me to be among the poorest people I saw in Xinjiang. And there might well have been some political reasons as well: Later in the year, I read Chinese press reports indicating that in the late summer of 1988 Chinese police had arrested a sizable number of Kazakhs in the Ili region, accusing them of having organized secret bodies, operating on both sides of the Sino-Soviet border, to agitate for Xinjiang's independence. I wondered whether the legacy of Osman Bator's armed resistance against the Communists after 1949 had left any significant legacy or residue of resentment among the Kazakhs in the region. I also speculated about whether there had been deliberate Han political discrimination against the Kazakhs because of their early resistance against the Communist takeover. I never came to any definite conclusion about such questions.

When I examined the data I gathered in Xinjiang on local leadership, I learned that of the region's top nine Party leaders and eight leading government officials (groups that I will discuss later), two were Kazakhs. One was a deputy Party secretary, and one was a deputy chairman of the regional government. This representation was not remarkable, yet in light of the Kazakh share of the regional population, it was not out of line. I never was able to obtain a detailed ethnic breakdown of the leadership at lower levels. Nevertheless, I left the region with a suspicion that some of the Kazakhs in Xinjiang might be getting a raw deal—perhaps in part because of Chinese memories of the resistance of Ili rebels in the 1940s and of Osman Bator and his supporters in the 1950s. I did not get the impression that Urumqi and the area around it was in any sense a powder keg of potential resistance against the Han Chinese. From everything I learned, I concluded that, to the extent there was active political opposition to Han rule among the Kazakhs and Uighurs in Xinjiang, it was centered mainly in the southwestern part of the province, near the Soviet border and in the Ili region, not in the Urumqi area. Reportedly, however, there were some dissident intellectuals in Urumqi.

*   *   *

My second trip in 1988 outside of Urumqi was to Turfan. This oasis city developed many centuries ago as an important stopping point on the ancient Silk Road, and it was a key strategic point, located in southern Xinjiang on the northern edge of the huge Tarim Basin. Two of the principal branches of the Silk Road went through this general area. The main stopping points on the northern route were Hami, Turfan, Karashahr, Kucha (Kuqa), Aksu, Tumshuk, and finally Kashgar (Kashi). The main southern route went through Miran, Cherchen, Khotan, and Yarkand before finally reaching Kashgar. Kashgar was the largest and most important oasis city in the west. From it (as well as from the cities of Yarkand and Khotan), several routes led to what are now India, Pakistan, Afghanistan, and Central Asia, and from there the Silk Road went on to Tashkent, Samarkand, Bokhara (the first two of which I had visited on earlier travels) and then to the Middle East and to the West.

The history of Turfan has been extremely complex, mirroring the turbulence of two millennia of constant migrations and conflicts in that part of the world. Several ancient kingdoms had been established at different times in its area, and periodically, from the first century B.C. on, when the military forces of the Han dynasty first conquered the area, Chinese garrison forces had been stationed there. Several times, Turfan was destroyed and then rebuilt.

Buddhism, imported along the Silk Road from India, had a very significant impact on Turfan. Later, the influences of many other religions were also extremely important. Eventually, most of the population was converted to Islam, but Manichean believers and Nestorian Christians continued to be fairly numerous in the area for many years. About the time that the Tang rulers were ascendant in China, the Uighurs established a kingdom centered in Turfan, but its power peaked during the eighth century, and it was destroyed by the Kirghiz in the ninth century. The Uighurs continued to occupy many influential positions in the area, though, and when Genghis Khan conquered the region, he borrowed the Uighur alphabet and employed many Uighurs in his civil administration. Later, during the Ming and Qing periods, the Chinese regarded Turfan as one of the most important strategic oases in the entire region. Partly because of this history, Turfan has continued into the modern period to be regarded as one of Xinjiang's most important oasis cities. Together with Kashgar and other major southern oases, it continues to be viewed by many people as representative of the essence of Uighur Muslim life and culture in Xinjiang.

The old camel caravans are now long gone, and when I made my trip to Turfan I traveled on an excellent two-lane paved highway. Most of the road was quite smooth, but we did encounter several bumpy stretches, and in desert areas—through which we traveled most of the way—it was very dusty and windblown. The distance from Urumqi, according to our driver, was about 112 miles, although on a map that I obtained in Urumqi, an arrow pointing toward Turfan noted that it was about 75 miles. I never was able to clarify which was right, but I guessed that one of them may have been measured as the crow flies. After leaving Urumqi, we first drove through rolling, brown hills where we passed a number of scattered villages and some farmland. All along this part of the route, Bogda rose out of the lowlands on our left and was a magnificent sight. Then the road entered a wide valley; here there were quite high snow-capped peaks on one side and low, barren mountains on the other. For a short way, we paralleled the main Urumqi-Lanzhou railway. We also passed three large salt lakes—the color of which was a striking milky green. Near two of the lakes were urban settlements and a few isolated farms, and next to one of them was a chemical factory and a small town, with workers' housing. Most of the territory we went through, though, was extremely sparsely populated and desertlike—a mixture of rocky *gebi* and *huangmo,* with small clumps of grass, widely separated.

About halfway along our trip, we stopped at Daban, a sizable village or town inhabited mainly by Hui Muslims but with a mixture of other groups including Han Chinese, Uighurs, and Kazakhs. It was dominated by a large bazaar—enclosed and with a high ceiling—within which were many small shops, stalls, and little restaurants, most of them operated by Hui entrepreneurs. We stopped and had a very pleasant lunch, dominated—as most Hui meals are—by various mutton dishes.

After Daban, we entered a grassland area, where there were large numbers of sheep but very few villages. Before long, our road divided, with one branch going to the heart of southern Xinjiang and the other to Turfan. On the Turfan road, we immediately entered a gorge that cut through barren mountains, following a stream with small trees on its banks. When we emerged from the gorge, we entered a very wide valley, with low hills on our right and fairly high snow-covered mountains in the far distance on the left. This valley was one of the most forbidding areas of *gebi* that I had ever encountered. For as far as the eye could see ahead, there was nothing but gray rocks, most of them about the size of large pieces of gravel. Not a single living thing could be seen, not even a bush or a blade of grass. The area looked as if a cosmic dump truck had deposited endless miles of rock on the area. In the far distance, at the edge of the mountains, we could see huge rock slides—which I presumed had been the source of the gravel that had covered this entire valley. Ahead, all we could see, as far as the horizon, was the thin ribbon of our road, stretching mile after mile, gradually narrowing in the distance into a fine line stretching toward infinity. The sun beat down fiercely and was so debilitating that at one point our dyspeptic Uighur driver simply announced that he was tired and was going to take a nap: He stopped the car, stretched out in the front seat, and was oblivious to the world for 15 minutes—and then silently resumed his driving.

This awesome rock desert continued for the rest of the way to the Turfan oasis. The only signs of civilization anywhere along the road itself were telephone lines and, at one point, a branch rail line that connected with the main route going south toward the Tarim Basin. Finally, we saw in the far distance some trees, at the foot of the mountains to our right. This was the start of the

Turfan oasis, which thereafter continued for many miles. Eventually, we entered the center of the oasis and stopped at a small village. It was typical of the rural areas around Turfan. The atmosphere was totally Middle Eastern. Except for a single new, hard-brick, two-story house, all of the homes were very traditional, one-story mud structures. They were separated by narrow tree-lined lanes that wound throughout the village. Two-wheel donkey carts plodded along the dirt paths. At one point, a group of bearded elders came down a lane; they were returning home after a meeting at one of the local mosques. Following the men were a number of women and young girls, all wearing multicolored scarfs on their heads. On the outskirts of the main part of the village, there were many irrigated vineyards and melon fields, but beyond them the land was saline and uncultivable. We saw evidence of underground canals—typical of much of the Middle East—which were punctuated periodically by open wells; they provided the village's lifeblood, water. At several vineyards, there were structures built of lattice brickwork, through which breezes could blow; they were for drying grapes to make raisins. Some of the melon fields were covered with plastic sheeting, a relatively recent innovation.

Before entering the center of the city of Turfan, we made a detour to stop at Jiaohe Gucheng, the remains of a very ancient Chinese city. Built originally in the first century B.C. as a garrison city for Chinese troops, it was five kilometers (a little more than three miles) in circumference and was constructed on the pattern of a miniature imperial city, with an outer wall, a second wall within it, and still a third one further in—all encircling the city center. During the Tang dynasty, the city had been an extremely important center, and at one point, I was told, the Uighurs used it as their capital. It was abandoned in the fourteenth century, according to local people. I found the place to be a fascinating, ghostly relic of ancient times; its high mud wall and scattered buildings had been eroded over the centuries into very strange shapes.

The only other historic site that I had time to visit in Turfan was the Imin Minaret, a very impressive brick tower more than 120 feet tall with intricate brick designs on its surface. Built in 1777, during the Qian Long era of the Qing dynasty, it was named after a local Turfan leader who had helped the Chinese suppress a rebellion in the area but who also had strongly defended Islam. Reputedly, it was the tallest minaret in Xinjiang. (Unfortunately, I had no time during my brief period in Turfan to visit any of the numerous Buddhist sites located near the city, many of which are justly famous.)

*   *   *

When we finally arrived in the center of Turfan, I discovered that, like many cities throughout west China, it consisted of two distinct urban areas. In Turfan's case, the "old city" was immediately adjacent to the "new city."

We entered the old city first. It strongly resembled traditional Muslim towns throughout Central Asia. Its ancient city wall had disappeared but the streets in this part of the city were narrow and lined with tall, stately poplars. The buildings were almost all low, one-story structures. Modern transportation had only recently invaded the scene in this area, and motor vehicles passed donkey carts on the narrow streets; the result was an intriguing mixture of old and new. However, most people dressed in very traditional clothes, which gave the entire area a very Muslim atmosphere.

This old city merged quickly into the modern part of Turfan. Actually, I was told, although it was called "new city," this area had begun to develop many years previously ("perhaps a hundred years ago") on the edge of the old city, but it had been totally rebuilt during the previous years—mainly in the 1980s. According to the senior local Muslim leader who briefed me at considerable length about the city, in the early 1980s some of the local authorities began to construct buildings that were modern but were adorned with many features of traditional Islamic architecture—features such as arches, domes, and minaretlike towers. The earliest building constructed in this new modern Islamic style was the first modern hotel in the city. Started in 1983, the Turfan Hotel was a fairly gaudy but nevertheless quite attractive example of Islamic architecture. It was no longer considered to be the best place to stay in the city, but it was still the object of considerable local pride. However, as more buildings of this kind were built, some local Han Chinese officials began to criticize this hybrid architecture and, according to my informants, considerable controversy followed. But when Zhao Ziyang visited Turfan (in 1985, I was told), he strongly and publicly endorsed the architectural mixture of modern and traditional Islamic styles, stating that it effectively symbolized the merging of minority culture and modernization in a Chinese environment. Subsequently, there was a burst of new construction of many large buildings in this distinctive style. To beautify the center of the city, a large grape arbor was built over one of the main avenues, and local officials began to call Turfan the "grape city." It was a touch of PR sloganeering that reminded me of Alashan's designation of Bayanhaote as "camel city."

The core of the new part of Turfan City, where most of the modern Islamic architecture was located, consisted of only a few square blocks, but in it were many important buildings, including a new People's Congress building, the government headquarters, a local TV station, a huge and extremely colorful bazaar (the front of which looked very much like that of an elegant mosque), and many other quite attractive modern/Islamic public buildings. Also in this area was the city's newest hotel (opened in 1986), called the "Oasis" (Lüzhou)—but also referred to by many as the "New Guest House" (*xin binguan*). This hotel, where I stayed, effectively captured, I thought, the varying flavors of Islam, Han China, and the modern West. Designed mainly for Western tourists, it was surprisingly modern and comfortable; in fact, it came close to meeting the standards of the best Western-style hotels in east China. Its external architecture was distinctively Islamic, as was the interior decor. But it contained all the appurtenances of a very modern hotel. The food was excellent, and it mixed Chinese and Muslim dishes (kebab, mutton, pilaf, and so on) together with typical Chinese dishes. The waitresses—half of them Uighur and half of them Han Chinese—were extremely attractive young ladies, sporting permanent waves, calf-length skirts (red or black), white blouses, and high-heeled shoes (red, black, or white). One of them, whose hair was tied in a ponytail, wore jeans, a T-shirt, and a very "mod" jacket, together with red high-heeled shoes. During my brief stay there, I encountered several other foreign tourists, including four Japanese and two young Americans. The guests in the hotel also included a half dozen Uighur cadres.

Even though my visit was in the spring, the weather in Turfan was very hot. The temperature rose to the high eighties (Fahrenheit), and it was sticky. There was good reason for the heat: Turfan lies in a deep basin, about 200 feet below sea level. In summer the temperature rises very much higher—reportedly it is considered almost intolerable by most foreigners. However, the rooms in the new hotel were all effectively air-conditioned! In any case, I did not mind the heat. In fact, I am a genuine fan of dry, desert climate. Despite the heat, therefore, I thoroughly enjoyed wandering throughout the entire city and poking about in bazaars—and I learned a good deal about the existing situation from ordinary people as well as local officials.

Turfan, I learned, was a *diqu,* or prefecture, 1 of 16 prefecture-level units in Xinjiang. (In 1988, 11 of the 16 were regular prefectures, and 5 were autonomous prefectures *zizhi zhou.*) As I mentioned in an earlier chapter, in much of east China, prefectures have been gradually disappearing—replaced by enlarged municipalities that have incorporated numerous adjacent counties. This did not seem likely to happen in Xinjiang, though, in part because the counties and urban settlements are too widely scattered to fit logically into economic areas centered on a few large cities.

All five of Xinjiang's autonomous prefectures were in areas where minority groups other than Uighurs predominated. The comparable units, at the same level, where Uighurs were the majority, remained as regular prefectures. No *zizhi zhou* were established in Uighur areas because the Uighurs were the majority group in the entire region. Local officials in Turfan carefully explained to me the differences between regular prefectures and the *zizhi zhou.* Regular prefectures, they pointed out, were simply "administrative" (*xingshu*) units that were "dispatched organs" (*paichu jigou*) of the regional government—that is, they functioned, in effect, simply as branches of the government in Urumqi, and their leaders were appointed by the region and operated on the basis of direct instructions from above. In theory, at least, the *zizhi zhou* had more autonomy in making local decisions: They elected their own leaders and could decide on some issues themselves. In reality, however, differences were less than they appeared on the surface. The regional government in Urumqi still had a very large say in determining the leadership and in managing all affairs in the *zizhi zhou* as well as in the regular prefectures—even though Turfan officials went out of their way to emphasize that they did have some leeway in making decisions on local issues that most regular prefectures did not have.

The inhabitants of Turfan whom I interviewed showed obvious pride in the historic strategic position of their city and the fact that, because of its key location southeast of Urumqi, it had always been an extremely important stopping place on the old Silk Road. They also maintained that it continued to be a city of special strategic importance: They asserted that everyone recognized that it was the most important city in the entire area between Urumqi and Hami—and was located extremely near the main rail route. Local people made a distinction that I had not heard earlier. They said that whereas most of Xinjiang could be classified as either part of North Xinjiang (Bei Jiang—the heart of which is Dzungaria) or part of South Xinjiang (Nan Jiang—with the Tarim Basin as its center), Turfan was unique in that it belonged to neither of those two major areas but instead was the principal city of what they called East Xinjiang (Dong Jiang).

Originally, the area of Turfan consisted of three counties, I was told. But then one of the counties—the one containing the main urban center of the oasis—was granted the status of a county-level city, and the other two units remained as counties—Shanshan in the east and Toksin in the west. Under them were 17 townships (*xiang*) and 8 towns (*zhen*). The counties encompassed not only the fertile oasis land at the foot of the mountains but also a considerable area of *gebi* desert. Turfan Prefecture was one of the "smallest major administrative units" in Xinjiang, local officials said, but by the standards of other parts of China it was not small. The total territory of the prefecture, I was told, was a little more than 27,000 square miles—an area about the size of West Virginia. (Nothing in Xinjiang is really small!)

The population of the entire prefecture, according to the latest figures that local officials could give to me, was roughly 450,000. About 310,000 (or more than two-thirds of the total) were Uighurs. In addition, the inhabitants included roughly 90,000 Han Chinese, more than 40,000 Hui Muslims, and perhaps 10,000 or so Kazakhs (most of whom lived in nearby mountain areas). The majority of the Han residents of the prefecture, and a great many of the Hui, were relative newcomers. Before 1949, I was told, there were only "a few" Han Chinese in Turfan. But after 1949 they moved to the area in several different waves. One group came at the time of the Communist takeover; later waves included the young people assigned to help Xinjiang's "construction" from the 1950s on, demobilized army men, and cadres sent from the "interior" (*neidi*) at various periods. I was struck, incidently, by the fact that when people in Turfan—and, in fact, in the rest of Xinjiang—talked about provinces further east, although at times they referred to them as "coastal provinces," most frequently they categorized them as being in the "interior." This practice was the exact reverse of the use of the term "interior" by Chinese in eastern areas, who invariably used it to refer to places far from the coast, those in the west.

I was told that there had been relatively little intermarriage between Han Chinese and Uighurs. "It occurs sometimes, but we do not encourage it," one person said, adding that "when there are mixed marriages, it is important to have very clear arrangements or understanding, because customs are so different." Whether male or female, Han Chinese were expected to convert to Islam when marrying Muslims in this area.

However, almost everyone I met emphasized that the local policy in selecting leaders—not only political leaders but also leaders in economic units—was to try to mix different ethnic groups; in appointing cadres, the aim was to see that the numbers were roughly proportionate to the different groups' shares in the population. The Party secretary of the prefecture was a Han Chinese, but the Standing Committee had both Han and Uighur members. The head of the Turfan Prefectural Government was a Uighur. (The previous prefectural head, I was told, had subsequently become the major of Urumqi.) All of the county magistrates were Uighurs, my informant said; however, under them the cadres in subordinate jobs were ethnically diverse. I was given a number of examples of how the leadership in a variety of organizations was mixed in numbers roughly proportionate to ethnic representation in the population. The examples included government bureaus such as the Municipal Foreign Affairs Office, enterprises such as a local chemical factory, the Oasis Hotel where I was staying, and various others. On the surface, I saw no obvious signs of Han-Uighur tensions (but in Turfan, as elsewhere, I assumed that there must be some potential tensions existing under the surface because of past conflicts as well as recent demographic trends).

In Turfan, as in all of China, religion had come under severe attack in earlier years, especially during the Cultural Revolution. But local people asserted—convincingly, I thought—that in the 1980s, since the adoption of a relatively conciliatory policy toward religion, there had been a genuine religious revival. During the Cultural Revolution, I was told, "many" mosques were destroyed and almost all of the rest were taken over for use as factories, warehouses, and organizational headquarters. However, in the 1980s, not only were the mosques that had been destroyed or damaged rebuilt, but many entirely new ones were constructed. Some of these new mosques were "better" than the old ones, according to my informants, and "most had been built with local contributions, not government support." By 1988, there were "several hundred" operating mosques scattered throughout the prefecture—"more than before the Cultural Revolution."

*   *   *

At the time of my visit in 1988, I could see that the economy of Turfan was still basically agricultural, and in many respects traditional, but I saw many signs that "modernization" had begun to transform it. The city had recently established numerous links with the outside world—connections of a kind that would have been almost inconceivable in the years before 1949. Most of these links had developed very recently, since 1978. Moreover, the character of Turfan had obviously begun to be changed in very important ways by the prevalence of paved roads and TV and other modern communications as well as by the recently built modern buildings, obvious improvements in agricultural methods, the introduction of some modern factories, growing contacts with at least a few foreign businesses, and the burgeoning tourist industry.

The population of the prefecture remained mainly rural, however. Only 70,000 to 80,000 people (about a sixth of the total population)—workers, cadres, merchants, and so on—were classified as urban. These people were concentrated in the new part of Turfan City (which contained perhaps 40,000 people) and in the county seats and the eight towns (*zhen*) under the prefecture. Roughly five-sixths of the total population were still engaged in agriculture, raising grains such as wheat and sorghum, fruits such as grapes and "Hami" melon, cotton, and vegetables. Local officials asserted that agriculture had made notable progress and that the prefecture was now self-sufficient in grain, even though, since decollectivization, there had been a major shift from grain to cash crops. Except for people working in two state farms (which concentrated on growing fruit), all farmers—I was told—now operated under the household contract responsibility system. Some improved seeds, many new methods, and modern technology of various kinds had been introduced into agriculture. (Plastic sheets to cover fields were one very visible example.)

As a result of recent economic trends, there had been a significant increase in the per capita income of rural families; I was told that the average had been under Y 300 before 1978 and had risen to roughly Y 500 in 1987. The target for the rural population of the prefecture for the near future was Y 800. There were still some "quite poor" rural families, local officials told me, but there was also a growing number of quite affluent ones (including quite a few who earned more than Y 10,000 a year). The general level, in any case, had clearly risen significantly.

Irrigation remained the most crucial underpinning of agriculture—as always is true in desert areas. In the entire prefecture, I was told, there were more than 1,860 miles of waterways in numerous underground canals (of varying lengths). I had first seen this type of underground canal many years previously—both in Xinjiang and in Iran and other areas in the Middle East. They are impressive feats of simple engineering. Designed to convey glacial and stream water for long distances underground, with minimal evaporation, they are testimony to the skill of local engineers dating to very ancient times. In addition to these underground canals, Turfan had six aboveground canals—which brought substantial amounts of water from the Tian Shan—as well as more than 1,000 deep wells.

Animal husbandry ranked well below agriculture in its importance to the local economy, but local officials told me that there were about a half million sheep that grazed in the nearby mountains (tended mainly by Kazakhs) and almost an equal number of sheep owned by agricultural households. The prefecture's output of mutton and lamb now made it "almost self-sufficient" in the production of these meats, but Turfan still had to import a significant amount of pork (for non-Muslims) from other areas.

Modern industry was still limited in Turfan, but I was impressed that it at least had made a start. The largest local factory was a chemical plant, which used raw materials transported from Lake Aydingkol (Aiding), a salt lake not very far to the south that also provided raw materials for several smaller chemical plants and a salt processing plant. "Several dozen" small coal mines provided fuel for the prefecture's thermal power plant as well as for other local uses, and two main hydropower stations in the mountains—plus several smaller ones elsewhere—also provided some local power. In addition, there were many wineries in the area. Growing wine had been a centuries-old occupation, but it had been expanded and somewhat modernized recently. (I asked whether the Xinjiang Production and Construction Corps ran any farms or enterprises in the Turfan area, and local officials said: "No, most of their activity is in the north." But I was not sure that this was absolutely correct; I had been told elsewhere that the Corps did operate in some eastern and southern areas.)

I was given figures by local officials for the gross value of the entire economic output of the prefecture in 1987. The total, they said, was roughly Y 300 million. However, this was a figure that they cited from memory, and I did not have time to get them to check it and give me a precise figure. When I asked them about their budget, again they gave me a very general and rather vague answer. Local tax revenue, they said, was not sufficient to cover their expenditures, so they relied fairly heavily on subsidies from the regional government. They did not give me any specific figures.

Even though modernization in Turfan was obviously in a very early stage, it impressed me because it contrasted so much with my memories of Xinjiang in the 1940s. And I was genuinely surprised to hear about the degree to which new links had been forged with the outside world. "Foreign trade," I was told, was growing steadily and now "accounted for about 10 percent of Turfan's gross value of output" (although no one made clear to me exactly what this meant or even whether the term "foreign trade" meant only trade with foreign countries or included trade with coastal Chinese provinces). The leaders of Turfan clearly hoped to attract foreign business cooperation and investment. So far, two wineries had obtained some foreign capital and had purchased some foreign machinery—from Japan, the United States, and Switzerland. Refrigeration equipment had been imported from the United States, and some packaging technology had been purchased from Switzerland.

The most important new industry in Turfan that created significant links with other parts of China as well as with foreign countries was clearly tourism. Whereas in 1980—according to the head of the local Foreign Affairs Office—less than 1,000 foreign tourists had visited Turfan, in 1987 about 18,000 had come. The number of Chinese tourists had grown even more rapidly. By 1987 the total number of all tourists, including both Chinese and foreign, had risen to more than 100,000. To serve these tourists, especially the foreigners, Turfan had constructed three modern hotels, with about 500 beds, and it had acquired 30 imported vehicles (mainly Japanese cars, vans, and buses) with approximately 400 seats to take tourists on trips to nearby historic sites. The impact of tourism went far beyond the foreign exchange earned. Even more important, in my opinion, it greatly expanded contacts between the local population and people of all kinds from other areas, including foreigners. Moreover, the attempt to develop local services that could meet the standards expected by foreign tourists had compelled them to learn much more about the outside world than they had previously known. This inevitably had had a significant impact on the ideas, and even the values, of local people. I had no way to measure this impact, but my impression was that it was very significant. Geographically, Turfan was still a very remote place, but its sense of isolation was gradually being destroyed.

What I was able to see in Nanshan and Turfan—as well as in Urumqi—provided valuable insights into recent local history, the current situation, and, above all, the way in which modernization was steadily transforming Xinjiang. But I was acutely aware that what I was able to see was only one very small area in the north-central part of the region. I did not have an opportunity to visit Kashgar or any of the other major oasis cities in southern Xinjiang—nor did I see the vast Taklimakan Desert in the Tarim Basin in the south, Lop Nor in the east (where China's main nuclear weapons testing sites are located), the fertile valleys and rich grasslands of the Ili area in the northwest, the Gurbantünggüt Desert in the Dzungarian Depression in the north, or the Karamai oil fields on the edge of that area. Xinjiang is a region of almost continental or imperial size, and I could not hope to see more than a tiny part of it. To obtain an overview of the region as a whole, I was compelled to rely heavily on a variety of intense interviews that I had had with officials and scholars in Urumqi. When I began these interviews, I did have a fairly solid starting point, namely, what I had learned and written about in 1948. But I learned a great deal that not only brought me up to date but substantially expanded my understanding of the region.

*   *   *

As I have mentioned earlier in this volume, when I last visited Xinjiang in 1948, the province was embroiled in several serious internal and external conflicts. The internal conflicts were very complex, but in essence many of them were based on deep-rooted ethnic tensions, especially between the politically dominant Han Chinese and the majority ethnic groups in the area, especially the Uighurs and the Kazakhs. Yet it was not really that simple: More than just ethnic or other internal conflicts were involved. The Ili revolt was a good example of the complexities. Starting in 1944 with Soviet backing, the revolt detached the three northern districts of the province. The leaders, who had established what they called the East Turkestan Republic, were predominantly Uighurs, but they also recruited numerous Kazakhs. However, the Chinese, who still controlled almost all of the rest of Xinjiang, had been able to co-opt many minority leaders—both Uighurs and Kazakhs— and had appointed some of them to significant positions in the provincial government. Although Kazakhs had played a key role in the Ili military forces at the start, later many—including the forces led by Osman Bator— had shifted allegiance and in 1948 were on the Chinese side. Even the revolt's Uighur supporters were concentrated mainly in the northwest. Briefly, in 1947, the revolt had spread to Turfan and two other southern Uighur oases, but it had been rapidly suppressed in those areas. At the time of my visit in 1948, prominent minority leaders were on both sides of the struggle, and the situation was deadlocked.

The Academy scholars whom I met in 1988 gave me their account of that period in Xinjiang's history, which added some interesting details to what I had learned four decades earlier. I was particularly interested to hear their views on the ultimate merging of the Ili rebellion and the Communist revolution, which was reaching its climax in China when I had previously been in Xinjiang. At the start of the rebellion, they said, the leaders in Ili had no significant contacts with the Chinese Communist Party (CCP). Their roots were fundamentally local, but eventually they relied heavily on the support that they received from the Soviet Union. Their first important link with the CCP was forged in 1948, they told me. In that year, the Chinese Nationalists convened their first National Assembly, in Nanjing, and they induced one Uighur leader from the Ili region—a man named Abdul Karim Abasov—to attend the meeting. It so happened that he had a Han Chinese wife. In Nanjing, he and his wife made contact with Chinese Communist representatives, and when they returned to Xinjiang, a Communist contact man returned with them in the guise of being his wife's brother. There this agent established a radio station to obtain news reports from Yan'an, some of which he distributed in a Communist-oriented local publication.*

The Soviets initially supported the Ili rebellion, according to my informants, mainly because after Sheng Shicai had broken with Moscow the Soviets were very uneasy about what policies the Chinese Nationalists might pursue. Support of the Ili rebels gave Moscow leverage in dealing with the Nationalists. Over time, in the opinion of the Academy scholars in Urumqi, Moscow became increasingly suspicious of U.S. objectives and activities in the area, especially during 1947–1948, fearing that the United States was "intriguing to subvert the area in cooperation with Mohammed Imin, who was provincial Commissioner of Reconstruction." The Ili rebels then received less attention from Moscow, and the Soviets hoped that the CCP would be able to seize Xinjiang and put an end to U.S. activities in the area. Consequently, the Academy scholars said, Liu Shaoqi (the CCP's second-ranking leader) visited Moscow, in 1948, and Stalin reportedly urged the Chinese Communists to liberate Xinjiang sooner rather than later—hopefully in 1949 rather than 1950. Liu is said to have reported Stalin's opinion back to the rest of the Chinese Communist leadership when he returned, and the Party apparently concurred.†

In 1949, the Ili movement formed a new organization, I was told, called the League for Peace and Democracy in Xinjiang, and "really for the first time the Ili leaders acknowledged that their area was a part of China." The Chinese Communist Party sent Deng Liqun to Xinjiang. (Deng at that time was not yet a senior leader but subsequently he became one of the Party's major ideologists.) He invited top Ili leaders to attend a forthcoming important meeting that the Party planned to hold in Beiping (subsequently Beijing)—the People's Political Consultative Conference, at which the Communists intended to establish formally their new national government.

---

*This was not, by any means, the first Chinese Communist involvement in Xinjiang, of course. In the 1930s, one of Mao Zedong's principal rivals, Zhang Guotao, had urged that a Chinese Communist base be established there, but the Party decided against it. However, later in the 1930s, Xinjiang's warlord, Sheng Shicai, aligned with the Soviet Union and tolerated a Chinese Communist presence in the province—and, in fact, at times he welcomed Chinese Communist representatives. The Party opened an office of the Eighth Route Army in Urumqi, headed by fairly high-ranking leaders; Mao's brother, Mao Zemin, spent some time there. Ultimately, however, Sheng turned on the Communists and executed many of the Party members in the province, including Mao Zemin.

†Although this is what I was told, I had no knowledge of any trip to Moscow by Liu in 1948, and I found no reference to it when I subsequently checked several standard biographical sources. Either my informants were mistaken or they revealed new information that historians should investigate.

Deng Liqun then went secretly to Urumqi, where he reportedly stayed with Burhan and also contacted some leading Chinese Nationalist officials, including the Xinjiang garrison commander, Tao Zhiyue. (Tao, whom I met in 1948, had replaced Song Xilian as garrison commander; he impressed me as being an extremely able military man—far above the average Nationalist leader in that region.) Burhan, who had recently become governor, was a Tatar. He was playing an extremely complex balancing game throughout 1948. (When I met him in the summer of 1948, when he was still deputy governor, he said to me: "Xinjiang is like a guitar. All of the strings must be in tune for it to play.") The Nationalists had made him governor in December 1948. Burhan had been trying for some time to lay a basis for a peaceful turnover, and General Tao was sympathetic with the idea. Deng Liqun worked actively to bring this about, mainly with Burhan—but presumably also with Tao. However, several powerful Guomindang generals were strongly opposed to giving in to the Communists. They resisted at first. Then, when the civil war was reaching its climax elsewhere in China, these generals finally decided to flee from Xinjiang; some of them went to India and others to Taiwan. After they left, Governor Burhan and General Tao publicly announced, on September 25, a peaceful turnover. The First Army Group, commanded by Wang Zhen, reached Urumqi in late October. Some Ili troops also then came to Urumqi. In late December, Tao's forces were redesignated the Twenty-Second Army Corps, with Tao still nominally in command but with Wang Zhen, who was appointed its political commissar, really in charge. Ili troops were then incorporated into the Communists' forces.

After describing the military takeover, my Academy informants also gave me their account of the period immediately after the takeover; I found it, too, extremely interesting. Formally, they said, Peng Dehuai, who was headquartered in Xi'an, commanded all forces in the northwestern region (he was commander and political commissar of the Xinjiang Military District, which was established in December 1949), but, in fact, Wang Zhen, who was Peng's local deputy, exercised real power in Xinjiang, according to the Academy scholars, and eventually he was formally designated commander and political commissar in the area. Although Deng Liqun had played a very significant role in establishing the local Communist Party organization, Wang became the top Party leader in the province and became secretary of the Xinjiang Sub-Bureau of the Party Central Committee, which was the leading Party body there until a provincial-level Party Committee replaced it. (Wang Zhen continued as Party chief until he was succeeded by Wang Enmao in 1952.)

The Chinese Communists tried in Xinjiang, as elsewhere, to co-opt into the new ruling structure as many local non-Han leaders as they could, including both those who had achieved prominence in Urumqi and those who had led the Ili revolt. Initially Burhan continued as governor, and the Ili re-

gime's leaders rapidly accommodated to the new Chinese Communist regime. The Communist Party finally recognized and formally acknowledged
that the Ili regime was a "revolutionary" one and that it had been a "part of
the Chinese New Democratic Revolution," and it accepted most of the Ili regime's leaders into the Chinese Communist Party. (Some of them had earlier
joined the Soviet Communist Party.) These leaders were exempted from the
probationary period that was usually required. Many were almost immediately assigned significant roles in the new Xinjiang elite, in the Party, government, and military establishments.

Then, in the fall of 1949, a disaster wiped out a large part of the top eche-
lon of the Ili leadership. A group of the key leaders of that regime, headed by
a man named Akhmedjan Kasimov, started out for Beijing to attend the
scheduled September meeting of the People's Political Consultative Conference. En route, they went via Alma Ata, capital of Kazakhstan in the USSR;
then, when flying from there to China, their airplane crashed, and they were
all killed. The Chinese Communists attempted at first to suppress the news
of this disaster, I was told, but when the Soviets leaked a report of it, the Chinese felt compelled to make a public announcement about it. There was speculation at the time that the Chinese Communists might have wished to eliminate these Ili leaders, but there was no supporting evidence of this then (it
always seemed very unlikely to me), and my informants in Urumqi said that
it was absolutely untrue. In any case, according to my Academy briefers, "after consultation with the Soviet Consulate in Urumqi," the Chinese recognized Saifudin (Saif-al-din Azia) as the top Ili leader, and he and the other
surviving top Ili leaders assumed important roles in the provincial regime.
Later, in 1955, Saifudin succeeded Burhan as top leader of the government,
and at the time that Xinjiang was converted from a province into the
Xinjiang Uighur Autonomous Region he became chairman.

For a period of time, according to my Academy briefers, there was some
significant resistance to the Communist takeover in Xinjiang. The forces
that resisted most fiercely were the Kazakhs led by Osman Bator, who fought
hard for more than a year. After failing to persuade him to surrender, the
Communists labeled him a "bandit" and pursued him from Xinjiang into
Gansu and then into Qinghai. They finally captured him in Qinghai in February 1951, and, according to what I was told in Urumqi (which was somewhat different from what I had learned in Qinghai), took him back to
Xinjiang, where he was tried and executed in Urumqi in April 1951. (I was
inclined to accept the version I heard in Urumqi as more authoritative than
what I heard in Qinghai.)

*   *   *

As the Communists did when they took over everywhere in China, they
rapidly established, militarily and politically, a more effective basis for con-

trol over Xinjiang than the Nationalists ever had done. However, despite their co-optation of many minority leaders, and even though they proclaimed a variety of new policies designed to respond to minority groups' needs, Han Chinese continued—and even increased—their domination of the area, both politically and militarily. Moreover, serious ethnic tensions persisted, simmering under the surface; occasionally these tensions led to overt political eruptions. The most serious incidents involved Kazakhs, at least in the earlier years, but some of them also involved Uighurs and other smaller minority groups such as the Kirghiz and Tatars. That certain ethnic groups overlapped the China-USSR border also created a variety of problems, which occasionally were serious and gave both sides opportunities to try to manipulate the situation. Even in the 1950s, when Sino-Soviet relations were at their best, perhaps 10,000 or more people from Xinjiang who held Soviet passports and citizenship—including some very prominent figures—left Xinjiang for the Soviet Union, according to my informants. Most of them were Kazakhs, but some Uighurs also left. In contrast to later out-migrations, this one was "legal," the Academy scholars pointed out, and it therefore caused no major crisis. But it did seriously irritate the Chinese.

Then, in the early 1960s, at the height of the Sino-Soviet conflict, both China and the Soviet Union actively encouraged subversive activities across the border—the Soviets with greater success—and there was a major crisis. The Soviet consulates in Ining (Kulja) and Urumqi issued passports to thousands of people in Xinjiang—mainly Kazakhs—and in 1962 around 60,000 of them moved across the border, with Soviet assistance, into the USSR. There also were periodic disturbances, some of them fairly serious, in certain of the major Uighur oasis cities in southern Xinjiang. Many of these clashes were probably based mainly on cultural and economic frictions between Han Chinese and Uighurs, but some clearly involved political friction.

The officials I interviewed in 1988 made a great point of stressing that the present leadership in the region was strongly committed to implement policy designed to treat minorities with real equality and, in fact, to give them special preferential treatment in many respects. (I will discuss later some of Xinjiang's "affirmative action" policies.) But in some nonofficial conversations that I had, I received a strong impression that although the state of Han-minority relations in most of the region was not critical (in this respect, the situation in Xinjiang in 1988 seemed to me to be very different from that in Tibet), historically based frictions continued to pose problems, even in Urumqi. One man said, for example:

> Although Han Chinese and Uighurs mix reasonably well in normal times, there are some underlying tensions that can erupt as a result of incidents. In 1986, to cite one example, there were some fairly large student demonstrations in Urumqi. Some voiced a desire for independence as well as a demand for democracy. Also, periodically, Han-Uighur disputes break out and cause friction. For

example, several years ago there was an incident in which a Han shopkeeper built a structure on a neighboring Uighur's land, and this led to a dispute that ended with the Han shopkeeper shooting and killing the Uighur with a hunting gun. This led to riots. Then Wang Enmao—leader in the region at the time— handled it as follows. He first called together a group of Uighur leaders and urged them to cool their emotions, and then he did the same with a group of Han leaders. The offender was tried and convicted, and this cooled things down. Actually, Han leaders have leaned over backward to placate the Uighurs. Nevertheless, young Uighur students and intellectuals remain a source of potential instability.

There were reports in 1988, published in official Chinese journals, of several incidents of ethnic conflict in Xinjiang. Even Wang Enmao, who was no longer local Party chief but still headed the Regional Party Advisory Commission, was quoted as charging that Xinjiang faced a threat from "elements coming from outside to conduct acts of sabotage and separation." He reportedly named three subversive groups: the East Turkestan National Salvation Committee, the East Turkestan Popular Revolutionary Front, and the World Islamic Alliance. All three were accused of sending spies, instigating underground action, calling for "independence for Xinjiang," and trying to organize an East Turkestan Party. These charges were especially notable because their source was Wang Enmao, a man generally regarded by virtually all the people I met as a leader who had worked hard to promote good ethnic relations in the region. He had attempted, for example, to prevent destruction of mosques during the Cultural Revolution. On ethnic issues, he had the reputation of being a conciliatory moderate. There also were some reports in 1988 of arrests of a number of Kazakhs in the Ili region as well as some other reports of demonstrations in Urumqi in which students protested graffiti that was allegedly racially motivated.

I was unable to judge accurately how serious the underlying tensions might be or what the potential for political instability was. On the surface, Han-Uighur relations generally appeared to me to be quite "normal" in the limited areas that I visited. I sensed, though, rightly or wrongly, that this might be less true of Han-Kazakh relations. I had no doubt that historical and cultural differences still posed problems. Nevertheless, my overall impression was that the regime's policies during the 1980s had significantly reduced tensions at least in Urumqi and nearby areas.

*   *   *

One important set of questions that I tried to explore in Xinjiang, as elsewhere in China in 1988, concerned the changes in the political leadership that had occurred during the decade of the 1980s. In 1948 I had met virtually all of the most important leaders in Urumqi. In 1988 I was not able to do this, but I did have an excellent, long interview with one of the senior deputy chairmen of the Xinjiang Autonomous Region, a man named Mao Dehao, and I met a number of senior officials. They told me a great deal about both the leadership and the administration of the region. In 1988, leaders and officials in Xinjiang, as in the other provinces in autonomous regions that I visited, were willing to discuss such matters in considerable detail.

The region's top leaders, I was told, consisted, in 1988, of 15 individuals on the Party Standing Committee and 8 top government leaders. The ethnic balance and the career profiles of these leaders were similar to those I had learned about in other areas in the west that I had just visited. The secretary of the Party was a Han technocrat (Song Hanliang, formerly an engineer who had worked at the Karamai oil fields). His five deputies included two Han Chinese, two Uighurs, and one Kazakh. Of the nine other members of the Standing Committee, six were Han, two were Uighurs, and one was a Mongol. One of the Han members served concurrently as the political commissar of the Xinjiang Military District. The chairman of the regional government (who concurrently served as the ranking deputy secretary of the Party) was a Uighur; of his six deputies (one of whom also served as a member of the Party Standing Committee), three were Han (including Deputy Chairman Mao, whom I interviewed), two were Uighurs, and one was a Kazakh. The secretary-general was a Uighur.

In the leadership of the Xinjiang People's Congress, the chairman and 8 of the 12 deputy chairmen were of minority ethnic origin. If one added to all of the aforementioned leaders a few others who were classified by local people as "top leaders" (including the chairman and deputy chairman of the People's Political Consultative Conference), the total number of individuals listed as members of the "top leadership" totaled just over 50—and more than half of these (55 percent) belonged to minority ethnic groups.

A majority of these top leaders were people who had risen to high positions very recently, during Deng Xiaoping's nationwide campaign in the mid-1980s to promote younger, better-educated, and more technically qualified leaders. Deputy Chairman Mao Dehao was a good example of the kind of individual promoted. He impressed me as being competent, pragmatic, and a thorough professional—comparable to the majority of the technocratic and professional leaders I had been encountering throughout northwest China. Mao, 52 years old, had been born in Jiangsu Province and educated at Nanjing University, where he obtained a degree in geology. Assigned to Xinjiang right after graduation, he had spent most of his three decades there working in the Xinjiang Academy of Sciences. His research included a great deal of work on agricultural problems and rural planning but also involved investigation of glaciers. Ultimately, Mao rose to be president of the Xinjiang Academy of Sciences. Then, in late 1985, he was selected to be a deputy chairman of the region; his primary area of responsibility was culture and education, including science (the so-called *wenjiao* system). He im-

A typical traditional donkey cart in Urumqi (then called Dihua). By 1988 modern transportation had taken over and only a few donkey carts were left.

Two young Kazakh horsemen, down from their encampment high in the Tian Shan, visiting Dihua.

Uighurs selling melons at a street stall in Dihua in 1948. Their world-famous melons were so juicy that they were almost drinkable.

Public buildings, including those of the municipal government, in the center of Urumqi, which is now a major modern metropolis.

A tall skyscraper under construction in Urumqi in 1988.

Han Chinese and Uighurs mix at a local fair. The modern ambience is very different from that of 1948.

Above:
In 1948 I rode to the Tian Shan encampment of Osman Bator, the preeminent Kazakh leader in China (photo courtesy of Ian Morrison).

Below right:
A Kazakh woman in the Tian Shan.

Above left:
Osman Bator in 1948 at his Tian Shan headquarters, where I interviewed him. A huge man, he evoked images of ancient central Asian leaders such as Genghis Khan or Tamerlane.

An aerial view of the Tian Shan, including Bogda Ola, near Urumqi.

A Kazakh home in the foothills of the Tian Shan.

A Kazakh horseman showing off his riding skill to me in 1988, much as Osman Bator's men had done in 1948.

The barn of a Kazakh home. Because they are isolated, many Kazakh families lead hard lives (the children of this family walked several miles each way to attend school in 1988).

Snow-covered mountains on the road from Urumqi.

A yurt (ger) being erected in the Kazakh area of the Nanshan.

My view of a rocky gebi desert, which seems to stretch to infinity, en route from Urumqi to Turfan in 1988.

A street in Turfan's old city. This traditional Uighur scene looks as though it could be in the Middle East.

A blend of modernity and adapted Islamic architecture in a building constructed in the 1980s in Turfan's "new city."

A large new bazaar in Turfan, filled with shops and stalls with a strong Middle Eastern flavor.

pressed me as being a very different type of person from a majority of the provincial-level leaders that I had met either in the 1940s or during the Mao Zedong era.

In the bureaucracies and in the leadership at lower levels there also was a large representation of minority groups. For example, I was told that at both the regional and prefectural levels, more than 41 percent of unit heads within the bureaucracies were minority cadres. The percentage dropped at the county level to roughly 32 percent. However, in "autonomous counties," 53 percent of all cadres were said to consist of members of minority groups. In the region as a whole, the total number of minority people who were "state cadres" (*guojia ganbu*)—that is, functionaries and officials of all kinds—had risen to 210,000. One top official pointed out—and emphasized—that this was 70 times the number of people of minority origin who held any sort of official position in Xinjiang before 1949.

Of the total number of people in the province classified as "scientific and technical personnel"—around 200,000—more than half were said to be members of ethnic minorities. I was also given a variety of other figures, which I will not cite here, that highlighted the great increase in the number of minority people who had achieved cadre status since the Communist takeover. (Chinese Communist officials have a great penchant—in fact an irresistible impulse—to compare "before and after," with the dividing line usually being either 1949 or the Cultural Revolution.)

All of the statistics of this sort that were given to me clearly indicated that members of minority groups were playing a much larger role than in the past in both the leadership and the bureaucracies and that they had risen steadily also in the intellectually scientific elite of the region. National laws and regulations required that they hold certain top governmental positions, but they obviously had been rising into many positions that no laws or regulations required. However, their representation in a good many sectors was still somewhat lower than their percentage in the region's population. Moreover, as in most of the other areas of northwest China that I visited, it was fairly clear that Han Chinese still held the most powerful positions in the most important centers of power—especially in the Party and the military. I was told, for example, that probably under 10 of the top local Party leaders—that is, Party Committee secretaries in the major geographical-administrative divisions within the region—were minority cadres even though there were at least some minority cadres in all Party Standing Committees. Nonetheless, there was no doubt that the political roles and the political influence of the Uighurs, at least, were now substantial. One observer I met who impressed me as particularly knowledgeable about the local situation (he was a Han Chinese) said: "The Uighurs in high positions are by no means mere figureheads now; they *do* have real influence; actually, some Han Chinese increasingly complain about the discrimination in favor of minorities."

My strong impression was that the influence of minority leaders was greatest in day-to-day government affairs, particularly at subregional levels and especially in "autonomous" areas—most of all in areas that were relatively far from the capital. For centuries, even when the ruling dynasty in China exercised fairly effective overall control of Xinjiang, the military and civilian officials sent there often left the local political structure largely intact and worked to a great extent through local Uighur, Kazakh, and other non-Han leaders. Under the Qing dynasty, when the Lifan Yuan (roughly equivalent in some respects to a colonial office) was generally responsible for the area that is now Xinjiang, which was usually referred to at that time simply as the "western area" (*xiyu*), the region was controlled by "a general's headquarters" (*jiangjunfu*), and control tended to be very loose. Not until 1884 (after Zuo Zongtang's defeat of the Muslim rebellion led by Yakub Beg and the subsequent recovery of the Ili region from the Russians, who had seized it during Yakub Beg's rebellion) was Xinjiang finally incorporated formally into the regular Chinese administrative system. Thereafter, it retained the status and title of Xinjiang Province for seven decades, until 1955, when the Communist regime renamed it the Xinjiang Uighur Autonomous Region.

*   *   *

The organization of "autonomous" units in many areas of China in the 1950s was clearly designed to conciliate minority groups and to co-opt as many as possible of their leaders into the new regime. In some respects, it did have the desired effect. However, demographic trends from the 1950s on resulted in some fairly drastic changes in the ethnic balances in many western regions, which inevitably strengthened the position of the Han Chinese. As noted earlier, in the period just before the Communist takeover, Han Chinese made up less than 6 percent of the total provincial population of Xinjiang, which at that time was estimated to be about 4 million. Of the more than 94 percent of the population made up by ethnic minorities, the Uighurs alone accounted for about 75 percent. By 1986, not only was the population three to four times larger than in the 1940s, but of its total of close to 14 million, the Han Chinese now constituted two-fifths of the total, minority groups had dropped to around three-fifths of the total, and the Uighurs alone now accounted for a little under half of the population in the region.*

---

*The figures for 1948 that I cite are ones that were given to me by officials in Xinjiang at that time. The officials I interviewed in 1948 admitted that, not having conducted a real census, there was considerable room for error. Their overall figure of 4 million actually was somewhat lower than the estimate published at that time by the national government, which was closer to 4.5 million, but I was inclined to accept the local estimate. The figures that I received in Urumqi in 1988 were for the year 1986 (the latest year for which officials there could give me definite

Just how great the changes in the demographic profile of the area had been became especially clear to me when I compared specific figures on different ethnic groups for the years 1948 and 1986. In 1948, not only had the Uighurs accounted for roughly three-quarters of the entire provincial population, but their numerical predominance was even greater in the southern oases ringing the Tarim Basin, and at that time roughly two-thirds of the province's entire population reportedly was concentrated in that southern area. The Kazakhs, then the second largest group, whose numbers totaled between 400,000 and 500,000, made up about 10 percent of the total population, and they were predominant in a number of important mountain areas. Although the Han ranked third (with just under a quarter of a million people), they accounted for only about 6 percent of the province's population—and tended to be concentrated in certain areas in the north.

By the late 1980s, the contrasts with the 1940s were striking. By 1986 Xinjiang's population had risen to 13.836 million, but the proportion made up by minority groups had declined to just over 60 percent. The Uighurs remained the largest group, and in absolute numbers had more than doubled to 6.431 million, but their proportion of the total population had dropped to just under 47 percent. The Kazakhs, although they had more than doubled in absolute numbers to about 1 million, now constituted only a little more than 7 percent of the total population. The most dramatic change had been the direct result of large-scale migration by Han Chinese into the area. The Han population had soared from around 240,000 in 1948 to 5.386 million in 1986. Han Chinese had, in short, grown by more than 20 times, and their numbers were approaching those of the Uighurs—and they exceeded the Uighurs in many areas.*

Xinjiang continues to be one of only two provincial-level autonomous regions in China where ethnic minorities are still in the majority. (The other is the Tibetan Autonomous Region, where Tibetans still make up the overwhelming majority—96 percent, in 1986, according to official statistics.) Nevertheless, the "Hanification" of Xinjiang has gone very far in four decades, and if the trend continues, as seems likely, the Han Chinese almost certainly will become the majority group before long. Moreover, the differences between the northern and southern parts of the region have definitely increased. Although I did not obtain detailed statistics on the regional distri-

---

figures)—but scholars at the Academy of Social Sciences assured me that they thought these figures were accurate and had not changed greatly since then. I have rounded most of the figures I received to the nearest hundred thousand.

*In 1986, the only other really sizable group in Xinjiang consisted of Hui Muslims (mainly Dongan), with 612,000. The figures for other, smaller groups—rounded—were as follows: Mongols, 128,000; Kirghiz, 126,000; Xibe, 30,000; Tadjiks, 30,000; Manchus, 11,000; Uzbeks, 10,000; Dawuer (Daur), 4,900; Tatars, 3,700; and Russians, 5,200.

bution of ethnic groups, my strong impression was that a very large percentage of the Han newcomers are concentrated in the north, especially in cities
along the northern side of the Tian Shan and around the Jungarian (or
Dzungarian) Basin, where population growth has been extremely rapid. It
seems likely that the south will continue to be predominantly Uighur.

Urbanization in Xinjiang has increased substantially as economic development has progressed, and the number of persons engaged in occupations
other than agriculture and animal husbandry has steadily risen. However,
agriculture and animal husbandry still predominate, in basic respect.

In the mid-1980s, according to statistics that I was given for the year
1984, 74 percent of the region's population was still rural. Moreover, 68
percent were still engaged in agriculture, whereas only 32 percent were in
nonagricultural occupations. As these figures show, the majority of the population was still very much rooted in the past; nevertheless, the increase in
the urban population to roughly a quarter of the total, and the growth of the
nonagricultural population to almost a third, were revealing indications of
the important economic transformation that was under way as a result both
of the Chinese migration and of major efforts at local economic development—two trends that were clearly linked.*

The most important urban centers were now, as in the past, Urumqi, Ining
(also known as Kulja—the main city in Ili), and Kashgar (the largest city in
the south). However, Urumqi was in a class by itself—and had grown much
more rapidly than the others. It had become a quite impressive modern metropolis. By the mid-1980s, its population had risen to 1.147 million, four-
fifths of whom (922,000) were classified as urban and 83 percent of whom
were engaged in nonagricultural work.†

*   *   *

Urbanization and occupational changes were only two of many important
indices of the progress of modernization in Xinjiang in the years since my
first visit. The development of education was another important one. I had
not obtained detailed data on education in the province when I visited it in
1948, but it was clear at that time that, in general, modern forms of educa-

---

*By 1986, in the region as a whole, the total labor force had risen to 5.16 million, of whom
3.56 million were in agriculture, 680,000 in industry, 340,000 in commercial work, 270,000 in
construction, 265,000 in education, research, science, and technological work, 190,000 in
transportation and communications, and 160,000 in Party and government work (the rest of the
total were divided among various miscellaneous occupations).

†These were the figures given to me in Urumqi. National statistics (from the State Statistical
Bureau) for Urumqi in 1986 gave its population as 1,040,000, with 960,000 (92 percent) nonagricultural.

tion had barely begun to develop and did not reach most of the Uighur and Kazakh populations. By the late 1980s modern education had been significantly expanded, and official policies gave high priority to developing further the education of minority groups.

The latest official statistics available (most of them for 1987, but a few for 1986) indicated that in the region there were a total of 8,404 primary schools with an enrollment of 1.966 million students. Among these primary school students, more than 1.2 million were from minority groups—a figure that reflected closely the 60 percent share of the population belonging to minorities. At the middle school level, there were 2,147 schools, of which about two-fifths, or almost 860, had senior as well as junior middle school classes; the total enrollment of the middle schools was 955,000 students. The number of students who actually graduated from senior middle schools each year, I was told, was roughly 80,000—indicating a substantial drop-out rate. The percentage of middle school students who were members of minorities also showed a lower percentage compared to the population as a whole: Of the 955,000 middle school students, only about 310,000—or about a third—were students of minority nationalities. What all of these figures indicated was that in Xinjiang education consisted of a steep pyramid–as it did in most parts of China—and one in which the higher levels of the basic educational ladder were disproportionately populated by Han Chinese.

It is interesting, however, that this was less true in the region's institutions of "higher education." Officials from the Education Commission told me that in the region as a whole there were 20 such institutions (universities, colleges, and other institutions given a similar status), not counting a number of so-called part-time or worker and TV "colleges." The two leading institutions of higher education in Xinjiang were classified as "key" universities—a designation given to only a relatively few universities in China: Xinjiang University and Xinjiang Normal University. The majority of all the institutions given the label of "higher education" were concentrated in the region's capital city. Besides the 12 located in Urumqi, however, there were 3 in Shihezi and 1 each in Kashgar, Aksu, Ili, Khotan, and Changji.

Altogether, just over 30,000 students attended these 20 institutions; almost all of them were students studying at the undergraduate level, although throughout the region, in 1988, there were in local institutions of higher learning a total of 57 M.A. students and 21 Ph.D. students. I was told that approximately 55 percent of all students attending higher education in such institutions throughout the region were members of various minority nationality groups; this was a surprisingly high figure—close to the percentage of minorities in the total population—which clearly was a result of policies that made a special effort to enroll minorities and gave them preferential treatment in the entrance examinations. (The figures may have been skewed a little as a result of the fact that many members of ethnic minorities studying

at the university level spent five years rather than four years in college because many took remedial or special courses to begin with. Probably, also,
more Han students than minority students left the province to study in universities elsewhere—which also could have affected the statistics for those
within the province.*)

Wherever ethnic groups are mixed in an educational system, language issues generally become sensitive problems. In Xinjiang, this was obviously
the case, but it was also clear that important compromises had been made to
try to accommodate the linguistic diversity. In primary and middle schools
(and other secondary-level schools), classes were taught, I was told, in six
different languages: Uighur, Hanyu (Chinese), Kazakh, Mongol, Xibe, and
Kirghiz. There were textbooks in all six of these languages. Most of them
were translations of texts received from Beijing, although some minority language texts had been prepared locally. Not all schools taught all six languages; exactly what was taught—and the textbooks used—varied by
school. A few schools were "mixed," which meant that they taught in more
than one language, but most were not. In effect, the system was based on different language "tracks," and my informants asserted that about 95 percent
of the primary and middle school students attended schools in which the basic teaching was in their own native language track. However, from the third
grade on, I was told, minority students were expected to be able to use the
Chinese language (Hanyu and spoken Chinese, *putonghua*). Han Chinese
students were required to study a foreign language—but it did not have to be
one of the local nationality group's languages, and in recent years, my informants said, the study of Western languages (especially English) had become increasingly popular, and the number of Han Chinese studying minority languages had declined.

In Xinjiang, as elsewhere in west China, the local officials I met—minority
officials as well as Han Chinese—strongly stressed to me that preferential
treatment was being given to minority students, and to minority languages,
especially in higher education. In some institutions of higher learning the basic language was Hanyu, but in others it was Uighur (although even in these
schools all students had to study Hanyu). In the Normal College in Ili, both

---

*In Urumqi, I received more than one set of statistics on education enrollments, and there
were inconsistencies among them. The Xinjiang Foreign Affairs Bureau gave me the following
figures for 1987 (which differed somewhat from those given to me by the Education Commission): 8,104 primary schools, with 1.9482 million students; 2,360 middle schools and technical
secondary schools, with 1.1345 million students; and 18 "colleges," with 29,700 students. I had
no way to check the figures and determine which were the accurate ones, but I chose to accept
the figures from the Education Commission—whose officials were directly involved in the educational system.

the Uighur and Kazakh language (Turki) and Hanyu were considered to be "basic languages." Minority students were admitted to college-level institutions with scores that were lower than those required for Han Chinese students—usually 100 points lower—and I was told that most students took entrance exams in their own languages. If they were enrolled in an institution within Xinjiang where the basic language was Hanyu, they could, if their knowledge of Hanyu was below par, either attend a special language training course, given by the Education Commission, or spend their initial year at the college studying Hanyu (which extended their college program to five years).

A sizable number of students from Xinjiang were sent to universities elsewhere in China. I was told that roughly 4,000 went each year to attend universities in other provinces. Many of these students first spent two years in basic training at one of the two main minority institutes—in Beijing or Lanzhou—where their curricula focused on learning the Chinese language, and then they went on (or at least many of them did) to other universities in Beijing, Shanghai, Guangzhou, and elsewhere.*

For many years there had been—and continued to be—a serious "brain drain" problem, I was told, which was especially troublesome among the Han Chinese students. My informants said that whereas the majority of minority students from Xinjiang who attended universities elsewhere returned to the region, only about 40 percent of Han students from the region did so. Officials candidly admitted that many of the latter "do not like to live and work in the northwest"; in contrast, they said, most Uighurs and other ethnic groups (except, perhaps, the Xibe—for reasons they did not explain) "do not like to live and work in other provinces, as a rule." In early 1988, I was told, Beijing's State Council adopted a policy that required all Xinjiang students going for university education elsewhere to return to the region following graduation, but the people with whom I talked were uncertain as to how effectively this could be implemented.

From what I learned in 1988, it seemed clear that, in contrast to the pre-1949 period, the government was trying to extend basic education to most of the population. There was no doubt in my mind, though, that the quality of the education remained relatively low. Virtually all of the officials I met frankly admitted that this was the case and said that they were dissatisfied with the situation and gave high priority to improving it. I had no basis for judging exactly how low the quality was, but it was clear that Xinjiang shared this problem with most of the rest of China—perhaps in a somewhat

---

*Reviewing my notes on my interviews with Xinjiang Education Commission officials, I am uncertain whether the 4,000 figure they gave me included both Han Chinese students from Xinjiang and local minority students, but I believe it did include both.

more acute form. Nevertheless, certain basic knowledge, including literacy and mathematical skills, and some general knowledge about the society and the world, were being imparted to virtually the entire younger generation.

I speculated about what the possible political effects of greatly expanded education might be in the long run. Local Chinese leaders obviously hoped that their educational policies would not only raise the level of knowledge and skill of the minority ethnic groups but would also tend over time to integrate them more effectively into a unified society. They also hoped that their policies would, at the same time, satisfy the desire of ethnic groups to maintain their own languages and cultural identities. Whether these multiple goals are likely to be successfully achieved remains to be seen. It is also conceivable that, despite the preferential treatment given to minority ethnic groups, the simple fact of steadily rising educational levels may, over time, create a stronger base for "local nationalism." Moreover, there is no question that, as development makes progress, education will have to be upgraded, qualitatively, and all the local leaders I met fully recognized this. Nevertheless, the quantitative development of education since the 1940s had clearly played a very major and essential role in Xinjiang's recent development and modernization.

*   *   *

Although my interviews in Xinjiang covered a wide range of subjects and issues, by far the majority focused on how, and how much, Xinjiang's economy had developed in the four decades since my previous visit, and in general I was greatly impressed by what I learned. As I mentioned earlier, the detailed briefings that I received included one by Deputy Chairman Mao and many with a fairly wide range of government planners and academics. Virtually all of them were technocrats or economists. Among the most intelligent, well informed, and articulate of them were men who had originally come from the Yangzi valley. The backgrounds of the following three were typical in some respects of many of those I met. One came from Shanghai, where he had been educated at Fudan University and at the Shanghai Finance and Economics College. He had worked in the field of economic affairs in Xinjiang since 1953. Another was a man who had been educated at Beijing University and at People's University, also in Beijing, and then came to Xinjiang in 1960. He spent his first 20 years working for the Production and Construction Corps, then became a staff member of the local Academy of Social Sciences. Still another, a Uighur, came from the Lop Nor area of Xinjiang but moved to Urumqi to study agricultural economics at the so-called August One Agricultural College. All of these men, and the majority of others I met, impressed me as being strongly dedicated to the economic development of the region, competent in their fields, and extremely pragmatic rather than ideological in their approach to problems.

The economic development of the region, as they described it to me, had occurred almost entirely since the Communist takeover. As I mentioned earlier, when I visited Xinjiang in 1948, there were only four modern factories in the entire province. Although I heard a great deal at that time about the "fabulous riches" of Xinjiang, provincial officials told me that only 3.6 percent of the province had been systematically prospected, so really there was very little concrete knowledge about the resources in the area. Apart from the development of small oil wells at Wusu, some gold mines in the Altai region, a few tungsten (wolfram) mines, and a number of small coal mines, its resources remained largely undeveloped—and in fact largely unknown. No rail line had yet penetrated into the province, and all major roads were still unpaved.

Then, following the Communist takeover, the development of transportation, power plants, mines, and—above all—modern industry occurred quite rapidly. This development was the result of a deliberate central government policy, dictated by both strategic and economic priorities. From the start, investments from Beijing and assistance from the central ministries dominated the region's economy; in 1988 they still did. The most striking thing to me was the huge role played in the local development process by the army's Production and Construction Corps. Originally run by the People's Liberation Army (PLA), it was later transferred to civilian control, although it was still organized and run along military lines. The development of rail transportation also contributed in a major way to the modernization process; much of the industrial development had taken place along the routes of the rail lines. To me, the development of modern industry in the region was impressive, even though Xinjiang remained primarily agricultural in several basic respects.

Economic reform had reached Xinjiang in the early 1980s and was beginning to have a significant impact on the region, and the leadership had taken steps to implement most of the policy innovations that Deng Xiaoping and his colleagues sponsored. However, local leaders there—as in much of northwest China—were frank in acknowledging that their reform efforts lagged behind those in many eastern parts of the country. Nevertheless, Xinjiang's rate of economic growth recently had been accelerating, and its leaders articulated some very ambitious plans for the future.

The central government had a variety of motives for deciding in the early 1950s to allocate substantial investment funds to the region and to send a great many skilled technicians and workers there. One aim was to consolidate political control over a huge region of strategic importance that had almost always been under very loose control. Another was to explore the resources in the region, which were believed to be great but were little known; they were needed not only for local use but also for the development of the entire country. Still another reason was to use these resources to build a strong economy in the northwest, which was a strategic border region, to strengthen China's position in relation to the Soviet Union and Central Asia—and South Asia as well. In the period immediately following the signing of an alliance with Moscow in 1950, Sino-Soviet cooperation made a very significant contribution to the region's initial development. Two Sino-Soviet joint-stock companies were established in Xinjiang to exploit the region's petroleum and nonferrous metals, and a jointly run civil aviation company was created to provide air service between China and the USSR. But by the start of the 1960s, the Sino-Soviet split ended such cooperation.

During the 1950s, the PLA played an extremely large and multifaceted role in most of China's "borderland regions." The army's functions were much broader than simply military defense: After establishing control, military units set to work to develop the local economy. The PLA's Xinjiang Production and Construction Corps was similar to corps established in several other places, including Heilongjiang, Inner Mongolia, and Hainan Island, but the one in Xinjiang proved to be the most long-lasting and probably the most important of them all. The Corps initially put major emphasis on developing agricultural land—through land reclamation and irrigation—but it also started very early to develop industries.

After the first spurt of development in the area in the early and mid-1950s, a second followed, when investment and growth surged rapidly ahead in the period between 1958 and 1960, during the Great Leap Forward. In that era, additional technicians, skilled laborers, capital, and industrial enterprises were transferred on a fairly large scale from coastal China. For the most part, though, what was moved was not entire plants—as was the case in some other areas. As one expert there said to me, "A few, although not a very great many" factories were transferred at that time from Shanghai to Xinjiang. This period of rapid growth did not last very long, however. The boom was soon followed by a major bust—in Xinjiang as elsewhere in China—resulting in the post–Great Leap depression.

During the 1960s and the 1970s, Xinjiang's economy continued to develop, but at a slower pace. Xinjiang was no longer especially favored as it had been in the 1950s. As I discussed earlier, from the mid-1960s to the mid-1970s, in the period following the Sino-Soviet split, Mao Zedong personally promoted his so-called three-front strategy, and Beijing poured huge amounts of investments into industrial development in several selected interior provinces and regions in both southwest and northwest China to build new economic bases that ostensibly would be secure against outside threat. However, because Xinjiang bordered on the USSR, it was considered to be a vulnerable area, and therefore it was largely left out of this new plan. Strategic considerations, which had worked in Xinjiang's favor in the 1950s, proved to be a liability in the 1960s and 1970s.

The situation then changed fairly radically again in the 1980s, when—in the context of China's new policies of reform and "opening"—Sino-Soviet détente took place, and the old "three-front" idea was abandoned. Xinjiang now experienced another major surge of growth and modernization. This was spurred, in part, by the renewal of large-scale investment in the region by Beijing, but it was also a result of the radically new reform policies introduced by the central government in this period.

*   *   *

During the four decades of modernization in Xinjiang from the late 1940s on, the region had major ups and downs—but it made significant economic progress. Several things were crucial in the process of development. One was the extension of modern transportation—especially rail transportation—into the region. A large proportion of the new modern factories that sprouted within the region were built along the rail route. Construction of the Lanzhou-Urumqi line was begun in 1952—after the rail connection between Lanzhou and east China had been completed—and after a formal agreement to build such a line connecting China and the USSR was signed between Beijing and Moscow. The plan, from the start, had been to build a 1,182-mile line right up to the Soviet border, where it would then connect with the entire Soviet rail network including the main Trans-Siberian route. However, because of the deterioration of Sino-Soviet relations from the late 1950s on, and the rupture of economic ties in the 1960s, this plan had to be modified—and the last portion of it was shelved. The main part of the line was completed to Urumqi and then was extended from there to Wusu, but it stopped there—and was not resumed for many years. Finally, though, in the 1980s—when Sino-Soviet relations improved—China and the USSR again agreed on the desirability of completing this line, and work on the final stretch of it, from Wusu to the border, was resumed. During my 1988 visit, the big push to complete it got under way. When I met Deputy Chairman Mao, he told me that he had just come back from Wusu, where on the previous day—May Day—he had taken part in a major ceremony to kick off the construction of the final 149 miles of the line to complete it to the Soviet border. The schedule called for completing it within two years.

Besides the main trunk line to Urumqi and its extension to Wusu, a southern branch of the railway had also been built, starting from near Turfan. It went 295 miles southward to Korla. Leaders in Xinjiang told me that they hoped to be able to extend the line further into the southern part of the region before too long. They also hoped that eventually they could build a line to connect with Qinghai Province, but they admitted that funds to do this were not available and that they had not yet been able to make any definite plans for it—or to have the project included in Beijing's state planning.

Virtually everyone I met expressed optimism that once the link connecting with the Soviet network of railways was completed Xinjiang's economic growth would receive a major boost. This was a hope shared by officials I had met in some other areas in the northwest. What they expected was that it would result in an increase in Sino-Soviet trade (although, as I will note later, in 1988 they had only modest hopes for the immediate expansion of cross-border trade). More important, they hoped that it would provide an entirely new "bridge between China and Europe." They argued that this new route would be much shorter than China's two existing rail links to the USSR—from Heilongjiang and Inner Mongolia. What they anticipated was that the new line would enable China to increase its direct trade to Western Europe by a substantial amount. In particular, they hoped that large-container cargo trade would rapidly develop. They argued that this would be very competitive with sea trade; several pointed out that the new rail route directly to Europe would cut the distance from China to Rotterdam by perhaps as much as a half compared to the distance of the existing sea route from China to Rotterdam. This, one expert said to me, should cut transport costs of container cargo by perhaps as much as 20 percent. The more they talked about it, the more it sounded to me as if many hoped that this would, in effect, become a new Iron Road to Europe—a kind of modern equivalent of the old Silk Road—so that instead of being a remote back door, Xinjiang might again begin to be one of China's front doors. (I was impressed by their enthusiasm but was somewhat skeptical about the high hopes they had. Subsequently I have wondered how the disintegration of the Soviet Union has affected their planning and their estimation of what might be possible.)

In addition to building the first railways in the area—the length of which totaled 870 miles in the entire region by 1987 and would, they said, grow to about 1,000 miles by 1990—the local regime had given priority from the 1950s on to building a network of paved roads, connecting all major urban areas in the region. By 1987, I was told, this road network totaled roughly 13,000 miles, and the most important roads were paved. Officials stated that roads now reached every county and town in the autonomous region, and public bus service connected the most important centers of population—although the main use of the roads continued to be for trucking cargo rather than for passenger traffic.

Air travel had also been significantly expanded (it was extremely primitive before 1949). Urumqi now had direct scheduled air service to seven major Chinese cities (Beijing, Tianjin, Shanghai, Xi'an, Lanzhou, Guangzhou, and Chengdu). When I flew to Urumqi in 1948, it was like making an adventurous expedition into the unknown. Now that Urumqi is well connected with virtually the entire country, air travel is routine. This has been a much more profound change than those who have never lived in places without air travel may realize. Recently a local airline company, called Dunhuang Air, established regular links between Urumqi and other major cities within the region.

Even though Xinjiang's modern transportation system is still minimal in some respects, and clearly requires further development, by the late 1980s the isolation that had characterized the region in the 1940s had ended—forever. Moreover, in Xinjiang, as elsewhere in China, the great expansion of modern media that had taken place in the 1980s had created much closer communication links than had ever existed before, both within the region and with other parts of China and the entire world.

The press and other publications had expanded greatly (and newspapers were now published in all the major languages). However, because I did not have time to gather detailed information about every aspect of the modern media, I concentrated on trying to learn as much as I could about the growth of the electronic media, the prevalence of which I found so remarkable in every place that I visited in northwest China.

In the Xinjiang region as a whole, I was told, official estimates indicated that 70 percent of the entire population had access to, and listened to, the radio in 1988. (I remember seeing virtually no radios anywhere in Xinjiang when I visited it in 1948—except for a few sets owned by foreign consulates.) Apart from the major broadcasting station in Urumqi, 10 counties had built their own wireless radio stations, and each of them did some programming of its own as well as rebroadcasting many national and regional radio programs. Virtually all the settled population in the region, moreover, was linked into wired radio-speaker systems (somewhat similar to "rediffusion" in the West), which had been universally developed from the 1950s on. I was told that not only did all counties have such systems but 701 townships and 1,294 villages did, too. My informants asserted that all of these could originate local programs—or at least make local announcements over the loud-speakers—as well as rebroadcast programs from Beijing and Urumqi. On my own radio, I found the airwaves, both long and short wave, filled with an extraordinary variety of programs from all over China and abroad as well as the region itself. (For some reason, however, I had considerable difficulty finding any FM stations, and frequently the short-wave reception was poorer than I expected in this region—where I thought that interference would be minimal.)

But here as elsewhere it was the penetration of TV—which had occurred entirely during the decade of the 1980s—that struck me most forcefully. By 1988, I was told by informed local people, there were 1.1 million TV sets in Xinjiang; this amounted to about one per every three households, regionwide. In urban areas, I was told, virtually every household owned a TV set. It was estimated that about 65 percent of the entire population of the region was within geographic areas that were effectively reached by TV signals. Throughout the region, in addition to regular TV stations, there were

92 TV relay stations, mostly rebroadcasting the output of the stations in Beijing and Urumqi. Altogether, within the region, there were 23 local TV stations that had at least some capability to put out their own programming, but everyone stated that most of the programs were ones rebroadcast from national and provincial stations. I was told, though, that—in contrast to Inner Mongolia and Qinghai—Xinjiang had not yet actively promoted the sale and distribution of small windmill generators; as a result, many people in the grasslands, especially Kazakhs, had no source of electricity and therefore lacked TV. My informants mentioned among possible reasons the fact that local fluctuations in wind were quite large. My guess was that they simply had not yet pushed the idea. They said some study had been made of simple solar generators, but they were not in wide use either.

In Urumqi itself, there were 14 hours a day of TV broadcasting in the Chinese language (*putonghua*), and 12 hours a day in Uighur (Turki), but only 3 to 4 hours on a single day each week were devoted to special programs for Kazakhs. This allocation of programming obviously gave local Uighurs in the city a disproportionate amount of program time in their native language since only 12 percent of Urumqi's population was Uighur and virtually all of them spoke the Chinese language. But in light of the fact that Urumqi programs were relayed throughout the region, the time allotted was understandable. The Han Chinese, whose population made up 82 percent of the municipality's population (and roughly two-fifths of the region's population), had slightly more air time. Even though the Kazakhs constituted only 3 percent of Urumqi's population and only 7 percent of the population of the region, and even though most of them could understand Turki programs produced for the Uighurs, it nevertheless seemed to me that they were being shortchanged in the TV field—as in many others—in comparison with the Uighurs.

The mix of TV programs—national news (which contained some segments of local news), entertainment, educational programs, and advertising—seemed very much like that in Beijing. The nightly national news had a very large local audience, I was told (my impression was that this was true throughout China). I was impressed by the fact that the local newscasters closely imitated their national, and international, models: The co-anchors of news programs—usually one man and one woman—were smartly dressed in Western clothes and looked remarkably like their counterparts on the American networks (on whom they seemed to model their style). Political propaganda was largely absent in 1988. TV was full of images of China's most developed areas and of very modern areas in the West—especially the United States and Europe—and bombarded viewers with scenes of modern life in all of its varied aspects. Subtly, and not so subtly, both advertisements and regular programs strongly promoted consumerism—by urging everyone to buy every conceivable kind of consumer durable and many kinds of luxury consumables. A combination of all the messages being communicated by the electronic media (at least before the Tiananmen disaster in 1989), combined with the effects of modern transportation, created powerful new forces for modernization.

*   *   *

Compared to many areas of China further east, the growth of modern industry in Xinjiang since the 1940s was obviously still, as of 1988, in an early stage, but I was nevertheless impressed by what had been accomplished because of my memories of 1948 when modern industry had been almost totally lacking. The main industrial centers in Xinjiang had developed, as I noted earlier, mainly along the rail lines. Apart from the industries in Urumqi, some factories had been built in Hami, Turfan, Shihezi (an entirely new city not far northwest from Urumqi), and several other places along the rail lines. In addition, Karamai, further northwest, had become a major petroleum production center, and there had been some further development at Wusu, which was the most significant oil-producing center before 1949. A few industries also had been built in the southern oases and in the principal cities of Ili in the far northwest. In addition, in the area of southern Xinjiang east of the Taklimakan Desert, the Chinese had built their Lop Nor (Lop Nur) Nuclear Weapons Test Base (in the area that overlaps Turfan Prefecture and Bayingolin Mongol Autonomous Prefecture). This base had become China's main test site and a key part of the entire Chinese nuclear weapons complex, linked to other institutions in Beijing, Gansu, and Qinghai. (I was not able to learn very much on my 1988 visit about this aspect of Xinjiang's development. What I did know was based largely on what I had learned earlier from Western writings; in Xinjiang the subject was essentially out of bounds, at least for an academic visitor such as myself.)

As I did everywhere, I requested local statistics on the economy. The data that I obtained in Urumqi about the region as a whole highlighted several facts. In recent years, the rate of economic growth in Xinjiang had been good—"above the national average." Despite the region's huge size, however, Xinjiang's economy remained relatively small by national standards. In fact, the gross value of its industrial and agricultural output in 1986 constituted roughly 1 percent of the national total—ranking it fourth from the bottom among China's provincial-level units. (Only Tibet, Ningxia, and Qinghai ranked lower.) However, its per capita income was nevertheless relatively high—at about the middle level for the country as a whole. The improvement in local living standards resulted partly from the region's industrial development and partly from its expansion of agriculture.

Of the combined gross output of agriculture and industry in 1987, I was told, 40 percent came from agriculture (including farming, animal husbandry, forestry, fishing, and so on) and 60 percent came from industry (including mining)—even though only 26 percent of the population lived in urban areas. The 40 percent for agriculture was higher, according to figures from the State Statistical Bureau, than the percentage in all but the previously mentioned four other provinces or regions (namely, Tibet, Guizhou, Guangxi, and Anhui).*

The ratio between heavy and light industry in Xinjiang (also measured in value of output) was roughly 55 to 45 respectively. This percentage for light industry was higher than in many other provinces and regions in northwest China, but it was considerably lower than the ratio in China's coastal areas—where most of the country's consumer goods were produced. Petroleum and coal output accounted for a very high percentage (roughly a third, by value) of the region's heavy industrial output and, in fact, accounted for about one-fifth of all industrial output in the region. In sum, even though the region's industrial development—the first really modern development in the region's history—was significant, Xinjiang continued to be more dependent on agriculture than most areas in China; it still had relatively few large heavy industrial factories; and most of its heavy industry was simply extractive industry—particularly in petroleum and coal.

Both local officials and Academy scholars stressed that these were the general characteristics of the regional economy, and the statistics that they provided supported the generalizations. So, too, did the statistics that I later obtained from State Statistical Bureau (SSB) publications. As always, I encountered inconsistencies, but none of them undermined the general judgments arising from the overall statistical profile that I obtained.† The variations were not so great, it seemed to me, to invalidate any of the generalizations I had made.‡

------

*Although some of my informants in Urumqi also used this 40 percent figure, some of the detailed statistics that officials provided to me there indicated that the ratio between agriculture and industry was about 30 to 70. I never was able to reconcile the different figures on the ratio.

†When I later obtained SSB statistics and compared them with the local statistics I obtained in Urumqi, I spent a considerable period of time trying—without success—to reconcile the difference between the national and local statistics and also to reconcile inconsistencies within the various sets of statistics that I obtained in Urumqi. I was never able to do so to my satisfaction. I am convinced, though, that some of the inconsistencies were the result of differences in statistical methods used nationally and locally. The State Statistical Bureau volume that I consulted certainly hinted that this was the case when it stated: "The total product of society of each province ... is calculated according to its own method [and therefore the sum of provincial figures] differs from the national total."

‡For posterity—or for any readers who have a special taste for statistics—I will present a few of the different figures that I obtained. The regional Foreign Affairs Office asserted that in 1986, the "total product of society" in the region as a whole was Y 21.117 billion, which it said was an increase of 10.2 percent over 1985 (this implied a figure of Y 19.162 billion for 1985). Local planning officials, in an interview, gave me the figure of Y 24.7 billion for 1987 (in current

My informants in Urumqi also gave me a variety of figures about the rise in living standards during the 1980s. Although I was never able to pin down entirely to my satisfaction exactly what the calculations were based on, I nevertheless was convinced that there had been an impressive rise in incomes. Leading planning officials asserted that per capita "output" in Xinjiang doubled between 1980 and 1987, from Y 360 to Y 760. They also asserted that by 1986 the "net per capita income" of urban residents had risen to Y 890 and that of the rural population engaged in agriculture and animal husbandry had risen to Y 420. These figures were based in substantial part, I was told, on sample surveys—in addition to data on urban wages. I would have liked to have obtained some data on the per capita income figures of various ethnic groups but was not able to do so. My guess was that the income of some residents in pasture areas—perhaps especially some of the Kazakhs—was near the bottom of the scale; that the general level of Han Chinese and probably the Hui Muslims was probably near the top; and that perhaps the majority of Uighurs were in the middle. However, I did not get specific statistics to support these hunches. Moreover, it was possible that some of the people in pastoral areas were doing well—if their situation was similar to that of Mongols and Tibetans I had interviewed earlier in Inner Mongolia and Qinghai—because of the relatively favorable prices for animal products.

*   *   *

The industrial development in Xinjiang had, quite naturally, reflected the region's comparative advantages in resources of energy and minerals (including many nonferrous metals and other rare metals). However, even though Xinjiang was believed to have some of the richest underground resources in China, exploitation of most of them had really just begun. The region's remoteness, shortage of capital, scarceness of skills, and distance from major markets still posed very large obstacles to full exploitation and devel-

---

prices). They (and the deputy chairman of the region) said to me that their published figures, as well as the ones that they gave to me orally, included the output of the Xinjiang Production and Construction Corps but did *not* include the output of military industries in the region (just as was the case in Gansu) because, they said, military industry "fell under a different system." The figure published by the SSB in Beijing for Xinjiang's total product of society in 1985 was Y 18.458 billion. The breakdown by sectors was as follows: industrial output, Y 8.552 billion; agricultural output, Y 5.850 billion; construction, Y 2.078 billion; transport, Y 0.799 billion; and commerce, Y 1.370 billion. The Xinjiang Foreign Affairs Bureau gave me statistics on the region's gross industrial and agricultural output for both 1985 and 1986. In the former year, they said, it was Y 14.863 billion, and in the latter year it was Y 16.322 billion. I had neither the time nor the inclination to try to resolve all the differences; I will leave that to others. However, the figures nevertheless gave a good idea of the general dimensions of the region's economy.

opment of its resources. Nevertheless, the region had made a good start toward discovering and developing important resources.

Xinjiang's heavy industry (a category that in China includes mining as well as factories) was mainly concentrated in the fields of energy and nonferrous and rare metals. In the long run, petroleum and coal seemed destined to be crucially important. Oil production had begun on a very small scale in the pre-1949 period, mainly at Dushanzi near Wusu, but the discovery of oil at Karamai in the mid-1950s had led to major development and a rapid rise in output—even though the output remained much smaller than that at some other major oil centers such as Daqing in China's northeast and Shengli and Dagang in north China. Xinjiang's output of crude oil, according to official figures, reached 5.5 million tons in 1986 (roughly 4 percent of the national total). But local leaders felt—probably rightly—that the potential for petroleum output in Xinjiang was enormous if technical problems could be solved and if capital could be obtained to pay for the high cost (including the cost of pipelines to transport oil to the eastern parts of China).

Large basins of oil were believed to exist in varying parts of the region. Major foreign companies already had shown a strong interest in exploring the region, but the Chinese leadership in Beijing, though willing to ask foreign companies to give some technical assistance, was still showing a considerable reluctance about allowing substantial participation in production in the region. This reluctance contrasted with Beijing's active solicitation of foreign investment in China's offshore oil fields during the 1980s, perhaps because offshore operations could be less intrusive and presumably therefore less disruptive, politically and socially, within the country. However, local Xinjiang leaders, it seemed to me, were extremely eager to see much greater involvement by foreign oil companies in the region's development, and they told me that there was a real possibility of building a large oil pipeline from Xinjiang to Xi'an; this had been seriously considered, they said, even though concrete plans were still sometime in the future. My guess was that the pressure to bring in foreign oil companies to accelerate the development of the region's oil resources would mount over time—and eventually prevail. Local leaders in the region would almost certainly throw their weight in favor of such a development.

Coal production also has been very important to Xinjiang's economy; output in 1986 was 16.5 million tons. However, this output was still mostly for local use, mainly by power plants and other industries. The region's electricity output (4.285 billion kilowatt hours in 1986) was produced mainly in those places that had coal-fueled thermal plants. Local officials estimated that the region's coal reserves totaled about 1.6 trillion tons—which would make them among the largest in China. Therefore officials firmly believed that the region would be able to greatly expand its output and that if the railway's capacity to transport coal to other parts of China were improved, they should have a large market elsewhere. This may or may not have been an excessively optimistic view.

Other mining operations in Xinjiang included iron (to supply the small local steel industry), aluminum, copper, salt, manganese, and gold (from mines in the Altai region). Other heavy industries in the region included iron and steel, chemicals (especially ones using raw materials from the region's numerous salt lakes), some machinery, automobiles (on a very small scale), and cement. There were two iron and steel plants located in Urumqi, but their output—about 200,000 tons in 1986—was very small by national standards and was mainly for local use.

"Light industries"—accounting for almost a half of the value of Xinjiang's gross industrial output—were mainly agriculturally based. They included a number of textile plants, which used both local cotton—mainly good-quality, long-fiber cotton, the cultivation of which had been expanded greatly by the Production and Construction Corps—and some cotton bought from other areas. Sugar was also important; several sugar-refining plants (mainly using local sugar beets) also had been developed by the Corps. In addition, within the region there were several tobacco factories, plants producing fur and leather goods (mainly using the products of local animal husbandry), paper mills, and a variety of factories producing food products (meat, fruits, and so on) plus a number producing a wide variety of "daily necessities." There also were some factories producing consumer durables, including TVs, washing machines, and refrigerators, but output of these was small scale. Altogether, I was told, as of 1987 Xinjiang had a total of roughly 6,000 industrial plants; most of them were small, but more than 500 were classified as medium-sized or large. Among those classified as "key enterprises" were the Karamai Oil Company, the Xinjiang Petrochemical Plant, the August One Iron and Steel Works, the July One Cotton Textile Mill, and the Tian Shan Wool Knitting and Textile Company.

*   *   *

Agriculture had been significantly expanded and modernized since 1949, with the PLA Production and Construction Corps playing the central role in its development. In addition to the traditional farming centers in the southern oases and the Ili-Dacheng area, the Corps had developed some entirely new agricultural areas and expanded others; these included areas northwest of Urumqi, near the Manas River (close to the new city of Shihezi), and the Changji Hui Autonomous Prefecture (just a little north of Urumqi). By 1987, according to official local figures, cultivated land in Xinjiang totaled 8 million acres. Local officials believed that—in contrast to most other areas in east China—Xinjiang had large, arable, but still uncultivated areas. Water was the key requirement, but they felt that there were good potential sources of additional water. They asserted, in fact, that in their judgment the region still had more than 28 million acres of potentially "reclaimable" or developable farming land (in other words, 3.5 times what was already being cultivated). These local experts asserted that this reclaimable or developable land was mostly in the category of *huangdi*—that is, wasteland that is capable of being cultivated. (They contrasted this with *huangmo*—desert wasteland that can be used by animals but cannot be cultivated.)

Traditional grain crops continued to be very important in Xinjiang, and their output had steadily risen over the years. Wheat was still the largest crop, but rice, corn, and sorghum had become increasingly important. By 1986, annual grain output approached 5.5 million tons; this amount, my informants said, made Xinjiang self-sufficient in grain and, in fact, allowed it to "export" more than a half million tons to other parts of China. Output of cotton and sugar beets also had significantly expanded. The region now had a large surplus of cotton, local officials said; only one-fifth of its local output could be used by the region's textile industries, and the rest was sold elsewhere. (The small amount of cotton that they imported consisted of special types.) Sugar beets were mainly used locally, to supply the region's refineries; these refineries produced about 60,000 tons of sugar in 1986.

Output of oil-bearing crops had grown. Xinjiang also had long been famous for its melons; in fact, for centuries, "Hami" melons had been greatly prized throughout China. Xinjiang grapes (especially "Turfan grapes") were also renowned. Many other kinds of local fruits were of excellent quality and well known. (One of my most pleasant memories of my 1948 visit was consuming huge quantities of melons and grapes; the melons, as I remember them, were so juicy that one could virtually drink them.) Among the other notable agricultural products of the region were mulberry (used for making silk, especially in southern Xinjiang), hemp, and a variety of vegetables.

As I mentioned earlier, the climate in the region is so dry that irrigation is absolutely essential—it is the lifeblood—for agriculture in most of the region. (The only exceptions were certain parts of the northwest, in the Ili region.) Throughout most of the region, rivers and streams supplied by melting glaciers and snow had for centuries been supplemented by complex networks of underground irrigation canals. Irrigation was already well developed four decades ago (in fact, it had been developed centuries ago), but the amount of land irrigated had been substantially expanded since that time. This expansion had largely been the work of the Production and Construction Corps. Agricultural mechanization also had been promoted actively in Xinjiang—more than in most of China (except for northeast China)—and in 1987, I was told, two-thirds of all land preparation, over one-half of all seeding, and about one-fifth of harvesting in Xinjiang were handled by machines.

Animal husbandry also has contributed to the region's economy in very important ways. In 1988, the principal areas that were devoted exclusively to grazing animals were the traditional grasslands, which are mainly in the mountains inhabited by the Kazakhs, Mongols, and Kirghiz. Areas where animal husbandry is mixed with some farming had increased, and I was told that now many farming families raised some animals. Altogether, I was told, there were about 32 million animals in Xinjiang in 1988—more than double the number of human inhabitants in the region. Approximately 25 million were sheep and goats (roughly 21 million sheep and about 4 million goats); more than a million were horses, about 160,000 were camel, and there were large numbers of various other animals—cattle, donkeys, mules, hogs, and so on. With its 160,000 or so camel, Xinjiang ranked second only to Inner Mongolia in its camel population. Its officials said that it had the second ranking in sheep and goats—although actually SSB statistics showed Xinjiang marginally ahead of all other regions, including Inner Mongolia. According to local statistics, the pastureland areas in Xinjiang that were currently usable totaled roughly 127 million acres; however, much of this was still not in active use, so there was considerable room for expansion of animal husbandry.

The development of Xinjiang since the 1950s had been possible because of the investment of a very large amount of capital in the region—especially for its industrialization but some for modernization of agriculture as well—that had come from the central government, directly or indirectly. Even in 1988, the central government, and the Production and Construction Corps operating under its leadership, still managed much of the economy and provided much of the investment. Local officials estimated that of the gross value of the region's industrial output, roughly 30 percent was accounted for by enterprises still directly managed by the central government and its ministries; about 20 percent was accounted for by industries directly run by the Xinjiang Production and Construction Corps (which was under the supervision of Beijing's Ministry of Agriculture). The remaining 50 percent was accounted for by enterprises in the region that were directly under the region's government.

A great deal of the capital—even that needed by the regional government's own enterprises—actually had come, and continued to come, from Beijing, through central government investments and other kinds of financial support provided from the center to the regional government. Xinjiang was, therefore, like most of northwest China, heavily dependent on Beijing. Deputy Chairman Mao said to me that annual expenditures by the region had varied in recent years between Y 3 billion and Y 3.3 billion. Of this, local revenues had usually provided about half or less of what was needed. The annual subsidies provided by the central government had ranged between Y 1.2 billion and Y 1.7 billion. Xinjiang was subsidized more generously than Gansu, I was told (both by the governor of Gansu and the deputy chairman of Xinjiang), because it had a much larger minority population.

Xinjiang's officials were obviously pleased that they were getting this kind of special treatment from "the center." They pointed out, with satisfaction, that they were receiving better treatment than the nearby province of Shaanxi. Although the amount of subsidy given by the central government to both Xinjiang and Shaanxi was about the same, in per capita terms Xinjiang did better since its population was about half the size of Shaanxi's. Officials in Xinjiang obviously regarded themselves as competitors with Shaanxi as well as other provinces in the northwest. Deputy Chairman Mao attributed his region's better treatment, compared even to Shaanxi, in part to the large minority population in his region, but he also hinted that it might be related to the strategic location of Xinjiang and to the large continuing role of the PLA and the Production and Construction Corps in the region.

                              *   *   *

It did not take me very long, during my stay in Xinjiang, to realize that the Xinjiang Production and Construction Corps (which I will hereafter refer to simply as the Corps or the PCC) played a unique, extraordinarily important, and in many respects dominant role in the region's entire economy. It is common in Western countries to use the term "company town" to describe cities where one corporation or industry plays a dominant role. Before I left Xinjiang in 1988, I decided that it was quite valid to call Xinjiang a "company region." The Corps' employees and their families constituted about one-sixth of the region's entire population, and the economic clout and pervasive influence of the Corps were evident everywhere.

One of the first clues that alerted me to the extraordinary importance of the Corps was its headquarters building in Urumqi. Located a little south of my hotel, on the main boulevard leading to the center of the city, it symbolized an institution of enormous power. The building was a huge one, a sprawling, Russian-style structure built in the 1950s, with an air of faded elegance. Its architecture was clearly classical. And it was evident to me that this building housed an institution with power comparable to that of the Party and government. I had read a good deal about the Corps ever since the 1950s, but I had never fully grasped the extensiveness or the importance of its roles in Xinjiang. From the time I first asked about who occupied that building, I began to be told, bit by bit, a great deal about the extraordinary range of the Corps' activities. In virtually every interview that I had, the subject of the Corps' role came up, even when I did not ask about it.

The People's Liberation Army established the Production and Construction Corps in Xinjiang—as it did similar organizations in many other areas of China—right after the Communist takeover of power in 1949. Among the most important of these Corps were, as I noted earlier, those in Heilongjiang, Inner Mongolia, Tibet, and Hainan island; most important of all was the one in Xinjiang. According to one written source, all of these Corps were disbanded in 1975 but then the Xinjiang Corps was revived in 1982, the only Corps to be reestablished. The similar Corps elsewhere reportedly were not reestablished at that time—although I have seen some evidence that many of their components were converted into state farms and continued their existence in that form.

The Corps in Xinjiang, when it was first established in 1950, was headed by the top military leader in the region, Wang Zhen. From the start, it had multiple functions: military, political, and economic. Initially most of its personnel were military men, but over time, even though military men continued to hold many top positions, lower-level cadre positions were increasingly filled with demobilized military men. And gradually its rank-and-file workers came to be predominantly civilians, some of them local people but a great many (especially young people) of them sent from China's eastern provinces.

The Corps from the start was a paramilitary body, with some responsibilities relating to frontier defense, and it has always had responsibilities for helping to protect the Party's basic political power. In addition, from the start it also has undertaken major economic tasks, including land reclamation, building the region's economic infrastructure (including roads), promoting certain agricultural crops, and developing new industries and mines. Gradually the importance of its paramilitary responsibilities declined, and it became—as its name suggested—primarily an organization for production and construction.

From what I had read about the Corps in Xinjiang, I believed that it had remained under direct PLA military control at least into the 1970s. In Urumqi, however, I was told that as early as the mid-1950s a shift from military to civilian administrative control had begun when Wang Zhen left to assume the job of heading Beijing's Ministry of State Farms and Land Reclamation. Even though, I was told, Wang, and the PLA, continued for some time to play important roles in directly managing the Corps, authority over it was eventually shifted to the Ministry of Agriculture and Forestry in Beijing (which later was renamed the Ministry of Agriculture, Animal Husbandry, and Fisheries—and still later was divided into several parts). In 1988, at the time of my visit, the parent organization of the Corps in Beijing was the Ministry of Agriculture. These successive ministerial parents of the Corps provided, over the years, the bulk of its start-up capital for most projects. But I was told that gradually, over time, the Corps was able to generate an increasing amount of income from its own operations and therefore had larger resources of its own for investment. The parent ministry always exercised a great deal of direct control over the organization, though. (One person said to me that "most of the Corps' income" still went "directly to the ministry," but I was not able to confirm whether that was true.)

However, as is so often the case in China, the exercise of administrative control was very complicated. As of 1988, I was told, the Corps was under the "dual leadership" of the ministry in Beijing and the region's government in Urumqi. Apparently, though, the Party organization in Urumqi was actually the organization that made many of the key decisions affecting the Corps' activities. The regional government was then expected to implement these decisions, under central supervision.

The Corps was still organized, on paper at least, along military lines. Under its commander (a man named Liu Shuangchuan) and the Party secretary, who also served as political commissar of the Corps, the work force of the Corps belonged to farms and enterprises, all of which reported to overall umbrella units that bore military titles—divisions, regiments, and so on (which were the equivalents of prefectures, counties, and other civilian government units). The Corps formulated its own budget and prepared its own annual and long-range plans, but these then had to be approved by the ministry in Beijing and then integrated into Xinjiang's overall budget and plan. (The region's economic statistics did include, as I noted earlier, the Corps' output, even though it did not include the output of military industries.)

The Corps was described to me as an organization that "integrated agriculture, industry, and commerce" and "combined Party, government, army, and economic functions." It ran its own police force and courts as well as its own educational institutions and hospitals. As of 1988, under its headquarters there were 11 major "divisions"—1 industrial division and 10 agricultural divisions. The industrial division was considered to be a unit of "prefecture level" and was located in the city of Shihezi, north of Urumqi. (This city, mentioned earlier, was founded in 1950. It contained textile, sugar, and other plants that used mostly local Corps-produced agricultural outputs and raw materials.) Under all of the Corps' divisions, there were nearly 800 industrial and transportation enterprises and 170 state farms and state ranches. I was told that as a result of the national economic reforms introduced in the 1980s, the household responsibility contract system had been implemented, and much of its land had been divided among 17,000 household farms—although these apparently still operated "within the framework" of the state farms system. (I did not really understand what this change meant.)

Altogether, as of 1988 the Corps administered areas with a total population of almost 2.5 million—a figure that included employees plus their family members. This number amounted to roughly 18 percent of the entire population of Xinjiang. The gross value of its industrial and agricultural output varied between Y 3 billion and Y 4 billion. (In 1986, it was Y 3.1 billion.) In sum, its output accounted for between one-fifth and one-quarter of the entire agricultural and industrial output, by value, of Xinjiang. Its farms, ranches (animal husbandry areas), and industrial and other nonagricultural enterprises were located throughout much of the region in both northern and southern regions, although its activities were said to be considerably larger and more extensive in the north. Even though it had developed many of Xinjiang's industrial and nonagricultural enterprises, the Corps' main focus continued to be on agriculture and animal husbandry. Reportedly, over the years it had reclaimed about 2.5 million acres of land and had built more than 31,000 miles of irrigation canals and channels.

The reality was that the Corps operated, as it had from the start, as a special "economy within the regional economy"—even a "state within a state"—and it was indisputably the dominant economic organization in the region. It was distinctive because it was organized separately, along military lines, and continued to have especially close links with both the central government and the military establishment. No one I met seemed to think that this was likely to change in the foreseeable future. (According to one person with whom I talked, the formal name of the Corps had been changed, not long before, to the Xinjiang Agricultural, Industrial, and Commercial Corporation of Land Reclamation, and the title of its head was now "president" instead of "commander," but everyone I met, without exception, still referred to it by its old name, the Xinjiang Production and Construction Corps.)

*   *   *

The unique economic roles of the Corps probably helped explain the fact that, in 1988, the presence of the PLA—as well as that of the People's Armed Police and uniformed Public Security personnel, impressed me, as I noted earlier, as being more visible and obvious in Xinjiang than in other areas that I visited in the northwest. As I have said several times in earlier chapters, in most of west China I was forcefully struck by how little evidence I saw of military and security forces; in most places that I visited they were extremely inconspicuous, if not invisible. However, in Xinjiang I saw a sizable number of uniformed personnel, often in clusters, sometimes in substantial numbers, not only in Urumqi but also in other places that I visited. In Urumqi, in particular, I observed more uniformed personnel—most of them Peoples' Armed Police—than in any other western city I visited. And on my trips to both Nanshan and Turfan, I passed quite a few small military barracks and outposts. Even though all the top civilian officials I met heavily emphasized that the Party had supreme leadership in the region and that Party leadership was effective within the PLA, the unusually large military presence seemed to suggest that the PLA exercised an especially large influence on the society as a whole and probably exerted an especially large influence on both the Party and the government in this region.

To put this in perspective, few of the soldiers or uniformed men of any kind whom I saw were actually armed, and almost none of them were carrying military weapons or equipment. A majority of the uniformed persons on the streets were simply engaged in normal activities of daily life, and I did not sense or see evidence of any particularly serious tensions between army men and civilians, who seemed to mix quite freely and easily. The degree of militarization was much less than what I had observed in Xinjiang in the late 1940s. At that time, national and provincial forces were everywhere; they were engaged in two major international conflicts and were facing some serious domestic political problems as well. In 1988, I had no sense of that kind of militarization. In fact, the military presence that I observed in Urumqi in 1988 was considerably less than what I had seen in coastal Chinese cities during 1972–1973—in the wake of the Cultural Revolution and the alleged Lin Biao coup. Nevertheless, the PLA presence was notable and, I thought, significant. I could only speculate about the reasons for it, but several explanations seemed plausible: the region's long history of ethnic tensions, its strategic position vis-à-vis the Soviet Union, and the history of complicated international conflicts all around the area—as well as the extraordinarily important role that the PLA was playing in the region's economy.

The more that I learned about the role of the PLA and the Corps in Xinjiang, the more I suspected that Xinjiang would be a difficult place to implement many of the reforms that Beijing was trying to promote throughout the country at that time. Nevertheless, as I did everywhere that I visited, I attempted to learn as much as I could about the extent to which the new reform policies had begun to change the local economy and society. My conclusion was that although there had been efforts to implement many of the reforms, and they had brought some changes, Xinjiang—even more than most other areas in west China—lagged far behind coastal China in moving in the direction of structural reform.

What had changed in Xinjiang during the reform period, it seemed to me, was the general political, economic, and social atmosphere. As elsewhere in China, I found that the old political and social controls characteristic of the Maoist era had been greatly loosened in the 1980s; ideology had eroded and become much less prominent; people seemed to speak with remarkable freedom and frankness, even with a foreigner; and as the average standard of living had improved, expectations and hopes had risen. Important in all of this had been the rapid development of modern communications, which had helped to increase knowledge as well as raise expectations and had created new links with the rest of China and the outside world. Although Xinjiang was not as "open" as many eastern parts of China, by 1988 nine of its cities had been declared open to foreign travel, and the number of people moving in and out of the province had grown a great deal. The provincial leadership was trying hard to expand the region's external trade, but they were finding that this was not easy to do.

Top local officials readily acknowledged, as did local academics, that even though they were making serious efforts to try to implement major economic reforms, many of these reforms were extremely difficult to implement and were taking root very slowly. Almost everyone agreed that the area had not gone very far in changing the basic structure of the economy—to say nothing of the polity.

As of 1988, for example, even though the leadership had tried to encourage the growth of collective enterprises, state enterprises still accounted for 86 percent of the region's gross industrial output, the output of collective enterprises had reached only 14 percent and the output of private enterprises was negligible. Local leaders were acutely aware of how different this was from the situation in east China, where collective enterprises had become the most dynamic and fastest-growing elements in the economy. The main reason for the lag in Xinjiang, according to the leading local planners I interviewed, included the remoteness of the region, its lack of capital, the underdevelopment of local science and technology, and also deep-rooted "historical reasons." I suspected, and heard hints, that resistance by "conservatives" (probably, I guessed, especially some military men and leaders of the Corps), as well as the lack of local entrepreneurship, were among the major obstacles to "reform of the ownership system." Township enterprises were now being actively encouraged, I was told, and were developing somewhat more rapidly than in the past, but one local planner explained that "because we started late, we therefore are still far behind others on this." As of 1987, the gross output of township enterprises of all kinds (including those in industry, transportation, construction, commerce, and service industries) was only Y 1.67 billion—and of that output only about one-third came from township industrial enterprises. This was a very small amount by any standard—but particularly so compared to what was happening in eastern provinces.

In the region's state enterprises, I was told, the manager contract responsibility system (*chengbao zhidu*) had finally been adopted—although quite late compared to in other places. About 60 percent of the state enterprises' managers were said to have been selected recently by "open bidding" (at least in the formal sense)—that is, by competition—but the effects, everybody admitted, had been limited, partly because of "our basic shortage of talent." Most local managerial personnel had been educated mainly to serve as technicians (many were engineers), some leaders stressed, and therefore they lacked the kind of broad managerial experience and expertise that the region needed. Moreover, my informants said, people "hesitated to apply for managers' positions under the new system in part because of the risks that they would have to take."

Apparently, the reform policies arousing the greatest hopes in Xinjiang were those associated with China's new open policy. The leaders and officials I met in Urumqi, like those in other inland areas, were ambivalent—to say the least—about Beijing's coastal policy, and they feared the possible consequences of giving special economic privileges to east China. One scholar said—speaking diplomatically and cautiously but nevertheless frankly—that "Xinjiang of course supports this policy, but in the academic world, as well as in the government, there are very different views. If the coastal areas sell more abroad, this may open up the domestic market more for the interior areas ... however, it is possible [and clearly he meant "likely"] that Xinjiang will fall further and further behind. It is really a challenge to us."

Some economic officials said to me that because Xinjiang borders on the Soviet Union, Beijing had recently given the region some special trading privileges. Officials referred to a document that they called the "Nine Points," which they said permitted the regional government to engage directly, once again, in direct trade across the border, to hold trade talks with foreigners (meaning, in 1988, mainly the Russians), and to send trade exhibitions abroad. (Nobody explained precisely what the nine points were.) Clearly, these officials hoped to expand external economic relations as much as possible, as soon as possible. They also hoped to broaden Xinjiang's trade within China. Yet they felt that they were still far too limited by existing restrictions imposed by Beijing.

I received no statistical data on the growth of Xinjiang's economic ties with other Chinese provinces, but economic planners emphasized that ties had grown substantially in recent years. They emphasized that it would be highly desirable to increase collaboration among the five northwestern provinces and regions—and they favored the inclusion of Inner Mongolia into the group of northwestern provinces and regions—which had recently been proposed. Deputy Chairman Mao hoped, specifically, that the regular annual meetings of the leaders of these five (or six) areas would lead to much closer cooperation. He also wished to expand collaboration between bureaus, commissions, and other organizations at lower levels. He told me about how he had recently led a delegation from Xinjiang to Xi'an to meet officials from both Shaanxi and Gansu to discuss expanding cooperation in scientific and technical education as well as to exchange views on ways to solve the special educational problems of minority students. (These were issues that, within Xinjiang, were within Mao's special area of responsibility because he headed the so-called *wenjiao* system handling "culture and education.") Mao felt that this kind of regional coordination could be strengthened a great deal.

Even though Xinjiang's officials fervently hoped to develop broader foreign economic relations, it was clear that as of 1988 their efforts both to expand trade and to attract foreign business investments had accomplished relatively little. The Xinjiang Foreign Affairs Bureau informed me that in 1986

Xinjiang's exports had totaled US$205 million and that its imports totaled only US$79 million (the latter, for some reason, had declined substantially compared to 1985). I obtained no figures for 1987 or 1988, but officials said that the region's foreign trade had increased some but not very much. Border trade with the Soviet Union, which had been formally authorized by the central government and had resumed in Xinjiang in 1984, was starting to revive mainly at the Ili town of Korgas, but the volume of this trade was still small—considerably smaller, they said, than Sino-Soviet border trade in Heilongjiang. They complained because Beijing gave stronger support to the latter. In the local cross-border trade that was developing in Xinjiang, the Soviets were especially interested in obtaining Chinese consumer goods, but the Chinese, on their part, found relatively little that they wanted to buy from the USSR. I heard several estimates of the value of that border trade at the time I was there; Deputy Chairman Mao thought that it had reached the level of roughly 30 million Swiss francs a year.

Local planners said that as of 1988 there were only 27 enterprises in all of Xinjiang in which there was any foreign involvement of significance; these included both cooperative projects and equity joint ventures (mostly the former). There was only one wholly owned foreign enterprise in the region, I was told: a shoe factory. They mentioned one hotel that was an equity joint venture. But, they said, most of the projects involving foreigners were "cooperative ventures," with limited external involvement. The total amount of foreign capital involved was small. In 1986, according to the Xinjiang Foreign Affairs Bureau, it totaled only US$14 million. Compared to national statistics showing the rapid growth of foreign investment in China's coastal provinces, these figures were pitifully small. They highlighted the fact that Xinjiang's hope for expanded economic relations were still largely unfulfilled. However, some people expected that this could change after the completion of the new Sino-Soviet rail link—or, perhaps, when the central government changed its mind and decided to permit major foreign participation in petroleum production in Xinjiang.*

Xinjiang's overall economic targets for the rest of the century, as described to me, were very ambitious. The target set for the region's gross economic output in the year 2000, I was told, was six times that of 1980 (a target even more ambitious than the national aim of quadrupling output in the same period). Their hope was to raise per capita incomes accordingly. To try to achieve such aims, they said, they would continue to develop agriculture and animal husbandry; raise output of alloy metals and petroleum; intensify sur-

---

*During 1991–1992, Xinjiang's cross-border trade grew rapidly, and reportedly Premier Li Peng stated that China might soon authorize major foreign investment in petroleum development in Xinjiang.

veying of the region's underground resources; strengthen transportation, communications, and other infrastructure; and try their best to increase their earnings of foreign exchange. They expected the central government to continue providing large amounts of capital to Xinjiang, but their plans also called for an increase in the region's own investments, and they strongly hoped to obtain additional new capital from more affluent Chinese provinces—as well as some foreign investments (perhaps substantial foreign investment, if oil development could be opened up to foreigners).

*   *   *

Local leaders assumed that in the 1990s, as in the 1980s, the relatively relaxed international environment would encourage faster economic development. If post–Cold War trends—especially Sino-Soviet détente—continued, they said, the region could enjoy one of the longest periods without conflict in its modern history. When I asked whether there was any danger that old conflicts might be revived, they expressed confidence that this would not happen in the foreseeable future. But when I asked how close relations with the Soviet Union could become, they acknowledged that they thought there would be severe limitations. In passing, they mentioned that "the three big mountain passes" to the Soviet Union had still not been opened (in 1988) to normal traffic and stressed that "political factors" still limited Sino-Soviet contacts. But they insisted that the border was "calm." I inquired specifically about the dispute between China and the Soviet Union over the Pamir Mountains—a long-standing dispute involving about 20,000 square kilometers (approximately 7,700 square miles) of territory—and asked what the prospects for a total solution were. They had no answer, but they claimed that it was not a serious problem, even though the issue was unresolved. The area was quiescent, they insisted, and they expected that the status quo would continue to be maintained. (I got no clues as to what the prospect was for an eventual formal resolution of their conflicting territorial claims.)

The Chinese-Mongolian dispute over the Beidashan area—which was very active when I had visited Xinjiang in 1948—had been essentially settled, I was told. One member of the Academy's Institute of History said to me that the resolution was a result of a Sino-Mongolian agreement, the main basis for which was said to be compromise by the Chinese side. My informant claimed that whereas China "kept control of the mountain ridge," in return it "gave up its claims to the north slope and the Burgan [Bulgan] River area," which had been ceded to Mongolia. The explanation that this scholar gave for the compromise was interesting. The Chinese had long considered the area involved to be Chinese territory, he stated, even though both the Soviets and the Mongols considered it to be part of Mongolia. "However," he said, "in the late 1940s a Chinese Communist publication in Yan'an had published the Soviet position on this area, without challenging its validity, and this gave Moscow a strong basis for arguing that China had accepted its position." Whether this was in fact the most important explanation for the compromise, apparently the Chinese had given up some of the territory that they had claimed and, my informant asserted, had subsequently made further small border adjustments. As a result, this border was no longer considered to be an area of contention.

Deputy Chairman Mao asserted, flatly, that there were "no current tensions over the region's borders" because both sides (meaning all sides) were willing to maintain the status quo under existing circumstances. The hope in Xinjiang, clearly, was that there would be continued calm and further improvement of overall relations among all nations within the region—and that this would lead to a significant increase of trade—particularly with the Soviet Union but also through the Soviet Union with Europe. Whether or not these hopes for the future will prove to be justified, the relatively calm international environment during the 1980s had clearly been beneficial to Xinjiang's modernization.*

All in all, Xinjiang's leaders were obviously concerned when I met them in 1988 that their region still lagged seriously behind China's coastal provinces, and they feared that this gap could widen in the period ahead. They nevertheless seemed to have considerable optimism about the region's prospects for future growth. Their urge to catch up, and to compete with other Chinese provinces, was very strong. So, too, was their desire to expand external economic relations as much as possible, to speed the process of modernization. They felt under considerable pressure to proceed with structural economic reforms, but because of numerous special obstacles to the reforms in the region, they were cautious about introducing many of them. It was apparent that systemic changes in Xinjiang would be slower than in many other parts of China. One reason was the continuing domination of the PLA and the Production and Construction Corps. Another was the continuing complexity of ethnic problems and relations within the region.

---

*In the three years following my 1988 visit, the dramatic collapse of communism in both Eastern Europe and the Soviet Union changed the situation in fundamental ways. Initially, Beijing was seriously concerned, and in some respects alarmed, by these developments. However, the Chinese government continued to try to strengthen relations with the government in the Soviet Union during 1989–1991, and trade expanded. Then, after the dissolution of the USSR, China rapidly established ties with all the successor states. But there was continuing concern that there could be chaos in the Soviet Union, which could have unpredictable effects across the border in northwest China.

CHAPTER SEVEN

Inner Tibet

GANZI (SICHUAN)

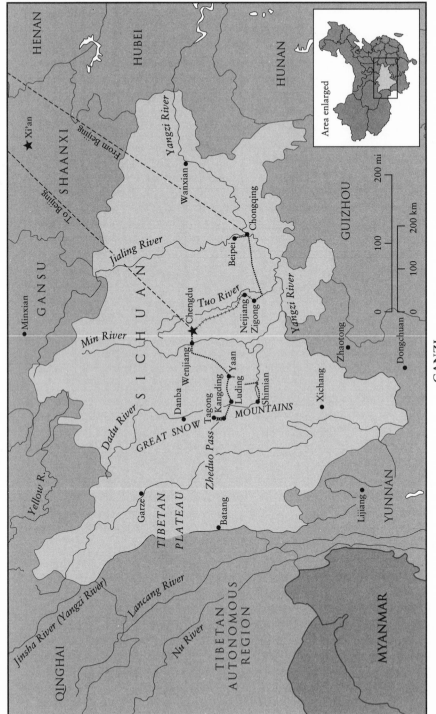

Area enlarged

HENAN

HUBEI

HUNAN

SHAANXI

Xi'an

From Beijing

To Beijing

Wanxian

Yangzi River

Jialing River

GANSU

Minxian

Chongqing

Beipei

GUIZHOU

200 mi

200 km

100

100

Chengdu

Tuo River

Neijiang

Zigong

Yangzi River

Zhaotong

Dongchuan

S I C H U A N

Min River

Danba

Wenjiang

Yaan

Xichang

Dadu River

Tagong

Kangding

Luding

Shimian

MOUNTAINS

Zheduo Pass

GREAT SNOW

Yellow R.

Garze

Batang

TIBETAN
PLATEAU

Lijiang

YUNNAN

Jinsha River (Yangzi River)

Lancang River

Nu River

TIBETAN
AUTONOMOUS
REGION

QINGHAI

MYANMAR

I HAVE ALWAYS liked to travel off the beaten track. For anyone with these predilections, Ganzi is the place to go. It was the most remote and difficult-to-reach area that I visited in 1948. Getting there in 1988 was a little easier, but it was still, by far, the most difficult trip that I made.

Once a part of Xikang (Sikang) Province, Ganzi was incorporated—some years ago, after the Communist takeover of China—into Sichuan Province as an autonomous Tibetan prefecture (*zhou*). Geographically, it still is—as it has always been—a part of the Tibetan plateau. Anyone who has visited any part of this plateau knows why it is called "the roof of the world": Virtually all of the plateau is above 10,000 feet high, and from this starting point many mountains rise much higher—in fact, some of them are the highest in the world. Ganzi, like the eastern part of Qinghai Province, is where agricultural China meets the Tibetan grasslands, and it is where Han and Tibetan cultures confront each other. Much of the territory is extremely rugged, and all of it is awesome. To reach Ganzi from Yaan (the westernmost city of any size in Sichuan Province before one climbs toward the Tibetan plateau), one must travel over the most intimidating and frightening roads that I have ever seen, going up and over Two Wolf Mountain (11,273 feet) to reach the capital city of the prefecture, Kangding, which used to be known as Dajianlu (Tachienlu) when it was capital of Xikang Province. Kangding is an extraordinary little town that lies in a tiny pocket-size valley, over 8,400 feet high, in the midst of the majestic Great Snow Mountains on the edge of the Tibetan plateau. Not far to the south of it is the towering peak of Minya Gongka (Gongga), 24,784 feet high, which is the tallest peak in this part of China until one reaches the Himalayas. Just a few miles to the west of Kangding, on the road that leads to Lhasa, one climbs up and over Zheduo (Chedo) Pass, 14,071 feet high, the gateway to the plateau and the grasslands.

When I visited this region in 1948, Xikang Province was a wild, primitive, cops-and-robbers frontier region. It was the private domain of one of China's most notorious warlords, Liu Wenhui. As a recognized political entity, Xikang had emerged gradually, during the first part of this century—following a sizable increase of Chinese migration into the fringes of the area. The leaders of the Qing (Manchu) dynasty called the area the "Sichuan Border Region" (Ch'uan Bian) at that time, and Beijing sent its own officials to govern the territory overlapping Sichuan Province and Yunnan Province. Subsequently, in the late 1920s, the Nationalist government appointed Liu Wenhui—then one of Sichuan's leading warlords—to be the military commander of the region. This, in effect, created a de facto new province. The area was officially made a province, with Kangding as its capital, in 1939, roughly a decade before my first visit. The province—and Liu's personal control of it—lasted thereafter until the start of the 1950s, when the Communist takeover occurred.

*   *   *

My 1948 visit was a memorable expedition (and it really was an expedition rather than simply a trip). I made the trek to Kangding and the grasslands with Philip Valdes, a Yale classmate who had just taken up his first foreign service post, in the American Consulate in Chongqing (Chungking). I asked Phil whether he thought he could get the use of one of the Consulate's jeeps and come with me to the grasslands. He was delighted to do so and was able to obtain permission because no one from the Consulate had visited that area for many years. It was a lengthy drive. We first went from Chongqing to Ziliujing (Tseliuching; now called Zigong), then to Neijiang, and on to Chengdu, the capital of Sichuan Province. From there we traveled southwest to Yaan. All of the roads were terrible. It took several days to get even to Chengdu, and we slithered almost all the way through mud. Then, on the one-day trip from Chengdu to Yaan, the gravel-and-dirt road was so rough that we destroyed three of our four jeep tires (and had to order replacements to be sent from Chengdu—which arrived several days before our return trip). On the entire trip, we drove through tightly packed villages, traditional settlements typical of the Sichuan rice area. There were virtually no other modern vehicles on the road, but the road was crowded with human traffic and every conceivable kind of traditional vehicle, including wheelbarrows (most of them loaded with huge, squealing pigs on their way to market), carts of all kinds, some rickshaws, donkeys, and occasional sedan chairs (carried by two or four men, depending on the load); the sedan chairs carried wealthy merchants wearing old-fashioned men's gowns. Most short-distance freight was carried by men using shoulder poles. Even bicycles were extremely rare in remote areas of China at that time; one saw them mainly in larger towns.

Along the way, except in Chengdu, we stayed in old-fashioned Chinese inns. We intended to do this in Yaan, but when we arrived there we encountered some local European Catholic priests who were delighted to have visitors and invited us to stay the night at their establishment. The offer of comfortable beds and homemade grape wine was more than we could resist. It was a pleasant stay, and we learned a great deal from them.

Then the adventure began, an arduous trip by foot through high and rough mountains to Kangding—which took five days going and four days returning—and then, from Kangding, a fascinating foray further onto the Tibetan grasslands, by horseback. For us to make the trip, it had been necessary to obtain the personal permission of Liu Wenhui in Chengdu. Actually, Chengdu, the capital of Sichuan, was Liu's real headquarters; from there he exercised remote control over Xikang, which he visited only occasionally.

Liu's personal army, which maintained control over part (but by no means all) of his province, was headquartered in Yaan. Only the provincial civil administration was physically located in Kangding, the official capital of the province. The Kangding government had been run by a small group of loyal subordinates of Liu's ever since 1939. Liu's army in Xikang was the real basis of his power, however: His forces, as well as the civil administration, were financed largely by illicit opium trade. Liu's military men purchased the opium—most of which was grown high in the mountains, a great deal of it by minority peoples—by providing rifles and other arms to the opium growers, and then Liu sold the opium elsewhere. Not surprisingly, lawlessness and banditry were rampant, and I was told that virtually every family owned arms of some kind for their own defense.

The five-day hike from Yaan to Kangding covered roughly 120 miles, most of it climbing. (The return trip took only four days because it was largely downhill.) A few years earlier, during the Sino-Japanese war, a narrow gravel-and-dirt road had been built to Kangding, but it had fallen into total disrepair—with many landslides blocking it—and was totally unusable. On our trip, we sometimes followed the route of the road, but often we went directly up over mountain paths. Virtually all traffic was by foot—although a few people traveled by sedan chairs and some cargo was carried by small donkeys. Red "brick tea," grown mostly around Yaan, was the main commodity going to Kangding, where it was sold to Tibetans (tea had long been a basic staple in the Tibetan diet, and all of it had to be "imported" from Chinese areas). Most of the tea bricks were carried in large baskets (some weighing over 150 pounds) strapped onto human backs. The carriers included many women and some young children, although their loads were generally lighter than those carried by men. Once the tea reached Kangding, it was transferred to leather containers and then transported on the backs of yaks to the grasslands. The main Tibetan commodities carried from Kangding to Yaan included musk (used mainly for perfume in the West) and medicinal herbs; since these items were lighter and less bulky than the tea, for most carriers the return trip to Yaan was relatively easy.

Because banditry was so prevalent in the area at that time, Liu Wenhui had insisted on assigning an armed guard to accompany us. So when we reached Yaan, the officers of his 24th Division selected an escort consisting of one young lieutenant and a squad of ordinary soldiers—all well armed. On the trip, these soldiers never had to fire their rifles in anger, but in some of the deep gorges through which we went along the way they considered it great sport to fire their rifles into the air, mainly to hear the shots echo but also to try to dislodge some of the high rocks at the top of gorges. They stopped only after I sternly protested and pointed out that the dislodged rocks might well hit one of us.

Initially we followed part of the old road, but when we had to climb over Two Wolf Mountain we abandoned the old road entirely and gingerly picked our way along tiny paths, just wide enough for one person—or at times two—to climb directly up over the mountains. These paths were cut into the side of high cliffs, with huge drops below. Along the way, we spent our nights at small, dark, traditional inns, used mainly by the tea carriers—virtually all of whom smoked opium in the evenings to relieve the pain and strain of their difficult work. The food in the inns was so bad—unsanitary and virtually inedible—that in several places we restricted our diet to tea and hardboiled eggs; I learned that eggs in their shells are among the world's best "naturally packaged" foods—and are always clean.

In 1948, when we finally reached Kangding, I was flabbergasted to see a bustling trade center—with a mixed Tibetan and Chinese population—whose shops were well stocked with a wide variety of goods, including British cigarettes and other consumer goods from the West that had been transported all the way from India across the entire Tibetan plateau. A small 500-kilowatt plant provided some electricity, and the town even had a movie theatre! As the key trading center linking Chinese and Tibetan areas, Kangding (which almost everybody there then called Dajianlu) had developed into a trading town very similar to Kalimpong, which provided a key trading link between Tibet and India.

From Kangding, we traveled by horseback through Zheduo (Chedo) Pass onto the grasslands, where we visited Tibetan villages and several homes. When we went through the pass, it was snowing—on July 4! Once over it, we entered an area of beautiful green grasslands, which looked to me very much like mowed lawns or even golf greens; they were covered with a profusion of breathtakingly beautiful wildflowers. On this trip, too, we had to take an armed guard; this time it was simply one rifle-toting Tibetan. The government of Kangding insisted on it, and even the local Tibetans we met argued that it was essential. After we had gone through the pass, we had one very brief scare, when a mountain patrol of armed Tibetans suddenly appeared, charging out of nowhere and galloping toward us. It turned out, though, that they were regular Tibetan militiamen, and after stopping us they were cordial and okayed our further travel; from then on we proceeded unmolested.

*   *   *

In 1948, Chinese maps showed Xikang Province stretching to a point quite near Lhasa, but these maps bore little relation to reality. Chinese influence in Tibet Proper has steadily declined for many years—a process that accelerated in the early part of the twentieth century—whereas the influence in Tibet of the British, based in India, steadily increased until it greatly overshadowed that of the Chinese. (Although the British usually acknowledged

Chinese sovereignty—or at least suzerainty—over the area, sometimes they simply ignored it.) For some years, China had had no official representation in Lhasa, but in the 1930s the Chinese reestablished an office there, which was under Nanjing's Commission on Mongolians and Tibetan Affairs. However, they were unable to exercise any very significant direct influence in Tibet proper at that time, and by 1948 the Chinese exercised no political control at all beyond the Gold Sand River (or Jinshajiang—the upper reaches of the Yangzi River in this region).

In fact, except for a few Chinese traders authorized to go to Lhasa, travel for Chinese was very severely restricted beyond Batang and Dege, the main towns just east of the river—which was about halfway to what the maps showed to be the province's western border. Beyond that, the town Qamdo (Chamdo)—and all the rest of what the map showed to be Xikang, to say nothing of Tibet proper—was for all practical purposes beyond the reach of Chinese political influence. The Tibetans maintained custom posts at Qamdo, just as the Chinese did at Kangding. In the regions between Kangding and the Gold Sand River, there was some Chinese presence, but even in this area Chinese control was relatively loose. Small garrisons (or at least a few soldiers) were stationed in virtually all towns of any size, and the county magistrates were Han Chinese, but at the township (*xiang*) level, all leaders, I was told, were Tibetan. The Tibetans maintained their own militia forces and generally managed their own affairs. In the southern part of Xikang, an area that I was unable to visit, there was a large concentration of Yi people coexisting with a sizable group of Han Chinese. These Yi—generally called Lolos (a derogatory term used by the Han Chinese)—were tribally organized. A few Yi also lived high in the mountains in the region between Yaan and Kangding. Most Yi were farmers, and one of their principal crops was opium.

When, in planning my 1988 trip, I asked to put Kangding on my itinerary, I was told that the area was still "closed" and that no foreigners had been permitted to visit the area in recent years. Eventually, though, I was told that the authorities would make an exception in my case and grant me special permission to revisit the area. It did not take me very long to see why Kangding and almost all of Ganzi were still considered by officials in Beijing as unsuitable places for foreigners to visit. Although modern paved roads had in recent years been built—or rebuilt—in the region, traveling into the area was still extremely difficult. My trip, though much easier than the one in 1948, nevertheless was by far the most rigorous of any that I made in 1988. To begin with, the roads were horrendous and the topography was just as daunting as I had remembered it. When I began the car trip from Yaan to Kangding, my first reaction was one of incredulity that I had actually hiked the route four decades earlier, but the farther I traveled, the more I began to feel that no sane person would choose to drive on such dangerous roads. At times, in fact, I was tempted to get out and try to walk again!

Once the trip was completed, however, I had no doubt that it had been worth the effort. I learned that even though the region was still extremely remote and difficult to reach, and even though the road links with the "outside world" were abominable, modernization had nevertheless penetrated the area in a very significant and fascinating way, and its economy had developed much more than I had expected. In real terms, the area obviously had become far more integrated into the Chinese nation than it had been four decades earlier—and linked much more significantly to the modern world as a whole than I expected. But it is not going to become a tourist area any time soon. Nowhere on our route were there any modern commercial accommodations or facilities considered usable by foreign travelers.

Nevertheless, the government guest houses where I stayed were equipped with many of the appurtenances of modern hotels, including TVs!—and they were a far cry from the primitive inns in which I had stayed on my first visit.

*   *   *

I began my trip from Yaan on an early morning in April with my young escort from the Sichuan Academy of Social Sciences and an Academy driver to pilot our shiny new Toyota sedan. My escort from the Academy was Zhang Xiangrong, a delightful 28-year-old man who was bright, curious, and open-minded. He had accompanied me throughout Sichuan for almost a month. Together, we had first gone from Chongqing to the north, to an area where in 1948 I had made a study of local village government and politics. From Chongqing, we had gone to the city of Zigong and then on to Chengdu. There I spent a significant amount of time in the adjacent prefecture of Wenjiang, where I was again able to make a study of local government in Sichuan. The son of a university professor of engineering who had retired and taken up traditional painting, Zhang also had studied mechanical engineering, at Chengdu's Science and Technology University. After graduating in 1983, however, he had decided to join the Sichuan Academy of Social Sciences and soon rose to be deputy head of its five-person Foreign Affairs Office. His wife worked in a candy factory, and they had a two-year-old child. His real love, I learned, was Western music; he played the violin (and said that he fervently hoped that his child might be able to become a professional violinist), and he spent almost all of his spare money on tapes of Western classical music.

The entire distance of our journey from Chengdu to Kangding was 322 miles, I was told. It took us the better part of two days to get there. The first leg, from Chengdu to Yaan (which had become a sizable city and was now capital of a prefecture) was 94 miles, and it took us three and a half hours.

After a short stop at Yaan for lunch, we proceeded on the next leg, which took five and a quarter hours to cover 129 miles. We reached the small town of Shimian, a county seat, arriving late in the afternoon. All of this part of the route on the trip going to Kangding was on the "new road"—which had not existed at all in the pre-Communist period. Unlike the "old road" (which I will have more to say about later), this one went quite far to the south of Yaan before turning north to the city of Luding, where it merged with the "old road." After spending the night in the county government's guest house in Shimian, we left very early the next morning, going via Luding to Kangding, a trip of over 100 miles—which took us five and a half hours. Along the way, we stopped for a while at the town of Luding, which I wanted to see again because it was so famous in Chinese Communist historical lore as the place where revolutionary troops—on the Long March—had fought their way across the Dadu River in 1935 in one of the most celebrated feats of heroism during that historic trek. We also felt that we could take a little while to relax since our trip was all but done; the final leg to Kangding was only 25 miles or so.

But then, just five or six miles before we finally reached Kangding, our car broke down. It simply expired, and nothing we could do revived it. Unfortunately, there was no AAA in Ganzi. Our driver—and I as well—fiddled with it for quite a while but we could never determine what the problem was. Our driver checked the carburetor, dissected the distributor, and then fiddled with almost every part of the car—but with no results. Mortified, he urged Zhang and me to try hitchhiking our way to Kangding while he continued to work on the car. We decided to do this, and when a small—in fact, tiny—motorized jitney crammed with eight local Tibetans dressed in traditional Tibetan clothing came by, we flagged them down and asked if we could somehow squeeze into the vehicle. They were mystified by seeing a foreigner and not very enthusiastic about giving us a ride, but finally they allowed us to sit on a small spot on the floor to the rear of the jitney. We arrived in Kangding about midafternoon, with a great sigh of relief. Since leaving Chengdu, we had gone through two municipalities (Chengdu and Yaan), three prefectures (Wenjiang, Yaan, and Ganzi), and nine counties (Shuangliu, Xinjin, Qionglai, Mingshan, Yingjing, Hanyuan, Shimian, Luding, and Kangding).

On this initial trip—going from Yaan to Kangding—we took the new road, I was told, because ordinary passenger cars such as ours simply could not travel on the old road; it was so rough that only vehicles with very high axles were permitted to use it. However, for our return trip the government of Kangding County loaned us a sturdy, high-axled Toyota Land Cruiser (our sedan was still out of commission), so we returned to Yaan by the old road, which followed the route that I had walked in 1948. On this route, the distance from Kangding to Yaan was only 165 miles—about 65 miles less than on the road that went via Shimian—and it therefore took only 7.5

hours (instead of almost 11). But, for me, most of those hours were pure terror. I had found the new road scary enough: It clung to the side of cliffs for much of the way, as we went over Two Wolf Mountain and wound our way through the mountains on the side of the Dadu River. But the old road turned out to be, without any question, the most terrifying one that I had ever traveled by car (it had been much less terrifying on foot). Partly because it was shorter, it went directly up and over Two Wolf Mountain, clinging to mountainsides, with huge drops below, and going through one tight hairpin turn after another. It turned most of my few remaining hairs one or two shades grayer.

Our original plans for the return trip called for traveling from Yaan to Chengdu on the same road that we had originally taken, but just outside of Qionglai we encountered a major truck accident (one of half a dozen or more that we saw on the entire journey), which entirely blocked the road. Since the prospects for opening up the road soon were extremely uncertain, we veered off and took an entirely different route, which went west and north before reaching Chendu.* Altogether, our route all the way from Kangding to Chengdu totaled 240 miles—roughly 82 miles shorter than the route out.

The opportunity to cover so much territory—along two different routes—in this remote area of southwest China, which I had not visited for four decades, was fascinating for me: It provided a remarkable opportunity to observe both changes and continuities in a region virtually unknown to most foreigners.

When we left Chengdu on the first leg of the trip to Ganzi, it was raining and was surprisingly cold and clammy for an April day. Fortunately, forewarned that we would encounter cold weather, I had put on the double-knit long johns that I had brought from the United States. The road on which we started was one of three that went from Chengdu to different Tibetan areas. One led to the south, via Leshan (near the famous sacred mountain of Emei). Another went further north, via Wenjiang and Guanxian (the location of some of the oldest large irrigation works in the world), eventually leading to other routes going both north to Qinghai and west to Tibet. The road we took was the main one to Yaan and Kangding and was, I thought, the most important of the three.

At the start, the road was impressive. Some sections of it were four lanes wide. But it soon narrowed to a two-lane road and continued that way for

---

*On our return trip, we went through the same two municipalities and three prefectures that we had on the trip out, but this route took us through three counties that we had not seen—Tianchuan County in Yaan Prefecture and Dayi and Chongqing counties in Wenjiang Prefecture.

most of out trip. The road was paved with a macadam surface and was mostly quite smooth, although in some places where it was heavily worn the surface consisted mainly of rough gravel. For almost the entire way to Yaan, we traveled through densely populated and generally fertile agricultural areas. This region was part of the famous Chengdu plain, which is one of the best agricultural areas in China. We did not reach hilly country until shortly before reaching Yaan. Most of the way, the road was very crowded with a remarkable variety of modern vehicles—trucks, passenger buses, civilian "jeeps" (Chinese made), small crawling tractors (used mostly for transport rather than fieldwork), and bicycles. We saw and passed some carts—either pushed or pulled—but these were mainly in the towns. Apart from the ubiquitous bicycles, almost all the vehicles on the open road were motorized, which represented a very great change from when I had traveled this road four decades earlier. Two kinds of heavy-duty trucks predominated: the "Liberation" model, made in Changchun, and the newer "East Wind" model, made in Wuhan. Both are tough vehicles, but the latter seemed to be the preferred one, at least in the minds of the drivers with whom I talked. At times, the traffic was so great that it created chaos, especially near some of the larger towns, where accidents were frequent. The first of many accidents that we saw was one where a truck had hit a bicycle and injured its rider. Public Security Police were trying to manage a large crowd of rubberneckers who had gathered to see what was taking place, and a well-marked modern police car with flashing lights arrived as we were leaving the scene.

In each of the counties through which we traveled, our road cut right through the middle of the county seat. Seeing these towns, I was impressed by all the evidence that they were rapidly developing and modernizing urban areas. However, the towns—and the surrounding countryside—were still a fascinating mixture of new and old. Each county seat had some areas that looked very traditional, yet each also had areas where recently built modern sections were full of "high-rise" apartments as well as new, modern-style office buildings—a great many of which were four, five, or six stories high. The apartments were of the kind that had sprouted throughout China in most urban areas—even in relatively small county seats. Everywhere I went, it was evident that urban Chinese were increasingly becoming apartment dwellers, even in fairly remote areas. In all the county towns, there also were many new stores—most of them with living quarters above them, in the traditional way, with the store portion of the building below. Not far from Chengdu we passed a large, refurbished Daoist (Taoist) temple, but in general we did not see very many really old historical buildings.

On this route we passed a great many small factories. The majority of them were in or near the county seats, but there were quite a few deep in the countryside as well. The number of factories was certainly less than in the Yangzi valley or the Pearl River valley areas; nevertheless, I thought the number of factories was impressive. Most of them here, as in coastal China, had been built during the 1980s. We also passed many very busy open markets. These, too, were mainly in the towns. They were full of goods of all kinds and masses of people. To my surprise we saw a number of newly built hotels in these county seats. The countryside that we passed through looked notably prosperous, especially in the "suburbs" of the county seats. In some of these areas, old-type rural dwellings were intermixed with new farmhouses, but in many areas, even some deep in the countryside, new farmhouses had transformed the appearance of the place. In general, the rural housing looked quite good. It was obvious that even many of those that were built in the traditional fashion were relatively new—built probably in the 1980s— and consisted of fairly large two-story brick structures. It appeared that almost all of the relatively affluent farmers now had such two-story farmhouses, many of which were in modern style.

The main crops in this area were rice, rape, beans, vegetables, and some sugar—as well as tea in the hills around Yaan. Everyone with whom we talked said that the rural economy was doing well, and everything I saw supported this. However, the preparation of the fields, then under way, was still being done mainly with buffaloes drawing plows rather than by tractors. Quite a bit of the work was still being done by human labor. In one place, for example, I saw a group of about 30 people who were transplanting rice by hand in the fields, in the time-honored fashion that has been used in China for centuries. My companions guessed that this group probably consisted of close relatives. (The old collectives no longer existed.)

Almost everyone we saw was well dressed. Although in this area the majority still wore fairly traditional clothing—cotton jackets and pants, mostly blue—nevertheless there were quite a few who wore "modern" clothing; some of these still wore Mao suits, but a sizable number wore Western clothing. There were quite a few men—many in the towns, but some even in the countryside—who wore Western-type suits. And I was struck by how many women—especially younger ones—wore Western-type slacks, blouses, and jackets. A few wore Western-type skirts. (There were more slacks than skirts because, I was told, women in Sichuan tended to wear slacks until the winter was entirely over and then switch to skirts in the summer. When we went it was still cold, even though it was April.) On the entire route, I saw only two people—both of them old men—wearing clothing that was ragged and patched. In the fields, there were a few, but not many, farmers who still wore traditional straw hats (conical ones in the first areas we went to, then round-capped ones later on). Most of the farmers, though, wore modern raincoats, made of thin plastic, which had hoods attached to them to pull over their heads. I saw only one group of people on the entire route who were wearing traditional raincoats made of coir (coconut hair), which had been virtually universal in the 1940s. The further we went toward the west, the more traditional the clothing became; however, even far into the hinterland, a great many people were wearing modern clothing in the larger towns. Especially striking were the many women dressed fashionably, in jackets, slacks, and high-heeled shoes.

*   *   *

On my first trip along this route, four decades earlier, this area had been extremely isolated, with virtually no sense of connection with the rest of the country, to say nothing of the rest of the world. Now, it was obvious, there were all kinds of links that tied this area to the rest of China and to the world. The road was one of the most important links. In addition, all along the way we saw telephone lines that tied the entire west to the eastern parts of the country (electric lines were ubiquitous). In this region—as in every other remote area of China I had gone through—I was amazed by the number of TV antennae in most areas, even in the countryside, and in one county seat we passed a local TV broadcasting tower. The density of the antennae varied along the route; they were less numerous in relatively hilly areas but were never completely absent anywhere along the road.

Since our road was one of the major military as well as civilian routes to Tibet, I was alert to see what signs I might observe of military vehicles, personnel, or installations or military activity of any sort. I was again surprised, as in other areas I had recently visited, by how few signs we saw of any military presence or activities on the route between Chengdu and Yaan (although, as I will note later, further on we did see somewhat more evidence of a military presence, both within Yaan and in Ganzi Prefecture—but even in those areas it was less than I expected to see). Shortly before we reached the town of Mingshan, the road took us through two large arches, both of which proclaimed that this was the road to Tibet. The signs on both of them called for "army-civilian cooperation" and for the building of "spiritual civilization" on the Tibet road. At this point there was one large area that looked as if it might be a military barracks and a compound full of big trucks—doubtless army trucks—yet even there I saw few people wearing uniforms. The area did not have the feel of being militarized in any sense, and it seemed to me that the road was ill-suited for military traffic. As we went through every town, we encountered serious bottlenecks and chaotic traffic jams—mainly connected with markets—which obviously would pose major problems for any attempt to move military vehicles through the area rapidly.

By late morning—from Mingshan on—we could see mountains in the distance; they were covered with mist. Before long, we began to climb, going through hills where terraced fields of rice and tea covered virtually all of the slopes. Many fields clung to hillsides that had a slant of 45 degrees or possibly more. Slightly before noon, we finally entered Yaan's "suburban area," where we saw quite a few small factories and many three- and four-story-

high houses, and then we soon reached the center of Yaan Municipality—
now a sizable city. Set in a valley surrounded by high hills, it had become the
seat of a prefecture.

Yaan had grown enormously since my previous visit. It now was a "real
city" in population and size and had the ambiance of one. In the 1940s, its
atmosphere was very much that of a remote provincial town—even though it
already was fairly large. By 1988, remote as it was, it looked quite modern.
Numerous newly built office buildings and apartment houses, many of them
multistory structures, were scattered throughout the city, and TV antennae
were visible everywhere. My escort, who had visited Yaan four years earlier,
said that most of the modern buildings had been constructed since his previous visit. He could easily distinguish these new buildings from the older,
post-1949 ones, he said, because the older ones were almost all stodgy, "So-
viet-type in style" buildings, dating to the 1950s and 1960s. The new buildings looked more "Western": There was much greater variation in their architecture compared to those built in the 1950s and 1960s, and there also
was more color in the materials used and in the decoration of the buildings.
Like large cities and towns throughout most of China, Yaan had experienced
a remarkable building boom during the 1980s—especially during the years
from 1984 or 1985 on.

We did not stay long at Yaan this time (we were scheduled to stop and stay
overnight there on the return trip). We did take time for lunch, though. We
ate in an old-fashioned restaurant where we ordered typical Sichuanese
dishes—eels, double-cooked pork, and peppery bean curd. The meal was excellent and relatively cheap (only Y 3 per person). After lunch we pressed on
toward Shimian. On leaving Yaan, we crossed a modern bridge that spanned
the small river along which Yaan had developed. There were armed guards
at both ends of the bridge (members of the People's Armed Police). This
seemed unusual, and I asked about it; nobody was able to explain why the
guards were there. They did comment on the bridge, though. It had been
built, they said, in the 1950s, according to specifications that had been presented to the Chinese by Soviet advisers. Local people now thought the
bridge was very poorly built—although it looked all right to me.

The driving became much harder after Yaan, and this continued to be the
case all the way to Kangding. As I noted earlier, our route out was via the
new road. This route was certainly less spectacular—or dangerous—than
the old road that I had seen in 1948 on which we traveled on the way back to
Chengdu. Nevertheless, traveling even on the new road was not lacking in
excitement.

Within 15 minutes of leaving Yaan, we entered an area of quite high
mountains. Although the road was paved, and ostensibly was two lanes
wide, it actually was very narrow. We climbed steadily for a substantial distance, winding along the edge of a mountain overlooking a streambed far be-

low. The road continued to narrow until it really was not more than one-and-a-half lanes wide. This width continued for most of the rest of the trip. Passing other vehicles therefore involved a good deal of courage. Almost always, two approaching drivers played the game of "chicken" to try to force the other to get to the side of the road, much to my discomfort. We usually won, which always gave our driver great pleasure but usually left me limp.

The road passed directly through a great many small villages—and between them an even larger number of smaller hamlets and tiny clusters of farmhouses. Most homes along the way were very traditional ones, made of mud bricks, sometimes whitewashed, and generally topped by sloping tile roofs. On virtually all mountains adjacent to the road, cultivated fields—some terraced and some not—crept high up into the mountainside. Many of them were on slopes between 40 and 50 degrees. I had remembered these incredible fields from my earlier trip. I could not really understand why the fields did not simply wash away whenever there was heavy rain. Then, for a short stretch, the valleys through which we were traveling shrank to almost nothing more than the road and a stream along it, yet even in these areas we saw tiny patches of yellow rape fields. (Rape seeds are used to make vegetable oil, which is the main cooking oil used in this area.) Nowhere in China is land really wasted. In this part of the country, this is even more the case, if possible, than elsewhere. Often one had to look almost straight up to see the sky, yet even in such areas one could see cultivation taking place on the hillsides, and in many places one could see wooded regions on the top of the mountains.

* * *

Less than an hour after we had left Yaan, the climbing road entered a series of tight hairpin turns, clinging to the edge of the mountains, where the land dropped precipitously to a valley far below. At one point, thick fog reduced visibility to almost zero. I was told that when visibility was good, from this point one could see Minya Gongka, the spectacular snow-covered peak that is the tallest in this part of China. I very much wished to see it because in 1948 the mist made it impossible—despite the fact that I walked through various areas where this peak was supposed to be visible. On this trip, once again the thick fog prevented me from seeing Minya Gongka, though we saw many other very high snow-covered mountains.

Thereafter, the roads went steadily down, down, down, again following a series of fairly terrifying hairpin turns, until again we reached a narrow valley. Following this valley for a considerable time, we passed through many traditional villages and hamlets. On this stretch, there were few modern vehicles on the road—only an occasional cargo truck. Eventually, though, a little more than an hour from Yaan, we drove through an area where again we saw quite a few small factories and approached another county seat, the town of Yingjing, the first real town that we had seen since leaving Yaan. Set in a small valley, surrounded by agricultural fields, it proved to be—like every county seat that we passed through—a town with quite a few modern, multistory, flat-topped buildings, mainly four-story apartments or two-story shops and business offices. There were parts of the town in which the predominant buildings were still traditional, one- or two-story, tile-roofed structures. But modern buildings were rapidly taking over.

The next two-and-a-half hours or so, from Yingjing to Hanyuan, we did a great deal of climbing, but the mountains were interspersed with agricultured valleys. Immediately after leaving Yingjing, we drove through a valley with many small villages—located at frequent intervals—where the road narrowed and also steadily deteriorated. Now much of the road was not paved, and the gravel was very rough. Moreover, it narrowed further, until it was really only about one lane wide. Although most of the homes in this area were traditional, we continued to see a great many TV aerials. Much to my astonishment, we passed several areas along the road where young men were playing pool, on Western-style pool tables. Throughout much of China, pool had become a fad in recent years, and I had seen pool tables on roadsides in many widely separated parts of the country. I was nevertheless surprised to see them here. (About 20 years earlier, I had been struck in a similar fashion by how pool tables had spread throughout the countryside in Taiwan.)

Eventually the road again went steadily down, through another series of hairpin turns, to a small valley paralleling a stream. In this area villages consisted of about 20 to 40 homes. From time to time, we would pass on the road groups of small schoolchildren, always very colorfully dressed, and obviously walking very long distances to return from school to their homes. For some reason, the volume of truck traffic increased substantially in this area. We also passed, for the first time since leaving Yaan, many people carrying large and heavy freight loads in long baskets on their backs—exactly as they had done when I was in the area in the 1940s. I was told, however, that no long-distance freight was carried in this manner anymore. But this method of carrying goods was still widely used for short distances.

Our road—and the stream we were paralleling—eventually joined the Dadu River at Hanyuan, and from this point on we saw many small rope or chain-link suspension bridges, most of them precarious and usable only for pedestrians crossing streams single-file—exactly as I had remembered from my trip four decades earlier. At one point, the road dropped very low and was at river level, and there we passed a town with five-storied apartment houses, located near a tiny hydropower station. Also nearby was a pumping station, and we could see the pipes from it climbing high up the mountain behind the station, carrying water for distant fields. The hydropower station was producing electricity, and adjacent to it was a transmission station.

Once again, we climbed up through a narrow valley. In this one, though, there were neither houses nor cultivation, only some rock quarries where the workers were removing, by hand in small baskets, sizable rocks that had been blasted from the mountainside. Their living quarters were flimsy shacks constructed of bamboo and reeds. As we climbed up and up, the weather became worse, and we entered an area of clouds in which the fog was so dense that, to my dismay, we could barely see the hairpin turns in the road. Everywhere in the road, moreover, fallen rocks littered—sometimes almost blocking—the roadway. Some were huge boulders. The driver told us at that point that we were then going over a high point on Two Wolf Mountain. He himself complained that the altitude was making him woozy, which was not very reassuring to us. (Assuming that the driver was right, this clearly was a very different part of Two Wolf Mountain from that on the old road that I had seen in 1948 and that we crossed again on our return trip—where the views were much more spectacular.)

After we emerged from the clouds, we again descended into a small valley, where we saw very few vehicles. We did pass, for the first time, several large trucks carrying huge logs, which had come from far beyond Zheduo Pass. (We were to see a great many of them later.) The few villages in this region were obviously extremely poor, and because of the altitude, the small terraced fields that we saw were still brown and barren in April. (I was told that farmers could only raise one crop a year in this area, whereas in most of Sichuan the majority of farmers grew two or even three crops every year.) As we kept descending, though, the land gradually improved as the altitude dropped, and eventually we reached an area where the fields were green, the villages were much more numerous, and the houses were generally well built; by the time we reached this area we again saw many TV aerials. As we approached the next county seat, Hanyuan, there were many signs that we were entering an area of greater prosperity. As in Yingjing, this county town had a new skyline of multistory apartment buildings; most of them were four stories high. The people were better dressed, and in the "suburbs" we saw many brick farmhouses, most of them surrounded by fruit trees, which obviously belonged to relatively well-off farmers.

Hanyuan straddles a tributary that flows into the Dadu River—which also is a tributary of the Min River; the Min eventually joins the Yangzi. This county town, I was told, is a major stop on the route that goes to the southern part of Sichuan Province, to the city of Xichang, and then on into Yunnan Province. (A second road going south starts at Shimian and joins the one from Hanyuan as it goes to Xichang.) The newest part of this new road is really the section between Hanyuan and Shimian, and then from there to Luding. After leaving Hanyuan, we paralleled the Dadu River, on its north side, following it all the way to Shimian. Even though, on this final stretch of the road to Shimian, we occasionally went through narrow valleys with scattered villages and towns, very large areas appeared to be almost totally unin-habited. For much of the way, in fact, the road was literally cut into the side of mountains high above the Dadu. In some places, the river was a celadon color; in others, it was a light milky green. But in many places it was turbu-lent white water.

The traffic was very light in this area, which led our driver to conclude that he could step up our speed. He was wrong. Within a period of about an hour, we were involved in three "incidents." In the first, the driver failed to see a barrier stretching across the road, which proved to be a checkpoint where loggers' trucks were stopped and examined by officials who tried to enforce safety standards. I yelled to the driver to warn him that a barrier was ahead, and he tried at the last minute to brake, but we nevertheless went straight into—and hit—the iron bar that was across the road. Fortunately the damage was minimal. Not long thereafter, our driver, who again was driving much too fast, blithely ignored a man on the side of the road who rather frantically was waving a red flag to us. The driver simply ignored it and did not halt, until many yards down the road several other men even more frantically waved to him to stop. He finally did. Their reasons for stop-ping us were excellent: A dynamite charge was just about to go off a short distance ahead of us. We braked and stopped just as the charge exploded. It was a rather close call. The third incident was one in which we simply ran into a large rock in the middle of the road. The noise was alarming when the rock hit our undercarriage. Again, though, we were lucky and there was no really serious damage. (Actually, we hit quite a few smaller rocks along this part of the road, and on each occasion our driver stopped and solemnly ex-amined the undercarriage of our car, but in each case he then proceeded on-ward at a breakneck pace.)

*   *   *

As we neared Shimian, we passed a large area of flowering *tong* (*tung*) trees, which had beautiful white blossoms. Sichuan is famous for these trees, the nuts of which produce a very valuable vegetable oil that is highly prized all over the world for its value in making paint. (It was once a major Chinese export, and a great deal of it was sold to the United States.) For centuries, the Chinese have regarded soot made from *tong* wood ("China wood"), com-bined with soot from the wood of pine trees, to be one of the best forms of the carbon that is needed to produce *mo,* the black ink used in Chinese cal-ligraphy and painting.

Across the Dadu, we could see, at various points, several coal mines lo-cated halfway up the mountains. And on the top of one peak was a TV relay station. I kept seeing things that surprised me. At one point, near the place where the TV station was, for example, we passed quite a few very fashion-ably dressed young women, wearing high heels, casually walking on the road. Finally, we reached our destination for the day, Shimian. The town's name means asbestos, and even before crossing the river to the town we could see, high up on the mountainside, a large asbestos mine, below which, next to the river's edge, was a large white pile of the mine's product. Next to the town was the asbestos plant, which was surrounded by five-story apartment houses for workers. One reached the town by crossing the Dadu on a modern, steel, automobile bridge—well built but so narrow that traffic could go only one way at a time. Shimian proved to be a small but remarkably modern little town, resting at the foot of mountains. Its raison d'être was obviously the production of asbestos. I do not know how long it had been mined there, but the mining had clearly been developed mainly since the Communist takeover. Another explanation for the location of the town was that it was located at the juncture of the road coming from Yaan, in the north, and the roads going both northwest to Luding and south to Xichang. I was also told that there were valuable medicinal herbs that came from nearby mountains—which doubtless had been gathered even in early years.

Small as it was, Shimian had quite a few modern apartments and office buildings, some as high as seven stories, and its main streets were broad and paved. Most people on the streets were dressed very much like those in larger cities, even those in east China. Partly because of its asbestos plant, it was well supplied with electricity from a local power plant. The town also had developed into a significant political and administrative center—the seat of government of the southernmost county of Yaan Prefecture.

The population of Shimian, I was told, consisted almost entirely of Han Chinese, but on the streets I saw some colorfully dressed people of the Yi minority who had come into town from the mountains. Local people said, though, that the number of Yi people had declined in this area—even in the deep mountain regions where they traditionally had lived. Since, as I noted earlier, the Yi people had obtained much of their income decades ago from opium, I asked both my driver, who was familiar with the area, and a local man whether—to their knowledge—any opium was still grown in the area. They asserted no, saying it had been stamped out years ago, and I saw no evidence of either poppy fields or opium smoking. Both of them said, though, that they had seen some legal cultivation of poppies for opium (for medical use) in the Aba Autonomous Tibetan Prefecture, far to the north, in another remote area of Sichuan Province.

In Shimian, we were provided accommodations at the Shimian County Guest House (*jiaodaisuo*). It was a simple place, but quite "modern" and clean. It was full of Chinese officials (cadres) of various ranks; most of their vehicles, parked in the guest house courtyard, were either Toyota minivans or "Chinese jeeps" (that is, jeeplike indigenously made Chinese vehicles— not the Cherokee jeep that by this time was being manufactured by a joint venture enterprise in China). Needless to say, the guest house was hardly in the league of the recently built, modern hotels that by 1988 had proliferated throughout east China and major cities elsewhere, but it was far superior, by any standard, to the Chinese inns that I had stayed in on my 1948 trip. I was given room number one—the best in the house—and was impressed by it; I had expected much less. It had a double bed with a soft mattress and sheet (unheard of in traditional inns), a comfortable pillow covered with a clean towel (standard in Chinese sleeping accommodations now—for cleanliness), two traditional Chinese quilts (*beizi*), two easy chairs, and a small desk. In addition to a thermos bottle containing boiling water (also now standard equipment in Chinese accommodations), cups, and packages of tea, the room had some striking and rather unusual decorative touches, including a little *pengjing* (a diminutive garden in a flat pottery dish—similar to bonsai in Japan), some plastic flowers in a vase, and two poster-size prints on the walls, one of them depicting a waterfall and the other a portrait of a well-known Chinese movie starlet.

The room also contained a reasonably good color TV set (by 1988, these too seemed to be essential equipment in first-class guest houses as well as in virtually all hotels, even in the most remote areas that I visited). I discovered that despite the surrounding mountains, the TV reception was quite good. Even more important, the room had its own bathroom; this was virtually unheard of in remote Chinese guest houses—even in the 1980s. Shimian was obviously determined to show its Chinese VIP cadre visitors how modern it had become. My enthusiasm about the bathroom, however, was soon tempered. The good news was that it had a bathtub, with hot water and soap, which was unusual, and even a private urinal. The bad news was that, for serious business, one still had to go outside—taking one's own toilet paper—to a separate public outhouse, a dimly lit building with open stalls, where, as elsewhere in such establishments, everything smelled to high heaven. In the 1940s, such outhouses were the only toilet facilities available when traveling in the deep interior; I discovered in 1988 that although some places had developed bathroom facilities within major buildings, in a great many places far off the beaten track—such as in Hainan Prefecture in Qinghai, and, I was soon to learn, in Kangding—even visitors staying in the best guest houses still had to use outhouses located some distance from the main buildings. I also discovered that—as in the 1940s—good heating of buildings was rare. Generally one was compelled to cope with changing temperatures by adding or subtracting from one's clothing. The Shimian Guest House had no heat. Even in April, I was chilled to the bone. I suspect that in winter it was extremely cold—although tolerable if one wore very warm clothing (padded clothing in the old days; knitted thermal underwear in the 1980s).

Like most traditional hotels or inns in China the guest house had no chests of drawers or closets; in fact, my room had no place at all to put anything in the way of baggage or belongings. This was still the norm throughout China except in very modern hotels. But it did not seem to bother Chinese travelers very much. I was always impressed that most Chinese "travel light," with very few clothes or other belongings of the kind that most Westerners carry when they travel. (Actually, after visiting a great many Chinese apartments and homes, even those of relatively affluent people, it was apparent to me that the majority of Chinese simply do not accumulate, even at home, the plethora of belongings that Westerners generally do—although now a great many of them do possess a variety of basic consumer durable goods.)

The guest house in Shimian contained two dining halls. One was a small VIP room, where we ate; the food in it was certainly edible but was by no means memorable. The service was notable, nevertheless; we were served by smartly dressed young women who wore tailored white jackets and black slacks and sported permanent waves. In the dining room, there were copies of the *Sichuan Daily,* a provincial Party organ, that were only two days old. In the back of the guest house was the main mess hall, where almost everyone else ate. It was a very large room, and the ambiance was extremely noisy and lively. The atmosphere was considerably more interesting than that of the small VIP room since I could hear—even just passing by it—snatches of interesting gossip passing among the cadres.

*   *   *

After dinner, which was served very early (about 5:45 P.M.) I walked the streets of Shimian. But I soon discovered that it was a very small town, and in a few minutes I exhausted the sight-seeing possibilities, so—like local people—I went to bed early. As I noted in an earlier chapter, the daily schedule and pattern of life in most remote Chinese towns as well as villages is essentially diurnal, determined largely by the rhythms of sunrise and sunset. This was not quite as true in 1988 as in 1948, when there was no electricity, but even with electricity people retired very early—although many now watched television in the evening. In most small towns, including Shimian, the day began when the cocks crowed. For some, it ended when it became dark, but now, for many, TV had transformed their evenings and provided their principal entertainment as well as source of information.

I tuned in to my TV set at 6:30 P.M. and ruminated on the possibility that at that moment perhaps more people were watching TV in China than in any other nation in the world—at least, so it seemed to me in light of how pervasive TV had become even in remote areas. I also pondered the implications of the end of the kind of extreme isolation that had characterized most areas of China until recently. The programs that I saw on TV in Shimian raised a wide range of unanswerable questions in my mind about the likely impact of the unprecedented exposure that people in remote areas of China now obtained to images and ideas coming from very distant places, not just from China's major metropolitan centers but from faraway foreign cultures and societies. The first program that I saw when I turned on my TV at 6:30 P.M. in Shimian was one in which a Chinese commentator was discussing Western paintings—specifically landscapes painted in oils, a medium with which most Chinese have been unfamiliar. A series of Western paintings flashed onto the screen, and each was accompanied by a commentary presented by a very modern young Chinese woman. In the background, Western symphonic music played softly. The next program that I watched was the nightly national news (more about that later). Then, when it was finished, I watched a Western movie, dubbed in Chinese, of a kind that I found astonishing in this remote area. It was a British comedy of manners, set in the 1920s. It seemed bizarre that it was showing on the TV in Shimian.

In the national news, consisting of broadcasts and rebroadcasts from Beijing (which came after the program on Western painting and before the British comedy), there were several segments about the important National People's Congress sessions then going on in Beijing. I was able, in early April, to watch fairly extensive TV coverage of this meeting, over a several-day period. I found some of the interviews, and discussion by commentators, quite remarkable. This was a time when openness in China probably reached its peak before the Tiananmen tragedy in 1989. There was unprecedented coverage of several plenary sessions as well as special discussions, interviews with officials, and reporters' commentaries. I had not seen anything quite this open in the years before 1988—and certainly TV has not had comparable programs since 1989 (although in my opinion they doubtless again will, in due time).

As I watched the TV coverage of this National People's Congress session—in several places in west China—I was reminded of my experience 40 years earlier, in the spring of 1948, when the Chinese Nationalists convened their "First National Assembly," which I had attended as a newsman for several days in Nanjing and then tried to follow from a distance—from the local newspapers—as I traveled throughout many areas of Sichuan. In 1948, the National Assembly meeting was a serious and in several respects fascinating affair. As a newsman, I attended the first few days of the meeting and interviewed many of its delegates and reported on it back to the United States. It, too, was unprecedented in many respects: There was much more open political debate than in any comparable meeting previously, and there was an open challenge to Chiang Kai-shek by Li Tsung-jen (which now would be romanized as Li Zongren) and others. However, when I left Nanjing and traveled throughout Sichuan, I found that very few people in Chongqing or elsewhere had any real interest in or knowledge of what was going on at the National Assembly meeting.

In 1988, I found that the level of interest in the National People's Congress meeting was considerably higher, and the level of knowledge about it in remote places was much greater—largely, I think, because of the TV coverage of the meeting. However, even in 1988, I did not see much evidence that people really felt "involved"; there was still considerable validity to the ancient adage that the "emperor is far away." The people with whom I discussed the meeting did not seem to see any direct link between the discussions and debates going on in Beijing and their own lives or problems. The top leaders chosen ("elected") by the National People's Congress were mainly Party elders from the Long March generation. There had been a fairly dramatic and far-reaching generational change throughout China in many political positions, especially of the provincial and lower levels. Younger men had been elevated to responsible positions. However, this was not reflected in the choices made in Beijing at this National People's Congress meeting. At breakfast at the guest house in Shimian, I asked my tablemates what their reaction was to the selection of such old leaders. The answers I received were interesting and indicated the growing gap between generations in China. (I was repeatedly impressed wherever I went in China in 1988 by evidence of this growing gap, and I felt that it would inevitably have important, probably profound, long-term political implications.) One man at my breakfast table in Shimian (a man in his fifties) replied to my question: "It is of course very appropriate for older men to hold these positions, because they have experience." The reaction I received from a young man, who was in his twenties, was exactly the opposite: "No-no-no; they are of course too old."

When we were preparing to leave Shimian, I asked about paying my bill. I was told that I did not need to do anything about it. The county government, the people at the guest house said, would bill the Academy of Social Sciences headquarters in Chengdu for both my room and board, and I would then settle my accounts with them. This was the way my bills were handled at most of my stops during 1988. Although I carried enough cash in U.S. dollars and traveler's checks to pay all of my expenses, almost invariably my local host—as well as my Academy escort—preferred either that the bills be sent to Chengdu or that my escorts pay for my local expenses—after which I would repay them.

This was different from my experience in most places in 1948. At that time, I was essentially on my own and had to carry enough acceptable legal tender of a kind locally acceptable to pay all my bills myself. Because of the runaway inflation in China at that time, Chinese paper money was absolutely of no use and was not accepted in most places because its value evaporated literally by the hour. During my travels at that time, therefore, in east China I generally carried U.S. currency in fairly large bills and concealed most of it in a money belt under my clothing. In remote places, however, I found that it was necessary to carry most of the money that I needed in the form of Chinese silver dollars or small gold bars. On one of my trips—it so happened that it was my trip to Kangding—I miscalculated what I would need and ran completely out of funds. Desperate, I asked the local government officials in Kangding if I could obtain a loan from them for the money I needed. They rapidly worked out the necessary arrangements for this. (In this case, what happened was very similar to the modus operandi that I followed almost everywhere four decades later in 1988.) The officials in Kangding immediately telegraphed Governor Liu Wenhui, and he authorized them to give me a considerable number of silver dollars. I simply signed a chit (a promissory note for their loan), and then when I returned to Chengdu I repaid Liu. It was obvious that no one had any doubt that a person who borrowed money from Liu, or any of his officials or generals, would rapidly repay it. Similarly, in 1988 no one seemed to have any doubt that anyone who signed chits for debts would repay them rapidly.

*   *   *

The last lap of my trip in 1988, from Shimian via Luding to Kangding, started inauspiciously. The initial stretch of road after we left Shimian, like certain portions we had already passed where the road was cut into the mountains high about the Dadu River, seemed to me to be frighteningly precarious—even more so than the earlier portions. Moreover, the surface of the road was abominable: It was a washboard, so bumpy that it made our teeth rattle. Eventually, however, we reached an area where there were intermittent stretches of paved road, and finally, when we rejoined the old road (from Yaan), the surface greatly improved. From then on to Kangding, although the road was narrow, it was paved virtually the entire way. I was still disconcerted, though, when we went through areas—which we frequently did—where there were huge drops to valleys far below, with no guardrails anywhere to be seen along the road. (Nowhere on the entire route—even in the most dangerous spot—were there any guardrails of any kind.)

As we went along, the mountains on both sides of the river rose higher and higher, and my companions kept saying that Minya Gongka was only a few miles to the west. But we still could not see it, in part because of the clouds and mist but also because we drove through deep gorges much of the way. On the final part of the trip, however, we did see many other very spectacular snow mountains, which rose high into the clouds. My companions kept stressing that this, too, was an area where one should be able to see Minya Gongka, at least on clear days. But never were we able to see it. They were as disappointed as I was because they wanted to show off their famous mountain. They then kept stressing that I certainly should be able to see it on the way back since, they said, on the old road there were half a dozen spots that were really the best places to see the mountain. But I never did see it. It proved to be as elusive a mystery in 1988 as it had been in 1948.

Along the road after we had left Shimian, the population was sparse, but we did see a few farmhouses; most of them were old-fashioned and poor, with mud walls, but with tile roofs. We did see a few relatively new and well-built ones, however, and we even passed a few that were made of brick and were two or three stories high. Shortly after Shimian, our driver pointed to a small town across the river that, he said, was called Anshunchang, a place famous for two things. In 1935, during the Communists' Long March, elements of their First Division, which was commanded by Liu Bocheng with Nie Rongzhen as his political commissar, were able to cross the Dadu River on small boats and began harassing their Nationalist opponents. The crossing here was only a small one, though, so the bulk of their forces had to go further and cross upstream, at Luding. The other thing for which the town of Anshunchang was famous was that in 1864 a famous leader of the Taiping Rebellion, named Shi Dakui (Shih Ta-k'uei), had suffered a major military defeat at this point. (Wherever one travels in China, one encounters many ghosts of past history, and the majority of local people are aware of major historical events at least in the place where they live.)

Beyond Anshunchang, we encountered no significant towns until we reached Luding. I looked forward with special anticipation to seeing Luding again (I had seen it first in 1948) because of its special role in Chinese Communist history and mythology. I found that Luding was still a fairly small town but nevertheless was an extremely interesting place. Surrounded by mountains (as virtually every urban settlement in this region is), the town itself is called Luqiaozhen. It had become the county seat for Luding County, which was now a part of the Ganzi Tibetan Autonomous Prefecture; Luding was located right on its eastern edge. Although the population of the town had not grown very much—in 1988 it was still only about 12,000, I was later told by prefectural officials in Kangding—it nevertheless was the second most populous urban center in the entire prefecture, second only to Kangding itself.

One part of the town was still very traditional; there the typical buildings were two-story, open-front shops and homes—their walls generally built of mud and lattice, and their curved roofs made of dark gray or black tiles. Another part of town consisted of modern, recently built, three- to six-story concrete or brick apartments and office buildings. The centerpiece of the town was still—as it had been in 1948—its famous bridge. In 1935, in one of the most celebrated incidents in the history of the Long March, a Communist unit fought its way across the Dadu River over this bridge. Supported by 13 long iron chains, it was the largest and most important suspension bridge crossing the Dadu anywhere. It remained, in 1948, the most important suspension bridge of a traditional kind in the entire area, but by 1988 a series of modern, strongly built bridges, which crossed the Dadu in several places, were much larger and more important. But this famous chain bridge was still celebrated and had become a major tourist attraction. There was a large plaque on one side giving its history. When I was there, a major refurbishing job was under way.

When we resumed our trip, starting the last leg from Luding to Kangding—a distance of 25 miles or so—we immediately crossed the Dadu on a very modern, two-lane bridge. At that point we passed a gas station—the first that I had seen (or at least noticed) since leaving Yaan—although I was told that all sizable towns along the way (or at least all county seats) had someplace where one could purchase gasoline. From then on we paralleled the river on its other (west) bank for 10 to 15 miles, on a stretch of road that was very similar to the one between Shimian and Luding. Above the narrow gorge, high mountains—many of them snow-covered—rose on both sides. We continued to pass occasional villages, adjacent to small patches of cultivated land, and in this area the houses were mostly made of stone (a few of them were new and quite a few were two-story). Even in this area I was again amazed to see that some of the houses had TV antennae; it was remarkable that TV transmission could reach such deep valleys. Later I learned how this was possible: All along the way, some mountaintops had relay stations, the signals of which could reach into the valleys.

Eventually the Dadu was joined by a much smaller river coming from Kangding. At this point the main road turned west, and we continued on it; a branch turned north at that point, paralleling the west side of the Dadu all the way to Danba in the far north. The scenery on the rest of our route to Kangding was—as I remembered it from 1948—fairly spectacular. Towering rock crags, with scrub bushes clinging to their sides, rose on both sides of the white-water stream. Occasionally we passed a few tiny cultivated plots, with clusters of farmhouses around them, but in general the population was extremely sparse. Traffic on the road was very light, but as we approached Kangding we did pass an increasing number of trucks carrying huge logs, many of them snow-covered because they had just come from distant logging areas high on the plateau, far beyond Kangding. Some of these logs went by road—on the old road—all the way to the Sichuan plain, but some of them, when they reached the Dadu River, were floated downstream to lumberyards located on the river edge.

Shortly before reaching Kangding, we passed a small hydroelectric station, and almost immediately thereafter our car began to sputter and then broke down completely. Further out on the grasslands, I later learned, there were quite a few small army posts—reportedly located every six or seven miles—where truckers whose vehicles had problems could go for assistance or at least could telephone more distant places for parts or assistance if they could not get help there. But, we found no help on the outskirts of Kangding so, as I said earlier, we hitchhiked the final few miles of our trip.

*   *   *

Before I recount all that I learned in Kangding and the grasslands beyond, I will complete my saga of the perils of traveling in the far west of Sichuan

Province by describing my return trip to Chengdu. After our driver had worked for a long time, trying everything he could think of to repair our car, he finally concluded that he simply would not be able to do it, so he, too, hitched a ride to Kangding. There he hired a truck to take him back to where our car was, and somehow they were able to hoist our car onto the truck and haul it into the city. Mechanics in Kangding then worked on the car but finally determined that our generator was "finished," and they said that there was no way that they could repair or replace it there. Our driver then spent several days trying to determine, by telephone, whether any auto shop in Chengdu had a usable replacement in stock that they could send by car to Kangding. The answer, finally, was no. The only thing that we could then do, the driver decided, was to again hoist the car onto the back of a truck and take it all the way back to Chengdu as freight—to await the arrival there of a new generator sent from east China. The car's return trip took place on the same day as my escort and I returned to Chengdu in another vehicle—loaned to us in Kangding. As we wound our way over the mountains, at several points we saw our inoperable passenger car, lumbering along on the back of a truck. It looked very much like a huge wounded animal. (In an earlier chapter, I noted that China essentially is still in the railway age—though its rail network still needs to be greatly expanded. It has begun, haltingly, to enter the automobile age as well. But it has an extremely long way to go to acquire not only the roads but also the gas stations, service stations, and everything else required to support a comprehensive system of motor transport. This is still true over most of China, and obviously it is especially true in remote areas.)

Since our original car was hors de combat, our principal host in Kangding—the county magistrate there—came to our rescue and loaned us a new car. Actually it was a far better vehicle, a larger Toyota Land Cruiser that, because of a higher undercarriage, was able to return on the old road. We took it all the way to Chengdu. The county driver who was assigned to take us back was delighted to have this chance to visit the big city.

I, too, was delighted because it would enable us to retrace my travels of 1948 and go back on the old road. Once we were en route, though, I had steadily growing doubts, and eventually I spent much of my time silently praying that we would make it and that I would see another day.

The first part of the return trip repeated the last part of our trip out, but then, after joining the old road, just a short way beyond Luding, the road first briefly followed the Dadu River and then entered a wide valley in Tianchuan County (still in Yaan Prefecture). Soon after that, instead of skirting the edge of the mountains, as the new road had, the old road climbed almost straight up and over Two Wolf Mountain. The old road was located in the region that I remembered well from my 1948 trip, but at that time, because the road was impossible, we had not always followed its twists and turns but often had simply climbed straight up over the mountains. Now, I saw, with some incredulity, that the road did essentially the same thing.

Once we began climbing the mountains, the entire route consisted of an unending series of tight hairpin turns going up and up; then there was another series of equally unbelievable turns going down on the other side. The road was mostly unpaved, and in places it was badly rutted and extremely rocky. I finally decided that, despite the discomfort of the road, I was glad that it was filled with rocks and ruts, because they were lifesavers. They forced us to slow down, and they reduced our skidding—the surface was extremely slippery, especially near the top (the peak was 11,273 feet high), where the road was snow-covered.

This old road was far too narrow for two-way traffic, so the part that went over Two Wolf Mountain was restricted to one-way traffic. Every morning it was open to vehicles going from Kangding to Yaan, and every afternoon the traffic flowed the other way. As a result, long lines of trucks had to wait on one side or the other for the road to open. Along the road itself, there were a few pull-off areas where one vehicle could get out of the way so that others could pass it, but they were few and far between. The hairpin turns, both on the section going up and that going down, were fantastic. At any point, one could look out, or back, and see several layers of winding roads far below, looking like tiny ribbons attached to the side of the mountain and crowded with what looked like miniature toy vehicles. Here, as elsewhere, there were no guardrails or barriers of any kind on the road's edge, and the drops to the valley below were often thousands of feet. I constantly felt that we were less than a yard from oblivion.

The traffic on the road gave me additional reasons to feel something close to panic. Almost all of the vehicles were large, heavy trucks. Many of them carried huge logs, some of which had a diameter of roughly three feet or so. Others were large army trucks carrying oil tanks, returning empty from the grassland area. The rest of the vehicles carried a variety of products and people. Going up the mountain, we passed a dozen or so trucks filled with uniformed soldiers who, we learned, were men returning home after completing their tours in Ganzi. Halfway down, on the Yaan side, we also passed a small army post, presumably responsible for road security. These few army men did not seem to be doing anything to facilitate the road traffic.

On the Yaan side, the hairpin turns ended when we reached the small village of Xingou ("new gorge"). From then on, the route followed the valleys of rivers and streams. From every valley, cultivated fields climbed up the mountains to great heights. Some of them were terraced; others had small rock borders to prevent the land from being washed away. The first large town we reached was the county seat, Tianchuan, located in an agricultural area on a river that flows toward Yaan. Like almost all the other county seats I saw in this region, it was a bustling place, half traditional and half modern.

After we left Tianchuan, the valley widened, the land flattened, and we soon entered a good agricultural area. Almost every area we went through had its own characteristics and peculiarities. In this region I was struck particularly by the very large number of intercity travelers riding on bicycles. On the way we stopped at a simple roadside restaurant where all of the patrons except ourselves were truck drivers. The meal that we had there was surprisingly good—typical Sichuanese dishes that were very well cooked and tasty.

Finally we reached Yaan, where this time we stopped and stayed overnight. As I mentioned earlier, Yaan had developed, since my last visit, into a fairly large and quite modern city. It had become capital of a prefecture. Much of it was now filled with buildings that had been built during the 1980s. There was little to remind me of what I remembered from the 1940s except one thing: To my surprise, the prefecture's guest house where I stayed turned out to be a building located in the Catholic mission compound where I had slept in 1948. I concluded, in fact, that my room this time was in one of the old buildings that had been part of the compound when I first visited it.

Once restricted to relatively high-ranking Party cadres, the guest house had recently been opened to the public and was serving as a hotel for anyone who wished to stay there and could pay for the room. My room was typical of what I had by this time come to regard as "standard guest house accommodations." The only distinctive and unique thing about it was that my bed was covered by mosquito netting—typical of lowland areas in China's southern areas. The guest house had a huge dining hall; at mealtime it was jammed with people, and a cacophonous roar came from it. It was definitely what the Chinese call *renao*, meaning "hot and noisy"—or lively and good fun.

Actually, the entire city of Yaan was *renao* when we reached it. The reason, I learned, was that the city's "spring fair"—one of two large annual trade fairs—was in full swing. I spent the entire evening walking through the crowded streets and expansive fairgrounds, which were filled with innumerable shops and stalls, most of which were run by private (*geti*) entrepreneurs. They were selling everything under the sun. There was a carnivallike atmosphere; big speakers blared loud music most of the time, and the music was occasionally interspersed with announcements of various sorts. The music was mostly "Western pop." I also noted that quite a few food stalls had, in addition to traditional Chinese fare, various types of foods that had come from the West and had obviously become popular in this region; they included coffee and Western-type buns. I stopped at one large state liquor store to buy a bottle of *baigan* (liquor made of sorghum), which I wanted to get as a gift for our car driver. I discovered that in Yaan, as in most other places that I visited in 1988, the state trading stores were losing out to private and collective enterprises. The manager told me that he was not allowed to sell me a bottle of liquor because I did not have the necessary coupon to give him, but he then immediately pointed out that a private shop just down the road would certainly be able to sell one to me without any coupon. I proceeded to that shop and bought a bottle, but it cost Y 38 (very expensive—perhaps a third of the average monthly salary of some Chinese). It was a very enjoyable evening, and it was quite late when I turned in. The people at the guest house reminded me to put my watch back an hour because it was the Sunday in mid-April when all of China changed to daylight savings time.

On the final leg of our return trip from Yaan to Chengdu, we at first followed the same route that we had traveled when going to Yaan, but, as I mentioned earlier, after encountering an accident in which two trucks had collided and totally tied up all traffic we backtracked (with great difficulty) to Qionglai and traveled a route that went through Dayi, Chongqing, and Wenjiang counties. I knew almost nothing about the first two of these counties, and did not learn a great deal about them on this rapid trip, but Qionglai and Dayi did have, in one respect, a particular significance and historical resonance for me. I had long had a strong interest in Chinese pottery and porcelain, and in a book that I had read several years earlier I had learned that Qionglai and Dayi had, during the Tang dynasty, kilns that had produced a very famous type of pottery. My understanding was that it was no longer produced there, and in any case we had no time to stop.

The main impression that I received as we traveled through this entire region of Sichuan was one of a society and an economy that were definitely "on the move" in an impressive way and were developing and modernizing rapidly. Like most of the rest of this province, the area was one of very intensive agriculture, inhabited by masses of people living in numerous closely linked towns and villages. The roads were jammed with every conceivable type of vehicle, almost all of them motorized. Most of the towns looked quite modern. Local farmers clearly had benefited from the reform policies of the 1980s, and the entire area had a general appearance of prosperity; many farmers had built new homes that were totally unlike those I remembered from the past. Some of them were two or three stories high and contained six to eight sizable rooms. The designs of the homes varied, and many had imaginative decorations. On some of them, there was considerable use of colored tile; others had walls that were painted with bright colors.

For most of the way from Qionglai to Wenjiang, the roads—and the towns they went through—were being rebuilt and transformed, and signs of new construction were everywhere. What had originally been a two-lane road was being widened to a broad four-lane highway (on the pattern of a broad four-lane highway that had previously been built connecting Wenjiang and Chengdu—a Chinese version of a superhighway). Driving conditions were in many respects terrible because everything was "under construction": For much of the way, the road was torn up and large numbers of people were working on it. We—and all others using the road, including those riding bikes—had to pick our way gingerly over large areas of gravel or rock on incompleted portions of the new road. But, to me, despite the discomfort, it was fascinating to see an entire new transportation network taking shape. This was an area, I decided, that would enter the motor age fairly soon—sooner than most of the country, including many areas in the east. Moreover, as the roads were being constructed, new shops and houses were rapidly being built along them. In some places these new shops totally dominated one side of the road whereas traditional shops were left standing on the other—a striking juxtaposition of old and new.

Earlier, before I had started on my trip to Ganzi, I had spent some time in Wenjiang, interviewing a large number of local officials at all levels concerning the organization and functioning of local governments and issues in local politics. I had at that time been greatly impressed by the degree to which Wenjiang had become—at least in Chinese terms—a really modernized area, despite its location in the countryside. The same transformation appeared to be taking place in most of the other county seats that we passed through on the trip back to Chengdu. All of them were experiencing a building boom. In every county seat I saw a sizable number of factories. There were also many factories in the countryside between the towns. Even though this region was not as dynamic or prosperous as certain regions of coastal China—notably those in Guangdong Province and in the Yangzi valley—nevertheless I found the atmosphere dominated by a sense of change, development, and modernization that was impressive to me, particularly since it was such a great change from what I had seen four decades earlier in this distant area. The new roads and new modern communications, the modernized buildings starting up everywhere, the many new township factories, the ubiquitous free markets, the prevalence of modern clothing—these and many other things were dramatic symbols of the transformation under way.

And as we finally returned into the city of Chengdu, my overwhelming impression and feeling was that it had become a large modern metropolis. This was only partly because I had just returned from faraway Kangding. It was basically because Chengdu really had been transformed in recent years—especially in the 1980s—into a modern city, in many respects—dramatically different from the Chengdu I had seen four decades earlier. I suppose that some Chinese visiting Chengdu from the great coastal cities of China may still view it as a relatively parochial and unsophisticated place, but to me—as I remembered the Chengdu of the 1940s, or even the Chengdu that I saw in the 1970s—it was remarkable how rapidly the process of modernization had begun to change the place in the 1980s.

*   *   *

Now, having completed this extended account of my odyssey in getting to Kangding and back, let me return to the main point of my trip: learning what

I could not only about Kangding but also about Ganzi as a whole, including the Tibetan grassland areas to the west. I trust that my account of the trip has made it clear that even though important roads now exist where none were usable in the 1940s, travel to and from the region is still extraordinarily difficult—and requires a sense of adventure. Nevertheless, what I decided after having completed the trip was that without question what impressed me most was the degree to which—despite the difficulty of getting in and out of the area—modernizing forces of a powerful and impressive sort were beginning to change even this remote region in many ways. The area had undergone tremendous change since I had last seen it in 1948. Although in many respects Ganzi obviously remained relatively poor and backward—and still seemed distant indeed from the mainstream of modern development in China—it clearly had been brought closer to the rest of the country in every respect and was much more involved in the major transformation taking place in China than it had been in earlier years.

In Kangding, there was no modern hotel (although there were some traditional inns), so my host put me up at the official guest house of the Ganzi Tibetan Autonomous Prefecture. This was a small two-story structure that was considered to be the place offering the best accommodations in town. It was passable, but even by the standards of interior China (including the standards set by the guest house in which I stayed in Shimian), it was no better than passable. The room in which I stayed did have most of the standard features that I have noted earlier in describing other guest houses. However, my bedroom was a tiny cubicle (its size reminded me, in fact, of some of the miniature older Japanese hotel rooms that I had stayed in during the 1950s and 1960s). Crowded into it were a bed (this one had a pink quilt and pillow), a small easy chair, a small desk, the ubiquitous thermos bottle and packages of tea, and so on. It, too, had the by-now standard TV set—this one a small color set. One unique feature of the room was that it had a small electric stove. This appliance, with heating coils, was designed mainly to boil water; there was a kettle on it, and clearly it had been used on numerous occasions by Tibetan residents to make butter tea. As a result, a faint smell of rancid butter permeated the room. I found the heater useful not for preparing any food or drink but simply for providing a little heat.

My room had no regular heat, and since Kangding lies at an altitude of 8,400 feet,* the temperature was quite cold even in April—which made it very exhilarating and great for sleeping but provided problems for someone used to warmer weather in the spring. I constantly wore my long johns, as

---

*People in Kangding gave me two figures for the town's elevation, but the majority of my informants seemed to agree that it was 8,400 feet.

The armed guards whom Governor Liu Wenhui insisted should accompany me on my trip from Yaan to Kangding because of the lawlessness of this mountain area in 1948 (photo courtesy of Philip H. Valdes).

A typical poor mountain village on the road to Kangding—untouched by the modern world and desperately poor.

Above left: All cargo moving between Yaan and Kangding had to be backpacked or carried by ponies; these porters are traveling a typical mountain path.

Above right: The path over Two Wolf Mountain on my five-day hike from Yaan to Kangding, the return trip took only four days because more sections were downhill (photo courtesy of Philip H. Valdes).

Many white-water streams rushed out of the mountains; crossing most of them required perilous acrobatics over primitive rope "bridges" (photo courtesy of Philip H. Valdes).

Trucks carrying cargo in 1988 on the spectacular and often hazardous road be-tween Yaan and Kangding.

There are still some traditional villages on the new road to Kangding, but like this one, most are now relatively prosperous.

The modern town of Shimian on the road from Yaan to Kanding, where an asbestos plant has been built. Several towns in the area are now modernized.

Hairpin turns on the road between Yaan and Kangding.

A torrential mountain stream, called the Zheduo River, rushes through the center of Kangding. This 1948 photo shows old buildings hanging over its banks and the town's two streets paralleling the river, one on each side (photo courtesy of Philip H. Valdes).

This scene of a woman back-packing a heavy load, tradition-al shops lining the street, and Tibetans and Han Chinese sharing the street with dogs was typical in 1948. There were no modern buildings or vehicles.

Tibetans and Han Chinese trading at a street market in 1948 in Kangding, the meeting place for those from Han Chinese agricultural areas and those from the Tibetan grasslands.

The largest lamasery in Kangding and an important religious center for a large region. Tibetans and Han Chinese (including soldiers) mingled in the open space beside it (photo courtesy of Philip H. Valdes).

Above: Two Tibetans leaning on the new railing along the Zheduo River in Kangding in 1988. The center of town had been totally rebuilt and modernized.

Below left: A bird's-eye view of Kangding, by 1988 modern public buildings, apartments, and factories had moved up the valley toward Zheduo Pass.

Below right: A Tibetan woman shopping at an open-air free market. By 1988, such markets were outcompeting state stores in Kangding, as in China's eastern cities.

A young Han Chinese mother and her child, dressed in modish Western clothes, walk along one of the paved modern streets that have crept up the sides of the hills surrounding Kangding.

The largest lamasery in Kangding was badly damaged during the Cultural Revolution, but by 1988 its restoration was nearly complete.

did most local people, and I tried to warm myself by the stove whenever I was in my room. Nevertheless, I was usually cold. All around the town, high mountains rose almost straight upward, and the entire time that I was there—even though it was still April—a light blanket of snow covered the mountains.

Even though the guest house was in some respects "modern," like in a great many Chinese public buildings its corridors were extremely dimly lit, by very low wattage bulbs, and the entire interior seemed gloomy and dirty. On my floor (the second and top floor), I discovered that there was a young Chinese woman—who sat at a tiny desk next to my stairway—who was responsible for being a kind of concierge. She kept the keys to all rooms, and she was supposed to be helpful to the guests. Instead, she was extremely surly, incommunicative, and totally unhelpful. I never saw her doing anything except watching the TV at her small table and drinking tea during the daytime. On a couple of occasions I asked her for information and got only mumbled replies and no help at all. Later I learned that most of the people in Kangding—at least those that I met—were hardworking and friendly—and certainly the majority of them were extremely helpful to me. However, this woman was, I thought, a classic example of the sloth of many low-level cadres and bureaucrats in China during the Maoist period—when the traditional Chinese work ethic was seriously eroded and in some cases totally abandoned. During my stay in Kangding and Ganzi, I learned, there were many things undergoing far-reaching changes as a result of the winds of reform blowing from Beijing and east China. This particular woman, however, had obviously been untouched.

In theory, this guest house had a washroom located on the first floor—as well as an outhouse located beyond the main building for serious business. However, the washroom was almost always locked, and only once was I able to get the concierge to unlock it for me so that I could fill my kettle. Because that room was almost always locked, I had to use the outside outhouse. It lived up to—or down to—the standard of traditional Chinese facilities of that sort: It consisted of one filthy, open stall, and the smell was putrid.

The view from my second-story window was extremely colorful and very pleasing, though. Directly across the small river that rushed through the middle of town rose Paoma Mountain (Paomashan). It was famous throughout China, I was told, because it was the subject of a very popular love song. My young Academy escort, from Chengdu, was familiar with it. He thought that the song dated to the Song dynasty and had been recently revived; it was currently a hit tune throughout China. A pavilion painted in very bright colors had recently been built at the top of this mountain, and it was said to be a favorite spot for hiking and picnicking. To the left of my window—and very near—was one of Kangding's major lamaseries, which I remembered from 1948. It was undergoing major reforms (to repair serious damage inflicted during the Cultural Revolution), but it nevertheless was in active use, and lamas dressed in deep red robes were constantly going in and out of the lamasery's main courtyard and buildings throughout most of the day. To the right of my window was a small lane, on which was located an open market where small piglets were being sold. There was loud bargaining between sellers and buyers, accompanied by constant screaming from the piglets. The lane was filled at almost all times with a heterogeneous mixture of Tibetans and Chinese—men, women, and children of all ages—each of them dressed a little differently.

There was a great deal of variety in the Tibetans' clothing—more than I had remembered—and local people explained to me that this was because each locality, or clan, in the region had its own distinctive dress. Whatever their differences, all of the women wore multicolored clothing, and virtually all of the men wore felt hats, heavy leather boots, and sheepskin-lined jackets. Quite a few elderly Han Chinese wore fairly old-fashioned clothing or Mao suits, but the majority of younger Chinese were dressed, somewhat to my surprise because of the remoteness of the area, in Western-style clothes. The males wore suits with jackets, and the women wore slacks and jackets. I continued to be surprised in virtually every town of any size that I visited, no matter how remote, by how fashionably dressed many young Chinese women were. Bright red high-heeled shoes seemed to be the height of fashion in 1988—not only in this area but in many others that I saw. I had no doubt that all of this was testimony, above all, to the power of TV to spread fads and fashions in China in the 1980s—and not just fads relating to clothing.

Soon after my arrival in Kangding, I walked the length and breadth of the town, poking into virtually every nook, cranny, and byway to form an initial impression of what had changed and what was the same. This tour of the town did not take very long. Kangding is a pocket-size town. It rests in a tiny hole in the mountains, with a white-water river (really a stream) rushing at a great pace right through the middle of the town, next to its main street. This little river is called the Zheduo, which is the name of the mountain pass that leads to the grasslands west of Kangding. My hosts said that Zheduo is a Chinese phonetic rendition of the Tibetan name Zhedela. In the city, this stream is joined by another small one, called the Yada (which means "Yak River"). From Kangding, the Zheduo rushes out of the town and tumbles down the mountains and ultimately joins the Dadu River.

According to local leaders, the name Kangding dates only to 1908, when "Kangdingfu" was first established. (Fu was the title used during the Qing dynasty for prefectures; it was a fairly grand title to give to such a small place.) Before that, the town had been officially called Dajianlu (Tachienlu), and when I visited the town in 1948 virtually everyone was still using that name for it—and a great many still did in 1988. I discovered, as I did in many Chinese towns that I visited, that local people were able and very willing to explain in considerable detail—whether it was correct I was not sure—the historical origins of the town. The name Dajianlu, I was told, was closely associated with a famous Chinese general. One of my informants said that this general was Zhuge Liang (Chu-ko Liang). This informant said that Zhuge Liang had come to this area and "made a sword." He explained that the word *da*, which means "strike," referred to the making of the weapon and that the word *jian*, which generally means arrow, referred to the weapon that he made. By the time he finished his explanation, I was not very clear about the story—or about the weapon that reputedly was made—and found myself somewhat skeptical about this explanation. However, what was clear was that many local people continued to use the word Dajianlu, even though the town's name was officially changed to Kangding early in this century. Then, in 1951, after the Communist takeover, Xikang Province was abolished, the area was incorporated into Sichuan Province, and Kangding was converted into a county. Actually, the name of the town itself—that is, the small urban area—was simply Luchenzhen, or Luchen Town.

*   *   *

In 1948, the population of the urbanized part of the town was roughly 7,000—remarkably small for the capital of a province. By 1988, it was still small, but it had more than quadrupled to over 30,000. It was still a diminutive place, but it was growing and changing from a town into a small city. The main part of town was still extremely compact. In 1948, there had been only two main streets in the town, one on each side of the river. In fact, of the two, really only one of them could be considered a major street. It was named Shaanxi Street because many people had come from Shaanxi Province and had established shops on the street. By 1988, the town had spread out a little but not a great deal: There were now four important streets, two on each side of the river, and the town had begun to creep up onto the adjacent hills. In 1948, virtually all of the structures in the town were either old-style, two-story wood-and-stone buildings, with tile roofs, or were Tibetan-style structures, most of which were lamaseries. The only exception at that time that I remember was a small, gray brick building that housed the provincial government. This building was still in existence in 1988—and was pointed out to me—although it was surrounded now by many more modern buildings that housed the prefectural and county governments as well as many other official agencies.

By the 1980s very few of the old buildings remained, and most of the city now consisted of recently built, modern, multistory structures, quite a few of them rising as high as six stories. These buildings had radically changed the atmosphere and ambiance of the town. Some of them had been constructed immediately after "liberation," but only a few of these remained. This was because Kangding had been virtually destroyed and rebuilt twice during the first two decades after the Communist takeover. In 1955, a large earthquake, with its epicenter less than 10 miles away, leveled much of the town. And then in 1963 a large fire swept through the town, destroying most of the old wooden buildings. After both of those disasters, the town had been reconstructed—and in some respects virtually rebuilt. However, most of the best modern structures that I saw in 1988 were said to have been constructed during the building boom stimulated by the reforms of the 1980s. In fact, I was told, most of them had sprouted up since the mid-1980s. Some of the new buildings had been financed by the county government, but many others had been constructed by prefectural, provincial, and even central governmental agencies.

On one side of the river, government buildings and high-rise apartments now predominated. Both the Kangding County Government and the headquarters of the Ganzi Tibetan Autonomous Prefecture were located there. So too were many agencies run directly by the provincial and central governments. Even though Kangding was no longer a provincial capital, the number of governmental agencies in the town had multiplied greatly: By 1988, a total of 305 "government units and government-run enterprises" of all sorts were located there. Along the river's edge, on both sides, there were huge free markets for clothing and many other things.

The main area of shops was on the other side of the river, where two-story buildings predominated. In this area there were also many small open markets. The narrow streets were teaming with people, and the shops and markets were filled with a plethora of goods. In almost every area I traveled in 1988 I was amazed by the variety of goods I saw compared to the prereform period of the 1970s as well as the pre-Communist period. In the case of Kangding, however, as I noted earlier, I had been amazed even in 1948 by the variety of goods that had been carried by yak all across Tibet from India, or backpacked from Yaan. In 1988, I was more impressed by the things being sold. The shops and stalls catered to very diverse tastes and interests. In addition to Tibetan specialties, the shops sold virtually everything that one could find in towns in east China. I was astonished most of all, I think, to see stores specializing in TVs, radios, tape recorders, and other electronic equipment and gadgets. There were at least two stores devoted entirely to selling cassettes of popular music. The general price level for most goods, I was told, was roughly 20 percent above that in Yaan; even though trucks had reduced transportation costs, prices were still high. The difference was not as great as it had been earlier, though: In 1948 the price of goods had often been two, three, or four times what they were in Yaan.

As the town had grown, it had spread up into the valley leading toward Zheduo Pass, toward the grasslands. Virtually all of the buildings in this valley were modern. But despite all the development and change, much did remain the same. The rushing stream bisecting the town, and the mountains rising high on both sides of it, still dominated the setting, and the population was still an extraordinarily colorful mixture of Han Chinese and Tibetans. Tibetans no longer brought their musk and other goods from the grasslands to the Kangding by yak caravan, and the Chinese no longer carried red brick tea and other commodities on their backs from Yaan. Trucks had supplanted both animal and human transport. Yet much of what I saw reminded me of what I had seen in the 1940s.

*   *   *

During my stay in Kangding, I learned a great deal not only about the town but also about the county and the prefecture. I learned much simply from observation and casual conversations, but—as was true in most of the places that I visited—the most detailed information that I gathered came from systematic interviewing of a wide variety of local people, including top local leaders and other officials. Leaders of both the county and the prefecture were extremely helpful and very open in responding to my endless questions. None of them had been interviewed by a foreigner, and they seemed to be pleased to have the opportunity and were eager to tell me what they knew. Most of them were young, and the majority were well educated and had some kind of technical qualifications. All of them had risen to leadership positions recently. They impressed me as being strikingly different from most of the leaders and officials that I had met there in the 1940s. (They were very different, also, from most of the officials I met in China during the Maoist era.) I had some of my interviews in offices and government buildings, but I also learned a lot from long, relaxed conversations held over lunches and dinners in more informal circumstances. All of my interviews and conversations were almost totally lacking in formalities or protocol.

Some of the most useful discussions that I had about Ganzi Prefecture as a whole were with a man named Fu Keli, who was a deputy head (people referred to him as a deputy "governor") of the prefecture, who had long sessions with me together with many of his staff. Those present at my interviews and conversations with him included the secretary-general of the prefecture, the head of its foreign affairs bureau, and various other bureau heads. We met in the main prefectural government building—a sizable modern structure located in a compound that contained several government office buildings, all of which were relatively new except the one old brick building that dated back to 1948. Fu impressed me as being a competent, energetic, "modern," nonideological, and pragmatic leader, strongly committed to trying to raise the professional standards of public service in the area and obviously dedicated to the economic development of Ganzi. Educated to be a doctor, he had graduated from Southwest Medical College in Chengdu in 1964. After graduation, he had practiced medicine as a surgeon. Not long after his graduation, he had come to Kangding and worked in the town as a doctor for two decades until, in 1985, he was selected to become deputy head of the prefecture. (Fu's son, he told me, was studying to become a professional violinist—something, as I noted earlier, my young Academy escort hoped that his son also would become.) The other prefectural officials I met impressed me as being cut out of similar cloth.

My longest conversations while I was in Kangding were with the leaders of the county. I had very good sessions with both the county magistrate and the county's Party secretary. I found both of them to be competent and personally engaging people. The magistrate, my primary host, was an attractive 41-year-old woman named Wang Dingqing. She told me that she was one of only two women county magistrates in Sichuan Province—out of a total of more than 175 county magistrates in the province. She was a Tibetan who originally came from Daofu (Dawu) County, which was located on the grasslands to the northwest of Kangding, near Qinghai. However, she had been educated in the Chinese school system and in many respects therefore seemed quite Sinified—yet she clearly retained her Tibetan identity. She dressed in Chinese clothes and spoke excellent Chinese. She seemed equally at ease dealing with Han Chinese and her fellow Tibetans.

She told me that as a very young child she had been carried to Kangding by her mother on horseback, riding in the folds of her robes. Her mother was a singer and was chosen to be a cadre in the local Tibetan singing troupe. After attending primary school in Kangding, Wang Dingqing had been picked out as a talented young student and was sent to attend middle school in Beijing. Her hope at that time, she told me, was to become a doctor, but that hope was ended by the turmoil that disrupted all education during the Cultural Revolution. She was sent back to Kangding and worked for roughly a decade as a low-level cadre in the Kangding government. Once more she was selected—obviously because she was bright and had done well—to go to Beijing. This time she attended the country's most important minority nationality institute. Her major there was in the Chinese language, and she graduated in 1982. Immediately after graduation, she was assigned to work in the Ganzi Prefectural Party Committee and before long became head of its policy research office. In 1985, at the time when sweeping changes in personnel were taking place throughout China, she was chosen to be the county magistrate—which involved a dramatic promotion. (Her husband worked in the Kangding electric power plant, as a technician.)

She was my principal host, but my co-host was the Party secretary of the Kangding County Party Committee, a man named Lin Foshen. Although generally—throughout China—Party secretaries clearly outranked equivalent government leaders, when I met with Wang and Lin, Lin consistently deferred to the magistrate in our discussions in a way that did not seem to me to be either insincere or awkward. The two of them appeared to have an easy and relaxed relationship and to think well of each other. Lin, 44, was a Han

Chinese who, like the deputy head of the prefecture, was a professional who had only recently been appointed to a political position. A native of Sichuan, his home county was Changshou, which was now a part of Chongqing Municipality. As a young man, he decided to become a veterinarian, and he attended Sichuan Agricultural College, in Yaan, graduating in 1969 with his veterinarian degree. The following year, he was sent to Kangding to practice veterinary medicine, starting as an "ordinary cadre" but rising rapidly to become head of the local veterinary station in 1978. In 1980, he assumed his first bureaucratic position, as deputy head of the County Bureau of Agriculture and Animal Husbandry. Three years later, he became deputy head of the comparable bureau in the prefecture. Then, in 1985, he was chosen to be part of the Party leadership group in the county, first as a deputy Party secretary and then later in the same year as Party secretary—the top position in the county.

Several other county leaders and officials participated in my discussions with the magistrate and Party secretary. All of them were Tibetans. All but one of them seemed to be, like the magistrate, Tibetans who were perfectly at ease in a Chinese setting and were Sinified in some respects. The one exception was a man who, at age 58, was the oldest of the group. Named Jalazhangche (this is my inexpert attempt to transliterate his Tibetan name as he pronounced it), he was the only one of this group who dressed in traditional Tibetan clothes. His schooling had ended with junior middle school, but—doubtless because of his family background—he had risen to become one of the three deputy magistrates. His area of responsibility was religious affairs, together with other work included in the general "culture and education system," including health, sports, research on local history, and family planning. He came from a long line of Tibetan leaders, and his father was magistrate of Kangding in the 1950s. Jalazhangche had been deputy magistrate for many years. Other Tibetans privately said to me, though, that he was really not influential politically and that his position was in some respects more symbolic than powerful.

It was notable that not one of the local county leaders had risen to his or her current position through a career in Party organizational work, propaganda work, the army, or public security—the paths that often were the best stepping stones to power during the Maoist era. The majority of these new leaders were either professionals, technocrats, or people experienced in administration. Most of them were still young and had risen rapidly in the mid-1980s.

*   *   *

My discussions with the local leaders in Kangding covered a very wide range of issues. Some of the subjects that I found particularly interesting were local administration, the role of the Party, the development of the economy, educational trends, Han-minority relations, trends affecting religion, and the local role of the military. I started out, though, asking a little bit about local history.

The only historical subject that I was able to explore in more than the most superficial way was the history of the Communist takeover in Kangding. Only the 58-year-old Tibetan deputy magistrate was old enough to have personal memories of that period, but virtually all of the local officials I met knew something about it either from reading or from talking to older people. Everyone stressed that the takeover had been relatively smooth and facilitated by political deals, as had been the case in all but a few of China's outlying areas. The Party had earlier made some attempts to lay the groundwork for its ultimate takeover, but in the period just before "liberation," I was told, it did not make any significant headway. At that time there was a very small underground organization in Kangding that consisted, they said, of only four or five Party members (all of them "young intellectuals"). All of them were killed by bandits when they were making a trip between Kangding and Yaan. In short, the effort at that time was aborted. Many years earlier, of course, the Chinese Communists had, during their Long March in the 1930s, established temporary control of several areas in this region. Memories of their activities in that period were still strong—and a great deal of mythology had grown up about particular incidents—but in fact the Party had been unable to develop an effective underground movement that was lasting. Governor Liu Wenhui and his officials and military supporters were able to maintain firm control until finally, seeing that the Communists were winning the civil war elsewhere in the country, Liu decided to accept the inevitable and switch his allegiance, which he did in December 1949.

Thereafter, the transfer of power took place very rapidly. Liu was removed from his governmental position of leadership, and his 24th Army was taken over by the Communists and largely absorbed into the People's Liberation Army. But in 1950 Liu was given a position (essentially honorific) as a deputy chairman of the Sichuan Military and Administrative Committee, a position he held from 1950 to 1954. Liu's regime in Xikang had been one of the most oppressive (in my opinion, one of the worst) warlord regimes in China. However, the Communists, to facilitate their takeover, accepted him into their national governmental structure. From 1951 on, he was a member of the national leadership of the Chinese People's Political Consultative Conference, and from 1954 on he held a seat in the National People's Congress. He was appointed to head the Ministry of Forestry in Beijing in 1959, but he held that position only briefly. He died soon thereafter.

According to my hosts, because of Liu's decision to switch allegiance—which really meant simply to surrender—"there was really no fighting" when the Communist forces finally came in, although my hosts later acknowledged that there was some continuing resistance in distant areas. The

PLA quickly established direct control during 1950–1951. Administrative changes also began to be made in 1950, when the official capital of Xikang was moved to Yaan and Kangding was made an autonomous prefecture. Right from the start, the Communists installed new Tibetan leaders in top local government positions. (They gave me the names of some of them, but I despaired of transliterating them.) The Communist military forces then began their real takeover of Tibet proper in the fall of 1950, and at that time they set up a new administration to govern the area extending to the Gold Sand River (Jinshajiang), which is the present western border of Ganzi. The next year, 1951, the Communists compelled the Dalai Lama to submit, politically, to Beijing's authority, and PLA forces then moved into Lhasa. Finally, in 1955, Beijing decided to set up the Tibetan Autonomous Region west of the Gold Sand River, and in 1956 its preparatory committee was established in Lhasa. Xikang Province was abolished, and the Ganzi Tibetan Autonomous Prefecture was formally established as part of Sichuan Province. Kangding became a county under it.* (However, Yaan and six other counties that had belonged to Xikang were separated, but they too were returned to Sichuan Province.) The old border between Sichuan and Xikang had been near Jingjiguan, between Yaan and Mingshan. The new border between Yaan Prefecture and the Ganzi Autonomous Prefecture was moved to just east of Luding.

*   *   *

As of 1988, the Ganzi Tibetan Autonomous Prefecture was a very large administrative unit that stretched all the way from Luding in the east to Batang in the west. In the southwest, it bordered on Yunnan, and in the northwest it touched Qinghai. The area included was huge: Its 59,394 square miles made it considerably larger than a number of European countries, including Hungary, Bulgaria, and Austria, and comparing it to administrative units in the United States, it was slightly bigger than such large states as Michigan, Illinois, and New York. Even in the context of China's huge territory, this prefecture was larger than many important provinces, including such well-known ones as Jiangsu, Zhejiang, Shandong, Liaoning, and Fujian. However, its vast grasslands were so sparsely populated that its entire population was just about 800,000 (the specific figure I was given by prefectural officials was 799,300; I believe this figure was for 1987). In the eastern fringe of the prefecture, the population was slightly more dense than

---

*Later I learned that, in Ganzi as in western Qinghai, when the Chinese took steps in 1955–1956 to tighten political controls and accelerate economic and social changes, some Tibetans in these areas resisted, and there was major fighting. In 1988, no one in Ganzi or Qinghai mentioned this to me.

in most of the prefecture. (Kangding County had a population of 94,021, which was about 11 percent of the population of the entire prefecture.) The density of the population in the prefecture as a whole was between 13 and 14 people per square mile, which was very similar to the density of population in certain western American states such as New Mexico and Idaho.

Administratively, the prefecture was divided into 18 counties, which contained 16 towns (*zhen*) and 326 townships (*xiang*). In the entire prefecture, there was no urban settlement large enough to be classified as a municipality, and, in fact, all of the towns were really very small. Among them, the town center of Kangding was by far the largest, even though its population was only a little over 30,000. Among the others, the second largest was Luqiaozhen, the town center of Luding, which had a population of roughly 12,000. The town called Ganzi (or Garze), which lay to the far northwest and was the place for which the prefecture was named, and the town of Batang, on the western border, each had slightly under 10,000 people (and, at least in the case of Batang, this figure included not only the town center but also two nearby townships). Among the other "important towns" were Litangzhen (proudly proclaimed one of the "highest cities in the world"), which was located about halfway between Kangding and Batang and had a population of between 3,000 and 4,000, and Lengjizhen, the town where I observed a cement factory en route to Kangding, which had perhaps 2,000 inhabitants. All of the other seven towns were even smaller. In sum, this was one of the least urbanized areas in all of China, and its residents were overwhelmingly either animal herders or farmers.

The statistics provided to me by the prefecture indicated that of the total population, about three-quarters—or 598,000—were Tibetans. They were spread very thinly throughout the grasslands, although a few lived in the small towns. The Han Chinese accounted for just over one-fifth of the total population (or, to be more precise, about 180,000, or 22.5 percent). There were some Han people living in every part of the prefecture, but the large majority lived in the eastern fringe of it. Although among the rest of the population a total of 19 other minority groups were said to be represented, only the Yi (who totaled somewhere between 10,000 and 20,000) and, to a lesser extent, the Hui Muslims were numerically significant. The size of all the other minority groups was minuscule.

In Ganzi Prefecture, as almost everywhere in China, I found that local leaders were willing to identify very precisely for me who the "top leaders" of the local Party and government were. In Ganzi, they consisted of eight members of the Prefectural Party Standing Committee and seven top governmental officials. The Standing Committee members included: the secretary, four deputy secretaries, and three ordinary committee members. Only the secretary was a Han Chinese; the other seven were all Tibetans. Roughly 200 cadres worked for the Prefectural Party Committee headquarters. Recently, in accord with national reform policies, the local Party structure had been simplified somewhat, but it still had three key departments (*bu*)—for organization, propaganda, and united front work—as well as a Discipline Inspection Committee. The Standing Committee also exercised authority over the local Young Communist League, labor unions, and the Women's Association. The Party's Armed Forces Department (*wuzhuang bu*) was responsible to the Party leaders of both the prefecture and the counties, I was told, but most of its actual work was said to be at the county level. (There was also a Military Sub-District in the prefecture, which I will say something about later.) Party membership in the entire prefecture totaled 27,422, or roughly 3.5 percent of the entire population—a slightly lower percentage than in many areas in eastern China.

The seven individuals identified for me as the top government leaders included the head of the prefecture and his six deputies. The prefectural head and five of the others were Tibetan (one of whom was a religious leader), and only one deputy (the individual whom I interviewed at some length—Fu) was a Han Chinese. (Their definition of and identification of the top government leadership was somewhat more narrow than that I had received in many other places, where the group often was said to include the government's secretary-general and the heads and deputy heads of the local People's Congress and People's Political Consultative Conference. It was apparent to me, though, that their short list did include all of those they felt were really important in making major government decisions.) This group, I was told, met "almost every day."

The Chinese constitution and national regulations require that all top government leaders in autonomous minority areas such as Ganzi be elected officials, and they also require that the very top officials in such areas be representative of the largest minority group in the area. In practice, the election of such officials obviously was, in general, a pro forma process, and mainly symbolic. They were actually selected by Party leaders. The linkage between the Party and the government continued to be very strong. Of the top seven government leaders, two (the prefectural head and one of his deputies—the man that I met) belonged to the Party's Standing Committee.

Below the top leadership, the structure of the prefectural government was—as they described it to me in detail—virtually identical to that of regular governments at the prefectural level in other parts of China. As elsewhere (although there were some minor local variations), the organization of government at the grass-roots level was essentially the same as in nonminority areas, and was designed to carry out all major policies defined by Beijing and Sichuan Province in virtually every field of government activity. Ganzi Prefecture's government consisted of roughly 40 units of various kinds—offices (*shi*), commissions (*weiyuanhui*), bureaus (*ju*), and departments (*chu*). Altogether, the government of the prefecture employed roughly 900 people, about 60 of whom worked in units located at the headquarters building of the prefecture. The total number of "state cadres" (that is, officials or cadres paid by the government) in the entire prefecture, at all levels, totaled roughly 20,000, but about three-quarters of these consisted of teachers, medical and health personnel, and technicians. I was told that the total of those who held "administrative" positions was roughly 5,000.*

*   *   *

As in virtually every place I visited in northwest China in 1988, except Xinjiang, I was struck in Ganzi by how relatively inconspicuous military personnel were in areas where I expected to see much more evidence of the People's Liberation Army. As I noted earlier, I did see some evidence of the military presence in the area. On my trip to and from Kangding, I passed several small army posts and barracks, and on the roads I saw a few soldiers traveling in trucks and some military oil tankers. On the outskirts of Kangding, on my way to the grasslands, I also passed the headquarters of the Ganzi Military Sub-District, which was clearly labeled with a sign at the gate, but I was surprised to see that there were no guards at the entrance of the military compound and few soldiers visible within it. On my fairly long trip into the Tibetan interior, on the grasslands beyond the pass, I saw several small army posts of the kind that people had told me dot the entire route to Lhasa, and on the way to Tagong we passed through one town that clearly had become the site of a significant—but still relatively small—military base; we saw quite a few Han Chinese in uniform there, most of them simply shopping at the busy open markets on the main street. Yet even in this region— where I had assumed that the military presence would be quite visible, since it is on one of the main routes to Lhasa—I saw virtually no soldiers who were carrying any arms, and almost no military equipment. Moreover, even though I was everywhere extremely alert to try to judge the extent to which the military establishment might be interfering with civilian life, I found little

---

*Although the deputy prefecture head whom I met, Fu, used a figure of 36 units when describing the government, I later obtained a detailed breakdown (which I recorded in my trip notes) from the secretary-general that listed 31 prefectural government organizations—and he said that this list did not include 9 other organizations that were "directly run" by the prefectural government (he did not explain what these were). Neither of the lists I received was complete; they did not include a considerable number of enterprises (and factories) about which I was told that were owned by the "state" and run by various bureaus under the prefectural government. As I stated earlier, although the structure of the government in Ganzi was essentially similar to that elsewhere in China, like many other local governments it varied in details. What struck me about the Ganzi organization was the much greater attention, in comparison with most areas, given to animal husbandry, forestry, minority and religious affairs, and earthquakes (which are a major problem in the area).

evidence that it was very intrusive—to my surprise—and, in fact, after having observed major roads to Tibet in both Ganzi and in Qinghai Province, I left somewhat baffled about how the Chinese were supporting and sustaining their very considerable military establishment in the Tibet Autonomous Region.

I was told by local leaders that because Ganzi is a subdistrict (*fen chu*) of the Chengdu Military Region, the local military forces were in no sense commanded by the local political authorities but were under the direct leadership of the regional command. Kangding's local political leaders stressed to me—as the majority of the political leaders I met throughout the northwest had—that the Chinese military establishment was an entirely "separate system," but—also like Party leaders I talked to elsewhere—they asserted that there was "very close liaison" between the Party and local military forces. The commander of the subdistrict, they told me, was a member of the Party's Prefectural Standing Committee (but he was the only military man on that committee). In normal times, local leaders said, the major responsibilities of the subdistrict were to handle conscription, the training of some new recruits, and the care of retired army men. In cooperation with the prefectural government, they also, however, supervised the Armed Services Departments (*wuzhuang bu*) of all the counties. Both prefectural and county officials strongly maintained that the subdistrict had no responsibility at all for handling ordinary, day-to-day, law-and-order problems and issues; these were dealt with solely, I was told, by the Public Security authorities.

Both the prefecture and the counties had, under them, Public Security Bureaus, and these bureaus recruited, trained, and managed the local People's Armed Police (*wuzhuang jingcha*). Separate units of these armed police were under the administration and control of the prefecture and each of the counties. Even they, though, were inconspicuous, and I saw few of these semimilitary policemen anywhere in the area. I saw a handful in Kangding, one in the village of Tagong, which I visited on the grasslands, and a few along the way, on the road. The situation contrasted greatly with everything I had read and heard about the situation in Lhasa and nearby areas in the Tibetan Autonomous Region, where obviously both the PLA and various semimilitary and other police units play a very visible controlling role. In contrast, it seemed to me that in Ganzi the maintenance of ordinary law and order did not seem to present serious problems. The regime's basic instruments of coercion were obviously there, but it appeared that they were generally used with a fairly light hand in dealing with the population.

*   *   *

Ganzi is widely considered, with considerable justification, a very backward area. It clearly is still in the very early stages of modernization. Nevertheless, I was impressed by the degree to which it had changed and progressed economically since my last visit to the area. Despite the fact that the population—mainly Tibetans—is still dispersed throughout the grassland area, the prefectural government's statistics showed that by 1988 roughly 460,000 people were classified as engaged in farming whereas only 200,000 were classified as people still engaged solely in animal husbandry. In explaining these figures to me, officials dealing with economic affairs pointed out that most people—including Tibetans—in all areas in the prefecture now engaged in both animal husbandry and agriculture. The prefecture classified only a single county (Luding) as being entirely agricultural, and it classified only two counties in the far northwest as being exclusively pastoral; the rest were classified, in occupational terms, as "mixed."

"Most Tibetan families," my informants said, "now raise some animals and also farm a little," and "all now have fixed dwellings, even those who move their animals to better pastures and live in tents part of the year." I was told by officials that there were close to 5 million animals of all kinds in the entire prefecture—more than 6 per man, woman, and child in the area. Almost half of them—2.3 million—were yaks, which were regarded as the most valuable, all-purpose providers of the Tibetans' needs—including milk, cheese, yak hair (to make tents) and wool (to make heavy clothing), and transportation. In addition, there were perhaps 2.4 million sheep and goats in the prefecture as well as an estimated 300,000 or more horses. The prefecture's farms produced mainly grain.

Barley was the major crop; as in the past, it was the necessary staple for making *tsamba* (roasted and powdered barley), which is a fundamental staple of the Tibetan diet. Normally, *tsamba* is made into a kind of paste, by moistening it, and it is eaten together with rancid butter tea; in my opinion, it is, without question, one of the most unappetizing staple foods that I have encountered anywhere in the world. It looks a little like Portland cement, and—to my untutored tastebuds—to the extent that it has any taste, it seems very much like what I think Portland cement would taste like. In contrast to *tsamba,* some of the other Tibetan food items that I ate—especially their version of fried crullers, and various cheeses and small snacks—were very tasty. Perhaps that helps to explain why most Tibetans, I was told, have eating patterns somewhat different from those of the Chinese. Instead of eating a few regular large meals, many Tibetans were inclined to eat small snacks much more frequently—perhaps five, six, or even seven times a day. Apart from the predominant crop, barley, the other major crops in the area were wheat, corn, and beans.

Grain output reportedly had increased substantially in the 1980s, yet it was still insufficient to meet local needs. Moreover, droughts continued to be a major problem; so too, from time to time, were earthquakes, which sometimes had a devastating impact on agriculture. The prefecture's requirement for grains of all kinds had recently varied, I was told, between roughly

220,000 tons and 275,000 tons, but the local output had averaged around 193,000 tons. The shortfall was made up by purchases of wheat, flour, and rice from the provincial government; the Grain Bureau of the prefecture managed these purchases and then handled the sale of the grain to consumers. In recent years, the amounts purchased (at relatively low state prices) had averaged about 44,000 tons annually, but in some years it had been as high as 72,000 tons.

When discussing economic development in Ganzi, local officials emphasized, rightly, that one of the most important stimuli that had helped pushed forward growth and modernization in the region had been the construction of new roads and the penetration of modern communications into the region. Before 1949, there had been no usable motor roads—at least in the period immediately before 1949 (as I said earlier, during World War II a road to Kangding from Yaan had been built, but it was only briefly operable). By 1988, roads of some sort linked Kangding to all 18 counties and to about 230 townships (about 70 percent of the total). By far the majority of the new roads were fairly simple ones, made of gravel, but a few were paved. From Kangding, the major road going east to Luding had important branches that led north to Danba and south to Shimian. The principal road from Kangding to Tibet went almost straight west via Yajiang, Litang, and Batang. From a junction about halfway between Kangding and Yajiang, as well as from Yajiang and Litang, other major roads led north and south. In the east of the region, the road system provided linkages among four counties, and in this region the road network totaled about 250 miles in length. The roads in the northern part of the prefecture provided links among eight counties and totaled more than 390 miles. Those in the south connected six counties and totaled about 300 miles in length. The ability of trucks and other motor vehicles to reach all of these areas represented a very major change from the past.

Equally important had been the revolution in communications that had taken place in Ganzi as throughout almost all of China. Small battery-operated radios seemed to have spread throughout most of the prefecture, and TV had begun to penetrate into some of even the most remote areas—although, in this respect, Ganzi still seemed to lag at least somewhat behind many of the other areas in the west that I had visited, in part because so much of the area lacked electricity. "We have just started to experiment with windmill generators," I was told. "Even though they are now affordable, at about Y 2,000, and despite the fact that the winds are usually favorable in many areas in the prefecture, Tibetan families are still waiting to see if they work well." However, I thought the degree to which TV had spread in some of this remote area was nevertheless rather remarkable. In addition to the TV station that had been built in Kangding, there were 28 TV relay stations scattered throughout the prefecture as of 1988, and in large areas reception was reportedly "good." However, actual ownership of TV sets, I was told, tended to be concentrated around the urban or semiurbanized areas—the towns and township centers—and had not yet spread very broadly into the hinterland because of the lack of electricity and the failure, to date, to promote small windmill generators (such as those that had become much more prevalent in certain areas of northwest China). Ownership of sets was restricted to small towns and township centers that had access to some sort of electricity—some from small hydroelectric stations and some from other kinds of generators.

*   *   *

Modern industry had begun to develop in the area (four decades earlier there had been virtually none there). However, local officials emphasized that industrialization had just begun, and they were right. It was still relatively small in scale and was concentrated in a relatively few places. The principal extractive industries were located beyond the pass in the grassland areas—in *guanwai*. The principal one was lumbering, which was done in fairly remote mountain areas. Although a few woodworking factories or shops had been developed in the prefecture, there were no really large lumber mills. The majority of the logs cut were therefore sent for processing to other places, fairly distant, in Sichuan, including Leshan and even Chengdu.

The majority of the industries that had been developed in towns and townships in the grassland areas consisted of handicrafts, although in Danba and the town of Ganzi there were a few other kinds of factories. Clearly, though, the main factory areas were in the east—in Kangding, Luding, and Lengji, and even in these places the process of industrialization was in its very early stages. Electricity capacity had increased gradually. Before 1949, in the entire region there was only one 5,000-kilowatt power station. After 1949, output grew, especially from the 1970s on. Most output was from small hydrostations; the largest one had a capacity of 6,000 kilowatts. All 18 centers had at least some electricity. However, I was told that by 1988 total capacity in the prefecture still was only 40,000 kilowatts.*

Among the modern factories in the province, there were a few producing textiles (wool fabrics and clothing), cement, and tiles. The bureaus of the prefectural government ran a total of 17 industrial factories, and there were some others under county government bureaus. The majority of the modern factories were in Kangding. According to local people, the "most important" factories in the entire prefecture were a major wool textile factory in Kangding and four cement factories (two in Lengji and one each in Kangding and the town of Ganzi).

---

*These figures on electricity capacity were received in my interviews and recorded in my notes. They seem too low, but I have been unable to check them.

The prefecture unquestionably has within its territory substantial raw material resources, as well as many hydroelectric power sites, which could be developed to support much more extensive mining and industrial development. But the government's economic plans for the future, as they were described to me in 1988, did not stress rapid industrialization, and for very good reason. The shortage of capital and technicians, and the continuing relative backwardness of transportation (especially transportation into and out of the region), still posed huge—in some respects almost insuperable—obstacles to more rapid industrialization. Instead, the government's plan emphasized, most of all, further development of animal husbandry and agriculture. The prefecture estimated as of 1988 that it contained about 17 million acres of good pastureland—much of it not fully used—and also very sizable forest areas that could be developed.

Even though industrialization and modernization had just begun, the prefecture's official economic statistics revealed that average living standards in the area had been gradually raised—quite significantly, in fact—to a level considered to be "average" for China as a whole. For the entire prefecture, according to Deputy Prefecture Head Fu, per capita income had risen to Y 431 in 1987.

It was no surprise to me to find that issues relating to reform of the economy were not a major preoccupation of the local leaders in Ganzi. Economic growth was their clear priority, and, because they lacked a large modern industrial sector, many of the reform issues that appeared to be most pressing in more advanced areas of China seemed much less relevant to this remote spot. In the early 1980s, when the entire nation decollectivized, the household responsibility system was introduced in both agriculture and animal husbandry, and this stimulated growth. Moreover, in Ganzi as elsewhere, business enterprises of all kinds—obviously most of them small—had developed rapidly in the 1980s (I saw them everywhere) and this, too, had helped to boost the economy. A great many of the shops in the area were now privately owned and privately run. (In the Kangding area alone, I was told, there were now about 500 "private enterprises"—including shops and even smaller operations.) Most of the local officials I met clearly favored moving further toward more complete marketization.

A few changes had taken place in local factories. In those in Kangding, efforts had recently been made to "separate enterprise management from government and Party," and some steps had been taken to begin implementation of the manager contract responsibility system (*chengbao zhidu*). Three factories in Kangding, I was told, had attempted to choose new managers by "open bidding," but these efforts did not seem to have had much effect. In one case, my informants told me, several new people applied, but a man who already was working in the factory as a deputy manager was finally chosen to be the new manager. The process did, however, remove two persons who previously had been in charge in other factories. Inflation, which by 1988 was a serious problem in many parts of China, clearly had had some effect in Ganzi, but for some reason it did not seem to be as high on the local leaders' list of concerns as it was in many other areas of China—even though local prices already were relatively high because of high transportation costs.

The nation's open policy had had very little impact in Ganzi. The region's horizontal economic ties with other parts of China had grown somewhat, but local leaders, being quite realistic, saw very little prospect of attracting any foreign interest or foreign investment, although one UN organization had given a significant grant—US$200,000, I was told—to help the government develop a modern language laboratory for its school system. Local leaders were generally skeptical about whether the benefits of Beijing's coastal policy would trickle down to them any time soon, as, in theory, Beijing hoped it would. In dealing with both Beijing and Chengdu—especially with Chengdu—it was clear that the prime objective of local leaders was to obtain as large an amount as possible of subsidies and investments from the national and provincial governments. One Kangding County leader said bluntly: "Whenever we go to provincial meetings, we always argue that they should give more money to Kangding." And the deputy head of the prefecture said to me: "We think that some day the government [meaning higher-level government] will give more attention to us because we are rich in resources, including mineral resources, even though we lack transportation, energy, and specialized personnel." He said that in recent years the central government had given an annual subsidy to Ganzi, channeled via the provincial government, of approximately Y 36 million for major projects—two-thirds of it earmarked for agriculture and industry and one-third for education.

Local leaders were generally realistic, I thought, and openly recognized that the extreme difficulty of transportation in and out of the area was probably the greatest single obstacle to more rapid development They recognized that improving major transportation routes, though extremely difficult, should be a top priority. I was told that at one point plans had been drawn up to make the old road between Kangding and Yaan a two-way highway by widening it wherever possible (in many areas, its location, cut into the mountain, made widening impossible) and by building a separate, parallel road in certain other parts of the route. They stated, in fact, that some work on this project had already begun in certain places. But, I saw no signs of it taking place, and I suspected that it would be a long time before this hope could be realized. After having traveled the old road on my return trip, I had some doubts as to whether it would be possible at all—at least in the most difficult and dangerous parts of the route over Two Wolf Mountain.

*   *   *

I inquired at some length about education in the area and concluded that this was one area in which there really had been substantial progress—at least quantitatively—compared to when I last visited it. In 1948, the number of schools in grassland areas was minuscule, and almost all teaching everywhere was done in the Chinese language. At that time, both the Tibetans and the Chinese I met told me that a great many Tibetan parents resisted pressure to get them to send their children to school because they felt it was a waste of time; in their view, measures to compel them to do so seemed analogous to government efforts to conscript adults into military service. By 1988, it was obvious that the basic attitudes had changed fundamentally, and the school system had been substantially expanded and now extended over the entire prefecture. It also had been adapted, to some extent at least, to serve more adequately the needs of Tibetans as well as Han Chinese. Nevertheless, everyone I met frankly recognized that the school system was still inadequate—not only qualitatively but even in terms of quantity—and local leaders gave high priority to improving the system.

In the entire prefecture as of 1988, there were 902 primary schools, with more than 60,000 students; 24 junior middle schools, with about 7,000 students; and 18 senior middle schools, with roughly 3,000 students. The prefecture also had 7 "technical secondary schools"—3 to train teachers and 1 each for agriculture, industry, public health, and accounting; altogether these had roughly 1,500 students. They also had one "teachers college" for Tibetans (a *dazhuan* institution, teaching at a level somewhere between middle school and college, with a three-year program). Institutions of this level had about 400 students. Both the central and provincial governments helped to subsidize Ganzi's education. From 1981 on, I was told, the provincial government had given subsidies to pay all of the expenses for some Tibetan students; in 1988, these funds were used to pay for 47 specialized classes, with about 4,500 students, in primary, junior, and senior middle schools. As I noted earlier, about one-third of the Y 36 million subsidy given by the central government was earmarked for education. The provincial government of Sichuan also provided financial support for a Buddhist seminary, located in Daofu.

In some primary schools, teaching was in the Chinese language (Hanyu), whereas in others it was in Tibetan (the latter included most schools out on the grasslands). In many, both languages were used. The Tibetan textbooks used in the primary schools came mainly from the Education Commission in Beijing. But as of 1988, there still were no regular senior middle schools run by the prefecture in which all of the teaching was in the Tibetan language. In Daofu, however, there was one middle school, run by the province rather than by the prefecture, that taught in the Tibetan language, and some prefectural middle schools taught part of their classes in Tibetan—especially for students who had graduated from Tibetan-language junior middle schools.

Local leaders deplored, however, that despite the school system's substantial development, it still did not reach a very large proportion of the population. In the prefecture as a whole in 1988, I was told, only 53 percent of the children of primary school age were enrolled in schools. Although in some urban areas the figure was close to 100 percent, in some very poor and remote areas (especially those where there were no roads) the figure was extremely low—sometimes not much above 20 percent. The percentages for older students and for higher-level schools were even lower. As in so many areas in a developing country such as China, whether one sees a glass as being half full or half empty depends on what one uses as a basis of comparison. I was impressed at how much education had developed since the 1940s. At the same time, I—like local leaders—was daunted by how far they still had to go. The leaders I met from the prefecture, and also those from Kangding County, were extremely frank in discussing the real situation and the urgent need to continue broadening—and raising the standards for—all levels of education in the region. They clearly recognized the importance of improving education to accelerate economic development, and in more than one of my conversations they discussed it at some length. I had no doubt that they would keep trying.

In Ganzi, as in most other parts of west China, local leaders I met were also frank in stating how difficult it was not only to attract talent from elsewhere but also to prevent a brain drain of local talent—that is, local people educated elsewhere. The government was trying to prevent the brain drain by providing various kinds of special financial incentives to educated, local, young people—and people from other areas—that included higher salaries and better housing and other perquisites. A new university graduate starting work in Ganzi received, I was told, at least one salary grade higher than he or she could obtain elsewhere. But such incentives so far had only limited results. Most educated Chinese from other parts of the country simply considered the living conditions in an area as remote as Ganzi too *ku* (bitter).

Compared to the 1940s, Ganzi had made some progress in developing medicine and health care, but in this too it had a long way to go. At the time of my 1948 visit, the outreach of modern medicine was extremely limited. There was, even at that time, one hospital in Luding (a 320-bed facility run by foreign missionaries) and a small provincial-supported hospital far away in Batang. But most people in the grasslands had no access at all to any modern medicine—and very little access even to simple, local, traditional medicine. By 1988, the prefecture ran four sizable hospitals. The largest one still was the hospital that had existed before 1949 in Luding. There was now another fairly large one that had almost 200 beds (and had acquired a considerable amount of quite modern and sophisticated medical equipment) as well as two other ones, which were smaller. In addition, and probably equally or more important, the prefecture had established 19 smaller "hospitals"— which I concluded were really clinics—as well as 19 special maternity and birth control stations. These smaller institutions were widely scattered throughout the prefecture, and they had been able to extend modern care to a much larger number of people than in the past. Altogether, I was told, there were 2,304 beds in all of these institutions (not a large number for such a huge area but an improvement over the past), and the medical personnel totaled more than 4,300, of whom between 200 and 300 were doctors (mainly "middle-level" doctors). In terms of both personnel and facilities, what existed as of 1988 was obviously still inadequate to provide the health care needed for such a huge area with a population of more than three-quarters of a million. Nevertheless, modern medicine reached a great many more people than it had when I was last there in the 1940s. Also, in general my impression was that the people I saw looked healthier than the majority had in 1948.

*   *   *

Among the questions I wanted to explore during my visit in Ganzi, those relating to Han-Tibetan relations, and the state of religion in the area, were high on my agenda for inquiry. Although I was not able to learn all that I would like to have learned, by the time that I left I had acquired, through my interviews and observations of various religious institutions, at least some basis for reaching general judgments—though very tentative ones. Many of the most basic and important questions regarding attitudes and beliefs that I would like to have learned about are ones that obviously could not be easily answered on the basis of one relatively short trip and a few interviews. But I did form some very definite judgments on the basis of visits to several religious institutions, both in Kangding and in the grasslands (especially in the township of Tagong) as well as from my interviews. What I saw and learned about religion in Ganzi was consistent with, and generally reinforced, the impressions that I received elsewhere in west China.

In this region—as in other Lamaist and Muslim areas in west China—the attack on religion that was carried out by Red Guards during the height of the Cultural Revolution had been incredibly brutal and destructive. However, I was convinced, as I had been in other areas, that in Ganzi the regime's policies had undergone a profound change in the late 1970s and that in the subsequent years—the period of Deng's reforms—government policy had been notably conciliatory and accommodating and had aimed at trying to repair the recent damage to Han-minority relations. As a result of such policies, there had been a real revival of religion and religious practices in the area, and what I saw and heard convinced me that in this area the government genuinely was not only tolerating a revival of religion but was actually encouraging and in some respects supporting it. Considerable progress had been made in rebuilding religious institutions and returning them to fairly normal operations (although it was clear that all this was still under general state supervision). The government in Ganzi—as throughout much of the

northwest—was also pursuing policies of "affirmative action" aimed at reducing the inequalities among ethnic groups and was trying to reduce minority groups' grievances by giving them preferential treatment in education
and in many economic activities.

One crude measure of the change that had taken place was provided by
the number of religious institutions and what had happened to them during
and after the Cultural Revolution. In the prefecture as a whole, I was told,
there had been between 400 and 500 lamaseries before the Cultural Revolution. Of these, 27 major lamaseries of particular importance had been partially "protected" by intervention from higher authorities (usually either
provincial or central government authorities), but even all of these had been
damaged, and "most of the others had been either completely destroyed or
extremely badly damaged." It was hard to grasp the ferocity of this assault
on religion—and on all old traditions (including those of Han Chinese) by
these young fanatics, encouraged by radicals in Beijing and even by Mao
himself. In the decade following the initiation of reform in the late 1970s,
however, 440 of the lamaseries had been rebuilt or repaired and had been re-
opened, I was told. The central government had contributed about Y 10 million for this purpose—mainly for the 27 most important lamaseries—and
the prefecture and county-level governments had given a significant amount
of financial help as well, mainly to other lamaseries. But ordinary people had
made very large contributions—probably the majority of the funds needed.

In Kangding County, officials told me, there had been 24 lamaseries operating before the Cultural Revolution. They all had been destroyed or damaged, but they all had been rebuilt. Three of the 24 were located in the town
itself, and all 3 were back in operation, although the reconstruction of the
one that I remembered from 1948 was still under way. The central, provincial, and prefectural governments had contributed significant sums—totaling Y 1.23 million in 1987 alone, I was told—to the repair and rebuilding of
lamaseries in Kangding. I was told by both the Tibetans and the Han Chinese
I met that a substantial number of Tibetans were now again worshiping at
the lamaseries, especially on major religious days.

In Kangding, five major sects of Lamaism were represented. The largest
number of believers within the county belonged to the Yellow Hat sect.
However, the Red Hat sect and the Flowery (or Multicolored) Hua sect were
also well represented. Only a few, I was told, belonged to the White sect or
the Black sect.* All believers were said to view both the Dalai Lama and the

---

*The romanized terms that I use here are my translations of the Chinese forms of the sect
names. I am indebted to Professor Melvyn G. Goldstein of Case Western Reserve University for
the Tibetan names of the sects: Yellow Hat sect—Gelugapa; Red Hat sect—Nyingmapa; Multicolored sect—Sakyapa; White sect—Kagyupa; and Black sect—Bon.

Banchan Lama as important religious leaders. My Tibetan informants maintained that the differences between the sects were really not extremely large (although I suspect that some people would dispute that). When I asked local Tibetans what they felt about the fact that the Dalai Lama supported the idea of Tibetan independence, they said (in some cases no Han Chinese were present) that local people in Ganzi did not endorse the idea and did not think it was feasible. I, of course, had no way to be sure what their private thinking was; some may well have secretly sympathized with the idea. Nevertheless, my impression was that many genuinely did feel that the idea of independence was unrealistic—at least at the present time—at least as far as Ganzi was concerned. Nevertheless, believers in this area had renewed significant contacts with Lhasa and other parts of Tibet proper. I was told that when lamas in Kangding reached a certain rank they were expected to make a pilgrimage to either Lhasa or Xigaze; the former was described as being in Front Tibet (Qian Zang) and the latter was described as being in Rear Tibet (Hou Zang). Some were expected to make pilgrimages to both of these religious centers. In recent years, I was told, quite a few (but not all) lamas in Kangding had been able to make such trips. (Although all of the Tibetan political leaders that I met in Kangding County and Ganzi Tibetan Autonomous Prefecture had at one time or other visited Beijing, none of this particular group of men had ever visited Lhasa or Xigaze.)

Because Kangding lay next to a Tibetan area, Lamaism was the predominant religion in the region. However, three other religious institutions existed in Kangding. All of them predated 1949, and all had been closed in the 1960s. In the 1980s, they had been reopened and were once again operating. One was a mosque, another a Protestant church, and the third a Catholic church. The mosque already had a resident Ahong, but the Protestant church still had no regular pastor and was operating with lay leadership. I did not learn whether the Catholic church had a priest.

In the small township of Tagong (which I will describe later), I visited one of the important outlying lamaseries. It was a large establishment, with several buildings built around a big courtyard. It was the heart of the life of the village—and probably of a broader district. A total of 70 lamas were resident there; in addition, the lamasery ran a religious school (a kind of seminary) in which approximately 30 young students were studying under three full-time teachers. This lamasery belonged to the Hua, or Flowery (Multicolored), sect. This sect was predominant in that particular area, although Tagong also had a few believers who belonged to the Red Hat sect and the Yellow Hat sect.

Beijing's policies toward religion in the 1980s were, as I noted earlier, part of a broader policy of "affirmative action" aimed at minority peoples. In Ganzi, as elsewhere, for most of the decade of the 1980s preferential treatment had been given to Tibetans in appointments to governmental positions, in entry into institutions of higher learning, and in hiring for some kinds of jobs (including certain factory jobs)—and also in family planning policies (which were much looser for Tibetans than for Han Chinese). Local officials said that in Ganzi a three-child family was considered the norm for rural Tibetan families, and a two-child family was supposed to be the norm for Tibetan families living in urban areas. Urban Tibetans were "encouraged," however, to have one-child families. I could not judge how effectively these policies were being implemented. However, figures that I obtained for the population in Kangding (as I will note later) suggested that many families exceeded the specified norms.

*   *   *

As I stated earlier, the longest, and in many respects the most rewarding, conversations that I had while I was in Ganzi were with the leaders of Kangding County. With them I was able to probe more deeply, and obtain more extensive data, than I was able to do in regard to the prefecture as a whole. Although in some respects Kangding County was typical of—or at least representative of—the entire region, in others it obviously was unique. Not only did it contain the largest town (small as it was) in the prefecture, it served as the seat of political power for both the county and the prefecture. It was by far the most important transportation juncture; located just inside Zheduo Pass, it was the key link between Tibetan and Han Chinese areas. It was also, in economic terms, the best-developed area. Moreover, it was really the only place in the region that was, literally, half Chinese and half Tibetan in its population and—I would say—in its culture as well.

Earlier, I briefly described the appearance of the center of the town (Luchenzhen) and the characteristic of this center for 30,000 residents. Let me, at this point, add a few comments on the county as a whole. The size of the county was 4,400 square miles, roughly the size of Connecticut. Although this constituted only 7 percent of the prefecture's huge territory, it was by no means a small area. For example, it took the magistrate a full day traveling by car to reach some of the county's most distant places.

The population of the county as a whole totaled 94,021 in 1987. This total was about 12 percent of the population in the entire prefecture. (I should note, though, that it was considerably less than 1 percent of the total population of Sichuan Province, to which it belonged.) Administratively, the county was divided into 1 town, 7 districts (*chu*), and 237 villages (*cun*). In most of China there were, at one time, districts (*chu*) between county-level governments and local township governments (they were, administratively, really branches of the counties [*paichuso*]), but some years ago they were abolished in most of the country. The leaders in Kangding explained to me, though, that because the county's territory was so large, its population so small, and its transportation so difficult, it was still felt to be desirable to have these intermediate levels of administration to help the county supervise lower levels of administration.

The population density in Kangding County, which was roughly 21 people per square mile, was above that of the prefecture as a whole (which was about 13 per square mile), but this was only because there was a fairly large concentration of people in the town of Kangding; much of the county was almost as sparsely populated as much more distant areas on the grasslands.

The county's ethnic mixture was, as I noted, unique, because it was the principal meeting place of Han and Tibetan cultures and had a population mixture in which almost exactly half were Tibetans (51 percent) and half Han Chinese (49 percent). (Virtually all areas to the west were overwhelmingly Tibetan, and all those to the east were predominantly Han Chinese.) The only other significant ethnic group in the county consisted of about 800 Hui Muslims; the Yi and other minorities were extremely small. Despite the half-and-half division of the population in the county, Han Chinese were more numerous in the town itself.

County statistics classified a surprisingly large percent of the population as agricultural rather than pastoral. Of the total number of people listed as "rural residents" (which came to 8,153 households, with 53,000 or so members*), 85 percent (6,918 households, with 46,500 members) were classified as "agricultural households" and only 15 percent (1,235 households, with 6,500 members) were classified as "households in animal husbandry." These figures provided some clues about the degree to which, in this area at least, many Tibetans had shifted to or engaged in some agriculture. The statistics also revealed that the average family size far exceeded the regime's stated norm: The average for the "rural" population was 6.5, that for agricultural families was 6.74, and the figure for those in animal husbandry was 5.16. Because relatively permissive state policies toward birth control among minority groups allowed the Tibetans to have larger families than the Han Chinese, these figures were somewhat surprising and may have underestimated the size of Tibetan families. Or they may simply have shown that the local enforcement of the regime's population policies were not very strict or effective in regard to all ethnic groups.

*   *   *

I discussed at some length with the county's leaders, as I had with prefectural leaders, the organization, the leadership, and the functioning of the local party and government. They described the county leadership in terms of

---

*The figure of 53,000 for the "rural population" in the county implied that the urban population was about 41,000—or 10,000 or so more than the official number cited for Luchenzhen. Perhaps certain suburban or other areas were also classified as urban.

three layers: an inner core of 7, a larger group of 21, and a somewhat larger group of 25. The core, they said, consisted of the Party secretary of the county, his 2 deputies (1 of whom was the county magistrate), and the 4 deputy magistrates. The larger group of 21 included, in addition to these 7, the head and deputy head of the county Party's Discipline Inspection Commission, the chairman and 3 deputy chairmen of the county People's Congress, and the head and 7 deputy heads of the county People's Political Consultative Conference. The broadest definition of the top leadership group—the total of 25—included, in addition to all of the preceding, 2 other members of the Party's Standing Committee (including the head of the Party's Armed Forces Department) plus the heads of the local government's court and procuratorate. I found it interesting, and unusual, that they defined the leadership elite in this particular fashion—as a group combining Party and government personnel—rather than treating them separately. However, after outlining for me this conception of the top leadership, they then proceeded to describe the leadership of the Party and government separately rather than as one group.

The top leadership of the Party itself consisted, as almost everywhere in China, of those who belonged to the Standing Committee. In Kangding, this committee had eight members, four of whom were Han Chinese and four of whom were Tibetan. Almost all of them were in their forties. The eight included the Party secretary (age 44), his two deputies (age 42 and 41, the latter of which was County Magistrate Wang), and five other members (all of whom held significant posts; they included the heads of the Party's Discipline Inspection Committee, the Party's Armed Forces Department, and the government's People's Court; the other two held lesser positions). Only three of the eight—the Party secretary and his two deputies—including the magistrate—had graduated from "institutions of higher learning," although some were fairly well educated, at lower levels, and the government was trying its best to raise the general education of the leadership.

Under the Standing Committee of the Party, the structure of organization included a general office; departments for organization, propaganda, and united front work; the Armed Forces Department, and the Discipline Inspection Committee. (The previously existing departments for economic work had, in this area, been abolished, as reform policies had called for.) Altogether, these units under the Standing Committee had about 40 employees.

The Party membership throughout the entire county was grouped into 259 Party branches, 79 of which were within urban areas—within other organizations located in urban areas—and 180 of which were in rural areas. The Party's membership totaled 2,071, of whom 55 percent (1,144) were Tibetans and 45 percent (927) were Han Chinese. Compared to most areas of China, the size of the Party membership was unusually small as a proportion of the total population: It consisted of only 2.15 percent of the entire population in the county, which was far below the figure in more-developed areas. Local Party leaders told me that they were currently trying to carry out a variety of Party reforms, as requested by higher Party authorities, and they maintained that they had had some success. For example, they said that they had made progress toward "separating Party and government." In addition, they had already abolished Party *dangzu* or "core groups" in local government organizations. This was something Beijing had proposed some time previously but had not been very widely implemented, at least in the areas in which I visited and interviewed Party officials in 1988.

I could not help but be rather skeptical, however, about how real the separation of Party and government was, since Party Committees still existed in all government organization and since the Party secretary said (with the magistrate agreeing) that "we in the Party have responsibility for personnel and also for major policies, especially economic policies, as well as for insuring the implementation of all policies; the county government is responsible for actually carrying out the policies." This statement left no doubt about the primacy of the Party even though (as I stated earlier) in the conversations that I had with both the Party secretary and the magistrate, the magistrate generally took the lead in the discussion and the Party secretary politely deferred to her.

Among the county government's top five leaders—the magistrate and her four deputies—four were Tibetans and only one was Han Chinese. The government structure consisted of 30 major units—offices, commissions, and bureaus—plus two subordinate offices and a number of companies.* I was told that a total of 2,082 "state cadres" worked for the county government; of these, 905 were said to be administrative cadres, 964 were classified as professional and technical cadres (the largest number of whom were teachers), and 213 were cadres employed by major enterprises under the county government. Only about 100 of the 2,082 were graduates of institutions of higher learning. The magistrate herself decried this and talked at some length about the government's desire to raise the average educational level of officials. The goal of the government, she said, was to have all the top county positions filled as soon as feasible by "well-educated" people. But she admitted that this was going to be extremely difficult to do and would take time. The magistrate said, in fact, that even though recent regulations—set by higher governmental authorities—required, in theory, that cadres in a great many lower-level positions had to be graduates of at least middle school, even at this level qualified people were in very short supply, and it would take quite a while for the county to comply.

---

*In Kangding County, as elsewhere, I recorded in my notes a detailed list of the units in the county government as of 1988, as they were given orally to me, but I will not list them here.

*   *   *

One reason that the county government could not meet the standards that had been set for the educational level required of local officials obviously was that despite the substantial progress in developing education since 1948, the educational system was still clearly inadequate to meet local needs. As of 1988, in Kangding County, there were only 10,500 students attending school—in 91 schools, including both primary and middle schools. Among the 91 schools, 87 were primary schools, and of the 4 middle schools, only 1 was a senior middle school. Kangding's schools taught in both the Tibetan language and in Hanyu, but clearly there was a tilt toward the Chinese language. Of the 87 primary schools, only 31 (all of them in the grassland districts of the county) used Tibetan as their basic language but also taught Hanyu. Of the 4 middle schools, only 1, with 115 students, used Tibetan as its basic language of instruction. As a proportion of the county's total population, the children attending school in 1988 came to only a little over 11 percent; this percentage was less than half of the national percentage of children attending both primary and regular middle schools as a proportion of the total population. These figures highlighted the fact that even though I was impressed by progress compared to 1948, Kangding still had an enormous way to go to catch up with even the rest of China.

Kangding's economy, likewise, still had a very long way to catch up with many other areas in China; as I said earlier, it had begun, but only just begun, the process of modernization, and in many respects clearly was still backward. There were some obvious reasons for this: the area's overwhelming geographical and topographical disadvantages as well as the lag in education and transportation. The economy had grown substantially, in quantitative terms, since the 1940s, but it remained mainly nonindustrial—and relatively underdeveloped. In 1987, according to the local government's statistics, the gross value of the output of both agriculture and industry in the county was Y 29.65 million. Of this total, only Y 9.45 million came from industry whereas Y 20.20 million came from agriculture and animal husbandry combined. (Of the latter, a little over Y 11 million came from agriculture and about Y 9 million came from animal husbandry.) The recent rate of growth (as estimated, rather crudely, on the basis of the rate of growth of agriculture and industrial output) had been fairly high—8.9 percent in 1987, for example. But this rate of growth resulted in large part from the fact that the figure for agriculture was fairly high because it was in a period of recovery after a very bad year due to drought in 1986. Because of this recovery from drought, the rate of growth of the grain output in 1987 was very high—20.14 percent—and officials expected the total grain output to reach somewhat over 18,000 tons in 1988. This was the main reason why statistics showed that "agriculture as a whole"—including animal husbandry and farming and all other agricultural output—had a growth rate of over 10 percent in 1987 whereas, in contrast, the gross value of industrial output grew only 3.07 percent that year.

The official figures for "per capita income" of the rural population of the county showed a standard of living that was relatively low. I was told that the average in 1987 was Y 389. This was above the level of China's poorest counties. However, it was significantly below what I had been told was the average for the total population of the prefecture (Y 431)—as well as considerably below what officials in Beijing stated was the national average—Y 425.* I was given additional figures, which broke down the per capita income figures in the county into that for various groups. The figures showed that the figure for the farming population was extremely low—only a little over Y 300. In contrast, the figure for the population engaged mainly in animal husbandry was considerably higher—Y 560. Statistics that I had received in some other areas, such as Qinghai Province, had also shown that people in pastoral areas enjoyed higher incomes than those in farming. But the size of the gap between these two groups in Kangding County surprised me. The explanation, I was told, was the same as that I had received in Qinghai—namely, that the prices of animal products were substantially higher than those for agricultural products, which had been kept low by the government, to the detriment of the farmer. The price ratios, therefore, definitely favored those who raised animals.

Kangding's budgetary situation, and its dependence on subsidies from higher levels of government, fit the pattern that I had found at all levels throughout west China. In 1987, I was told, the county's own revenue totaled Y 9.35 million (roughly Y 100 per person), but its expenditures totaled Y 16 million (Y 140 per person). The deficit of Y 6.65 million was made up by subsidies from higher levels of government.

The ratio of "industrial output" (including mining and extractive industries) to economic output as a whole in Kangding County was also somewhat lower than I had expected in light of the fact that it was the industrial center of the area. The gross value of industrial output, according to the figures given to me, accounted for less than one-third of the combined value of agricultural and industrial output, whereas the value of agricultural output (including animal husbandry) accounted for more than two-thirds. These

---

*My own calculations for per capita output of the entire population in the county, derived by dividing gross agricultural output plus gross industrial output by the population total, produced a per capita figure of Y 315. I should say, though, that neither in Kangding nor elsewhere on my travels in the region did I see obvious evidence of extreme poverty. Most of the people I saw in towns *and* in rural areas and remote villages looked reasonably well fed, well clothed, and healthy.

figures produced a ratio that was almost the reverse of that for industry and agriculture in the national economy of all of China. And this was so despite the fact that Kangding County was considerably ahead of the rest of the prefecture in industrialization, as I noted earlier. The county had two of the largest factories in the prefecture—a cement plant and a printing plant. It also had an electric power-generating plant, factories producing building materials, and a number of small plants or shops producing clothing, leather goods, and jewelry. There was also a fairly large logging operation in the county, at Jintang, which was a one-day trip from the town of Kangding. And there were several mines within the county that produced coal, lead, gypsum, and tungsten; they were located in fairly remote mountain areas.

Because it was the crucial juncture between the high grassland areas and agricultural Chinese areas, Kangding continued to be—as it had been in the past—an important trading town. The value of the county's total trade turnover in 1987, I was told, was Y 53.52 million. State trading channels still predominated in interregional commerce, but they had declined in local trade because both free markets and private shops had expanded so rapidly in recent years; the private entrepreneurs now handled a very large percentage of local trade. It was clear that in Kangding, as in much of China, one of the most important results of the "decade of reform" in the 1980s had been "reform from below," involving the very rapid growth of small-scale private and quasiprivate entrepreneurs at the grass-roots level.

As I noted earlier, also, because it was the hub of the prefecture's road system, Kangding enjoyed at least somewhat better transportation facilities than most of the prefecture, and its communications (telephone, telegraph, radio, and television facilities) were by far the best in the entire area. The town's local TV station had been built in 1985, and by 1988 there were three TV relay stations in the county, two of which were in the most mountainous area and one of which was out on the grasslands. Wired radio networks had also been extensively developed, and there were several regular radio broadcasting stations. Some radio programs originated within the county, and others rebroadcast programs from elsewhere. Within the county were 10 township "broadcasting stations." I was told that the local radio stations carried some programs in the Tibetan language, but the majority were in Chinese. And I was told that none of the local TV programs were in the Tibetan language.

*   *   *

After my interviews in Kangding, I was eager to travel out in the high grassland areas, beyond Zheduo Pass. I had made such a trip in 1948, by horseback (really, I should say, on a small pony), and it had been one of the most memorable of all my expeditions in the 1940s. At that time, the Kangding government had insisted that I be accompanied by an armed Tibetan escort—a man who worked for the provincial government—"for my protection." The trip was a difficult one then. We climbed up the long valley to the 14,071-foot pass at Zheduo. Even though it was July, I had been warned that it would be cold, and it certainly was. The local people loaned me some warm clothing—including a wide, white felt cape and a wide-brimmed Tibetan hat—which made me look a little like Pancho Villa. But a light snow was falling as we went through the pass and onto the plateau. I still remember very vividly my first sight of the grasslands out beyond the pass. Ahead of us was a wide valley, with mountains rising on both sides, and in many respects the scene was breathtaking. No one had explained to me what the grasslands in this region looked like. I suppose that I expected to see tall, messy, yellowish blades of grass. Instead, what we saw looked very much like an endless, bright-colored golf green, except that from the grass sprouted a profusion of beautiful wildflowers. Because the course we traveled by horseback was difficult and slow, we did not go very far into the grasslands on that visit, but we did go far enough to visit some villages and to stop and see a relative of my Tibetan escort (we spent the night there, in a traditional Tibetan farmhouse built of stone—a two-story building, with the lower one used as a barn for animals). It was at that time that I was first introduced to *tsamba* and butter tea. It was all memorable.

My trip in 1988 was quite different. Accompanied by the young woman who was magistrate of Kangding County, we—my escorts and I—traveled in a comfortable Toyota Land Cruiser, on a good macadam road. Our destination was the village of Tagong, 67 miles from Kangding. What might well have required several days of travel in 1948 took only three-and-a-half hours each way in 1988. For the first 20-plus miles, from Kangding to the pass, we traveled through a series of narrow valleys, steadily climbing and twisting through one hairpin turn after another. The climb took us 5,000 feet higher than Kangding. Just outside of Kangding, we passed a sizable number of very modern buildings (including, as I noted earlier, the headquarters of the military subdistrict), which stretched quite a way up the valley, but then there were only scattered Tibetan stone farmhouses, and just before the pass we entered an uninhabited area. Construction of this road, in its modern form, Magistrate Wang said, had begun in the 1950s (the PLA built it), but most of the paving was not completed until the 1970s. Among the passenger vehicles that we passed were two long-distance buses; by the 1980s, such buses had routes that went all over the country, even to some of the most remote areas. We also saw a great many freight trucks on the road. The majority of them were carrying huge logs from mountain areas rising from the grasslands, but we did pass, also, one long convoy of PLA oil tank trucks on its way out to the grasslands.

It did not surprise me (in light of my experience of 1948) when, soon after leaving Kangding, we encountered snowfall—in April. It was light at first, but as we approached the pass it became heavier. Shortly before reaching the pass, we encountered a scene of a kind that etches itself into one's memory. Suddenly, in the middle of nowhere, we saw a barefoot man, running in the snow in the middle of the road. He was a bearded and wild-looking person, lightly dressed in very ragged clothes, with long matted hair, and he was running wildly, flailing his arms, seemingly without purpose. He did not try to flag us down; in fact, he clearly was lost in some other world and simply ignored us. "He is a crazy man, out of his mind," our driver said; his explanation was unnecessary because it was obvious that the man was, in some respects at least, a mad person. My own instinct was to stop and try to do something to help him, but we did not stop. The magistrate said that he would be helped. Actually, when we returned, we passed the same man again. "Do not worry; others will take care of him," I was told. Perhaps they eventually did. The welfare assistance for China's poorest people had, in fact, expanded tremendously throughout the country in recent years—even in this region. I suspected, though, that people regarded as "crazy" still fell through the gaps in the Chinese "safety net." As I ruminated on this man, I came to the realization that I had seen very few such people in all of my travels either in northwest or southwest China.

Virtually all of those I did see—and they were a very small number—were people such as this man who were obviously emotionally disturbed. I had seen one ragged group of men on the streets of Wenjiang Prefecture in Sichuan, and later I saw a few such people in Kunming, but there really were not many. All of them reminded me, in fact, of the "street people" (particularly those who are mentally disturbed former inmates of institutions) that one sees on the streets of American cities, including my home base, Washington, D.C. I actually saw fewer such people in Chinese cities than I have in American cities. However, the image of the man near Zheduo Pass was seared into my brain indelibly, in part because, in that setting, barefoot in the snow, alone in the middle of nowhere, he seemed to epitomize the lost souls of the world—whether in China or elsewhere.*

---

*I had one comparable image that had been permanently engraved on my mind many years earlier. In early 1945, when I was a young Marine Corps officer on Okinawa, I had to make periodic flights to small outlying islands, and I vividly remember one flight in a Piper Cub from Okinawa to an outlying island called Kume. We passed over a tiny little sandspit—perhaps a 100 yards long—in the ocean, miles from anywhere, and standing on it was one lone Japanese soldier, with no equipment, no shelter, nothing. How, I wondered then, did he ever get there? What was he doing? Where would he go? He looked up at our little airplane but did not even wave. Later, we sent a message to headquarters reporting our sighting of this lost soul, but I have no idea what they subsequently did, and in my memory he is still standing there on that sandspit, all alone. I feel the same way about the barefoot man in the snow at Zheduo Pass.

When we finally reached Zheduo Pass, the snowy roads were extremely icy, and the pass was blocked by a messy pile-up of trucks that had skidded into each other. We had to wait until all of these trucks put heavy chains onto their tires, after which the mess was gradually untangled and we were able to proceed. We had no chains, though, so the trip from there on, winding down onto the plateau on very icy roads—without any railguards—was another hair-raising experience. We had to go down from the pass to reach the first major plateau in the grasslands, but we did not have to go very far down because virtually all of the grasslands in this region lie at an altitude of 10,000 feet or more and have high mountains rising to much greater heights around them. Our destination, Tagong, lay slightly above the general level of the plateau, at an altitude of 11,610 feet.

*   *   *

The 47-mile ride from the pass to Tagong took us close to three hours. Right after the pass, the vista was a spectacular one. Out of the broad snow-dusted valley rose high snow-covered mountains. It was very much as I had remembered the scene from 40 years earlier, except that now, in April, the grass was either purple or brown instead of bright green. (It was not until early summer that it turned green, I was told.) Beyond the pass, the road first went almost straight westward. Then it divided, with one road continuing west (it was the one we followed) and another leading to the south. Eventually, the latter one linked up with the road to Xichang. A little further on, our road divided again. One route continued west; it was the main road to Batang and from there to Chamdo, which, our driver said, was "about 1,000 kilometers further on." The driver told us that when he was an army truck driver he had used this road frequently and had followed it all the way to Lhasa. This was not the only road to Chamdo, though; another, in the north, went via the towns of Ganzi and Dege. On this trip, we turned north on the road toward Ganzi.

The entire atmosphere in the countryside on the Tibetan plateau in this region—which everyone used to call *guan wai* ("outside of the frontier" or "outside of the gate")—was very different indeed from that in Han Chinese agricultural areas inside the pass. The feel was entirely Tibetan rather than Han. This was true even where the Tibetans no longer depended mainly on animal husbandry but had become essentially farmers. Actually, our route took us through a series of valleys, paralleling streams, in most of which the local Tibetans both farmed and raised animals. Not until we were near Tagong did we reach an area that, I was told, was devoted entirely to animal husbandry.

The first valley that we went through was uncultivated and mostly treeless. There were many animals in the valleys and on the hillside; the majority were yaks, but there were also sheep, goats, and horses. In the distance we could see a number of large, black tents (made of heavy black felt, from yak hair). There also were occasional stone Tibetan houses, but not many in this area. Although I was impressed by the number of animals that we saw, my companions said that in the summer there were many, many more. A large number of local people, they said, had taken their yaks elsewhere for better winter grazing and had not yet returned. Soon we entered into a series of valleys where farming was more prevalent. In many small cultivated fields we saw men, women, and children—all Tibetans—engaged in plowing and preparing the land for planting. In these valleys we saw an increased number of houses, and, although some of them were isolated, most were grouped into small hamlets or villages, each of which typically consisted of a half a dozen to a dozen or more houses. Most of the homes were made of stone, and their architecture was typical, traditional Tibetan: They all were very square, built of stone, with flat roofs and distinctive sloping walls, and most of the homes were two stories tall (although some were three) and had barns in the lower level and living quarters above. All of the stone Tibetan homes had very distinctive, white-framed, slanting windows—one of their trademarks.

Even in the valleys where there were many cultivated fields we saw numerous animals, especially on the hillsides above the fields. I was told that the household responsibility system had been effectively implemented throughout this area and that it was applied to the management of both agricultural land and grazing land. Local township (*xiang*) governments now had the responsibility of deciding on the boundaries separating different parts of pastureland. In winter, I was told, because of the scarcity of good pastureland, people were fairly strict in observing such boundaries, which divided the pastures that were assigned to different families. But in summer, when good pastureland was more plentiful, the authorities were said to be a good deal more relaxed. In some circumstances, I was told, the township demarcated pastureland according to villages (*cun*) rather than individual households. My informants talked to me about the townships and villages and said that, in reality, they really were organized in ways that were not very different, at least in this area, from the ways in which traditional Tibetan units of social organization had been organized. The townships were said to be comparable to traditional Tibetan units that they called *tusi* (my transliteration), which usually had included several dozen families. The villages were comparable to traditional Tibetan units at a lower level, which had been called (as best I could try to transliterate and record the title they used) *garonjie;* these generally, my informants said, included up to a dozen or so households.

The final part of our trip to Tagong was through another district (*chu*)— one of seven in Kangding County. This district contained five townships, and we passed through, and stopped at, the village headquarters of one of them. It was simply a small cluster of houses, in this case Chinese-style buildings.

As we proceeded, we had the road to ourselves for the most part; all that we passed was an occasional bicycle or crawling tractor. About noontime, however, we reached—and briefly stopped at—a real town, which was called Waze, where we talked briefly with the local leadership. The town had a population of between 2,000 and 3,000 people. Magistrate Wang said that it would probably soon be large enough to be classified as a real town (that is, a *zhen*). This town had not existed before 1949, I was told; only four or five houses had been located there at that time. Now it was the governmental headquarters of a district that had a population of more than 10,000 people, who lived in five townships and three villages. Its raison d'être was obvious: There was a small army base located just outside of town, and uniformed (but unarmed) soldiers were much in evidence within the town—shopping in the markets and local shops. Although we saw quite a few Tibetans on the streets in this town, the appearance of the place was essentially Han Chinese—in architecture, clothing, and general ambience. My guess was that the population was predominantly Chinese because of the presence of Chinese military personnel. Both the town center and the countryside elsewhere in the township were, according to my informants, supplied with electricity. Partly because of this electricity, a TV relay station was located there, and I was told that local TV reception was excellent. The cultivated fields near this town were larger than those of most of the other areas we went through, and at the time of our trip the fields were being plowed with tractors. This was the only town of any significant size that we passed on our entire trip, and as such it clearly had a more "modern" and developed appearance than the smaller townships and villages that we passed through.

Just beyond Waze, we turned north and proceeded toward Tagong. Our route took us through Dangwale Township, where the township center was a cluster of perhaps 20 or so buildings, part of them built in Tibetan style and part in Chinese style. The road then wound through a series of valleys, where some areas were almost exclusively agricultural and others were almost exclusively pastureland—although a few still were mixed. On a number of hillsides, there were evergreen conifers. We also saw two lamaseries, in the distance, and passed a number of other small religious structures, including a white stupa or dagoba (these are pagodalike structures used as depositories for religious relics) as well as one large tentlike religious center. As we climbed from the flat agricultural land into a more hilly area, we passed two installations where a sizable number of Tibetans had built huts along the stream and were actively panning for gold. After that point, the paved road ended and we entered a narrow valley, with fir trees covering the hillsides beside it. There was no systematic logging in this area, I was told, but local people could, with permission, cut down trees to use in the building of their own houses. Vehicular traffic was nonexistent on the last stretch as we approached Tagong—but, much to my surprise, suddenly out of the blue a modern ambulance appeared and passed us going very rapidly in the other direction. Nobody seemed to know where it might have come from or where it might be going. Possibly, it was an ambulance based at the army town that we had passed a few miles back. It was, in any case, fairly convincing evidence that at least some health services were reaching into this remote area.

*   *   *

We finally reached Tagong in the early afternoon and were warmly welcomed by the local leaders, who had been alerted beforehand, by telephone, of my impending visit. They had prepared a fairly elaborate, Tibetan-style lunch. As we ate, I engaged in uninterrupted conversation with a fairly large group of local leaders, trying to learn as much as I could about the place. After lunch, while wandering with my hosts throughout the village, I learned a good deal more about local governments and the local economy.

Tagong was the seat of government of one of Kangding County's districts. It was also a township—one of two into which the district was divided. Its residents were also organized as a village, and they constituted 1 of 18 villages within the district. So, in fact, three levels of governmental organization were located there. The district's population in 1988 totaled 6,502 individuals belonging to 1,262 households. The average household size—5.15 persons—was almost exactly the average number for Tibetans engaged in animal husbandry in the entire county of Kangding (according to the statistics I had been given earlier). Only 350 or so people actually lived within the village center.

The place had a real "frontier town" atmosphere. Homes, and the few public buildings, were widely scattered. The highway, passing through the middle of the village, was the "main street." Dominating the area was a large lamasery—Tagong Si (mentioned earlier when I was discussing religion in Ganzi). This was a Hua sect institution. According to local people, it had first been built in the Tang dynasty. It was obvious that the lamasery and its religious school were very much the center of most of the life of the community. Just outside of the village itself was a large, white stupa, after which Tagong had been named. (*Ta* means dagoba, stupa, or pagoda). It was evident that the village had grown up where it did because of the location of the lamasery and the stupa.

In the village, on or near the "main street," there were several small buildings that housed public institutions. Most of them were fairly new; a few were two-story "modern" structures. In these buildings were the government and Party headquarters and also three county-run institutions (a primary school, a clinic, and a grain sales station) and also two prefecture-run organizations (a branch post office and a credit cooperative, which served as a kind of local bank). Also in this area were four shops—all that there were in the village. One was a "large" state-run establishment, and three were

In 1948 I rode a pony to Zheduo Pass, gateway to the Tibetan grasslands. Because it was snowing (on July 4!), I was lent a yak-hair cape and hat.

Tibetan men, traveling the grasslands, stop to eat lunch. They use the small eating bowls that Tibetans always carry when traveling.

My Toyota Land Cruiser stuck in the snow on Zheduo Pass in 1988. A snowstorm in April created a massive traffic jam (but travel by motor vehicle was nevertheless a big improvement over travel by horse).

Sheep on the Tibetan grasslands, beyond Zheduo Pass. Thousands of sheep, goats, yaks, and horses can be seen everywhere, even where Tibetans farm.

Typical Tibetan homes in 1988 were larger and better built than most in 1948, and many had modern appliances. These are in a Tibetan farming area; the women are working in the fields.

The large lamasery at Tagong was clearly still, in 1988, the center of life in this small Tibetan township.

Tibetans clustered around a public building on the modern paved highway that now is Tagong's main street.

In many respects, yaks are the most important all-purpose animals for Tibetans on the grasslands.

In the late 1980s, the game of pool swept through much of China, and by 1988 it had become one of the main recreations in Tagong.

smaller, private shops. In this village there was no real entertainment center, such as the small movie theaters that some places had. However, in the center of the village, right in the open air, there was a pool table; it was surrounded by young dudes, and this seemed in effect to serve as the principal recreation center. In addition to the public institutions I have mentioned, there was, in the village, a tiny Public Security station (*paichuso*), which, I was told, was a branch of the county Public Security Bureau. Three uniformed policemen were stationed there, and these three men were responsible for maintaining law and order in the entire district—and among all of its 6,502 inhabitants. (In most of my travels through remote areas of China in 1988, I was constantly surprised by how few policemen there were in most rural areas.)

The government of the district was in the hands of a group of 12 cadres. It was obvious that the idea of "separating Party and government" had not penetrated to Tagong. When I asked the district Party Committee secretary and the head of government there to describe the district's leadership and political organization, they first discussed the Party and government officials as if they were members of a single organization. (These two top leaders, both in their early forties, were eager to tell me all they could about the district; they had never met and talked with a foreign visitor before.) When I said that it seemed to me as if the Party and government were almost merged, they said no, this was not entirely the case, and then began to discuss the organizational structure of the two, separately. But it was evident that they really did not differentiate them very clearly.

The 12 cadres working in the district, they said, included the Party secretary and his deputy; the district government head and his deputy; two *mishu* (clerical-type secretaries in this case) who served both the Party and the government (one helped with Party organizational work and the other with economic matters); a Party cadre who was in charge of women's work generally (a Party responsibility) and also for family planning (primarily a governmental responsibility); two other government cadres who were in charge, respectively, of civil affairs and statistics; two party cadres responsible for propaganda and youth work (working mainly through the local Young Communist League)—plus a cook, who fed all of them together, at work. Of these 12 cadres, 6 were local people, but 6 had come to Tagong from other areas. I had never, anywhere else, heard the Party and government organizations and personnel described in this fashion with so little differentiation between governmental functions and Party work, and I was struck by how large a percentage of the cadres were "outsiders" (although most of them were from areas nearby and were natives of the region).

Under this "top leadership," however, the Party did have its own separate organizational branches, located throughout the district, and the government did deal directly with subordinate government cadres who were stationed in the 2 townships and the 18 villages in the district. In the Party, in addition to a district-level Party Committee there were Party Committees in each of the two townships. The district Party Committee's staff was very small. It had no "departments" of its own, but four of its cadres dealt with traditional areas of work—organizational work, propaganda work, women's work, and youth work (things that were handled by Party departments at a higher level). Altogether there were 15 Party branches in the entire district; 3 of these were located in the town that was the headquarters of the district and township, and 12 of them were "rural" branches scattered throughout the district's rural areas. Total Party membership in the district was only 114, which amounted to a mere 1.7 percent of the population—a percentage far below that of most of China and, in fact, most of Kangding County. The local township government structure, which was subordinate to that of the district, was, as I said, also located in the town (or village) center. It had 11 cadres working for it. I did not, however, obtain any details about their backgrounds or responsibilities.

From talking with local leaders—and watching their interactions with the people from Kangding who had accompanied me—it was apparent to me that the magistrate of Kangding County and Tagong's local leaders knew each other well and seemed to have a very easy relationship with each other. They all said that there were frequent direct contacts between the county and district governments; these included frequent visits by county personnel to Tagong and occasional visits the other way. Magistrate Wang emphasized to me that "the work of the county is *mainly* at the district and township level, so naturally we send personnel very frequently to the local level." Often, she said, the county dispatched small groups of five or six cadres who together went to learn all they could about particular local problems as well as to monitor the work of local governments. By happenstance, two such visitors arrived while we were having lunch. One was a deputy head of the Organization Department of the County Party Committee, who was visiting a number of local Party branches; the other was a uniformed Public Security policeman, who was making an "inspection trip" on behalf of the County Procuratorate. They, too, seemed to have a fairly easy relationship with local Tagong leaders.

The lunch that I had with the local leaders was a very pleasant affair. It was held in a large tent on the edge of the village, near the white stupa. The tent had been pitched on a flat area of grassland, with snow-covered mountains in the background. Unlike most traditional Tibetan tents made of heavy black yak hair, this one was white and made of light cotton fabric. It looked very much like a small circus tent. These white tents were increasingly used, I was told, in the period between spring and fall because they were cooler and cheaper (they cost about Y 300 each, compared to about Y 1,000 to Y 2,000 for a good traditional yak hair tent). During lunch, we sat on the floor, squatting at low, long tables, and we were served a wide variety of Tibetan delicacies and dishes, many of them new to me—and many of them very good. At lunch, my hosts discussed mainly the economy of Tagong (it was later, going around the village, that I asked them about governments). The economy, they said, was based almost entirely on animal husbandry—although many people supplemented their incomes by a variety of sideline activities. Tagong was one of the relatively few districts in the county that was officially classified as being based exclusively on animal husbandry. Their statistics on animals were even more precise, therefore, than those I received in Kangding or elsewhere. The latest local animal census, I was told, had shown that there were 52,226 yaks, 5,519 horses, and 6,699 sheep in the district—a total of 64,444 animals, or almost 10 for every man, woman, and child in the district. That four-fifths of the animals were yaks seemed quite remarkable to me; I took it to be a sign of considerable affluence in the district.

*   *   *

After discussing animal husbandry as the foundation of the local economy, they went on to say that a great many families in the district obtained substantial amounts of supplementary income from a variety of sideline activities, and they gave me a number of examples of this. After lunch, I learned more specifically about some of these secondary occupations when I visited three families in the town.

All three of these families lived in quite spacious, well-built, two-story stone houses, constructed in traditional Tibetan style, with living quarters upstairs and barns for animals downstairs. These houses were very solid, with whitish stone as the main construction material, and with solid wood frameworks. I could see that virtually all of the local homes were built in this fashion. The district head (a relatively young man, age 43) accompanied me as I wandered throughout the village (or town). He said that building the kind of homes that I saw was a fairly new development, during the last 10 to 20 years; before that, he said, most of the local homes had been built of bricks made of mud with straw to reinforce them. All three of the homes that I visited were quite comfortable. In fact, all were furnished with a variety of low tables and cabinets and colorful rugs—which were not only on the floor but also hanging on the walls—and a variety of "consumer durables." In each of these homes, there was a variety of "manufactured" modern items. Every one of them, also, had some electronic items. Even though there was no electricity in Tagong, battery-operated equipment was widely used by people. All three homes had at least a radio.

In each of the homes, I was greeted effusively: All members of the family who were present gathered around me, and I was ceremoniously seated at a low table, where I sat on rugs and was able to lean against pillows of various sorts. Tables were generally about the height of a low coffee table in the West or a typical table in a traditional Japanese home. Despite my protestations— we had just finished our lunch a short time earlier—in each of the homes the family insisted on plying me with food (a wide variety of Tibetan snacks) and drink (including buttered tea, which is not one of my favorite beverages). The Tibetans are a very hospitable people (so, too, I should note, were virtually all the other people I met in distant places as I traveled around the west, including Mongols, Uighurs, Kazakhs, and also Han Chinese).

The families I met were obviously quite well off, but only one family head was a local official (he headed the *cun,* or local village, located within Tagong). The other two family heads were ordinary, nonofficial people. Their houses were not by any means unique; in fact, from the outside they looked very much like most of the other houses in the village.

The first home we visited belonged to the village head, who was 51. He told me that his *cun,* or village, contained 83 families with 340 family members. (This indicated an average of 4 persons per household, which was smaller than I would have expected.) The family living with the village head was obviously atypical, being considerably larger than the average. Altogether, he said, his household included 14 people—he and his wife and their children and a brother and his children. He had built this house 17 years previously, in the early 1970s. He owned 73 yaks and 3 horses (this amounted to only 4 to 5 per person—below the average in the district). In one corner of the living room in his home, on the second floor, I saw a radio and a tape cassette player. The radio was obviously battery operated. I was not sure what powered the cassette player, but it might have been a battery as well. The room also had some pressure-operated gas lights, with double filaments— very much like the Coleman lamps that were common in the United States a couple of generations ago. When I asked about his family's livelihood, he seemed delighted to describe in some detail their activities and income. (The same was true not only of the other family heads I met here, but also of people that I met throughout China.) The bottom line, he said, was that the "annual income per family member" (that is, what the local leaders referred to as the "per capita family income," calculated by dividing the total family income by the number of family members) was Y 900, a figure well above the average income in rural China as a whole and also higher than the average income in Ganzi.

In the second home that I visited, the family was even more affluent than those in the first. Also, their home was a newer one. The head of the family said that he had built the home four years previously. It, too, was well furnished. A total of five people belonged to this household. Their per family member (that is, per capita) income was Y 1,100, and they owned 36 yaks and 3 horses (close to 8 per person). Their income from raising animals was supplemented by important additional outside income. The household head explained to me that in the nearby mountains there were very valuable herbs, and all the members of the family earned a good deal by gathering these herbs and selling them.

The third household that I visited was the most affluent of the three. The family was a relatively small one—a man, his wife, and their two children. The father of the family was a Han Chinese, but he had settled permanently in Tagong; his wife was a Tibetan. They owned 40 yaks and 1 horse (10-plus animals per family member). But the main explanation for their relative affluence was the supplementary income that the head of the family earned. In addition to raising animals, he said, he was a cabinetmaker, and this was quite lucrative. As a result, the per capita income of this family averaged Y 1,900. (All of these figures were for annual income.)

I thoroughly enjoyed these family visits—and my entire visit to Tagong. The people were friendly. The air was invigorating. The setting was attractive and particularly interesting because of its cultural difference from most areas of China. And—for good reasons—I had the feeling that I was "close to the earth" and was seeing "real life" in this distant Tibetan grassland area. (I would not try to maintain that this was a typical Tibetan village. In fact, I doubt if there is such a thing as a typical one, because the variations are considerable from place to place.) I have always, on all my travels, found distant, out-of-the-way places of particular interest.

When it came time to leave, I expressed my great, and genuine, thanks for their hospitality. We then entered (mounted) our Toyota Land Cruiser, started to drive cross-country to get to the main road, crossed a very small stream—and promptly fell through the ice and got stuck. With embarrassment, but with great aplomb, the village leader mobilized some neighbors, who found two small but long logs and then jacked up the car and pushed it onto hard ground. We then took off for Kangding.

The trip back was uneventful. Light snow was still falling in the pass, but there was no traffic jam this time. Over the pass, as we drove down into the valley, we again passed the ragged, mad, lost soul that we had seen on the way up, and again my impulse was to stop and see if we could do something to help him. Again, though, the county magistrate assured me that she would see that something was done to help him later and that we should not stop now.

In the evening, the weather worsened, and I was told that the icy rains made it too dangerous to try to go over the old road on Two Wolf Mountain under such conditions. We should therefore, they said, wait a day. I quickly agreed, and the next day I spent relaxing, lying in the bed in my small room, reading a book I had brought with me. It was the first really free day that I had had in weeks, and I took good advantage of it to recharge my batteries. The following day, the weather improved, and we started our trip back, via Yaan, to Chengdu—a memorable journey, which I described earlier. Soon thereafter, I departed from Sichuan Province, flew to Beijing, spent a few days there, and then started another long journey to a different part of the huge country called China.

*   *   *

As I left this area, I reflected on what I had observed and seen in Sichuan's far west—especially in Ganzi Prefecture but also in the area around Yaan, both of which had belonged to the now-defunct Xikang Province. I was not absolutely certain whether the continuities or the changes had impressed me more.

This area remained one of the most difficult ones to reach—and therefore, in some respects, one of the most isolated—of any region in China. Certainly it was the most difficult to reach and isolated of any area that I visited—in 1988 and 1948—because of the extremely rough mountain terrain and the extreme difficulty of travel by road. (In contrast, by the late 1980s the Lhasa area of Tibet had good air service, a sizable flow of tourists, and a Holiday Inn! Ganzi had none of these, and it seemed unlikely to have any in the foreseeable future.) Not surprisingly, therefore, there was much that was unchanged.

Yet, on balance I decided that I was more impressed by the changes than by the continuities. The area was very different in important respects from what I had seen four decades earlier because of the construction of roads in the area (poor as most of them were); the dramatic improvement of modern communications (including TV); the steady expansion of trade and contact with other parts of China; the large expansion of modern education; the penetration into the area of modern facilities for public health and medicine; the obvious improvement in methods of raising animals and crops; and the beginnings (even though they were still small beginnings) of industrialization. In the 1940s, poverty and poor health were almost universal and were highly visible, and the general atmosphere and appearance of the region was reminiscent of the distant past. Even then, there were faint signs of the intrusion of the modern world into the area—mainly the goods in the shops of Kangding that had come all the way from British India—but in general it was easy to imagine that one was in some earlier century. By 1988, not only was the area much better connected with the rest of China and the modern world, but its appearance had been undergoing constant change, and it looked very different from the way it had appeared in the 1940s. It was evident that modern influences were inexorably intruding into, and altering, even this very remote pocket of the country. This was most true inside the pass, but the force of modernizing influences was visible outside the pass as well. It was obvious that the average standard of living had improved substantially. This was true of some groups more than of others (and, it was interesting that some of those who had improved their living the most were Tibetans in good pasture areas of the grasslands).

What impressed me, in short, were the changes I saw in comparison with situations that had existed in that area four decades earlier, in the 1940s.

Comparing the area to present conditions in the most advanced areas of China, however, western Sichuan obviously is still relatively backward and poor. Moreover, the gap between it and eastern China—particularly coastal China—seemed almost certain to continue, and it is easy to foresee circumstances under which this area could lag even further behind the more rapidly developing areas in the east.

I could also imagine—in theory—some circumstances in which the development and modernization of the area might be accelerated. If, for example, it was found that the area possessed large resources of vital raw materials needed by rapidly developing areas to the east (mineral raw materials, timber, and so on—substantial amounts of which are already known), and if governments and enterprises elsewhere in China were prepared to invest in them, and if—probably most important—the extreme difficulty of transporting goods into and out of the area could somehow be overcome or at least alleviated (for example, by building a long tunnel through Two Wolf Mountain and constructing a much better road system in other vital areas), then I could well see the possibility of more far-reaching and rapid modernization of the area. However, these are huge ifs. And I certainly do not think that this is likely in the near future. Nevertheless, I concluded that the process of modernization, already started, would continue, inexorably, in this area as in most areas even in outlying China. I felt that the process was unstoppable and that it would gradually bring this area into the modern world and would steadily improve the life of its inhabitants.

Politically, there was no question that this area was already much more closely integrated into the Chinese policy than it had been when I visited it in the 1940s. It seemed to me likely—in fact, almost inevitable—that this integration would continue and that it would be driven by a combination of economic and political factors. A key question, of course, is what the relationship between the Han Chinese and the Tibetans will be as these processes unfold in the period ahead and whether, in the years ahead, the area is likely to be politically stable or rent by ethnic tensions and struggles. In 1988, it seemed to me, the situation was remarkably stable in fundamental respects, and, at least in the areas I visited, relations between Han Chinese and Tibetans seemed generally amicable—more so, I will say, than I expected. In this respect, the area appeared to me to be different from everything I had heard and read in the late 1980s about "Outer Tibet"—especially the Lhasa area of what is now the Tibetan Autonomous Region. Tibetans in the Ganzi region obviously feel strong cultural and religious links with that area, yet politically and economically they are much more closely linked to areas of China to the east—that is, to Han China. In 1988 it also seemed to me that they tended, in almost every respect, to look more to the east than to the west, partly because of the immense distance to the Tibetan Autonomous Region.

Although I was, as I have said, favorably impressed by what seemed to me to be generally good relations and interactions on a personal level between Tibetans and Han Chinese, I nevertheless assume that there continue to be some tensions under the surface. Because of the profound difference between Han culture and Tibetan culture, this has always been the case. Moreover, I also assume that the savage rampages of the Red Guards during the Cultural Revolution left resentments that are still strongly felt by some. Such resentments still exist all over China, not only among minority people but also among many different types of Chinese groups who were victimized at that time. But it seemed to me in 1988 that even resentment about the Cultural Revolution period had begun to recede into the background. The reason, I believe, was that the affirmative action programs and policies adopted by Beijing in the late 1970s and early 1980s, after Deng Xiaoping's reform program got under way, had—in fact as well as in theory—had a significant impact on the area. During the 1980s, many young Tibetans were brought into the leadership; educational opportunities were expanded; and the livelihood of Tibetans clearly improved. In the years ahead, it seems to me, there will probably be increasing contacts and interactions of many sorts between Tibetans and Han Chinese, and it also seems probable that gradually the educational and economic gaps between these groups—and in some respects the cultural gaps as well—will be narrowed.

However, such trends are not inevitable, and it is easy to imagine ones that would be different. If, for example, there were to be much greater open conflict between Han Chinese and Tibetans in the Tibetan Autonomous Region, this would doubtless reverberate and have a significant impact on Ganzi. Whether it would impel Ganzi's Tibetans to become more involved with politics in the Tibetan Autonomous Region is difficult to predict.

However, when I left Ganzi I felt that, over time, as the Tibetans in Ganzi become better educated, improve their economic status, and interact more with other parts of the country, it is likely that, instead of losing their sense of ethnic identity, they may well assert it more strongly. They probably will be further integrated into the political and economic fabric of the rest of China, but at the same time they could well become more politically activist and perhaps exert increasing pressure for a greater degree of real political decentralization—and for greater autonomy (although, I would guess, probably not for total "independence"). Such trends are likely, I think, throughout most areas of west China that possess large minority populations. (Comparable trends have gained force in many parts of the world since the late 1980s.) If this happens, it will pose a major challenge to Beijing and to Han Chinese leadership everywhere. What the long-term effects will be will depend on how willing China's future Han leaders will be to be flexible, accommodating, and responsive to aspirations of the Tibetans and other minority groups as the western areas of China develop and are modernized.

CHAPTER EIGHT

South of the Clouds
YUNNAN

YUNNAN

T HE FINAL STOP on my long odyssey in 1988 was Yunnan Province, in China's far southwest. Yunnan means "south of the clouds" in Chinese; folklore has it that it was so named because Sichuan Province, just to its north, is so frequently covered by haze and mist. In ancient times, the area was called Dian, after a kingdom that ruled the area at that time.

Han Chinese penetrated the area two millennia ago, but they did not migrate there in large numbers until the Ming dynasty, starting from the late fourteenth century, and Yunnan was one of the last areas of "China proper" to be incorporated into the regular administrative system of the Chinese empire. Originally populated entirely by diverse groups of non-Han tribal peoples, it has continued, right to the present, to be one of the most ethnically complex provinces in the country. The more than 11 million minority people now inhabiting the province belong to 24 different ethnic groups, which today make up close to one-third of the province's population but occupy at least two-thirds of its territory.

Like so many of China's outlying provinces and regions, Yunnan is large and much of it is isolated, and it is among the most underdeveloped and poorest areas of China. Its remoteness and inadequate transportation, as well as its complicated ethnic composition, help to explain its relative backwardness, but doubtless the most basic reasons are rooted in its topography. It is an area dominated by tall mountains, high plateaus, and deep ravines. According to one estimate, only about 6 percent of the province's territory is cultivated, and the conventional wisdom is that not very much land that is really good for agriculture is uncultivated. The western part of the province is a spur of the Tibetan tableland, most of which lies to the northwest. In the east, the Yunnan plateau extends into Guizhou Province; many geographers refer to this region, in fact, as a single area and label it the Yunnan-Guizhou plateau. In the south, Yunnan reaches into the Indochina Peninsula.

To simplify—in fact, oversimplify—the topographical characteristics of the area, the province has two main topographical regions: (1) the Yunnan plateau in the east and (2) an area of high mountains in the west, running north and south, which are divided by deep river canyons. The average elevation in the province as a whole is about 6,000 feet, but it varies greatly, especially between west and east. As the plateau slopes downward to the east, in the direction of Guizhou, it decreases from an average height of about 6,000 feet in the area near to its capital, Kunming (which lies at 6,232 feet), to about 4,000 feet in Guizhou. Much of this area, as one goes east, is forested. Even the plateau is very rough territory, broken by many river gorges and mountains. Numerous grabens (basins, some of which have lakes, such

as the Lake Dianchi* at Kunming) and many areas of karst (limestone formations characterized by deep fissures, jutting pinnacles, and caves) dot the
region. Three major rivers course through the eastern area: the Jinsha (Gold
Sand), which runs, in this area, northeast as it makes its way to join the
Yangzi River; the Nanpan, which flows east and ultimately merges into the
Xi (West) River en route to Guangzhou; and the Yuan River, which becomes
the Hong (Red) and ultimately reaches Hanoi in Vietnam.

Yunnan's westernmost area—especially the area beyond the Yuan River—
is very different and much more inaccessible than areas to the east. The population in this area, which is very sparse, consists mainly of tribal groups
that have relatively little contact either with the outside world or with each
other. If the Tibetan plateau is called the "Roof of the World" (as it frequently is), this region ought to be called the "Mother of Rivers." Several of
Asia's greatest rivers originate in the highlands of Tibet and Qinghai, but
they become significant rivers in this area of Yunnan, where they carve deep
north-south canyons through the high mountain ranges, some of which rise
to 16,000 feet or more. All of these rivers run north to south between the
high north-south mountain ranges. The alternating ranges and rivers are the
Gaoligong Mountains on the China-Burma border (in the far west), separating the Nmai and Nu rivers, the former of which runs into the Irrawaddy in
Burma; the valley of the Nu River (which becomes the Salween in Burma);
the Nu Mountains; and the Lancang River (which becomes the Mekong and
courses through Laos, Cambodia, and Vietnam).

To the north, the Yunling Mountains divide the Mekong and Gold Sand/
Yangzi rivers, and to the south the Wuliang Mountains divide the Mekong
River and the Babian (Black) River, both of which enter Vietnam. In addition, as noted earlier, the Red River descends from the plateau and, after several name changes, also flows into Vietnam. Few, if any, regions of the world
have so many major rivers and mountain ranges in such close juxtaposition.

Although the topographical differences between east and west in Yunnan
define the major regions in the province, each of the two major regions has at
least two important subregions. The northeastern part of the province is the
longest settled and most populous area. It also has a large percentage of the
province's agricultural land as well as much of its industry, most of which is
concentrated in the flat areas around Lake Dianchi, where Kunming lies on
the plain, and around the copper center of Dongchuan on the plain near the
Gold Sand River. In the southeast, which is an area of limestone mountains,
karst outcroppings, and small valleys, lie two sizable cities, Gejiu (Yunnan's

-----

*The word *chi,* which is part of the name Dianchi, means pond or pool, so in a sense the word
lake in the name Lake Dianchi is redundant, but I believe that for Western readers its use is desirable.

tin mining center) and Kaiyuan. The climate in this area is subtropical, and rain is plentiful, but agriculture is difficult because of the terrain. In the northwest lie the highest mountains and many of the wildest areas. Farming in that region is concentrated in very limited areas around Lake Erhai, where the cities of Dali and Xiaguan are located, and in a few river valleys. Tea and some other crops are grown on the mountainsides, and there are good grasslands in this region at higher altitudes. The southwest of the province is lower and warmer (mostly subtropical and tropical), and it has more rainfall. There is farming in many valleys, but it is less advanced in farming methods than areas in the east. Some people classify the four areas I have just described as the province's major economic regions, but Yunnan's provincial planners, when I talked with them in 1988, actually divided the province into five economic regions (which I will discuss later).

*   *   *

Yunnan Province borders on three foreign countries (Burma, Laos, and Vietnam) as well as two autonomous regions and two provinces within China (Tibet, Sichuan, Guizhou, and Guangxi). Historically, Yunnan has usually been regarded by the Chinese as a frontier area, far from the mainstream of Chinese life. It has always been significantly influenced by a variety of external pressures and influences from adjacent areas. Old trade routes cross it, connecting the Yangzi region to Burma and linking Tibet to Tongking. Buddhism reached the area from India quite early (relics from the first century A.D. have been found there). During the Han dynasty—roughly 2,000 years ago—the Chinese, moving southward, established a vague suzerainty over the Yunnan area, and thereafter many Chinese expeditions (including one led by the famous Chinese strategist Zhuge Liang in the third century A.D.) entered the area. However, other important kingdoms that rose and fell in the area exercised real power before the Chinese established lasting control. The most important (after the Dian state) was the Nanzhao Kingdom. This Tai (Thai) state (inspired by the Tang dynasty in China) was established in A.D. 740 with its capital at Dali, and after it merged with the Dali Kingdom in the tenth century A.D. it ruled much of the area until it was conquered by the Mongols in A.D. 1253.

The Mongols, after defeating China's Song dynasty and establishing a new dynasty of their own in what is now Beijing, moved south and incorporated the Yunnan area into China, really for the first time—or at least they were the first to establish really firm control on the area from the outside. (The ubiquitous Marco Polo visited the area and wrote about it at that time.) Yunnan's Mongol conqueror was one of Kublai Khan's generals, named Uriangqatai. He established an effective, centrally controlled administration, dominated by Mongol officers. However, he left some authority to local Tai princes, and he hired a fairly large number of able Muslim officials from

Central Asia to help administer the region. From then on, Yunnan increasingly became a stronghold for Islam in China. From about that time, also, the Tai people began to move further south, finally establishing, in the fourteenth century, a state of their own in the area that is now Thailand, far to the south of Yunnan.

In the fourteenth century, Zhu Yuanzhang, a monk who had become a rebel, defeated the Mongols and established the Ming dynasty; he drove the Mongols out of Yunnan in 1382. It was during the period of Ming rule that a sizable flow of Han Chinese to Yunnan really began. This flow continued during the subsequent Qing dynasty and thereafter. Some of the migration, in earlier years, was voluntary, but some was forced (the Ming resettled at least a quarter of a million soldiers from the north in Yunnan). Gradually the Chinese settled most of the best lowland agricultural areas and pushed a large percentage of the minority peoples into the mountains. Because the majority of these Han Chinese migrants were from the north (they now make up the majority of the population), most Yunnanese have from the start spoken excellent Mandarin (better than in almost any place in China other than the Mandarin-speaking heartland in north China).

At the end of the Ming dynasty, Yunnan came under the control of a Chinese general named Wu Sangui, who ruled it as a semiautonomous region for many years. Wu first fought on the side of the Ming rulers against other Chinese rebels but then joined the invading Manchus and helped them to establish the Qing dynasty. Wu pursued the Ming remnants all the way to the southwest, into Burma. Then he stayed in Yunnan and ruled it as a private domain for a long time. Later, he openly rebelled against the Qing rulers in the 1670s, but Manchu forces defeated him and established their own control in Yunnan, which continued, despite sporadic opposition, until the collapse of the Qing in the early twentieth century.

The Qing rulers took various steps to try to integrate the province more fully into their imperial system. Most notably, they began in the eighteenth century to replace local, hereditary, tribal chiefs (*tusi*) with appointed officials to strengthen direct rule. (Because of continuing resistance, however, the *tusi* system was not totally replaced until the midtwentieth century, following the Communist takeover.) Opposition to the Qing increased in the nineteenth century, as the dynasty's power waned, and tensions between Han Chinese and Muslims increased until they exploded in midcentury. Several Hui revolts kept the province in turmoil for roughly two decades, from the 1850s to the 1870s, and resulted in huge casualties (according to some estimates, at least a million people died). Widespread destruction occurred in many parts of the province until Qing forces were finally able to supress the rebels.

In the nineteenth century, the British and the French, operating from newly acquired footholds in Southeast Asia, exerted growing pressure on

Yunnan. One goal of the British, who already had achieved control of Burma, was to open a trade route to Yunnan; they paid scant attention to Chinese claims of suzerainty over Burma and exerted growing pressure to obtain special rights in Yunnan. The French, based in Indochina, pushed even harder and more successfully for special rights in southern Yunnan. Sino-French disputes led to war in the 1880s, and the Qing dynasty had to bow to French demands. By the end of the nineteenth century the French had succeeded in making much of Yunnan a special sphere of interest of France. They began at that time to build a railway to Kunming from Indochina. This line—called at the time the Dianyue Line—was completed in 1910. Thereafter, most of Yunnan's trade flowed south, into Indochina. As a result of French pressures, several Yunnanese cities, including Kunming, Mengzi, and Simao, were opened for foreign trade; Simao, in particular, became a special center of French economic activities.

With the collapse of the Qing dynasty in 1911, Yunnan, like much of China, entered a period of chaotic warlordism. A series of military leaders— Cai Ao, Tang Qiyao, and then Long Yun—acquired their own military forces, achieved political dominance, and ran the province with little central government interference. The last of these three, Long Yun, was a member of the Yi minority; he dominated the area for almost two decades, from 1927 to 1945. His power began to be undermined, however, in the late 1930s and early 1940s, when the Sino-Japanese war forced the Nationalist government into southwest China and thousands of Chinese from eastern and northern China migrated to Sichuan, Yunnan, and other areas in the southwest. They brought with them not only troops but also factories and skilled personnel. The Guomindang government moved to Chongqing, in Sichuan, but Kunming became the second most important headquarters for the Nationalists in their war against the Japanese—it was the terminal for both road traffic over the newly built Burma and Ledo roads and the airlift over the "hump" from India and Burma, which became the main routes over which supplies flowed to the Nationalists. It also became the headquarters of the U.S. 14th Air Force operating in China. Transportation and communications within the province improved substantially in this period. Eventually, the central government's military forces outmaneuvered those of Long Yun, and Nationalist officials steadily expanded their control over the province. Finally, almost immediately after the war's end, Chiang Kai-shek ousted Long, replacing him with one of Long's more compliant relatives, Lu Han (who also belonged to the Yi minority group).

Lu Han was still governor when I visited Yunnan for the first time, in October 1949, but his days were numbered, and he knew it. The smell of imminent revolutionary change was in the air. The Communists had just established their new central government in Beijing, and their forces were rapidly spreading over the country into those areas that had still not been taken over.

Yunnan was ripe for picking. Actually, ever since—following the end of World War II—the struggle between the Nationalists and the Communists had erupted into open civil war in 1946, Yunnan had undergone a process of steady deterioration similar to that which undermined Nationalist rule nationwide—even though Yunnan was far from the main battlefields until right at the end. The local economy had been dealt a major blow when, at the end of the Sino-Japanese war, most of the people and the factories that had been transferred there during the war returned north; then, the runaway inflation afflicting all of China steadily eroded the foundations of Yunnan's economy. And in several areas of the province, Communist guerrillas gradually built up areas of Communist Party control. As Lu observed the power of the Communists growing elsewhere, he began to position himself for a switch of allegiance. As a step in this direction, he attempted to assert greater autonomy from the Nationalists; this was evident when I was there. But Chiang Kai-shek was able temporarily to halt this trend; he struck back and forced Lu to accept greater Nationalist control for a while. However, the capitulation of Lu to Chiang did not last long. In December 1949 (soon after my visit), Lu declared allegiance to the new Communist regime, and—like many local leaders elsewhere—he was rewarded with some impressive-sounding regional and national government titles but at the same time was deprived of all real power.

*   *   *

When I discussed the takeover period with local officials and academics in Kunming in 1988, almost everyone said that "essentially, the turnover of power was peaceful." But then several proceeded to describe continued opposition that lasted for several years. There was scattered resistance to the Communists that took several years to "mop up." The military guerrillas that did this were mainly ones from the north, but they were helped by local guerrilla forces. They mopped up first in the south—and then in the west. The task was complicated, though, because of periodic incursions by Nationalist troops who had fled into Burma. (These Nationalist forces, it was claimed, also bribed minority groups to continue resistance against the Communists.) One senior provincial official whom I interviewed in Kunming in 1988 said that "fighting in mountain areas continued for two to three years, and one of Long Yun's sons played a key role in it." But the consolidation of political control was essentially completed by 1952 or 1953.

In the years that followed the province's "liberation," Yunnan's experience was, in many respects, basically similar to that in most other areas of China. The Communists proceeded to establish an unprecedented degree of centralized control and extended the Party's and government's outreach to the grass roots to an extent that no previous regime had been able to do. All of the major economic and political campaigns promoted by the Party, nationwide, were carried out in Yunnan, including land reform, the campaign against counterrevolutionaries, collectivization, socialization, the anti-Rightist campaign, the Great Leap Forward, communization, the Cultural Revolution, and the reform policies of the 1980s. However, not surprisingly, the political developments in the province were significantly influenced by the province's special historical, geographical, ethnic, economic, and political background, and the new provincial leadership had to adjust their priorities and approaches in many ways to deal with the distinctive local problems.

Elements of the Communists' conquering 2d Field Army, which played key roles in Yunnan at the start, continued to do so for many years thereafter, although gradually an increasing number of local Yunnanese were raised to leadership positions. In carrying out national campaigns, the leaders in Yunnan consistently lagged behind more developed areas. Because of the province's long history of tensions between Han Chinese and minorities, local leaders always had to give special attention and high priority to "minority policies," designed to placate non-Han groups. Over time, minority areas were in many respects integrated into the regime's centralized political system more than ever in the past, but then, starting in the early 1950s, minority areas were organized into "autonomous" prefectures and counties, and special efforts were made to train minority cadres and raise them to leadership positions. Furthermore, because of the economic backwardness of the minority areas, both the province and the central government had to invest fairly large resources to try to promote the development of these areas. The province also had to cope with continuing problems in areas bordering Burma and Vietnam. In the early years, such problems were greatest along the disputed Burma border—until a Sino-Burmese border treaty was signed and cross-border pressures from former Nationalist forces slackened. In later years, Sino-Vietnamese tensions grew, until they finally exploded in war at the end of the 1970s.

The fundamental economic problem facing the province's new leaders was poverty. When Beijing launched an ambitious national development program, by initiating its First Five Year Plan in 1953, Yunnan also attempted to put primary emphasis on economic development. However, unlike the stress in the national plan, the development program in Yunnan could not do very much in heavy industry. The province simply lacked the essential prerequisites. Instead, in Yunnan emphasis was placed on agriculture, transport, communications, and on mining (in areas where it was already started)—plus small-scale industry that could serve rural areas. A few sizable industrial enterprises were built, however, in Kunming and several other cities. Railways were built, creating new connections with Sichuan Province and Guizhou Province, and the road network within and out of the province was substantially expanded. Major attention was paid, also, to the expansion of education. Despite all efforts, however, and despite the fact that some economic progress was made, Yunnan continued to be relatively backward and poor compared to most of the country, and poverty remained its greatest and its fundamental problem.

Throughout the Maoist era, the province confronted special political problems as well. Han-minority tensions were by no means eliminated, and minority areas continued to lag enormously, in almost every field, behind other areas. Yunnan's relations with Beijing also were periodically strained, and central leaders repeatedly charged that some leaders in Yunnan were guilty of "local nationalism" and were trying to build an "independent kingdom." This was not surprising; even more than in most provinces, local leaders in Yunnan faced unsolvable dilemmas, created by competing pressures from below, from within the province, and from Beijing.

Yunnan suffered during the Cultural Revolution, in the late 1960s and early 1970s, even more than most other areas. The struggle there was especially complicated and intense, factionalism was rife, and the physical conflict was particularly violent and destructive. Thousands were killed. At almost every stage, Yunnan was one of the last provinces to carry out Beijing's instructions; for example, it was one of the last to establish a so-called Revolutionary Committee, and it later was one of the last to rebuild the Party's organization. Beijing summoned Yunnan's leaders to the capital on several occasions, to try to end local conflicts in Yunnan, but restoration of even a semblance of order was slow. Finally, in the early 1970s, economic recovery did begin to take place, and political stability was gradually restored, but the aftereffects of the earlier struggle continued to complicate local politics in Yunnan until the end of the Maoist era.

When I made my second visit to Kunming (my first since the Communists took over), it was the autumn of 1977, a year after the death of Mao and the purge of China's radical "Gang of Four." The aftereffects of the Cultural Revolution were obviously still crippling the area. Nevertheless, even then I could see that Kunming had changed a great deal since my visit three decades earlier. The city had grown substantially. Broad new avenues and numerous Soviet-style, modern buildings had altered its appearance. And in and around the city, I saw a sizable number of factories, built since the Communist takeover, and visited a large one. My overall impression at that time, however, was of a city still traumatized by its recent history, attempting to recover from the bitter conflicts of the 1960s and 1970s. Local leaders who had been associated with the Gang of Four had just been purged, but the pall of Maoism still hung over the city. The American delegation with which I traveled—which was one of the first to visit that area of China after the restoration of U.S.-China contacts—was treated politely, but local leaders were obviously very uncomfortable receiving an American delegation, and they told and showed us very little. Their instinct was simply to mouth slogans and to keep a tight rein on the travel of foreign visitors. Although we interviewed a number of local leaders, visited a machine tool factory, and talked with people at a major minority institute and several other institutions, our hosts insisted that we spend a great deal of time in pure tourism. Kunming still was essentially a closed city, wary of outsiders. It also was a gloomy city. There was little sign of any vitality. The traffic on the roads was extremely light (and consisted mainly of bicycles). The large factory we visited was obviously run down, overstaffed, and inefficient. Broken windows and other damage incurred during the Cultural Revolution remained unrepaired. The nearby village areas that we saw looked very poor.

*   *   *

Memories of my visits in both 1949 and 1977 were in my mind when I flew to Kunming from Guangzhou in 1988. Guangzhou, the capital of Guangdong Province, was, by 1988, an extraordinary place, the most dynamic and rapidly developing area of China at the time. I did not know what to expect in Yunnan. I knew it would not be like Guangzhou. But I did not know whether to expect a city revitalized by the reforms of the 1980s or one comparable to what I had seen in the 1970s.

My flight to Kunming was in a Boeing 737. It was one of the most comfortable trips that I made in 1988. The aircraft was commodious (with much more room between seats than in most aircraft in China), and, even though no regular meal was served, the hostesses were polite and professional and offered us coffee and peanuts. Immediately after our takeoff, we flew over the rice paddy fields of the delta of the Pearl River and the West River. Even though it was not possible from the air to see precisely how the villages and countryside had been transformed, I could see that the changes had been enormous. Earlier, and subsequently, I saw these changes on the ground. Most peasant houses were sturdy new buildings—the majority of them two or three stories high. There were numerous township and village factories visible throughout the area. Many villages looked like small modern towns rather than traditional rural settlements.

Before long, hills and low mountains dominated the landscape; although there were a few high mountains, the terrain was mostly rough or hilly rather than mountainous. We flew too high to see very much, but I could discern how the nature of the topography had shaped the society in this area, as everywhere in China. Between the hills were numerous rivers, and along their banks were scattered villages, towns, and occasional factories. We did not see any large forested areas, but most of the hills at least had green cover. Red clay predominated in areas where there was no green. The landscape was very different from the brown plains of north China and the lush Yangzi River delta. Ever since my 1947 air trip to China, which took me over Europe, the Middle East, and South Asia—and was the first long flight I had made over land—I had been fascinated and intrigued by what one could learn about societies simply by observing the pattern of land use from thousands of feet in the air.

Once we were over Guangxi, we began to see many areas of karst, where thin, rocky pinnacles rose from relatively flat areas. (Guilin, which in recent years has become a major tourist attraction, is probably the best-known example of karst on a large scale.) About halfway to Kunming, the clear sky gave way to cumulus clouds, then to haze, and finally to a general cloud cover that totally blocked our view of the ground—except when there were occasional breaks in the clouds. I found myself mesmerized, as I often am when flying, by the intriguing variety of clouds that we saw. At various points they looked like soft white quilts, or like cotton candy; at other times they looked like whipped cream or like ripples on a white lake.

The flight took us almost due west, and our flying time was only one hour and 47 minutes to cover 974 miles. It was certainly a big improvement compared to 1949—and was much better even than in 1977. As we neared Kunming, we descended through the clouds to see a lush, green plateau that was crowded with villages and towns; we passed Lake Dianchi and then set down gently on the airport just south of Kunming. I marveled at how jet air travel had shrunk space and time and made it possible to hop quickly over old barriers yet remain encapsulated in a warm cocoon of modernity. However, on landing at the airport (where we saw numerous military planes but almost no civilian aircraft), when I saw Kunming's air terminal, I was immediately reminded that Yunnan was one of China's least-developed areas. The air terminal was very small and primitive. (I learned later that a new air terminal was scheduled to be built "soon," but during its four decades under Communist rule, Kunming—a large city, and a provincial capital—had had to make do with an air terminal comparable to that in many very small towns in the United States.)

At the airport, I was greeted, cordially, as always, by my hosts, who were leaders from the Yunnan Academy of Social Sciences; they drove me rapidly (a 25-minute trip) to my hotel in town. Early the next day, we talked about my itinerary for my stay in Yunnan, and then I set out to get reacquainted with the city of Kunming. By car and by foot, I soon was able to explore virtually all parts of the city. The recent changes (during the 1980s) had been far-reaching and impressive. They had changed the basic appearance of the city, not only in comparison with 1949 but also with 1977. The surge of modernization in the 1980s—and the effects of reform—had had a visible impact. The city looked far more "modern" than it had previously. As in most Chinese cities that I visited in 1988, an extraordinary building boom had taken place during the past few years. Modern high-rise buildings had sprouted in many parts of the city, creating a new skyline and a new atmosphere.

The majority of people I saw while traveling to all parts of the city looked well dressed and well fed. When I saw a handful of ragged beggars on one of the main streets (a very common sight in the 1940s), they stood out like sore thumbs in contrast to the general appearance of people on the streets. Traffic on the main streets was sparser than in major cities to the north, but Kunming nevertheless seemed to me to be much more alive and bustling than it had been a decade earlier.

Some of the changes in the city were obviously the product of the long, painful, and costly process of development that had been under way ever since the Communists first consolidated their power in Yunnan. However, many of the changes that struck me most forcefully were clearly the result of the rapid development, and the reforms, of the 1980s. During this decade, economic growth had spurted ahead, and living standards had risen quite remarkably, by two to three times. Yunnan was still one of China's poorest provinces and faced enormous problems; I spent most of my stay there learning about these problems. But the city of Kunming unquestionably had made very significant strides toward modernization. Kunming was ahead of other areas in the province for several obvious reasons. It was the provincial capital. It was the province's transportation hub and its principal cultural, commercial, and industrial city. And it was located in one of its best agricultural areas. But when I traveled elsewhere in the province I discovered that modernization had also changed other areas that I saw significantly.

*   *   *

Kunming is located near the center of the eastern part of the Yunnan plateau, in a small basin that surrounds Lake Dianchi (one translation of the lake's name is "the pond that overflows"). The first town built there reputedly was founded in 109 B.C., during the early Han dynasty, and thereafter its economy gradually developed on the basis of agriculture on the surrounding plain, fishing and salt extraction from the lake, and some gold and silver mining in hills nearby. The importance of the town increased in the eighth century, when the rulers of the Tai Kingdom of Nanzhao (first headquartered at Dali) seized it, enlarged it, changed its name to Tuodongcheng, and made it a secondary capital. The rulers of Nanzhao controlled it for roughly five centuries, until the Mongols captured it in the thirteenth century. The Mongols then made it their capital of the Yunnan area, and called it Zhongqingfu, but their domination was brief. Ming forces took it in the fourteenth century, and they built a new walled town three miles from the lake (and some distance from the old location of the town) on a site where it has remained up until the present. They called it Yunnanfu. The present city is their legacy; subsequently it grew rapidly, especially during World War II.

Near the end of the first decade of the twentieth century, Yunnanfu's population was still considerably under 100,000. (I have seen two different figures for the population in the early decades of the century—85,000 and 45,000—and I am not sure which one is closest to being correct.) Then rapid growth began during World War II. By the end of the war, its population had risen to almost 300,000. It continued to grow rapidly after the Communist takeover. By 1988, it had doubled again, by comparison with the 1940s, and exceeded 600,000 in urban areas of the city itself. (Administratively, the urbanized area of the city, as of 1988, was divided into four districts, two of them urban districts within the city itself and two in suburban areas.) Moreover, Kunming had become a major municipality, and by 1988 its territory had expanded so that it included 6,060 square miles, an area larger than Connecticut, and its boundaries included eight counties. The total population administered by the municipality, as of 1988, was 3.3 million; roughly 860,000 were classified as urban, and 2.4 million as rural people. (Like other major cities, in recent years Kunming had expanded its territories as a result of the new policy to try to link economically municipalities and nearby rural areas more closely.) The territory of the entire municipality in 1988 was almost three times what it had been in the early 1980s, when its boundaries had encompassed 2,407 square miles and its population had been just under 2 million.)

The city rests on the Yunnan plateau at an altitude of over 6,000 feet. (A brochure published by the municipal government stated that its altitude was 1,900 meters, or 6,232 feet.) Because of its altitude, and its southern latitude, Kunming is famous for its salubrious climate. The weather is generally mild all year round, although at the time of my 1988 visit, which was in November, the temperature was unusually chilly—definitely sweater weather. My hotel was in the northwest part of the city. It rested on the edge of an attractive little lake, which was called Cui Hu (Green Lake); not surprisingly, the hotel was called Green Lake Guest House. It was an attractive and comfortable hotel, located near three of the city's major institutions: the city zoo, its Nationalities Institute, and its Engineering Institute. I was told that in 1988 it was the best of three modern hotels in Kunming that were considered suitable for foreigners. In 1977, I had stayed in one of the other major hotels, called the Kunming; it had been a very gloomy place. The third of these three hotels was some distance from the center of town, in Kunming's Western Hills, which was used by some as a vacation spot.* The Green Lake Guest House was a sizable tourist hotel (344 rooms) that had recently been modernized with advice from abroad. Its lobby was quite elegant, and its large dining room was lined on both sides with columns and had a slightly Euro-

---

*On a later visit to Kunming, in 1992, I stayed in a new hotel, the King World, which was as luxurious as leading hotels in the United States.

pean atmosphere. Compared with most other hotels in west China, it was, in my opinion, one of the best equipped for attracting foreign tourists. The rooms were quite comfortable; mine, which I think was typical, had a private bathroom, a heater, a radio, a telephone, a color television set, and a small refrigerator. Although on my travels throughout west China I found many of these appurtenances (especially TV) virtually everywhere, the heater and the refrigerator were very unusual. At the time of my visit, there were some tourists at the hotel, but only a few, and most of them were Hong Kong Chinese.

In the small lake adjacent to the hotel, there were several islands, and the surrounding shores had been developed into an attractive city park. Next to the hotel was a fairly large, old, foreign-style house that my car driver *believed* had been a residence of the former governor, Lu Han. (It did not seem grand enough to me.) The one jarring note in this attractive setting was the fact that outside of the front gate of the hotel there were a number of young Chinese men, hippy-types, and several old women as well, who accosted each hotel resident who left the hotel building, whispering "change money?" In my travels throughout China in 1988, I had encountered a growing number of such people outside of most hotels that served foreigners in major cities. They were trying to obtain any foreign exchange they could (or the special Chinese currency that foreigners were supposed to use) at black market rates. They were a disturbing, visible sign of the times—and of the spread of corruption.

*   *   *

Like many large Chinese cities, Kunming in 1988—as I noted earlier—looked very different from the past, and the core of the city had acquired a much more modern overall appearance. The city still was a mix of old and new, but it was the new that struck me most forcefully. The new buildings reflected two very different architectural styles. Those built in the 1950s and 1960s were mostly fairly low office and apartment buildings (4 to 6 stories), squat and gray. In contrast, many of the buildings constructed in the 1980s were much higher, sleeker, and more colorful; they included a considerable number of tall office buildings, some of which rose to between 10 and 20 stories. They were much more "Western" than any of the buildings previously built; quite a few reminded me of some buildings constructed a few years earlier in places such as Hong Kong. (My guess was that Hong Kong architecture had had a very significant influence on Chinese architects on the mainland when they began to remake almost all of China's cities in the 1980s.)

The central area of Kunming was dominated by several wide boulevards, running both east to west and north to south. Typically these boulevards had four lanes for motor traffic plus two side lanes for bicycles. Most were lined with tall, attractive fir trees. Starting from near Cui Hu, Dong Feng (East

Wind) Road, one of the city's major thoroughfares, wound eastward to the center of the city. Landmarks along the way included one of Kunming's modern department stores (also named Dong Feng) and the Yunnan Provincial Museum (built in a Stalinesque style, it originally had been a PLA museum but in 1988 was a fascinating repository of artifacts from most of Yunnan's incredibly complex minority groups.) Traveling Dong Feng Road, I reached—about halfway down the road, in the middle of the city—a large circle around which were a number of modern buildings, including the city's largest department store and a modern hotel. Before the Communist takeover, this was an area where foreign banks and office buildings were clustered; a few of them remained. The most impressive new modern high-rise buildings were to the southeast of the circle, at the intersection of Jinbi and Beijing roads, the latter being the major north-south avenue in the eastern part of the city. At this intersection was a concentration of recently built, tall, and quite elegant modern skyscrapers, some of them almost 20 stories high. This area in particular looked strikingly similar to Hong Kong's business district as it appeared several years ago—and to the most modern areas of China's eastern cities in the late 1980s.

From a strictly economic point of view, the pros and cons of the explosive growth of costly, modern, high-rise office buildings and hotels in major Chinese cities in the 1980s were debatable. The large investment in "nonproductive" structures was an important factor contributing to an excessive rate of local investment, which was one of the root causes of rising inflation by the late 1980s—and inflation was a key factor in China's economic crisis during 1988–1989. However, the new buildings clearly had become highly visible symbols of modernization, and personally I believe that, as such, their psychological impact, though difficult to measure, was important. I believe they also had some very practical, positive effects: Many old Chinese office buildings were extremely inefficient to use, and most of the new ones were much better in this respect. Although this, too, is difficult to measure, I suspect that they improved productivity and efficiency in many instances.

Although the new skyscrapers had, for me, changed the atmosphere of the city, by no means all of the city had been transformed by them. Between the major boulevards, the streets were narrower, and the buildings were a mixture of modern and traditional. In many areas, the modern predominated, but there were still many remnants of the past. And in a few areas (as I will note later) pockets of buildings in the city looked entirely traditional.

In several areas that mixed old and new, I passed buildings that evoked dim memories. On one street, Baoshan Road, my driver pointed out to me a building that he thought had been General Claire Chenault's headquarters during World War II. My brother, Bob, had been Chenault's intelligence briefing officer for an extended period during the war, and I imagined Bob giving Chenault daily reports in the building.* On another street, near the city's largest "night market" (which was open until midnight and had a number of restaurants that were open 24 hours a day, I was told), I passed the former YMCA building, on a small road called Dingxing Road. (My father had spent 26 years in China, from 1910 to 1936, as a Y secretary, and colleagues of his from Kunming had often stayed with us when visiting Shanghai.) I was told that the Y building had, after 1949, become a "children's palace" and then a cadre dormitory.

In the far southeast of the city, where the city's main railway station was located, the area looked very similar to comparable areas in many east coast cities before the construction boom of the 1980s. There were still a few areas of the city, such as that around the Nanqiang Road Market, that had a very traditional atmosphere. In these areas, buildings were generally tile-roofed, old-style, two-story structures; usually the lowest floor of the building was used as a shop, which opened directly onto the street, and the upper floor served as living quarters for the owner and his family. In the 1940s, most of Kunming—as I remember it—consisted of areas and buildings such as these. In 1988, these areas, and such shops, stood out as leftovers from the past; some of them, in fact, seemed almost like small old-fashioned villages or towns embedded in the more modern parts of the city.

One of the most traditional areas was the main Muslim district, along Chengjie, a small street south of and parallel to Deng Feng. I spent quite a while wandering through this area on foot, and I found that its narrow, crowded, and lively streets still had the feel of "old China." Bearded elders monopolized the tables at the open tea shops, where, with steaming cups in hand, they conversed and smoked large, old-fashioned bamboo pipes. I had no doubt that these men much preferred the ambiance of this area to that of more modern parts of the city. I was told that for many centuries this street had been the heart of the Hui Muslim area of the city. Nearby, I had lunch in a small noodle shop that served a kind of noodle called *guoqiao mixian* (meaning "crossing-the-bridge rice noodles"), which reputedly originated in the city of Mengzi in southern Yunnan. These noodles, a tasty concoction, were prepared at one's table by the shopkeeper, who dropped rice noodles, together with pork and vegetables and a large dash of peppers, into the boiling water in each customer's large bowl.

Throughout the city, the shops were full of goods, and along many streets there were crowded free markets, with open stalls, selling almost everything under the sun. One of the largest free markets occupied a long section of

---

*Later, my images of these briefings dissolved when my brother told me that the headquarters where he had briefed Chenault was at the main airfield outside of Kunming.

Qingnian Road, a wide, tree-lined boulevard stretching north from Dong Feng Road. Its name—meaning "Youth Road"—was chosen because the Young Communist League's members had been mobilized to build the road in the 1960s. The stalls that lined the street sold, among other things, clothing from Hong Kong, Shenzhen, and Guangzhou; numerous items imported from Burma; and various other consumer goods from almost all parts of China. Although some of the shoppers were dressed in traditional clothing or in Mao-era suits, the majority, including virtually all young people, wore Western-style clothing, mainly slacks and jackets (some of the latter, made of leather, looked like World War II flight jackets). Much of their clothing was very colorful (red was the favorite color, as it was in many other places in China that I had visited). Most young women dressed quite fashionably and many had permanent waves or other modern hairdos. Quite a few wore high heels. Mixed in with the urbanites, however, were some Han Chinese peasants; among them, the women wore electric blue jackets (embroidered in front), black pants, and old-fashioned caps or headgear of some sort. There was also a scattering of minority peoples at this market; all of them were dressed in very colorful native clothing. They too, I would say, were well dressed. That virtually everyone was well dressed, not only in this area but throughout the city, was an important indicator, I thought, of how the living standards of ordinary people had risen significantly in the 1980s. In this area—and throughout Kunming and some rural areas as well—there were many, many signs that consumerism had really taken hold in Yunnan, as elsewhere in China—for better or for worse.

*   *   *

After exploring the city, I spent most of the rest of my time in Kunming interviewing officials and scholars—especially those responsible for economic development and reform—rather than visiting factories, educational institutions, and farms, which I had seen in great numbers elsewhere in China. Once again, I was struck by how different from old officials (even the cadres I had met in the 1970s) these new, modern-minded technocratic, pragmatic men who had emerged into positions of authority in the 1980s were. Brief biographical data on just a few of those I interviewed in Kunming will illustrate the kinds of backgrounds and qualifications they had. The provincial deputy governor I interviewed (named Zhu Kui) was aged 58. A native of northern Jiangsu Province (his original home was near Xuzhou), he joined the Communist Party in the 1940s, when he was very young. He did some underground work in Shandong, then joined the 2nd Field Army, in which he engaged in political work during most of the postwar civil war. (Although he served under Deng Xiaoping, who was political commissar of the 2nd Field Army at that time, he never met him then. He had met Deng in recent years when he visited Yunnan, though.)

In 1950, he left the army—immediately after the end of the civil war—and began a career dealing with economic matters, in a variety of positions and a variety of institutions. His first job was in an industrial enterprise in Guizhou, where he was demobilized, but then in 1954 he was transferred to Yunnan Province, where he worked in the metallurgical industry. Because he was not an engineer or a technician, many of his positions were political (he was Party secretary in several enterprises). However, over time he learned a great deal about the metallurgical industry simply from direct experience. He worked first in iron and steel plants and then in a number of enterprises in the nonferrous metal industry. In some of his positions, he was involved in designing. In the early 1970s, he was assigned to work in the tin industry in Gejiu, in southern Yunnan (I will have more to say about Gejiu later). Working for the Yunnan Tin Corporation, he steadily rose until he became general manager as well as Party secretary in this huge enterprise, one of the largest in the province. In 1980, he became mayor of Kunming, and in 1983 he rose to be a deputy governor. When I met him he was the executive deputy governor (*changwu fushengzhang*) of the province—a position in which, ranking just below the governor, he had to deal with all provincial issues and matters, across the board, as the right hand of the governor. (Originally, I had been scheduled to meet the governor, but during my visit he had to go to a remote part of Yunnan to organize relief in an area hit by a bad earthquake— which I will also have more to say about later.)

The director of the provincial Planning Commission (a man named Yang Jianqiang), aged 40, was a member of the Bai minority and came from the Dali region. A native of Yunnan, he had gone to northeast China to study physics and had graduated from Jilin University in 1976. (Later he took advanced work in his field at Qinghua University in Beijing.) From the mid-1970s to the mid-1980s, he had held technical positions in factories in Yunnan. Then, in 1984, while he was still in his thirties, he became mayor of Dali. In 1986, he moved up to head the provincial Planning Commission.

One of the deputy directors of the provincial Economic Commission (named Wang Ning), aged 58, was a member of the Bai minority who came from Jianchuan, near Dali. He had "joined the revolution" about the time of the Communist takeover of Kunming. After a period of service in the army, he was demobilized and went to work for the government as a civilian. Subsequently, almost all of his positions had been in economic work—although some of them were generalized leadership positions. He rose to be a county magistrate and then was promoted to be an economic planner (handling industry) in a prefecture. From 1978 to 1986, he was deputy head and then head of Baoshan Prefecture in Yunnan. Subsequently, he was promoted to deputy head of the provincial Economic Commission, in 1986 (two years before I met him).

One of the deputy directors of the provincial Structural Reform Commission (a man named Zhang Jiatai), aged 55, was from Hangzhou in Zhejiang Province. After completing his primary and middle school education in Shanghai, he joined the PLA in 1949 and was sent to Yunnan in 1950. The PLA enrolled him in an "institution for advanced education"—which he said was considered to be equivalent to "higher education"—that was run by the military itself. After being demobilized in 1952, he spent several years in Party youth work in Yunnan, first in a county and then in the prefectural government of Yuxi. Thereafter, he became, in succession, a Party secretary on a farm, the head of a vocational school, and Party secretary in Huaning County, just before the Cultural Revolution. Following that debacle, he was appointed to the provincial Bureau of Construction Materials, and then in 1986 he became one of the three deputy directors of the provincial Structural Reform Commission (the head of which was the governor). Zhang's knowledge of economic development issues came more from experience than from formal education.

One of the deputy directors of the Administrative Office of the Structural Reform Commission was remarkably young—only 33 years old. He was a native of Kunming. After spending four years in the army, in the early 1970s, he worked for five years as a factory worker. Because of his outstanding performance, he was selected in the early 1980s to attend Yunnan University, from which he graduated in 1985 with a degree in economics. After graduation, he joined the Structural Reform Commission.

I would call all of these men pragmatic technocrats. They all impressed me as being able, realistic, forthright, and genuinely concerned about the economic development of the province. Ideology never arose in our conversations unless I raised it. Like most of the leaders and administrators I had been meeting throughout west China, they were mostly in their fifties or forties, and some were in their thirties. Many were local people, but a significant number of those dealing with the economy had come from more advanced areas of China, especially the lower Yangzi valley. Although many of these men had served for a period of time in military units, their subsequent work had been in civilian jobs, and most of them had spent almost their entire careers in technical and economic work. Often, though, they had moved up from essentially technical work into administrative and political positions but still dealt with the economy. A significant number of them had graduated from universities, and some others had taken various types of advanced training. Among those who lacked higher education, many had had extensive, hands-on experience dealing with economic matters.

By no means all officials in Yunnan in 1988—not even all those I met—had these characteristics. The leadership—and the bureaucracies—still included large numbers of people who reflected the outlook and priorities of earlier periods; most of them had risen in the ranks through military service,

Party organizational work, ideological and propaganda activities, or work in the security apparatus. The lower levels of the bureaucracies were still loaded with timeservers and careerists, whose ability to deal with the problems of a modernizing society were limited. Nevertheless, I was impressed— in Yunnan, as in most other areas I visited in China—by how much the level of competence of those handling economic affairs had risen in the 1980s compared to what I had seen in the 1970s. The growing level of competence was a result of the promotion to leadership and administrative positions of an increasing number of younger, better-educated, technically and professionally competent individuals. From those with whom I had extended interviews—not only those I mentioned but others as well—I was able to piece together what I believe to be a fairly accurate picture of general conditions in the province (especially economic conditions). And, from them and those I met on a long trip to southern Yunnan, I learned much about Yunnan's local problems as well as its leaders' accomplishments and hopes.

*   *   *

Wherever I went in my extensive travels in 1988, the sheer size of China and its subunits awed me. One of the great political and cultural achievements of Chinese rulers, over most of the past two millennia, has been their ability to hold together in one political unit so many disparate areas, many of them larger—in territory, population, or both—than most countries in the world. In no other region of the world of a comparable size has this been possible. Although China had periodically virtually fallen apart for fairly long periods of time, new leaders had always put it together again.

Compared to other provincial-level administrative units in China, Yunnan is smaller than many, and a number of them exceed it in population. Nevertheless, Yunnan is a very large entity. As of 1988, it had an area of 150,540 square miles, which made it slightly larger than Japan. As of 1987, the year before my visit (the last year for which I obtained population statistics), its population was 34.56 million—close to that of Poland. The growth in the province's population since my first visit in 1949 had been remarkable; it had almost tripled in those four decades. In 1949, I had been told that the population in the province was around 12 million; then when I made my second visit in 1977, local officials said that it was roughly 28 million. By 1987, I was told, Yunnan's 34.56 million people belonged to roughly 9 million family households. (If those figures were correct, they meant that the average size of households in the province was slightly less than 4, but I was later told by some local demographic specialists that the average size of households in the province was approximately 5. I never learned the reason for this discrepancy.)

The density of population for the province as a whole in the late 1980s was about 230 persons per square mile. This density was lower than in many other large Chinese agricultural provinces, but it was much higher than in China's largest autonomous areas in the northwest. But the figure for Yunnan is extremely misleading. Provincial planning officials told me that they classified 94 percent of the province as mountainous, and because large portions of the mountain areas are uninhabited or have very small populations, a large proportion of the 34.56 million people in the province are jammed into relatively small areas—in the limited agricultural areas where farming is possible and in urbanized areas, principally in the east. Roughly 10 million people were classified by provincial planners as urban residents in 1988 (these constituted 29 percent of the total population—which was not a small figure, for China), but most of the urban population was located in the eastern fringe of the province. Moreover, a very large percentage of the 24.5 million people (71 percent of the total population) classified as rural also were in the eastern part of the province since a large proportion of the province's good agricultural land was in that area.

The imbalance in population between east and west in Yunnan seems likely to continue, even as modernization progresses, but the provincial planners I met expected that the urban-rural balance will gradually change as a result of industrial development. The rate of growth of the population as a whole, I was told, had dropped to around 1.5 percent a year in the late 1980s, although, among the minority groups, it continued to be around 2 percent a year. The minority populations, which totaled 11.1 million (32 percent of the total population), continued to be overwhelmingly rural: About 85 percent of all the minority people were said to live *outside* of urbanized areas, whereas the Han Chinese predominated in virtually all of the significant cities.

Administratively, Yunnan has undergone frequent changes in recent decades: reclassification of areas, name changes, and boundary adjustments. As of 1987, the province contained 15 prefectures (7 regular prefectures and 8 autonomous prefectures); 11 cities (2 large ones—Kunming and Dongchuan—with administrative status equal to that of prefectures, and 9 county-level cities); and 114 counties (29 of which were autonomous counties). As in most of China, regular prefectures were essentially branches of the provincial government, and autonomous prefectures formally enjoyed greater local rights. But in Yunnan, as elsewhere, the distinction between regular and autonomous prefectures was less significant in practice than in theory. (Some regular prefectures enjoyed considerable operational flexibility even though they were branches of the provincial government, and the autonomous prefectures were unquestionably subordinate to the provincial government and subject to its control on most matters.)

Economic development within the province had varied considerably between different areas. As I noted earlier, the economic differences between regions closely reflected topographical and ethnic differences. The provincial economic planners whom I met, instead of seeing the province as divided essentially into two main regions (east and west), or even into the four geographical divisions I discussed earlier, told me that they generally divided the province, for the purposes of economic analysis, into five economic regions. The first—and by far the most important of these five—they said, was the central economic region (*dianzhong jingjiqu*). With Kunming as its center, this region included five subareas. The most important was Kunming, and the other four were clustered around it and included the copper center at Dongchuan in the northeast, Qujing in the east, Yuxi in the south, and Chuxiong in the west. This one region, with its five subregions, contained about 60 percent of Yunnan's population and accounted for about 70 percent of the gross value of the province's industrial output. (The percentage of total provincial output from small townships and other rural industrial enterprises was even higher.) The municipality of Kunming alone accounted for roughly 55 percent of the value of the province's industrial output. This region also was the principal "base" for output of grain, tobacco, and sugar.

A second economic region was called the west Yunnan economic region (*dingxi jingjiqu*). Centered on Dali, it included Lijiang, Nujiang, and Deqen (a Tibetan autonomous area) to the northwest. This region was noted for its pastureland and forests in mountain areas, and it contained some nonferrous metal deposits (including tin and lead). Modern industry had not developed very much in this area, but planners, both within the province and in Beijing, saw the hydroelectric potential in the region as a basis for future development. I was told that the State Council hoped to develop this hydropower potential and use it to expand production of nonferrous metals and metal products in the area. How and when this might be feasible was not clear.

A third economic region was called the Kai-Ge economic region. Named after its two principal mining and industrial cities, Kaiyuan and Gejiu, it was in some respects the second most important economic region. Gejiu was China's largest center for the production of tin, and this industry had great importance for the entire provincial economy. Kaiyuan also was a center of considerable industry. Within the region, in addition to these two very important cities, there were some other cities or towns of significance. Perhaps the most important was Mengzi, located on the rail line to Vietnam.

A fourth economic region was in the southwest; it was called, simply, the frontier economic region (*bian jingjiqu*). Most of the region paralleled the Burma border. Its major cities included Baoshan and Lincang in the west and Simao and Xishuangbanna in the south (where the region borders Laos). There was very little industry in this region. The basically agricultural economy produced tropical and mountain products such as bananas, rubber, coffee, tea, and sugar. Plans for the future called for expanded output of these products and increased exports of some of them. Cross-border trade was quite important in the local economy.

A fifth economic region, called the Zhaotong *jingjiqu,* was named for one of Yunnan's prefectures lying in the far northeast of the province. This prefecture was, in effect, a geographical extension of Yunnan Province, squeezed between Guizhou and Sichuan. Most of this region was mountainous, and partly for this reason it was an especially poor area. The territory in the Wumeng Mountains, next to Guizhou, was said to be the poorest area in Yunnan. Animal husbandry was the main local occupation. In addition, a small amount of coal was mined there.

                              *   *   *

Despite the great regional variations, and the serious poverty of some remote areas, the overall economy of Yunnan was sizable, and it had grown a great deal since the Communist takeover. According to the deputy head of Yunnan's Economic Commission, the gross value of industrial and agricultural output in the late 1980s was more than 12 times the output just before the Communist takeover (of course, output in the year just before the Communist takeover was abnormally low because the civil war was then under way). The deputy head of the Economic Commission gave me statistics for 1949 and 1987. They showed that in 1949 the gross value of the province's agricultural and industrial output was Y 1.87 billion, of which agricultural output accounted for 85 percent and industrial output for only 15 percent. There were 1,400 industrial enterprises in the province in 1949, almost all of them small, and their employees totaled only 60,000 people. Both agriculture and industry were very backward technologically.

In contrast, according to the official statistics, the gross value of industrial and agricultural output in 1987 was Y 23.1 billion (more than 12 times the 1949 figure). By 1987, the province had roughly 12,000 industrial enterprises, and industry accounted for 65 percent of the gross value of output (Y 14.9 billion) whereas agriculture accounted for only 35 percent (Y 8.2 billion).

To assess these figures, several factors must be taken into account. As I stated earlier, 1949 was an economic low point. Many factories that had moved to Yunnan during the Sino-Japanese War had left, to return to other areas, and the chaos created by the civil war and runaway inflation had hit hard in Yunnan. Moreover, when growth is stated in terms of changes in gross value of industrial and agricultural output, the resulting figures are less meaningful than figures of growth stated in terms of national income or GNP. The reason, as I have stated earlier, is that figures on gross agricultural and industrial output include the value of intermediate products and therefore involved double counting that inflates the real value of net output. (Although I believe that these figures are in "constant yuan"—that is, that they take inflation into account—in reviewing my notes, I did not find clear evidence that this was the case.) Nevertheless, the figures show—correctly, I think—that there had been very significant economic growth in Yunnan between 1949 and the late 1980s.

Despite such growth, though, Yunnan still lagged far behind much of the rest of the country, as it always has. The State Statistical Bureau (SSB) figure for the gross value of agriculture and industry of all provinces in 1986 indicated that, despite its large population, Yunnan's output (which the SSB figures showed to be Y 24.3 billion in 1986) was eighth from the bottom among the 29 provincial-level administrative units on the China mainland. In per capita terms the SSB rated it even lower—among the bottom three.

None of the leaders, planners, or administrators whom I met in Yunnan tried to conceal or obscure the province's comparative economic backwardness and relative poverty. In fact, most of them, from the deputy governor down, made a special point of highlighting the fact that, on a per capita basis, Yunnan was "one of the three poorest" provincial-level units in China. (The other two were said to be Guizhou and Guangxi, although most statistical studies placed Gansu at the bottom. Perhaps my Yunnan informants were talking about just southwest China.) They discussed at great length the multiple reasons for the province's backwardness: its mountainous topography, its ethnic complexity, its poor transportation, its shortages of skilled personnel and capital, and other factors. But all of them also discussed their plans and hopes for the province and their determination to try to accelerate across-the-board modernization of the economy.

More than once I have commented, earlier in this volume, on the way in which statistics have become almost an obsession with local officials in China. In Yunnan, as elsewhere, I was given a wide variety of figures by officials from the commissions on planning, economics, and structural reform as well as by the deputy governor. Having earlier struggled to make sense of the varying statistics I had obtained in other parts of China, I knew that the reliability of local figures varied from place to place and that trying to interpret their meaning accurately required a great deal of information—more, in many cases, than it was possible for me to obtain on short visits. Nevertheless, the figures given to me in Yunnan (plus figures that I obtained later from SSB publications) did provide one basis for understanding the general characteristics of the province's economy.

Over the four decades between the late 1940s and the late 1980s, the rates of growth—especially industrial growth—in Yunnan had been quite impressive. According to provincial planners, the "total product of society" (gross output of industry and agriculture plus the value of construction, transportation, and commerce—which, like the figures for "gross output of industry and agriculture," included a great deal of double counting) had grown since 1949 at an average annual rate of 8.7 percent. The province's GNP (a mea-

sure that is based on net figures rather than gross figures, attempts to eliminate double counting, and also includes services and depreciation) had
grown, they claimed, at an even more rapid rate of 13 percent. In 1987, the
gross value of industrial output alone had grown at a rate of 16 percent; the
gross value of agricultural output had grown at a rate of 5 percent; and the
gross value of industrial and agricultural output combined had grown at a
rate of 8 percent. The province's "national income" (net material product—
that is, value added—which eliminates double counting but does not include
services and depreciation) was said to have reached Y 14.8 billion in 1987.

Of the many figures that I obtained in Yunnan and from SSB sources,
those on the province's "national income" were the most useful and revealing in many respects, I thought, because they were broken down by sector.
These figures indicated (which the figures on gross industrial and agricultural output did not) that despite the fairly rapid rate of industrial growth,
Yunnan's economy continued to be mainly agricultural, and industry accounted for a lower percentage of the province's economic output than that
in a majority of China's provinces (only in Tibet was the percentage much
lower; in Guangxi it was a little lower, and in Qinghai and Inner Mongolia it
was about the same). The breakdown of Yunnan's "national income" in
1985 (which totaled Y 13.9 billion) showed that even in the mid-1980s, agriculture still accounted for Y 6.5 billion, close to half (47 percent) of the province's total output; industry accounted for Y 4.6 billion, about a third (33
percent); and other sectors accounted for smaller percentages (for example,
commerce accounted for 11 percent, construction for 6 percent, and transportation for 2 percent).

As one would expect, the figures on productivity of the labor force showed
that laborers in industrial enterprises were much more productive than those
involved in agriculture. As of 1986, the total "labor force," urban and rural,
in the province totaled 17.48 million (roughly half of the total population).
Of the 17.48 million, 13.59 million (78 percent) worked in agriculture
(broadly defined, including animal husbandry, forestry, and fishing),
whereas only 1.28 million (a little more than 7 percent) were employed in industry. Applying these figures to those for the value of output (as measured
by "national income" in 1985), the per capita output of workers in agriculture was only Y 478 whereas the figure for industry was Y 3,594.

                    *   *   *

In discussing the development of Yunnan's industrial sector, those I interviewed stressed how dependent this sector still was on central government
support. There had been two main periods of expansion of industry in Yunnan. One was in the 1950s and early 1960s, when the State Council gave

high priority to the development of heavy industry; in Yunnan special stress
was placed on the expansion of production of tin and copper plus the development of power to support these industries "to make Yunnan a major nonferrous metal base." The second major period of economic growth in the
province, I was told, was in the 1980s following—and as a result of—Deng's
reform program. In this period, greater effort had been made to develop agriculture (including tobacco and sugar), textiles, and other light industrial
products, especially those using agricultural raw materials, "to raise living
standards and strengthen the basis for later expansion of heavy industry, at
which time nonferrous metals would again be given priority." I was told that
Yunnan had been largely left out of economic plans for expansion during the
period of Mao's three-front strategy, when a great deal of industry was transferred to other interior provinces—Sichuan, Guizhou, Shaanxi, and others—
"because it is a frontier [border] province."

Provincial planners said that in the late 1980s, in fact as well as in theory,
increased priority was being given to developing agriculture, especially cash
crops. They stressed that the province was still relatively backward in agriculture, for all the reasons they had discussed for the relative backwardness
of the entire provincial economy. But some progress in agriculture had been
made, they said. Reportedly, the province had been essentially self-sufficient
in grain for some years (and they expected it to continue to be, except in
years of very bad drought). Its output of "grain" (a term that included beans
and potatoes) generally totaled between 8 and 9 million tons, I was told, but
at times had exceeded 10 million tons. In 1987, however, because of severe
natural disasters, the province had had to purchase "about a half million
tons" from "the State." Rice continued to be its main grain crop, with corn
second; in addition, some farmers grew wheat and a substantial amount of
potatoes.

Priority in the late 1980s was given to expanding output of tobacco and
sugar. In tobacco, it already had become—local planners said—one of the
two principal producing areas in China (Henan was the other); they claimed
that the quality of Yunnan's tobacco was superior to that produced in
Henan. They also believed that tobacco output could be substantially increased. About half of the production was now being used to manufacture
cigarettes within the province (in 1987 Yunnan's cigarette output totaled
about 3 million cases, each of which contained 2,500 packages, and the central government rated 9 Yunnan cigarette factories as among the 13 best in
the country); the rest of the tobacco output was sold to other areas of the
country. In its production of cane sugar, Yunnan (whose output in 1987 was
540,000 tons) was still far below the output of Guangdong and Guangxi;
nevertheless, Yunnan had become one of the half a dozen provinces that

were major producers, and planners in Kunming said that they expected
production to rise significantly in the future. The State Council, local officials said, wanted Yunnan to become a major "base" for sugar. By the 1980s,
Yunnan had become second only to Hainan in production of rubber, local
officials told me. The province was also trying to increase its output of tea
and fruits. Overall, however, Yunnan still had a fairly long way to go to
modernize its agriculture. In the past decade, agricultural productivity had
improved to some degree, partly as a result of decollectivization, but the
province remained relatively backward in farming methods. Major efforts
were being made to improve agricultural productivity because expanded agricultural output was essential to increasing the output of light industry by
any substantial amount.

*   *   *

The development of Yunnan's industry in the years since 1949 had, as the
figures cited earlier suggest, been fairly rapid. Progress had been made in a
wide variety of fields: power, coal, metallurgy (including steel), nonferrous
metals, chemicals, electrical appliances, construction materials, forestry
products, textiles, and other light industry. But only in the nonferrous metals
industry had Yunnan been a leader nationally. In tin, Yunnan continued to
be, as it had long been, China's principal producer (with the main mining
center at Gejiu). It was also a major producer of copper (the principal center
of which in Yunnan was at Dongchuan) as well as a significant producer of
lead and several other minerals. Its planners underlined how great the potential was in the province for further expansion of output of minerals, asserting that, in terms of reserves, the province was first in China in lead, second
in tin, and third in copper. To develop these minerals further, however, they
would first have to expand, substantially, the output of their power industry,
both thermal power and hydropower (in the latter, they said, Yunnan had
the third largest potential in China, after Tibet and Sichuan).

As modern industry had developed in Yunnan, a large percentage of industrial enterprises was very concentrated geographically, and the industrial
sector that developed was overwhelmingly dominated by state-owned enterprises, especially by large, heavy industrial enterprises. It was partly for this
reason that in the late 1980s special stress was placed on the need to speed
up the growth of the light industrial sector. Sorting out and trying to understand provincial statistics can be a numbing process; readers who cannot endure it can skip the next page or two. Unfortunately, however, it is necessary
to try to sort out the figures if one wishes to arrive at any valid generalizations about the economy.

Official statistics showed that in 1986 there were 12,581 industrial enterprises in Yunnan, with 922,000 employees and a gross output of Y 12.13

billion.* Of the total number of enterprises, state enterprises accounted for 2,664 (21 percent); these had 735,000 employees (80 percent of the total) and a gross output of Y 9.586 billion (79 percent of the total output). Collective enterprises accounted for 9,586 enterprises (79 percent), 182,000 employees (20 percent), and a gross output of Y 2.45 billion (20 percent). Put simply, although only one-fifth of all industrial enterprises were state owned, because most of these were large, they accounted for four-fifths of both workers and output. Although collective enterprises accounted for four-fifths of the total number of enterprises, they were generally much smaller and therefore accounted for only one-fifth of industrial workers and industrial output. The official statistics included a category labeled "other," which was undefined but clearly included small private industrial enterprises, the total of which was only 39, with 5,000 employees and an output of Y 96 million. In short, private enterprises had barely begun to grow in this area. The statistics were probably misleading in some respects since many collective enterprises operated very much like private enterprises; in fact, some people called them quasiprivate enterprises. Nevertheless, Yunnan was lagging behind the most advanced and most rapidly reforming provinces in east China in the development of both collective and private enterprises.

Official statistics also classified industrial enterprises by size and type of industry (heavy or light). The figures showed that heavy industry was totally dominated by large state enterprises, but state enterprises were also important in light industry. In my interviews, I was told that 250 large, key enterprises produced about 70 percent of the province's total industrial output. In addition to the Gejiu tin mines and the Dongchuan copper mines, the largest heavy industrial enterprises included Kunming's iron and steel works, machine tool plant, and lathe plant; the Yangtao coal mine; the Kaiyuan power plant; and the Yijiang sugar refinery. Official statistics showed that, as of 1986, 49 enterprises classified as large (a fraction of 1 percent of all industrial enterprises) accounted for an output value of Y 3.56 billion (29 percent of all industrial output); 163 medium-sized industrial enterprises (just over 1 percent) accounted for Y 2.99 billion of industrial output (25 percent); and 12,369 small industrial enterprises (98 percent) accounted for Y 5.58 billion of output (46 percent). Heavy industrial enterprises, both large and small, throughout the province totaled 5,761 (46 percent of all industrial enterprises). They employed 598,000 people (65 percent of all industrial employ-

*These figures differ somewhat from ones that I cited earlier for Yunnan's gross industrial output and the industrial labor force because of differing *definitions* used in official publications for different sectors. I also received from one source in Yunnan a different figure on the number of industrial enterprises in the province—11,825—although this was for 1987, not 1986. Why the figure for 1987 was smaller than that for 1986, I do not know.

ees) and had an output value of Y 6.34 billion (52 percent of gross industrial output). The corresponding figures for light industry were 6,820 enterprises (54 percent of the total number of enterprises), 324,000 employees (55 percent of the total), and an output value of Y 5.80 billion (48 percent of the total).

In sum, despite the greater emphasis in recent years on and encouragement of collective enterprises and light industries, as a result of the reforms of the 1980s, and despite some growth of such industries, heavy industry in Yunnan still accounted for over one-half of the province's total industrial output. And a handful of large enterprises classified as either "large" or "medium-sized" totally dominated heavy industrial output and played a large role even in light industrial output. This pattern was unlike that in coastal areas of China in the 1980s, but it was similar to that in many other western provinces and regions.

I was told by local officials in Yunnan that the preceding figures on industrial output did not include strictly military production. They said that Yunnan (like some but not all other provinces) did not include military-industrial output in its published industrial statistics. However, my informants insisted that production of military equipment in the province was relatively small (a claim that I could neither confirm nor challenge).

Both the deputy governor and the provincial planners I met admitted—and decried—the fact that there were still relatively few rural township enterprises in Yunnan, and they looked with envy at the coastal provinces where such enterprises, and small private enterprises, had become the most dynamic economic sector in the 1980s. I was not able to get specific statistics on township industries in Yunnan. Perhaps many or most of them were included in the statistics that I did receive on "collective enterprises" (a category that also included urban collectives). Urban collectives in Yunnan varied greatly; some had semistate characteristics, whereas others were semiprivate in nature. The Yunnan government clearly would like to accelerate the growth of small-scale township enterprises, but most of the officials I met did not seem very optimistic about the prospects because of many factors that they described; the major obstacles included the basic poverty and low educational levels of many rural areas, the serious lack of capital and technical and entrepreneurial skills, and poor transport. Some middle-level officials I met felt, also, that the provincial government had not given sufficient support and encouragement to the growth of township enterprises—at least until very recently.

*   *   *

In almost every conversation that I had on the provincial economy, my interlocutors recognized, and frankly acknowledged, the inadequacies of the provincial transportation system and stressed the determination of the province to modernize the system. Before World War II, apart from the French-built narrow-gauge railway to Vietnam, and a few urban roads, modern transportation was almost totally lacking. The road system began to be developed during the war. It was at that time that the Nationalist regime built the Burma and Ledo roads to provide outside links on which military supplies could be brought to China. (The roads went through incredibly rough terrain, which made truck driving on them extremely dangerous, but they did provide links that were of crucial importance during the war—though less important now.) At that time, a number of other roads were constructed within the province, and military airfields were built.

From the time of their takeover in Yunnan, the Communists gave high priority to the building of both roads and railways. By the 1970s, roads of some kind (as well as telegraph and telephone lines) reportedly reached every county in the province and almost 9 out of 10 communes (which are now townships). In addition, a radio network covered most of the province. In the 1980s, a TV network was added.

Expanding the rail network in Yunnan was more difficult than building roads, and even in the late 1980s the number of rail lines was minimal. However, the narrow-gauge railway to Vietnam was restored, and two important new lines were built, one north to Chengdu (in Sichuan) and the other northeast to Guiyang (in Guizhou). The latter also had a short branch that went to Dongchuan's copper mines and also to Baiguo (a town in Guizhou near the Yunnan border). Altogether, as of 1988, the rail network totaled over 1,000 miles. Construction of new lines was still a priority objective for provincial leaders, but even though preliminary planning had been done for several new lines, construction was not yet in sight: In every case, because of the difficulty of the topography and the high cost of construction, provincial leaders had simply been unable to get approval from the state Planning Commission to include construction of most of the hoped-for rail lines in specific plans to which national resources would be contributed. Construction of most of the lines would be impossible without the central government's major financial help.

The deputy governor told me that planning was under way, nevertheless, for three new lines. One of them would go to Nanning in adjacent Guangxi Province (this was regarded as especially important because it would connect Yunnan with the route to the southern Guangdong port city of Zhanjiang and give Yunnan much easier access to the sea). Another line that they hoped to build would be a second line to Sichuan; it would link up with the main Chongqing-Chengdu rail line at Neijiang. A third line, this one within Yunnan, would link Kunming and Dali. No one could predict when these three lines might be built, however. In the meantime, efforts were being made to improve existing lines. Electrification of the line to Guizhou was already under way, and plans had been drafted to electrify the existing line to Chengdu in the early 1990s.

The road network in Yunnan had developed more rapidly than the rail system, but provincial leaders recognized that it was still very inadequate for a province that had more than 150,000 square miles of territory. By 1986, the latest figures for which I obtained road statistics, the total length of roads in Yunnan was slightly more than 30,000 miles. It was claimed that almost 24,000 miles were paved. However, only one-fifth of the miles of paved roads were classified as being of "top and secondary grade"; roughly two-fifths were said to be of "medium grade," and two-fifths of "lower grade." In 1988, at the time of my visit, I was told that four new major highways were "under construction"; most were actually improved versions of existing lower-quality roads. These highways would nevertheless make the links between Kunming and all major regions in the southeast, south, southwest, and northwest much better. The deputy governor was enthusiastic when he discussed how much these roads, when completed, would improve interregional transport within the province.

A revealing clue about how far Yunnan still had to go in modernizing transport was the figure given to me on the total number of civilian motor vehicles in the province: roughly 100,000, of which about three-quarters were trucks and only one-quarter were passenger vehicles of all kinds (mainly buses)—to serve a population of almost 35 million. Everyone said that the importance—in fact, the necessity—of expanding modern motor transport could not be overemphasized. The links that had been built in recent years had begun to bring Yunnan into the motor age—but the province was still in the early stage of that process. By the late 1980s, most long-distance cargo was being transported by truck (which was a big change from four decades ago), but a large percentage of short-distance cargo was still being carried by carts of various sorts (many of them drawn by crawling tractors).

Yunnan's air service, not surprisingly, was even more rudimentary than its surface transportation. In 1988, Kunming had regular, though not frequent, airline connections with several other major provincial cities, and the provincial government hoped for a renewal of some transiting international flights (at one time it had been a fairly important stopping point for flights between China and Burma). Kunming's airfield, as I noted earlier, still left a great deal to be desired, and its terminal was one of the smallest of all provincial air terminals that I visited in 1988. But the new air terminal and new runways that were being built would soon convert it into a real "international airport" capable of handling Boeing 747s. In addition to being served by national airlines, Yunnan had some local air services, which connected Kunming to Simao in the south and to Baoshan in the west. I was told, also, that provincial plans called for initiating service soon to Xishuangbanna in the far south and Zhaotong in the far northwest. (There also were a number of military airfields in the province, including ones at Dali and Mengzi, but they were not being used for regular civilian flights.)

Although the lack of modern transportation created huge obstacles to the integration of various regions within the province, modern communications, especially radio and TV, had obviously had a profound effect on the area. They had broadened everybody's horizons, and they had created much closer links between outlying areas and Kunming. I failed to obtain detailed statistics on the ownership of radio and TV sets in Yunnan, but I was told that radio blanketed virtually the entire province and TV reached much of it. In my travels through large areas of the countryside to the south, the number of TV aerials that I saw was perhaps fewer than in some other interior areas, but I saw at least a few virtually everywhere, and it was clear that the coverage was very broad. I did obtain statistics in one area, around Gejiu, in southern Yunnan: In that area there was one TV station and 23 TV relay stations, which local people said reached 65 percent of the local prefecture.

As these comments and data indicate, Yunnan has begun to modernize, across the board, but it is still in the early stages of modern development. Local officials emphasized the need to improve just about everything. Obviously, though, they regarded some actions as more urgently needed, and of higher priority, than others. When I asked the deputy governor what he thought the most urgent need was, he stated: "development of a commodity economy" (meaning, further marketization) and the "changes in attitudes" that this would require, "but also modernization of education, transport, agriculture, and light industry."

* * *

Because of its underdevelopment, Yunnan remained, in the late 1980s, as I noted earlier, one of China's poorest provinces. The officials I met talked at considerable length about their efforts to cope with the worst poverty. Per capita annual output in the province as a whole, I was told, averaged Y 428, but this figure obscured great variations, including the great gap between rural and urban areas. According to provincial planners, in 1987 the annual per capita income in rural areas was Y 365 (per farmer, not per family in farming), whereas in urban areas it was Y 1,700 per worker (a figure based just on salaries and not including bonuses or other extra income). The relatively high figure for urban workers helped to explain why, in Kunming and other cities and towns I visited, almost all the people seemed to be quite well clothed, well fed, and generally fairly well off by Chinese standards.*

The statistics on rural incomes unquestionably reflected very real and very serious poverty in many areas of Yunnan. But even figures on rural areas required very careful analysis. As I discuss later, in traveling more than 400 miles by car through Yunnan's countryside in 1988, I failed to see many people who appeared to be desperately poor. Much of the area through which I traveled was relatively poor—compared to coastal China and even compared to some other western areas that I visited. The standard of living was obviously far below that in most developed East Asian countries, to say nothing of that in most Western industrial countries. Yet even in rural areas such as those in Yunnan, most people I saw seemed to be reasonably well fed and well clothed; they clearly were better off than they had been in the past. I concluded, just as I had in other areas of west China that I visited in 1988, that the worst poverty was concentrated in extremely remote areas, beyond the reach of modernized towns and transport. After a great many interviews in Yunnan, I eventually obtained data, from both economic planners and officials responsible for minority affairs in the province, that strongly supported my hypothesis. These officials stated that the worst problems of extreme poverty were concentrated in remote mountain areas inhabited by minorities.

In 1988, provincial planners told me, the worst poverty was in roughly one-third of the province's counties (not a low proportion). Altogether, there were 41 counties in the province classified as "the poorest," and these had a population of about 3 million, composed mainly of minority groups. (The people in these counties constituted more than a quarter of the entire minority population in the province but under 10 percent of the province's total population.) The average per capita income in these counties classified as the poorest was extremely low, averaging about Y 150, which was far below a subsistence level. To prevent disastrous starvation in such areas, the central government was providing food as well as special antipoverty subsidies. Special funding included about Y 60 million in grants and Y 210 million in low-interest loans. This financial aid was channeled through the provincial gov-

---

*As I mentioned in an earlier chapter, by this time I had concluded that in trying to determine Chinese living standards it was very misleading to convert yuan figures to U.S. dollars at the official exchange rate. In fact, my strong impression was that many Chinese urbanites seemed to be living far more comfortably than they could have in most Western countries on comparable salaries—even if their income figures were converted to U.S. dollars on a basis of one to one. When converted to dollars at the official exchange rates, most Chinese incomes simply would not be sufficient for survival. As I have said several times, I was favorably impressed by the general level of livelihood, judged by food availability and the character of clothing; housing for most people was still tight but less so in Yunnan than in crowded eastern China.

ernment and went to 26 of these extremely poor counties; the provincial government itself gave subsidies to the other 15. (As I will elaborate on later, this funding was only a part of the general support given to autonomous prefectures and counties in Yunnan.) In other minority areas containing a population of more than 4 million minority inhabitants, local food production met basic needs, but even in these areas average living standards remained well below those of most of the Han population. However, in other minority areas, which contained about a third of the population of minorities in the province (4 million), average living standards were close to those of the average for Han farmers.

Even among the Han Chinese the variations also were substantial. Not only were the average incomes of urban workers much higher than those of the Han farming population in general, but those Han farmers who lived near urban areas were considerably better off than most farmers in remote areas. Near cities and towns, the per capita income of the Han rural population was generally about Y 400, I was told, and often it was between Y 500 and Y 600; in many remote areas the average was nearer to Y 250 (and in some very remote areas, it was even lower). Poverty, in short, was extensive but localized.

In light of Yunnan's poverty, it was no surprise to learn that, like all of China's western provinces, it was fiscally dependent on subsidies from the central government. Even after I received a briefing on the province's finances, I was not sure that I really understood the situation as it was described to me—or the specific meanings of the data given to me—but one thing that was clear was that the province depended heavily on funds received from Beijing. As in other provinces, the government in Yunnan actually collected almost all revenue, but it remitted a large percentage of it to the central government and then received allocations of funds and subsidies from Beijing. I was told, at one point, that the province expected its revenues to total Y 3.74 billion in 1988—but, hard as I tried, I was unable to clarify how much of that they would keep, how much they would send to the central government, and what their total local budget really was. However, officials did give me quite a bit of data on some specific elements in the budget. One new factor in 1988, they said, was the requirement that they pay about Y 800 million to the central government specifically as a quid pro quo for Beijing's decision to increase the prices of cigarettes made in Yunnan (from which the province profited). At one point they talked of a general subsidy from the central government to Yunnan in 1988 that would total Y 700 million—in addition to what they would obtain in special subsidies earmarked for aid to poor minority areas and a sizable amount of central government investment in enterprises in the province. Exactly what the balance sheet would look like by the end of the year I never was able to determine. One official said, "We get great financial support from the central government; it gives us much more than we give to it," but I was never able to pin down exactly how much more.

A significant amount of the central government's subsidies to Yunnan was designated specifically for support of poor minority areas. Officials from the Minority Affairs Commission told me that the budgetary expenditures of all Yunnan's autonomous prefectures and counties totaled Y 1.82 billion in 1987; that they raised only Y 980 million in local revenues; and that most of their budgetary shortfalls, which totaled Y 840 million, were made up by central government subsidies that were channeled through the provincial government. These figures suggested that Beijing paid for roughly one-half of the annual expenditures of these areas. In addition, in 1987 the central and provincial governments reportedly invested a total of about Y 1.4 billion in these areas; of this, about Y 600 billion was used for capital construction.

                              *   *   *

I found that the principal preoccupation of leaders in Yunnan was the necessity for accelerating economic growth, and—like other leaders in west China—they were frank in admitting that the process of reform in their area lagged significantly behind what was taking place in advanced coastal provinces in the east. Nevertheless, Yunnan's leaders were attempting to carry out most of the reform policies being promoted by national leaders, and, even in Yunnan, it was possible to see how the economic system was gradually being transformed. Some of the economic changes were of a kind that were readily visible; for example, free markets were numerous in all the places that I visited, and they were very lively indeed. Other kinds of changes were not readily visible, but I was told about them by local people. I could also sense significant changes in the general political climate compared with what I had seen during my last visit in the 1970s, and it was evident from what I was told that this change had taken place as a result of the reform program of the 1980s (before the Tiananmen crisis of 1989). The level of political tension seemed very low to me, and the general atmosphere in 1988 was one of relative stability. Maoist ideological sloganeering was almost totally absent, and political and social controls were much looser than they had been. Most people I met were willing to talk freely and openly and express their own personal opinions to an extent that would have been almost unimaginable in the 1970s.

Much of what I learned about economic reform in Yunnan came from officials who worked in the provincial Structural Reform Commission. They discussed in considerable detail the evolution of the reforms in Yunnan and highlighted reforms that were currently receiving priority attention. In this province, as in the country as a whole, they said, economic reform began with a focus on agriculture, which was given the highest priority during 1979–1984. The return to family farming had a very positive effect in Yunnan. Then the focus shifted, in the mid-1980s, to urban and industrial reform—and it was reforms in that area that they wished most to describe and provide details about. Finally, after the 13th Party Congress in 1987, they said, political reform became an important part of the local agenda in Yunnan, and what had been called the Economic Structural Reform Commission became, in Yunnan, simply the Structural Reform Commission, and it was given responsibility for both economic and political reforms in the province. It was evident that real political structural reform had not yet taken place, in any lasting or major way. The deputy governor was frank to acknowledge that political reform had been slow in the province. But he argued that some significant changes had taken place—guided by the Political Reform Small Group that had been established under the Structural Reform Commission. Several similar small groups had been established under the commission, he said, that dealt with administrative reorganization, enterprise reform (he chaired the small group for that), and other specific areas of reform. The most important political changes, in his judgment, had been in the realm of personnel policy and characteristics of the leadership, and he discussed how the Party and government in Yunnan had elevated to positions of authority large numbers of younger and better-educated people, which had changed the nature of the system in important ways. (Everything I heard and saw tended to confirm this judgment.)

In organizational terms, the focus was currently on "separating Party and government" as well as separating "Party and enterprises," he said. Two of the Party's economic departments (those for finance and trade and for industry and communications) had been abolished; the Rural Work Department continued to operate, however. Also eliminated from most government departments (*ting*) were the Party core groups or fractions (*dangzu*), which previously had been embedded in, and had exercised very direct and close control over, the government as a whole, including most departments. As a result, the intervention of the Party apparatus into economic affairs had been substantially reduced, and the role of government specialists and technical people had definitely been enhanced. At the top levels of provincial leadership, there continued to be a fairly large overlapping between Party and government leaders, that is, people who simultaneously held high positions in both Party and government hierarchies. There was more of this overlap, it seemed to me, in Yunnan in 1988 than there was in many other areas that I visited. For example, in most provinces the usual pattern now was for only two top government leaders—the governor and one other, usually his executive deputy governor—to be concurrently members of the Party Standing Committee. However, in Yunnan, a short time before I was there, two other members of the Standing Committee had been assigned to government positions, creating a situation in which there was an overlap of four people. This increase in the number of leaders holding top jobs in both the Party and the government appeared to be working in a direction opposite from that called for by the policy of separating the Party from government and enterprises. When I noted this, local officials acknowledged that this was the case but argued that it was likely to be a temporary situation.

Officials from the Structural Reform Commission told me that they were, at that time, working on proposals for other reforms that they said would be introduced in 1989. Among these proposals were calls for further administrative changes designed to strengthen "comprehensive departments" in the government—that is, those departments that exercised broad coordinating functions—and other proposals to reduce the size and number of operating departments. My impression was that although the adjustments or changes in the Party's roles were not insignificant, none of the political or administrative steps taken to date—or planned for the immediate future—had begun to change the political *system* in any fundamental way.

*   *   *

It was no surprise to learn that officials in the Structural Reform Commission considered their major priorities to be in the field of economic reform rather than political reform—and, since 1984, local leaders had stressed reform in the urban and industrial sectors in particular. They said they were currently trying to achieve what by 1988 were recognized to be priority objectives throughout China and were taking measures to improve the efficiency of large state enterprises, decentralize more decisionmaking and give greater authority to enterprise managers, begin to separate management from ownership, put greater emphasis on profits as the criterion for success of enterprises, and so on.

In Yunnan, officials said, they began to introduce the contract responsibility system in 1987 in large and medium-sized industrial enterprises. By 1988, the system had been put into effect in all 250 key enterprises, they claimed, and in close to 80 percent of all industrial enterprises of any kind in the province. They argued that this system had basically changed the relationship between enterprises and the government's industrial departments, which formerly had exercised direct control over enterprises but now only "supervised industrial sectors" in a "looser and more indirect" fashion. As one official put it, "Formerly, what the government bureaus ordered, the enterprises had to do, but now relationships are contractual." Yunnan had also made some progress in developing markets for materials, and my informants said that the number of materials directly allocated by the government under mandatory plans in Yunnan had been reduced to 7; 26 others were under guidance planning, and the rest were sold on the market. They estimated that perhaps half of the raw materials trade in Yunnan was no longer under direct state planning (however, the percentage varied by commodity); they admitted, however, that the state still controlled the most crucial items.

Some steps had been taken toward diversification of ownership and management. The government had sold or leased 4,316 small state industrial enterprises, mostly to other enterprises (usually collectives). Within state enterprises, they had been working to improve the effectiveness of management; one method, they said, was to encourage more competition for managerial jobs by "bidding" (that is, encouraging people to apply for managerial positions in open competition). They asserted that bidding for managerial jobs had been carried out in 30 percent of all state industrial enterprises, including more than 70 of the largest 250. This process involved competition for the post of director, or manager, and also very hard negotiations between the new or prospective managers and the government about the precise requirements of the contracts under which they would operate. Most contracts signed in Yunnan were for three-year periods. In signing a contract, a manager had to agree to certain targets, which were then written into his contract. In theory he suffered penalties if he did not achieve these goals, and he and his employees obtained larger incomes if they exceeded them.

In my discussions about the system, one official told me about several specific cases. One involved a factory where 18 people had applied in the competition for the manager's job (it was a large Kunming enterprise). The man who won the competition promised to raise the amount of profit that the enterprise paid to the government annually from Y 5.5 million to Y 7.1 million. (No wonder he won the job!) Generally, however, there was "very tough bargaining because managers tried to *reduce* the set profit targets, as well as other targets, whereas government departments tried to increase them." The basic aim of the bidding process, obviously, was to find and select the best possible managers. Apparently, though, the majority of managers selected under this system, where it had been adopted, actually were insiders (that is, people within the enterprise who were promoted to the manager's position) rather than outsiders. My informants estimated that about 60 percent of all those chosen through bidding had been incumbent managers; about 30 percent had been new people but had come from the government departments that were supervising the enterprises; and only about 10 percent of the new managers had come from outside both the enterprises and their supervising departments. The pool of able potential managers who represented really new talent—that is, ones who were not already employees of a factory or its supervising department—was disappointingly small, they said.

The manager contract responsibility system had been adopted, I was told, in 98 percent of all state industrial and commercial enterprises in the province. Under this system, managers were required to fulfill the obligations embodied in the contracts that they signed with government departments. But the system also aimed to give managers more "independence" from the Party's control and to give them more decisionmaking authority, more flexibility in deciding certain targets in running their enterprises on a day-to-day basis, and greater leeway in deciding how best to use that part of the enterprises' profits that they were allowed to retain.* Of the profits that an enterprise was allowed to keep, up to 63 percent, my informants said, could be used for "technical renovations"—that is, reinvestment—but some could be used for increasing wages and bonuses and improving programs for workers' welfare. The new policies were supposed to impose penalties on enterprises that failed to meet their targets as well as give rewards for success. Local officials were fairly frank in admitting, however, that even though regulations on bankruptcies were now on the books, not a single enterprise had been declared bankrupt. Recently, 16 enterprises whose debts exceeded their assets had been "taken over" by larger and more successful enterprises. I was not given any specific examples of managers who had been punished for not meeting targets; I got the impression that the new policies put much greater emphasis on rewards for good performance than on penalties for bad performance.

As a result of the steady reduction of the scope of state planning, and because the new policies were trying to promote a "socialist commodity economy," managers "no longer can simply sit back and wait to receive state plans and then just sell their products to the state," one of my informants stated. "They now must try to produce for the market and make what consumers need." But, local planners said, developing markets had not been easy, in part "because of Yunnan's special characteristics." Nevertheless, they said, recently a total of 2,723 "consumer goods markets" of all kinds had been organized (although they did not explain what, exactly, this term referred to). It seemed clear, from everything I heard and saw, that collective and private commercial enterprises (shops, peddlers, and so on) were gradually outcompeting the state shops—but more gradually than in eastern provinces. Between 1978 and 1986, I was told, sales by collectives rose from 34 percent to more than 40 percent of all retail sales in the province, and individual (*geti*) sellers increased their share of sales from less than 5 percent to about 16 percent of the total. As a result, retail sales by state commercial enterprises had declined from a little over 60 percent of all retail sales to a little over 40 percent. Rural markets were very active throughout the province,

---

*One of the planners I met asserted, flatly, "Formerly, the Party Committee constituted the only leadership in an enterprise, and the manager had to obey what the Party secretary decided. Now, the director is in charge." I had no opportunity to check how true this was in practice, but I found the statement to be plausible—at the time. It may have been less so from mid-1989 on: After the Tiananmen crisis, there were some reports that in at least certain places the Party attempted to reestablish greater control over enterprises. However, by 1992 the trend toward loosening controls and granting managers greater authority accelerated again.

everyone said, and they operated daily in most areas near cities and on a traditional periodic basis (varying from one every three days to one every seven days) in more remote areas.

The development of both labor markets and financial markets was on the agenda of Yunnan's planners and reformers; they made a little progress in these fields by 1988. In late 1987, one unit called the Labor Service Company, under the provincial Department of Labor (which had been separated from the old Department of Personnel and Labor), had organized a job placement program. But only 3,000 or so workers had even registered as job seekers, and only about a third of them had actually been placed in jobs, I was told. Some steps had been taken to modify the old wage system, and my informants said that their stated goal was to end, eventually, the system of guaranteed lifetime security (the "iron rice bowl") and introduce new systems that would provide many more incentives for hard work and efficiency. In the past, all workers in the urban sector of Yunnan had been paid on the basis of the standard, national, eight-grade wage systems, under which rank and seniority played major roles in the determination of wages. But since the start of reforms, some new systems had been introduced, several of which were now operating in parallel in different places and enterprises. Many workers were still paid on the old system, but now some were paid on a piecework system and others were paid under a system in which their pay was decided partly by standard base pay regulations and partly on the basis of piecework-based supplements to their pay.

In a few select industries—including metallurgy, tobacco, and textiles—a total of 347 enterprises had adopted a system that they said combined a basic salary with extra "efficiency [productivity] pay." Under this system, for every 1 percent increase in productivity, the enterprise could increase workers' pay by between 0.3 percent and 0.7 percent. In 1987, Yunnan had also begun to introduce a system of "contract labor" for new employees in state enterprises. Workers hired under this system signed contracts for employment for a specific period of time (in contrast, in the Maoist period it was generally assumed that a job would be for one's lifetime). By 1988, my informants said, 17 percent of all labor in state enterprises in the province were under this system of "contract labor."

In the sphere of banking, Yunnan had recently established 20 of what they called "financial markets." As they tried to describe to me what this term meant, I concluded that it was only a very modest step toward developing a real financial market. Apparently the term referred to new policies under which the five major types of state banks—agricultural, industrial and commercial, and so on—were no longer rigidly restricted to making loans within their particular fields but could broaden their operations into other fields. This easing of restrictions facilitated interbank lending and borrowing (including transactions with banks in other provinces). The banks were also developing, I was told, a new network for the exchange of information between banks. Deposits in Yunnan's banks had grown substantially in recent years, and by the end of 1987, savings deposits in banks within the province totaled Y 5.54 billion. Provincial planners wanted to devise new ways of using this pool of capital more effectively for investment in projects that would help the province's development. In 1988, they said, Yunnan also had begun to establish some "stock markets." These were really, as they described them, bond markets that sold mainly government bonds, but they had begun to sell some enterprise bonds as well. They admitted that these were still in a very early stage of development.

Housing reform was also on the agenda of the Structural Reform Commission. The hope was that eventually Yunnan could move toward privatization by making housing a "commodity." Relatively little had been done so far to make progress toward that goal. Officials from the commission said they were "studying how to do it." They had, however, begun some experiments in the sale of houses (mainly individual apartments within large apartment buildings) in three cities and three counties. Some housing owned by selected enterprises and schools also was scheduled to be sold. Not many houses had actually been sold yet, though. The main action that they had taken recently in regard to housing had been the decision to increase some rents; however, in many cases the higher rents had been accompanied with increased housing subsidies. (In the long run, for housing reform to achieve the stated goal of commercialization, such subsidies would have to be reduced and eventually eliminated.)

When I asked officials in Yunnan what they thought about the prospects for comprehensive price reform—which, by 1988, a great many reform leaders and academics in Beijing believed was the most crucial but also the most difficult and risky reform needed in the period ahead—everyone I posed the question to immediately stated that they thought it was extremely important but that they doubted if it was in the cards soon. The general view was that it would not be attempted until inflation was under much better long-term control. I was surprised that those I interviewed did not, on their own, raise the subject of prices or volunteer their own views or express great concern about the dangers of inflation. But once I raised the subject it became clear that they were seriously concerned about the rising rate of inflation.

The official figures I was given indicated that Yunnan's rate of inflation (based on the local retail price index) had been 6.6 percent in 1987 and then rose to about 14 percent during the first three quarters of 1988. (The real rates were probably higher.) Urban areas were most affected. Moreover, in August 1988 the rate rose—even by official calculations—to above 20 percent in Kunming and to close to 13 percent in rural areas. Even if the figures understated the real rate of inflation, they were high enough to create real worries. They showed that the rate of price inflation had more than doubled in one year and had risen well above the level that many Chinese leaders—and ordinary people—considered tolerable.

Yet despite the fact that they clearly were concerned, I did not sense that leaders in Yunnan were as worried about inflation as many of those I met in eastern coastal areas and in Beijing. In those areas, even more than in the interior, the tolerance of leaders—and ordinary people—for inflation was severely limited. Many leaders with whom I discussed inflation in 1988 in Beijing and coastal China stated frankly that inflation above 10 percent or so was intolerable because it could lead to destabilizing political and social effects. The level of 10 percent, of course, is far below what many countries—especially developing countries—have had to accept in recent years. Whether the extreme sensitivity of Chinese leaders about anything above 10 percent was justified, they had strong feelings that any higher rate was dangerous. (Clearly their fear of inflation was based on China's experience with hyperinflation in the 1940s, which helped undermine the Nationalist regime and paved the way for the Communists' rise to power.)

* * *

In my discussions with leaders and planners in Yunnan, I found that the policy of opening, which was a key element in the policies of reform initiated by Deng in the late 1970s and early 1980s, was one that aroused great hopes but also serious apprehensions—mainly because of the current coastal policy that gave preferential treatment to the provinces in east China. In Kunming, when I began questioning officials about their views on the coastal policy, invariably they first gave a standard response, which echoed Beijing's official view. This view was articulated as follows in Kunming (which was similar to the way it was articulated in most places I visited in the west): The aim of China's policies is to develop all of the country. However, the country is so large that this cannot be accomplished all at once. Therefore, it is logical—in light of the fact that coastal areas have many advantages that they can use to accelerate growth, including advantages of location, skills, entrepreneurship, and so on—for policies to give coastal areas preferential treatment at first to ensure that they will accelerate their development but at the same time try to ensure that they help the interior provinces to develop at a later stage. In the initial period, the interior provinces, most of which are rich in raw materials, can benefit a great deal by selling their resources to coastal areas and obtaining in return greater amounts of capital, technology, and advice. Moreover, so the argument went, because the coastal areas will increasingly stress exports, the interior provinces should be in a better position to expand their sales in the domestic market. Then, at a later stage, the interior provinces will receive much greater attention and help—not only from Beijing but from the more advanced coastal provinces; this should enable them, over time, to catch up.

This was an obvious and in some respects understandable rationale for the open policy. It was a variation of the well-known trickle-down theory familiar to anyone who has been concerned about economic development in less-developed parts of the world. Yet in Yunnan, as in other western areas, the longer I discussed this subject the more it became evident that local leaders were quite fearful that, in reality, the gap between their areas and coastal areas was likely to steadily widen. Leaders in all the interior provinces that I visited were trying, as best they could, to be actively involved in the new foreign economic relations that China was developing under the open policy, and they were lobbying for policy adjustments that would give them many of the privileges granted to coastal states to engage in foreign trade and attract foreign investment. I also found, though, that when leaders in the interior discussed the open policy, they were talking not only about foreign economic relations but also about expanding what they called "horizontal economic ties"—that is, greater trade, exchange of technology, and other kinds of cooperation with other parts of China.

In his discussions with me, the executive deputy governor of Yunnan placed very special importance on the need to increase cooperation with both governments and specific enterprises in other Chinese provinces—especially coastal provinces. He emphasized this, I believe, because he saw that, realistically speaking, the opportunities would probably be greater in the immediate future for the expansion of interprovincial collaboration than they would be for the promotion of foreign trade or the attraction of foreign investment—although he felt that the latter would be extremely desirable, to the extent possible. Ties with several coastal provinces had been expanding significantly, he said, and already they had resulted in "exchanges of great mutual benefit." Yunnan's "most important horizontal relationships," he asserted, "are with Shanghai."

In recent years, he said, more than 1,000 cooperative arrangements had been worked out with Shanghai, both with the government (including not only the municipal government but also local governments down to and including the counties) and with enterprises. Some of them, he said, involved "long-term" relationships. Of the 1,000 plus, a few had not yet gone beyond letters of intent, but the majority were already under way, and he expected all of them to be operational soon. To facilitate closer economic cooperation, Yunnan and Shanghai had established special organs—called Economic and Trade Coordination Associations—which had appointed a variety of specialized committees to promote economic and technical cooperation in specific fields. There were no regular joint meetings between these associations, but each year Yunnan and Shanghai exchanged delegations to try to broaden their economic cooperation. (The deputy governor noted in passing that he was just about to leave with an economic mission on

Left:
*Constructed during the
1980s building boom,
skyscrapers such as these
have transformed the ap-
pearance of many parts of
Kunming.*

Right:
*Many major avenues in Kunming
have four or more lanes—some
for autos and trucks, others for
bicycles—and are crowded with
vehicles; many are also lined
with trees.*

*This street, lined with traditional shops and houses, is in the small Hui Muslim dis-
trict of the city, one of the few areas that still resembles what most of Kunming
looked like before 1949.*

Above left: A new two-story peasant home on the road from Kunming to Gejiu. Such homes, which were almost universal in many parts of east China in 1988, were spreading in Yunnan.

Above right: Minority women at an urban market en route to Gejiu. Many minority women still dress in traditional clothes, but in urban areas few minority men do.

A traffic jam on market day in a town on the road between Kunming and Gejiu. Note the fascinating mix of modern and traditional forms of transport.

Top:
A modern Gejiu cityscape. By 1988 the city had been almost entirely rebuilt and modernized and bore little resemblance to the pre-1949 city.

Middle:
In Gejiu, as in other major cities, urban Chinese had by 1988 become apartment dwellers. These apartments are generally more spacious than those in east China.

Bottom:
This street scene highlights the contrast between old (traditional shops) and new (modern apartments). In Gejiu in 1988 the old was rapidly disappearing.

Remnants of the old tin mine-shaft that I visited in 1948. The old mine was superseded by more modern ones.

A large mountain area near Gejiu is now covered with modern mines and mine-related installations such as this.

a trip to Japan and that he planned to stop, on his return trip, in Shanghai to talk with "the top leaders" there about economic cooperation.)

The deputy governor also discussed and gave me his views on the "group of six provinces" of southwest China—which was comparable to the similar group I had learned about in northwest China, and, like it, was "informal" (that is, although it was acknowledged and accepted by the central government, it was not formally authorized or established by the State Council). He said that once a year there was a meeting of the top leaders of Sichuan Province, Chongqing Municipality (which recently had been granted economic decisionmaking authority equivalent to that of a province), Xizang (the Tibetan Autonomous Region), Yunnan Province, Guizhou Province, and Guangxi Province. "We have a kind of permanent organization, but our meetings rotate annually among our members; it is basically a liaison organization." In 1987, the meeting convened in Yunnan, and in 1988 it was held in Sichuan. Each year, the group's chairman was the head of government (that is, the provincial governor, regional chairman, or, in the case of Chongqing, the mayor) in the place where they met, and the group's "staff" consisted of people sent by each province or region to the place of the meeting. "The most important function of this group is research and coordination of economic development." He added, "After discussing an issue, the group sometimes makes proposals to the State Council." My own guess was that one of the group's most important functions was lobbying in Beijing.

Despite their realistic acceptance of the fact that in trying to promote foreign economic relations Yunnan faced great problems and suffered from obvious disadvantages, Yunnan's leaders were trying actively to promote, as much as they could, foreign trade and investment. But to date they had had only limited success. Starting in 1978, I was told, Beijing had given Yunnan some limited authority to conduct direct trade with foreign areas, and in the 1980s the local government had established several provincial trading companies, but most of the province's foreign trade still had to go through central government ministries, trade agencies, or corporations. Nevertheless, Yunnan had developed some trade with "more than 90 foreign countries and regions." They exported, among other things, nonferrous metals and other minerals as well as farm products, and they imported technology and a variety of other goods. But the volume of foreign trade, provincial planners said, was still "very small." (I obtained no definite figures.)

Because Yunnan was a frontier area, it was, I was told, given authority— in theory—to keep half of its foreign exchange earnings "within the plan" and 70 percent of "above plan earnings." They said that in practice it did not work out that way. In the case of their exports of certain commodities that were controlled by the central government, they were really allowed to keep only a small percentage of the foreign exchange earnings, and, they said, they obtained no foreign exchange from their barter trade with East Euro-

pean countries. So, according to one of my informants, the province had actually been able to keep—in the recent past—only about US$80 million of
foreign exchange a year (a figure so small that I wondered if it was correct).
In dealing with foreign investments, Yunnan was authorized to make decisions only on very small projects, valued at US$5 million or less. Statistics
for 1986 showed that from the time foreign investment had begun up
through 1986, only a trickle of foreign capital had come to Yunnan. The figures given to me—US$3.79 million in direct foreign investment and US$2
million in foreign loans—seemed extraordinarily low to me (perhaps that
figure did not include everything). Whatever the correct dollar total, by
1988 only 22 cooperative ventures involving foreigners had been initiated in
the province, I was told; most of them, moreover, provided only very small-
scale assistance to existing factories or to the construction (or management)
of modern hotels. A few were said to be equity investment projects, but most
were for other types of cooperation.

If these figures were accurate, they indicated that Yunnan had not yet been
able to attract any significant number of foreign businesses to become seriously involved in the province. Probably the greatest effect of the opening so
far had been something much less tangible but nevertheless important:
greater exposure to both the rest of the country and the outside world. Outside contacts had greatly stimulated hopes and raised aspirations. But the
limited concrete results had also created disappointment and frustration. I
had little doubt that Yunnan (and other interior provinces) would lobby persistently for increased authority and opportunities to try to attract more foreign capital and investments and expand foreign trade. But even if the central
government eventually was more responsive to such lobbying, I could see little basis for great optimism—at least as of 1988—that Yunnan would in the
near future obtain much direct or large-scale benefit from China's open policy. In the long run, it could be different.

Although the leaders in Kunming were obviously trying to look outward
more than in the past, circumstances still compelled them to look primarily
inward and to devote most of their attention to solving—or at least managing—the province's internal problems, many of which were rooted in its past
and in its geography, topography, and demography.

*   *   *

The policies pursued by leaders in Yunnan to deal with ethnic problems
had varied over time, but it was apparent that since the start of the reform
decade there had been quite vigorous efforts to raise the educational and
economic levels of minority groups by implementing a wide variety of affirmative action policies. In contrast to many past periods of harsh political
repression and/or benign neglect, the regime's policies in the 1980s reflected

those of new national policies toward ethnic groups that were much more conciliatory.

Yunnan, as well as its two adjacent southwestern provinces—Guizhou and Guangxi—have had ethnic mixtures quite different not only from areas of China where Han Chinese have predominated but also from other areas of west China. In Yunnan there has never been a situation in which one or two minority groups were clearly predominant in numbers, and it has therefore been quite different from those areas that have been dominated by Tibetans, Mongols, Hui, or Uighurs. It is true that a thousand years ago the Tai people (who established the kingdom on Nanzhao) achieved supremacy; it is also true that certain other minorities (including the Yi) have established effective control over certain parts of what is now Yunnan for considerable periods of time. As I said earlier, even in this century Yi warlords such as Long Yun and Lu Han were able to achieve military supremacy and control of the provincial government for short periods of time. However, for most of the region's history, what is now Yunnan had, in effect, been divided into numerous small areas inhabited by different ethnic groups, and each minority group, historically, had tried to go its own way, maintain its own identity, and exercise autonomy to the extent possible.*

Only in very recent decades—and especially since 1949—have all of the small ethnic groups in the area been effectively incorporated into China's larger body politic, and a great many of them have by no means been culturally assimilated but have continued to maintain their own separate identity.

In Kunming, I was briefed at length about Yunnan's minorities and government policies toward them by three scholars at the provincial Academy of Social Sciences (one of them was a Naxi, another was a Bulan, and the third was a Han Chinese). They all impressed me as being knowledgeable and competent. As of 1988, the ethnic situation in the province, as they described it to me, was as follows. The 11.1 million members of minority groups in Yunnan made up roughly one-third of the province's population, and they belonged to 25 different ethnic groups (including the Han). Although some were scattered throughout all areas of the province ("every city, county, and township has some ethnic minority people"), the majority lived in the 8 minority autonomous prefectures (*zizhi zhou*) and 28 minority autonomous counties that had been established following the Communist takeover. All of these areas contained a mixed population. (According to law and policy, I

---

*Even in the 1940s, when I visited southwest China, a sizable Yi area that overlapped southern Sichuan (with its center at Xichang) and Yunnan was often referred to as an "independent Lololand" ("Lolo" was a derogatory term for the Yi that was commonly used by Han Chinese at that time). And they exercised a substantial degree of autonomy up until the Communist takeover.

was told, any area where minorities constituted 30 percent or more of the total population could be designated a minority autonomous area and named after the largest minority group in it.)

As of 1988, the total population living in these autonomous jurisdictions (both prefectures and counties) was about 18 million (a little more than a half of the province's population). Of the 18 million, 9.44 million—or just over one-half—belonged to minority ethnic groups, and roughly 8.5 million were Han Chinese. About 1.7 million minority people lived outside of the autonomous areas. The ethnic map of Yunnan, therefore, showed at least small pockets of minority people in every part of the province (two of Kunming's counties were, for example, labeled autonomous counties). Actually, roughly two-thirds of the total territory of the province belonged to prefectures and counties labeled autonomous areas (although the largest concentrations of minority peoples were in the south and west).

Linguistically, the minority groups in Yunnan had been classified as belonging to three main linguistic groups, my informants said: the Tibeto-Burmese, the Dai (Tai), and the Mon-Khmer. There was tremendous cultural diversity even within each group, they said.*

The largest of Yunnan's minority groups was the Yi, with 3.5 million members in 1988. Next in size were the Bai and the Hani, each with over a million people. The others were generally smaller, most with under a million members, and some were much smaller than that. The scholars I interviewed talked at some length about the differences in the levels of development of these various groups. Although the criteria that they used in defining the levels were never entirely clear to me, my impression was that all three of the scholars (including those of minority origin) essentially judged the levels of development of specific groups to a large extent on the basis of how big a gap existed between their living standard, economies, and even culture and those of the majority Han population.

Several minority groups, they said, were "advanced"—that is, close to the Han standards; these included, in their judgment, the Bai, Naxi, and Zhuang, and most of the Yi (especially those in the south), as well as the Hui Muslims. They labeled a number of the minority groups as "fairly backward," and most of the groups that they put in this category were ones that

----

*In addition to such well-known ethnic groups as the Han, Hui, Tibetans, and Mongols, the groups in Yunnan included the following: Yi, Bai, Hani, Dai, Lisu, Wa (Va), Lahu, Naxi, Jingpo, Bulan (Blang), Achang, Pumi, Nu, Benglong, Dulong, Juno (Jino), Miao, Yao, and Zhuang. (I was not able to identify the two missing from this list.) At least a little anthropological and ethnological research has been done on most of these groups, but a dozen Margaret Meads could spend their entire lives in fieldwork in Yunnan and only begin the task of learning about all these ethnic minorities.

had lived until recently under tribal *tusi* (chieftains). The groups that they put into this category included the Dai, Lahu, Hani, and Yunnan's Tibetans as well as part of two other groups, which included the Naxi (as noted earlier, they put the majority of this group in the more advanced category) and Pumi. They considered the Yi in the northwest of the province (there were about 100,000 there) to be essentially backward because many in that area had lived in slavery until relatively recent times. They placed a few groups "somewhere in the middle." And they labeled seven groups as the "most primitive" ones (these were labeled primitive, they said, in part because in the pre-1949 period they had never developed private ownership of land and still, at that time, considered all land the property of the community); these groups, in their categorization, included the Dulong, Lisu, Nu, Jingpo, Wa, and Juno (they also put some of the Bulan in this category). Most of this last category of groups—the "most primitive" ones—lived west of the Nu River (Nu Jiang), near the Burmese border.

As my informants described these categories and groups to me, the taxonomy did not sound very scientific to me. However, I am fairly sure that if they had had more time to educate me on the subject, I would have discovered that they had a plausible basis for their categorizations. I suspect, though, that I might have found that their criteria for judging whether the groups were "advanced" or "primitive" reflected Han Chinese cultural predispositions.

My informants then proceeded to discuss, at some length, the poverty that was characteristic of many of Yunnan's minority areas, and they identified three general levels of poverty (which I noted earlier). They then linked their analysis of levels of poverty with their classification of minority groups according to their levels of development, from advanced to primitive. They also discussed the linkages between general levels of poverty and the overall characteristics and demographics of the eight autonomous prefectures in the province. In their analysis, the poorest and least advanced peoples were mainly in the most sparsely populated and remote areas. For the most part, the better-off and more advanced peoples were in areas of larger populations and areas that were less remote.

They pointed out that most of the population contained in autonomous prefectures in Yunnan was concentrated in four of these prefectures, which were located in two areas. One stretched northwest of Kunming and included the Chuxiong Yi Autonomous Prefecture and the Dali Bai Autonomous Prefecture. The other area of concentration was in the southeast, where the Honghe Hani-Yi Autonomous Prefecture and the Wenshan Zhuang-Miao Autonomous Prefecture were located. These four autonomous prefectures, each of which had between 2 million and 3.5 million people, together contained a population of 11.2 million (83 percent of all people living in autonomous prefectures). In contrast, each of the other four autonomous prefectures (the Dehong Dai-Jingpo Autonomous Prefecture in the far west, the Xishuangbanna Dai Autonomous Prefecture in the far south, the Nujiang Lisu Autonomous Prefecture in the west, and the Deqen Zang [Tibetan] Autonomous Prefecture in the far northwest) had less than a million people. All were located in very remote areas, and altogether they had a total population of only 2.23 million people, of whom 1.55 million belonged to minority groups. In each of these four remote prefectures, the proportion of the total population made up by minority peoples was at least half or more, and in three of them it ranged from 70 to almost 98 percent.*

Among the many things that these figures reveal is the direction of Chinese migration, historically, into Yunnan's minority areas. The figures showed that the main thrusts of Han Chinese migration—after they had settled the northeastern part of what is now Yunnan and the area around Kunming— had been toward Dali in the west, toward Gejiu, Kaiyuan, and Mengzi in the south, and in the areas that bordered Guangxi and Vietnam in the southeast. The ethnic map showing where the population had shifted in favor of Han Chinese also revealed the areas in which political integration and economic development had gone the farthest.

                              *   *   *

After describing the ethnic profile of Yunnan, the Academy scholars discussed some of the special policies toward minorities implemented in the province, especially those that had been energetically carried out in the 1980s. The policies they described were very similar to those I had heard about elsewhere in west China, but there were some local variations.

In Yunnan, I was told, as of 1988 the heads of all autonomous prefectures and counties (and the heads of the local governmental congresses in all of these places) were members of minority groups. As I pointed out in an earlier chapter, designating an area as "autonomous" meant that leaders from ethnic minorities in such areas should occupy the highest governmental positions in the area. It also meant that areas with this designation could be allowed to exercise somewhat more flexibility in applying national or provincial policies and could take special action to preserve national languages and customs. However, only limited real authority was granted to

---

*The specific figures given to me for the total population in each of these eight autonomous prefectures, and the percentages made up by minority peoples, were as follows: Honghe, 3.4 million total population (53 percent of them minority people); Dali, 2.84 million (48 percent minority); Wenshan, 2.76 million (46 percent minority); Chuxiong, 2.2 million (28 percent minority); Dehong, 830,000 (50 percent minority); Xishuangbanna, 700,000 (70 percent minority); Nujiang, 400,000 (almost 98 percent minority); and Deqen, 300,000 (80 percent minority).

these areas. But minority leaders did occupy leadership positions. (Even the governor of Yunnan was a member of a minority group—the Naxi—despite the fact that laws and regulations did not require this since Yunnan Province as a whole was not classified as an autonomous region.) The provincial regime's policy was to make a major effort to train sufficient minority cadres so that their percentage in the local governmental bureaucracies would approximate their percentage in the local population. My briefers asserted, also, that in Yunnan's autonomous areas, a majority of the top Party secretaries were members of minority groups (if true, this was unusual; in many minority areas that I visited, although the top governmental leader was a member of a minority, Han Chinese still occupied the majority of key Party positions).

As elsewhere, the family planning policies applied to most minority groups in Yunnan differed from those applied to the Han Chinese. Instead of the stated norm being a "one-child family," most ethnic minority families in Yunnan were permitted to have two children, and in some situations, more than two. My informants stated that this did not apply to the three largest minority groups in the province—the Yi, the Bai, and the Hani. These three groups were subject to restrictions similar to those that applied to the Han Chinese, with an important exception: if they lived in remote mountain areas, they were permitted to have two children.

The Academy scholars were frank in admitting, however, that "policy is one thing, and implementing policy is another." It was very difficult to enforce family planning policies in remote areas, especially mountain areas, they said; this was true not only among minority peoples but also among Han Chinese living in such areas. One reason was the strong urge to have sons and to continue childbearing until a boy was born. Another reason was that contraceptives often were in short supply in remote areas. It was possible to enforce family planning policies fairly strictly in cities, they said, but it was simply not possible to do so as effectively in remote areas. When I asked what the rate of population growth in minority areas in the province was, they said that recently it had been about 2 percent—compared to roughly 1.5 percent for the province as a whole. (If those figures were correct, they showed that even though Yunnan's birth control efforts had not been as effective as in some other areas of China, they were fairly effective—certainly when compared to many other poor developing countries.)

Earlier, I described some of the special economic policies applied to minority areas in Yunnan—including the large budgetary subsidies given to these areas. The Academy scholars who briefed me also stressed that very high priority was given to expanding and improving the education of minority groups. Even basic literacy remained disturbingly low among many minority groups, they said, and the provincial government and local governments were committed to changing the situation. In some minority groups a large proportion remained illiterate. The Lahu had the highest illiteracy rates, they said: Over 80 percent of the Lahu were still illiterate. Among 10 minority groups that lived mainly in the most remote and poorest areas, over 70 percent of the people were still illiterate. Among all minority peoples in the province, their statistics showed that the illiteracy rate was 40 percent—considerably worse than the rate for the entire population of the province. They said that the provincial government estimated that about a third of everyone in Yunnan was illiterate (a large percentage of this figure was made up of minority peoples, and most of the rest were old people and women). The overall rate was considerably higher than the average for the country as a whole. (My informants in Kunming said that it was their understanding that the national illiteracy rate was about 25 percent; I have seen varying figures, but that is a plausible one.)

Confronted with an extremely serious educational problem among minority peoples, the provincial government had allocated substantial resources to raising their educational level, and, as a result, the numbers of schools and students in the minority areas had been substantially expanded since the 1940s. (Educational institutions for Han Chinese had also expanded greatly.) By 1987, they said, in the province's autonomous minority areas there were 2.58 million primary school students (of whom 1.6 million belonged to minority groups), 570,000 students in junior and senior middle schools and vocational schools at that level (of whom about one-half belonged to minority groups), and 3,454 students (one-half of them minority students) in postsecondary institutions located within autonomous areas. In the poorest areas, the government was providing food (and in some cases also housing and clothing) to students in about 3,000 primary schools and 40 middle schools. The principal institution of higher learning for these groups within the province was the Yunnan Institute of Minority Nationalities, located in Kunming (but some students also went to attend Beijing's Central Institute of Minority Nationalities or to the Southwest Institute of Minority Nationalities). Other students from minority areas were sent (often after completing a special preparatory year in the Kunming Institute) to large comprehensive universities, not only in Yunnan but elsewhere.

As was true in other provinces in the west, the minority students in Yunnan could gain admission to higher education with lower entrance examination grades than those required for Han Chinese; generally, I was told, the requirement was lower by 20 points or so. (None of the special educational policies, I was told, applied to the Bai, Hui, or the Naxi because their educational level already approximated that of most Han Chinese.) After discussing these preferential policies, though, the Academy scholars went on to say that because the educational level of some minority groups was so low in general, even with such special treatment only a few were able to gain entrance to China's major "key universities."

In the schools attended by minorities, both the Chinese language (Hanyu) and minority languages were used, but compared to some other minority areas that I visited there seemed to be a greater use of Chinese and less of minority languages. One reason for this, the scholars briefing me explained, was the great diversity of languages. Some minority groups—such as the Tibetans and Dai—had long used their own written languages. So too, to a lesser extent, had the Naxi and Yi. Foreign missionaries had helped to develop written forms of indigenous languages in the case of some other of the minorities in Yunnan, including the Jingpo, Lisu, Lahu, and Miao (they had also helped the Yi). However, according to my Academy informants, many of these written languages were still relatively underdeveloped and unstandardized at the time of the Communist takeover in the late 1940s. They asserted that for most minority languages, standardization had taken place mainly after 1949. Even after standardization, though, it was extremely difficult to provide school materials—or qualified teachers—to teach in so many different languages.

In any case, whatever the reasons, real bilingual education in Yunnan's schools was restricted to the first three grades of primary school, where native languages were the primary medium of teaching and the Chinese language was secondary. (Where there were not adequate written materials in minority languages, Chinese books were used, they said, but oral teaching was in the minority languages.) In grades four through six, the native languages were still taught, but as a second language, and the Chinese language was the primary one. From the start of junior middle school on through higher education, the teaching was essential in the Chinese language (although some special classes were taught in minority languages).

This pattern obviously posed serious difficulties for minority students as they progressed up the educational ladder. It also, however, contributed to a gradual, albeit partial, assimilation or acculturation of minority groups into the dominant Han culture—although, it seemed clear to me, many other factors continued to work strongly against full assimilation. (One small sign of the partial acculturation of many minority people was the spread of Chinese and/or Western clothing among them. Except in some remote areas, I was told, traditional clothing was worn mainly by women, and some of them only wore their native clothing on special occasions.) In one sense, the language policies implemented in Yunnan simply reflected the difficulties of educating such a multicultural population. However, the situation clearly left much to be desired from the point of view of the minority groups, and I felt that it was almost inevitable that in time they would press for greater use of their own languages in the schools.

Newspapers were published in Yunnan in several minority languages; these included the Lisu, Dai, Jingpo, and Naxi. Papers in the Tibetan and the Yi languages were obtainable from Tibet and Sichuan.

The Academy specialists who briefed me on all of these matters relating to minority affairs were very frank, I thought, in discussing existing problems and in stating how serious they were, but when I asked them to characterize Han-minority relationships in general, they asserted that the relationships had improved a great deal during the 1980s and now were relatively stable. In the areas that I visited, what I observed and heard tended to support such a judgment. But I knew that there had been some clashes in recent years between Han Chinese and minorities in isolated parts of the province. And there was no way that I could really know to what extent there were tensions under the surface (I was sure that there were some, in at least some areas of the province). Nevertheless, I was persuaded that the provincial government was making a good-faith effort to raise the economic and educational levels of minority groups. The more I learned about the complexity of the ethnic situation in the province, the more I felt that it was unlikely that, in the foreseeable future, any strong political opposition based on ethnic conflicts could develop to the point of posing a threat to the regime. There were simply too many divisions among and between the minority groups.

*   *   *

My final interview in Kunming was with two young army officers. Soon after my arrival in Yunnan, I was very pleased to hear that, in response to my request to meet a top local military leader, an interview had been scheduled with the chief of staff of the Yunnan Military District. But at the last minute the chief of staff had to leave town because of the earthquake in the area near the Burma border. But my hosts were able to arrange on short notice an interview with two young colonels, which turned out to be very interesting. One of them (named Chen Daotong) was a 40-year-old lieutenant colonel from Hunan who had come to Yunnan immediately after joining the army in 1968. When I met him he was director of the Command Headquarters of the Military District. Despite the fact that senior middle school was as far as he had gone in his formal civilian education, his crisp, confident manner was that of a disciplined military professional. The other, 37-year-old Li Xinghuo, also was a lieutenant colonel, in the same headquarters, and his native province was Shandong. He had joined the army as a young man, in 1969, and was soon thereafter sent to Yunnan. In the early 1970s, he was assigned to attend Yunnan University, where he studied foreign languages (he could speak a little English, but with difficulty—it was not enough to carry on a conversation), and after graduating in 1975 he returned to active duty. I would describe him as an "army intellectual"—that is, a new type of officer, of whom I had met several in China, who seemed to me to be the military equivalent of the new technocratic intellectuals who were coming to the fore in the civilian sector). Both men were articulate, and both were very forceful in stating their personal opinions.

My principal motives for wishing to meet with military men were not only to get a sense of the characteristics of the rising generation of young professional officers, but also to learn something about the perspective of officers on the evolving civil-military relationships and changing roles of the military establishment in Chinese society as a result of the reforms of the 1980s. In Yunnan, specifically, because of the major military clashes and continuing hostility that characterized Chinese-Vietnamese relations in the late 1980s, I also wished to learn what I could about the impact of that conflict on the province. What I was able to learn was limited but was nevertheless interesting.

These two lieutenant colonels impressed me, as had similar young army officers I had encountered in Beijing and elsewhere, as being no-nonsense types, essentially nonideological and notably professional—and also nationalistic—in their approach to most problems and in their answers to most questions that I raised. Although they shared some of the characteristics of the young civilian technocrats who were rising in the administrative and political hierarchies in China in the 1980s, they also were different in that their demeanor and style were distinctively military. In this sense they were similar to military professionals in many Western countries.

In our conversation, they began with comments on organizational matters, and then, without prompting from me, went on to discuss reform within the military establishment. Describing their chain of command, they said that although the Yunnan Military District was clearly subordinate to the Chengdu Military Region, it also functioned under the dual leadership (actually it was multiple leadership) of the Provincial Party Standing Committee—and, they said, of course they also had to look to the leadership of the Military Affairs Commission of the Party Central Committee, in Beijing, which was the ultimate authority over all military units in China. The primary responsibility of the Yunnan Military District, they stressed, was frontier defense, but it also handled training and management of reserves and other matters within the province. The border that their forces in Yunnan had to defend was very long; they cited, from memory, fairly precise figures not only on its total length but also on the length of key segments. The length of their border with Vietnam, they said, was 836 miles. And Yunnan's part of the border with Burma (not counting the small portion that abutted on Tibet) was 1,240 miles. Yunnan's border with Laos was 435-plus miles. I asked how many troops it took to protect the 2,500 miles of Yunnan's international borders. They quickly stated that they were not authorized to reveal military information, including figures on how large the Chinese forces defending these borders were. But they were willing to discuss many other subjects.

The military forces in Yunnan fell into two categories, they said: Group Army forces (*jituan jun*) and local forces (*difang budui*). All of the Group

Army forces, they said, were under the direct command of the Party's Military Affairs Commission in Beijing. They maintained that such forces were not numerous in Yunnan. These Group Army forces, moreover, were not permanently stationed in the province and were easily transferable elsewhere; their "principal function" in Yunnan, they said, was "to train other forces." One of the two officers then said, "Actually, there really are no important Group Army units in Yunnan; our forces are almost all 'frontier troops' (*bianfang budui*), and almost all are local forces." He added: "I really do not know a great deal about Group Army forces, because ours are local forces—frontier forces." Coming from a senior officer in the Yunnan district headquarters, this statement was revealing and very surprising to me.

They went on to explain that the bulk of Yunnan's troops operated under the "dual leadership" of the Yunnan Military District and higher authorities. On strictly military matters, they said, both the Chengdu Military District and the Central Committee's Military Affairs Commission provided leadership. The provincial Party Committee's involvement, they stated, related mainly to the management of the reserves and the militia. Having spent many years trying to understand the multiple lines of authority in China, I did not think that this clarified the situation very much for me, and I was not sure that it reflected the real relations among various levels of authority with accuracy, but I decided not to pursue this particular matter further.

The majority of troops in Yunnan were soldiers recruited within the province itself, but some had come from Sichuan and Guizhou and other more distant areas. Their troops included "quite a few" minority people (they did not give any specific numbers). Language did pose some problems, they said, especially in units that had minority people in them, where not all spoke Chinese well, even though all had had Chinese language instruction in school. The educational level was rising, and by 1988 the majority of even ordinary soldiers, they said, were graduates of at least junior middle school, and some had completed senior middle school. New recruits were inducted annually and all of those who were 18 years of age or older were eligible. However, since educational and physical requirements were now fairly high, "we choose only the best." In recruitment, their policy was to recruit men between 18 and 22 and women between 17 and 21. New recruits received three to four months of basic training, and the standard length of service for most of them was three years. Thereafter, if they were demobilized they became part of the reserves, and all of them had to join the militia. (Some militia units received a month of training each year.)

*   *   *

Reform within the PLA really began, they said, in 1985. "Thereafter, the size of forces was reduced, the structure was reorganized (with the number of offices cut), and the ratio of officers to men was reduced to a rational

level. We also started to improve our equipment." Perhaps the "most important recent changes [reforms] in Yunnan" had been those "in our officer
corps." During the Cultural Revolution years, many soldiers without much
education were promoted to be officers. In contrast, by the late 1980s one
had to be a graduate of a military academy—or the equivalent—to become
an officer, and Yunnan had its own academy. Moreover, the Military Affairs
Commission had adopted new policies that set age limits for various ranks of
officers. The top age for persons with various commands were, I was told:
platoon, 30; company, 35; battalion, 40; regiment, 45; division, 50; and
army, 55. In the case of an army commander, the top age limit could be
raised somewhat, to 60, if the unit commanded was part of the "fighting
forces" (*dzuojan budui*). They added that the forces stationed right next to
the Vietnamese border were all "fighting forces." In Yunnan, as a result of
changed policies, a majority of older, higher-ranking officers had been retired in recent years.

Ranks had been restored (they had been abolished during the Cultural
Revolution). "This was completed a month ago, and all officers now have
definite ranks based on their positions and responsibilities and length of service." Length of service was still important: "Sometimes it can result in a difference of two or even three grades for people holding similar positions."
(New uniforms had also been introduced, in 1988.) Also, a regular retirement system had been introduced. When retired, officers were given a boost
in rank (this resulted in an increase in their retirement pay, which often
added the equivalent of one to two months' salary per year). All retiring officers were also awarded one of four medals: First Red Star, Second Red Star,
Victory, or Independence medals, depending on their length of service but
also taking into account the positions they held at the time of retirement.

Transfers of officers between Yunnan and other areas (including Beijing)
had been numerous, but recently few new officers had come to Yunnan from
other areas, "because they are not needed here now." Decisions on transfers
of lower-ranking officers could be made by authorities at the army level and
above, but the Military Affairs Commission was responsible for transfers of
high-ranking officers.

Officers spent a considerable amount of time studying theory because
"without theory, armies cannot develop; this is true all over the world." Pres-
ently, they said, study focused not only on how to improve the fighting ability of their forces through study of strategy and tactics, but also on reform
within the PLA and how the PLA can "best serve the nation's economic construction."

Financially, "Yunnan [its military establishment] is special; we are different from most other provinces. Because we are a frontier area, we get strong
support from the Military Affairs Commission and the State Council, so we
do not confront the financial constraints that many other areas do."

One of my informants added, "Apart from our main function, namely frontier defense, another major responsibility is to provide assistance at the time of disasters." In Yunnan, this was particularly important because the province lies in a major earthquake belt. He said, "When earthquakes occur, we are the first to help." Local forces also helped to fight forest fires.

The People's Armed Police were not directly under the Military District, my interlocutors said. These forces were led, and trained, by the Public Security system. However, "We maintain close liaison with them."

Although I was unable to meet the highest military leaders in Yunnan (which I had hoped to do, partly to ask them to describe the command relationships and in particular the relationship of the military to the top political leadership in the province), the two colonels I met did answer some of my questions relating to military-civil relations. The military commander of the Yunnan Military District, they said, was a local Yunnanese (named Wang Zhuxun), who was about 50 years old and was a major general. Like many of the recently appointed junior officers, he had begun his career as an ordinary soldier and then rose through the ranks. The political commissar of the Military District (named Zhao Kun) was a lieutenant general (outranking the military commander partly because of his long service); his native province was Jiangsu, and he was just over 50 years old. The political commissar belonged to the provincial Party's Standing Committee, and, in fact, he was the ranking deputy secretary under the Party secretary. This made possible "very close liaison" between local military and civilian leaders, the colonels said, and this link was "the main form of liaison." Under the Party Committee was an Armed Forces Commission (Wuzhuang Weiyuanhui), headed by the governor, with the political commissar as his ranking deputy; this commission was the civilian group responsible for dealing with military affairs in the province. (There was no organ within the provincial government, they said, that had this basic responsibility.)

All that these colonels said was consistent with the impressions I had received about the changing nature of civil-military relations throughout China in the 1980s. In Yunnan, as elsewhere in China, the military forces clearly constituted a special, separate organizational system. Although they maintained close, high-level liaison with the local Party and government leaders, the relationships that they had with local political leaders were far less important than those with higher authorities within the military establishment to which they were responsible. Their local liaison was primarily with the Party, moreover, rather than with the government.

Like other institutionalized hierarchies in China, the armed forces had undergone important changes in the 1980s. Many of the "reforms" seemed to me to be primarily aimed at regularizing the forces and raising the morale of officers and troops. However, I was impressed by what I learned about the far-reaching changes that had occurred in the officer's corps; such changes were laying the basis, it seemed to me, for a much greater change in the military establishment in the future—change in the direction of increased professionalization, which might or might not lead to further depoliticization. I was surprised to be told that "Group Army forces" played a relative small role in the province and that "local forces" carried the main responsibilities for frontier defense. (In fact, I left with some doubt in my mind as to whether they misspoke or that I misunderstood what they were trying to say.) However, I was convinced that, even though rank-and-file recruits came mainly from within the province and nearby provinces, "local forces" were very different from the local forces under warlords in the pre-1949 period. The Military District clearly operated as a part of a controlled national military system and was under effective control—it appeared to me—exercised by the Military Affairs Commission in Beijing as well as by the Chengdu Military Region. (When I had visited Kunming in 1948, the military situation was extremely complex: Some forces were loyal primarily to the local warlords, and some were controlled by Chiang Kai-shek, and military relations between them were extremely uneasy, to say the least.)

*　　　*　　　*

In Yunnan, as throughout most of the northwest, I was impressed by the low visibility of military forces and the apparent demilitarization of civilian society. This struck me with particular force in Yunnan, I think, because Yunnan was the front-line province in the country's continuing conflict with Vietnam. Because that conflict had not been ended, I expected to see much more evidence of the army's presence than I did. In all the areas that I visited, I saw very few troops and practically no equipment. This was true not only in the Kunming area (the fighter aircraft that I saw at the airport were the main sign of military activity that I saw there), but also on the long motor trip I made to Gejiu, located far to the south, near the border of Vietnam. I asked the two colonels I met why I did not see more evidence of the forces engaged in the conflict with Vietnam. They laughed and gave several reasons. Although some forces were scattered throughout the province, they said, most were concentrated very near the border. Those stationed elsewhere, moreover, were located, for the most part, well away from main population centers.

Obviously, the low visibility of troops did not mean the PLA presence was small. In Yunnan as well as in other parts of the country, the PLA continued, in the late 1980s, to play very important roles in the civilian sector—such as handling calamities—in addition to their defense function. Even when they were in the background, they provided important basic support to the Party and government, and in times of crisis they could suddenly emerge and become very visible indeed to the civilian population (as I had observed in the early 1970s, following Lin Biao's alleged coup). Nevertheless, I was struck by the degree to which, in ordinary circumstances, the PLA tended to stay in the background and avoid obvious, direct intervention into civilian society. The long-term trend had been to transform China's military establishment into a professional national defense establishment and to reduce its functions as a political army and domestic garrison force. (This process was obviously set back, in 1989, by the military intervention at the time of the Tiananmen crisis in Beijing. But my judgment is that the long-term trend will resume before long.)

At the end of my conversations with the two colonels, I asked for their views on the conflict with Vietnam. It was no real surprise that the account they gave was totally one-sided and highly nationalistic. None of their comments were phrased in ideological terms, however; they spoke as intense Chinese patriots. In discussing the causes of the fighting in the late 1970s, they argued that the Vietnamese did three things in 1978 that led to open conflict: (1) they signed a treaty with the Soviet Union and obtained large-scale military support from Moscow, (2) they sent troops into Kampuchea (Cambodia), and (3) they expelled more than 60,000 overseas Chinese from Vietnam. (More than 30,000 of those expelled came to Yunnan, they said, where they had been settled in existing rural villages—and this had been a great burden on local farmers, even though the provincial and local governments provided them with financial aid. Most of the others went to Guangdong and Fujian.) The two colonels felt that conflict may have been inevitable, also, because the Vietnamese leadership wished to create an Indochina Federation, which was totally unacceptable to China.

Toward the end of 1978, they said, Vietnamese forces made attacks across the border, killing and injuring many people. Then, in February 1979, the Chinese "counterattacked in self-defense." Thereafter, the level of conflict was reduced somewhat, but it had by no means been ended. The second (and latest) period of large-scale battles, they said, was in 1984, when Chinese forces were "compelled to defend themselves and counterattack in several mountain areas—Laoshan, Zheyoushan, and Balihedong." But "the Vietnamese would still not accept defeat": In 1984, they attacked on six occasions, deploying forces as large as expanded divisions, to try to take back key territories. In addition, on more than 20 occasions they attacked with units of battalion or company size, and made a great many small incursions with platoons or squads. Vietnamese artillery attacks were almost constant, the colonels said; often they fired 1,000 to 10,000 shells a day. The Vietnamese still had two to three divisions along the border and another eight divisions backing them up along a "second line." Again, I asked, "How many Chinese were there facing them, in 1988?" Their answer was: "Enough." It was still "not a quiet border," they said, and small clashes, incursions, and artillery duels happened "almost every day."

"Vietnam is China's biggest enemy," they asserted. "Their leaders now say they want to improve relations with China, but so far we have seen no improvement." No improvement would be possible, they argued, until Vietnam totally withdrew from Kampuchea and "ended attacks on the border." Improvement of relations "depends on whether their *attitude* changes." In their view, the economic situation in Vietnam was "very difficult," which should eventually compel Hanoi to be more compliant. They praised Gorbachev for having adopted a sensible attitude toward Vietnam, and they said they hoped that he would end all Soviet support of Hanoi. However, they were pessimistic about any quick resolution of the conflict because of the "stubbornness of Hanoi's leaders." Most of what they said in discussing Vietnam echoed the tough line that was still being articulated by Beijing. (In 1988, this tough line toward the Vietnamese contrasted with Chinese foreign policy toward almost every other area in the world.) But I had no doubt that the officers were not just parroting Beijing's line; they clearly were also expressing their own, highly nationalistic feelings. At the same time, their perspective, as revealed by what they said, clearly was that of professional officers following orders from above.*

What surprised me most about the military situation in Yunnan, I suppose, was how little effect the continuing border conflict with Vietnam seemed to be having on the economy of the rest of the province, even in the areas that I visited that were very near the border. Yunnan's executive deputy governor and the planning officials I met argued, also, that there really was very little adverse effect on the local economy. I did not fully understand why this should be the case, but I presumed that a major explanation was that Beijing seemed to be providing most of the resources needed by the troops facing the Vietnamese.

*   *   *

The highlight of my 1988 visit to Yunnan was my trip to Gejiu, the center of the tin industry, located near the Vietnamese border. I had made the same trip four decades earlier, traveling then on the tiny, narrow-gauge, French-built railway, which was jam-packed with farmers. The train's route wound slowly through a succession of valleys and crawled through a seemingly endless series of tunnels cut straight through the mountains. When I had visited Gejiu in 1948, it was a small and very traditional kind of town. Even though it had long been China's major tin production center, there were only a few signs of modernity. Most notable were two fairly modern mine shafts, high

---

*Not very long thereafter, there were signs of a real thaw in Sino-Vietnamese relations, and over time it led to a steady reduction and then a virtual end to border tensions. By 1991, major efforts were under way to repair the overall Sino-Vietnamese relationship.

in the nearby mountains, but the majority of tin mines were nothing more than tiny holes in the ground, where all of the miners were young children, and the mining methods were medieval. One of my main objectives in revisiting Yunnan in 1988 was to see how—and how much—modernization had changed Gejiu.

I told my hosts in 1988 that I wished to make the trip by train, as I had in the 1940s, but they insisted that I travel by car. The reason, they said, was that the train took much more time to reach Gejiu because it stopped frequently along the way to pick up and deposit local passengers, mainly peasants making short trips but also people engaged in business. I was irritated at the time, but in retrospect I suppose I should have thanked them for their decision. Not only was it much more comfortable traveling by car (again, our vehicle was a Toyota), but it enabled me to see much more of the countryside than I would have if I had gone by train. The entire trip was almost 400 miles, going and returning. We traveled to Gejiu by one route, and returned by another, so I saw a great many of the small towns, and the countryside, in a large area of Yunnan. On the way to Gejiu, we went east and then south; our route took us through three counties—Yiliang, Lunan, and Mile—as well as through the city of Kaiyuan. On the return trip, we went west and then north, traveling through five counties: Jianshui, Tonghai, Jiangchuan, Jinning, and Chenggong. We covered much of central-south Yunnan.

The 205-mile trip to Gejiu took us nine and a quarter hours (including a 45-minute stop for lunch). The road clearly was one of the best in the province; it started, in fact, as a four-lane, paved highway, a superhighway by Chinese standards. However, it soon narrowed to two lanes, which it was for the rest of the way, but it continued to be well paved. At our starting point, in Kunming, we were at an altitude of 6,232 feet. We ended at Gejiu in a valley where the altitude was lower—5,524 feet, but en route we had no sense that we were descending because we were constantly going up, and then down, and then up again, going over mountains, plateaus, and through valleys.

On the first stretch, from Kunming going east to Yiliang county seat, we traveled over a large, flat, agricultural plain. Once we turned southward, though, the road constantly went up and down, through small valleys and over hilly areas.

A little more than 80 miles from Kunming, we stopped at Shilin ("stone forest"), an area of fairly spectacular karst stone outcroppings, which had become a major tourist attraction. On the day of my visit, the area was full of Chinese tourists, and I was the only foreigner. Everyone was having a wonderful time, climbing over the tall stone spires and meandering through narrow paths between the sheer stone cliffs that rose around them. In addition to climbing they were resting and chatting, having their pictures taken on camels and ponies, talking with the very colorfully dressed young women attendants (who were natives of various minority groups), eating in small restaurants or at small food stalls, and acting almost exactly like tourists do all over the world. We did not eat there, but we did stop at a roadside restaurant a little bit farther on on our trip. (The food there was anything but memorable.)

After Shilin, the road went over a long stretch of high plateau, from which one could see many isolated spires of karst outcroppings. The land on the plateau was obviously poor, and the population was sparse. After the plateau, we went over a series of hills, interrupted by small valleys, before reaching the city of Kaiyuan. Kaiyuan proved to be a sizable city. Located a little north of Gejiu, it was an outpost of modernity, with numerous factories, some quite large, and a surprising number of modern high-rise buildings, including one new hotel that rose 15 stories. The final leg of the trip to Gejiu took us through more rough mountainous terrain.

Although for most of the way the road was two lanes wide and was fairly good, for two short stretches it was really miserable. Repair crews were working on it by hand, hauling crushed rock in baskets attached to shoulder poles. I saw no modern machinery. Traffic between the towns was generally sparse, and it consisted of a mix of old and new vehicles. We passed some trucks and occasional long-distance buses, but where the traffic thickened—especially near towns—it was a jumble of bikes, carts drawn by oxen, ponies, buffaloes, and men carrying loads on their shoulder poles. There were also a few people on motorcycles. In the towns there were more trucks. It was evident that modern vehicles were carrying most of the heavy cargo, especially on long stretches between towns, but in the towns and the areas immediately around them a great deal of cargo was carried by traditional transportation methods. On the entire trip we passed fewer than a dozen passenger cars (several of those we did see carried men in uniform). Whether we were in areas that looked traditional or modernized, our driver was determined to keep us in touch with the modern world: Our Toyota van was equipped with a tape player, and he periodically played tapes of modern music, all of it Western; many were Strauss waltzes, but not all—he played *Carmen* at some length.

The region through which we went was principally agricultural, but once we had left the plain near Kunming much of the land was poor. In the northern part of our trip, the crops were mainly beans and corn, but further south we saw a good deal of rice, considerable sugar cane, and some bananas and fruit. Terraces climbed up many of the the hills, but the majority of the fields were located in the narrow valleys. Plowing was under way, and almost all of it was being done with ox-drawn plows rather than with tractors. Some areas we passed were among the poorest that I had seen anywhere in west China, and the majority of the villages were very traditional—especially those that were distant from towns. However, most peasant homes in the villages were built of mud brick, and the majority of them had gray tile roofs, except in the poorest areas, where a few still used thatch. All of the county seats had a more modern look. The roads in these towns were paved, and there were many brick or concrete buildings in them. Quite a few towns had numerous "standard" modern apartment buildings, several stories high. In some areas, particularly near county seats, the village homes were a mix of new and old, and there were quite a few recently built brick houses. My impression, though, was that there were fewer new brick peasant houses in this area than in many other areas I visited in 1988—including other areas in west China.

Most of the county towns had at least a few modern factories, but in between the towns there were not many; in this respect it was quite different from the rural areas in coastal China, especially the Pearl River and Yangzi valleys. Nevertheless, electricity seemed to reach almost all of the rural areas that we passed through. In every town we saw TV aerials, and in Mile county seat we passed a TV tower. Even in the most remote rural areas I saw at least a few TVs, although in the poorest areas they were relatively scarce.

We saw bustling free markets everywhere, especially in and near towns, but in some places in the countryside too. They were full of food and consumer goods of all sorts. Moreover, most people, including peasants, were fairly well dressed. In many areas in the countryside, traditional clothing still predominated. Most older women wore blue jackets and black pants and had bright cloth bands wound around their heads. In much of the countryside, many men wore either traditional jackets and pants or Mao suits. Even in this poor region, however, quite a few people (including the majority of young people) wore modern clothing, and such clothing predominated in and around the towns and was not uncommon in rural areas—even in remote places. Once again, I was startled to see some young women, even in remote villages, dressed in quite fashionable, colorful, modern clothing, and wearing high-heeled shoes, testimony to the spread of fashion as a result of modern communications, especially TV. Only twice on the entire trip did I see a few people in ragged, patched clothing. Even in this relatively poor area, it was obvious that the standard of living had risen, and clothing was *much* better than it had been in the 1940s. (In many towns and villages, some minority women were dressed in traditional, multicolored clothing, but I saw no men wearing traditional minority dress, and outside the towns I did not see any minority peoples wearing traditional clothes.)

*   *   *

As I noted earlier, I was once again struck—as I was throughout most of west China—by how little evidence there was of any military presence, either on the roads in the countryside or in towns. In addition to the men in uniform whom I saw in some of the few passenger cars we passed, we saw one compound that appeared to contain a military barrack, but otherwise the military presence in the area was out of sight. Even in Kaiyuan and Gejiu, both of which were major cities on the route to Vietnam, I saw few people in uniform. (It is possible, of course, that I did see some military men and did not know it, since there may have been some not wearing uniforms.)

On our return trip from Gejiu to Kunming, we followed another route, some distance to the west. It was slightly shorter (180 miles), but it went over more mountainous terrain and therefore took us about the same time (nine and a half hours). Along much of this route, the road was winding and had numerous hairpin turns. Repeatedly we climbed up mountains, where the views often were spectacular, and then descended deep into canyons, where the roads paralleled small rivers and streams. Here, as on the earlier route, the clothing, housing, and transport that we saw were a mix of new and old; somehow, though, on this route the contrast between new and old seemed even more striking. One could, in effect, observe the modern world infiltrating, blending with, and transforming the traditional society. We passed a larger number of crawling tractors, almost all of them being used for transport, and saw a greater number of motorcycles, but we also saw a larger number of ponies and pony-drawn carts than we did on the different route we took going from Kunming to Gejiu. Until we neared Kunming, we passed even fewer passenger automobiles than we had on the earlier trip. However, in one town, where there was a large vegetable market crowded with buyers and sellers, we encountered a massive traffic jam, and in the jam there was an incredible mixture of every conceivable kind of vehicle.

We passed quite a number of people working in the fields in the farming areas between towns. Many were colorfully dressed young women—quite a few of them wearing modern clothes. Some of these field-workers actually were school-age children. All were using hand tools, such as hoes. The mix of housing and clothing in this area was about the same, though, as on the first trip. So too was the distribution of TV aerials. (In Jianchuan we passed another TV tower.) We also, for some reason, passed more policemen on this return trip than on our trip out; some of them were riding in vans or in motorcycle sidecars. We also passed several ambulances in or near towns. In contrast with the trip out, we did see a few soldiers in uniform; some were in market towns, simply shopping, but when we approached Kunming we passed one sizable group traveling in a truck going toward the city.

The highlight of our return trip was a stop at the town of Tonghai, which is located about halfway between Gejiu and Kunming. Located in a wide agricultural valley, it was well known as a major "vegetable base" and was obviously relatively prosperous. An old, Chinese-style pagodalike building (built, local people said, in the Ming dynasty) marked the town center. The main streets were paved and lined with modern—and obviously relatively new—buildings, some of them several stories high. Yi people made up a fairly large proportion of the local population, and nearby there were some Mongols who had lived there ever since the Mongol conquest. Because there was a lake nearby, Tonghai had become a major Chinese tourist attraction, and on the day of our visit its streets were jammed with Chinese and minority visitors, most of them dressed either in modern Western-style clothing or in minority costumes. We stopped and had an excellent lunch in a local restaurant. (The pièce de résistance was a local specialty—small cakes made of fried goat's milk. I found them interesting but nothing I would put on my own list of the great culinary creations in the world.)

A little north of Tonghai we passed through the Hui Muslim town of Najiaying. It had the reputation of being a town with a "high cultural standard," one that reputedly had "produced many intellectuals." It was also famous, I was told, for the knives and swords that it had once made. (For one brief period, also, it had made guns, I was told.) We passed two small mosques in the town. The architecture of one was very Middle Eastern; the other was built in a traditional Chinese style.

As on most of my road trips in China, this time I passed one accident, which was on the stretch between Najiaying and Kunming. Apparently there were no serious injuries, but several policemen and a large crowd of onlookers surrounded it. It reinforced a view that I had formed much earlier on my travels, namely, that anyone who would try to be in the auto insurance business in China would be out of his or her mind.

When we approached Kunming, the countryside gradually melded into the city, as the countryside does on the edges of most Chinese cities. The roads extending outward from the cities are like ribbons of modernization that creep into the countryside. Returning to the cities, one sees the impact of modernization gradually becoming greater and greater until, in the center of major cities, one experiences the feeling of being in the modern world. Modern factories are one of the hallmarks of these areas around cities. On this return route, we saw many more rural township enterprises in the suburbs of Kunming than we had on the earlier route. And, as we approached Kunming on this route, old-style peasant houses gradually gave way to quite modern brick homes. When we approached near to the city, buildings gradually increased in height, rising to 6 to 8 stories in close-in suburbs and then, once we entered the city, soaring to 10 to 15 stories. As the buildings rose in height, the road gradually widened, from two lanes to four, then to six, and finally as we entered the main part of the city to eight (six for motor vehicles, and two for bicyclists).

*   *   *

My trip to and from Gejiu, like the other long forays into the countryside in places far off the beaten track in west China, gave me quite a good sense, I think, of both the persistence of tradition and the inexorable outreach of modernization, even into remote and poor areas of rural China. My stay in Gejiu itself dramatically illustrated, also, how modernity can leap over backward rural areas and create remarkable enclaves of modernization in very remote places. Within minutes of my arrival at Gejiu, I could see that the city had been transformed since my previous visit from a small traditional town into a large and remarkably modern city.

I arrived at Gejiu in the late afternoon, and the chilly November air (the temperature was in the forties, Fahrenheit, despite Gejiu's southern latitude) roused us from the torpor resulting from a long automobile trip and heightened my anticipation about being in this unique mining town again. A large circle—in the road at the edge of the town—announced the start of the city, and from then on we traveled on a wide boulevard, lined with trees and high overhanging street lights, which led directly into the heart of the city. On both sides of the boulevard were modern buildings, apartment houses, and headquarters of various organizations; some of them were about eight or nine stories high, but they did not block the view of the hills surrounding the small valley in which the city nestled.

We drove straight to the hotel where I was to stay, and we were met there by a middle-aged man and a young woman from the local Foreign Affairs Bureau. Both of them were obviously on edge: I was the first foreign visitor that they had received, because Gejiu had just been "opened," formally, for visits by foreigners in the previous month. (I learned later that the Tin Corporation had received a small number of foreign tin experts and diplomats who had been granted special permission to visit Gejiu to see the tin mines even in the period when the city was "closed.")

My hotel, the Jin Hu (meaning Gold Lake), had been opened in 1987 presumably on the assumption that the opening of the city would bring a flow of foreign visitors. But I was the first foreign visitor, I was told. The hotel was a remarkably modern structure, 10 stories high—the highest building in town, now. The rooms, I soon learned, were very spacious and furnished with comfortable modern beds and other furniture. My room had a sizable bathroom, a TV set, a radio, and all the appurtenances of modernity, and it was decorated in the style that I earlier decided to call "Chinese Provincial Victorian." Thick red curtains framed the windows, doilies adorned the arms on overstuffed chairs, and maroon rugs covered the floors. I was located on the top floor and had a great view of the city. Young women attendants quickly brought boiling water for tea. They were members of several local minorities and wore colorful minority clothing; it was obvious that I was the first foreigner they had seen. It soon became apparent, also, that the Jin Hu had quite a distance to go before it was likely to be listed in a Western tourist guide. There was no heat, no hot water in the bathroom, and neither the toilet nor the TV set worked. I was impressed, nevertheless, that such a hotel even existed in Gejiu, and, all things considered, it was really quite comfortable.

I was dead tired after our long trip from Kunming, so I went to bed immediately after an early supper. Less than an hour after I had fallen asleep, I was woken up by vigorous knocking on my door. My hosts, somewhat distraught, told me excitedly that we had just been hit by two shocks from an earthquake, which had made our building sway, and that we had to evacuate. (I had slept through both shocks.) So, together with all the other hotel residents, we walked rapidly down to the ground floor, where people were debating loudly what they should do. One group of young men decided that they wanted not only to leave the hotel but to drive to the countryside to get away from any tall buildings, and they departed hastily. The majority of people could not make up their minds about what they should do.

Someone then suggested that we telephone the staff of the prefectural office in Gejiu that was responsible for earthquake monitoring and detection to see what they suggested. We did so and were told that there had been, indeed, a major earthquake, which was estimated to be around seven on the Richter scale, but that its epicenter was probably about 300 miles away. We should expect several more aftershocks, they said, but there was really no danger to us.

I was greatly impressed that the local earthquake office knew as much as it did so soon after the earthquake began. I decided to go back to bed and immediately fell asleep. After I returned to Kunming, I learned from provincial officials that later analysis of the earthquake had concluded that it had been one that rated 7.6 on the Richter scale. This was a very large quake, even by Yunnan's standards. With its epicenter in Lincong County, near the Burmese border, it had been a major disaster, wreaking destruction on 5 autonomous prefectures and 13 counties. According to a preliminary estimate, about 700 people had been killed and over 2,000 injured. It was the most serious earthquake, they said, that Yunnan had experienced since a large one further north had devastated areas in Baoshan and Dehong prefectures, which also lie near the Burmese border, several years earlier. Provincial government leaders felt that the earthquake I experienced was so serious that a very high-ranking delegation, composed of leading figures both from the central government and the provincial government, immediately flew into the area (presumably to a military airfield there) to assess the damage and determine what help was needed. The delegation included a member of the State Council in Beijing, Song Jian, several others from the capital, the provincial governor, the commander of the provincial Military District, and other leading local figures. The entire episode revealed how rapidly the government could respond to disasters. Also, I learned what the geography books I had read meant when they labeled Yunnan a part of a major "earthquake zone." I also learned that the Chinese system for monitoring earthquakes was remarkably good (something I had heard from American seismologist friends of mine).

*   *   *

The next morning, all was calm in Gejiu; people went about their business as if nothing had happened. Looking out of my hotel room at 6:30 A.M., I could see, far below, about 100 men and women lined up in the cold, listening to announcements and doing exercises. In the Maoist period, I had seen such early morning group calisthenics almost everywhere I went, but in the 1980s this practice had declined in east China. At 7:00, I had a quick breakfast and then toured the city in a car provided by my hosts. My driver was a local man who was an exceptionally friendly, practical, and helpful guide. Although he had only a primary school education, he impressed me as being extremely knowledgeable. I thought to myself that he clearly had the intelligence to go far, so I asked him what he aspired to be in the future. He stated, without any obvious rancor, that being a driver was probably the best that he could hope for because he was not well educated. Being a driver, he said, was not bad because the pay was quite good. Actually, many drivers in China, including truck drivers but perhaps especially those in charge of passenger cars, were accorded very considerable respect. Many of them had learned to drive in the army; a few (including my Gejiu driver) used their personal savings to pay for training courses.

My tour of the city confirmed my initial impression, namely, that Gejiu really had become a new city, very different from the one I had visited four decades earlier. The great majority of buildings in the city now were modern, multistory structures built of concrete or red brick; most of them had been built very recently. The majority were at least 3 to 6 stories high, and some were between 8 and 10 stories high. The architecture of many was fairly attractive—more so than in many industrial areas in big eastern cities. The main streets were broad, well paved, clean, and lined with attractive fir trees; on many there were modern streetlights (not something one expects in most interior Chinese cities). The layout of the city was on an east-west axis. To the east, modern buildings predominated along a major boulevard and its side streets as well. Although a few old houses still existed, most had been torn down and replaced by spanking new apartment houses.

To the south lay a small lake, with a park located on a little peninsula jutting into it; children were floating on the lake in small motorboats and recreational rowboats. A dredge was operating in the middle of the lake, bringing up tin ore, I was told. In the 1940s, the spot where the lake was now located had been the center of the old town. Intense fighting had occurred there, my driver said, at the time of the Communist takeover in 1950. Then, in 1954, the center of the town had simply disappeared. As a result of a torrential rain, it had suddenly collapsed into a limestone cave that lay below it, and the area became a lake. Virtually all the buildings in that area of town, obvi-ously, had been built since then—most of them in the 1980s. In the west, there was still one area of 8 to 10 streets that had been part of the old city, and in this area a majority of the buildings were traditional—tile-roofed, two-story shops and buildings. They appeared much as I remember virtually all buildings in the city appearing when I visited it in 1949. As I traveled around the city, I now saw new buildings, especially modern apartment buildings, almost everywhere. The mayor of Gejiu later told me that between 1950 and 1988 the amount of per capita housing in the city had more than doubled, rising from 2.7 square meters to about 6 square meters (roughly 65 square feet). He also said that more than half of the new space had been con-structed in the 1980s. Even in the old area that I mentioned earlier there were numerous new buildings mixed in with the old.

Driving through the city, we passed many schools, and my driver pointed out one and said it was the "best middle school" in the city. We passed nu-merous government buildings and several medical institutions (mainly small clinics). Among the most impressive buildings were a new modern structure housing the municipal government, the prefectural government headquar-ters (which was in an older building), and a large compound where the local Party headquarters was located. When I took a picture at the gate of the Party headquarters, the young armed member of the People's Armed Police who was at the gate got quite agitated and loudly protested, saying it was not permitted to take photographs there. He clearly had not gotten the word about Gejiu's "opening."

The clothing worn by most people in the city was—I concluded—less "modern" than in eastern areas, but many if not most young people wore Western-style clothing. Quite a few Yi and other minority women walked the streets clad in colorful traditional clothing, but men from minority groups were indistinguishable from the Han Chinese population. In and around Gejiu, I saw a sizable number of factories; the largest was the area's leading tin smelter (moved from its old site near the center of town, which had collapsed). Another smaller smelter could be seen on a hillside adjacent to the city. All in all, Gejiu seemed to be an entirely different city from the one I had seen earlier. Mostly new, it had a very modern atmosphere.

                                    *   *   *

During my stay in Gejiu, my most useful interviews in the city itself were with leaders and officials of both the Gejiu Municipality and the Honghe (Red River) Hani-Yi Autonomous Prefecture (to which Gejiu belonged). I met the mayor (a man named Yu Zhengyun) and the prefecture's head (a man named Li Xianyou) separately in their offices. Both of them had with them a considerable number of aides and subordinate officials. The mayor, I learned, was a native of Sichuan Province and had obtained a university degree in electrical engineering from Jiaotong University in Xi'an, Shaanxi. As-signed in 1961 to work in an industrial plant in Gejiu, he, in time, became plant manager, and he had held this post from 1980 to 1983. In 1983 he was appointed head of the municipality's Economic Commission (but continued to serve as secretary of a Party committee in a major factory). He then be-came mayor in 1986. The head of the prefecture was a Yunnanese and a member of the Hani minority. His native place was in the Yuanjiang Hani-Yi-Dai Autonomous County, to the west of Gejiu. After graduating from the Number 8 Middle School in Kunming, he then obtained a university educa-tion in Beijing, where in 1968 he graduated from the Central Institute of Mi-nority Nationalities. Returning to Yunnan, he headed the Education Com-mission in a prefecture for several years, and then, from 1986 to 1988, was magistrate of Luchun County in Honghe Hani-Yi Autonomous Prefecture. He was promoted to be head of Honghe Prefecture just four months before I met him. Both were relatively young and well educated; their promotions in the 1980s reflected Deng Xiaoping's nationwide drive to replace old leaders with younger technocrats. The mayor and the prefectural head, with the help of their staffs, briefed me in some detail about local conditions, both in the county and in the prefecture.

The reason for Gejiu's existence, and the basis of the economy of the entire region, was the location of tin there. The flatland around Gejiu was a farm-ing area, but the farms were poor. The region's income came mainly from tin, and most employment was associated with the tin industry. Tin mining had started many centuries ago. According to the mayor, mining in this area dated to the Han dynasty (206 B.C. to A.D. 220); the mining of tin, silver, and lead was begun in this area at that time, he said. I do not know whether he was exaggerating. On my previous trip to Gejiu, in 1949, local officials had talked to me about their "400-year tin mining tradition," and they had told me at that time that significant output had been under way for between 100 and 150 years. In any case, in 1883 the Qing dynasty established a tin enter-prise at Gejiu, and in this century the Nationalist government organized a modern tin mining company, in 1940. In the years just before the Commu-nist takeover, even though some modern mining methods had taken hold in Gejiu, most tin extraction was still done by very traditional and primitive methods. Since 1949, however, the tin industry had been almost entirely modernized and greatly expanded, and Gejiu had grown along with its in-dustry.

When I visited the city in the 1940s, Gejiu was already fairly large, even though it was still a very traditional sort of town. The population of the city itself, I was then told, approached 100,000 (if one included both the urban inhabitants and farmers in its immediate environs), and if one included the adjacent mining areas, the population exceeded 180,000. By 1988, the population of the municipality had roughly doubled, rising to 356,000—roughly two-thirds urban and one-third rural.

The area around Gejiu had always had a large minority population. In recent years, however, the number of Han Chinese had risen substantially and they now predominated in the municipality. In 1988, the Han Chinese in the municipality totaled roughly 250,000, or 70 percent of the total population. The 30 percent, or roughly 106,000, people who belonged to minorities were split between various groups. The Yi, totaling roughly 70,000, were by far the largest group. Next in size were the Hui, totaling roughly 13,000, followed by the Zhuang, with about 11,000. The Miao, the smallest significant minority group, came to roughly 8,000. All of the other minority groups were very small.

The territory of the municipality had expanded over the years, and in 1988 (according to the mayor) it covered 613 square miles, comprising seven towns and three townships. Its administrative status had also repeatedly changed. As the mayor described the changes, my mind boggled at the thought of how complex the competition and lobbying must have been in the local politics as these changes were considered and debated.

*   *   *

Before 1913, the mayor said, Gejiu was not a separate entity but fell under the authority of Mengzi—a nearby city that at that time was the main urban center in the region. One of Mengzi's departments (*ting*), which was responsible for mining, was in charge of the administration of Gejiu. In 1913 Gejiu was classified as a city. Almost four decades later, after the Communist takeover, its status was elevated again, in 1951, to that of a city of prefectural level (a status acquired by only a few cities in Yunnan or elsewhere); it joined Kunming and Dongchuan as one of three cities of that status in the province. Also in the early 1950s, the seeds of what later was to become the Honghe Hani-Yi Autonomous Prefecture were planted; a Honghe Hani Autonomous County was first established in 1953, and in the following year the Honghe Hani Autonomous Prefecture was established, with its capital at Yuanyang. Gejiu was not yet incorporated into it at that time. Finally, in 1958, there was a major administrative reshuffle: A greatly enlarged prefecture was established and was now called the Honghe Hani-Yi Autonomous Prefecture, and the three major cities in the area—Gejiu, Kaiyuan, and Mengzi—were incorporated into it. Gejiu was then designated as its headquarters; however, at the same time Gejiu City was reduced to that of a county-level city. (Mengzi and Kaiyuan continued to be classified as counties rather than cities, although later, in 1983, Kaiyuan—which had become more important as an industrial center—was reclassified and became, like Gejiu, a county-level city under the prefecture.) Shortly before my visit, one additional change had taken place, in 1988: Gejiu had been granted "economic management authority" equal to that of a prefecture, even though in administrative terms it still remained a county-level city under the jurisdiction of the prefectural government of Honghe. (The only other county-level city in Yunnan granted such authority was Dali.)

During the Maoist period there were repeated changes in the administrative structure of many parts of China, which must have been extremely destabilizing and confusing for many local leaders. However, the changes that local leaders described to me in this area seem to have taken place even more frequently than in most areas. Every one of these administrative changes must have involved complex calculations about costs and/or benefits for local leaders, but it was beyond my ability to try to sort out what they might have been and what the local consequences were of these changes. The net result, in any case, was that by 1988 Gejiu had emerged as the main political and administrative—as well as economic—center in southeast Yunnan. It was the headquarters of both the prefecture and the city government of Gejiu and was the supervising authority over nearby counties. The growing economic importance of Gejiu was symbolized by its new economic powers.

The dominance of the tin industry in the local economy was overwhelming. Local leaders were very proud of the industry and constantly referred to Gejiu as China's "tin city" or "tin capital." The city was a striking example of a company town. In this respect, it was comparable to Baotou in Inner Mongolia (which its leaders constantly call the "steel city"), but the dominance of tin was even greater in Gejiu. The economic statistics that the mayor gave to me made it amply clear that tin was king. The gross value of Gejiu's "agricultural and industrial output" in 1987 was Y 820 million, he said. Of this, industrial output accounted for Y 780 million. About Y 270 million of the industrial ouptut came from the mining of tin, and Y 130 million from tin refining and related activities. If one then added the output value of all other economic activities related in some way to the tin industry, the mayor said, then the industry accounted for about 70 percent of the value of the city's industrial output. The figures that the mayor gave me on employment in the municipality also highlighted how much the tin industry dominated the economy. Of an industrial work force totaling about 73,000, he said, roughly 53,000—or more than two-thirds—were in mining and industrial enterprises that were part of the tin industry.

The gross value of agricultural output was insignificant in the total economy, to judge by the figures given to me. I expected the figures to be low because four-fifths of the municipality's territory was mountainous and soils even in the places where farming was possible were said to be very poor. However, the figures given to me were so low that I wondered if there was miscommunication on this in our interview.

Despite the strength of Gejiu's tin industry, the municipality's budget still depended on funds from the central government, the mayor said, because Gejiu had to turn over most of the tax revenue from the tin corporation to the central government. He provided a number of figures to me to demonstrate this, but I confess that, once again, I could not fully understand what the statistics meant. What he told me, in essence, was the following: Gejiu's revenue totaled Y 170 million; most of it, not surprisingly, came from taxation of the tin industry. The specific taxes that produced most of it, he said, were the "product tax" and the "profit tax" levied on the tin company. Of the revenue from the product tax, about 70 percent went to the central government and Gejiu kept about 30 percent. Of the profit tax, he said, 43 percent went to the central government, 12 percent went to the company's Kunming headquarters, and some of it went to the province. Altogether, the mayor said, of the total revenue that they collected, Gejiu sent almost Y 100 million to higher authorities (and most of this, he indicated, eventually reached the central government), and it kept only Y 72 million for local use. In short, Gejiu was a major contributor to higher-level government's revenue. (As he described all this, it sounded as if Gejiu's financial situation had many similarities with that of Baotou.)

Although the mayor did tell me something about the tin industry and its role in the local economy, I actually learned much more about these subjects by talking later with people in the tin corporation. The mayor was not an economist, and he was better informed on noneconomic subjects, many of which he wanted to talk about. One was progress in education. What he told me highlighted the extent to which education had been expanded and developed since the 1940s. He described the changes mainly in statistical terms, as Chinese officials are prone to do. In 1988, he said, the municipality had 310 primary schools, 27 middle schools, 2 vocational schools, and 6 "professional schools." Modern education at the basic level was close to universal, he asserted, and he claimed that 99 percent of children of primary age were attending school, that roughly 90 percent of primary school graduates went on to junior middle school, and that about 85 percent of junior middle school graduates went on to senior middle school. He also said that close to a third of middle school graduates subsequently took some kind of postsecondary training; if true, the progress in education was impressive and certainly was superior to that in most places in China. I could not judge the accuracy of his figures, but I ultimately decided that they probably were plausible. They certainly put Gejiu far ahead of most of the rest of the province in the development of local education. The basic reason, clearly, was that the economy, based on the modern tin industry, required an educated work force, and the tin-based economy (even after large contributions were given to higher levels of government) possessed the resources to provide support for an educational system that was far above average.

*   *   *

In addition to talking with the mayor, I met the head of the Honghe Hani-Yi Autonomous Prefecture, and he gave me a more extensive briefing about the prefecture than the mayor had about Gejiu City. The territory of Honghe, he said, covered 12,699 square miles (roughly the size of the state of Maryland). In addition to its two important cities, Gejiu and Kaiyuan, it contained 11 counties, 3 of them autonomous counties. In contrast to Gejiu City, the minorities slightly outnumbered the Han Chinese in the prefecture. In 1987, of a total population of 3.48 million, 1.62 million (47 percent) were Han Chinese, and 1.86 million (53 percent) belonged to minority groups, the largest of which were the Yi, who accounted for 769,000 people (22 percent), and the Hani, who made up 539,000 (or 15 percent). The rest of the population consisted of relatively small numbers of a variety of groups, including the Miao, Dai, Yao, Zhuang, Hui, and others.

Although the tin industry was the foundation for the economy in the prefecture, as well as in the city of Gejiu, tin was less dominant in the prefecture than in Gejiu because there had been gradual industrial diversification, much of which was outside of Gejiu. Kaiyuan ranked second to Gejiu as an industrial center, and there was some modern industry in Mengzi as well. Industrial plans called mainly for further expansion of output of nonferrous metals, but the prefecture also hoped to expand the production of chemicals. Agriculture was insignificant in Gejiu but quite important in the prefecture. The main grain crops grown were rice, corn, and wheat. Farmers also grew several other crops, including tobacco, sugarcane, tea, and a variety of fruits (oranges, pears, tropical crops such as bananas and pineapples, and others). The prefecture's agricultural plans called especially for expansion of output of fruits and tropical crops.

The prefecture was dependent on financial contributions to its budget from both below and above—that is, from the tin industry and Gejiu but also from the province and central government. A sizable proportion of what it received from these various levels of government was earmarked for programs designed to help minority groups. The prefecture's head said, though, that the subsidies from above were less than he hoped they would be. "Because the tin industry makes the area relatively prosperous," he said, higher levels of government did not feel it was necessary to give them as large amounts in subsidies as he thought they really needed. According to the prefecture's head, the subsidies received from the central and provincial government accounted for only about 5 percent of the prefecture's budget.

The impact of national reform policies on the prefecture had not, it seemed to me, been very great. One reason, I thought, was that it was dominated by one huge industrial enterprise; large state enterprises were the most difficult things to change in China. Nevertheless, the prefecture's head said that he and his government had tried to promote the development of small township enterprises, with some success. By 1988, Gejiu alone reportedly had 234 township enterprises. Of these, 199—mostly small ones—were collective enterprises or enterprises run by township governments, and 35 of them were semistate collectives; a few of the latter were quite large and had close links with the Yunnan Tin Corporation (among these, some were small mines and processing enterprises). The total output of nonstate enterprises within the prefecture, he said, had risen to around Y 100 million.

I had found in almost all of west China that the local leaders, though approving in general of Beijing's economic reforms, were uneasy about the coastal policy. "We support it, but it poses problems," said the head of the prefecture. Despite the importance of tin as an international commodity, Beijing's open policy had not—at least up until then—had much effect on Honghe. Gejiu and four other cities in the area had just recently been opened, but this did not mean very much (what it really meant was that they were open to foreign visitors). The prefecture had not been given any authority to engage directly in foreign trade. All of the trade from the prefecture, I was told, still had to go through national trade corporations. Local leaders were trying to expand their economic ties with coastal cities, with some success. Their most important ties, they said, were with Shanghai and Wuxi in the Yangzi delta, but they were also beginning to develop greater ties with Guangzhou and Shenzhen in the south and with Dalian in the northeast. However, local officials said, unless and until Beijing was willing to relinquish some of its control over the tin industry, Honghe and Gejiu could not expect to get very much benefit from the open policy.

The prefectural head emphasized Honghe's commitment to the achievement of universal education in the prefecture, and he claimed that 94.1 percent of children of primary school age (including 90 percent of minority children) attended school. (These figures included the very high averages for Gejiu and the lower ones for other rural areas.) He also stressed the importance of the changes taking place in the region as a result of modern communications. Gejiu's TV station and 23 relay stations in the region covered 65 percent of the prefecture's area, he said, and every county had its own local radio broadcasting facilities. (It was not clear to me how many of these were wired systems and how many were wireless broadcasting stations.)

*   *   *

The highlight of my trip to Gejiu was my return to the tin mining area that I had visited in the late 1940s and the long discussions I had about the tin industry with leaders of the Yunnan Tin Corporation. When I had first visited Gejiu, getting to the mountains required a difficult trek through fog-bound mountains on extremely poor roads. But even then it was worth the effort. In the 1940s China was already one of the world's major tin producers, and

Gejiu was clearly China's major tin center. The industry had only begun to be modernized in the late 1940s. In 1949 I was told that Gejiu's annual output of refined tin at that time was between 3,500 and 4,000 tons. However, only about 1,200 tons, or roughly a third, were produced by the two mines run by the modern tin company.

This company, then called the Yunnan Consolidated Tin Corporation, was headed by a man named Y. T. Miao, who was almost invariably called the "tin king." (I interviewed him in Kunming in 1949.) The company had been founded in 1940 as a result of a merger of three older companies. After the merger, it was jointly owned by a semigovernmental organization under the provincial government and two central government bodies. Staffed by well-qualified modern engineers, it had a total of 4,500 employees, most of them working at two main mines, the New Mine (Xin Chang) and the Old Mine (Lao Chang), and at its semimodern concentrating facilities located at the Old Mine and its smelter in Gejiu. Much of the output of even the modern mines still had to be transported by mule pack down the mountains, but one aerial tramway had been built before my 1949 visit. I interviewed Y. T. Miao and some of the managers working under him, and it was clear that they had had some success in introducing modern management practices, and, although their labor practices were far different from those in Western countries, they were, it seemed to me, paternalistic and in many respects enlightened. During my visit at that time, I went to the major installations and descended the Old Mine to 600 feet down into the bowels of the mountains, where, to my untutored eye, facilities seemed surprisingly modern.

I also visited many of the old, traditional mines at that time. They still produced two-thirds of Gejiu's total tin output. Most of this came from roughly 50 very small "native mines," where age-old methods prevailed. I visited several of these and the contrasts between them and the two modern mines was striking. The old ones were incredibly primitive, and the conditions under which their laborers—all of whom were small children—worked were abominable. In fact, I think they were about the worst working conditions that I have ever seen anywhere. A typical mine looked like nothing more than a tiny hole in the mountains, with an opening measuring perhaps two-and-a-half to three-and-a-half feet wide. From the opening, a narrow shaft slanted downward along a long slippery slope. Some of the shafts descended several hundred feet into the mountains, and horizontal shafts branched off from the main ones at frequent intervals. Because the shafts were so small, only children aged 15 or younger could be lowered into them, and each child had to make several trips a day, dragging up each time 40 to 50 pounds of red ore. The ore was then crushed in crude stone grinders, and subsequently it was concentrated by repeated splashing with water in simple sedimentary "mud flats" until the concentration was sufficient to send it on mule back to smelters elsewhere.

The contrast between what I saw at the mines in 1988 and what I had seen—particularly at the small native mines—40 years previously was tremendous. The tin industry had been totally modernized. Although there still were a few relatively small mines in the area, I was told, I saw none, and people said that they were nothing like the native mines that I had seen in the 1940s. The old tin corporation had been transformed into a huge, modern, state-owned conglomerate—which was called, simply, the Yunnan Tin Corporation. By 1988, it had become an extremely large operation, as I learned by visiting several of its major facilities as well as by talking at great length, at the headquarters in Gejiu, with the corporation's leaders. Everyone I met who was connected with the mines impressed me as being very "modern"; most of them were well-trained engineers who seemed to be very competent professionals. (At the corporation headquarters, they screened for me a slick, but well-done and informative, videotape that gave basic data about the operations of the corporation.)

I was told a little about the history of the corporation after the Communist takeover. The old corporation was rapidly converted into a new, state-owned enterprise, and the central government decided, soon thereafter, to make it one of China's "key projects." At that time, Beijing made huge investments in developing Gejiu's tin production, and large numbers of technicians and skilled industrial workers were transferred to Gejiu from other parts of China. From the start of the 1950s to 1988, I was told, new investments in tin mining in the area had totaled roughly Y 4 billion. (Until the reforms of the 1980s, the central government's investments were in the form of grants, but after the start of reforms, Beijing gave only loans, which the corporation was expected to repay eventually.) For a brief period, Soviet specialists came and provided some advice—for example, advice on how best to modernize and expand the concentrating and smelting facilities—but for the most part it was Chinese technicians, I was told, who developed the mine and all of the facilities associated with it, and the corporation was strictly on its own for most of the years after 1960.

*   *   *

I met the corporation's leaders at their headquarters in Gejiu, which was a large modern building that looked a little like a ministry in Beijing. The men I interviewed were very proud of their accomplishments and were very aware—with justification—of the national as well as local importance of the corporation. "Without the tin corporation, there would be no modern Gejiu," one of these men said, emphasizing that the city of Gejiu had developed mainly because the corporation had grown so large. Moreover, they said, the corporation had produced not only a large amount of tin but also many of the political leaders who had risen in recent years to high positions in the governments of the city, prefecture, and even the province.

The corporation, my briefers said, was administratively led by the Yunnan Bureau of the central government's National Non-Ferrous Metal Corporation. This had been true since 1983; before that, the corporation had reported to a provincial department subordinate to the Ministry of Metallurgical Industry. The change was the result of the "policy of separating government and enterprises," they said. (I could not judge how much real change had resulted from this administrative reshuffling.)

The corporation and all of its associated factories and mines constituted a mammoth industrial complex that ran 11 large modern tin mines (5 of them were underground mines, and 7 were surface mines) as well as 10 dressing (concentrating) plants, 3 smelters, and 2 machine plants. The corporation's annual output of tin in recent years had averaged between 10,000 and 15,000 tons of refined product. Although Gejiu was not the largest tin producer in the world, one corporation leader asserted, "We believe we are the largest tin complex in the world." He went on to say that one large tin smelter in Malaysia produced more tin, with many fewer workers than they did. "We are not efficient." He acknowledged that the Malaysian smelter (which he had recently visited) employed only 400 to 500 workers but produced more tin than their smelters did with over 2,000 workers. The Yunnan Tin Corporation was both huge and modernized. But it obviously suffered from the overstaffing and inefficiency endemic to almost all large state-owned enterprises in China. Its management was very aware of this situation and hoped that they would be able to change it.

The corporation operated a large transportation system of its own, including an extensive network of aerial tramways and 1,300 trucks to transport ore. In moving tin from Gejiu to both domestic and foreign destinations, it still had to use the primitive French-built railway, with its narrow gauge tracks (0.6 meters in one section, 1.0 meters in another—which compared to 1.47 meters on most standard lines in China). There had been some discussion, I was told, about building a new rail line that would link Kunming and Gejiu, but as yet there had been no definite decision to go ahead with it.

At the time of my visit, the corporation employed a total work force of 41,000 (all of them "state employees"), and 15,000 other workers were employed by collective enterprises associated with the corporation. Including the families of workers, for whom the corporation—in paternalistic Chinese fashion—were responsible, the corporation directly supported well over 100,000 people. In its early years, I was told, many of the workers were hired locally (most had been farmers), but workers were later recruited from all over Yunnan and more distant places. Of the 41,000 state employees, roughly 4,700 were technicians (of whom 480 were senior technicians, more than 1,000 were geologists, and the rest were technicians of lower grades). The administrative staff totaled approximately 7,000 (a high figure, but one typical of Chinese corporations). Technical personnel had been recruited from a wide range of universities, but the majority were natives of Yunnan and had graduated from universities within the province. Ordinary mine workers were generally recruited at age 18, worked 15 to 20 years in the mines, and after that were shifted to easier work (such as transportation).

Both the standard eight-grade pay scale (plus bonuses) and a piecework system were used by the company. Average worker wages, they said, were about Y 81 a month—or roughly Y 972 a year, but, if bonuses were included, the figure would be about Y 1,830 a year. The employees of collectives associated with the corporation (which they said had been developed fairly rapidly in the reform period starting in 1979) had mainly been jobless young people before joining the collectives. These collectives were generally small—most had under 10 employees—but they produced almost 10 percent of the gross value of the corporation's output.

As the corporation had grown, electricity had become a serious problem, even though the supply of power had been greatly increased. Apart from local electric production, they now obtained a substantial amount of power from a power plant in Kaiyuan. However, in some years as much as one-and-a-half months of production was lost as a result of power shortages. Water also had become a major problem. Some of their needs were met by local wells, but they also had been compelled to build pipes—at great expense—to bring water from Kaiyuan and Mengzi.

Over time, mining of tin in Gejiu had required deeper and deeper mines, and this was one reason why the corporation had decided to diversify its mining by increasing its output of other minerals, including lead, copper, bismuth, antimony, zinc, and tungsten. Tin and lead were generally found at the highest altitudes, and other resources at lower altitudes. The corporation also had diversified by producing other kinds of products, including plastics; by 1988 it had 13 important subsidiary enterprises. Much of Gejiu's tin output was exported, as it had always been, but the corporation itself was not directly involved in the exportation: It had not been given authority to engage directly in foreign trade, so all imports had to be handled by the central government's trading organization.

The corporation was a classic example, it seemed to me, of what the Chinese referred to as a "small society" (although, in this case, I think the term "large society" would be more appropriate)—that is, it was a huge enterprise that incorporated not only everything necessary for production, but also everything relating to the lives of its employees. The "tin mining district," where most of the corporation's facilities were located, was a very large administrative area, covering about 965 square miles. Although the corporation was not given top administrative authority over the district, it did have "some administrative authority." In fact, it had its own Public Security Office, whose policemen were employees of the corporation and could arrest people, although it could not try them. ("We have everything but a court," one top corporation leader said.) The corporation operated a large school system, with 33 primary and middle schools, and more than 1,000 teachers. It also ran hospitals, hotels, and shops. And it provided housing for its employees.

The annual output of all the corporation's activities, as of 1988, was expected to total Y 500 million (calculated, they said, by "the GNP method"— that is, eliminating double counting). Corporation leaders stressed how important the revenue they paid was to central and provincial governments; they said it was also absolutely crucial to the local government. Officials of the corporation confirmed that 70 percent of the product tax collected from them went to the central government and 30 percent to the local government. They also said that the tax rate of the profit tax that they paid was 55 percent of profits, of which 43 percent went to Beijing and 12 percent to Kunming. They also paid a variety of miscellaneous taxes—for example, a transportation tax that went mainly to the local government.

*   *   *

After extended conversations with the top management of the corporation, I spent one day visiting many of its major installations, including one of its largest mines, deep in the mountains; its largest tin concentrating plant, at the foot of the mountains; and its largest tin smelter, which was in Gejiu City. The trip to the mining area involved driving over 57 miles of winding roads that went high into the mountains; the roads were built and maintained by the corporation itself. Knowing that I had visited the area in the 1940s, they insisted on taking me to where I had been—which I wanted to do anyway— namely, the Old Mine, and then they took me to a more modern mine. The trip to the Old Mine was 14 miles; going west of Gejiu, we climbed up and up, over a route that was very scenic, into the mountains. After passing through a small area of forests (tall firs), we reached a foggy, cloud-covered area where we could barely see the road, but we finally broke out above the clouds, reaching an area where the landscape was bleak and treeless. Along the route, we passed a small lake and a reservoir, which they said provided some of the water needed by the mines. We also passed several small mines that were not owned by the corporation. As we neared our destination, one young man who was accompanying us became sick—from the altitude, he said—and we had to stop the car to let him regurgitate his breakfast. (We were well under 8,000 feet at that point.)

Finally, we reached the mining area that was our destination; among its mines was the Old Mine that I had seen years before. A sizable and quite modern town had grown up around the shaft entrances. Spread along the mountainside was a large complex of multistory brick apartment buildings—housing for workers—and a number of administrative buildings as well. On one edge of this little town in the mountains were two old mine shafts: One was still being used to transport construction material down into the mine, and the other was simply a relic of the past. At the other edge of town was a new mine shaft, which we were shortly to descend. This new mine had been built between 1979 and 1986; the initial cost had been Y 100 million, and another Y 100 million had been invested in it subsequently.

After receiving a thorough briefing from the mine's chief engineer, we all donned the special clothing required for anyone entering the mine. I put on large rubber boots (which were very uncomfortable because they were too small for my big feet), baggy pants and jacket (pulled over one's own clothes), a gauze face mask, and a yellow hard hat. We first walked a considerable distance, horizontally, into the mine and then took a long elevator ride down. At the first level, we got out and walked a short distance and then traveled on a small train for more than two miles. This horizontal shaft was roughly 9 feet high and 13 feet wide, just large enough for the small train, which was used to transport both men and materials into the mine and to bring ore out. The train consisted of three tiny cars, each of them having three small compartments, in each of which four people could be seated. (I could barely squeeze in; my head touched the ceiling, and my legs bumped the edge of the compartment.) We then went down another elevator, to a lower level, and walked further into the mine; the train we took there crawled very slowly, and it took us more than an hour to go three more miles into the mountains. Numerous side tunnels, with active mining under way, branched off of the main shafts. In all of the shafts, there were electric power lines as well as pipes for water and for oxygen.

When we reached our final destination, we had descended 928 feet: from an altitude of 7,659 feet to 6,731 feet at the lowest level—where it was, as I expected it would be, cold, wet, and muddy. In the heart of the mountain, I ruminated—as I always had on all previous mine trips I had made—on how hard the life of miners all over the world is. This time I could not help but wonder also, since I had recently felt one of Yunnan's earthquakes, what would happen if a major quake—or even aftershocks—occurred when one was deep inside the mountain. It was obvious that the engineers accompanying me were unconcerned, so I tried to look nonchalant. In general, I was genuinely impressed by what I saw as well as by the people I met. I certainly am no expert on mines, but having visited several in China—not only in this area, years ago, but more recently elsewhere in China—I felt I had some basis for making a layman's comparison, and this mine impressed me as being very modern and well run.

After exiting the mine from the back of the mountain, we drove another 17 miles over high mountain roads down to the corporation's largest concentrating plant, which was at the foot of the mountains. Along the way we passed a number of other mines, and a variety of modern mining and processing installations, as well a network of aerial tramways that crisscrossed up and down the mountains carrying ore. The signs of development were everywhere, and most of the installations looked new. We also passed several small farming villages, which were relics of another era. They were very poor. All of their houses were built of mud brick and had thatched roofs. The women who walked along the road were carrying heavy loads of wood in baskets on their backs. Clothing was entirely traditional—some of it old-style Chinese apparel and some of it minority clothing—and the contrast between their appearance and the modernity of the mining installations was striking.

Back in Gejiu, we visited the number one smelter—the largest of the corporation's three tin smelters. The final process of producing refined tin took place in these installations. I was told that the ore contained only about 0.3 percent of tin content when it first came out of the mountains; then, in concentration plants, the content was raised to about 40 percent. Finally, it was sent to a smelter for the last process of refining.

This smelter had had a long history. Founded in 1902, it had undergone steady development and in recent years had been greatly expanded and modernized. The smelter had moved to its current site following the collapse, in the 1950s, of the center of old Gejiu, where it had originally been located. At the time of my visit, it had, I was told, 2,250 employees, who worked in several large buildings. Although its main output was refined tin, it also produced lead, arsenic, and various other mineral products. To my untutored eye, it looked much like many other metal-producing plants that I had seen elsewhere in China—large, gloomy, and messy. But there was no mistaking what it produced: Adjacent to the main building were high stacks of shiny ingots of refined tin—the precious end product of an effort that required billions of yuan of investment and the labor of a small army of workers, toiling in many sites scattered throughout Gejiu's huge mining district.

*   *   *

The trip to Gejiu was a fitting climax, I felt, to my extended wanderings in west China. From Gejiu I drove back to Kunming, flew to Guangzhou, and finally exited China through Shenzhen, to Hong Kong.

The impressions and feelings that I took with me as I left Yunnan were very mixed. Yunnan was still, as it always had been, one of the most isolated and poorest provinces in China. Despite the economic growth and general modernization that had begun to change it in recent years, modern transportation was still very limited, and to reach most of the province was still difficult. The mountainous topography and complex ethnic mixtures still posed huge obstacles to development. And the province was still plagued by serious poverty, which ranked it near the bottom of all areas of China in its average living standards. The province still lagged far behind most of the country in industrialization, and some of China's reforms had had much less impact there than in coastal China. I did not have much doubt that Yunnan would continue in the years immediately ahead to be one of the least-developed areas of China.

Yet despite all these facts, I left the province impressed by the changes that I had seen, many of which had taken place in the very recent past, and I was confident that the process of modernization would continue in the years ahead. In the four decades since my first visit, some areas of the province had been transformed in many respects. Moreover, modernizing forces clearly were penetrating even into very poor and remote areas. Backward as transportation generally was, now roads had penetrated most of the province and reached even distant places. Modern communications, including TV, now linked the majority of the population to the world beyond Yunnan's borders in an unprecedented way. Basic education had been extended to the majority of the population and now reached most people except for the poorest groups—mainly minority groups—in the remotest areas.

The entire province clearly had been integrated, administratively and politically, into China's body politic more than at any time in the past. In certain areas, industrialization had made notable progress. Cities such as Kunming and Gejiu had changed tremendously: They were no longer essentially traditional towns or cities but had been transformed into modern urban centers. They and some of the other larger cities had become pockets of modernity in the vast area that was still primarily agricultural and comparatively backward. Moreover, it was clear that modernizing influences were flowing out of virtually all the cities into rural and remote areas of the province.

Even though Yunnan trailed far behind the most advanced parts of China, its leaders were trying to catch up by following the lead of Beijing and the coastal provinces. All of the major waves of change in China had reverberated there. The mass campaigns all had started elsewhere, but all had been implemented—in varying ways and to varying degrees—in Yunnan, even though often they were a little late and were modified to fit local conditions. In the 1980s, Yunnan's leaders, like those in other provinces, had given priority to the task of accelerating economic growth. From the start they had been compelled, by realities, to pursue special policies targeted at the province's basic problem of poverty. As I compared conditions with those I saw in the 1940s, I was genuinely impressed by the improvement in the diet, clothing, and health (and, in some areas, the housing) of most of the population.

Because of its complicated ethnic mix, leaders in Yunnan had faced special problems, but like most leaders in western China, they appeared to have given high priorities in recent years to improving relations between the Han Chinese and minority groups—and also to improving the living conditions of the minorities. Dealing with the latter problem had always been difficult since the majority of minorities inhabited distant areas—many of them mountainous. I left, though, with little doubt that the province's policies toward minorities in the 1980s had, wisely, given preferential treatment to minority groups in many respects. However, I also left with no doubt that poverty was still close to desperate in sizable minority areas. Even though I did not see such areas, official statistics—as well as what I was told—made it clear that in some areas the conditions were still dreadful. Yet from what I could see, in most areas there had been a reduction in the incidence of hunger and disease, and people no longer lived on the edge of total economic disaster—as many had before. From what I was able to see and hear, also, it seemed to me that despite the long history of Han-minority tensions and conflicts, and the residue of resentment about the brutality of the Red Guards during the Cultural Revolution, relations among and between the provinces' diverse ethnic groups had improved and appeared in 1988 to be relatively stable.

I was also impressed in Yunnan—as I was elsewhere in China during 1988—by the results of the generational change in the leadership that had occurred during the decade of the 1980s. The change had brought into positions of authority a new technocratic elite, whose members seemed to be genuinely committed to modernization and were clearly more competent than most of their predecessors. Although I saw no evidence that members of this elite gave high priority to democratization—at least in the Western sense—those I met impressed me as being essentially nonideological, pragmatic, development-oriented individuals. It seemed likely that in time they would throw their weight in favor of both economic pluralization and gradual political liberalization of some kind.

The impact of the reform policies promoted by Beijing's leaders in most of the 1980s was obviously not as great in Yunnan as it was in coastal provinces. Large state enterprises were still overwhelmingly dominant in the industrial sector; collective and township enterprises were developing but at a rate much more gradual than in coastal areas; and the open policy had, so far, not had very dramatic effects there. Nevertheless, the officials I met in the province accepted the need for such reforms, and they were trying to carry them out as best as they could, even though local conditions stacked the odds against rapid change.

Despite Yunnan's long history of localism, and the pre-1949 dominance of local warlords who for many years were able to keep the national government at arm's length, I saw little evidence that Yunnan's leaders might be inclined to—or able to—strongly assert their local power and resist central control. Like provincial leaders over most of China, they were trying their best to promote local interests, both in their dealings with Beijing and in their competition with other provinces. However, like leaders in most of the poor provinces in west China, their leverage and room for maneuver were limited by their financial dependency on Beijing.

I was struck, as I was in most of west China, by the "demilitarization of society"—at least by comparison with what I had seen in earlier years. Operating essentially as a distinct "system," separate from the civilian hierarchies (albeit with close liaison at top levels), the military establishment in Yunnan maintained a low profile that was notable, I thought, particularly in a province located on the front line of the festering conflict between China and Vietnam.

My overall impression, therefore, was of a relatively poor and backward area that was struggling to enter the modern world and was making some real progress despite the enormous problems facing its leaders. In the province, there were some quite remarkable pockets of modernization, and there were signs of creeping modernization in many areas. Yunnan was eager to catch up with more advanced areas. But its leaders feared, still, that it might fall further behind.

CHAPTER NINE

Reflections

MY TRAVELS throughout China during 1988 covered so much territory—equivalent to roughly six coast-to-coast trips across the United States (half the mileage covered was on the ground)—that I had few opportunities then to digest and think about the meaning of what I had learned. Virtually all of my time was spent recording everything that I saw and heard. Only after returning to the United States was I able to piece together, organize, and reflect upon the information that I had gathered and on my vivid impressions of people and places. In the previous eight chapters of this volume, I recorded facts that I gathered and judgments that I made about situations and trends in each place that I visited. In this final chapter, I will make some broader generalizations about overall trends, particularly as they throw light on the extent and nature of economic, political, and social change in west China between the 1940s and the 1980s, and on the impact of Beijing's reform policies in the 1980s. These were the core questions that guided my search for understanding in my travels throughout all parts of China in 1988. Although my generalizations will relate particularly to China's far western regions and provinces, I will also present some of my views about likely trends affecting all of China in the future, based on all of my observations not just in west China but throughout the country in 1988.

It should be clear to anyone who has read my earlier chapters that by the end of my extensive travels in west China in 1988, I was deeply impressed by the extent to which powerful forces of modernization were changing these remote areas. Many continuities with the past were obvious, but, on balance, I was much more impressed by the changes under way than by the drag of tradition.

When I first visited west China in the late 1940s, almost all the area was ruled by semiautonomous warlords who controlled their own semimodern armies and ruled with an iron hand. The primary aim of these leaders was political survival, not modern economic development. The societies they ruled were heavily militarized. Relations between Han Chinese and most minority groups were strained, and often hostile, throughout much of the west. Economically, the west was essentially premodern in every sense of the word. Transportation and communication were still primitive. Only three railways even touched the region: the one to Baotou, one reaching from east China toward Lanzhou, and the other running from Indochina to Kunming. The few roads were mostly unpaved. Little economic development was under way. Modern industry was almost entirely absent, and production almost everywhere was still largely by handicraft methods. Even electricity was lacking in most cities. Agriculture was based on centuries-old methods of cultivation. Modern education had barely begun to develop in urban ar-

573

eas, and the great majority of the rural population was still illiterate. Poverty was glaringly evident everywhere; it was visible in the poor food, clothing, housing, and health of most of the population. In short, west China had barely begun to enter the modern world. Most western areas looked much as they must have appeared centuries earlier. The few Westerners who visited and wrote about China's far west generally gave the impression—with considerable justification—that they had traveled through the area as explorers of exotic and ancient places.

I did not know what to expect when I revisited China's far west in 1988. During the four decades since my previous travel in that part of China, I had read a handful of journalistic reports by Western travelers, many official Chinese press reports about the western regions and provinces, and a few—but not many—scholarly monographs on the west. These had been sufficient to keep alive my interest in west China but did not begin to satisfy my desire to understand what the trends and events had been in these areas since the 1940s.

*   *   *

When I finally reached west China again, I was genuinely astonished by how much had changed in the previous four decades. There were some things, which I have reported in previous chapters, that were vivid reminders of the past; it could hardly be otherwise in a country with such deep-rooted historical traditions, cultural values, and attitudes. Yet my most powerful impression was that the changes had gone quite far in transforming many areas in China's west and propelling them along the road toward modernization. Most obvious were the material changes—the consequence of substantial and growing industrialization through much of the region and of the general process of modernization that was the result. However, it also seemed to me—as far as I could judge—that the attitudes and values of both the Han Chinese and many members of minority groups were also undergoing significant change—not as rapidly as the material changes, but at an accelerating rate, and more rapidly in the 1980s than in any previous period. My judgments about attitudes and values obviously had to be impressionistic, but as more scholarly studies in depth are made in the years ahead (a number of young American scholars already are doing important fieldwork in western areas), I am confident that they will show that economic modernization has been producing far-reaching social and cultural changes.

The material changes were highly visible everywhere that I visited. To me they were impressive. However, as I discussed in earlier chapters, I was also awed by the size of the problems and the enormity of the tasks of bringing these areas fully into the modern world.

Judgments about development in any area depend, of course, on what one uses as a basis of comparison. I am sure some Westerners visiting these areas might be less impressed than I was. Compared to the dynamic and rapidly developing eastern provinces along China's coast, most areas in the west are still relatively backward and poor. Leaders in the region are acutely aware of this fact and recognize that whatever progress they make, they still may fall further behind some areas in the east. And, if one compares modernization in west China to that in Japan and the so-called four little dragons in East Asia (South Korea, Taiwan, Hong Kong, and Singapore), the gaps are still very large, and it is difficult to see how areas in west China can catch up in the foreseeable future.

Nevertheless, I was impressed by what I saw because, in my opinion, the most valid standard of comparison to use in judging the process of economic modernization that has gotten under way in west China is that which compares its present situation with its own recent past—not comparisons with better-endowed, more favorably located, and more rapidly developing, modernizing areas to its east, which today are the most dynamic and rapidly developing areas in the *world*. The changes I saw in 1988—especially in cities such as Baotou, Lanzhou, and Urumqi but also in smaller cities and even in rural areas throughout much of the region—left a deep impression on me.

*   *   *

The economic transformation of China's west began in the 1950s and was propelled by many factors. The development of modern transportation and communication was among the first and most important. Starting almost from scratch, the Communist regime first built several key trunk railways, then constructed paved trunk roads radiating out from the railways, and thereafter built a fairly extensive network of unpaved roads that reached into very remote areas. The spread of modern industry followed the path of development of this still small, but crucially important, new system of modern transportation. Together with the spread of modern transportation and industry, new modern cities grew, modern education developed, and agriculture in surrounding areas was improved. By the time of my visit in the late 1980s, all of these important aspects of modernization had made substantial progress and had penetrated even into many of the most remote areas, though in varying degrees. Not surprisingly, the impact of modernization was most striking and visible in the major political and economic cities, which had grown enormously and were now the hubs of modern transportation. These cities now had much improved links with the rest of China and the world primarily because of recently built railways but also because of new scheduled passenger air service.

From the relatively few large cities in the region, modernization had spread steadily to medium-sized and small cities and to mining centers. Most of these places, too, developed mainly in the zones along the new rail lines. From the railway zones, modernization, including industrialization, had then spread to smaller towns and rural areas, especially those located along new motor roads. The outreach of modern influences was less in deep interior areas, but, as I saw on my travels, they had some outreach to all areas that had even poor unpaved roads. It was easy to see, wherever I went outside of major cities, how the spread of modernization had followed the railways and roads and then tended to peter out in areas where modern transportation was least developed.

In the initial stage of the construction of modern transportation in China's west, progress was rapid. Between the 1950s and the 1980s, west China compressed into one brief period the changes that in Western countries had taken place much more gradually. West China entered the rail age, the motor age, and the air age almost simultaneously. However, it was clear to me—and obviously clear to local leaders—that all of these forms of modern transportation would have to be substantially expanded to meet the needs of future development. This expansion will require new investment by both the central government (which in the past has financed the most important new transportation routes) and regional and provincial governments, on which the burden of financing is likely to fall more heavily in the future. Government leaders in western regions will face some difficult choices in setting priorities for further modernization of their transportation system.

New rail lines are badly needed. One of the great hopes of leaders almost everywhere in the west is that they can promote more rapid general economic development by accelerating the exploitation of rich raw material resources located in the west, and for this hope to be realized, a number of new rail lines will have to be constructed. National as well as local leaders recognize that the construction of rail lines will be an important prerequisite for the expansion of mutually beneficial economic relations among regions and provinces in the west and between them and China's coastal provinces. The relationships now developing are based on the exportation of raw materials from the west to industrial centers in the east in return for various kinds of financial and technical assistance from coastal cities (as well as a great increase in two-way trade). More rail lines will be essential for this, and if the petroleum resources in the west are to be developed, major pipelines will be necessary. But building new rail lines and pipelines will be very expensive, and it is by no means clear where the funds will come from. Preliminary planning has been done for several new lines in the west, but they have not yet been built because of the lack of funds. A great deal will depend on what priority the central government is willing to give, in its financing of infrastructure throughout the country, to the urgent need for better transportation in the west. The serious fiscal problems that Beijing now faces—resulting from a decline in the share of budgetary income controlled by Beijing largely because of some unwanted side effects of broad economic reforms—make it difficult for Beijing to do what is needed to improve the country's infrastructure in the near future. The pressure on local governments to assume a larger part of the burden of financing transportation and other infrastructure projects will probably increase. However, as I indicated in earlier chapters, the financial dependence of every government in the west on Beijing limits what these governments can do.

For all of these reasons, despite the urgent need for new railways and pipelines, governments in the west may well be forced to rely heavily on the extension and improvement of their road system. Roads are less expensive to build than rail lines. In the past, the central government financed the major trunk motor roads but local governments themselves were able to build many secondary roads. Moreover, cargo trucking could reach much larger and more remote areas of the west than will—at least in the foreseeable future—be served by railways. Commercialization is developing rapidly in the west, as it is throughout China, and as this process proceeds the demand for improved road systems will probably lead the governments of western provinces and regions to give higher priority to their construction. Improving the road systems will require not only the building of numerous new ones but also the paving and widening of existing roads and improvement of the now rudimentary facilities that exist for fueling and repairing trucks and other vehicles along all routes. Some high-speed, multilane highways connecting major cities, and linking them with major mining centers, will also be needed in west China; a few such roads have been built in coastal Chinese areas in recent years, but almost none have been built in the west.

Airlines have developed a small but important passenger traffic linking western areas with other parts of the country. But they are unlikely, in the foreseeable future, to play anything like the important role that they do in Western industrial countries in carrying either cargo or large-scale passenger traffic because of the relatively high cost of air transportation. However, both the national government and local governments are fostering some expansion of airlines, including local provincial-run branches. The existing air service, rudimentary as it is in the west, is nevertheless important because it provides rapid connections with Beijing and other parts of eastern China.*

*   *   *

---

*I have said little in this volume about water transportation. The reason is simple: Nowhere in west China is water transportation significant. National statistics, in fact, list no water transportation in Xinjiang, Ningxia, Inner Mongolia, Qinghai, and Tibet; an insignificant amount in Gansu; and slightly more, but not very much more, in Yunnan. Even in Yunnan the volume of cargo and passenger traffic carried by waterways amounted in the late 1980s to only a tiny fraction of 1 percent of the total of such cargo and passenger traffic in China.

The development of modern transportation in west China from the 1950s on was paralleled by the growth of modern communications as well. In the 1940s, even telegraph, telephone, and radio links with, and within, western areas were poorly developed. After 1950, high priority was put everywhere on the need to build, as rapidly as possible, telegraph and telephone lines reaching throughout even very remote areas and to construct radio stations and wired radio systems that could blanket the country. I was also impressed, but not very surprised, by the extent to which the print media—newspapers, journals, magazines, and books—had developed in the west. Everywhere in China, during the early period after their takeover, the Chinese Communists considered it essential to develop all of these media rapidly, because of their importance in propaganda as well as education; west China was no exception.

What really amazed me, however, everywhere I went in west China in 1988, was the astonishing degree to which television had spread, reaching even extremely remote areas. This development had occurred in less than a decade. Before 1980, there were virtually no TV sets anywhere in China; I suspect that they were almost totally absent in the west. By the late 1980s, both the coverage of TV and the ownership of TV sets approached that of much more highly developed countries. This was something I had *not* expected to see in the west. Traveling throughout western areas, in virtually every place that I visited, no matter how distant, I saw many TV aerials in rural as well as urban areas. The statistics on TV coverage and the ownerships of TV sets indicated that an extraordinarily large percentage of the population could and did receive TV programs. TV relay stations extended the areas of coverage into distant grassland and mountain areas. I was most flabbergasted when, on some trips to faraway grassland areas, my escorts pointed out tiny windmills in the distance, and I learned that they were attached to small generators that produced enough electricity to power a TV set as well as a light bulb.

By the end of my travels in 1988, I had no doubt that in west China during the 1980s—as in almost all of China—a true communications revolution had taken place. It was essentially a TV revolution. It had ended, forever, the traditional isolation of most of west China. It had also helped to fuel a fairly dramatic explosion of information. No one, in my opinion, can yet predict with any accuracy what the long-term consequences of this revolution may be. My impressionistic judgment was that the effects already had been very far-reaching. Even though this judgment was based on anecdotal evidence and fragmentary data, I had little doubt that if and when in-depth studies can be made of the effects of all of the electronic media in general, and TV in particular, throughout China, they will show that TV has been, and is likely to continue to be, an extraordinarily powerful agent of change.

One of the most profound effects of the spread of TV, in my opinion, was nothing less than the creation of a whole new world for millions of ordinary people, not just in cities but in many rural areas as well. It seemed to me that this was as true in west China as it was in more developed areas in the east. Millions of people in remote areas, who a few years ago had no real idea what even the modern areas of China were like, have been bombarded with images not only of those places but also of the most advanced Western nations. I cannot help but think that the resulting transformation of their world must have been, for many people, a fairly bewildering shock.

By the late 1980s, television in west China, as throughout the country, was playing a large role in the lives of a huge number of people. TV had become an important educational medium—even though some viewers with whom I talked complained about the dullness of strictly educational programs. (Their comments sounded very much like those of Americans criticizing PBS.) Tens of millions of Chinese watched national TV news, broadcast from Beijing; I found this to be true not only in cities but also in many quite remote areas in the west. This had created an entirely new kind of link between Beijing and the entire country. For a brief period during 1988, it appeared that TV was rapidly becoming a politically important channel for communicating new ideas and attitudes. Series such as "River Elegy" carried provocative, even radical, ideas with major political implications, and they attracted huge viewing audiences throughout the country. In several places in my travels, I watched the TV coverage of the 1988 session of the National People's Congress; it included press conferences and interviews with participants and observers, which represented a significant innovation. (When I asked people in various places, some of them quite remote, about their reaction, they reported that they had watched the coverage, but they seemed less impressed by it than I was.) This trend ended abruptly following the political clampdown by Beijing after the Tiananmen tragedy in 1989. I have little doubt, though, that when there is another change in the political climate and the process of liberalization resumes, as I believe it will before very long, TV could move once again toward playing roles that have increased political significance.

From both my own viewing of TV programs and from comments about them that I heard Chinese make in 1988, I was convinced that, for better or for worse, the impact of TV was affecting—and probably significantly changing—people's thinking and behavior in a wide variety of ways. I had absolutely no doubt that TV was a major factor fueling a revolution of rising expectations—and the rapid growth of consumerism. Everywhere, TV programs exposed ordinary Chinese to affluent modern life-styles. Most of the TV advertising that I saw promoted the purchase of either expensive consumer durables or luxury foods and beverages. In many places in west China, as well as in coastal provinces, I heard some elderly people decry the growing materialism among the young, which they often explicitly blamed on the effect of TV. The changes in people's expectations and aspirations clearly had already begun to be a major factor that Chinese political leaders could not ignore. There was evidence from the leaders themselves that they increasingly recognized that they were being judged—and would continue to be judged—by their ability to meet the population's rising economic expectations. As the strength of old ideological beliefs waned (TV contributed in a major way to the decline by showing how much China lagged behind more modern nations), the regime's political legitimacy appeared to be increasingly dependent on its economic performance. TV was only one of many factors involved in this, but in my judgment it was an important one.

By the late 1980s, also, TV was exerting a powerful and growing influence on life-styles. For a majority of Chinese, it also was now the principal source of entertainment. Much of this entertainment consisted of serial dramas ("soaps"), variety shows, movies, operas, and similar entertainment programs—some of them produced in China but many imported from foreign countries. Many such programs that I saw impressed me as being as puerile as similar programs in the West, but, even more than in the West, they played a dominating role in the entertainment of millions of Chinese, most of whom previously had almost no way to relieve the drabness of their humdrum lives. In cities, I heard some young intellectuals who were parents deplore—as many parents in Western countries do—the way in which TV monopolized their children's time and competed with homework.

TV had also become a medium that had a powerful influence on the spread of fads and fashions throughout China with remarkable speed. I was constantly surprised, in fact, astonished, when I saw in very remote areas signs that local people were trying hard to keep up with the latest fads and fashions originating in east China. In the case of women and girls, this was most obvious in their clothing and cosmetics. In the case of boys and men, often the visible evidence was the way in which they took to newfangled games—including pool and electronic games.

Although it is not easy to predict what the long-term effects of the TV revolution in China will be, I have no doubt that, broadly speaking, it will continue to accelerate the general process of modernization, in both obvious and subtle ways, by expanding the knowledge of ordinary Chinese, by raising their economic expectations and demands, and by linking them in entirely new ways to both the larger world of Chinese national life and to the world beyond China's borders. Already, the horizons of millions of Chinese have radically expanded because TV has been able to jump over all barriers of time and space. Any attempt to understand the process of modernization now under way must take full account of the effect of television.

*   *   *

The term *modernization* can be defined in a variety of ways. Some people object to the term for precisely this reason because it can mean different things to different people. Without attempting here to discuss my own views in detail, I will simply say that there is a fairly broad consensus, which I share, that economic modernization generally is based on a number of things: application of science and technology to production, the substitution of mechanical power and machines for human labor, the development of factory production, the introduction of new forms of production management, greatly expanded education, and new kinds of training for laborers, all of which contribute to increased productivity—and to the development of manufacturing and new services, first of all in new urban centers. In the process of modernization, industrialization has been accompanied by growing commercialization of the economy and urbanization of the population, which have led to far-reaching changes in society and important modifications of traditional values. Ultimately, almost everywhere, modernization has resulted also in major political changes—including growing political mobilization and participation—and in many societies it has led eventually to some kind of "democratization," although the nature and extent of such political change has varied greatly from place to place. A great many of the changes associated with economic modernization have been subsumed under the term *industrial revolution,* or, simply, *industrialization.*

When I visited China in the late 1940s, the industrial revolution had not begun in most western areas. When I returned in the late 1980s, industrialization clearly was quite far advanced in some areas in the west and had at least touched almost all areas. It had begun a major transformation of the nature of the local economies throughout most of the west. For me, it was fascinating to see how much the industrial revolution had affected such a remote region in so short a period of time.

As I reflected on the development of the industrial revolution all over the world, it seemed to me that the spread of industrialization in west China should be viewed as part of an inexorable global process that seems destined in time to reach virtually every area of the world and has been spreading in recent years at an accelerating pace.

It is easy to forget that industrialization does not have a very long history anywhere. Until a little more than two centuries ago, the entire world was preindustrial, and in China real industrialization is less than a century old. As is well known, the industrial revolution began in England in the eighteenth century, then took hold on the European continent and in North America in the early nineteenth century, and thereafter spread to other countries, including China, in the late nineteenth and early twentieth centuries.

When I grew up in China, most production throughout the country was based on manpower and used centuries-old technology. Even in Shanghai, China's largest industrial center then and now, only a few industries—

mainly textiles and other light industries—were yet well developed, and most production within the city still used traditional handicraft methods (which I used to watch with fascination in small shops scattered throughout the city). When one went into the nearby countryside, (the richest rural areas in China), one saw only farming methods that were strikingly premodern. For example, irrigation of the fields relied almost entirely on wooden water-wheels, powered either by the legs of men or boys or by lumbering buffaloes.

Gradually, industries grew in China in the first half of the twentieth century, yet at the time of the Communist takeover, industrialization was still limited. Most industry was concentrated in a few major cities—mainly coastal centers such as Shanghai and Tianjin, industrial centers in the northeast such as Mukden (Shenyang) and Changchun, and a handful of interior cities, notably Wuhan and Taiyuan. Outside of these industrial enclaves, few modern industries existed. By the late 1980s, the Communist regime had successfully constructed a very large and diverse industrial base, with many industrial centers scattered widely throughout the entire country. By the 1980s, industry accounted for a substantially larger portion of the country's national income than agriculture did—despite the fact that agriculture still employed a majority of the Chinese labor force.*

During the 1970s and early 1980s, I traveled widely, visiting many major Chinese cities, and had seen for myself how the growth of industrial plants all over the country had changed the face not only of urban China but of many rural areas as well. At that time, however, I was unable to visit west China and therefore knew little of its development. Although I had read press reports about industrial development in the west, I had no sense of the extent to which modern industry had spread into there. The area was essentially a blank until I revisited western areas in 1988. I will not repeat here the specific statistics on industry that I obtained in each place that I visited; nor will I discuss further the differing meanings and interpretations that can be made of these statistics. However, I have no hesitation in stating that, no matter how one assesses the specific figures, the general picture was clear. The figures—as well as what I myself saw in western areas—convinced me that in a remarkably short period of time there had been an impressive growth of industry in a surprisingly large number of places in west China.

---

*By 1986, according to State Statistical Bureau figures, industry accounted for 46 percent of China's national income and agriculture for 35 percent (construction, transport, and commerce accounted for the rest). However, of the country's labor force, which totaled 513 million, 60 percent were still employed in agriculture. More specifically, in 1986, of the country's total labor force of 513 million, 305 million (close to 60 percent) were employed in agriculture, close to 133 million (over 25 percent) in industry and other work in urban areas, and 75 million (almost 15 percent) in rural industry and other nonfarming jobs in rural areas.

The figures I received showed, also, that by the 1980s, in many western areas the value of industrial output was greater than the value of agricultural output. Typically, local statistics indicated that of the combined value of agriculture and industry, the value of industrial output varied between 60 percent and 75 percent of the total. In only a few places did I obtain figures on local "national" income, but where I did, the percentages made up by industry were lower. Nevertheless, all the figures showed, convincingly, that the industrial revolution was in full swing in much of west China.

I have long been very interested in the history of industrial growth in China (in college I wrote my senior thesis on the subject, in 1942)—and of the ways in which the industrial revolution has spread from some areas to others. Earlier, I noted, in passing, the key roles played by expertise and capital from European countries, the United States, and Japan in the development of China's first industrial centers in the Yangzi valley and northeast China (and in Taiwan). In the years immediately after the Communist takeover of the mainland in 1949, I observed, when I lived in Hong Kong, the process by which entrepreneurs and workers from Shanghai moved to Hong Kong and launched that British colony on its road to rapid industrialization. Then, in the 1980s, the direction of influence was reversed. Chinese entrepreneurs in Hong Kong played the most important roles in the rapid industrialization of coastal south China, particularly in Guangdong and especially Guangzhou and Shenzhen.

The spread of industrialization throughout most of China, including its far western regions and provinces, really began in the 1950s, following the Communist takeover. Beijing's leaders and economic planners decided at that time what industries to build and where, and the central government provided almost all of the capital required and arranged for the transfers, where needed, of skilled technicians and workers. In effect, the central government financed, through the national budget, a large-scale transfer of resources westward. It did this, essentially, by using a sizable proportion of the receipts it obtained from taxes and enterprise profits collected in relatively well developed regions in east China—above all, from Shanghai—to finance the construction, mostly from scratch, of factories in underdeveloped areas in the interior. Most of the expertise initially required to develop modern industries in the west came from more developed eastern areas and areas in the northeast. Shanghai and other cities in the Yangzi valley played an especially important role by providing much of the qualified personnel, including large numbers of skilled laborers as well as technicians and scientists. In certain periods and in certain places, a considerable number of complete industrial plants were transplanted from major eastern industrial centers to selected locations in the west. At other times and places, the process was piecemeal.

Gradually, the infrastructure necessary for industrial development was built in many western areas: Educational systems were expanded and improved, and local training of technicians and workers was begun. Gradually, cities in the west began to develop a significant number of skilled persons who had indigenous roots. However, in 1988 I was struck forcefully by how much the modern industrialization in west China still depended, very heavily, not only on Beijing for new investments and fiscal support but also on east China for a wide range of technical skills and for personnel with experience and competence in economic planning and management. People from the lower Yangzi valley played an especially prominent role in many western areas. I met many such people, and I was impressed by how the majority had apparently sunk fairly deep roots in the west and seemed to identify strongly with the areas where they lived and had committed themselves to local economic development. What I saw convinced me that although many western areas were gradually strengthening their local foundations for future industrial development, their dependency on Beijing and east China for various types of help was likely to continue for a fairly long period of time.

The pace and nature of industrialization in different places in the west varied, as I have indicated in my discussions in each of the earlier chapters. For most areas, the first surge of industrial development came during China's initial Five Year Plan, in the mid-1950s. This was the heyday of the Sino-Soviet alliance. Machinery and blueprints imported from the Soviet Union provided the basis for some major factories built in the west, and Soviet advisers and technicians provided extremely important assistance on a number of key projects. This ended, however, when the Sino-Soviet split came into the open, and Moscow withdrew its technicians in China in 1960. A second surge of industrial development occurred in most of the west during the Great Leap Forward—in the late 1950s and early 1960s. However, the post-Leap "depression" that followed had an extremely damaging effect on industry and agriculture throughout most of west China, as it did throughout most of the country as a whole.

A third surge of industrial development affected only certain areas. This was the period of the so-called three-front strategy, in the late 1960s (it continued into the early 1970s). The policy was based on Mao Zedong's idea that for strategic reasons there should be a major acceleration of industrial development in selected areas of west China that he thought were relatively secure from either a Soviet threat from the west or a U.S. threat from the east or the south. In a few years, many entire plants were transferred and large sums of new investments were poured into the areas designated by Mao as ones deserving priority.

In the judgment of most knowledgeable Chinese I met in west China, however, in many respects the most important period for rapid industrial development in the region as a whole was the one following the start of major economic reform in China, on the initiative of Deng Xiaoping, in 1978–1979.

Industrial development accelerated almost everywhere in the west, as it did throughout the rest of the country. In some places in the west, in fact, the rate of industrial growth was notably higher than the national average—although nowhere was it nearly as high as the rate in the most rapidly developing southern coastal areas (a fact on which many people in the west commented to me because it disturbed them). Everywhere I went in the west, I could see visual evidence of the expansion of industry in recent years, especially in the decade of the 1980s. Industrialization had spread throughout west China and had reached even into fairly remote areas, to a much greater degree than I had expected. In a fundamental sense, it seemed to me, much of west China was well on its way toward incorporation into the modern industrial world, for the first time.

The growth of industry in the west struck me with particular force because I remembered the appearance of even the major cities in the area in 1948 as being almost medieval and certainly premodern in every sense. The new, huge, modern, industrial metropolises that had sprouted from virtually nothing—places such as Baotou and Lanzhou—surprised me, and in some respects they amazed me. (So too did a number of other major cities that I visited in the interior of China, in or close to the west, including Xi'an, Chongqing, and Chengdu. They are not described in this volume because they were outside of the major western areas on which this book concentrates.) I was also impressed by the spread of industry beyond the largest cities. Every middle-sized city that I visited throughout the region had constructed an industrial base in the years since my previous visit. I was constantly surprised when I visited cities such as Yinchuan, Xining, Urumqi, Kunming, and others by how many modern factories they contained and by how modern the general appearance of the cities had become. Even more surprising to me was how modern industrialization had at least begun to spread to smaller and more remote places. It was apparent, from what I saw, moreover, that from all these pockets of industrial development, modern influences of a wide variety of sorts were spreading steadily into more distant agricultural areas—even into grassland areas.

*   *   *

The more I learned about industries in west China, however, the more I discovered that, impressive as their development was, the problems that many of them will face—in part because so many of them were artificial transplants from other areas—will be enormous. The problems will probably become increasingly serious as China moves further toward a market economy. Some of the problems are rooted in the basic geographical and topographical facts of life—the remoteness and isolation of the areas where they are located. But in the case of many industries, the problems derive from the fact that they were built in places arbitrarily decided upon by central planners, without careful feasibility studies and often on the basis of noneconomic objectives. As a result, many have been extremely inefficient, even by the standards of state enterprises elsewhere in China. A sizable number will almost certainly prove to be unviable when they face real market competition, without large-scale subsidies to sustain them. What I saw and learned about industry in west China, therefore, led me to a mixed verdict. There was no doubt that it had raised the overall economic output substantially in most of the west. Industrialization had accelerated general modernization, and I had no doubt that this would continue. But I also concluded that many of the industries in the area will face very painful adjustments if they are to survive in the future. Some of them probably will not survive.

In most of the leading industrial centers in the west, as of the late 1980s, industry was dominated by large and medium-sized state factories, especially ones in the field of heavy industry. Such heavy industries were among the most inefficient everywhere in China; if anything, my impression was that they were probably more inefficient in west China than in most other places. Beijing's central planners' decisions to locate industries were sometimes made on a rational basis, but often they were not. In particular, some industries producing military products were located, for security reasons, in very remote regions, far from raw materials or good transportation. During the three-front period, both the transfer of factories from east China to the west and the building of new factories in the west were often based on hasty decisions.

Another characteristic of industrialization in the west was its high degree of geographical concentration in a few major urban areas. Earlier, I stated that I was struck by the degree to which industrialization has spread beyond the major cities; that was true. However, most of the largest factories were built either within a few major cities or nearby, along rail lines or in mining centers. As a result, when measured by the value of output, a very large percentage of industry was concentrated in relatively few places. In several previous chapters, I gave data on this. The situation in Lanzhou illustrated the problem. In the late 1980s, industries in Lanzhou accounted for close to one-half of the total provincial industrial output of Gansu, and within Lanzhou, roughly nine-tenths of the municipality's industrial output came from large and medium-sized state industrial enterprises (even though they accounted for a relatively small percentage of the total number of factories in Lanzhou).

In a few areas in the west, the growth of township and village industries was beginning to speed up in the late 1980s, but the development of such rural industries had begun relatively late in most western areas, and nowhere in the west had they developed nearly as rapidly as in Guangdong or the lower Yangzi valley, where the explosive growth of township and village rural industries during the 1980s had, for all practical purposes, "industrialized the countryside" in many places. Local leaders in several western areas, when discussing their own economic development with me, expressed admiration for the way in which small rural industries—especially cooperative and private ones—had become the most dynamic element in economic development in much of coastal China. Most said they were trying to accelerate the growth of such industries in their own areas. However, progress had been relatively slow. Few rural areas in the west possessed the capital, the skills, or the tradition of entrepreneurship that existed in Guangdong and the lower Yangzi valley.

Almost all local leaders and economic planners I met throughout the west regarded the existing imbalance between heavy and light industries in their areas to be a serious problem. They hoped to diversify industry and encourage greater growth of light industries producing a wider variety of consumer goods. Most of them also recognized that their areas were lagging behind east China in the development of high-tech industries, and they emphasized the need to increase the number of skilled personnel in many technical fields because they felt that it would be impossible to catch up with east China unless they could do this. Some expressed the hope that, to strengthen their immediate capabilities to develop high-tech civilian industries, they could draw more than in the past upon the knowledge of highly qualified experts already living in their areas but working for military industries and institutes. They also discussed the need to make greater progress in upgrading local institutions of higher education and research, and they all wished to expand cooperation of various kinds with enterprises and institutions located in east China.

* * *

The recent economic development in west China—its industrialization in particular—has been closely associated with major demographic changes; these changes have been both causes and effects of the broad process of modernization. One of the most important demographic developments between the 1940s and the late 1980s was the large-scale migration of Han Chinese to western areas. This migration resulted in growing urbanization and in the growth of some major cities. In a very general sense, also, the demographic trends were closely linked to the entire process of economic development.

To what extent China's central government deliberately promoted Han Chinese migration westward, not only for economic reasons but also because of the regime's desire both to strengthen borderland defenses and to tighten control on minority groups, is debatable. Clearly, strategic considerations were involved in some of Beijing's transfer of certain groups of people to key border areas, in Xinjiang (and Tibet). In addition, some people who were sent to the west were prisoners. Others (including large numbers of youths), whose assignments were a form of punishment, were sent to work on large public works and development projects.

My overall impression, however, was that probably the large majority of Han Chinese who migrated to the west in the years after 1949 were assigned to the area by central government agencies because they were needed to support development projects, especially those related to industrialization. They included large numbers of administrators, technicians, and regular workers. My impression also was that the majority of these would probably not have gone on their own initiative; they went because they were assigned by the government. But starting in the 1980s there was an increase in the number of people going from east to west China on their own, strictly for economic reasons. They included many small traders and some laborers. This kind of population movement is likely to increase in the future as economic reform progresses and as the Chinese economy is increasingly marketized, commercialized, and decentralized.

In any case, however one analyzes the varied reasons for the movement of people to the west, the data that I gathered in 1988 showed that there had been some fairly dramatic demographic changes in almost every place I visited. These changes had significantly altered the balance between Han Chinese and minority groups and had strengthened the numerical position of the Han Chinese in almost all areas in the west. In recent years, there had been some counterflow of people eastward. This began in the 1980s, when one result of reform was a loosening of population controls. Some easterners resident in the west who wished to return to their native provinces in the east were allowed to do so. More important, in certain places—for example, Gansu—there was a sizable movement of peasants and unemployed workers from very poor areas to eastern provinces, in search of employment; many of the people of this kind who went eastward, like most of those moving west, were Han Chinese.*

The information I gathered in 1988 by no means answered all of my questions about population changes, but they did make clear certain important trends. One was the quite rapid growth of the total population in almost all areas in China's far west between the 1940s and the 1980s; in general, the population growth rates in these areas were substantially higher than in most of the rest of China. Some of this growth resulted from the relatively high rates of population increases among minority groups, in part because of the Communist regime's less restrictive birth control policies applied to

---

*In 1988, some official publications stated that in China as a whole, the country's "mobile population" had grown to about 50 million; by the early 1990s, some estimates put the total at 80 million or even more. I have not seen any good estimates of how many of them were migrants from west China either searching for short-term employment or trying to move permanently. The total probably included a significant number of people who came from poor areas in the west—but the majority doubtless consisted of migrants moving around other parts of China.

them. But the large movement of Han Chinese to western areas clearly accounted for a large percentage of the population growth. Since the majority of the Han migrants settled in cities, the migration of Han Chinese was one major factor that accounted for the rapid rate of urbanization in the west. Even before 1949, the majority of cities in the west were populated mainly by Chinese, and by the 1980s virtually all of the large, newly developed urban centers in the west were essentially Han Chinese cities.

As I stated many times in previous chapters, I was impressed almost everywhere by how modern western cities looked. They were one of the most striking visual symbols of the progress of modernization. In the 1940s, even the largest cities that I visited in west China were relatively small and underdeveloped; the majority of urban dwellers still lacked electricity, paved roads, or sewage systems. Not a single city that I visited in the west at that time could be classified as a modern urban center. By the late 1980s, in contrast, all cities of any size in the west had acquired the essential infrastructure required for a modern urban center—including electricity and paved roads. In all cities of any size, moreover, there was a remarkable building boom in the 1980s. There were at least some high-rise buildings in even medium-sized cities, and in larger cities there were quite a few real skyscrapers.

Some of the new cities were now large company towns, dominated by huge state enterprises that managed virtually all aspects of their employees' lives. Although authoritarian political control of urbanites had clearly been significantly loosened in the 1980s, in west China as in the east, China's "bureaucratic welfare state" dominated by large state enterprises was much in evidence in all medium-sized and large cities. Reform had not had much effect on this aspect of the urban industrial system. Even in small industrial centers, by the late 1980s a large percentage of the urban population lived in multistory apartment buildings, most of which were owned by government organizations or state enterprises. Even in relatively small county seats in remote areas of the west, urban Chinese were increasingly becoming apartment dwellers.

The migration of Han Chinese to the west had done more than change the nature of most cities: It had altered the overall demographic balance between Han Chinese and minorities in almost every western region and province. In the late 1980s, only in two autonomous regions in the west did non-Han ethnic groups still constitute a majority of the population. In every other provincial-level administrative unit, whether autonomous region or province, numerical predominance of Han Chinese was striking.

Among all regions and provinces in the west, the Tibetan Autonomous Region (which, as I stated earlier, I was not able to visit) now is the only one in which a single non-Han ethnic group still enjoys an overwhelming predominance numerically. As of the start of the 1990s, official statistics kept by the autonomous region indicated that its total population was 2.19 million, of whom 95 percent—or close to 2 million—were ethnic Tibetans. Compared to populations in other western areas, also, the residents of Tibet were uniquely homogeneous; in every other area there was a more complex ethnic mixture. Local figures indicated that in Tibet only about 100,000—roughly 5 percent of the total population—were Han Chinese registered as long-term residents of the region. This low figure undoubtedly did not tell the whole story, however. It probably did not include Chinese military personnel stationed in Tibet—mainly Han Chinese, whose number was not publicly revealed but may have totaled about 100,000 or more. Nor did it include the growing number of Han traders and businessmen who were temporarily resident in the region—perhaps another 100,000. Because of these omissions, the official figures did not accurately reflect the degree to which Han Chinese were a very important part of the population in many, if not most, Tibetan cities.

In recent years, many Tibetans have expressed strong concern about the growing number of Han Chinese in the region. Their concern is probably justified for several reasons. Han Chinese already play leading roles in the modern economic development of Tibet, especially in urban areas, because they tend to monopolize the skills required. If the flow of Han traders and businessmen to Tibet continues to grow, Chinese could become even more dominant in the economy. However, it seems very unlikely (at least to me) that Han Chinese will constitute more than a relatively small percentage of the total population of the Tibetan Autonomous Region—at least in the foreseeable future—for two basic reasons. Most Han Chinese find areas at high altitudes extremely difficult to live in, and most of Tibet is very mountainous and high. Moreover, Tibet's grasslands and deserts, as well as its mountains, offer few attractions to the majority of Chinese, whose cultural predisposition make them favor either urban life or traditional farming. Nevertheless, it is not impossible that the number of Han Chinese going to Tibet could grow, and unrestrained migration to the region, even if it was confined mainly to cities and towns, would probably evoke a fairly strong negative Tibetan response and add to social political unrest.

The only other autonomous region in west China in which ethnic minority groups still make up a majority of the population is Xinjiang. However, between the 1940s and 1980s, the population of Xinjiang more than tripled and the ethnic balance underwent very great change. In the late 1940s, when I first visited Xinjiang, Muslim ethnic groups (of which the Uighurs were the largest, by far, and the Kazakhs were the second largest) made up roughly 95 percent of the region's entire population of about 4 million. Han Chinese at that time constituted less than 5 percent of the total population, and they were concentrated for the most part in relatively few areas.

By the time of my visit in 1988, Xinjiang's total population had grown to 13.8 million, and the Muslim ethnic groups constituted only 60 percent of the total. The number of Han Chinese had meanwhile grown to almost 40 percent, because of large-scale migration. If this trend continues—and it seems likely that it will, as Xinjiang's modernization and economic development proceed—before very long the Han Chinese will almost certainly become the majority. Even if this does happen, however, Han Chinese will probably not overshadow minority groups in all parts of the region. Almost certainly, the Uighurs will continue to predominate in most of the oases of southern Xinjiang, and the Kazakhs will probably still constitute the majority of the population in certain mountain areas in central and northwest Xinjiang. In contrast to Tibet, Xinjiang is an ethnic mosaic. This is likely to continue to be the case, even if the Han-minority balance in the total population continues to change.

*   *   *

In every other region and province in the far west, the migration of Han Chinese—starting long before 1949 but accelerating thereafter—resulted in situations where, by 1988, the Han Chinese were overwhelmingly dominant numerically. By the late 1980s, the statistics I collected showed that Han Chinese made up four-fifths of Inner Mongolia's total population of 20-plus million; the 3.4 million Mongols in the region constituted less than one-sixth (although they still outnumbered by more than 50 percent the 2.2 million Mongols in Outer Mongolia). In Ningxia, Han Chinese made up almost two-thirds of the total population, whereas Hui Muslims accounted for only a third of the region's total population of 4.24 million. In Qinghai, which by the late 1980s had a mixed population of 4.13 million, Han Chinese accounted for roughly 60 percent of the total, Tibetans for 20 percent, and Hui Muslims for 14 percent. In Gansu's much larger but also mixed population of 20-plus million, the Han Chinese made up a very large majority—more than 92 percent—of the total. And in Yunnan, which remained the most ethnically heterogeneous province in China, by the late 1980s more than two-thirds of the total provincial population of very close to 35 million were Han Chinese.*

The migration of Han Chinese to most of these areas began centuries earlier, but the flow started to increase several decades ago, and then it accelerated greatly after 1949. By 1988, except for Tibet and Xinjiang, the rest of west China could no longer be viewed, in demographic terms, as minority

---

*In another minority area that I visited in both 1948 and 1988, the Ganzi Tibetan Autonomous Prefecture (formerly Xikang), roughly two-thirds of the population of approximately 800,000 in 1988 were Tibetans. But now Ganzi belongs to Sichuan Province, and in that province the total Tibetan population—located mainly in Ganzi and Aba—is literally a tiny drop in the bucket since the provincial population now totals more than 100 million.

areas into which Han Chinese were moving. They clearly had become Han Chinese areas, in which there were still minority groups of varying size and importance, occupying major portions of the west but greatly outnumbered by Han Chinese in agricultural development and in urbanization. The post-1949 demographic trends reinforced the political and economic measures taken by the Communist regime to integrate western areas more closely into China's polity and economy than at any time in the past.

However, the overall population figures—and the generalizations I have just made—can be misleading. As I noted earlier, by 1988 Han Chinese in the west dominated in most cities and in many major developed areas along railway lines and river valleys—including most areas suitable for traditional Chinese agriculture. But most of the territory in the west was still occupied by minority ethnic groups.

The centuries-old traditional dividing lines between Han Chinese agricultural areas and the grasslands inhabited by non-Han peoples who are pastoral (even though many now engage in agriculture, too) have shifted to some extent in recent years, and the boundaries are now less clear-cut and more porous than they once were. Nevertheless, these dividing lines still have considerable significance. By far the largest percentage of territory in the western regions and provinces, therefore, is still primarily the domain of minority ethnic groups, who are spread thinly over vast areas, even though the Han Chinese are numerically predominant in all but two regions and provinces. (As I noted earlier in this volume, figures for China as a whole show that although ethnic minorities make up only 8 percent or so of China's population, almost 60 percent of China's territory contains significant numbers of minority people.)

Since the recent collapse of European Communism, and the breakup of the Soviet Union, there has been considerable speculation about what impact the revival of ethnic-based nationalism not only in the former USSR but also in Eastern Europe and many other places in the world might have on China's far west. China's leaders are clearly concerned, especially about the possibility that the new regimes in Central Asia—Kazakhstan, Tadjikstan, and Kirghizstan—and in Outer Mongolia as well might stimulate unrest and lead to political agitation for greater autonomy or independence in Chinese minority areas across the borders. Throughout history, Han-minority relations, especially in the far west, have always been extremely complex, have often caused very serious problems, and have periodically led to conflicts. Changes across China's western borders could well intensify the tensions that cause serious problems in the region, as I will comment on later. However, in my judgment there is little possibility of a political collapse or fragmentation in China's western regions comparable to that which occurred in the former Soviet empire (unless there were to be a disintegration of the political center in Beijing, which is unlikely). One fundamental reason is that the basic demographic balance in China's west is now—as I have already stated—very different from that in the former Soviet Union, where there was almost a 50-50 balance between Russians and minority groups in the USSR as a whole, and where minorities were clearly dominant in many regions. In China, the Han Chinese predominance in most areas, including all important urban centers, means that the principal levers of modern development are in Han hands.

*   *   *

As I emphasized earlier, the growth of industrial centers created the foundations for broader modernization in the west. The main forces for change were generated in the cities and then spread to more distant agricultural areas. Nevertheless, the modernization of agriculture—both farming and animal husbandry—was another essential element in the post-1949 economic development of western areas. It was apparent, from what I saw in 1988, that rural modernization still had a very long way to go, and all western leaders I met recognized that the persistence of extreme poverty in certain areas posed some of the largest obstacles to achievement of their economic goals. Yet I saw evidence of significant agricultural improvement in many areas, and the local statistics on overall agricultural growth were quite impressive. One thing I learned that really surprised me was the fact that in several areas that I visited the average per capita incomes of minority ethnic groups engaged in animal husbandry had risen more rapidly than those of nearby Han and Hui farmers; by 1988 they were considerably higher in some pastoral areas than in many farming areas. The main explanation for this was that herdsmen were able to sell animals and animal products at relatively favorable prices—although, local people said, improvement in animal veterinary services, plus the end of collectivization of animal husbandry, had also helped greatly.

In most of the farming areas that I visited personally, there had clearly been significant increases in productivity in the years since the 1940s—as a result of improved irrigation, better seeds, and more modern farming methods—although there had been tremendous ups and downs in agriculture, some caused by changing weather conditions, some caused by political storms. Overall regional and provincial figures on per capita agricultural output were relatively low, but one major reason for this was that the averages were pulled down by the extremely low productivity of the poorest areas, especially those in mountain areas and where rainfall and irrigation were insufficient.

I saw very few of the poorest agricultural areas in the west; most such areas were located in areas even more remote than the places I visited. However, officials and scholars told me a good deal about these poor areas—which included not only distant dry and mountainous farming areas but also some very poor pastureland areas as well. In such areas, there were large numbers of people who had incomes below the standard "poverty line" set by the Chinese government—which was extremely low (about Y 200 a year). I was never able to determine, from the local figures I received, how many of the total number of people in China that Beijing said lived below the national poverty line—which central leaders in 1988 said totaled roughly 70 million—lived in the western provinces and regions that I visited, but from what I was told I concluded that it must be a sizable percentage of the total. The fact that I saw so few of them, despite travels to many distant areas, highlighted for me something that I already knew—that in a country as huge and complicated as China, trying to find the "truth" and generalize about it is full of pitfalls. Reading documents is not enough. But neither can one make sweeping generalizations simply on the basis of what one sees and hears in travels through the country, no matter how extensive those travels are.

In the 1980s, the rural reforms implemented all over China—including the far west—had a very positive effect on output in both farming areas and the grasslands. Earlier, the major organizational changes that had been carried out throughout rural China—cooperativization, collectivization, and communization—had, on balance, in the judgment of agricultural specialists I met in the west, had more damaging than helpful effects on overall agricultural growth. I was not able to learn a great deal about precisely what each of those organizational changes had involved in the west—although I learned a little about them. However, local people argued—plausibly—that all of the collective forms of organization had damaging effects on the incentives of both farmers and herdsmen and that the restoration of incentives, resulting from decollectivization and the return to family-based farming and animal husbandry in the 1980s, was probably the most important single factor that boosted agricultural productivity and output in the period. The result, everyone agreed, had been significant rises in the living standards of almost all rural groups, except for those in the poorest places who were still living below the poverty line in areas that were least touched by the surge of growth and modernization in the 1980s.

Although I returned from my 1988 travels with an acute awareness of the enormous problems of poverty that still afflict some areas in both the northwest and the southwest, one of my strongest personal impressions was of the visual evidence, in most places I visited, of the substantial rise in living standards in recent years. Compared to what I had seen in the 1940s, the visible improvement was striking. Without exception, everyone I met agreed that people's living standards had risen greatly, and they asserted that the improvement had occurred mainly during the 1980s. The overwhelming majority of people I saw appeared to be—as best as I could judge—well fed, well clothed, and healthy. (From what I had read, I knew that there were still some very serious health problems in western areas, but few were apparent in the places I visited. Forty years earlier, a great many of the people I saw in those places were afflicted by trachoma and other very visible diseases.) In 1988, people wearing ragged or patched clothing were so rare that each time I saw one I recorded it in my notes. Food was abundant everywhere that I went, in free markets as well as in state stores. Personally, I saw almost no evidence of extreme poverty, although I learned much about it from both officials and academics.

In the cities, most apartment houses and other living quarters I saw had been built since 1949; a very large proportion of them had been built in the 1980s. Although in some respects many of these apartment houses are quite depressing to a Westerner such as myself, they are clearly an improvement over most housing in the west 40 years earlier. And although by American standards the majority of apartments are very cramped, in general the space allocated to individuals or families is larger in western cities than it is in the east, basically because the population density is considerably less in western cities than in eastern urban centers. A great many people of all kinds—including ordinary workers as well as people of higher economic status—have benefited from "hardship pay" and many kinds of special bonuses designed to attract and keep them working in the west. In the west, as in the east, there was a rapid increase into the 1980s in the availability of consumer durables of all sorts—televisions, radios, cassette machines, washing machines, refrigerators, and so on—and everywhere the demand for them in 1988 was very high. In a period of less than a decade, the buying public's standards had risen rapidly, and many people were demanding higher-quality goods. For example, in several western places people told me that black-and-white TV sets were being rapidly replaced by color TV sets in the apartments of relatively affluent urban workers and even in the homes of some poorer rural residents. Yet the more information that I obtained, the more I realized that an accurate mapping of the differences in living standards would result in a very complex picture. Some farmers in well-irrigated areas, and many herdsmen living in areas with good pasturage, were better off than many nearby city dwellers. And within the cities there were considerable differences in the living standards of varying groups. Once again, I learned that broad generalizations about China rarely have universal validity; one has to see how true they are in particular areas.

*   *   *

Everywhere I went, I tried to assess the extent to which Beijing's economic reform policies of the 1980s had been implemented. In most of my conversations with leaders and economic planners on this subject, my interlocutors usually began with self-criticism and stated that they were concerned that they were lagging behind east China in implementing reforms because of a wide range of particularly difficult obstacles that they faced. They made it clear that they were very worried about the possible long-term consequences if they could not accelerate both economic reform and development.

Their concern was justified, and in many respects their self-criticisms were correct. Yet, somewhat to my surprise, the more I learned about the attempts being made to implement national reform policies in these western areas, the more I concluded not only that serious efforts were being made to implement at least some of the economic reforms but also that, as a result, the economic system was clearly undergoing significant changes, even in these remote areas.

In many places, the manager contract responsibility system had already been widely introduced. Various sorts of profit-sharing systems were in effect almost universally. Steps had been taken in most places to improve incentives for both managers and workers. The scope of central planning in its original form, in which mandatory planned targets had been set by Beijing's central planners, had been greatly reduced—much more, actually, than I expected. Even the scope of "guidance planning"—in which targets were set but were not mandatory—was being substantially reduced. "Marketization" (that is, real reliance on market forces) of the purchase and sale of consumer goods—and to a lesser extent many intermediate goods and raw materials—was steadily changing the system. "Diversification of ownership" was also being pushed in some places, and collective enterprises were growing more rapidly than state enterprises. Many of the new "collectives"—especially in townships and villages—were very much like private enterprises. "Free markets" had sprung up everywhere, and they were clearly outcompeting state retail stores; these free markets were meeting consumer demands for goods of all sorts much more effectively than the old state retail stores had. These and other economic reform policies were being put into effect throughout a large part of the west.

Nevertheless, local leaders were basically right when they emphasized that they were lagging behind coastal provinces in reform as well as in growth. In some places, local leaders frankly admitted that they were "followers" of Beijing and other parts of the country, not initiators of change. They were also right in recognizing that in certain crucial areas of reform, including the encouragement of collective and private township and village industries, they were far behind most coastal provinces and that this fact helped to explain why they had so far been unable to inject into their local economies anything like the kind of dynamism that was driving reform and development in provinces such as Guangdong.

In 1988, China as a whole was at a halfway house on the long and difficult road to economic reform. The fact that it was far more advanced in its economic reforms than the USSR or East European countries did not, however, make any easier the enormous problems of reform that it still faced. Several problems in particular posed huge difficulties, and there was still no consensus in 1988 on how best to cope with them. These problems included the extreme inefficiency of many large state industries and their resistance to change; the economic distortions (and corruption) that resulted from the country's transitional dual or multiple price system; the inadequacy of the country's fiscal and monetary mechanisms for managing economic change; and the lack of developed markets for capital and labor.

Some of these problems were particularly acute in west China. Most difficult was the problem of reforming large state enterprises, which dominated the industrial economies in the majority of large cities in the west. Some problems, however, seemed to be less destabilizing in the west than in coastal China. In Beijing, and in other major cities in the east, there was rising concern in 1988 about inflation—and the corruption that accompanied it. In many respects, both inflation and corruption were by-products of the reform process and probably were unavoidable to a certain extent. However, they were increasing in 1988 to levels that both leaders and ordinary people found unacceptable. As a result, Beijing adopted a tough austerity program in late 1988, and it led to a serious recession that lasted well over a year. Popular dissatisfaction with inflation and corruption was intensified by the results of the economic recession and led to very widespread political malaise. These trends were among the most fundamental underlying causes of the political crisis that China experienced in mid-1989, which culminated in the tragic massacre on June 4 in Beijing. The rapidly increasing concerns about inflation and corruption were high on the list of worries that people in east China expressed to me in 1988. In west China, it was obvious that inflation was increasing and that it was regarded as a serious problem, yet nowhere did I encounter the level of concern that I felt existed in the east. In a number of places, local people pointed out that although inflation was increasing, the level of prices was still significantly lower than that in major eastern cities.

I was not able to learn much in west China about how serious the corruption problem was—or what impact it had on public attitudes. This did not surprise me very much: Corruption is a very sensitive issue, and most people did not wish to talk about it with a short-term visitor. (In east China, I learned a good deal about the seriousness of corruption from people whom I had known for some time.) I assumed, though, that the problem in west China was probably comparable to that in the east since the underlying factors producing corruption (the loosening of ideological and political controls, the erosion of ideology and traditional values, and the greatly increased opportunities for corruption) were similar throughout the country at that time. However, I did not sense that corruption had had as serious a political impact in the west as it had had in major eastern cities.

From many meetings with leaders in west China, I concluded that as the reform process progressed in the 1980s, one lesson that most of them had learned was that to join the modern world, and to catch up with the rest of the country, they had to do everything possible—despite all obstacles—to bring an end to their traditional isolation and broaden their economic ties with other parts of China and that they had to try, to the extent possible, to expand relations with foreign countries. Almost all the new economic reform policies introduced in the 1980s were controversial in one way or another because they affected different regions and groups in different ways. In west China, clearly one of the most controversial reforms was the open policy, initiated by Deng Xiaoping, especially as it was later elaborated on by Zhao Ziyang in his coastal policy.

*   *   *

The open policy put an entirely new (for China) emphasis on the necessity of rapidly developing foreign trade, expanding exports to pay for imports, borrowing from foreign countries, trying to attract foreign investment, and learning and adapting many aspects of foreign economic management. Soon after adopting the open policy, Chinese leaders authorized the establishment of several special economic zones in south China, and then gradually, step by step, it opened up cities along China's coast, authorized a fairly wide variety of special zones, and granted many special privileges to coastal areas, giving them unprecedented authority to develop foreign trade and to attract foreign investment.

All the leaders I met in west China were envious of the special privileges granted to coastal areas and were very concerned about the possible consequences of the coastal policy. They believed, understandably, that the policy would enable eastern cities and provinces to move rapidly ahead and to shift their economic orientation toward foreign countries and away from the interior, which would probably widen the gap between eastern and western areas. All of them were lobbying Beijing to grant western areas greater privileges to engage in foreign trade and attract foreign investment, but as of 1988 none of them had achieved very much success. Most of them had begun to increase foreign trade with the major industrial nations, but only by very little. A few enterprises were purchasing new equipment abroad, but on a very small scale. Regions in the far northwest bordering on the Soviet Union (which had not yet collapsed at that time) were hopeful that cross-border trade would grow substantially—the new extension of the Xinjiang railway to Kazakhstan reinforced their hopes—but, as of 1988, cross-border trade was still relatively small.

In many places in the west, local leaders believed that for them to be able to develop their potential for foreign economic relations in a significant way, it would be necessary for Beijing to put much greater emphasis on—and to change policies to allow greater foreign participation in—development of energy and raw materials in the west. They hoped that it would be possible in the 1990s, but this had not yet happened. However, as of 1988, the benefits of the open policy to western areas were still meager. Western leaders saw that coastal China was expanding its foreign economic ties at an extraordinary rate and was rapidly being integrated into the East Asian–Pacific market economy. Although they were realistic about the obstacles they faced in trying to promote their own foreign economic ties, most of them hoped that Beijing would not give such preferential treatment to the coast and would modify national policies in ways that would give more help to the west.

Whenever I asked leaders in the west about the coastal policy, they usually began by summarizing Beijing's rationale for it. It was based, they said, on the assumption that in time the effects of rapid economic development in coastal areas would surely trickle down and assist the development of interior regions. It was also argued that western regions and provinces should be able to find larger domestic markets in areas that used to be served primarily by coastal provinces. Moreover, it was maintained, development in the west and the east, although different, should be complementary and mutually beneficial, and this should lead to more extensive economic ties between east and west China.

After discussing this official rationale, though, leaders in the west invariably made it clear that although they did not totally reject the central government's arguments, they were, at best, deeply skeptical about the reputed benefits for the west and feared that in reality the policies would lead to a growing gap between east and west.

In many conversations with western leaders, I learned of specific examples of the lobbying they were doing in Beijing to try to protect and promote their own interests. I concluded that virtually all western leaders engaged in such lobbying in Beijing much of the time. In many instances, what they were asking for was treatment equal to that given to richer eastern areas. However, in some instances it was clear that they were really asking for special treatment for the west, on the grounds that they were relatively poor areas and depended on Beijing fiscally in a way that made their entire economic situation very different from that of the eastern provinces.

My guess is that such lobbying will continue and steadily increase in the period ahead and that, eventually, Beijing will find it necessary to modify present policies and to increase the privileges as well as the financial aid granted to western areas. In many respects, Beijing's coastal policy has been extremely successful; it clearly is helping to accelerate the growth of many east China areas in a fairly dramatic way. However, there is little doubt, despite the trickle-down theory, that it will widen the gap between east and west China, and this will probably not be politically sustainable for a long period of time. At some point, Beijing, on grounds of equity, will probably feel compelled to grant to the regimes in west China greater privileges and increased economic aid, especially to facilitate faster development of raw materials in the west, perhaps with foreign participation, and to improve the transportation and other infrastructure through the west.

Although the leaders I met in the west were not very optimistic about their prospects for rapidly expanding foreign economic relations, they seemed more optimistic—justifiably, I felt—about the possibilities for expanding what they called "horizontal ties" within China, that is, interregional trade and economic cooperation of many sorts. Before the start of the reform policies of the 1980s, China's central planning system discouraged interregional trade; the most important ties of almost every region and province were the vertical links it had with the State Planning Commission, ministries, and other agencies in Beijing. In certain periods, moreover, the central leadership placed great importance on the goal of maximizing local self-sufficiency. In the 1980s, however, as the scope of central planning was steadily reduced and as China's national economy was increasingly commercialized and marketized, the incentives for expanding interregional trade and other economic ties were much stronger, and people everywhere were encouraged to expand their horizontal ties.

There were also important countertrends at the time, however. As more decisionmaking authority was decentralized, both to provincial-level governments and to enterprises, competition between provinces intensified, and some local leaders attempted to erect various kinds of protectionist barriers to support local producers and traders. I had read quite a few reports in Chinese newspapers about provincial protectionism in 1988, and in some of my interviews in coastal provinces I was told of specific examples. However, in most parts of the west, my impression was that there was much less protectionism there than in the east. The majority of local leaders I met emphasized that they were trying hard to reach out and broaden their horizontal ties with other parts of China. A variety of economic factors impelled individual enterprises, as well as local government in the west, to do this. A great many enterprises, including some of the largest state industrial enterprises, were now compelled, because of the economic reform policies, to purchase, on relatively free markets, a sizable proportion of the raw materials and intermediate goods that they needed for their own production. They then had to sell a roughly equivalent proportion of their products on nonstate markets— or on markets supervised by the state but permitting fluctuations of prices. I found everywhere that these changes had compelled both local governments and individual enterprises to develop new links with other parts of China. This was an important new trend: It had begun to change traditional patterns of economic orientation, even though some old patterns were still important.

*   *   *

In each place that I visited, I asked what ties with other parts of China local leaders regarded as their most important ones. In every region and province in west China, it was clear that ties with Beijing were still of paramount importance. Ever since the Communist takeover, Beijing had been the main source, for all of them, of investments and financial subsidies that covered a large percentage of local budgets. (In south China, especially Guangdong, economic ties with Beijing had become much less important by the late 1980s. The decentralization of economic decisionmaking had benefited the east much more than the west. In the west, it had not reduced the financial dependency of most areas on Beijing.) Western leaders were clearly ambivalent about their economic relationships with Beijing. They wanted more economic autonomy and freedom of action, yet they also wanted more—not less—financial support from Beijing. At times they lobbied Beijing to allow them greater latitude in dealing with many problems. (For example, they wanted more power to raise the selling prices of major raw materials that they sold to eastern provinces. But this was strongly opposed by leaders in eastern areas, who, if anything, wanted prices to be lowered.) However, even while lobbying for greater autonomy and decisionmaking authority, western leaders could never forget that Beijing provided the bulk of investments required for development of the west as well as budgetary subsidies that were essential for their very economic survival.

Compared to the pre-1949 period, the western areas were obviously *more* dependent on and tied to the "center" than they had been in the past. Because of this fact, no leaders in the west, it seemed to me, could seriously consider any major plans and projects without first obtaining Beijing's support—or, at a minimum, its acquiescence. In contrast, by the late 1980s coastal provinces enjoyed very considerable leverage in their bargaining with Beijing over economic issues, in part because Beijing depended heavily on them for foreign exchange earnings and (especially in the case of Shanghai) for the bulk of the central government's tax revenues. The western provinces and regions operated under much greater constraints, and had much less leverage, because of their economic dependency.

Because China is so large, there have been periodic attempts throughout history, including the period since the Communist takeover, to devise mechanisms for regional coordination. Some of these efforts in the Communists' early years represented central government efforts to enhance its ability to control, coordinate, and supervise local regions by grouping several provinces together. Others seemed to represent, at least in part, local initiatives— although they never went very far without central government approval and support.

In the early 1950s, powerful regional military, Party, and government bodies were established at the time of the Communist takeover, and they exercised great power of all kinds—including power over economic matters—in several large regions, each of which contained several provinces. Soon, however, Beijing moved to recentralize power, and the regional Party and government bodies were abolished, although in the military hierarchy the regime continued to maintain (and still does) coordinating regional military bodies. This situation remained essentially unchanged throughout the Maoist era. (Briefly, in the 1960s, regional Party bureaus were reestablished, but only for a very short period.) It was clear that China's central planners did not want to re-create any broad coordinating economic organizations at the regional level. During these years, however, there were still a few interprovincial coordinating bodies dealing with some specific problems—such as allocation of water from rivers.

Then, in the 1980s, when China's reform policies began to produce far-reaching changes in the old patterns of central-local relations and also interregional and interprovincial relationships, there were a number of experiments in establishing new mechanisms for interprovincial economic cooperation. One of the first ones of importance was the Shanghai Economic Zone established in 1983. It was a regional group encompassing five provinces—Jiangsu, Zhejiang, Anhui, Jiangxi, and Fujian—as well as the Shanghai Municipality, which enjoyed provincial status. The State Council appointed a former mayor of Shanghai, Wang Daohan, to head the Shanghai Economic Zone Office, and with a State Council mandate the office was given the task of promoting interprovincial cooperation to solve a fairly wide range of economic problems. On two occasions (the last one in 1987), I had the opportunity to talk at length with Wang about his office and the Economic Zone. He exuded enthusiasm and optimism and discussed with me a variety of specific plans and projects, but it was clear that he was not finding it easy to translate general plans into real cooperation and to ensure implementation of new policies. The State Council had not given the Zone Office any authority to make decisions that would be binding on the governments that were involved in the zone; its task, therefore, was to persuade provincial leaders to agree on voluntary cooperation within their areas of common interest. Its actual accomplishments were very limited.

Before starting my travels in 1988, I heard that there were attempts at regional cooperation in other parts of the country, but I was never able to learn much about any of them. Everywhere I went, therefore, I asked top local leaders what mechanisms existed for economic cooperation or coordination and how important they thought they were. I was told about a variety of efforts to develop economic cooperation, which I mentioned in earlier chapters; clearly the most important ones were regional groupings in both northwest and southwest China, which involved regular meetings among top leaders. They struck me as being similar in some respects to the Shanghai Economic Zone. One difference, though, was that neither the body in northwest China nor the one in southwest China had been officially authorized by the State Council—although everyone told me that the State Council looked favorably upon their activities. The one that I heard most about was the northwest China group. Every governor or deputy governor I met in the region was willing to comment on it. Organized only a few years earlier, this group brought together the leaders and the most important economic officials of five provinces: Shaanxi, Gansu, Ningxia, Qinghai, and Xinjiang (the group was considering, at that time, adding Inner Mongolia even though it was, for most purposes, regarded as part of north China). The governors and their advisers met once a year, and the place of meeting was rotated among the provincial and regional capitals. The purpose of these meetings was to exchange information, identify common problems, and agree on cooperation in certain specific areas or on certain projects.

It was interesting to listen to how the leaders in different places described and assessed the value of this grouping. Some of them obviously placed very considerable importance on the annual meetings and on the potentialities for broadening cooperation. Others, for reasons that I never fully grasped, seemed much less enthusiastic about the potential for cooperation through this particular group. After many conversations, I concluded that although it had an important potential for becoming a significant player in developing the economy of the northwest, its potential had not by any means been fully developed yet. Although some of the projects under way that were described to me were useful, the accomplishments of the group impressed me as being fairly limited.

I had fewer opportunities to discuss the group in southwest China, but I did learn some facts about it. At that time, I was told, the group included the leaders of Sichuan Province, Chongqing Municipality (which had recently been given economic authority equivalent to that of a province), the Tibetan Autonomous Region, Yunnan Province, and Guizhou Province. It obviously was very similar to the group in northwest China: Its leaders met once a year, rotating the place of meeting between capital cities, and dealt with a wide variety of problems. In both the northwest and southwest, I was told, there were small staffs that provided each member government with assistance in handling the meetings, but there was no large bureaucracy, and the staffing of the meetings, I was told, tended to be ad hoc, in the place where each annual meeting was held.

My overall impression was that these tentative gropings toward new forms of regional economic cooperation had not yet accomplished a great deal but had the potential of developing into more important mechanisms for cooperation, and I thought that the effects of economic reforms might eventually push Chinese leaders to place greater importance on such regional mechanisms.

In 1992, long after my travels in west China, Beijing revealed that in south and southwest China a new mechanism for regional economic cooperation had been established—one that sounded as if it would have much greater authority than any established in the recent past. If it proves to be a model for other areas, it might have far-reaching effects throughout the country. In early 1992, China's top economic planner, Zou Jiahua (who was a deputy premier as well as head of the State Planning Commission), traveled to the Guangxi Zhuang Autonomous Region, taking with him leaders from 11 central ministries, and they met with the heads and leading officials of five provinces and regions. The membership in this group was different from that of the group that had existed in southwest China in 1988. The new group included Sichuan, Guizhou, Yunnan, Hainan, Guangdong, and the Guangxi Zhuang Autonomous Region. The changes in membership were significant. Now a significant linkage was made between the relatively affluent and rapidly developing areas of south China—Guangdong Province and Hainan Province—with the less economically advanced areas of the southwest. (The exclusion of Tibet seemed to indicate that Beijing wished to continue to deal with it as a unique and special area; why the municipality of Chongqing was excluded, I do not know—perhaps it was again to be placed under the supervision of Sichuan Province, in which it is located.)

The report on the meeting, published in the Chinese press, said that it resulted in an "agreement of intent" in which all the members agreed that they "will join a regional plan for common economic development." Reportedly, Zou also said that integrated planning of regional economic development would be a major factor in the nation's production plans for the 1990s. It was not clear whether this seemingly unprecedented step toward regional economic planning represented a very bold move by Beijing toward economic decentralization or a grudging response to pressure from south China (especially Guangdong) for less central control. Perhaps it was both. If, in fact, greater responsibility for economic matters is given in the period ahead to regional bodies, starting with south and southwest China, the consequences could be far-reaching. However, south and southwest China may be regarded as a special case: It appears that Beijing may now expect Guangdong to assume greater responsibility in leading and giving assistance to other areas in the south and southwest. This is a pattern that could be applied to the Yangzi valley region, where Shanghai could lead and assist the entire region (in some respects, it already does). It is a pattern that would probably be more difficult to apply to northwest China, however, since there is really no place in that area capable of leading and assisting all the others in the region.

It is difficult to see how west China can reduce its dependency on Beijing in any dramatic way in the foreseeable future. However, as I stated earlier, I concluded that there will be a major effort, both by local political leaders and by enterprise managers in the area, to expand economic ties with other parts of China. This trend was already well under way in some areas.

I was told about many specific, newly established "horizontal links" with cities and provinces in east and north China. Most of them involved agreements either between bureaus in the governments of two or more provinces or between enterprises in the west and counterpart enterprises in the east. The nature of the new links varied. In general, what partners located in the west most wanted were technical assistance, machinery and equipment, capital investment, and—in some cases—management help from their eastern partners. What eastern provinces wanted most of all was assurance of supplies of critical raw materials at reasonable prices. Almost everywhere in the west I found people especially interested in reaching agreements with partners in Shanghai and other areas in the Yangzi valley. Increasingly, though, I was told, they were also looking to Guangzhou, despite the poor transportation connections between the northwest and the south. In searching for new economic partners, different industrial cities in the west were pulled in different directions. For all areas located along the railway leading from Lanzhou to Baotou, Beijing, and Tianjin—terminating at north China's most important industrial city and port outlet to the world—the pull toward the north and northeast was strong. There were exceptions, however: Yinchuan, the capital of Ningxia, regarded its economic ties with Shanghai as most important in many respects.

Local people elsewhere told me of many other special linkages with particular cities; many were based on unique historical and personal ties. Among the places mentioned—by government officials and enterprise managers I met in different places—as being especially important because of personal and historical ties linking particular western areas with specific cities elsewhere were Changchun and Shenyang in the northeast, Zhengzhou and Shijiazhuang in north China, and Wuhan in central China. There were few places I visited in the west that had not at least begun to establish some special links with the Shenzhen special economic zone adjacent to Hong Kong. Shenzhen, and in fact most of Guangdong, were new magnets that were exerting increasing force in many places around China, including remote northwestern areas. In most of southwest China, the pull toward Guangdong, Shenzhen, and Hong Kong was particularly strong, but more traditional ties to Shanghai, China's largest economic center, were also important. Sichuan was different: Because it is located on the upper reaches of the Yangzi River, the pull toward Wuhan as well as Shanghai is particularly strong.

*   *   *

In each of the previous chapters, I reported some of the things I learned about the development of modern education throughout the west. On all of my stops, I spent some time discussing with educators and local officials responsible for education their major accomplishments and the most serious problems facing their educational systems. The majority of people were pleased to talk about the growth of the educational system and were also remarkably frank in stressing the seriousness of their problems. I was genuinely impressed by the quantitative expansion of education and by the unprecedented outreach to remote areas in the west. At the same time, though, I was awed by the serious qualitative problems and by how much still had to be done to build a modern educational system really capable of meeting the future needs for development of the west.

In the 1940s, as I noted earlier, only a tiny proportion of children of school age actually attended schools throughout most of the west, and the majority of people were illiterate. By the late 1980s, a sizable majority of the population was literate. (Most young people were literate. Most of the remaining illiteracy was among old people and very poor people living in remote areas.) Attendance in primary schools was nearly universal in the cities. At the middle school level, the proportion of persons of school age who were enrolled in school dropped significantly; nevertheless it was much larger than in the past. A start has been made toward developing some "institutions of higher learning," but a great deal needed to be done to expand such institutions. However, the existence of any educational institutions above the middle school level represented an important step forward for those places where there had been none before 1949.

In many of my sessions with officials responsible for education, professors, teachers, and students, my interlocutors began by giving me a statistical summary of the growth of schools and students but then spent much of the rest of our interviews discussing in considerable length the educational system's serious shortcomings and problems—which were numerous. The persistence of illiteracy in some areas was particularly distressing. In some of the worst pockets of illiteracy, as many as a half or more of the total population was still illiterate. Almost everywhere, I sensed that the need to develop new programs to make literacy universal—or at least close to universal—was high on the local agenda. People seemed to take great pride in the development of their primary school system, and their goal was to ensure that soon the entire school-age population finished primary school.

However, in some poor and remote areas there was still a critical shortage of both schools and teachers, and school attendance was relatively low. Most people were also very frank about the fact that the quality of teaching was far from satisfactory, not just in poor and remote areas but almost everywhere. A great many primary school teachers were simply graduates of local junior middle schools that were not very good. A sizable number of these teachers failed to meet even the most fundamental requirements for competence, but it was impossible to replace them because the pool of fully qualified teachers was still so small.

Above the primary level the educational pyramid narrowed sharply. In the 1940s there had been very few middle schools anywhere in the area, and by the late 1980s the number had multiplied many times. However, the percentage of school-age youths attending middle school was far below what everyone I met considered to be desirable. The pyramid narrowed even more at the postsecondary level. Nevertheless, local leaders were proud of the institutions of higher education that they had been able to establish, and these at least provided a small base on which a better system of higher education could be built. Improving higher education was important everywhere I went in the west. It was an aim, though, that will take a long time to achieve. In the meantime, west China will have to continue depending heavily on well-educated people from the east and on those young people sent from the west to major universities in the east to obtain their training. Attracting easterners with the skills they need to move west is no simple matter, though, and it will probably get more difficult as the central authorities in Beijing assign fewer college graduates to definite jobs and allow an increasing number to find their own jobs on the "market." Western areas also face a serious brain drain. Many of the local boys and girls sent for higher education in the east do not return because they see greater opportunities in richer and better-developed areas of the country.

Some of the most complex educational problems in the west are those relating to minority populations. From what I learned in 1988, I concluded that a special effort had been made—especially during the decade of the 1980s—to expand educational opportunities for minority groups and to implement affirmative action policies that, among other things, provided special subsidies for education in minority areas, gave preferential treatment to members of minority groups in admission to universities, and in general tried to reduce the gap between the educational levels of Han Chinese and most minority peoples. Both Han Chinese and minority leaders were frank, though, in acknowledging that although the educational level of minority groups had been significantly raised in recent years, the lack of educational opportunities was still acute in some areas, and for a variety of reasons (cultural as well as economic) a troubling gap still existed.

In west China, as in most multicultural societies—such as those in Malaysia, India, and many other countries—although a serious effort had been made to find viable solutions to the educational problems posed by linguistic diversity, few people claimed that their solutions were ideal. In virtually all such multicultural and multilinguistic situations, minority groups feel

strongly that, for cultural as well as political reasons, it is important to ensure that their children are fluent in their native language. This clearly is true
in west China. Yet not only does the Han leadership feel strongly that minority peoples should learn the Chinese language (Hanyu) in order to be able to
operate effectively in a country where over nine-tenths of the population are
Han Chinese, but many members of ethnic minorities recognize that to improve their situations, politically and economically, it is important—probably, in fact, imperative—that they learn Hanyu, which is the lingua franca of
the country.

I was told, in different places, of a fairly wide variety of attempts to teach
both Hanyu and one or more minority languages and to use different combi-
nations of languages for general instruction at differing levels of the educational system. In most places, I felt that a serious effort was being made to
cope with the unavoidable problems of complicated linguistic situations.
However, I did not feel that the basic problems really had been "solved" in
many areas. Too often, it seemed to me, the balance between Hanyu and minority languages was still weighted too much in favor of the interests of the
Han Chinese. I have little doubt that a great deal more experimentation will
continue to take place, that pressures from minority groups for different patterns of instruction will probably grow, and that achieving a better balance
between different languages in local school systems will take a long time.
However, I saw no evidence in 1988 that problems rooted in linguistic nationalism are likely to develop soon into explosive political issues, as they
have in India, for example, but I have no doubt that they already are sensitive issues and will continue to be for a long time.

As is apparent throughout this volume, I spent a great deal of time and effort in every place that I visited in west China in 1988 gathering data and impressions on economic development and reform—and on other changes that
are visible and measurable: the growth of modern transportation and communications, increasing migration and urbanization, industrialization in its
various forms, agricultural improvement, expansion of external economic
ties, the growth of education and training of the labor force, and the degree
to which developments in all of these areas have improved living standards.
In all of these areas, I could base my judgments both on changes that I could
see and on statistical data that local leaders and officials gave to me. I was
very aware of the huge gaps in what I learned. I also plead guilty to having
focused too much on economic and material changes in society and too little
on changes in political, cultural, and social relations; values; and ways of
thinking. The explanation is not that I was disinterested in such matters. I
have spent my entire adult life studying them. But it was much more difficult
to gather data and form judgments about nonquantifiable changes than it
was to learn about measurable material changes. I was fully aware that because I spent only a few days in most places I could not hope to probe very

deeply into behind-the-scenes politics or pretend to understand complicated and subtle changes in attitudes and beliefs. Nevertheless, I was able to gather a good deal of data—and to form some fairly strong impressions—about both political and social changes.

*			*			*

Among the things that struck me most strongly were certain broad political changes that, it seemed to me, were really fundamental and historic. I suspect that some of these changes may appear to be so self-evident and "expectable" to many Chinese as well as to foreigners who did not personally observe or experience China's travails in the first half of this century that they might totally overlook them. In this category I would put the unification of China and the integration of the west into the national polity high on my list of the most important changes. As I have stressed repeatedly, earlier in this volume, when I visited west China in 1948, most of it was ruled by old-fashioned warlords whose ties to the national government were tenuous at best. When I returned in 1988, the area, despite its remoteness, was fully integrated into the national polity. Without this basic change, the progress made in west China toward modern economic development would have been impossible.

Future historians will have a difficult time sorting out the accomplishments and failures of the Chinese Communist regime during the Maoist era. The catastrophic failure of many of Mao's policies from the late 1950s on—including the Great Leap Forward and the Cultural Revolution—will weigh heavily on the minus side in any balance sheet. The regime, using totalitarian methods, mobilized the population to an unprecedented degree and built the foundations of industrial power, but in human terms the costs were very high, and it is not clear how historians will assess costs versus accomplishments. However, I have little doubt that future historians will agree that the reunification of China, accomplished in a very short period of time after 1949, was a major milestone in China's twentieth-century history.

In some respects, this accomplishment clearly was comparable to the founding of earlier dynasties. What is now China has not always been united, but Han Chinese have always preserved an ideal of national unification—ever since the establishment of the Chinese empire in 221 B.C. The reality, however, has often diverged greatly from the ideal. China experienced repeated dynastic cycles that began with a strong ruler unifying the country and ended in disintegration and a period of troubles that often led to fragmentation. Many of the greatest dynasties lasted for two to three centuries, but eventually even the strongest of them went through a period of decay, and often China fell into chaos. In the modern period, the years from the Taiping Rebellion in the midnineteenth century to the Qing dynasty's collapse in 1911—and even beyond 1911, during the so-called Republican period and years of Nationalist rule, until the Communist takeover—were just such a period of disunity.

The conventional dating for the "warlord period" is 1911 to 1928, but that is very misleading. Although the Nationalist regime did start to reunify China in the late 1920s and early 1930s, the Sino-Japanese War from 1937 to 1945 not only halted the process but led to the undermining of the Nationalist regime. The Communist victory in the civil war following World War II applied the coup de grace. Then, within a very few years after 1949, the Communists were able to establish the strongest central government in Chinese history and restored central control over almost all of "historic China."

I have never accepted simplistic analogies between the Chinese Communist regime and traditional imperial dynasties. Nevertheless, there were some significant similarities. The Chinese Communists, like many of the founders of past dynasties, emerged in a time of troubles as a peasant-based movement led by intellectuals and reunified a fragmented country by force, reestablishing strong central rule.

What I saw in west China in 1948 clearly bore similarities to past periods of fragmentation and disintegration. From Inner Mongolia to Yunnan, west China consisted essentially of almost-independent states. Most of them were led by local despots who gave lip service to the central government but really went their own way; this was true even of the best of them—Fu Zuoyi, who ruled in Suiyuan—and it was even more true of Ma Hongkui in Ningxia, Ma Bufang in Qinghai, Liu Wenhui in Xikang, and Lu Han in Yunnan. One explanation for the ability of all these local leaders to maintain their power was, of course, the fact that the country as a whole was then engulfed in civil war between the Nationalists and the Communists.

The reunification process in the late 1940s and early 1950s, which was remarkably rapid at the end, after World War II, was testimony to the military as well as political power that the Communists had been able to build up over many years during their struggle for power; it was also testimony to the decay of the Nationalist regime. In 1988, I tried—on each of my stops in the west—to learn a little about the Communist takeover. What I could learn in a few interviews was limited, but what I did learn was interesting. In many places in the west, the leaders of the Communist forces that moved west were able to negotiate peaceful surrenders and political turnovers. This became the pattern in most places. Everywhere, though, whether the turnover was peaceful or not, the People's Liberation Army moved quickly to establish military control and to disband (or absorb) the old warlord armies. They then established new Party-army regimes and began to build local Party organizations and mass organizations. The inherited government structures were transformed, step by step, into larger and more complex political bodies. In most cases, the Communists attempted, with considerable success, to co-opt some leaders from the previous regimes, who they appointed to positions that were symbolic but lacked political power, in the new structures of government and mass organizations. This approach minimized military and political opposition to the final Communist takeover.

However, in many places there was some continuing resistance, which took several years to overcome. The Kazakh supporters of Osman Bator in Xinjiang, and the Muslim cavalry loyal to Ma Bufang in Qinghai, posed the most serious challenges to the Communists, but even their resistance was relatively short-lived. Before the mid-1950s, Communist rule had been firmly consolidated in almost all of west China, and by the end of the 1950s the Communists had created strong foundations for their new Party, government, and mass organization structures, which provided solid foundations for the regime's extension of effective power and authority in an unprecedented way to the grass-roots level, in west China as well as elsewhere in the country.

Nowhere that I went in the west in 1948 did the Nanjing government exercise firm political control. In contrast, it was clear everywhere I went in the west in 1988 that Beijing's mandate was effective even in the most remote areas that I was able to visit. However, it was also clear that central-local relations continued to be complex. This was no surprise. In every large polity this is true. And throughout China's history central-local relations have posed great problems, and relations between the center and the provinces have undergone many changes. In the west, as in most of China, even under strong Communist rule, decisions made by the "center" often underwent significant modifications—and in some cases fairly far-reaching transformation—in the process of implementation by the time they reached the grass-roots level. I expected to find, if anything, that this would be even more true in west China than in the rest of the country. However, I decided that this was not necessarily the case. In few if any areas in the west (certainly none that I visited) were local governments able to change the central-provincial balance in their own favor in the way that certain southern Chinese areas were able to do in the 1980s. In some places in west China, I could see how certain policies that had emanated from Beijing looked rather different at the local level, but nowhere did I sense that local leaders felt that they could ignore Beijing or directly challenge it. In this respect, the situation in 1988 was completely different from that in 1948.

In recent years, there have been some significant changes in relations between Beijing and the provinces. Many of them have been the result of the process of economic reform in China. Some of them have been deliberate; others have been unwanted side effects of reform. Some Western observers have speculated, especially since the Tiananmen tragedy of 1989, that recent trends might lead to a new kind of "warlordism"—at least to some kind of "economic warlordism." A few have predicted that the trend will be fatal to the Communists and result in the collapse of the Communist regime—if not immediately, in the near future.

Nothing that I saw on my travels in west China in 1988—or, for that matter, in other areas all over China that I visited then (and subsequently)—led me to such a conclusion. In fact, my own judgments were very different. Even after several visits to China following the Tiananmen crisis, I saw no basic reason to change my judgments on this. It is clear that the process of adjusting central-provincial relations will continue for a long time, and its outcome will be decided by competing pressures for centralization and decentralization. In the short run, I suspect that the pressures for more decentralization will move Beijing somewhat further in that direction. However, I believe that the competing pressures—and needs—for centralization will limit how far the changes go. The effects of decentralization, to date, have had very different effects in different parts of China. The speculation that a new kind of "economic warlordism" may be emerging is based almost entirely on trends in one area of south China, Guangdong Province. Local leaders there have shown remarkable initiative and have achieved uncommon freedom of action in dealing with their own economic affairs. However, even in Guangdong there are important constraints on how far local leaders can go in asserting their freedom of action. Moreover, their situation and experience cannot be used as a basis for sweeping generalizations about very different areas of China.

During the past few years, the devolution of decisionmaking authority has given most provinces—albeit in greatly varying degrees—some greater scope for initiative, but in this respect I have been struck as much by the differences between provinces as by the general trend. Clearly, provinces in coastal south China have benefited most from this trend. Some other coastal areas to the north have also been among the major beneficiaries. In contrast, the majority of inland provinces have not been affected nearly as much. And, as my previous chapters indicated, all of the regions and provinces in west China are so dependent on Beijing for fiscal support and development assistance that it is difficult to see how, in the foreseeable future, they will be able to achieve much greater freedom of action, even on economic matters. It is difficult to imagine circumstances in which they could directly challenge Beijing's political authority in any serious fashion.

In my opinion, as China's reform program moves the country closer to a market economy, Guangdong, and to a lesser extent other coastal provinces, will doubtless press, with some success, for even greater latitude for local decisionmaking regarding economic matters. Yet in my judgment it is very unlikely that even leaders in the south will directly challenge Beijing's ultimate authority: They recognize that their own economic health will depend, in the long run, on that of the country as a whole—and on Beijing's basic economic policies. Moreover, they do not have, and are not likely to acquire in the foreseeable future, the political or military basis for challenging Beijing directly. I believe, therefore, that even "economic warlordism" is highly unlikely. And warlordism in the pre-1949 sense will be impossible, unless there were a total collapse of the regime at the center.

Some observers have asserted that such a collapse is on the horizon, arguing that what happened in the Soviet Union and Eastern Europe will prove to be a model for China. These judgments are wrong, in my opinion, because they ignore some very fundamental differences between China and European Communist states. Economic stagnation, leading to insoluble economic problems, were fundamental causes of the changes of regime in the USSR and East European countries. In contrast, China's overall economic record during the 1980s was good—in some respects, in fact, spectacularly good. China was in the forefront of economic growth among all developing nations and in the lead in economic reform within the Communist world.

Moreover, in European Communist countries the legitimacy of the Communist Party ultimately evaporated. In Eastern Europe, the regimes' legitimacy was always very weak because they had been imposed from abroad, and in the USSR the failures of the 1970s and 1980s destroyed the regime's legitimacy. In China, although the Communist Party's legitimacy clearly was weakened by the regime's failures in the 1960s and 1970s, it was by no means destroyed. In addition, China's ethnic problems, though serious, were in no sense comparable to those in the Soviet Union or even to those in some Eastern European countries: The ethnic situation in west China did not threaten to fragment the country as a whole. In China, also, the People's Liberation Army continued to be a disciplined military establishment—despite the strains in the society and even in the military itself during the 1980s—and it remained committed to maintain political stability and to support economic modernization. And Beijing's power to appoint local leaders continued to be essentially unchallenged (although, in a few cases, Beijing's decisions on appointments were obviously influenced by local leaders).

For all of these reasons, although the trend toward greater decentralization of power—mainly to the provincial level—is important in China, it is not likely to lead to any contemporary version of warlordism that would radically change the political and military relationship between Beijing and the provinces. Also, in the foreseeable future the impact of decentralization will probably continue to have very different effects on different parts of the country, with the south China coast benefiting the most and virtually all of west China benefiting the least.

Although these are the most likely trends, one cannot totally exclude the possibility of fragmentation if there were to be a total collapse of political power and legitimacy of both the Communist Party and the government at "the center" accompanied by splits within the top civilian leadership, which could lead different military and provincial leaders to align with competing groups at the center. However, those who judge this to be likely in the fore-seeable future ignore, in my opinion, many important lessons from Chinese history. Both my reading of Chinese history and my personal experience in China in the years immediately before 1949 have convinced me that changes of regimes in China—especially ones aimed at fundamental changes in the political system—almost never occur easily or quickly. They are the result of a prolonged period of decay and disintegration of an ancien regime that leads to a profound social and economic crisis, during which opponents create organized political opposition backed by military force. Coups that affect only the top leadership are not likely to result in far-reaching changes of regimes or systems.

What I saw in China in the 1980s was not a country undergoing decay but rather one engaged in a historic process of economic and social transformation. The immense problems that resulted, which were apparent to everyone, were not likely to lead the country toward a political explosion that could suddenly change the political system or regime. Rather, they were inevitable birth pangs as China went through what Deng called its "second revolution." For some time, the most significant changes are likely to be economic and social, but eventually these will begin to transform the political system as well—although probably only after a lag of some years. I have no doubt that the forces unleashed in the 1980s are both powerful and irreversible. I also have no doubt that for a fairly long period of time they could create serious tensions and result in considerable intellectual ferment, social unrest, and instability. The extent to which these consequences will be destabilizing will depend on the quality of China's future leadership and on their ability both to move forward on reform and to cope with the inevitable side effects. The problems and eruptions in the 1980s—including the tragic Tiananmen crisis—should be viewed in this perspective.

The Tiananmen crisis was a damaging blow to China. But in time it will be viewed as a costly but only temporary setback to the process of economic—and ultimately political—reform in China. By 1991, less than two years after the massacre, there already was convincing evidence that the setback was temporary: Economic growth began to revive, and further steps were taken along the road toward economic reform. As the leadership prepared for the Communist Party's 14th Party Congress scheduled for fall 1992, there was intense, behind-the-scenes debate on future policies—and on who should lead the country after all of the founding fathers have died. What seemed probable was that the Party Congress would give increased impetus to the process of economic reform—and that, in time, this would lead to a gradual process of political liberalization.

On the basis of my visits to east China in late 1989, 1990, and 1992, I was able to form judgments about the direction of trends in the most developed areas of the country. However, I was not able to return to the west to observe trends there in the post-Tiananmen period. However, my belief is that as in the recent past, trends in China's far west have probably paralleled, in most ways, trends in the east. As more than one leader in the west said to me in 1988, they really have been followers, not leaders, in the promotion of development and reform. I assume, therefore, that the trends in the west since 1989 have not differed in any fundamental way from those in eastern parts of the country and that after a period of economic recession, both growth and reform have resumed. I also assume that after the crisis of 1989 political trends also have paralleled those in the east. If so, there has been repression of all signs of active dissidence, but the attempt to tighten political controls, reinvigorate ideology, and reemphasize ideologically motivated values has not succeeded except in a most superficial way (temporarily inhibiting public expression of individual views but not preventing great frankness in expression of such views privately). My visits to east China after Tiananmen convinced me that although the political retrogression was serious, especially as it affected dissident intellectuals, it would not be permanent and was unlikely to halt the broad forces working toward gradual political liberalization that emerged in the 1980s.

*　　*　　*

I stated earlier that when I compared conditions in west China in 1988 with those in 1948, one change that struck me as fundamental was the integration of the west into a unified China, which was a prerequisite for modernization in the years after 1949. Another change that had altered the situation in far-reaching ways was the demilitarization, or civilianization, of political life. This, like the consequences of reunification, may seem unexceptional to anyone who has no personal memories of the warlordism, civil war, and armed revolution that engulfed China in the decades before 1949. But because I did have vivid memories of that period and was revisiting China's far west for the first time in 40 years, the greatly reduced military presence throughout most of the west made the situation seem very different. Military forces still play more important roles in China than they do in developed countries, but as I traveled throughout west China in 1988 it became clear to me that they no longer penetrated and dominated civilian society in the way that they did before 1949. If this change proves to be lasting—which remains to be seen—it will be a change of historic significance.

Military forces have dominated the Chinese polity for most of the past century and a half, beginning at least from the time of the Taiping Rebellion in the midnineteenth century. At the end of the nineteenth century, the development of modern and semimodern armies was the precursor of both warlord armies and mass revolutionary armies. In 1948, almost all of west China was under the military rule of warlords, and Nationalist and Communist armies dominated the bulk of central and east China.

The initial period of Communist rule, after their new regime was established in 1949, also was characterized by military rule—albeit rule by a new kind of Party-led army. Almost everywhere, the Communists established "military control commissions," which monopolized political authority until all opposition forces were suppressed and the Party decided it was ready to reorganize the government and revert to civilian rule. The time required to make this shift from army to civilian rule varied: In some places it was relatively short, but in others it took several years.

On the national level, soon after establishing a new central government on October 1, 1949, Party leaders began discussing demobilization, and, in early 1950, Chinese leaders announced publicly that they would cut the size of their armed forces and shift their priorities to economic development. Soon thereafter, however, these plans had to be put aside when, in June 1950, North Korea attacked the south, U.S.-UN forces joined the battle, and Beijing decided to enter the war in October. During the ensuing three years of war, military affairs continued to dominate the political scene in China.

After 1953, when a truce was signed in Korea, the salience of the military establishment in Chinese society and politics began to decline, and the nature of the Chinese military establishment itself began to change. The PLA did not suddenly fall into the background. It marched into Tibet to reassert China's control, prepared to invade Taiwan, and then, during the 1950s and 1960s, was engaged in a series of crises on China's borders with Vietnam, India, and the Soviet Union as well as on its eastern flank, opposite Taiwan. Yet significant changes took place nevertheless. Beijing's top leaders, who throughout the years of revolutionary struggle had consisted of men who combined Party, government, and military roles, now were gradually differentiated into those managing civilian affairs and those responsible primarily for military affairs. As this took place, the number of career military officers in the leadership of the Party and government declined. Within the military forces there was increasing pressure to convert the PLA from a highly political revolutionary army into a more modern, professional, national defense force. This trend created tensions between those who stressed professionalization and those who emphasized the importance of ideology and politics in the PLA; these tensions continued throughout the Maoist era. The relative stress that the top leadership placed on "redness" (ideological and political correctness) or "expertise" (professionalism) shifted many times.

In the 1960s, Mao tried to revert to early revolutionary traditions and values, revive old traditions of the "people's army" and "people's war," and hold up the PLA as a revolutionary model for society as a whole. Then, at the height of the Cultural Revolution in the late 1960s, when political order broke down and resulted in near-chaos, the PLA stepped in to fill the resulting vacuum, and military men assumed leadership roles in the government,

in economic enterprises, and in the Party itself. As order was gradually restored, the PLA began, during 1969–1970, to withdraw from civilian affairs, but after Lin Biao's reputed coup against Mao in 1971, the PLA suddenly seemed to be everywhere, and no one could have any doubts that it
intended to support Mao. (When I visited many of China's major cities during the winter of 1972–1973, I was astonished by how conspicuous the presence of the PLA was: In every city, men and women in uniform were more
visible on the streets than they were even in the 1940s.)

Following Mao's death, and especially after Deng Xiaoping's return to
power, the new Chinese leadership clearly was determined to return the
armed forces to their barracks and reassert civilian control. Deng took the
lead in revising China's priorities, restoring civilian primacy and putting economic development in first place. This process was interrupted by the brief
but costly military conflict with Vietnam in 1979. However, by 1980 there
began to be significant cuts in the military budget, and the overall trend
clearly pointed toward greater separation of military and civilian affairs.
The political roles of the PLA were cut back, and within the PLA the emphasis was on modernization and professionalization rather than on ideology
and politics—but PLA leaders were told that they would have to do the best
they could with less resources.

During my travels in 1988, I saw remarkably few military men anywhere
that I went in China, and it appeared that, in a basic sense, the PLA had been
returned to its barracks. I had expected to find that military forces were
more visible in west China than in the east, because long-standing disputes
with both the Soviet Union and India were still unresolved and the Sino-Vietnamese conflict remained unsettled. Moreover, ethnic tensions had led to violence in the Lhasa region of Tibet, and there was evidence of increasing tensions in southwest Xinjiang. One of the things that surprised me most,
therefore, was how the PLA was almost invisible in most of the areas I visited—even areas that obviously were very important to China's national defense. In Xinjiang, I saw more men in uniform than elsewhere; I was not sure
why, but I decided that it was because of several things: the unusually large
role that the PLA was still playing in the local economy of the region as well
as the importance of Xinjiang to China's national defense and the complexity and volatility of some ethnic relationships there.

Elsewhere, even in some places where national defense considerations
were obviously of great importance, I saw much less evidence of the military
presence than I had expected. This was true even in southern Yunnan, near
the Vietnamese border, and on two of the major roads leading to Tibet, in
western Sichuan and in Qinghai. (I was told by friends of mine who visited
the Tibetan Autonomous Region in 1988, however, that in the area around

Lhasa the presence of Chinese military forces was very visible.) I knew that there were large military forces in several areas of west China—and that there were also important military facilities in the region, including numerous military factories and nuclear and missile sites; some of the forces and facilities were reportedly located in or near places that I visited. This was one reason that I was so surprised that I saw almost no sign of them. It eventually became clear to me that this was a result of deliberate policy: The regime's policy was to keep military personnel and facilities separate from civilian society and, to the extent possible, out of sight. I was told, also, that when military personnel were stationed in urban areas, or visited cities, most of them wore mufti and tried to be inconspicuous. The aim, apparently, was to reduce the extent to which military personnel intruded into normal, day-to-day civilian life. When I asked civilians about local military forces, the majority of ordinary people said they had little or no contact with the military establishment and knew little about it.

Everywhere I went, I questioned government and Party officials I met—as well as the few military officers I was able to interview—about civil-military relations. Without exception, they stressed that there was a fairly clear line separating civilian and military affairs and that the military establishment operated as a separate, distinct organizational "system." Liaison between the top leaders of local military forces and local Party and government leaders was nevertheless close, I was told, but the links were mainly among the highest leaders, and there was relatively little day-to-day interaction between civilians and military personnel at lower levels. In time of disasters, this changed, and the military forces were mobilized to give direct assistance to the civilian population. Moreover, local governments regularly provided a variety of goods and services to the military forces—including some grain and living quarters. But the PLA generally was inconspicuous.

The most important links between local military commanders and local civilian leaders were with the Party, not the government. Even these, though, were far less important to local military commanders than the vertical military chain of command through which orders passed from the Central Committee's Military Affairs Commission down through military regions and districts to local levels.

The limited number of military men I did meet (a few in Beijing, a few in the provinces) impressed me as being examples of a new kind of officer who clearly were younger, better educated, and more professional than most of the officers I had met in earlier years. Like the new technocratic civilian leaders, they seemed preoccupied with the tasks of modernization—improving military training and updating military doctrine as well as modernizing weapons and equipment. Those I met seemed to have little interest in ideology; they strongly supported the general thrust of Deng's reform policies. (In Beijing, however, it was clear that the PLA, though generally understanding and accepting Deng's stress on civilian development, was nevertheless lobbying for a larger military budget. After Tiananmen, China's military budget did begin to rise.)*

In the late 1980s, all the signs pointed toward further separation of military and civilian affairs, and many Western specialists on China began to argue that if trends already under way continued through the 1990s, perhaps China would see the end of the kind of military domination of political life that had plagued China for so long. I was one of those who thought this was possible. I did not have any illusions about the possibility of these trends rapidly leading to a new pattern of military-civilian relations in China that would be comparable to those in most developed Western industrial nations. However, in 1988 it did seem possible that there could be an important, long-term demilitarization of political life in China. Then, in mid-1989, Beijing's conservative Party elders ordered the PLA to fire on unarmed civilians to reestablish control over the increasingly chaotic situation on the streets in Beijing. The Tiananmen tragedy highlighted once again that the PLA was still the ultimate prop for Party rule and the final guarantor of political order in China. This fact was further underlined when, in 1992, the Party began to prepare for its 14th Party Congress; almost everyone seemed to agree that the PLA would play a crucial role—in the background if not in the foreground—in determining the outcome of the political succession in China.

Yet the use of the PLA for internal political purposes in 1989 did not necessarily negate or reverse the long-term trends. Both at the time of the Tiananmen crisis and later, there was evidence that at least some PLA leaders—perhaps many—were dismayed by, and opposed, the decisions that led to a violent confrontation between the PLA forces and the civilian population—for the first time since the Communist takeover. My personal opinion is that the long-term trends—both within the PLA and in Chinese society as a whole—will continue, despite the setback in 1989, to work toward greater separation of military and civilian affairs, toward further professionalization of the PLA, toward a reduction of the roles of the military establishment in nonmilitary matters—and therefore toward the steady demilitarization and civilianization of Chinese politics. Tiananmen showed that there are likely to be limits on how far this goes, and there may be setbacks along the way, but continued modernization and reform will inevitably alter old patterns of civil-military relations.

*　　　*　　　*

---

*The military budget grew rapidly in the early 1990s, when increased emphasis was placed on military modernization.

Another focus of my investigations everywhere I went in 1988 was on how the political system had changed, or not changed, and on the evolution of China's bureaucracies—questions that have been of great interest to me for many years. I concluded that in a basic sense several fundamental changes in the political system had taken place during the four decades since my previous visits. In 1948, the old-style military autocrats who ruled in west China were more interested in using their power simply to survive rather than in using it to promote economic development and social change. Not all of them were the same; some warlord regimes had borrowed modern totalitarian methods, and others ruled in very traditional ways. But none of them had developed bureaucracies capable of promoting broadly based modernization. Moreover, nowhere in the west at that time were there mass parties operating at the grass-roots level; neither the Guomindang nor the Communist Party had been able to build strong Party organizations in the west.

This changed very rapidly after 1949. Immediately after its takeover, the Chinese Communist Party proceeded, in west China as everywhere else in the country, to build a modern totalitarian system. Everywhere, they established Party committees and branches that reached to the lowest level of society and penetrated all existing social organizations. What I was told by Party leaders I interviewed indicated that by 1988, in most of the areas that I visited, the ratio of Party members to total population was comparable to that in more-developed eastern provinces—although in a few places the numbers were slightly lower. The new Party organizations, once established, took the lead in building an extensive structure of mass organizations similar to that built in eastern provinces.

My judgments about what took place in west China during the Maoist period is of necessity secondhand since I was unable to visit the west at that time. However, everything I was told indicated that the Communist Party succeeded in rapidly imposing a structure capable of controlling and mobilizing the mass of ordinary people in ways that were unlike anything in the past. The Chinese system in the Maoist era developed what in some respects was a unique mix of instruments of coercion, persuasion, and mobilization—and they did this even in the most remote areas inhabited by ethnic minorities, although the results in such areas were not always exactly the same as in eastern Han-inhabited areas. Everywhere, though, starting in the 1950s, they recruited large numbers of local cadres, and these were drawn from ethnic minority groups as well as local Han Chinese. Han Chinese— some of them local people but many of them "outsiders" who went to the west after "liberation"—generally held the key positions of power in the Party apparatus. But many members of ethnic minorities were absorbed into the Party, and in the government and mass organizations they eventually took over many important positions.

Starting in the early 1950s, Beijing launched a series of massive nationwide movements or campaigns, and from what I was told, all of them were implemented throughout west China as well as in the east. As a result, people in the west rode the same roller coaster as people in the east did. Periods of intense mass mobilization and political "struggle" alternated with periods of relative political relaxation. The impact on ordinary people's lives was unlike anything Chinese—or minority groups—had experienced. In the Maoist era, the Chinese brand of totalitarianism differed significantly from that in the USSR under Stalinist rule. For one thing, the Chinese Communist Party relied heavily on "coercive persuasion" to try to "remold" people's thinking, and the pursuit of political, social, and economic goals through mass campaigns was distinctive. At the same time, the Chinese Communist Party developed all of the apparatus necessary for a "police" state, but it never dominated the political system in the same way that the instruments of police coercion did in the Soviet Union. Nevertheless, the Party and its subordinate organizations penetrated Chinese society and intruded on people's thinking and behavior, as much as—and in some respects even more than—was true in Communist systems elsewhere.

My time in west China in 1988 was insufficient to learn all that I wanted to know about how political organizations and political campaigns in the west were similar to or different from those elsewhere in China. They clearly were different in some respects, especially in remote areas populated primarily by ethnic minorities. However, my strong impression was that in most of the west, the organization and mobilization of the population was very similar to that elsewhere in China. My guess was that many of the revolutionary changes carried out through mass campaigns during the Maoist period have had even more traumatic effects in the west than in better-developed areas in the east. Without doubt, the establishment of Party rule and the extension of mass organizations to the grass-roots level helped to integrate west China into China's national policy in an unprecedented way. There is also no doubt that although this brought benefits to the west, it also involved high political and human costs—especially during the heyday of the Cultural Revolution. The rampages of the Red Guards at that time ripped huge tears in the social fabric throughout the west. Post-Mao leaders had to give high priority in the 1980s to the task of trying to repair the damage done at that time.

Whereas rule through campaigns was one distinctive characteristic of Communist rule in the Maoist era, another major—and in a sense contradictory—trend in the years after 1949 was the enormous growth, in both size and functions, of governmental bureaucracies. From the mid-1950s on, especially after Beijing began to build a "socialist planned economy," the number and size of bureaucratic organizations all over China rapidly expanded. The effects of this expansion in the west were particularly striking to me because before 1949 the bureaucracies there were clearly less well developed than in the east. The bureaucracies of all the civilian organizational pillars of the new political system—the Party, government, mass organizations, and state enterprises—all grew enormously.

Various figures have been published in China on the total number of cadres in the country; the figures vary, in part because they do not all classify cadres in the same way. In an interview with me in 1988, Zhao Ziyang's principal adviser on political reform, Bao Tong, told me (speaking from memory, and using rounded figures) that at that time, the total of all "state cadres" (people receiving their salaries from the state) totaled 29 million.* Of the 29 million, he said, approximately 5.5 million were paid employees of the Party, government, and mass organizations (about 600,000 in the Party apparatus at all levels; roughly half a million in mass organizations; and approximately 4.4 million in government jobs). Approximately 13 million state-paid cadres worked in the fields of education, science, and medicine (the largest number of these were teachers). And about 10.8 million were state cadres holding leadership positions in economic enterprises. From the data I gathered in 1988, I concluded that the size and complexities of the bureaucracies in west China were comparable—judged by the number of bureaucratic organizations and the number of state cadres as a proportion of the total population—to those in the east.

One might argue that the national total of state cadres is not unreasonable for a country with a population of well over 1 billion; after all, 29 million is less than 3 percent of the population as a whole. However, the figure for state cadres does not reveal the total number of people on the government's payroll in China. As a matter of fact, by the end of the 1950s—after industry and commerce had been socialized and agriculture had been communized—virtually everyone in China, in a sense, worked for bureaucratic organizations (if one included state enterprises) that were dependent directly on the state in varying degrees and ways. By the end of the first decade of Chinese Communist rule, China had become a society of *danwei* (organizational units) that managed virtually all aspects of almost everyone's life.

Large bureaucracies are, of course, nothing new in China. The Chinese "invented" bureaucracy (the Europeans borrowed the idea from China, and from Europe the idea spread worldwide). In the immediate pre-Communist period, the Nationalists' bureaucracies were anything but small. However, after the Communist takeover the number of bureaucratic organizations

---

*These figures on state cadres did not include individuals holding cadre positions that were not paid by the state—or ordinary farmers in rural areas or ordinary factory workers in cities. The majority of Party members—who Bao Tong said totaled 46 million at that time—were not actually state cadres, even though many of them held positions in local non-Party and nongovernment organizations.

multiplied, and they steadily grew in size—in many cases, enormously. One of the main reasons for this was that the central government assumed steadily widening responsibility, encompassing not only every aspect of the country's economic life but virtually every other sphere of human activity as well, and virtually all the bureaucracies in Beijing were duplicated at lower levels. All political structures in China were organized as vertical hierarchies, with their headquarters in the national capital, and at every important lower level of government—province, prefecture, county, and so on—there had to be, in the Party, government, and mass organizations, bodies that carried out functions similar to those of the Beijing headquarters.

In 1988, in most of the interviews in which I attempted to learn the details of bureaucratic organizations and operations, I focused on the level of regional and provincial governments. As I suspected, the picture I obtained was one in which regional or provincial governments were in some respects virtual carbon copies of the central government. And each of the constituent parts of the government at this level was responsible not only to the top local leaders but also to their counterpart organizations in Beijing. Consequently, the bureaucratic structures at this level had to be much more comprehensive, larger, and more complex than they had been before the Communist takeover because they were now expected to manage or regulate virtually every aspect of the economy and society. In principle, the bureaucracies in the majority of provincial governments in the early 1950s had not been fundamentally different: They too had belonged, in theory, to vertical hierarchies responsible to the central government, and they too had duplicated many of the bodies in the central bureaucracy. In reality, however, at that time the local bureaucracies had been much smaller and simpler and had not even tried to carry out many of the functions that had become standard by the 1980s.

The mushrooming of both the central and local bureaucracies in the mid-1950s was probably inevitable once China embarked on a program of socializing the entire economy, but it nevertheless deeply disturbed many Chinese leaders—above all, Mao, who feared that growing bureaucratism would triumph and undermine his revolutionary goals. From the mid-1950s on, therefore, the Party launched a series of campaigns to combat bureaucratism—and periodically tried to streamline, reorganize, rationalize, and cut the size of the bureaucracies. The results were usually limited and short-lived.

Soon after Deng Xiaoping launched China on a new course of reform in the late 1970s, priority was again given to the goal of bureaucratic reform, and early in the 1980s Deng pushed hard for a reduction in the number of bureaucratic agencies and for personnel cuts.

Everywhere I went in west China in 1988, I found that local governments had tried to respond to Beijing's reform proposals, and in varying ways they had attempted to streamline the bureaucracies. I was given figures on the number of bureaucratic units cut and on the reductions in personnel rosters. But nowhere was I convinced that the effects had been significant. In many cases, it seemed clear that—as had been the case in many past campaigns to reform the bureaucracies—many of the organizational changes had simply involved a reshuffling of the deck. Sometimes several government units were merged, but they continued operating much as before. And many "cuts" in bureaucratic personnel turned out to be more like a game of musical chairs than genuine force reductions. It clearly was extremely difficult for leaders of the bureaucracies (just as it was for enterprise managers) to fire people. Members of the bureaucracies, like workers in factories, had come to view their "iron rice bowls" (guaranteed lifetime employment) as a right. Moreover, since in most places there was no real labor market, there was no place for excess or redundant people to quickly find alternative jobs, and since China had not yet developed an effective unemployment compensation system, there was no safety net to sustain them. Therefore, even those at the local level who genuinely wished to carry out Beijing's policy of bureaucratic retrenchment hesitated to do so for fear that newly unemployed people— whether bureaucrats or workers—might cause trouble and contribute to social unrest. For all of these reasons, the effort to carry out bureaucratic reform had had only very limited results.

                              *   *   *

More important than bureaucratic reform in Deng's reform efforts in the early 1980s was the campaign to retire older cadres and replace them with younger men and women—and at the same time to change personnel policy and define a new set of criteria for choosing and promoting leading cadres. I had read a good deal about this and was impressed, but I had not fully grasped, until my travels in 1988, the historic significance of the sweeping changes of leadership that had occurred in the 1980s throughout the whole country in governmental and Party bodies, and in military units as well, at all levels. What had taken place, in just a few years, was a planned, orderly, generational change (except at the very top, where a handful of Party elders clung to power). The new policy required that leading positions now be filled by cadres who not only were younger but also were better educated and more technically skilled than those they replaced. The old Maoist idea that it was better to be "red" than "expert" was now reversed: Emphasis was now on technical and professional competence rather than on ideological correctness. In addition to fundamentally redefining criteria for appointments and promotions in this fashion, the Party also began to decentralize responsibility for many personnel decisions.

In 1988 I met a great many of the new leaders—at provincial, county, and township levels—and I was impressed by most of them I encountered. In earlier chapters I commented on some of those I met in the west—particularly provincial leaders—and described their backgrounds. (Those I met in other parts of China were very similar.) It was clear, everywhere I went, that a genuine and far-reaching generational change had taken place and that it had involved a profound transformation of the nature of leadership in most parts of China; it had brought to power a new breed of leaders, except at the very top, in Beijing.

Over the past 40-odd years, I have met literally hundreds of Chinese leaders in every part of China. In the 1940s, most of them were either Guomindang leaders or leaders in outlying warlord regimes. In the late Maoist era, those I met were mainly Communist Party leaders in government jobs, both in local governments and in Beijing. Some of those I met, in varying times and places—even in warlord regimes—were able men. The Guomindang had many talented men, but the best educated and most forward-looking of them were concentrated in a few areas—at the capital in Nanjing and in the lower Yangzi valley—and at the end of the 1940s most of them moved to Taiwan. The leadership of the Communists when they took power also included some extremely talented people. Some of them had emerged from the intelligentsia and were well educated; others were for all practical purposes self-educated. However, under both the Guomindang and the Communist Party when they came to power, the majority of leaders and bureaucrats were poorly equipped to deal with the tasks of economic development and modernization in a country such as China. During the last years of the Guomindang, in too many places the tone of the regime was set by old-style military men, conservative traditionalists, or neo-Confucian authoritarians rather than by the regime's well-educated modernizers. Moreover, by the late 1940s, corruption was endemic; hyperinflation made this inevitable.

When the Communists came to power, there was a sweeping change in the leadership at all levels, and at the start the discipline and incorruptibility of both the leadership and the lower-level soldiers and cadres were impressive. So too was the quality of some of their top leaders. However, it became clear before long that the Party had only a very thin layer of well-educated people with the knowledge and skills required for China's modernization. It was essentially a peasant Party, and the bulk of its members, leaders and cadres alike, reflected this fact. Moreover, within a few years, the Party's old cadres, especially at the local levels, became—despite all of Mao's efforts to combat bureaucratism—an entrenched, highly stratified, privileged, bureaucratic elite. Seniority, measured by length of service in the Party, was often the most important criterion for career advancement. By the 1960s, Mao was so disturbed by what had happened to the Party since it had come to power that he decided to try to shake it up in an extremely radical way to try to revive revolutionary values. The result was the Cultural Revolution, in which the youth of the country were mobilized to attack both the Party and the government bureaucracies, and the result was a breakdown in the political system.

After Mao's death, when Deng emerged as China's supreme leader, he too recognized that to move China forward something fairly drastic had to be done about the system's aging bureaucracies and bureaucrats. His answer, however, was entirely different from Mao's. And it was much more sensible and successful. He engineered a remarkably peaceful transformation of the leadership and the bureaucracies that brought to power a new generation of people who were much better qualified to deal with the challenges of modernization.

I believe that my earlier thumbnail sketches of a few of the leaders I met in the west reflect fairly accurately the characteristics of the new generation of leaders. The majority I met were substantially younger than the people they replaced—often 10 or more years younger. The careers of most of them had focused on economic problems—and were very different from the careers of the majority of the older generation. In the Maoist period, the ladder of success in the political system was clogged by people experienced in Party affairs, military matters, propaganda and indoctrination, and public security and other security work. The majority of the new leaders were essentially economic technocrats. Many had graduated from universities—and therefore were much better educated than the men they replaced. Those who were not graduates of universities generally had acquired economic or technical expertise through long practical experience. A remarkable number of those who had risen to leadership positions were trained as engineers. Others had been educated in a variety of professional or technical fields; some were doctors and veterinarians, others had been professors, and so on.

I decided that the term *technocrat* is the most appropriate label for this new generation of leaders in China, if one uses the term in a laudatory rather than a pejorative sense. Those I met impressed me as being strongly and genuinely committed to the goals of economic development and modernization. For most of them, the Party's revolutionary struggle to achieve power was past history, not part of their own experience. With few exceptions, they seemed uninterested in ideology or dogma or revolutionary values rooted in the past. In a basic sense, their approach to problems, it seemed to me, was essentially pragmatic. I am sure that most of them would endorse Deng's often-quoted comment that the color of a cat is not important as long as it can catch mice.

I cannot claim that I learned what the inner thoughts of any of these leaders were. However, my impression was that all of them were strong supporters of the kind of economic reforms that Deng had promoted and wished to carry them further. It was more difficult to judge what their real views on political reforms were. Nevertheless, my guess was that their views were close to those of China's top reform leaders at that time—namely that political stability had to be given highest priority and that economic reforms should precede political reforms but that cautious steps toward political liberalization were both necessary and desirable because they were required for economic modernization.

It was remarkable, I thought, that Deng and his closest supporters were able to engineer such a far-reaching generational change so rapidly and with relatively little serious resistance. Choosing the new leaders must have been an extremely complex and competitive process, and I did not learn very much about the details of how it was carried out. However, I did learn a good deal about how Deng and his reformist supporters were able to minimize the resistance by old cadres. The strategy they adopted was very shrewd. Simply stated, they "bought off" the Party's old cadres (except a few at the very top of the regime) by giving them very generous retirement pay, granting them a very wide range of perquisites and benefits, treating all of them with great respect, appointing some of them to advisory and honorific positions, and establishing special Party organizations throughout the country to ensure that retired cadres, especially senior cadres, were treated well and provided with special facilities (which included a nationwide network of old cadre recreational centers, one of which I described in an earlier chapter).

The pace of change affecting the rank-and-file cadres staffing the middle and lower ranks of the bureaucracies was slower than in the case of senior cadres. Attempts to bring in new blood were under way, and in many places I saw evidence that some upgrading of the quality of cadres at lower levels had taken place. However, to raise the general level of the majority of the cadres would obviously take a long time. The shortage of well-trained people meant that it might take a generation or more to change the basic character of middle- and lower-level bureaucrats.

Beijing's reform proposals called for changing not just personnel but also the personnel system. Two kinds of changes were called for. One aimed at transferring decisionmaking power on many personnel matters—including appointments, promotions, and so on—to lower levels. Another called for reducing the responsibilities and sphere of control of the organization departments within the Party and granting greater responsibilities to personnel offices within the government and to enterprise managers in state enterprises. Where I was able to gather information about the implementation of these policies, it appeared that although personnel offices in government agencies and enterprise managers had acquired a degree of greater power, nowhere—as far as I could see—had the dominance of the Party in personnel matters been reduced sufficiently to alter the fundamental system.*

---

*After the Tiananmen crisis, conservative leaders pushed for greater rather than reduced Party control, and new regulations were issued that recentralized control over many appointments. My guess is, though, that this retrogression will be temporary because reform of the personnel system, which the leadership recognizes is clearly needed, *requires* greater decentralization.

*   *   *

In the 1980s, the conventional wisdom—certainly among most foreign observers but also among some Chinese I knew—was that although great progress was being made in economic reform, there was very little political reform. Some people argued that there had been *no* political reform. I disagree. It was certainly true that political change was lagging behind economic change. Deng Xiaoping and most other leading reformers stressed that at least in the initial period of reform, although structural change in the economy should move ahead, it was essential to maintain political stability, and this should be given priority over structural political reform. Virtually all of the top leaders warned that a two-party system might lead to chaos and maintained that continued leadership by the Communist Party was essential. Soon after economic reform was initiated, Deng himself put forward, in 1979, what were called the "four cardinal principles," which he said must undergird China's polity. The regime must uphold, he said, the socialist road, the people's democratic dictatorship, the leadership of the Party, and Marxism–Leninism–Mao Zedong Thought.

These slogans drew a line severely limiting political reform. However, as economic structural reform proceeded in the 1980s, the meanings of the socialist road, people's democratic dictatorship, and Marxism–Leninism–Mao Zedong Thought were increasingly ambiguous; they were constantly debated and redefined, and over time the principles looked increasingly elastic. They could be, and were, evoked by conservatives to justify periodic campaigns against "bourgeois liberalization," "spiritual pollution," and the danger of "peaceful evolution" (meaning the gradual subversion of the socialist system and reemergence of a capitalist system). They were also evoked by Deng himself to justify tough policies when he thought this necessary to preserve political order. Nevertheless, of the four principles, three gave a great deal of wriggle room for reform leaders to push ahead with economic reforms—and some political liberalization. The three principles were simply stretched to fit new realities and justify new policies. Only the principle of Party primacy seemed reasonably clear, and even it did not deter reformers from pressing for some political reforms, starting within the Party itself.

It was unquestionably true, nevertheless, that in the 1980s the majority of China's leaders, including the majority of even the Party's most ardent economic reformers, gave highest priority to political stability and were very cautious about political reform. This was certainly true of Deng, and it was even more true of some of the Party's most conservative elders, who were obsessed with the danger of chaos.

Yet in my judgment it is not correct to say that no significant political changes were taking place in China in the 1980s. Structural political change of the kind that would alter the basic political system in China had barely begun. Nevertheless, after traveling all over the country in 1988, I saw that some important political changes were under way and already had changed the way the political system operated, even though they had not changed the structure of the system. In the Maoist era, the political system in China was clearly *totalitarian;* by the late 1980s it already had evolved into a much looser form of liberalized *authoritarianism.*

In the late 1980s—before Tiananmen—many Chinese intellectuals and some leading reformers close to Party general secretary Zhao Ziyang were attracted by a concept that was labeled "neoauthoritarianism." The idea was formulated on the basis of the experience of Taiwan, Singapore, and South Korea. Chinese leaders, like people throughout the world, were greatly impressed by the economic performance of the regimes in all three of these places. They noted that all of them had strong leadership and fundamentally authoritarian regimes during the initial period of their economic growth and then moved toward political liberalization and ultimately to fairly far-reaching political reform at a later stage. Those Chinese who believed that this was a model appropriate for all of China argued that what was needed, during the initial period of modernization and rapid economic growth, was strong leadership and only cautious, controlled liberalization—a transitional period of paternalistic, benevolent authoritarianism leading at a later stage to more far-reaching political reform. (Although supporters of the idea of neoauthoritarianism had in the forefront of their thinking the experiences of Taiwan and the other "newly industrializing economies" in East Asia, the concept resonated also with Sun Yat-sen's idea of "political tutelage," promoted in the early part of the twentieth century.)

During the 1980s, many ideological, economic, and social changes were beginning to reshape Chinese society, and they were taking place in a political context that was very different from that of the Maoist period. The change from Mao-style totalitarianism to a looser form of liberalized authoritarianism involved significant alterations in the relationship of state and society, and, in my judgment, had begun to lay the basis for greater political changes later. I saw evidence of this all over China. Clearly the "center of the action" was in the coastal provinces, especially in the south; nevertheless, I felt that similar changes were taking place in west China, but somewhat later and with less far-reaching short-term consequences.

The redefinition of ideology, and—more important—its decline, were striking wherever I went in 1988. The decline was just as evident in the west as in the east. Everywhere, ideological slogans had virtually disappeared. I found that in most bookstores, Mao's writings had been shifted to the back shelves, and in some bookstores they had disappeared. As I said earlier, the leaders I met seemed preoccupied with practical economic problems and uninterested in ideology; this was even more true among ordinary people. The attention given to Mao, and to ideology in general, in curricula and textbooks in educational institutions at all levels had been drastically reduced. Even Party propagandists seemed to have redirected their attention from old ideological issues to propaganda in support of economic reform and mass education on things like the causes of inflation and the meaning of "commodity economy."

Intellectuals in Beijing in 1988 were engaged in lively debates about virtually every problem in China. They seemed to be much less constrained and inhibited than they had been for many years—perhaps since the Anti-Rightist Campaign in 1957. I met a number of intellectuals who were in the forefront of efforts to redefine ideology to fit the new reform policies. I also talked with some of those who were actively urging greater political reform and discussing alternative routes to reform. Among some, I sensed an undercurrent of anxiety about what might happen to them if there were to be major political retrogression under conservative leaders. However, most of those I met seemed determined to take advantage of the loosening of controls to speak out, and many were audacious in publicly supporting unorthodox opinions. China's policy of opening to the outside world, though motivated primarily by economic aims, opened China to a remarkable exposure to information and ideas of all sorts, and the rapid development of electronic media in the 1980s meant that new information and ideas from abroad were circulating throughout the country. Artists were experimenting with formerly banned styles. Filmmakers were producing entirely new kinds of movies. Journalists were pressing the limits of censorship. Educators were trying to expand their ties with academic institutions and scholars abroad and to reform their own teaching methods and curricula.

Among youths, I found virtually no interest in 1988 in traditional Marxist–Leninist–Mao Zedong ideology. University and middle school students were avidly reading the writings of well-known Western thinkers. In east China, there was a remarkable revival of religion—especially Christianity, which attracted many young people (by the late 1980s, there were more Christians in China than there had been before the Communist takeover). In west China there was also a revival of interest in religion, although it varied from place to place. My impression, however, was that probably the majority of young people were basically cynical and agnostic. I frequently heard criticism from older Chinese of the seeming preoccupation of youths with money and foreign ideas.

Most of the places I visited in west China in 1988 were far from the main centers of intellectual ferment and ideological change in east China. Many of the intellectuals, journalists, and students I met obviously felt their isolation acutely, and some of them talked plaintively about their sense of isolation. But with the loosening of political controls and the development of modern communications, they were trying to keep up with changing trends in China and the outside world. Everywhere I went in the west, moreover, I saw signs that changes in the east were at least reverberating in the distant western areas. For example, journalists in Inner Mongolia described their efforts to develop "investigative reporting"; they had been inspired by the audacious reporting and commentary of journals such as the *World Economic Herald* in Shanghai. Even though their efforts were a pale reflection of the real thing, they obviously wanted to try to keep up with changes in the east.

Professors and graduate students in Lanzhou discussed the contacts they had developed with scholars and institutions abroad and described how they were trying to reshape programs and courses, on the basis of what they were learning abroad, to make higher education more relevant to China's needs in an era of reform. In Qinghai, Party propagandists discussed how, even in that remote province, young people were fascinated by the ideas of a wide variety of Western thinkers, such as Freud and Sartre. The Party no longer banned the writings of such thinkers, but the task of the propaganda apparatus now was to convince young people that they were false idols. Everywhere I went in 1988, even in the remotest areas of west China, I saw some signs— not necessarily dramatic ones, but significant ones nevertheless—that the winds of change coming from the east were reaching the far west. (There were winds of change coming from the west too, and I have no doubt that they increased significantly during 1989–1991 as a result of the dramatic political changes in Eastern Europe and the Soviet Union. However, in 1988 there was no doubt that the strongest winds were coming from the east, and my guess is that that is still true.)

The Tiananmen crises in 1989, followed by the efforts of conservative Party elders to reimpose ideological and political controls, immediately changed the political climate in China, and the repressive policies adopted cast a pall over the main centers of intellectual ferment in China. In my judgment, for a wide variety of reasons (some of which I have discussed earlier in this volume and others of which I will elaborate upon later), the leadership no longer had the ability to impose controls as tight as those in the Maoist era. And the effects were therefore relatively limited and superficial, even on those groups who were the main targets—intellectuals, students, and workers who had been involved in leading demonstrations in 1989—and the effects on ordinary Chinese throughout the country were extremely limited. The opening of China, the communications revolution, and the information explosion had let a genie out of its bottle, and there was no way that the conservative octogenarians in Beijing could rebottle it. I had no doubt that unrelenting pressures from below, as well as the winds of change from abroad, would lead future leaders to relax controls again and return to a path of cautious political liberalization. In 1988, I felt that the pressures for change in west China were similar to those in the east, although not quite as strong as in the east, and the processes of change there were a little slower.

*   *   *

Something else that I observed everywhere I traveled in China in 1988 was a steady widening of the gaps between generations, which almost guarantees an acceleration of change in the future. I use the plural word *gaps* with good reason. The growing generational differences and tensions now are not just between "young people" and "elders": There are numerous cleavages between different age groups. At the top, the differences between the last remaining Communist Party elders from the initial revolutionary generation and the technocratic leaders now coming to power impressed me as being much wider than it seems to be on the surface. These differences will become more apparent, I believe, once all the founding fathers have disappeared.

Below the top, there now are many "generational" layers of Chinese; their attitudes vary, depending on what their experiences have been in the most important formative periods of their lives. China's history has been so tumultuous during the twentieth century that age differences of even a few years often created "generations" whose experiences and outlooks were quite different.

Some elderly Chinese seem to be trapped in the past—frozen in amber. A large number of middle-aged people who have lived through both the endless campaigns of the Maoist era and the rapid changes of the post-Mao era seem to be highly ambivalent about how to draw a balance sheet of China's past triumphs and tragedies. Among those now in their late thirties or early forties who joined the Red Guards during the Cultural Revolution, there are some, often labeled a "lost generation," who remember the exhilaration of worshipping Mao and "making revolution" but are now disillusioned and bitter about having lost their education, having been tossed aside, and having been ultimately sent down to the countryside. Others, of that same age, have been able to make up their lost education, and some of them now feel that they have special insight into China's problems. Almost all of them have acquired experience in political activism; some may soon begin to rise to leadership positions. Many other "generational" differences are also important, for example, the difference between those who were educated in the Soviet Union in the 1950s and those who were educated in the West in the 1970s and 1980s.

By the late 1980s it was clear that perhaps the greatest generational divide now is between young Chinese in their teens and twenties and everyone older than that. This is China's first "TV generation," and they have been bombarded by Western pop culture imported from abroad—or perhaps it should be called the contemporary "world youth culture"—which has somehow mysteriously jumped over all political and other barriers and spread to virtually every part of the globe. From those I met in 1988 it became clear that they are fascinated by everything to do with foreign countries and foreign cultures. Many are inclined to reject a great deal of China's own traditional culture. Almost all of the middle-aged Chinese intellectuals that I know bemoan the attitudes of almost all youths below their thirties. A cliché, which I heard numerous times in 1988, criticizes the entire younger generation for having "a horizontal rather than a vertical perspective." Translated, this means that the younger generation seems to be hypnotized by foreign cultures (that is, they have a "horizontal perspective") but are seemingly contemptuous of China's own society and culture (that is, they lack a "vertical perspective").

In 1988—before Tiananmen—most older Chinese also accused the younger generation of being crassly materialistic, uninterested in education, and politically apathetic. These characterizations seemed valid for many of the younger Chinese that I met at that time. Less than a year later, though, many of these same young people were among those who created the most dramatic political explosion in the entire period since the Communist takeover in China.

Although in 1988 young people in coastal cities were in the forefront of all of these trends, I was repeatedly startled to see evidence of the spread throughout the country, even to very remote western areas, of foreign influences, particularly Western pop culture as well as Western fads and ideas. The visual evidence that the younger generation, even in the west, was growing up in a very different world from that of their elders, was ubiquitous: breakdancing in a small town en route to a remote lamasery in Inner Mongolia; high-heeled young Uighur waitresses trying to keep up with Western fashions in the ancient city of Turfan in Xinjiang; middle school–aged children in southern Yunnan singing love songs popularized by a Taiwanese singer; disco dancers gyrating under strobe lights in Lanzhou and elsewhere; young cadres watching a Mexican TV soap opera in Qinghai, not far from the Tibetan grasslands; and a group of young people watching a British comedy of manners on TV in a remote town in western Sichuan, not far from panda country; and so on.

In 1988, when I attempted to engage young people in discussion of politics—or ideology—most of them with whom I talked (apart from students in a few major universities) did seem politically apathetic and showed relatively little interest in the state of political affairs in China. As I stated earlier, most older people with whom I talked were disturbed by this fact. The majority of older people—even those who were only a little older than China's first TV generation—were clearly bewildered by the impact of all the new cultural influences that were shaping young people's lives (much as many older Americans were bewildered by the effects of the "cultural revolution" in American universities in the late 1960s).

It is probably too early, in my opinion, to predict what the long-term effect of this "modern cultural revolution" on China's youths may be. Intellectual

trends can change rapidly, in China as elsewhere. I can think of many different countries where young people below a certain age seem to be totally out
of phase with their elders, but then these same young people, when they are
slightly older, seem remarkably similar to the generations that have gone before. The great differences between the prevailing perceptions of China's
young people—among older Chinese as well as foreigners—in 1988, and
what actually happened in 1989, argues for caution in predicting how China's first TV generation will act and what impact it will have on Chinese society and Chinese politics once they are older.

Having said that, I have little doubt that the 1980s will prove to be an important dividing line between generations in China. The generation that has
grown up in the 1980s has been exposed to and shaped by external influences, as well as by the reformist trends changing Chinese society, to a much
greater extent, in my opinion, than past generations. Their knowledge of the
rest of the world, or at least the world immediately around China, is greater,
and their expectations for China are higher in many respects than any generation in the recent past. It is almost certain, I think, that it is a generation that
will favor far-reaching change—motivated, if nothing else, by the feeling
that China must try to catch up with the major developed countries. If future
Chinese leaders try to cling to the past, they are unlikely to find much support among the younger generation and might well encounter either passive
or active opposition. Conversely, if future Party reform leaders try to mobilize support from the younger generation, my guess it that they will be at
least partially successful in doing so. I also suspect, though, that no matter
how much progress is made, it is unlikely to satisfy many young Chinese,
who I expect will push for even faster change and greater progress, which future leaders will find it difficult to achieve.

                        *   *   *

Many of the changes in China that struck me as being most important in
the late 1980s were economic ones. But I thought the generational changes
and trend toward political relaxation and liberalization were also extremely
important. I also saw small but nevertheless significant social changes that
pointed toward increased pluralism of society. In recent years, academic specialists on China in the West, and some scholars in China, have debated, in-
conclusively, the questions of how important nongovernment and relatively
autonomous social organizations have been in China in the past and what
the prospects are for the emergence in the future of greater social pluralism
that would change the relationship of state and society and lay the basis for
democratization. My own view, simply stated, is that in imperial China, despite the clear domination of state over society, there nevertheless was considerable social pluralism, and nongovernmental organizations, including
clans, guilds, secret societies, religious organizations, and "associations" and

"societies" of varied kinds, played important roles in society. In a sense, they constituted a kind of "informal government" that regulated many areas of economic, social, and even political life—even though they themselves were subordinate to and regulated by the state. Many—perhaps most—of these organizations (with the notable exception of some of the secret societies) were never fully autonomous and rarely attempted to challenge the dominance of the state. Many of them functioned, therefore, as adjuncts to government. Nevertheless, they were able to protect and to promote local and group interests, and at the local level they often performed some of the functions of political interest groups.

In the period of Nationalist rule, while there were important changes in government and politics at the national level, in much of rural China traditional social organizations continued to be active, and in many places they still dominated the local political scene. (I learned this in 1948 when I studied local government and politics in Xiemaxiang, a township in Sichuan Province, where the centuries-old "secret society," the Gelaohui, together with gentrylike landlord groups, dominated government and politics and the Nationalist Party played a very minor role.)

Following its takeover of power, the Chinese Communist Party, as part of its program to revolutionize Chinese society, systematically and rapidly dismantled and destroyed the pre-1949 structure of nongovernmental organizations in China. To replace old economic and social institutions, the Party rapidly built a new structure consisting of Party committees and branches and mass organizations at the grass-roots level under Party control. Special organizations were established for virtually every important major social group in China—peasants, urban workers, women, youth, students, each major religious group, and intellectuals as well as all important subgroups of China's intellectual and cultural elite, such as artists, writers, every professional group, and so on. The old social structure was atomized; what replaced it was a highly politicized and centralized structure under Communist leadership and control. As a result, the political system was transformed into a modern totalitarian polity, which, in contrast to traditional authoritarianism, intervened into virtually every aspect of social life.

As the reform process unfolded in China in the 1980s, even though there was little structural change in the political system—that is, it remained a monolithic, one-party system—nevertheless many things affecting the relationship between state and society did change, some obviously, some subtly. By the end of the decade the Party no longer dominated society to the extent that it had in earlier years. Although the legitimacy of the Party was not totally destroyed, as was the case in the USSR and Eastern Europe, the prestige of the Party declined, and its authority was weakened. This was a result of trends that had started many years before and reached a climax during the Cultural Revolution, when the Party's role in China reached its nadir. Although the Party was rebuilt during the 1970s and early 1980s, its prestige and authority were eroded again by the widespread corruption that was a by-product of the reforms of the 1980s. In the new circumstances of the 1980s, the loosening of political controls, and the opening of China's doors to foreign influences, contributed to a further weakening of the monolithic Communist structure that had been built in the early days of the regime and to the growth of both intellectual and social pluralism.

Most important, the spread of economic reforms resulted in greater economic pluralism, especially in the nonstate sectors. This was the result of decentralization, the growth of collective (semiprivate) and private enterprises, and the crystallization of new economic interests and groupings. Even though these trends did not immediately result in any dramatic growth of political pluralism, they gradually lay the foundations for greater political pluralism in the future. Trends in the 1980s were a little like the effects of a thaw on an ice cap. What previously had been fairly uniform and homogenous began to show cracks and fissures, and even though the ice cap did not break up, it began to move and change its shape.

The signs—or at least the hints—of growing economic cum intellectual and social pluralism in the 1980s were numerous. They were most evident in major cities, especially in coastal provinces, but in some interior areas too. There was, for example, a remarkable proliferation of intellectual and professional organizations and journals. Newly emerging economic interest groups—especially those involved in the rapidly growing collective and private sectors of the economy—began actively lobbying central leaders on issues relevant to their interests. Bureaucratic politics, which had always been important in the Chinese Communist system, now intensified and new alignments and alliances emerged within the bureaucracies. New entrepreneurs, some of them with very substantial economic clout, attempted to promote their interests—sometimes with the help of foreign businessmen—by lobbying Party and government officials at various levels of the system, including the very top.

In west China, even though the signs of increased intellectual, economic, and social pluralism were less palpable, they nevertheless were recognizable—for example, in the new citywide association organized in Baotou to represent the interests of the 5,000 or so entrepreneurs who had established small industrial factories or workshops; in the emergence in Qinghai of 50-odd associations, societies, and institutes listed as members of the developing "social science" community; and so on. These were only small cracks in the iceberg, which were far less important than many of the trends toward pluralism evolving in east China, but I felt that they were hints of things to come.

We will probably see, in the period ahead, a steady—and probably accelerating—development of economic pluralism as China moves closer to a market economy. This will produce greater social pluralism, and I have no doubt that in time it will eventually result in greater pressure for a more pluralistic political system.

The Tiananmen crisis of 1989 did not, in my opinion, reverse these trends; it did not even stop them from going forward. On visits to Beijing and Shanghai in the early 1990s, I saw new signs of trends toward greater pluralization. For example, I learned about several newly established foundations. They were extremely interesting organizations of a new type—funded by a variety of sources, including some of China's rich, new private entrepreneurs as well as some government agencies. These foundations were developing programs of research and publications that dealt with economic, social, military, and foreign policies. The foundations I learned about were attempting to promote further reform, and they were independently formulating and putting forward new ideas about how best to proceed with reform. I do not wish to exaggerate the significance of such trends—or straws in the wind; so far their political impact has been limited. Yet they are potentially important. I believe that when future leaders shift from political repression back to political liberalization, as I am confident they will at some point, there will be a more rapid development of interest groups in China, and in time this will have a significant impact on politics. Some Chinese reformers whom I know have predicted that the development of stronger interest groups in society will probably lead first to the emergence of interest-based factions or opinion groups within the Party and government and that these may eventually lay a basis for a multiparty system.

*   *   *

The political change that impressed me the most in the 1980s was one that was difficult to describe. In 1988, when I tried to define the most important political difference between what I observed and felt at that time with what I had seen earlier, both in the pre-1949 period and in the late Maoist period, I decided that it was simply the change in the overall political atmosphere. I remembered the conversations I had had in the 1970s, before the start of reforms in China—even those I had with Chinese I knew well, some of whom I had first met in the 1940s. All of them were extremely cautious in what they said, and it was obvious to me that the deadening effects of totalitarian control continued to constrain and inhibit everyone and prevented them from giving their own personal views if they varied in any way from the official Party line. It seemed that almost everyone was anxiously looking over his or her shoulder. It was totally unacceptable for people to discuss personal feelings and hopes, especially if they betrayed "bourgeois" desires to live better or to avoid politics. Unrelenting social pressures were exerted on everyone to submit and conform.

In short, in the 1970s the totalitarian apparatus of social and political controls that had been developed during the Maoist period still dominated not only the political system as a whole but also the lives of ordinary people throughout the country. The Party-controlled mass organizations and "small groups" at the grass-roots level enmeshed the population in an organizational web that exposed them to relentless propaganda and indoctrination and guaranteed that they would be pressured by their peers if they showed any signs of nonconformity or deviance. In the background, the coercive apparatus of both the Party and the state stood ready to punish everyone who got out of line.

During the 1980s, the political temper of the country underwent profound changes. Some of the trends at that time—including the gradual steps toward the creation of a new legal system, the leadership's efforts to regularize and institutionalize decisionmaking, attempts to make the political process both more predictable and more "transparent," and even, in some places, the efforts to make local elections meaningful—pointed toward changes that were potentially important even to reform of the basic structure of the system. But such changes were only in their early stages, and they were not, in my opinion, what had the greatest immediate impact on ordinary people in the 1980s. What altered the political climate was more subtle: People's fear began to dissipate. They began to open up and speak out. There was change in the air. I found this change in the climate all over the country, in the far west as well as in the east.

It is difficult to characterize the overall thrust of political trends in the 1980s. It was a period of steady loosening of ideological and political controls. Political decontrol led toward social relaxation, and some people clearly had a sense of political liberation. By the late 1980s, the penetration of Chinese society by the Party and the state had been substantially reduced. Many areas of life were almost totally depoliticized and decontrolled. The force of ideology declined greatly, and many people simply ignored old dogmas—something they could not do in the Maoist era. The majority of ordinary people could once again—for the first time in several decades—pursue their own private, nonpolitical goals, without guilt or fear of retribution. The regime no longer attempted to carry out major Maoist-style mass campaigns of the kind that had engulfed and convulsed almost all of China during the Maoist period. The campaigns that were launched in the 1980s had much more limited objectives, affected fewer people, and had less far-reaching consequences. The propaganda apparatus devoted less time to Marxist dogma and more to economic problems—except during the periodic but relatively brief campaigns against "bourgeois" liberalization. Formal indoctrination efforts were greatly diminished, and, for most people directly involved, they became increasingly routinized.

The Party no longer deified any of Beijing's leaders. At the grass-roots level, there was a similar trend, and local Party leaders no longer seemed omnipotent. Recruitment of new Party members continued, but increasingly it seemed as if few of the new recruits were "true believers"; more and more of them appeared to be careerists who joined the Party because Party membership was a kind of union card, necessary for jobs in the government or in the Party itself. But young people now had a variety of career options, and some of the best and brightest turned away from the Party to business and other careers in which they could make more money. In rural areas, the army as well as the Party found it increasingly difficult to recruit the ablest young people.

The regime's coercive apparatus was still there, but more and more it seemed to stand on the sidelines, watching but not doing very much about trends that in the Maoist era would have provoked a tough clampdown and effort to restore control and end deviation. Gradually, as reforms progressed and controls were loosened, the majority of the population turned their attention away from the Party and politics and concentrated on improving their lives.

The process of political change in the 1980s did not follow a straight line, nor was it smooth. As the economy experienced alternating periods of rapid growth and retrenchment—a boom and bust pattern—so too did politics. The political cycle was described by some Chinese as consisting of alternate periods of *fang* (release or relaxation) and *shou* (a tightening). Every few years, relatively conservative people in the leadership who were concerned about both the pace of reform and the side effects of reform were able to launch ideological campaigns designed to combat "bourgeois liberalization" and "spiritual pollution" and to prevent "peaceful evolution." What was noteworthy about these campaigns was that they were relatively brief and had limited effects. At the start, the campaigns frightened Chinese intellectuals, who dreaded the possibility of a return to Maoist-style control, but over time it became clear that Beijing's conservatives were either unable or unwilling (or both) to return to the past and reestablish old controls and revive old dogmas. Moreover, the political campaigns in the 1980s had relatively little effect on the mass of ordinary people (although the campaigns for birth control and against crime did).

As the regime's ideological grip loosened, its use of coercive instruments of rule slackened. All Chinese were still very much aware that these coercive instruments—the army, the People's Armed Police, the uniformed police, the secret police, the prisons, and the labor camps—were still there. Even when the general trend toward political liberalization was at its height, the regime did not hesitate to use coercion to suppress open political dissidence, to combat crime, and to deal firmly with any trends that seemed to threaten social stability. Nevertheless, during most of the 1980s—until 1989—coercive instruments were used more sparingly than was the case in the Maoist era, and they impinged much less than they had in the past on the day-to-day activities of ordinary people.

In 1988, I found that the processes of political liberalization and the relaxation of political controls were just as evident in west China as in the east. If anything, in fact, it seemed to me that ideological and political controls were even looser in the west. From Inner Mongolia to Xinjiang to Yunnan, the majority of people I met were remarkably uninhibited in expressing their personal opinions; the majority seemed to have turned away from politics and ideology. Almost none of them, as far as I could tell, were fearful of speaking out frankly. This surprised me. I had expected that in such distant places local people might feel uneasy about talking to a foreigner; I assumed that I would be under constant surveillance. I knew that foreign correspondent friends of mine had felt that they were constantly bugged, watched, and followed, not just in Beijing but even more so when they traveled to remote places. They were probably right—and their experience inevitably colored their view of China. However, my experience was quite different, and I concluded at the end of my travels in 1988 that as a result of the steady process of political liberalization during the 1980s, both Party and police controls had loosened greatly and that most ordinary people, particularly those in rural areas, had relatively little contact with the instruments of coercion and in general could ignore them.

Knowing the experience some of my correspondent friends had had, I made a special effort, everywhere I went in 1988, to be alert for any evidence of bugging or surveillance. I saw virtually none. I also tried to be particularly alert to any sign that my interlocutors were fearful about speaking frankly to me, and as I said earlier, I concluded that most of them were not. If any reader feels that this shows that I am either naive or unobservant, I will simply say that I have experienced bugging and surveillance on a number of occasions in the past, both in China and elsewhere, and therefore, although I claim no expertise about such matters, I am at least aware of things to look for. Of course, I recognize that local authorities could keep track of me, in a general way, quite easily, without any special surveillance, since my academic escorts were with me most of the time. However, none of my escorts were anything like the traditional Communist enforcers of ideological and political discipline, and their presence never seemed to inhibit local people I met—and certainly did not inhibit me. In sum, by the end of my travels in 1988 I was convinced that the gradual process of political liberalization in China had significantly changed the political climate throughout the country, in the far west as well as in the east.

*   *   *

Then, in mid-1989, the Tiananmen tragedy brought to an abrupt halt the liberalizing trend of the previous period. Conservative ideologues in Beijing reimposed strict controls over the media, tried to reemphasize ideologically based values, and attempted to intensify reindoctrination efforts. The police apparatus came out of the shadows, and its presence once again was very evident, at least in Beijing. Intellectuals hunkered down; public debates stopped. On the surface, the political mood again appeared to be one of silent conformity.

However, I soon concluded—after several post-Tiananmen trips to China, starting in fall 1989—that the real effects of the clampdown were much more limited than they appeared on the surface. The repression was real, but it focused on a relatively small group of intellectuals, students, and workers who had played leading roles in the 1989 demonstration, and its effects on the majority of the population were limited. The intensified propaganda and indoctrination campaigns stopped intellectuals and students from public debate and criticism of the Party, but they had very little effect on what they thought or said privately; those undergoing indoctrination expressed contempt of the process, and they had little hesitation in talking to friends. Relatively few intellectuals were arrested, or even lost their jobs. And there was no general purge within the Party and government. Virtually all the leading reformers, except for a small group closely linked to Zhao Ziyang, continued to sit in their old seats, kept their mouths shut, and bided their time. Most of the Chinese I knew were convinced that the process of political liberalization would resume, sooner or later—after future changes in the leadership, if not before—and they differed mainly on whether it would be sooner or later.

My own view was that even though the Tiananmen crisis had delivered a grievous blow to China, it had not stopped the process of economic reform, and the setback to political liberalization was only partial and likely to be temporary. It seemed to me that the majority of Chinese leaders—at least the majority of reform-minded leaders, of the kind that I thought were likely to dominate in the post-Deng period—recognized that economic and political reform were unavoidably linked. They differed on exactly what kind of political reform should be fostered, and at what pace. They also differed on whether political and economic reform should be carried out in tandem or whether economic reform should precede political reform (very few, it seemed to me, felt that it was wise to push ahead with political reform first, as Communist leaders in the Soviet Union and Eastern Europe had done).

In the period just before Tiananmen, there had been very lively debate on political reform in China. Some intellectuals had called for rapid steps in the direction of Western-style democracy. However, relatively few people, even among China's urban elites, felt that this was feasible, and this view appeared to have almost no resonance in rural China. I think the desire for political liberalization of some sort had, by 1988, become very widespread, certainly among intellectuals but also among broader urban groups. Many ideas were floated. My impression was that the majority of the proponents of political reform recognized that gradual incremental reform was more likely to succeed than attempts to carry out drastic, sudden changes of the political system. Not only within the Party and government, but also within a great many groups of reform-minded intellectuals, there was a feeling that sudden, drastic reform might lead to social instability and political backlash and that therefore gradual, step-by-step reforms were preferable. I think that the disintegrating effects that rapid political change had in the Soviet Union and Eastern Europe confirmed a great many Chinese in their view that incremental political reform was preferable.

Before Tiananmen, of the many ideas about political reform that were discussed, the concept that was labeled "neoauthoritarianism" gained fairly wide support, both within the Party and among intellectuals. Supporters of the idea argued that the experience of the four "little tigers" in East Asia— Taiwan, Hong Kong, Singapore, and South Korea—provided models that might well be applicable to China. The experience in these four places demonstrated, it was argued, that it was desirable first to emphasize economic development and reform. During this initial period, which some argued might last perhaps two, three, or more decades, there was a need for strong leadership. Cautious steps toward liberalization could be taken, but what was most important was to maintain political stability. Then, after economic development had produced higher living standards, a better level of education, and a new middle class, there would be a basis for more far-reaching structural political reform. This concept of neoauthoritarianism attracted support from the Party's General Secretary Zhao Ziyang and Party reformers close to him, and even Deng Xiaoping seemed to find it tolerable—although his "four cardinal principles" placed much more emphasis on political stability than on political reform. Gradually a consensus seemed to emerge among the reformers closest to Zhao on a strategy to push political reform forward, in a cautious, incremental fashion.

At the 13th Party Congress, in October 1987, Zhao Ziyang, in his report to the Congress, first emphasized the need to push forward economic reform, but then he asserted that it was "high time to put reform of the political structure on the agenda of the whole Party." Crediting Deng for starting a process of political reform in 1980 when he called for reform of the "system of Party and state leadership," Zhao then stated that the Party's aim was "socialist democracy" and that "without reform of the political structure, reform of the economic structure cannot succeed in the end." The basic purpose of political reform, he said, was to support economic development. He then proceeded to put forward a seven-point program for "gradual, cumulative" political reform. The seven points call for (1) separating Party and government, (2) delegating powers to lower levels, (3) reforming government organs, (4) reforming the personnel system, (5) promoting political consultation and dialogue, (6) improving the basis for socialist education, and (7) strengthening the socialist legal system. He discussed, briefly, what each of these planks in his platform meant. Zhao made clear that what he was proposing was reform from within the existing political system. He insisted that continued leadership by the Communist Party was essential, and he specifically rejected the Western model of multiparty competition and a separation of powers, saying that they were inappropriate for China. The reform program he proposed fell far short, obviously, of what supporters of Western-type democracy called for. It sounded similar in many respects, in fact, to what Mikhail Gorbachev tried—but failed—to do in the Soviet Union. However, many of the reform-minded Chinese I knew felt that a process of incremental reform such as Zhao proposed probably had better chances of succeeding in China than the kind of change taking place in the Soviet Union. They also felt that if even modest political reforms could be effectively implemented, they could start a process of political change that could go much further than the initial proposals.

*   *   *

In April 1988, half a year after the 13th Party Congress (and roughly a year before the June 1989 crisis), I had a long interview in Beijing with Zhao's principal adviser on political reform—Bao Tong—who had played a large role in formulating the political reform program put forward by Zhao. Explaining the background to the reform proposals, Bao Tong said that in September 1986 Zhao had established a small group to formulate a specific program of political reform: the Political Structural Reform Research and Discussion Small Group; Zhao himself headed it, and Bao Tong was in charge of the most important office under it. Just "one year and 10 days later," this study group was replaced, at the time of the 13th Party Congress, by a formal organization called the Office of Political Structural Reform. Bao Tong was appointed head of this office, which had a staff of about 20; of these, 2 were brought by Bao Tong to the meeting with me. The office made recommendations that were sent straight to the Politburo's Standing Committee—although some also went at the same time to the Party Secretariat. Bao Tong outlined for me, in some detail, what he believed to be the most important features of the program for political reform. What he told me is worth reporting in some detail. His views clearly reflected the views at that time of the leading reformers in the Chinese Communist Party—before the Tiananmen disaster. I believe that when political reform moves forward again in China, Bao Tong's plan of action could well be revived and have a significant influence on future trends.

In the early stages of political reform, Bao Tong said, highest priority was being given to the "separation of Party and government" and the "separation of Party and enterprises." The Party hoped to complete this relatively soon at two levels—the very top and the very bottom of the political system, that is, in Beijing and in townships at the lowest grass-roots level. Carrying it out at the "middle levels" of the political system—in prefectures and counties—would come somewhat later. The basic aim, he said, was to differentiate the functions of Party and other institutions much more clearly than in the past not only to eliminate conflicting and overlapping responsibilities but also—most important—to put an end to the Party's excessive day-to-day interventions into economic and other non-Party affairs.

In carrying this out, a number of specific steps were required. The regime had started to abolish the Party's "core groups" ("fractions") in government bodies and the leading bodies of mass organizations in Beijing. The first core groups to be abolished were those in ministries and other top-level bodies that were responsible for the systems (*xitong*) responsible for all economic matters. After this was done at the central level, it would be done at all local levels. They had not yet decided, but were considering, when and how to abolish the core groups in central government bodies responsible for the political-legal and cultural-educational *xitong*. Discussing the importance of abolishing the core groups, Bao Tong stated that before the 13th Party Congress, Party core groups in all the central ministries were appointed by, and received direct orders from, the Central Committee and Secretariat. Already, the old system had been changed, and the Secretariat no longer was trying to supervise day-to-day governmental matters. And once the economic "core groups" in government bodies dealing with economic matters were abolished, the way in which the government ran economic affairs would have changed in a major way.

The Central Committee had always kept a very tight control of the cultural-educational and political-legal fields, and the core groups would continue to function in these fields for some time. However, he said, most of the responsibility for supervising these fields had recently been transferred from the Central Committee to the State Council—although their core groups had still not been eliminated, and would not be until sometime later. Eventually the core groups would disappear from all ministries—and later on, all organizations. Once this had been accomplished, the role of the premier would be strengthened. The premier would have primary responsibility for coordinating every functional system in the government, and the way in which he exercised this responsibility would be different from in the past. In the past, the State Council had under it a number of fairly large bureaucratic organizations responsible for coordinating and supervising every field. In the future, one state councillor would be designated to supervise each functional field; each would have a small staff and would report directly to the premier and, in effect, act as the premier's assistant for the field. Until recently, each of these coordinating points under the premier had been called *kou,* but this term was no longer used.*

Bao Tong said that once the political reform process really got under way at the provincial and lower levels, several significant changes would take place in the organization of leading bodies and their division of responsibilities. Formerly, he said, Provincial Party Committees tried to do too much and had intervened too much in government affairs. These Party Committees bore overall responsibility for everything in their areas, and until recently they each had had Party deputy secretaries responsible for every major functional field: political-legal affairs, cultural-educational affairs, industry and transport, finance and trade, and agriculture and trade. The Party Committees also had under them Party Departments, each with its own staff (sometimes fairly large), which exercised direct supervision of each functional field. The plan now was to cut the number of Party deputy secretaries and abolish all the Party departments responsible for economic affairs. The general pattern in the future would be for a Party Committee to have three deputy secretaries, one responsible for Party affairs, one for ideology and propaganda, and one for general supervision of "government work." Bao repeated that eventually all "core groups" at every level would be abolished. There would still be deputy governors (and deputy mayors and deputy magistrates) responsible for supervising the major economic fields—but not the political-legal and cultural-educational fields, which had always been directly supervised by the Party and would continue to be in the period ahead until they were abolished.

After spending a good deal of time discussing changes of this kind, I think Bao Tong sensed that, although I was very interested, I was a little skeptical about the significance of such changes. I said what I had been thinking: that although I could see the rationale for such changes, it seemed to me that they really did not change the structure of political power in any fundamental way. Perhaps not, he said, but he then went on to say why he thought the changes were really important. "In the real world," he stated, "to carry out

---

*Bao Tong was aware that in an interview with me in July 1984 then-premier Zhao Ziyang had told me that at the pinnacle of the political system in Beijing, top-level policymaking had been shifted in the early 1980s from the Politburo and its Standing Committee to the Party Secretariat—probably about the time of the 12th Party Congress in 1982. Bao Tong confirmed that this had been the case, but he then said that after the 13th Party Congress the locus of the most important day-to-day policy decisions had shifted back to the Standing Committee of the Politburo, which he said was meeting approximately once a week, and to the Politburo itself. However, he added, some extremely important issues were still decided by the larger Politburo, which usually met about once a month. The Secretariat had reverted to its earlier role; it now passed most important issues on to the Standing Committee for decisions.

work, the Party and the government must have specific entities assigned to do the work. If the entities are abolished, the work cannot be done. Then, functions change. The assignment of personnel to specific responsibility determines where and what work is actually done in the Party and government. The changes we are making are *real*." On reflection, I agreed that the changes *could,* under some circumstances, have important effects.

Another high priority aim, Bao Tong said, was "reform of the personnel system"; this was already under way. It called for a redistribution of power to make appointments, from Party to government and from higher levels to lower levels; setting new criteria for selecting and appointing personnel; and dealing with many practical questions such as adjusting cadres' salaries. The regime had also committed itself, he said, to a very important long-run objective: electing many of the key top officials and then creating a genuine civil service system to select the rest on the basis of examinations. The shift of appointment-making power to lower levels in the system was also important, he said, in part because overconcentration made it impossible for people at the top to do the job well but also because when personnel assignments were made at the level at which people would serve—or, at most, only one level above that—they should be better, because the people making appointments were better informed about the jobs to be filled and the qualifications required. To illustrate the problem of overcentralized appointment power, Bao Tong cited his own experience. When he worked for the Organization Department of the Party's Central Committee, he said, that department had a staff of about 200 to handle more than 10,000 top-level appointments at both the central and lower levels. They were not able to handle that many effectively. Recently, their workload had been substantially reduced, and now they had to appoint only "several thousand" (he was reluctant to try to give a specific figure from memory).

Bao Tong talked at some length, with great enthusiasm—in fact, I would say, with passion—about the importance of the change in criteria for selecting people for leading cadres positions, all over the country. Starting in 1983–1984, he said, the effort was made everywhere to find and promote to leadership positions cadres who were younger, better educated, and more professional. He cited a few figures to show how far-reaching the consequences had been. In the 1970s, he said, the average age of ministers and deputy ministers in Beijing had been over 60; by the late 1980s, it had dropped to a figure in the 50s. In the 1970s, county magistrates had been, on average, in their fifties; now the average was roughly 10 years younger than that. In most provinces, the majority of the top group of Party and government leaders were new appointees; usually in these provincial bodies there were only one or two holdovers from the 1970s. He cited Guizhou Province as one example: among the top 17 Party and government leaders, there was only one holdover from the 1970s. Of the old cadres who were retired, some of the ablest ones had become members of local People's Congresses or People's Political Consultative Conferences; the majority were fully retired.

One of the most interesting changes in personnel policy focused on the leadership in economic enterprises. Formerly, he said, at local levels the Party almost always chose the ablest young cadres to serve in the apparatus of the Party itself. Now, the Party was giving priority to economic development and reform, and under this new policy the position of enterprise manager was supposed to be more important than even that of Party secretary; the new policy, therefore, was to choose the ablest young cadres and encourage them to become enterprise managers. As a result, he said, the "central position" (that is, the most important position) in a great many enterprises was now the position of manager, and the quality of people selected to be managers was steadily rising. He estimated that in close to one-half of all large and medium-sized state enterprises in the country, the shift of top authority from the Party secretary to the enterprise manager had already taken place. This shift did not always involve the selection of a new manager, but in a great many cases it did. When the old manager was obviously capable, he generally kept his job. In perhaps a fifth or so of large and medium-sized state enterprises, the Party secretary was obviously the ablest person, and he was shifted into the job of enterprise manager. However, in a growing number of enterprises, there had been open competition ("bidding") for the manager's job. Bao Tong estimated that, so far, perhaps a tenth or so of all managers of large and medium-sized enterprises had been chosen this way, and the aim was to make it the usual procedure for choosing managers once all enterprises had adopted the manager contract responsibility system (*chengbao zhidu*).

The Party was greatly concerned about the morale of state cadres (and also those of intellectuals in general) partly because of the relatively low level of their salaries. As a result of economic reforms, there were many groups—both in rural and urban areas—whose incomes had risen much more rapidly than those of people paid by the state. This made it more difficult for the Party and government to recruit able young people. In addition, many able and experienced older cadres were finding it increasingly difficult to live on their salaries. There was an increasing number of complaints that the pay of cadres was not commensurate with the responsibilities they carried. The situation was one that seemed likely to contribute to growing corruption. Bao Tong gave several examples to illustrate the problem. In Shaoxing, in Zhejiang Province, the salary of the leading Party secretary in the late 1980s was approximately Y 2,000 a year, which was only double the income of an average peasant. In contrast, in the 1950s the Party secretary's salary of Y 300 to Y 400 a year was about six times the average income for peasants in the area. Not surprisingly, the current Party secretary felt that in light of his heavy responsibilities he deserved to be paid more than double an average peasant. In Wenzhou, also in Zhejiang, the average pay of cadres was about Y 200 a month, whereas the average pay of urban workers there had risen to between Y 250 and Y 300.

Bao Tong did not cite specific examples of how the salary of intellectuals had lagged behind the rising incomes of many other people, but traveling around China in 1988 I heard many intellectuals bemoan the inequity of their low salaries compared to manual workers. There were several stories that seemed to be circulating throughout most cities in China that, whether apocryphal or not, reflected the dissatisfactions of intellectuals. Some of them were about how ordinary laborers, and people such as restaurant waitresses and taxi drivers, were earning several times what professors earned. One cited figures to show that a traveling barber, who cut hair on the street, earned as much as a first-class surgeon in a hospital. Bao Tong said that it was imperative to adjust upward the salaries of both cadres and intellectuals, but he acknowledged that they had been unable to reach a consensus on exactly how to do this and how much the raises should be. Many people feared, rightly, that there were real dangers involved in adding these costs to the already large budget deficit of the government and that it was dangerous to add fuel to existing inflationary pressures. Therefore no specific decisions on what to do had yet been made.

*   *   *

All of these steps, Bao Tong maintained, were significant, and those who did not recognize their importance did not really understand what was necessary to start the process of political reform. However, he went on to say that far more important than these preliminary steps was the goal, to which his office was fully committed, of creating a new governmental system in which most leaders and bureaucrats would be chosen either by genuine elections or by a civil service system requiring competitive examinations. The civil service system, he said, would be similar to that in Western countries. (However, the Chinese also had their own long tradition of imperial examinations, which would influence any new system.) It would first be necessary to identify three different categories of people working for the Chinese government: those who should be elected; those who should be appointed (a category that would be similar to high-level "political appointees" in Western countries); and those—the large majority of all cadres—who should be members of the civil service system and would be selected by examination. Bao Tong stressed that, not only in his personal view but in the view of Zhao Ziyang and the Party's top reformist leaders, these changes would be absolutely fundamental in their reform program. But these leaders had no illusions, he said, about the difficulties involved and recognized that it would take a considerable period of time. "If we do not develop a civil service system," he said, "we will lose the opportunity to develop the country." But it would take 10 to 20 years, or even more, to put the system into effect, he said.

In the future, Bao Tong told me, all university graduates would be viewed as potential leading cadres. But for quite a long time, China would simply not have enough able, well-educated cadres to institute a civil service system covering all the bureaucracies. The shortage of qualified people, he acknowledged, was especially great in west China, but even in coastal east China the problem was serious. To help train people qualified for government service, there were plans to establish a special college of government administration as well as to recruit from existing universities. Recognizing that it would be impossible to start all at once a system of civil service examinations for all the government bureaucracies, their plan was to do it in stages. The first people to be chosen under civil service procedures would be personnel involved in foreign affairs and the diplomatic service, judges and procurators, and tax officials. To introduce and perfect the system even for just these groups would take several years—perhaps as long as 10 years. To fully implement the civil service system for all the bureaucracies could well take as long as 20 or more years. (Compared to other countries, Bao Tong maintained, this would be fairly rapid. He said that those in China who had studied the introduction of civil service systems in other countries had told him that developing such systems had taken much longer than this in countries such as the United States and France.)

Bao Tong and the others who had drafted the Zhao Ziyang reform program believed that to get political reform off the ground in China it was necessary first to carry out reform within the Party itself; to change the relationship between the Party and government and other institutions; to change the criterion for recruiting and promoting cadres; to decentralize the personnel system; and to move to a new system under which top government leaders would be elected and the majority of the civil service would be selected by examination. However, the program also called for much broader reforms that could lay the foundations of a system in which elected representative bodies could play an increasingly important role. One of the first tasks was to make the National People's Congress (NPC)—and congresses at lower levels—more meaningful representative bodies, with real power to legislate. He and his colleagues believed, Bao Tong said, that the NPC, with about 2,900 members, was too large to be an effective legislative body, and its Standing Committee was too small. Moreover, the membership was too old, and in the case of the plenary NPC, the meetings were too infrequent.

There had been some positive developments in the 1980s. Despite all of its shortcomings, the NPC had gradually become involved in real legislation. He said that it was not right to dismiss the NPC as being nothing more than a "rubber stamp." In a few cases, it had initiated new laws: He cited as one example a law on the protection of juveniles. Moreover, he asserted that all laws passed since 1983 had been amended or modified in some way by the NPC, and in many cases—for example, the bankruptcy law and the enterprise law—they had been amended in important ways. They (those most active in pushing political reform) were urging it to take an even more active role in legislation.

However, Bao Tong acknowledged, for the NPC to become a significant legislative body, some major changes were required. First, he said, the NPC Standing Committee should be viewed as *the* body that should deal with most legislation, and the Standing Committee should be enlarged. The functional committees serving the NPC Standing Committee needed to be greatly strengthened and staffed by qualified people who were able to assist the Standing Committee's members deal with legislation in all important fields. The NPC Standing Committee should be developed into continuously operating legislative bodies. In recent years meetings had been quite regular, about every three months, but this was not enough. If it was to serve as a full-time legislative body, its members would have to become full-time legislators. Recently, some moves had been made in that direction. A decision had been made to bar NPC Standing Committee members from holding regular jobs in other institutions. This had been partially implemented, so only 30 percent of them still held any other jobs. Most of those who did hold other jobs worked for mass organizations or academic and research institutions, although a few still worked for the Party apparatus. A major effort was being made, also, to see that more young people were chosen for membership in the NPC and its Standing Committee.

Another recent decision that would be of great importance for the long-term development of the NPC into a stronger legislative body, Bao Tong said, concerned the relationship between the Party and the NPC. In the past, all Party members in the NPC were required, in their voting, to follow Party instructions, and since the majority of all NPC members were Party members, in a basic sense the NPC was not independent but instead was simply an adjunct to the Party. For the NPC to have real independence as a legislative body, this had to be changed. This idea was not new; changes had been proposed by a top Party leader many years earlier but had never been put into effect. In early 1988, Zhao Ziyang proposed, and the Party Central Committee decided, that Party members belonging to the NPC Standing Committee henceforth should make their own decisions on how to vote within the NPC and its Standing Committee except "on the most important issues on which the Party would still instruct them." This step to "loosen" Party discipline obviously was only a small one, and the NPC's independence could prove to be meaningless in practice if the top Party leaders classified many decisions as being "most important." Nevertheless, it did reflect the genuine desire of reform leaders such as Zhao and Bao Tong to see the NPC develop into a significant legislative body.

I knew that the top political leaders in China had publicly stated that they absolutely opposed a multiparty system, so this issue would be out of bounds even for a person of Bao Tong's rank. I also knew, though, that discussion of interest groups was no longer off limits and in fact was on the agenda of the regime's reformers. Zhao Ziyang himself, when discussing the need for a better system of "consultation and dialogue" in China in his report to the 13th Party Congress, asserted: "There should be channels through which the voices and demands of the people can be easily and frequently transmitted to the leading bodies." He went on to say that mass organizations should "carry out their work independently" and should "express and defend the specific interests of the masses they represent, while safeguarding the overall interests of the people." The meaning of the final phrase in that sentence was undefined, but, if interpreted narrowly, it would mean the freedom of action of interest groups would actually be very limited. However, I knew that many supporters of political reform in China believed that the development of significant interest group organization was an essential stage on the road to democratization in China. In 1988, moreover, the Chinese press—when reporting on meetings of mass organizations—indicated that there is fairly wide support for the proposition that mass organizations should now really represent the interests of their members and not simply enforce Party policies—which had been their primary role in the past.

When I asked Bao Tong what his view on the development of interest groups was, he said: "The meaning of 'interest groups' depends on how far we can carry out overall reform of the present system." This meant, he said, that after they had made substantial progress in changing the relationship between the Party and the government and the economic enterprises, they would then proceed to redefine the Party's relationship with mass organizations, starting probably with the labor unions and the Young Communist League. He acknowledged that, in the past, trade unions in China had been totally subordinate to the Party; in fact, he said, when leaders such as Li Lisan and Lai Ruoyu had tried to assert the "independence" of trade unions, the Party had carried out political campaigns against them. "Now we think that, while trade unions should, generally speaking, conform to the Party's will and should not become opposition organizations, neither should they simply be subordinate to the Party. ... Under present circumstances, the feasible way to be responsive to the interests of different groups is through increased consultation and dialogue" with them. The Party was trying to broaden consultative relations, Bao Tong said, with China's "democratic parties" (which always have been more like interest groups than parties), and it intends to consult more seriously with educators, economic managers, workers, ordinary urban inhabitants, and other groups.

China's reformers were now willing to recognize that there were real interest groups in China (which in earlier years the Party had generally denied) and to acknowledge that interest groups had a legitimate role to play in the Chinese political system. However, defining interest groups and their roles was still a very sensitive issue, and even people such as Zhao and Bao Tong, who were in the forefront of political reform, were very cautious in dealing with the issue. My own judgment was that as political reforms progressed, however gradually, the next generation of reformers would be compelled at some point to accept more explicitly and less ambiguously than anyone was willing to do in 1988 that it was both inevitable and desirable that independent and competing interest groups be important actors in Chinese politics. Some reform intellectuals I knew in Beijing were convinced that when this happened such interest groups would probably first form links with issue-based and interest-based factions within the Party and that the resulting coalitions might prove to be precursors of political parties.

Toward the end of our conversation, Bao Tong said that, in his view, China was "moving toward more free elections." One small step in that direction had been the decision, after the 13th Party Congress, to require that in all elections for either Party or government positions there be multiple candidates instead of the single slates that had been standard in the past. He told me of several cases in which this decision had produced unexpected results (and I had learned of several other examples during my travels in east China). However, Bao Tong said, just holding elections does not guarantee that they result in real choices. The Chinese people have to get used to the fact that they can make real choices through elections. Even having multiple candidacies was something that they would have to get used to before it had real significance.

Bao Tong also discussed, briefly, the increasing involvement and independence of many of China's newspapers and journals in the political process. The country now needed a good press law, he said, that could define press freedom—but also would make clear the limits of that freedom. A special group made up of journalists and academics as well as officials had started drafting such a law. I knew that many Chinese journalists looked on Bao Tong as a strong supporter of the idea of greater press freedom. However, on this as on so many other issues, it seemed to me, he was cautiously trying to define a course that was not simply pie in the sky but was something that was realistically feasible. During 1988, it looked as if passage of a press law might take place fairly soon, and in the first months of 1989 many newspapers and journals—and even TV stations—showed an unprecedented degree of independence in much of their reporting on the events leading up to the Tiananmen crisis. Then, as a result of the conservative backlash after that tragedy, the press was muzzled and tight controls were again put in place—and they remained in place in 1992.

*   *   *

During my travels throughout China in 1988, the Zhao program for political reform as it had been described to me by Bao Tong defined my own agenda for trying to judge whether, and if so to what extent, efforts to start political reform were under way at the provincial and lower levels. In earlier chapters, I reported what I learned in each of the places I visited in west China. I will not repeat those details here. However, a few general comments about the political reforms in the far west are in order. Almost everywhere in the west, when I asked local leaders to tell me what political reforms were being implemented, their initial replies were very similar to their first responses when I asked about economic reforms. Most local leaders began by acknowledging that in political reform, even more than in economic reform, they were lagging behind coastal China. This clearly was true. Yet, as I noted earlier, in the case of economic reform, the more I learned about the local political situation, the more I realized that some political changes were in fact taking place, and quite a few of them were far from insignificant.

Local leaders echoed the statements by people in Beijing that they were giving priority to steps to "separate the Party from the government" and "to separate the Party from enterprises." There was considerable variation, however, from place to place, in what they were actually doing. In some places, the Party's departments supervising economic "systems" already had been abolished; in other places, it was on the agenda—but not yet done. The same applied to the abolition of core groups in government bodies and mass organizations. In most places, there had been some efforts to reform the personnel system; however, the degree to which appointments had been decentralized, and the extent to which personnel responsibilities had been shifted from Party organization departments to government personnel offices and enterprises, also varied considerably. No leader I met—in either east or west China—yet had any idea of what had to be done to introduce a civil service system, and they obviously were wary about it. (All said that they were "waiting for instructions from Beijing.") Later, in 1991, I read that the State Council had just issued some instructions about the civil service system, but in light of what Bao Tong had told me about their timetable, I suspect that local leaders still regarded this as something that they did not have to do much about in the short run.

In some places I visited, elections with multiple candidacies had taken place, and in a number of places I was told of cases where the individuals elected had not been those with the strongest Party support. In most places, though, I did not get the sense that average people had yet begun to take the elections very seriously. One overall impression I had in 1988 was that even the reform agenda being promoted with great enthusiasm at that time by reform leaders in Beijing did not evoke much enthusiasm on the part of most local leaders, and the political impact of what was being done was still not very great.

The Tiananmen tragedy in mid-1989 obviously caused a major setback to political reform in China, and the Zhao-Bao program was shelved as conservative Party elders tried to tighten ideological and political controls. Zhao Ziyang was put under house arrest. Bao Tong's fate was worse: He was immediately jailed and finally, three years later, was tried and convicted on charges that he had incited revolutionary activities and had leaked state secrets at the time of the Tiananmen demonstrations. He was the highest-ranking supporter of Zhao singled out for such treatment. He was obviously being made a scapegoat.

The short-term consequences of the Tiananmen crisis were politically repressive and retrogressive. However, as I stated earlier, there was never any major reversal of the process of economic reform. By late 1989 and early 1991, new steps toward economic reform began to be taken on a piecemeal basis. Then, at the start of 1992, Deng Xiaoping threw his full weight into accelerating economic reform, and both economic growth and reform took off again. The concern, as in similar periods in the past, was that things might be changing too fast and that the economy would become overheated.

The political situation was frozen immediately after Tiananmen. But those who predicted, after the revolutionary changes in the Soviet Union and Eastern Europe, that China would follow the same path—toward either disintegration or collapse or both—were soon proven to be wrong. However, those who hoped for a fairly rapid return to political liberalization also were disappointed. Even though the effects of the post-Tiananmen repression were, in a basic sense, superficial, they persisted during 1989–1991. Hope for a return to political liberalization began to pick up at the beginning of 1992, however, when, with the 14th Party Congress scheduled for the fall, an intense struggle began, the outcome of which would determine who would lead the Party for most of the 1990s and what the main direction of Party policy would be. Deng's strong endorsement of accelerated economic reform raised hopes that this would lead to a resumption of political liberalization as well.

By 1992 few people had any doubt about the irreversibility of economic reforms. There was a strong consensus in the Chinese leadership that the country should move further toward a market economy; even conservative Party elders seemed to accept that this was inevitable, and they offered no alternative road. Moreover, movement toward a market economy was being driven by strong pressures from below—by irresistible changes in the economy and the society that were proceeding with little reference to what leaders in Beijing thought.

There was no such consensus on political reform. In fact, few people doubted that major political reforms would lag far behind major economic reform. Nevertheless, I believe that a great many Chinese assumed that as China moved closer to a market economy, pressure would mount for further political change and greater political liberalization would result. This was also my view. The far-reaching economic and social change that I observed taking place in China throughout the 1980s, and especially what I saw during my travels in 1988, convinced me that there would be growing demands from below not only for continued economic reform but also for political liberalization—and eventually for structural political change.

In the 1990s, China's prospect is not for regression toward a totalitarian system or for rapid progress toward a multiparty democratic system. What is probable, first, is a resumption of gradual, cautious movement toward a liberalized authoritarian system. It would not be surprising if the initial steps in that direction follow a course not very different from that recommended by Zhao Ziyang and Bao Tong. Whether or not it is labeled "neoauthoritarianism," it may well deserve that label. There will probably be an emphasis on the need for strong leadership and political stability. But there will probably also be strong and growing pressures for political change—from above (from new technocratic leaders), from below (from new groups and interests produced by economic and social change), and from outside China.

The nature and pace of political reform will depend on the regime's ability to feed, clothe, house, and educate China's growing population and on its ability to cope with some of the most difficult ecological and environmental problems in the world. Its success in dealing with these problems will determine whether it can modernize and at the same time maintain social and political stability. If it fails, what will replace the present regime is unlikely to be a democratic system; instead, it is likely to be a more repressive regime, possibly a military dictatorship. But that is not what I predict. I believe that despite the enormous difficulties that the Chinese face, the present regime will not collapse or disappear—but it will undergo major changes. In the near future it will probably evolve into a more liberalized authoritarian regime, but in the long term it will move gradually *toward* greater democratization. However, because of the size of its population, the immensity of its problems, and its authoritarian traditions, it is unlikely to opt, in the foreseeable future, for anything that closely resembles the multiparty systems in the major Western democratic nations.*

——-

*In early 1992 (after I had completed the main writing of this book), Deng Xiaoping strongly endorsed more rapid economic growth and a speedup of economic reform. His action initiated an extraordinary boom; as a result, China's GNP grew at a rate of over 12 percent in 1992. A debate on future policies and leadership continued throughout the year, reaching a climax at the 14th Party Congress in October. The Congress represented a major victory for Deng and for the supporters of his reform policies. For the first time, the Party endorsed the goal of achieving a "socialist *market* economy," and there were sweeping changes in the Party's top leadership, greatly strengthening the support for reform. Almost half of the membership of the Central Committee was changed. There was also a major turnover in the Politburo, and the new seven-man Standing Committee was dominated by pro-Deng reformers. Deng appeared to have succeeded in setting China's course—at least for the years immediately ahead.

*   *   *

Although the bulk of this book has focused on west China, in this final chapter I have tried to look ahead and forecast major economic and political trends in China as a whole. Because since the 1940s west China has been integrated into the national economy and polity to a far greater extent than ever in the past, its fate is now inextricably linked to that of the rest of the country.

In the 1940s, not only were the links between the rest of China and the premodern economies and semiwarlord regimes in west China very tenuous, but the lives and worlds of the Mongols, Tibetans, Uighurs, Kazakhs, Hui Muslims, and most other minority groups were still rooted mainly in the traditional cultures of non-Han Central Asia and southwest China—and in Islam, Lamaism, and animism. Neither their religions nor their cultures had been fundamentally changed by their long contacts and interactions with traditional, Confucian, Han society, and the entire area was virtually untouched by twentieth-century modernity.

Since then, there have been fundamental changes. For better or for worse—and perhaps it has been both for better *and* for worse—west China has been integrated into China and drawn into the modern world. It now *looks* very different from what it did before 1949—and it clearly *is* different. I have no doubt that the forces for change unleashed since 1949, in west China as well as in the country as a whole, will continue to transform the regions and provinces in the west in far-reaching ways in the years ahead. The migration of Han Chinese, and their domination of cities and also much of the arable land in the west, are likely to be inexorable. Migration will be driven by economic forces, whatever government policy may be. By the start of the twenty-first century, Han Chinese probably will outnumber minority groups even in Xinjiang, leaving the Tibetan Autonomous Region as the only region where a minority ethnic group predominates. Industrialization will continue, with the Han Chinese playing crucial roles in the process. However, I believe that minority peoples will be gradually drawn into more important roles in the development and modernization of the west.

The course, and the pace, of economic modernization will continue to depend fundamentally on Beijing's policies—and on the central government's support. Because large state enterprises still dominate the industrial sector in much of the west, the transition to a market economy will probably be particularly difficult there. Because every region and province in the west is still dependent on outside assistance for its development, the pace and characteristics of future economic development in the west will depend fundamentally on Beijing's willingness and ability to provide major investment and budgetary support, although gradually the west may be able to obtain more assistance from east China and possibly increase its own investment in development. Perhaps it will be able to attract some foreign investment. There is no doubt that the development of the west would be given a major boost if Beijing were to decide to invest more in the production of petroleum and raw materials throughout the west and also to permit—or even encourage—active involvement by foreign investors.

The industrialization and other development that has already taken place in the west has raised living standards significantly among most groups in the west. This will doubtless continue. However, leaders in the west will face very difficult and special problems in trying to eliminate the large pockets of extreme poverty within their areas of jurisdiction. Moreover, if the west continues to lag behind the east in both economic development and reform—which seems likely—the widening of the gap between east and west could create serious political problems. Probably leaders in the west will increase their lobbying and pressures on Beijing to modify their policies. I believe that eventually Beijing will find it necessary to do so, increasing the attention to the west and reducing the special privileges given to the east.

Both demographic and economic trends will continue to increase the dominance of Han culture in the west. In urban areas, the Sinification of some minority peoples will doubtless continue, and the number who are fully assimilated into Han culture could well rise. However, I believe that the majority of people of ethnic origins will try to—and I think will be able to—retain their strong sense of identity and preserve many aspects of their distinctive traditions and cultures. Probably the majority will still speak their own languages (although it is also possible that the majority will be bilingual, and know Hanyu as well) and retain their religion and many other cultural traditions, including dietary ones. In the vast grasslands, deserts, oases, and mountain areas in the west—which account for most of the territory and are the areas where the largest numbers of ethnic minority peoples still live—although the spread of modernization will have an increasing impact on their lives, minority people will doubtless continue to have a very strong sense of their distinctiveness and will maintain much of their traditional culture, although modernization will change it in many ways. As living standards rise, there will be an increasing number of people from minority groups who have become well educated, have acquired modern skills, and have moved to cities.

In many respects, the course of modernization in the west is likely to parallel, or follow, what is happening in the east. Both Beijing and coastal provinces will push or pull the west along the path of development chosen for the country as a whole, and the west will be brought along. However, almost always, I think, change in the west will be a little later, a little slower, and a little different from that in the east. Because of its location and topography, its problems will be different—and most of them will be more difficult. The west will always face especially difficult problems because of its complicated ethnic mixtures.

Over the centuries, the relations between Han Chinese and ethnic minorities in the west have had their ups and downs, but for long periods relations have been very troubled, and ethnic tensions have frequently led to conflict. When I visited western areas in the 1940s, some areas were in the grip of interethnic conflict; other areas were tense; and very few were calm or "normal." And, on the borders of both the Soviet Union and Outer Mongolia, mini-wars were going on. In the ensuing decades of Communist rule, relations between the Han Chinese and minority groups have varied greatly, and Beijing's "minority policies" have changed many times. People I met in the west told me that one of the best periods, when relations were fairly good, was soon after the Communist takeover in the 1950s. Clearly the worst period was during the height of the Cultural Revolution, from the late 1960s to the early 1970s, when the antireligious, antitraditional rampages of young Red Guards were incredibly destructive. The Red Guards' targets were not restricted to minority groups. They included most Han Party and government bureaucrats as well, and they targeted *all* religious and traditional values. But this fact did not make the attacks on minority groups and their religious institutions any less brutal.

In light of that background, I was impressed on my travels in 1988 by the degree to which interethnic relations seemed to have been repaired and normalized. As I stated in almost every earlier chapter, I saw few signs of obvious tensions or conflicts in the minority areas that I visited, and I found that fact to be quite remarkable. Clearly, it was the result in part of a major change of Communist Party policy in the late 1970s and of the efforts to conciliate minority groups, tolerate (and in some areas actively encourage) a revival of religion, and pay special attention to problems in minority areas. I have already described at some length the wide-ranging "affirmative action" policies implemented throughout the west, which provided special subsidies to minority areas for many purposes—to repair religious institutions, to subsidize economic development projects, to raise the level of education, and in general to narrow the gap between the Han Chinese and minority groups. In most places that I visited, I was impressed by these policies and by what I learned about their effects. I had no doubt that they were, as intended, having a favorable impact on Han relations with ethnic minority groups and were gradually improving conditions in many minority areas.

Despite the progress being made, though, I saw a number of signs that bitterness over the past, and particularly about persecution during the Cultural Revolution, had by no means totally disappeared. It was also clear that some very difficult special problems persisted; both the Han Chinese and the members of minority groups whom I met talked frankly about them. Although minority people now held the top government positions in "autonomous" administrative areas, and the number of cadres recruited from minority groups was impressive, Han Chinese still occupied most of the top Party positions, where real power rested. Even though there had been economic and educational progress in minority areas, many still lag seriously behind areas where the Han population is predominant. It will take time—probably quite a long period of time—to close the gaps.

These problems, and the differences, will not soon disappear. I left the area convinced, though, that if current policies continue for a reasonable period of time, the problems should be manageable and the gaps should gradually diminish. However, even though I did not see obvious signs of interethnic tensions, I felt that some tensions must still exist under the surface. Moreover, my guess is that as more well-educated and prosperous minority leaders are drawn into the mainstream of political and economic life, they are likely to exert more, not less, pressure for larger political as well as economic roles. It would not be surprising if rising new leaders from the minority groups push for more real autonomy. This has been the pattern of development in comparable situations in many other countries; I would expect it in China. In my judgment, future reform leaders in China will be compelled to give serious consideration to new forms of decentralization of power—and perhaps find it necessary to experiment with federalism, or something like it, not just in minority areas but in Han areas as well. In the long run, as China modernizes, the Chinese predisposition toward highly centralized political power will probably have to be modified.

Despite the many problems that I saw in minority areas in China's far west, nowhere did I feel that tensions had risen to dangerous levels that were likely to result in major political eruptions. In several places, I got the impression that certain minority groups probably felt that they were victims of political discrimination—perhaps because of their strong opposition to the Communists at the time of takeover—and I believe that all along China's western borders from Outer Mongolia through Kazakhstan to India there is a potential for external influences to stimulate political agitation and some unrest.

My own belief, though, is that there are only two areas in the west where anti-Han feeling is serious enough at present to cause major political unrest and conflict in the near future. Neither of them did I personally visit in 1988, but I learned a good deal about them secondhand from people I know and trust. First, and most important, is the Tibetan Autonomous Region. It will probably continue to be unstable, and experience periodic political eruptions, until some new agreement between Beijing and Lhasa becomes possible. In fact, a prerequisite to mutual accommodation between the Han Chinese and the Tibetans there probably must be a formal agreement of some sort between the Dalai Lama and the central government in Beijing. The other area where I think there may well be political eruptions in the period ahead is southwest Xinjiang, especially the area around Kashi (Kashgar), where in 1990 there was a violent clash between Uighurs and Han Chinese, followed by a tough Chinese military clampdown. However, nowhere in China's far west—including Tibet and southwest Xinjiang—are there likely to be circumstances prevailing in the foreseeable future that would make it possible for local people favoring secession or independence to succeed.

Beijing's present reform leaders believe, in my opinion, that moderate and conciliatory policies, where possible, are the best approach to dealing with minority populations in the west, and I would expect that future Chinese reform leaders will be inclined to pursue "affirmative action" policies aimed at improving the lives of minority groups wherever political and social conditions are relatively stable. Nonetheless, I have little doubt that future leaders will not hesitate to use force whenever and wherever there are direct challenges to Beijing's ultimate authority or Chinese sovereignty.

Most of the trends that I have described are likely, I believe, to continue in "the foreseeable future"—with one caveat. That caveat is important. I do not claim to be able to see very far into the future, and I think this is true of other China specialists as well. Now that west China has been integrated into the Chinese economy and polity more than ever in the past, and has been launched on the road to modernization with the help of Beijing and other parts of China, its future will be determined to a very large extent by the nature of China's future leadership and policies and by the overall success of the country's modernization. I believe that the reform policies launched by Deng Xiaoping in the late 1970s will continue to chart the main direction of China's modernization and development in the period ahead. It is a course that I think the far west as well as coastal China will follow. The problems China faces are so great that its path will zig and zag and undoubtedly be bumpy. However, I believe that China in the 1990s will make major progress toward creating a market economy and toward gradually liberalizing its political system. And I believe that China's far west will also move in these directions, though it will probably always be a little behind.

About the Book and Author

China's Far West is a rich portrait of China's least-known provinces by one of America's leading China scholars. Based on A. Doak Barnett's unrivaled travels in and study of some of the most remote areas of the country in both the late 1940s and the late 1980s, this sweeping work vividly portrays a China few outsiders have seen. Born and raised in China, the author brings unique insights to his analysis of the profound changes that have taken place over four turbulent decades of Communist rule.

Barnett's work builds on decades of experiences in China. He began writing about the country in 1947 and chronicled the Communist takeover in 1949. More than any other Western observer of the time, he followed the fortunes of China's distant provinces in the far west, most of which were then ruled by old-style warlords. His observations were distilled in *China on the Eve of Communist Takeover* (available from Westview Press). *China's Far West* is a successor to that classic work.

Returning to China in 1972, right after the U.S.-China "opening," Barnett resumed his travels. Then, when the doors to the interior areas opened more widely as a result of Deng Xiaoping's economic reform, he decided to retrace journeys that were now four decades in the past. In 1988, he revisited Inner Mongolia, the arc of Hui Muslim areas in the northwest, the Uighur and Kazakh regions in Xinjiang, the Tibetan enclaves in Qinghai and western Sichuan, and Yunnan's multiethnic regions. Everywhere he went, he probed for answers to two basic questions: How much had these distant areas changed over four decades? And what had been the impact of the economic reforms and accelerating processes of growth and modernization spurred by Deng in the 1980s? Like a modern Marco Polo, he attempted to record everything of significance that he saw and learned. At the same time, as both scholar and journalist, he tried to order, evaluate, analyze, and provide historical perspective for the information he gathered.

Containing remarkably comprehensive profiles of each area the author visited, the book is full of detailed information about government and politics, economic development, social changes, and relations between ethnic groups. Barnett comments on continuities, but he is clearly most impressed by the extent of the changes he saw, which far exceeded his expectations. In the 1940s, almost all of China's far west was poor and undeveloped, clinging to centuries-old life-styles. But by the late 1980s, most of the region was undergoing a profound transformation. The spread of industrialization, a remarkable communications revolution, rising living standards, and increasing contacts with the rest of China and the world had catapulted it into the modern world. Although many western areas were still among the poorest in China, the economic reforms of the 1980s were taking hold.

No other contemporary study of these little-known areas of China begins to match the scope and detail of *China's Far West,* and no other author has the experience to analyze the book's themes with Barnett's breadth and depth of historical perspective.

This book will help bring to life for Westerners many of the most fascinating, out-of-the-way provinces and regions of China.

Barnett's travels in the 1970s and 1980s as well as in the 1940s took him to every part of China, and although this volume concentrates on China's far west, the author discusses in both the Prologue and the final chapter the broad processes of modernization and reform that have been transforming every part of China during the past four decades.

A. Doak Barnett is professor emeritus of Chinese studies at the Johns Hopkins School for Advanced International Studies and is senior fellow emeritus at The Brookings Institution.

book will help bring to life for Westerners many of the most fascinating, out-of-
way provinces and regions of China.

arnett's travels in the 1970s and 1980s as well as in the 1940s took him to every
of China, and although this volume concentrates on China's far west, the author
usses in both the Prologue and the final chapter the broad processes of modern-
on and reform that have been transforming every part of China during the past
decades.

Doak Barnett is professor emeritus of Chinese studies at the Johns Hopkins
ool for Advanced International Studies and is senior fellow emeritus at The
okings Institution.

administrative areas, and the number of cadres recruited from minority
groups was impressive, Han Chinese still occupied most of the top Party positions, where real power rested. Even though there had been economic and
educational progress in minority areas, many still lag seriously behind areas
where the Han population is predominant. It will take time—probably quite
a long period of time—to close the gaps.

These problems, and the differences, will not soon disappear. I left the area
convinced, though, that if current policies continue for a reasonable period
of time, the problems should be manageable and the gaps should gradually
diminish. However, even though I did not see obvious signs of interethnic
tensions, I felt that some tensions must still exist under the surface. Moreover, my guess is that as more well-educated and prosperous minority leaders are drawn into the mainstream of political and economic life, they are
likely to exert more, not less, pressure for larger political as well as economic
roles. It would not be surprising if rising new leaders from the minority
groups push for more real autonomy. This has been the pattern of development in comparable situations in many other countries; I would expect it in
China. In my judgment, future reform leaders in China will be compelled to
give serious consideration to new forms of decentralization of power—and
perhaps find it necessary to experiment with federalism, or something like it,
not just in minority areas but in Han areas as well. In the long run, as China
modernizes, the Chinese predisposition toward highly centralized political
power will probably have to be modified.

Despite the many problems that I saw in minority areas in China's far
west, nowhere did I feel that tensions had risen to dangerous levels that were
likely to result in major political eruptions. In several places, I got the impression that certain minority groups probably felt that they were victims of
political discrimination—perhaps because of their strong opposition to the
Communists at the time of takeover—and I believe that all along China's
western borders from Outer Mongolia through Kazakhstan to India there is
a potential for external influences to stimulate political agitation and some
unrest.

My own belief, though, is that there are only two areas in the west where
anti-Han feeling is serious enough at present to cause major political unrest
and conflict in the near future. Neither of them did I personally visit in 1988,
but I learned a good deal about them secondhand from people I know and
trust. First, and most important, is the Tibetan Autonomous Region. It will
probably continue to be unstable, and experience periodic political eruptions, until some new agreement between Beijing and Lhasa becomes possible. In fact, a prerequisite to mutual accommodation between the Han Chinese and the Tibetans there probably must be a formal agreement of some
sort between the Dalai Lama and the central government in Beijing. The
other area where I think there may well be political eruptions in the period

ahead is southwest Xinjiang, especially the area around Kashi (Kashgar), where in 1990 there was a violent clash between Uighurs and Han Chinese, followed by a tough Chinese military clampdown. However, nowhere in China's far west—including Tibet and southwest Xinjiang—are there likely to be circumstances prevailing in the foreseeable future that would make it possible for local people favoring secession or independence to succeed.

Beijing's present reform leaders believe, in my opinion, that moderate and conciliatory policies, where possible, are the best approach to dealing with minority populations in the west, and I would expect that future Chinese reform leaders will be inclined to pursue "affirmative action" policies aimed at improving the lives of minority groups wherever political and social conditions are relatively stable. Nonetheless, I have little doubt that future leaders will not hesitate to use force whenever and wherever there are direct challenges to Beijing's ultimate authority or Chinese sovereignty.

Most of the trends that I have described are likely, I believe, to continue in "the foreseeable future"—with one caveat. That caveat is important. I do not claim to be able to see very far into the future, and I think this is true of other China specialists as well. Now that west China has been integrated into the Chinese economy and polity more than ever in the past, and has been launched on the road to modernization with the help of Beijing and other parts of China, its future will be determined to a very large extent by the nature of China's future leadership and policies and by the overall success of the country's modernization. I believe that the reform policies launched by Deng Xiaoping in the late 1970s will continue to chart the main direction of China's modernization and development in the period ahead. It is a course that I think the far west as well as coastal China will follow. The problems China faces are so great that its path will zig and zag and undoubtedly be bumpy. However, I believe that China in the 1990s will make major progress toward creating a market economy and toward gradually liberalizing its political system. And I believe that China's far west will also move in these directions, though it will probably always be a little behind.

This
the-
B
part
disc
izati
four

A
Sch
Bro

About the Book and A

China's Far West is a rich portrait of China's least-known pr
ca's leading China scholars. Based on A. Doak Barnett's
study of some of the most remote areas of the country in bo
late 1980s, this sweeping work vividly portrays a China f
Born and raised in China, the author brings unique insights t
found changes that have taken place over four turbulent dec

Barnett's work builds on decades of experiences in China.
the country in 1947 and chronicled the Communist takeover
other Western observer of the time, he followed the fortunes
inces in the far west, most of which were then ruled by old-st
vations were distilled in *China on the Eve of Communist T*
Westview Press). *China's Far West* is a successor to that class

Returning to China in 1972, right after the U.S.-China
sumed his travels. Then, when the doors to the interior areas c
result of Deng Xiaoping's economic reform, he decided to ret
now four decades in the past. In 1988, he revisited Inner M
Muslim areas in the northwest, the Uighur and Kazakh regi
betan enclaves in Qinghai and western Sichuan, and Yunna
Everywhere he went, he probed for answers to two basic que
these distant areas changed over four decades? And what had
economic reforms and accelerating processes of growth and
by Deng in the 1980s? Like a modern Marco Polo, he attempt
of significance that he saw and learned. At the same time, as
nalist, he tried to order, evaluate, analyze, and provide histor
information he gathered.

Containing remarkably comprehensive profiles of each area
book is full of detailed information about government and pc
opment, social changes, and relations between ethnic groups.
continuities, but he is clearly most impressed by the extent c
which far exceeded his expectations. In the 1940s, almost all c
poor and undeveloped, clinging to centuries-old life-styles. I
most of the region was undergoing a profound transformation
trialization, a remarkable communications revolution, rising liv
creasing contacts with the rest of China and the world had cata
ern world. Although many western areas were still among the
economic reforms of the 1980s were taking hold.

No other contemporary study of these little-known areas of
the scope and detail of *China's Far West*, and no other author
analyze the book's themes with Barnett's breadth and depth of

Index